MARY I

JOHN EDWARDS is Modern Languages Facu
Spanish, University of Oxford. His recent boo.
Inquisi

Also in the Yale English Monarchs Series

* Available in the U.S. from University of California Press

MARY I

ENGLAND'S CATHOLIC QUEEN

John Edwards

YALE UNIVERSITY PRESS
NEW HAVEN AND LONDON

Published with assistance from the foundation established in memory of Oliver Baty Cunningham of the Class of 1917, Yale College.

First printed in paperback in 2013

For information about this and other Yale University Press publications, please contact:
U.S. Office: sales.press@yale.edu   www.yalebooks.com
Europe Office: sales@yaleup.co.uk   www.yalebooks.co.uk

Set in Baskerville by IDSUK (DataConnection) Ltd
Printed in Great Britain by Hobbs the Printers Ltd, Totton, Hampshire.

Library of Congress Cataloging-in-Publication Data

Edwards, John, 1949–
    Mary I: England's Catholic queen/John Edwards.
       p. cm.
  Includes bibliographical refrences and index.
    ISBN 978-0–300118100 (cl: alk. paper)
  1.   Mary I, Queen of England, 1516–1558. 2.   Queen—Great Britain—Biography.
  3.   Great Britain—History—Mary I, 1553–1558.   I. Title
DA347.E39 2011
942.05'4092—dc22
[B]
                                                                2011005096

A catalogue record for this book is available from the British Library.

ISBN 978-0-300-19416-6 (pbk)

10 9 8 7 6 5 4 3 2 1

For Vivien

CONTENTS

ILLUSTRATIONS

1 Hans Eworth, *Queen Mary I* (1554). © National Portrait Gallery, London.

2 Lucas Horenbout (attr.), medallion showing Mary aged about nine (*c.* 1525). © National Portrait Gallery, London.

3 Detail of Mary's funerary effigy. © English Heritage Photo Library.

4 Gold ryal minted in London (1553). © Trustees of the British Museum.

5 Silver sixpence minted in London (1554). © Trustees of the British Museum.

6 Illuminated initial of Mary enthroned, 1 Mary Michaelmas plea roll, 1553. National Archives.

7 Illuminated initial of Philip and Mary, 1 and 2 Philip and Mary Michaelmas plea roll. National Archives.

8 Manuscript illumination of Mary touching for the King's evil (undated). By permission of Westminster cathedral.

9 Titian, *King Philip II* (1550). Prado, Madrid / Giraudon / Bridgeman Art Library.

10 Pompeo Leoni, painted silver bust of Philip II (*c.* 1556–60. Kunsthistorisches Museum, Vienna.

11 Hans Eworth, marriage portrait of Philip and Mary (1554). Reproduced by kind permission of His Grace the Duke of Bedford and the Trustees of the Bedford Estates.

12 *Cardinal Reginald Pole* after Sebastiano del Piombo. Lambeth palace, London/ Bridgeman Art Library.

13 Stained-glass window portraying Philip and Mary for the church of Our Lady in Antwerp. Photo © Ulrich M. Alexander, cathedral of Our Lady, Antwerp.

14 'The description of the burning of Mayster Bucers and Paulus Phagi-us bones . . .', woodcut from John Foxe, Acts and Monuments (1570), p. 2151. By permission of the Master and Fellows of Trinity College, Cambridge (C.17.25).

15 Framlingham castle, Suffolk, view from the lower court. © English Heritage Photo Library.

16 Winchester cathedral, Hampshire, the west and north fronts. © Angelo Hornak Photo Library.

17 Greenwich palace from the north bank of the Thames from Anthonis van den Wyngaerde, *The Panorama of London* (*c.* 1544). Ashmolean Museum, University of Oxford/ Bridgeman Art Library.

ABBREVIATIONS

Accession, ed. Malfatti	C. V. Malfatti, ed., *The accession, coronation and Marriage of Mary Tudor as related by four manuscripts of the Escorial* (Barcelona: Sociedad Alianza de Artes Gráficas and Ricardo Fontá, 1956)
AGS	Archivo General de Simancas
AGS E	AGS Sección de Estado
APC	*Acts of the Privy Council*
ASV	Archivio segreto vaticano
BAV	Biblioteca apostolica vaticano
BL	British Library
BNM	Biblioteca Nacional de España, Madrid, Sala Cervantes
BPR	Biblioteca del Palacio Real, Madrid
BREscorial	Biblioteca Real de San Lorenzo de El Escorial
CMT	Eamon Duffy and David Loades, eds, *The Church of Mary Tudor* (Aldershot: Ashgate, 2006)
CODOIN	*Colección de documentos inéditos para la historia de España*, ed. M. F. Navarrete and others, 112 vols (Madrid: various publishers, 1842–95)
Commendone, *Accession*	Giovanni Francesco [Gianfrancesco] Commendone, *Regno d'Inghilterra incominciando dal Re Edoardo VI fino il sponsalitio seguito tra il Ser[enissimo] Principe Philippo di Spagna ey la Ser[enissi]ma Reina Maria*, in Malfatti, *Accession*, pp. 3–61, 99–131
CPR	*Calendar of Patent Rolls*
CRP	Thomas F. Mayer, ed., *The correspondence of Reginald Pole*, 4 vols (Aldershot: Ashgate, 2002–8)
CSPDM	*Calendar of State Papers, Domestic: Mary*
CSP Span	*Calendar of State Papers, Spanish*
CSP Ven	*Calendar of State Papers, Venetian*
Foxe, with date of relevant edition	John Foxe, *Acts and monuments of these latter and perillous days [. . .]* [commonly known as the 'Book of Martyrs'] (London: John Day, 1563, 1570, 1576, 1583)
Guaras, *Accession*	Antonio de Guaras, *Relación muy verdadera de Antonio de Guaras criado de la Serenissima y Catholica reyna de Inglaterra [. . .] como doña María fue proclamada por Reyna, y de todos obedescida y su coronación, etc.*, in Garnett, ed., *The accession of Queen Mary [. . .]*, pp. 33–75
HMSO	Her or His Majesty's Stationery Office, London
LP	*Letters and Papers, Foreign and Domestic: Henry VIII*

Mayer, *PP&P*   Thomas F. Mayer, *Reginald Pole, prince and prophet*
                        (Cambridge: Cambridge University Press, 2000)
n.s.   new series
RCMT   John Edwards and Ronald Truman, eds, *Reforming
                        Catholicism in the England of Mary Tudor* (Aldershot:
                        Ashgate, 2005)
RMT   David Loades, *The reign of Mary Tudor. Politics, govern-
                        ment and religion in England, 1553–58*, 2nd edn (London
                        and New York: Longman, [1979] 1991)
SyC   Real Academia de la Historia, Madrid. Colección
                        Salazar y Castro
Tellechea, *CyP*   José Ignacio Tellechea Idígoras, *Fray Bartolomé
                        Carranza y el cardenal Pole. Un navarro en la restauración
                        católica de Inglaterra (1554–58)* (Pamplona: Diputación
                        Foral de Navarra, 1977)

PREFACE AND ACKNOWLEDGEMENTS

Mary Tudor, daughter of King Henry VIII and Queen Catherine, was the first woman to achieve effective sovereign rule over all the lands of the English crown. Still, centuries after the controversies and conflicts of her own time, Mary I has a bad reputation in the eyes of many and is more than a slight embarrassment to some. John Foxe, a contemporary of hers who continued to write about her in the subsequent reign of her half-sister Elizabeth, caused her to become known as 'Bloody Mary' by detecting her hand behind the 'bloody murdering' of Protestants during her reign. In this context, ever more energy and space are being given to her restoration of the traditional Christian religion of England, which had been much revised in the reigns of her father and her half-brother Edward. Another traditional component of her bad reputation, since her own day, has been her marriage to Philip, a man who would become one of Spain's greatest kings. Philip, too, does not have an unblemished and uncontentious reputation, being seen by some, however much or little they actually know about him, as a cold and cruel tyrant. Recent biographies, in English and Spanish, have devoted extraordinarily few pages to his four years as Mary's husband, during which he experienced a vital apprenticeship in rule which would serve him for another four decades.

As a highly controversial ruler, for the fact that she was female and because of her religious policies and her choice of husband, Mary was much commented upon during her own lifetime and in the years which immediately followed.[1] Convinced Protestant or reformed Christians, who opposed her restoration of Catholicism in the English Church, sometimes questioned her right to rule on constitutional as well as gender grounds. Thus an anonymous author, in a pamphlet perhaps published in Zurich in 1555, not only launched a personal attack against Queen Mary, but exploited the constitutional theory that had developed in England and in continental Europe during the period before 1500, which distinguished between the physical person of the monarch and the abstract and practical entity of the 'crown'.[2] Thus he (it was almost certainly a 'he') asked,

---

[1] For a comprehensive survey of such writing, see Thomas Betteridge, *Tudor Histories of the English Reformation, 1530–83* (Aldershot: Ashgate, 1999).

[2] E. M. Kantorowitz, *The King's Two Bodies: A Study in Medieval Political Theology* (Princeton, NJ: Princeton University Press, 1957).

dangerously, whether it was possible to separate treason against the King's (and hence the Queen's) person from treason against the body of the realm, in other words the Commonwealth, or *Respublica*, of England. He also asked whether a King could pardon treason against the body of the realm, and indeed betray his own realm, and whether England belonged ultimately to Mary, as queen, or to her subjects.[3] The expected answer was that Mary was fair game for rebels. Robert Crowley, in his account of her reign, published soon after her death, clearly took her as his target in the most personal of ways. He, like the martyrologist John Foxe, focused on her two false pregnancies, seeing them as signs both of her rejection by God and of her falseness in everything else, as well as of the corruption of her regime, which needed to be reformed and purged once her reign had been providentially brought to an end.[4]

Other contemporary writers, of course, took the contrary view. The play *Respublica*, attributed to Nicholas Udall and written in a traditional morality style, portrayed Edward VI's Council as allegorical vices, and their successors under Mary as 'virtues'. The central message of the drama was that Mary's arrival on the throne, like Christ's advent on earth, would not only reform abuses in England, but also prevent their return. The Queen was entirely good, and at least verged on ushering in Jesus's second coming, as foretold in Scripture in the New Testament Book of Revelation or Apocalypse.[5] In a more directly political work about Thomas Wyatt's rebellion of 1554, John Proctor portrayed the courageous Mary as the Nemesis of evildoers and the leader of a loyal country, which nonetheless contained impudent subjects, whom she had to face down.[6] Miles Hogarde's poetry, on the other hand, eulogized Queen Mary in religious terms. For him, the arrival of Mary on the throne did not immediately bring her loyal and Catholic subjects to the 'tower of perfection' of which he wrote, but simply made an inherently difficult journey a little less perilous. The pathway to perfection was open, but only to the chosen and godly who accepted her religious reforms.[7] Is it possible, at the beginning of the twenty-first century, to advance beyond these Tudor polemics?

In 2005 I agreed to undertake this biography at the suggestion of Heather McCallum of Yale University Press, with whom I had previously worked on my short study of Mary's maternal grandparents, Ferdinand

---

[3] *Certayne questions demanded and asked by the noble realme of Englande, of her true natural chyldren and subiectes of the same* (Zurich?, 1555), sigs A.ii, A.iiii.v; Betteridge, *Tudor Histories*, p. 31.

[4] Robert Crowley, *An epitome of chronicles [. . .] continued to the reign of Quene Elizabeth* (London, 1559), sig. G.ggg.2; Foxe, 1563, p. 1014; Betteridge, *Tudor Histories*, pp. 170–1, 177–8.

[5] *Respublica* [attr. Nicholas Udall], ed. W. W. Greg (Early English Text Society, old series, 226, London, 1969); Betteridge, *Tudor Histories*, pp. 136–44.

[6] John Proctor, *The historie of wyattes rebellion, with the order and maner of resisting the same* (London, 1554); Betteridge, *Tudor Histories*, pp. 144–7.

[7] Miles Hogarde, *The assault of the sacrame[n]t of the altar* (London: 1554), and *A treatise entitled the Pathwaye to the towre of perfection* (London: 1554); Betteridge, *Tudor Histories*, p. 158.

and Isabella of Spain.[8] Mary's husband Philip was, of course, the obvious link, but the offer touched on views and concerns of mine which go back many years. These involve the history and identity of England and of the Tudor dynasty – which was always of such interest, and disappointment, to a historian from a Welsh family – as well as the apparent frustration of the hope, in the 1960s, for a greater degree of Christian unity which first arose from Pope John XXIII's calling of the Second Vatican Council and then was largely dashed in its aftermath. I continue to hang on, despite everything and because of the deep and reasoned faith and decency which continue to distinguish it, in what has become known, somewhat arbitrarily and perhaps presumptuously, as the 'Catholic' part of the Anglican Communion. Study of the sixteenth century in the Modern History Faculty at Oxford, in the late 1960s, and participation in the life of the university as a whole, produced in me a strong urge to find out how we had come to this sorry pass. Subsequently, teaching and doing research while at the University of Birmingham on the Catholic Inquisition, particularly in Spain, have not increased my patience with oppression, but have, I hope, prepared me at least to attempt to enter the mindset of the churchmen and rulers in Mary's time, including the 'bloody' Queen herself, who felt compelled to enforce their understanding of Christian faith and practice in a restrictive and often violent way. If this is a 'methodology', then it is intended to be a tool and not a master, since no one can seriously claim to know the minds of women and men who lived several centuries ago.

I am grateful to many in Church and academia for bringing me to the writing of this book, among them my fellow students, most of them not historians, at The Queen's College, Oxford, and elsewhere in the University, as well as colleagues and students in the School of History at the University of Birmingham. I continue to be influenced by my life in the French research centre at Madrid, the Casa de Velázquez, during the last years of General Franco's rule, and more recently in the Real Academia de la Historia, also in Madrid, which elected me as a *miembro correspondiente* in 2003. I am of course grateful to helpful staff in numerous libraries and archives, including the Bodleian Library and the History and Modern Languages Faculty Libraries at Oxford. In Cambridge, I am equally grateful for excellent service received in the Manuscripts Room at the Cambridge University Library and in the Wren Library of Trinity College. Also of particular help have been the pleasant and efficient staff of the Manuscripts Room of the British Library, and of its equivalent, the Sala Cervantes, in the Biblioteca Nacional de España, Madrid, as well as kind and efficient people in other Spanish libraries, in particular the Biblioteca del Palacio Real, Madrid, the Real Academia de la Historia, and the Real Biblioteca del Monasterio de San Lorenzo de El Escorial,

---

[8] John Edwards, *Ferdinand and Isabella* (Harlow: Pearson Longman, 2005).

which was Philip I and II's own personal foundation In some places, help received has gone a long way beyond the call of duty. I owe a special debt to the staff of the Knights of Columbus Vatican Film Library, in the Pius XII Library at Saint Louis University, and to the Center for Medieval and Renaissance Studies there, which in the autumn of 2007 elected me to a National Endowment for the Humanities Visiting Fellowship to study its rich collection of Vatican archives on microfilm. I shall always remember with affection that time in St Louis, and in particular the friendship and support of Thomas Madden and Teresa Harvey, as well as Damian Smith, and numerous graduate students. I am also particularly grateful, for vital help in identifying likely sources, to the superintendent of the reading room of the Archivo General de Simancas, Sra Isabel Aguirre. In Valladolid, whence Philip set out in 1554 to meet Mary of England, I especially acknowledge the help of Javier Burrieza Sánchez, archivist of the Royal College of St Alban the Martyr ('El Colegio de Ingleses'), and of my long-standing colleague María Isabel del Val, who organized research facilities for me in the Arts Faculty Library of the University of Valladolid. A special highlight was my visit to the Library and Archives of Winchester College, where I was welcomed and greatly helped by the archivist, Suzanne Foster, and the librarian, Geoffrey Day, and to the Westgate Museum in Winchester, which was specially opened up by Geoffrey Denford for the three of us to see, as Philip and Mary no doubt once did, Warden, later Bishop, John White's 'painted ceiling'.

Many people, in England and abroad, have encouraged me in the writing of this book, producing ideas and new angles which have all gone into the mix, though none but I, of course, can take responsibility for the outcome. In Spain, I am particularly grateful for the support of my old friend and colleague, Miguel Ángel Ladero Quesada, who has always backed my projects, and to the Permanent Secretary of the Real Academia de la Historia, Eloy Benito Ruano, who as well as being a friend over many years, did the signal service of alerting me to the existence of the biography of Mary by María Jesús Pérez Martín, and securing a copy for me, through the kindness of the late author's sister. As the rest of this book demonstrates, I owe a great debt to Father Ignacio Tellechea, who devoted his life to a man who became one of Queen Mary's closest advisers, Friar Bartolomé Carranza, as well as to Thomas Mayer, without whose work and learning it is fairly impossible to say anything sensible about Cardinal Reginald Pole, who was another such adviser. In England, I am especially grateful to Dr Alexander Samson for generously sharing with me his work on Philip and Mary, and for a considerable meeting of minds. While working on this project, I have generally avoided pronouncing on its subject in public, but I greatly value the enlightenment gained from outings to speak to the British Reformation History seminar and the Spanish Research seminar at Oxford, as well as the 2009 Cambridge conference of the Society for Reformation Studies, and before that on two occasions in the Center for Medieval and Renaissance Studies at Saint Louis University.

I owe a special debt to Steven Gunn, who read a draft text before it was submitted to the Press. His vigilance and insights have enabled me to avoid some errors and improve this work in numerous ways, though of course he bears no responsibility for any inadequacies which may nonetheless remain. The same applies to the two anonymous readers for Yale, whose perceptive and meticulous comments have challenged and stimulated me in the process of revision, as well as warning of further pitfalls, which I have tried to avoid. In many respects, their views reached an interesting consensus with those of two people who are not professional historians, Helen Gordon and my wife Vivien, who very kindly read the same draft as representatives of the wider public. This too was a salutary exercise, and Viv, in particular, has perforce lived and breathed the life of Mary I for the last few years, providing endless encouragement and some challenging criticism. At Yale, Heather McCallum, who first had the vision of a 'Life' of Mary with a continental dimension, has been a tower of strength throughout. For all this I am most grateful, as I am to my efficient and friendly helpers in the final stages of preparing the book for publication: Rachael Lonsdale, Candida Brazil and Tami Halliday.

Oxford, Epiphany 2011

Chapter 1

SENTIMENTAL EDUCATION
OF A PRINCESS, 1516–1525

On 16 December 1485, at Alcalá de Henares in central Spain, a daughter
was born to Queen Isabella of Castile and King Ferdinand of Aragon.
She was to remain their youngest child, and was named Catalina, after her
English great-grandmother, Catherine of Lancaster. The future Catherine
of Aragon, Princess of Wales and Queen of England, first saw light
during a winter lull in her parents' war against the Muslim emirate of
Granada, which they would conquer seven years later.[1] Some months
afterwards, in the early hours of 20 September 1486, Elizabeth of York,
wife of King Henry VII of England, gave birth prematurely to their first
child, a precious son. He was named Arthur, after the famous and
legendary King of Britain, from whom Henry Tudor claimed descent.
The new prince's birthplace, Winchester, was believed at that time to have
been King Arthur's capital, and his supposed Round Table was still in the
castle there. While the infant Catherine had other siblings, Prince Arthur
had the hopes of his parents and the nation immediately thrust upon him.
He would be Catherine's first husband. Then, on 28 June 1491, a second
son was born to Elizabeth and Henry. He, notoriously, would be
Catherine's second husband.

By the time that Catherine came to England and married Arthur, in
St Paul's Cathedral, London on 14 November 1501, there was a long tradition of dynastic and economic relations between Henry VII's kingdom
and Spain. Dispatched to Ludlow Castle, on the border of England and
Wales, to serve an apprenticeship for rule, Arthur and Catherine's married
life was brief, since the young prince of Wales died unexpectedly, perhaps
from a pulmonary or bronchial infection, on 2 April 1502. As custom
dictated, his widow did not attend Arthur's mourning rites in Ludlow
parish church, or his burial in Worcester Cathedral, but returned to
London with an uncertain fate ahead of her.[2] From then until Henry VII's
death, on 21 April 1509, Catherine remained in London, while cynical
negotiations took place between her former father-in-law and her own
father Ferdinand, who considered only their own perceived political

---

[1] Tarsicio de Azcona, *Isabel la Católica: Estudio crítico de su vida y su reinado*, 3rd edn (Madrid:
Biblioteca de Autores Cristianos, 1993), p. 647.
[2] On these events, see *Arthur Tudor, Prince of Wales: Life, Death and Commemoration*, ed.
Steven Gunn and Linda Monckton (Woodbridge: The Boydell Press, 2009).

interests.[3] Everything changed for her when Arthur's younger brother immediately chose her as his wife. The new King Henry VIII announced to the world that, in marrying Catherine, he was fulfilling a deathbed command from his father but, whatever his motive, he brushed aside all existing disputes with Spain over her future, and summoned her to Court. The wedding took place at Greenwich, in the Observant Franciscan church beside the palace, on 11 June 1509, and the couple were crowned together in Westminster Abbey, on Midsummer Day, 24 June.[4] There followed a period of nearly seven years during which Henry and Catherine seem to have been genuinely in love, indulging in lavish Court entertainments and co-operating in the formulation of policy in political and military matters, particularly the wars of 1513–14 against France and Scotland.[5] Yet a shadow hung over their idyll, in the form of a queen's fundamental duty to produce a male heir for her husband and the kingdom.

On 31 January 1510, during the extended honeymoon which followed her wedding, Catherine miscarried a daughter. This sad event was kept within the circle of her husband, her Spanish confessor, Friar Diego Fernández, and her personal servants and physicians. Confusingly, her belly remained swollen after the tragedy, perhaps as the result of an infection, and her doctor foolishly suggested that she had lost a twin and was still bearing the second baby. Amazingly, this belief continued to be held even after she began to menstruate once more, and Henry declared Shrove Tuesday (13 February) of that year to be a day of celebration before his wife went into confinement once again. On 24 February, the Court moved to Greenwich, and Catherine duly took to her chamber during the following month. After some agonizing days of waiting, the swelling of her belly went down, and it finally had to be admitted by all that there had been no pregnancy.[6]

The couple's efforts to conceive were, of course, undiminished by this disappointment, and on New Year's Day 1511, the Queen gave birth to the longed-for son, who was christened Henry, amid immense rejoicing. The joy was short-lived since, within eight weeks, on 22 February, the boy was dead, and questions were inevitably asked, at home and abroad, about the possibility of her ever producing a healthy heir. The situation was not helped when, in January 1515, Catherine gave birth, about one month prematurely, to a stillborn son. Yet such difficulties were common in the conditions of the period, and she and her husband did not give up

---

    [3] S. B. Chrimes, *Henry VII*, 2nd edn (New Haven CT and London: Yale University Press, [1972] 1999), pp. 282–1; Garrett Mattingly, *Catherine of Aragon*, 2nd edn (London: Readers Union, [1942] 1944), pp. 70–101.
    [4] J. J. Scarisbrick, *Henry VIII*, 2nd edn (New Haven, CT, and London: Yale University Press, [1968] 1997), pp. 12–13; David Starkey, *Six Wives: The Queens of Henry VIII* (London: Chatto & Windus, 2003), pp. 106–13.
    [5] Scarisbrick, *Henry VIII*, pp. 13–40; Starkey, *Six Wives*, pp. 114–54.
    [6] Starkey, *Six Wives*, pp. 115–20.

hope. Finally, on 18 February 1516, a living daughter, Mary, was born at Greenwich.[7]

The girl who turned out to be Henry and Catherine's only surviving child, and heir to the English Crown between 1516 and 1537, was apparently named Mary after the King's favourite sister, the dowager queen of France and now duchess of Suffolk, though the name hardly required explanation or justification in Catholic Europe. Despite the acute disappointment of both parents that she was not a boy, the baby princess received their ample love and devotion.[8] Yet Princess Mary was born into a world redolent with male prejudice against women, and an almost modern scale of external instruction and interference in childbirth and parenting. When she was older, Mary would suffer as much from these pressures as her mother had done.

The danger of low fertility or, worse still, sterility perhaps caused by inbreeding, loomed particularly over royal wives, and Catherine's difficulties in pregnancy fed powerful prejudices and fears, not least in her husband. Educated and upper-class households in early sixteenth-century Europe had at their disposal a collection of handbooks offering miscellaneous advice, both theoretical and anecdotal, on conception, pregnancy and birth, as well as the subsequent nurture of children. Inevitably, Catherine's gynaecological history, up to the birth of Mary in February 1516, and her child's survival beyond a matter of days or weeks, had forced her, Henry, their own subjects and interested foreigners to confront the fear of a permanent failure to conceive again. The prevailing view, in the texts then available, was that the primary blame for low fertility or sterility lay with the woman. Apart from any misogynistic influence, there were pragmatic reasons for holding this view in the conditions which prevailed in Europe at the time of Mary's birth. Given the state of medicine, it was very likely that a woman – particularly if, as in Catherine's case, she repeatedly became pregnant – would suffer from injury or infection. Intellectually and practically, it was impossible even for an educated and royal woman, such as Mary's mother, to escape the prevailing view that reproduction was essentially 'women's work', even though the biology of the period, still based largely on Aristotle, emphasized that, in the sexual act, the woman was merely the passive receptacle of the activity of the male. As a corollary, terms such as 'barrenness' or sterility were generally applied to women, but not to their husbands. This was a particularly dangerous situation for those who found themselves in such a case as Catherine's. Most medieval works on fertility had much more to say about women than about men, even though it was generally acknowledged, as a commonplace, that both parties must have some responsibility when things went wrong. The man was, of course, expected to provide the

[7] CSP Ven II, p. 555; Scarisbrick, Henry VIII, p. 27; Starkey, Six Wives, pp. 120–3, 164.
[8] David Loades, Mary Tudor: A Life (Oxford: Blackwell, 1989), p. 14; Starkey, Six Wives, p. 164.

sperm which would effectively fertilize the egg, but after that single action, the mother took over responsibility for the whole lengthy process of gestation and parturition. Thus, while it was recognized that the man might be sexually inadequate, there seemed to be far more chance of things going wrong once the woman had become pregnant. This placing of the burden of responsibility for the unborn child on the woman had two main results. Firstly, it had the effect of turning the feminine zone of gestation, birth and initial nurture into yet another area of female 'weakness' to add to the perceived problems of temperamental instability and the capacity of women to lead men 'astray'. Secondly, in practice this meant, and nowhere more so than in the case of royalty, that a husband with a wife who was perceived to be 'barren' might seek to replace her. Advice manuals might advocate practical measures to be taken, in a such a case, by the husband as well as the wife, but the fundamental blame was still placed inescapably on the woman.[9]

Women in late medieval and early modern Europe did not, of course, submit to this state of affairs without a fight. Studies of the situation in Italy, for example, reveal a bitter battle between 'professional' medicine, dominated by male university graduates, and 'traditional' healing and gynaecology, which were commonly practised by 'unqualified' women. In the Italian peninsula, as elsewhere in western Europe in the early sixteenth century, there was a perceived hierarchy of medical studies and skills, in which male physicians were at the top and 'cunning women' or healers at the bottom. The 'profession' was largely unregulated, and wealthy urban patients, in particular, were offered a wide range of choices of practitioners and procedures. If nursing at home, with the advice of friends and relatives, proved inadequate, help might be sought from a barber or apothecary, and if possible a medically qualified physician.[10] Yet, even in major cities, there was still a role for female practitioners of medical arts using traditional methods, not least in the area of gynaecology. The situation in England was no different, with the result that queens such as Catherine, having all possible resources granted to them in pregnancy and childbirth, could not escape the constraints of social and medical prejudice.

Indeed, no mothers were more carefully controlled and heavily instructed in these vital matters than queens in general, and English queens in particular. Given her own personal and marital history, and the continuing insecurity of the Tudor dynasty, it was inevitable that Catherine should have been under particularly strong pressure to produce an heir as soon as possible. No doubt out of personal devotion as well as in accordance with public expectation, Henry's first queen paid several visits to the 'Holy House

[9] Joan Cadden, *Meanings of Sex Difference in the Middle Ages: Medicine, Science and Culture* (Cambridge: Cambridge University Press, 1993), pp. 249–52.

[10] Katharine Park, 'Medicine and Magic: The Healing Arts', in *Gender and Society in Renaissance Italy*, ed. Judith C. Brown and Robert C. Davis (London and New York; Longman, 1998), pp. 129–49.

of Nazareth', at Walsingham in north Norfolk, where some of the breast-milk of the Virgin Mary was believed to be preserved, and where women prayed to have children, and gave thanks when they were born. In this respect she followed in the footsteps of Henry VI's queen, Margaret of Anjou, and Edward IV's consort, Elizabeth Woodville. In Catherine's time, the main guide to practice for royal births was still the fifteenth-century *R[o]yalle Book*, which had been drawn up in Edward IV's reign and further developed in Henry VII's time under the influence of Lady Margaret Beaufort. In contrast with other major incidents in a queen's life, confinement for childbirth was a primarily feminine activity, from which men were largely excluded. Once those who claimed to know, with male physicians tending to prevail, for better or worse, over the 'unlettered' wisdom of midwives, deemed that the birth was imminent, a chamber was furnished to which the mother would formally retire until she emerged, forty days after the birth, to be 'purified' or 'churched'. The *R[o]yalle Book* specified that this natal chamber should be carpeted throughout and its walls and ceiling hung with blue arras cloth, all the windows except one being similarly covered. The only decoration on these cloths was to be the fleur-de-lys, which symbolized both English royalty with its claim to the French Crown, and also the prime model of both queenship and mother-hood, the Virgin Mary herself. In the chamber were the main bed, for the Queen, and a pallet bed at its foot, the latter probably being used during the day and canopied like a throne. In addition, the room was equipped with two cradles. About a month before the birth was expected, the Queen would begin her preparations for 'confinement' by attending Mass, before entering the larger outer, or 'great' chamber, in the company of her privy household and other courtiers, including males. Here she would sit in a 'chair of estate' and be offered wine and spices, but all this would take place in the absence of her husband. The men and women who had been with her at Mass would now accompany her into the darkened inner chamber, where more prayers would be offered for her, before the men were finally shut out. Thereafter like women of all other social classes the queen would be surrounded by female relatives, friends and servants and, not without good reason, male physicians were kept away as far as possible, so as not to alarm the incipient mother unduly. Queens were provided with profes-sional midwives, while other women performed the normal tasks of male servants – as butlers, servers, and so on. This little feminine world would remain secret unless, as in Catherine's case on more than one occasion, medical problems made external intervention necessary, and stimulated the interest, and gossip, of courtiers and foreign ambassadors alike.[11] On 23 January 1516, Catherine's father Ferdinand died near Seville in southern Spain but, although solemn requiems were celebrated for him in England, she was not told, for fear of endangering the birth.

[11] J. L. Laynesmith, *The Last Medieval Queens: English Queenship, 1445–1503* (Oxford: Oxford University Press, 2004), pp. 110–14.

When Mary was born, on 18 February 1516, every effort seems to have been made to conceal the disappointment of parents and people that she was not male. Thus there were appropriate celebrations at Court and in the country. The rumours that had been more or less surreptitiously spreading, not least at the French Court, that Catherine could not bear children and would soon be put away by her husband, were temporarily laid to rest. Henry announced, to all who would listen, that he and his wife were still young and could produce more children, preferably sons, and in the meantime love, affection and pride were lavished on the infant princess. Two days after her birth, the baby was carried in solemn procession, in accordance with the rules in the *R[o]yalle Book*, to be baptized 'Mary' in the Observant Franciscan church at Greenwich, using the silver royal font which had been brought from Canterbury for the purpose. The ceremony was suitably magnificent. A canopy was carried by four knights, including the fathers of two future queens of England, Sir Thomas Parr and Sir Thomas Boleyn, while the child's godparents were Cardinal Thomas Wolsey, Princess Mary's great-aunt, Catherine Plantagenet, daughter of Edward IV, and the duchess of Norfolk. Following royal tradition, the sacrament of confirmation, making her fitted to receive Holy Communion, was administered to Mary immediately after her baptism, and her godmother, or sponsor, was Margaret Plantagenet, countess of Salisbury, widow of Sir Richard Pole and mother of the future Cardinal Reginald. Queen Catherine did not attend these ceremonies, instead, in accordance with royal etiquette, remaining in her 'inner chamber'. After confirmation, Mary was carried back in procession, preceded by her christening gifts, to be presented once more to her mother and returned to the royal nursery. There, the team responsible seem to have been chosen by Catherine, the crucial wet-nurse being Catherine Pole, granddaughter of Margaret, and the 'Lady Mistress' being Margaret Bryan, who was also strongly supported for that role by King Henry. The Queen remained in her chamber until her churching forty days later. This religious rite represented both thanksgiving for the birth of a child and ritual 'purification' of the mother, after the bloody business was over. Then, once the Queen had returned to her duties, and while the quest for a male heir continued, without success as it turned out, immediate attention turned to the upbringing of the infant princess.[12]

Mary remained at Court with her mother for the first few years, and her servants were paid by the treasurer of the chamber. In the larger palaces, she had her own miniature chamber, this being a small set of rooms which adjoined those of the Queen. There was an inner room, in which the princess slept in her normal cradle, and an outer room where she might 'receive' visitors in the larger, and more elaborate, cradle of estate, with a canopy and royal arms. The lady mistress, the laundress and

[12] BL Harleian MS 3504, fol. 232.

the chaplain were also provided with separate accommodation but, as the number of male servants attached to Mary's household increased, already totalling twenty-two by the time she was one year old, it became necessary to accommodate her separately from her parents when the Court occupied smaller houses. While Catherine and Henry resided at Windsor, for example, Mary was set up two miles away, at Ditton Park.[13] At the end of 1519, Wolsey carried out a full review of the organization and expenses of the royal household and, as a result, Mary's household was allocated an annual income of £1,100. In addition, Lady Bryan ceased to be the mistress of her household, and was replaced by the countess of Salisbury. The countess, as well as being a close friend of Queen Catherine, would be a strong influence on Mary in her formative years, not least in the area of education. At a very early age, Mary became accustomed to putting on public performances, for the Court and its visitors. On 23 February 1518, for instance, when she was just two years old, the little princess was brought into an audience, at Windsor, of the Venetian ambassador, Sebastiano Giustiniani. Before her delighted parents, her hand was kissed by Wolsey, Giustiniani and other lords, and the Venetian record notes that she then caught sight of the court organist, the Venetian Friar Dionisio Memo, and, by repeatedly crying 'Priest, priest!!', induced him to put on an impromptu performance.[14] In June 1520, when she had attained the age of four, Mary performed at another state visit, this time by a party of French gentlemen, who met her at Richmond Palace. They later reported that they had met the princess in the Presence Chamber, where she was accompanied by her governess, the countess of Salisbury, her godmother, the duchess of Norfolk, and other noble ladies. By this time Mary had become a keyboard player, and she entertained the company on the virginals and by apparently making a creditable effort to speak French.[15] Also, serious consideration was being given to the manner in which the girl who was still the heir to the throne should be tutored.

Her mother Catherine had been exceptionally well educated in Spain.[16] Her own mother, Isabella of Castile, had of course learned to read and write Spanish and, as she had a Portuguese mother, she was also extremely familiar with that language. Later in life, she added at least a partial knowledge of Latin to her 'feminine' arts of dancing and sewing.[17] Isabella was an accomplished musician, and in general there was a vibrant cultural life at the Castilian and Aragonese courts of Catherine's youth. Thus while the Catholic Monarchs' primary effort was to educate

[13] *LP* Addenda, I, i, p. 259; *LP* III, i, p. 970; *The Privy Purse expenses of Princess Mary, daughter of Henry VIII*, ed. F. Madden (London: William Pickering, 1831), p. xxii; *LP*, II, p. 1477.

[14] *LP* II, ii, 4326 (ii); *LP* III, iii, 1539–43; *CSP Ven* II, p. 434.

[15] *LP* III, i, 895–96, 970; *LP* VIII, 263.

[16] David Starkey (*Six Wives*, p. 17), strangely claims nonetheless that there were 'gaps' in Catherine's education.

[17] Mattingly, *Catherine of Aragon*, p. 15.

their male heir, Prince Juan, all the royal children, including Catherine, were given an academic education which included Latin, as well as, in the case of the girls, dancing, drawing, sewing and embroidery. Successively, Antonio and Alessandro Geraldini taught Isabella and Ferdinand's offspring to read Christian Latin literature, such as the works of Prudentius and Juventus, and earlier Church Fathers including Ambrose, Augustine, Gregory the Great and Jerome. The children were also taught about pagan Roman writers, such as the distinguished Spanish philosopher Seneca, as well as Roman history and civil and canon law.[18] The Spanish monarchs were major patrons of both ecclesiastical and secular music, and their involvement went well beyond employment and finance, both within and outside the Castilian and Aragonese royal chapels. Isabella made specific efforts to ensure that her offspring received the best possible musical education, in which the influence of the prevailing Franco-Flemish school was balanced by the deliberate fostering of native Spanish performers and composers. Thus one of the duties of Catherine's tutor and future chaplain, Alessandro Geraldini, was to teach music to the royal children, and they also received practical instruction from one of the leading composers of the period, Juan de Anchieta.[19] With this background, it is not surprising that Catherine should have taken a strong personal interest in her daughter's education, herself teaching Mary informally in her earliest years. It was in 1523, though, with Mary approaching the age of seven, that serious attention was paid to her future instruction. Already there was perceived to be a dilemma, since, as a woman, Mary would be expected to receive training only as a wife and mother, but she was still Henry VIII's sole heir, and hence could possibly become a sovereign ruler eventually, as her Spanish grandmother had done. In any case, given her own experience, Catherine naturally expected that her daughter should receive the full formal education that princes were customarily given. At a lower social level, she had before her the example of Sir Thomas More, who gave his three daughters a full classical education alongside their brother.[20]

To be the infant Mary's first tutor Catherine chose a friend of her personal physician, Fernando Vitoria. He was Thomas Linacre, who, with his Spanish colleague, had helped to found the Royal College of Physicians and was of course well able to help look after Mary's health as well as drawing up a plan for her studies. In 1524 he dedicated to her a basic grammar textbook, *Rudimenta grammatica*, which he had written specially, and which became popular outside the royal household. Linacre

[18] Ibid., pp. 15–16.

[19] Soterraña Aguirre Rincón, 'La música de la época de Isabel la Católica: la Casa Real como paradigma', in Julio Valdeón Baruque, ed., *Arte y cultura en la época de Isabel la Católica* (Valladolid: Ámbito Ediciones, 2003), pp. 281–321, at pp. 307–9.

[20] John Guy, *A Daughter's Love: Thomas and Margaret More* (London: Fourth Estate, 2008), pp. 59–65.

was elderly, though, by this time, and Catherine chose a compatriot of her own, Juan Luis Vives, to replace him as her daughter's director of studies. Vives was born in Valencia, probably in 1493, into a family of *conversos*, who were now Christian in religion although their ancestors had been Jewish. In 1508, he was at Valencia's grammar school (*gimnasio*), leaving the next year to study at the highly influential Collège de Montaigu, in Paris. He stayed in Paris, becoming a friend of the great French humanist and biblical scholar, Jacques Lefèvre d'Étaples. In 1514, Vives moved north to Bruges, where there was a large and well established Spanish community. He settled with one of the leading Valencian expatriate families there, the Valldaura, teaching three of their children and taking an active part in the city's flourishing intellectual life with various followers of Erasmus, such as Jean de Fevyn and François Cranevelt.[21] In 1517, probably on the recommendation of Erasmus, Vives became the tutor of Guillaume de Croy, a Burgundian aristocrat who, although then only nineteen years old, was already bishop of Cambrai and a cardinal. As a result of Charles of Ghent's accession to the Crown of Aragon in 1516 and of effective rule in Castile on his mother's behalf, Croy was designated archbishop of Toledo and primate of Spain in succession to the illustrious and formidable Cardinal Francisco Jiménez de Cisneros. His new post took Vives from Bruges to the university city of Leuven/Louvain, where he made a considerable impression, though he became involved in the bitter feuding between academic conservatives and humanists.[22] During his two years with Cardinal Croy, he produced many published works and then, in 1520, he seems to have met Thomas More for the first time, in the context of the meeting between Henry VIII and Charles V, which followed the 'Field of the Cloth of Gold'.

In January 1521, Bernardo Valldaura, patriarch of Vives's host family in Bruges, and young Guillaume de Croy died in the same week. Greatly depressed by these blows, Vives struggled to continue work on a commentary on Augustine of Hippo's *De civitate dei* ('City of God'), which he had taken over from Erasmus. Finally, in July 1521, the Spanish scholar completed the commentary, dedicating it to Henry VIII of England. As a result, herself needing a successor to Linacre and through the intercession of Thomas More, Catherine granted Vives a small pension, but his depression apparently grew during 1522 as a result of increasing conflict in Europe in general, and Spain in particular, where rebellion had affected both Castile (the *Comunidades*) and his native Valencia (the *Germania*). At last, on 5 April 1523, he dated his dedication, to Catherine, of a Latin tract entitled *Institutio foeminae christianae* ('Institution of a Christian woman'), which focused on the education of Princess Mary. Before he finished this work, Vives was offered a chair in the Arts faculty of Alcalá de Henares, the university which Cisneros had founded at the beginning of the

[21] Carlos Noreña, *Juan Luis Vives* (The Hague: Martinus Nijhoff, 1970), p. 54.
[22] Ibid., p. 57.

century. He set out for Spain, perhaps to take up this post, but arrived first in England, in May 1523, where Cardinal Wolsey offered him, instead, a lectureship, in Latin, Greek and rhetoric, at Corpus Christi College, Oxford.[23] Vives seems to have been a great success there and in October of that year he received a highly unusual personal visit from the King and Queen, who soon granted him a larger pension, and invited him to spend the following Christmas with them at Windsor castle.

In return for this royal support, Vives produced his first educational work, *De ratione studii puerilis* ('A plan of childish studies'), for Mary's use. He wrote the book with the help of Richard Fetherstone, a Cambridge don who no doubt hoped for advantage by collaborating. Its instructions for Mary would clearly influence an attentive and conscientious pupil. According to Vives and Fetherstone, she was to read the Gospels day and night, as well as the Acts of the Apostles and the Epistles and some passages from the Old Testament. She was also to read works by the Fathers of the Church, in particular Cyprian, Jerome, Ambrose, Augustine (the *City of God* but not the *Confessions*, which might have raised too many questions in a young mind), as well as by approved 'pagan' authors, such as Plato (the *Politics*), Seneca, Lucian, and selections from Horace, Valerius Maximus and Justin, the aim being to induce good living and not just good reading. Mary was also immersed in the works of Erasmus and Thomas More. Her tutors urged her to read 'histories' which included Christian doctrine and argument persuasive to belief. Vives's role was supervisory, and Mary was given two or three other girls from the nobility, who formed a 'class' with her. She and her friends were not, however, to be allowed to read 'pestiferous' romances of chivalry, which her male tutors, without a trace of irony or self-criticism, pronounced as corrupting of female morals. Vives's plan gave Mary rules for the pronunciation of Latin and Greek, the latter being an accomplishment highly unusual in England at that time, and particularly for a woman.[24]

He also put her, at least potentially, under a draconian regime of memorization, at an age when languages should have been comparatively easy to learn. She was asked to memorize her lessons and repeat them to herself several times, by reading, before going to bed. She was to concentrate on translation from Latin to English, using the best dictionaries available. Also in 1524, the *De institutione feminae christianae* ('Of the upbringing of a Christian woman') was printed and published by Michel Hillen in Antwerp. In addition, Vives provided Mary with a third work,

[23] Ibid., pp. 84–5.
[24] María Jesús Pérez Martín, *María Tudor: La gran reina desconocida* (Madrid: Ediciones Rialp, 2008), pp. 95–6. During Mary's infancy, her mother actively supported the introduction of Renaissance Greek studies in Oxford and Cambridge, particularly at Corpus Christi College, Oxford, where Vives lectured (James McConica, 'The rise of the undergraduate college', in *History of the University of Oxford*, iii, *The Collegiate University*, ed. McConica (Oxford: Clarendon Press, 1986), pp. 67–8).

the *Satellitum sive symbola* ('Satellite or symbols'), which consisted of improving proverbs and sayings in the manner so beloved of Renaissance scholars such as Erasmus. It was from this work that Mary acquired her personal motto, *Veritas temporis filia* (Truth, the daughter of time).[25]

Vives remained in London until January 1525, since Oxford University was not functioning because of disease. In April he was granted royal licences to export grain and import wine and wool, and these enabled him, with the help of the Valldaura in Bruges, to become self-supporting and to abandon his teaching post at Oxford. He stayed for a week with Thomas More, and then, having heard that his wife and his mother-in-law were both ill, returned to Bruges, where he remained until February 1526. By this time, though, English foreign policy had been reorientated away from Charles V and towards Francis I of France. As a compatriot and adviser of Catherine, the Valencian humanist was no longer *persona grata* at Court, and Wolsey had him formally removed from his Oxford lecture-ship. Nevertheless, Vives continued to oscillate between Bruges and England, providing some comfort to Catherine during the beginnings of her resistance to divorce and, from October 1527, teaching Latin to Princess Mary. At this time, the Queen urged Vives to settle in London, and wrote to invite his wife over as well, but he resisted such blandishments because he was now coming under increasing pressure from agents of Henry VIII. He felt that he was under surveillance, and in February 1528 Wolsey questioned him about his private conversations with Catherine. Vives agreed to answer on the basis that he had nothing to hide.[26] Nevertheless, he took the precaution of asking Charles V's ambassador in London, Iñigo de Mendoza, to inform Pope Clement VII of Catherine's difficulties. For this, both Vives and Mendoza were put under house arrest, from 25 February to 1 April 1528. At about this time, Vives was asked to produce a scholarly tract on the rights and wrongs of Henry's proposed remarriage, in which he reasonably pointed out that a second marriage might not produce a son either. Although this document was apparently suppressed, Vives was released from house arrest, for fear of reprisals from Charles V, and by 7 April he was back in Bruges, being surprised to learn that the English King would continue to pay his existing pension.[27] In October 1528, the Valencian humanist returned to England, in order to advise the Queen during her legatine trial, in which he urged her to take no part. Vives left England for the last time in November 1528, now losing his pension, and spent the rest of his life in poverty, ill health and despair, dying in Bruges in 1540.[28] To add to all his problems in England, Catherine's educational adviser was indeed a *converso*, and, during the period of his involvement with her and her daughter, his family in

---

[25] Pérez Martín, *María Tudor*, pp. 95–9.
[26] Noreña, *Vives*, p. 103.
[27] Ibid., pp. 103–4.
[28] Ibid., pp. 103–18.

Valencia was in very serious trouble with the Inquisition, on account of his relatives' supposed 'Judaizing'.[29]

In recent years, Juan Luis Vives has been recognized as one of the major contributors to the theory and practice of the education of women in Renaissance Europe on the basis of the works he produced for Catherine and Mary, in particular *De institutione feminae christianae* (1524). By 1600, this text had appeared in French, German, Dutch, Spanish and Italian, in addition to Richard Hyrde's English version, which was published in 1529. Hyrde's translation was reprinted several times in the sixteenth century, but largely dropped out of scholarly knowledge thereafter, until the second half of the twentieth century.[30] Inevitably, it is a matter of debate, in the context of this wide-ranging treatise, to what extent Vives adjusted himself to the practical probability, at the the time of its composition, that Mary would eventually become the reigning sovereign of England, and not just a queen consort. He never regarded women as the intellectual equals of men, and assumed that, being weak-minded, they would automatically be led astray by 'unsuitable' literature. Nevertheless, Vives believed that a good education for women would not subvert the social order, and that fathers of daughters, including Henry VIII, had nothing to fear from letting them have it. Such instruction would fit women for their proper role as hand-maidens of God and man.[31] Since his own family had suffered so much at the hands of the Inquisition, which was in part her creation, Vives could not have avoided being aware of the reality of the late Queen Isabella of Castile as a powerful executive ruler in his homeland, and during his time in the Netherlands he could observe Margaret of Austria in a similar role, though as regent. In the *De institutione*, though, he sets out rules for moral conduct which would be beneficial to society, but severely restrict the options of a princess and queen. Commenting explicitly on Sir Thomas More's earlier *Instruction of a Christian Woman*, Vives indicates that, while More saw learning as opening up the spiritual world to his daughters and to other women, the Spaniard saw it as a better way of preserving a woman's chastity, which was her most precious possession. Nevertheless, by the very act of detailing the education which Catherine's daughter should receive, Vives could not avoid going well beyond the restrictive rules of conduct which he purported to set down. In this sense, *De institutione* did at least open up the possibility of female learning in a way unusual for the period. The primary purpose of this education, though, was always better behaviour and the avoidance of sin. Any learning beyond what was needed for this purpose was redundant, and educated wives should be as silent before their husbands as their less learned sisters. Thus he distinguishes

[29] Angelina Garcia, *Els Vives: Una familia de jueus valencians* (Valencia: Eliseu Climent, Editor, 1987), p. 13.

[30] Ruth Kelso, *Doctrine for the Lady of the Renaissance* (Urbana, IL: University of Illinois Press, 1956), pp. 71–2.

[31] On this see, for example, Loades, *Mary Tudor*, pp. 31–2, and Starkey, *Six Wives*, p. 176.

clearly between the education that should be given to a boy and what should be taught to a girl:

> Though the preceptes for men be innumerable, women yet may be enformed with fewe wordes. For men must be occupied bothe at home and for the abrode, both in theyr owne matters and for the common weale. Therfore it cannot be declared in few bokes but in many and longe, how they shall handle them selfe in so many and divers thynges. As for a woman hathe no charge to se to, but her honestye and chastity. Wherefore, when she is infourmed of that, she is sufficiently appoynted.

Vives's educational system, as set out here for men as well as women, would breed conformists and put no value on independent reasoning and moral decision-making. For him, it is better not to give people a choice in matters of virtue or vice as the good will always choose the former, and the bad the latter. As an author, he requires his arguments to be accepted without question, and offers no analysis of moral and social problems, which might have allowed the reader to work out his or her own conclusions. Nevertheless, his book would have been of no use to Catherine and Mary, or to any other woman, if he did not at least allow that women were, in principle, capable of self-control.

Vives thus regarded reading and learning as a school for strengthening and enforcing good moral precepts:

> She that hath lerned in bokes to caste this and other such thinges, and hath furnyshed and fensed her mynde with holy counsayles, shal never fynd to do any vylany. For if she can fynd in her harte to do naughtyly, hauying so many preceptes of vertue to kepe her, what shulde we suppose she shuld do, hauying no knowleg of goodnes at all? And truly if we wold call the olde world to remembrance, and reherse their tyme, we shall fynde no lerned woman that euer was yll, where I coulde brynge forth an hundred good.

This argument suggests that women did in fact have a certain moral autonomy, and this is a paradox in Vives's argument. For while he sets out, in his treatise, the achievements of various distinguished women of the Classical period, his overall argument seems to discourage the women of his own day from following their example, on the somewhat feeble grounds that the modern woman 'nedeth it nat' (moral and practical independence, that is). Revealingly, Vives justified his low valuation of female intelligence by reference to that staple of misogynist argument throughout the Middle Ages, the 'Fall' of humankind according to the biblical account in Genesis chapter 3:

> For Adam was the fyrste made, and after Eue, and Adame was not betrayed, the woman was betrayed in to the breche of the commandement. Therfore bycause a woman is a frayle thinge, and of weake

discretion, and may lightly be disceyued, whiche thinge our fyrste mother Eue sheweth, whome the dyuell lyght argument.

Such would be Mary's ambiguous heritage when she came to reign.[32] In the meantime, if she followed diligently, as she appears to have done, Vives's instructions on syllabus in his *De ratione*, she would have learned how to read, and speak, Latin and Greek, getting some passages by heart, and have read and absorbed both the New Testament and Classical proverbs and adages, as well as some contemporary popular literature, such as the edifying tale, in terms of his own educational aims for women, of 'patient Griselda'.[33] Testimony to her ability and hard work, particularly in mastering Latin, is offered by Henry Parker, Lord Morley, in a prologue to his own translation into English, with a commentary, of the traditional Marian devotion, the *Angelus* (derived from Luke 1: 26–38). In it he says that already, in 1528, at the age of twelve, she was 'so rype in the Laten tongue, that rathe[r] dothe happen to the women sex, that youre grace not only coulde perfectly reide, wright and constrewe laten, but farthermore trans-late eny harde thinge of the laten in to ouer Englysshe tonge'.[34]

The solemn and high-minded instructions of Vives and his colleagues were not entirely followed, however. Catherine, as the daughter of a Trastamaran Court in Spain full of dances, music and revels, and like her mother Isabella a lover of rich clothes and massively applied jewellery, evidently believed that Mary would not be a proper princess unless she actively indulged in such things. Whatever Vives's anxiety to preserve her chastity against the seductions of chivalric romances and alluring songs, Henry's eldest child was a fine player of the lute and keyboard instru-ments. The King, as an accomplished musician himself, seems to have approved of all this, at least until Anne Boleyn came on to the scene, but Mary's Spanish tutor was not the only one to worry about the corrupting effect of music at Court. In *The boke named the governour*, produced at this time, Sir Thomas Elyot warned even men to be careful with music. It 'serveth fo[r] recreation after tedious or laborious affairs', and is 'necessary for the better attaining the knowledge of a public weal [good]', but it should not produce too much 'delectation' and thus distract from more important activities. The Roman emperor Nero is offered as an awful warning of the consequences, if this advice is not taken.[35] In view of all

---

[32] Pamela Joseph Benson, 'The new ideal in England: Thomas More, Juan Luis Vives and Richard Hyrde', in Pamela Joseph Benson, *The Invention of the Renaissance Woman: The Challenge of Female Independence in the Literature and Thought of Italy and England* (University Park, PA: Pennsylvania State University Press, 1992), pp. 157–81, at pp. 172–81.

[33] Starkey, *Six Wives*, pp. 177–8.

[34] BL Royal MS 16.C, fols 2r–v.

[35] Sir Thomas Elyote, *The book named the Governor*, ed. S. E. Lehmberg (London: Dent, 1962), pp. 22–3; Hyun-Ah Kim, *Humanism and the Reform of Sacred Music in Early Modern England: John Merbecke the Orator and* The Booke of Common Praier *noted* (Aldershot: Ashgate, 2008), pp. 101–2.

this high moral sentiment, full of the fear and anxiety which so often surround the bringing up of children, it is perhaps a relief to learn that Mary and her childhood friends were able to watch plays written especially for them by one of the finest poets, dramatists and musicians of the day, John Heywood. These childish 'interludes', which unfortunately do not survive in writing, apparently had titles such as *Morris Dancers, Carillons [sic] of Hobby Horses* and *Lord of Misrule*. They were acted by companies of children, directed by Heywood himself, and were accompanied by other charades and spectacles, including mock battles and sung ballets, which seem to be the ancestors of opera. The fun often culminated in a firework display.[36] In her childhood years, though, Mary had an essential duty to perform as a royal heir: to find herself, or rather to be found, a husband.

It was not long before the infant princess became a pawn in the European dynastic game, and she was first linked with the dauphin, Francis, eldest son of Francis I of France. During the first few years of Henry's reign, English policy towards the 'superpower' of the period had oscillated frequently. In October 1518, when Mary was just two years old, England and France, with the active involvement of Cardinal Wolsey, were attempting to draw up a treaty which would commit all the major powers of Europe to settling their disputes by means of diplomacy rather than war. As a part of this doomed scheme, on 4 October the two countries signed a treaty that restored Tournai, which had been Henry's proud conquest of 1513, to Francis, and also arranged a marriage between Mary and the Dauphin, who was even younger than his betrothed. On 5 October, in Catherine's chamber at Greenwich Palace, a French representative, Admiral Bonnivet, was indeed 'betrothed' to Mary on the Dauphin's behalf.[37] Despite the solemnity of such occasions, though, the ties which they represented were frequently provisional and subject to change as a result of political considerations. Mary's French 'marriage' was no exception, and her second betrothal resulted from Wolsey and Henry's efforts, in the early 1520s, to shore up the 1518 treaty of London.

By the end of 1520, relations between France and the new emperor, Charles V, had deteriorated considerably. In these circumstances, Charles began to seek a marriage with Mary of England, even though she was sixteen years his junior, which meant that cohabitation would have to be delayed for another eight years. Henry rightly feared that Charles would not wait that long, but seek a bride who was closer to his own age.[38] Despite these well-founded doubts, Henry saw the possibility of extracting a good financial settlement from Charles, given that Mary was his sole heir at this time.[39] There was, however, an older rival, Princess Isabel of

[36] *LP* III no. 2585; Pérez Martín, *María Tudor*, pp. 85–86.
[37] *LP* II, no. 4480; Scarisbrick, *Henry VIII*, pp. 72–3; Loades, *Mary Tudor*, p. 16.
[38] *LP* III, p. 1150.
[39] *LP* III, p. 1162.

Portugal, whose dowry of about £200,000 was around four times the amount that the English were offering with Mary. Henry and his agents argued that the English princess was worth at least as much as Isabel, because of the succession to the throne, and that it was more useful for Charles to ally in this way with England than with Portugal, given the overall European situation, but the French soon heard of these discussions and worked to preserve Mary's tie to the Dauphin. Not wishing to push England, the empire and Spain together, Francis objected only mildly to the Imperial plan, but diplomatic manoeuvres continued nevertheless. By July 1521, Pope Leo X had moved decisively to the Imperial side, this being crucial to any plan for Charles and Mary to marry, since they would inevitably require a papal dispensation because of consanguinity through Catherine. Thus on 29 July Wolsey started negotiations with Charles's officials and a treaty was concluded on 14 September. In addition to setting up a military alliance in case of future conflict with France, the treaty established that Mary would be betrothed to Charles with a dowry of £80,000, provided that, at the time of the marriage, she was still heir to the English throne, and £120,000 if a prince had been born to Henry and Catherine in the meantime. It was secretly stipulated, though, that the extra money would not necessarily be insisted upon in such circumstances, and, indeed, the treaty ('of Bruges') was not published.

The text of this treaty also provided that the Emperor should visit England, and he duly did so, landing at Dover on 26 May 1522 and remaining in England until 6 July. On 2 June, in the midst of lavish festivities, Charles was entertained at Greenwich by the Queen and Princess Mary. The six-year old danced for the Emperor, and his kindness towards her would be engraved on her memory. The age gap between the two could not be bridged, though, and Wolsey next came up with a plan for Mary to marry the nine-year-old James V of Scotland, whose mother was her aunt, Henry's sister Margaret. After many political and military manoeuvres, on 18 November 1524 Scottish negotiators arrived in London to make peace and agree the marriage. Although it would have meant that the Scottish king would, under current circumstances, sit on the English throne, it was increasingly realized that Charles was unlikely to fulfil his marriage agreement, while, in March 1525, the French began once again, with some hope, to pursue the tie with the Dauphin. Thus, at the age of nine, Mary once again became a pawn in an elaborate diplomatic game involving the main western European powers. It was hard to see any advantage for England in her deployment in this way, and her personal role in the proceedings was inevitably confined to occasional dancing and musical performances for foreign visitors. It is likely, as Loades argues, that she acquired early on a strong sense of her own royal dignity.[40]

---

[40] Scarisbrick, *Henry VIII*, pp. 126, 137–40; Loades, *Mary Tudor*, pp. 20–6; Starkey, *Six Wives*, pp. 179–83.

Meanwhile, the 'love' to whom she would later return emotionally, Charles V, was about to marry another.

From his birth, at Ghent in 1500, Charles had been promised, at various times, to several princesses. In accordance with the original preference of his father, Philip 'the Handsome', and his favourite, Guillaume de Chièvres, the first aim was to seek an alliance with France, but the resentment caused by Charles's election as Holy Roman Emperor made any agreement impossible. Nevertheless, at one time or another, his name was associated with Louis XI's daughter, Claude de France who would eventually marry Francis I, and Claude's sister Renée, as well as the latter's infant daughter Louise. Bad relations with France in the early 1520s increased the attraction of Mary as a future wife, distant as that future might be, but a continuation of the historic Trastamaran ties with Portugal also asserted itself as a possibility, and by November 1525 there was considerable support in Spain for a marriage between Charles and Isabel of Portugal, daughter of King Manuel. The Castilian cortes of Toledo, in 1526, petitioned the King to choose Isabel, or else her younger sister, and by this time Charles had come to the conclusion that it would be safer to marry within Iberia than risk a dynastic tie with England or France. An additional attraction was that Isabel could, and did, act as regent for Charles in his Spanish kingdoms while he spent time in other Habsburg territories, and this was something of which Mary would not be capable for some years. Unsurprisingly, therefore, the marriage with Isabel was duly agreed, and the wedding took place in Seville, in March 1526.[41] Mary's first serious matrimonial foray was over.

---

[41] Mónica Gómez-Salvago Sánchez, *Fastos de una boda real en la Sevilla del Quinientos (Estudio y documents)* (Seville: Universidad de Sevilla, 1998), pp. 22–36.

Chapter 2

A DYSFUNCTIONAL FAMILY, 1525–1536

In her teenage years, Mary continued to be the recipient of other people's actions, rather than taking initiatives of her own. Charles V's abandonment of Mary, and his subsequent marriage to Princess Isabel of Portugal, had considerable consequences beyond Iberia and the other Habsburg lands. The Emperor seems finally to have decided to make the change in 1525, when Henry VIII failed to provide him with military help against France. In the fluid political situation which then existed, it seemed unwise for Charles to tie himself by marriage either to England or to France, since whichever royal house was not chosen would be bound to seek revenge. Spanish documents indicate that, in order to extract himself from his betrothal to Princess Mary, Charles relied on her father's meanness. In a letter from Valladolid in Old Castile, dated 7 May 1525, Martín de Salinas told the Emperor that Commander (*Comendador*) Pedrosa had been sent to England to ask for funds to assist the war effort against the French.[1] Salinas wryly commented that, '[As for] the king of England, your Highness knows, and knows well, that he will not give a penny'.[2] In an earlier letter, dated 3 April 1525, Salinas indicates that, by then, Charles had already sent an envoy to Portugal to negotiate his marriage with Isabel. Spanish cynicism proved to be wholly justified when Henry VIII failed to hand over his agreed dowry payment on Mary's behalf. As a result, Charles's negotiations with the Portuguese continued purposefully, though they were delayed both by the consequences of Francis I of France's defeat at Pavia earlier in the year and by his subsequent captivity in Madrid, as well as by a dispute between Spain and Portugal over the Spice Islands ('Las Molucas').[3] The nine-year-old Princess Mary was thus 'jilted' for the first time, but would soon receive some degree of compensation from her father, even though she was hardly in a position to appreciate it.

Given that, in the summer of 1525, Henry still had no legitimate son, his wife Catherine was extremely unlikely to conceive again, and his only child, Mary, was at least temporarily out of the dynastic marriage stakes,

---

[1] Gómez-Salvago, *Fastos*, pp. 26–7.

[2] A. Rodríguez Villa, *El emperador Carlos V y su corte según las cartas de don Martín de Salinas, embajador del infante don Fernando (1522–1539)* (Madrid: Real Academia de la Historia, 1903), p. 278. Gómez-Salvago, *Fastos*, p. 27n ['El Rey de Inglaterra, V[uestra] A[lteza] sabe y conoce como no dará un real'].

[3] Gómez-Salvago, *Fastos*, p. 28.

he could choose between three options. He might accept his daughter as his heir, together with her future husband, who might be a foreign prince or else a potentially troublesome English subject, who would probably excite envy and even rebellion among the aristocracy. Alternatively, he might recognize Henry Fitzroy, his six-year-old illegitimate son by Elizabeth Blount, as heir to the throne, or, thirdly, he might take the most radical option, which was to repudiate Catherine and marry again in the hope of producing the longed-for male heir. Henry did not imagine, in the summer of 1525, that his daughter had definitively lost her chance of marriage with a leading European royal house, and the result of his ponderings was a typical compromise or 'fudge', which kept all his options open. On 18 June he made Henry Fitzroy, duke of Richmond and earl of Nottingham, with symbolic governmental responsibility in the north of England as titular Lieutenant. This move naturally infuriated his wife Catherine but at the same time he despatched Mary to exercise a similar 'office' in Wales and the Marches.[4]

Ostensibly, Henry took this action, which no doubt corresponded to the desires of his chief minister, Cardinal Wolsey,

> . . . forasmuch as by reason of the longe absence of any Prince making continued residence either in the Principalitie of Wales or in the marches of the same, the good order, quiet and tranquilitie of the countrys therabout hath greatly been altered and subverted, and the due administration of Justice by means of sundry contrarieties hitherto hindered and neglected.[5]

Thus Mary was sent initially to the Welsh Marches, as her mother's first husband had been in 1501, but, although she was quite commonly referred to thereafter as 'princess of Wales', she never received that legal title and, in his manoeuvres of June 1525, her father conspicuously failed to make any official pronouncement on the succession to the throne, either by his own prerogative or through parliament. This problem was left for the future as, in August of that year, Mary, accompanied by a large household, although it was not as large as that which went north with Henry Fitzroy, headed initially for the former seat of the late duke of Buckingham, at Thornbury in Gloucestershire. As far as much of the English, and no doubt the Welsh, population was concerned, Mary was now to be regarded as Henry's heir, though she had also been neatly separated from her mother at a time of growing tension in the royal marriage. This situation was useful also to Wolsey as, after the deterioration of relations with the Habsburgs, it appeared that Mary might be used as a diplomatic counter in a manner of which her mother would very much disapprove.[6]

---

[4] Loades, *Mary Tudor*, p. 37.
[5] BL Cotton MS Vitellius, C. 2, fol. 23; Loades, *Mary Tudor*, p. 36.
[6] Loades, *Mary Tudor*, pp. 37–9.

Margaret Pole, countess of Salisbury, was recalled to Court to become mistress of Mary's Welsh household after having briefly lost the king's favour at the time of the execution of the duke of Buckingham in 1521, for supposed treason, while Edward Sutton, Lord Dudley became chamberlain, and Walter Devereux, Lord Ferrers, was appointed steward. The ladies and gentlemen of the princess's entourage were provided with over ninety servants, and the whole household amounted to more than 160. At the same time, this being the main purpose of the enterprise, the Council of Wales and the Marches was re-formed, with Bishop John Veysey of Exeter as its president, or chancellor, and consisting in addition of six learned legal counsel and a secretary, who were assisted by a herald, a poursuivant, two sergeants-at-arms and over forty servants. In practice, there was no rigid distinction between the Princess's household and the Welsh Council, the whole body consisting initially, in July 1525, of just over 300 people, whose wages amounted to the considerable sum of £741 per annum.[7] Given the fact that only a few of the household members were previously known to her, notably the countess of Salisbury and her former chamberlain and governess, Sir Philip and Lady Jane Calthorpe, the experience must have been disorientating for a nine-year-old child, but such were the demands made of sixteenth-century royalty. Probably no more than a dozen of Mary's seventy-five chamber staff would have had familiar faces, but it no doubt helped that her now restored governess, Margaret Pole, brought a number of relatives, such as her granddaughter Catherine Pole and her daughter-in-law Constance Pole, as well as other sympathizers, into the princess's household.[8] Her schoolmaster in the Marches, Dr Robert Fetherstone, had been involved in her education previously. The primary purpose of Mary's expedition towards Wales was to assert English power, and about a quarter of her Ludlow household was Welsh or at least from the Marches, including the steward, the treasurer, the vice-chamberlain and the master of the horse.[9] Little is known about Mary's life during her two and a half years in the Welsh Marches, though Margaret Pole seems to have closely supervised her education, as a trusted deputy for Queen Catherine. On the King's orders, the Princess continued to study Latin, French and music, as well as benefiting from plenty of fresh air.[10] In the Marches, Mary's main base was at Ludlow castle, which had been expensively rebuilt for the purpose, after having scarcely been

[7] BL Cotton MS Vitellius, C. 2, fol. 123; Loades, *Mary Tudor*, p. 40.

[8] Loades, *Mary Tudor*, p. 40; Hazel Pierce, *Margaret Pole, Countess of Salisbury, 1473–1541: Loyalty, Lineage and Leadership* (Cardiff: University of Wales Press, 2003), pp. 42–4, 59.

[9] Maria Dowling, *Humanism in the Age of Henry VIII* (London: Croom Helm, 1987), p. 227; Loades, *Mary Tudor*, p. 41.

[10] BL Cotton MS Vitellius C. 2, fol. 123; BL Royal MS 17.C, xii, xii; BL Add. MS 17012; Dowling, *Humanism*, p. 228 & n; Loades, *Mary Tudor*, p. 42; W. R. B. Robinson, 'Princess Mary's Itinerary in the Marches of Wales, 1525–1527', *Historical Research*, lxxi (1998), pp. 233–52.

touched since Arthur's death in 1502, though she also lived at Thornbury (Gloucestershire) and Tickenhill (Worcestershire), which had both belonged to the late duke of Buckingham, as well as at Hartlebury castle in Worcestershire. She was also taken on what amounted to a royal progress to Coventry, and in September 1526 travelled to Langley, Oxfordshire, via Tewkesbury, to meet her father. After this, the two travelled together to Ampthill in Bedfordshire, via Bicester and Buckingham, before Mary left for the Marches once more, on 1 October.[11]

The meaning of Mary's Welsh episode, and of Henry's purpose in bringing it about, has been variously interpreted. The manoeuvre has been seen as the King's 'shrewdest blow' against his wife, since it separated Catherine from her child for the first time, as indeed it separated her from her husband for the longest period to date.[12] On the positive side, in the Marches Mary had, at a very young age, a miniature Court, which the Welsh council made into a government in miniature as well. Her councillors were generally of higher rank than those of Henry Fitzroy in the north, and she was effectively 'prince' of Wales though, as has been stated, her status was never legally defined. Although she was commonly referred to as 'princess', 'princess of Wales' or 'prince of Wales', she was never formally invested with the principality, presumably because this would have confirmed her position as heir to the throne. In any case, the ten-year-old Mary returned to the royal Court in London in September 1526, accompanied by a large and impressive retinue, and by the following year Henry seems to have abandoned his project of regional governments. Nevertheless, the Council of the Marches, exploiting the earlier departure from the scene of the two leading Welsh magnates – first Edward Stafford, duke of Buckingham and then Rhys ap Gruffydd, executed for treason in 1521 and 1531 respectively – continued into the 1530s with great effect, in Mary's name, under the chairmanship of Rowland Lee, bishop of Lichfield and Coventry.[13] During this period, Henry and Catherine's only child was entered once more in the European marriage stakes.

As a consequence of the warming of relations between England and France after Charles V's Portuguese marriage, in the autumn of 1526 negotiations over Mary's future began between the two hereditary enemies. By April 1527, she had been summoned back from the Welsh Marches, and on the 23rd of that month, St George's Day, she was shown to French ambassadors at Greenwich Palace. Under canon law and the contemporary law of nations, Mary, now aged eleven, was only a year away from cohabitation with a husband, but the Frenchmen recorded their concern that she was physically unready, something which had

---

[11] Loades, *Mary Tudor*, pp. 42–6.

[12] Mattingly, *Catherine of Aragon*, p. 189.

[13] Richard Rex, *The Tudors* (Stroud: Tempus, 2002), p. 68; John Guy, *Tudor England* (Oxford: Oxford University Press, 1988), p. 174; Starkey, *Six Wives*, pp. 200–2; Loades, *Mary Tudor*, pp. 22–3; *LP* IV, 1557.

already been noticed, of course, by those who surrounded her on a regular basis.[14] By then, the political situation of western Europe had been transformed by the return of Francis I to his kingdom, from captivity in Madrid, on 17 March 1526. In May, Wolsey gave enthusiastic support to the establishment of the League of Cognac. This supposedly united France, the Papacy, Venice, Milan and Florence, though not England, against Charles V, with the proclaimed purpose of forcing him to fulfil the terms of the treaty of Madrid, which had resulted from the Habsburg victory and the capture of Francis at Pavia, in 1525. In particular, the aim was to secure the release of the two French princes, the dauphin François and Henri, duke of Orléans, who had been kept in Madrid as hostages. As part of the English rapprochement with France, Wolsey revived the plans of early 1522, which had been abandoned when Henry formed an alliance with Charles. Thus it was proposed that Mary should marry Henri of Orléans, who was three years younger than her and would therefore offer time for her further physical development. By early July, Bishop John Clerk of Bath and Wells had been sent to France to begin negotiations. Two months later, Henry was offering to join the League of Cognac and even, extraordinarily, given his previous perception of himself as another Henry V, to renounce his claim to the Crown of France, if Francis paid him a pension (known in England as a 'tribute'), ceded Boulogne to England, and agreed to a French marriage for Mary, possibly to himself rather than to one of his sons. The first of these marriage proposals would have seemed somewhat grotesque to most, given that Francis was only two years younger than Henry and, although an eligible widower since 1524, was also a notorious philanderer. Despite these caveats, the lawyers hammered out the contents of a possible treaty to this effect, according to which, if Francis died before Henry VIII, with children by Mary, England would still remain autonomous. This was a vital factor for the English, as was generally recognized in Europe, since the French King already had two sons to succeed him, who might thus become kings of England at some future date. Realistically, both sides knew that, even if the French King outlived his English counterpart, his reign in England would be short. Francis himself hesitated when confronted with the marriage proposal, thinking it might be no more than an English ploy to regain Boulogne, but in November 1526 Bishop Clerk reported that he was enthusiastic. In fact, this marriage had by now become Henry's main aim, so that in December he announced that he was prepared to drop the demand for Boulogne, and well-informed people in France thought that such a marriage was likely. Francis was, however, still under a treaty obligation to marry Charles V's sister Leonor, the widowed queen of Portugal, yet despite this negotiations with England continued into 1527.

But after the French had seen Mary at Greenwich, in April of that year, they readily agreed with Wolsey that she would not be sent to France for

[14] Loades, *Mary Tudor*, pp. 45–6.

marriage until she was of 'full age'.[15] On 30 April 1527, an agreement was duly signed for an Anglo-French marriage, though the identity of Mary's future husband was not specified, the most likely candidate being Henri of Orléans, who would reside in England after the wedding. This agreement, signed in London, led to the treaty of Amiens of 18 August 1527, in which, once again, it was not stated whether Mary should marry Henri or his father. If Mary was betrothed to Henri of Orléans in 1527, either she would live, in which case England would have a French king, or else she would die young, and James V of Scotland would become king through the right of his mother, Henry VIII's sister Margaret.[16] In 1527, Henry's thought seems to have been that if Charles V started a new war against France, Mary would be married off to Francis himself, while, if he did not, she would marry Henri.[17] By this time, much darker clouds were appearing over Mary.

Henry had begun to have doubts about the validity of his marriage with Catherine as early as 1514. At the time of his own sister Mary's brief marriage to Louis XII of France, it was rumoured in French Court circles, and in the Rome of Pope Leo X Medici that Henry meant to repudiate Catherine on the grounds that she was supposedly unable to bear children. Instead, like his sister, he would marry in France, a likely candidate being a daughter of Duke Charles III of Bourbon. The documentary basis for this notion was formerly believed to be an entry in an index to the Vatican Secret Archive (ASV), in which Leo X appeared to refer to the 'nullity' of Henry and Catherine's marriage, but it now seems that this supposed entry note was erroneous, even though it remarkably foretold subsequent events.[18] The pressure on Catherine to produce an heir was, of course, partially reduced when she gave birth to Mary in February 1516, since at this stage her husband still declared himself to be confident of eventually having a son, but by 1520 it seemed obvious to observers that this was exceedingly unlikely to happen. At the deepest psychological level, as conditioned by the social and political values of the time, Henry seems scarcely to have regarded his daughter as his child, despite his continuing intermittent tenderness towards her, and this factor may well have contributed to his paradoxical treatment of his legitimate daughter and his illegitimate son in 1525. By 1527, though, it seems undeniable that a new woman, Anne Boleyn, had come into his life.[19] Henry now perceived himself as being in some kind of dynastic emergency. In his mid-thirties, he was still in his prime, but his wife could bear him no more children and his daughter had been jilted by the most eligible royal bachelor in Europe. As the notion of Mary eventually exercising sovereign power in England in her own, even sole, right seemed inconceivable,

[15] *CSP Ven* III, p. 1406; Loades, *Mary Tudor*, pp. 46–8.
[16] Loades, *Mary Tudor*, pp. 49–51.
[17] Scarisbrick, *Henry VIII*, p. 145.
[18] *CSP Ven* II, p. 188; Starkey, *Six Wives*, pp. 152–3.
[19] Starkey, *Six Wives*, pp. 197–8.

the prospect facing the kingdom was an unpalatable choice between foreign domination if she married a prince from abroad, and a repetition of the Wars of the Roses, but with improved military technology if her husband was an English aristocrat.[20] Thus by the time that Henry's desire to end his marriage with Catherine began to be known, in the first part of 1527, he had been concerned for some years that his only heir was Mary. Now, though, he doubted, in addition, whether he had been properly married to Catherine in the first place. In his mind, theological scruples now added to the pressures of European diplomacy besides the over-riding need to preserve the Tudor dynasty.[21]

Given the vast importance of the events which followed, not only for the lives of the couple themselves and their daughter, but also for English and international history, considerable attention has to be given to the legal and theological argument which underlay the case, as well as to the personal and political events themselves. If he and the Queen had indeed been married unlawfully, this would explain, in Henry's eyes, why Catherine had suffered a series of miscarriages, and failed to produce a son. God was punishing them, and He was doing so because they had defied His law, as set out in the five 'books of Moses', in Hebrew, the Torah. In particular, the Book of Leviticus sets out, in chapter 18, a list of sexual prohibitions ordained by God on Mount Sinai. It begins with the general pronouncement that 'None of you shall approach anyone near of kin to uncover nakedness: I am the Lord', and verse 16 states, in particular, that 'You shall not uncover the nakedness of your brother's wife; it is your brother's nakedness'. There is nothing in this passage to suggest that the brother in question had to be already dead for this precept to apply, and the surrounding verses appear to refer only to the living. Nevertheless, the prohibition on a man's marrying his brother's wife seems to be reaffirmed and strengthened in Leviticus 20: 21:

> If a man takes his brother's wife, it is [ritual] impurity; he has uncovered his brother's nakedness, they shall be childless.

In this case, too, nothing is said to imply that the brother in question was dead, and Princess Mary was most definitely a child of Henry and Catherine, even if daughters were seen as dynastically inferior. A more fundamental problem than this is, however, involved in the interpretation of Leviticus on the subject.

The fifth and final book of Torah, Deuteronomy, contains a passage, traditionally regarded as being of equal status in principle, which appears directly to contradict Leviticus in this matter and which specifically refers to the death of a husband as the context for a second marriage:

---

[20] Ibid., p. 199; Scarisbrick, *Henry VIII*, pp. 149, 150.
[21] Scarisbrick, *Henry VIII*, pp. 151, 152.

When brothers reside together, and one of them dies and has no son, the wife of the deceased shall not be married outside the family to a stranger. Her husband's brother shall go in to her, taking her in marriage, and performing the duty of a husband's brother to her; and the firstborn whom she bears shall succeed to the name of the deceased brother, so that his name may not be blotted out of Israel. (25: 5–6)

Following verses state that if the surviving brother refuses to take the widow in, she should go to the 'elders at the gate' and tell them what has happened. The elders should then summon the brother and, if he still refuses to marry her:

Then his brother's wife shall go up to him in the presence of the elders, pull his sandal off his foot, spit in his face, and declare, 'This is what is done to the man who does not build up his brother's house'. Throughout Israel his family shall be known as 'the house of him whose sandal was pulled off'. (25: 9–10)

This passage does indeed seem to cover the case of Arthur, Catherine and Henry, in which the Spanish princess's first husband had most certainly died, and the then duke of York had done what a good Jew would have done in the circumstances, though this was hardly a recommendation in the religious and social conditions prevailing in sixteenth-century Christendom.

As early as 1524, Henry had drifted away from Catherine, no longer sleeping with her in the hope of begetting offspring. He may indeed have been thinking of divorce by June 1525, when Mary was despatched to the Welsh Marches, and her illegitimate half-brother to the north of England. He was obviously deeply concerned about the succession, but still unwilling, at this stage, to settle it, although he had every expectation, on past form, that Clement VII would help him, should he bring his matrimonial 'scruple' to the attention of the Roman Curia.[22] What is definitely known is that in April 1527 Henry took his first formal step to divorce Catherine, thus permanently changing both her life and that of their daughter Mary. The resulting consultations with Wolsey and ecclesiastical experts were followed in August of that year by an application to Clement for dispensation for Henry to marry again, Anne Boleyn not being named in the relevant document. In the draft supplied by the English to the Curia, it was proposed that the Pope should dispense Henry not only from his marriage with Catherine, but also from any previous contract of matrimony with another woman, including one within the first degree of affinity to the King. This discreet phrase seems to refer to Anne Boleyn's older sister Mary, who had undoubtedly been Henry's mistress before she was married off to Sir William Carey.[23]

[22] Eric Ives, *The Life and Death of Anne Boleyn* (Oxford: Blackwell [2004], 2005), pp. 63, 83.
[23] Ibid., pp. 84–8, 375 n. 49.

What is known is that, in May 1527, Henry spoke to Wolsey, who then announced that, as a cardinal and also papal legate *ex officio* as archbishop of York (*legatus natus*), he too was now troubled about the validity of the Anglo-Spanish marriage, setting out some arguments against it. In a private hearing, with the King acting as defendant rather than plaintiff, under the inquisitorial procedure laid down by canon law, Wolsey briefly heard the case and then adjourned his 'legatine court', naming certain theologians to consider the matter further. Among them were three bishops, Fisher of Rochester, Longland of Lincoln and Stokesley of London.[24] By 18 May 1527, news of these comings and goings had reached the Imperial ambassador in London, Iñigo de Mendoza, who informed his master, Charles V, that Henry wanted to divorce Catherine, that Wolsey was assisting him, and that the Queen knew nothing of the affair. This message was sent just a day after Wolsey opened the legatine court, probably in his London house, York Place, soon to become Whitehall Palace. Henry was charged that he had unlawfully cohabited with the wife of his deceased brother Arthur and, according to inquisitorial rules, his counsel was required to argue in favour of the marriage and against the 'promotor', or prosecutor, Dr Richard Wolman.[25] In the previous April, Wolman had interviewed the eighty-year-old, and blind, former bishop of Winchester, Richard Fox, who had been involved, as one of Henry VII's councillors, in negotiating both of Catherine's English marriages. Crucially, Fox told Wolman that he believed Catherine and Arthur had indeed had sexual intercourse while at Ludlow castle. Partly on this basis, in the legatine hearing, the promotor developed a case against the validity of Julius II's 1503 dispensation, presenting this argument to the court on 31 May 1527. He then asked Wolsey to weigh the case and give judgment, but this did not happen.[26] During the latter part of May, everything seemed to be going smoothly for Henry, but Catherine remained unaware that her marriage was in danger, having been neither informed of the latest development nor summoned to appear personally in court. The adjournment of 31 May changed the situation drastically in that it denied Henry and Anne the quick result that they so much desired. From now on, interpretation in the King's favour of the relevant passages in Leviticus and Deuteronomy became crucial. It mattered whether or not Catherine had consummated her marriage with Arthur because both the papacy and the universities to which Henry turned for support had to work on the

---

[24] G. W. Bernard, *The King's Reformation: Henry VIII and the Remaking of the English Church* (New Haven, CT and London: Yale University Press, 2005), pp. 7–9; Scarisbrick, *Henry VIII*, p. 155.

[25] *LP* IV, ii, pp. 1426–9 (no. 3140); Starkey, *Six Wives*, pp. 205–6.

[26] P. S. and H. M. Allen, eds, *Letters of Richard Fox, 1486–1527* (Oxford: Clarendon Press, 1929), pp. 156–7; *LP* IV, ii, 3140 (p. 1429); *LP* IV, ii, 5792 (p. 2588); H. A. Kelly, *The Matrimonial Trials of Henry VIII* (Stanford, CA: Stanford University Press, [1976] 2004), pp. 25–9; Starkey, *Six Wives*, p. 206.

basis that if her first marriage had been valid, a dispensation for the second should not have been issued. In such a case, the whole debate over Leviticus and Deuteronomy would be irrelevant, and Catherine was right to think that she had to insist on her virginity at the time of her marriage to Henry, if she was to save it. Even on the most generous interpretation, papal power to dispense was limited in such cases, and Catherine's supporters, such as Fisher, recognized this.[27]

Henry and his supporters were fully aware of the text from Deuteronomy which appeared to contradict those verses of Leviticus on which they based their case. Those who thought the King's marriage with Catherine to be invalid put forward the argument that, as part of the 'ceremonial law' of the Jews, the precept that a man had a duty to marry his dead brother's wife applied only to Jews and, what is more, was no longer practised by the Jews of Europe in the sixteenth century. The Jewish 'Law' (Torah) had very low prestige among Christians in this period, being seen as outmoded and even wicked. Indeed, the Inquisition which had been revived and refounded in Castile and Aragon on the initiative of Catherine's parents, Ferdinand and Isabella, was at that very time engaged in the arrest, trial and punishment, often by burning, of Christians of Jewish origin, including members of the family of Mary's tutor Vives who were specifically accused of practising the 'ceremonial' law of Moses. Thus the debate over Henry's marriage was heavily loaded, and yet late medieval canon lawyers had already in effect come to a compromise, to cover the apparent contradiction between Leviticus and Deuteronomy in this matter. One could, they argued, follow Leviticus by acknowledging the general ban on a man marrying his dead brother's wife (a practice known as 'levirate' marriage, from the Hebrew *levir*, a brother-in-law), while making an exception when the dead brother was childless. In this interpretation, of course, it had been perfectly proper for Henry to marry Arthur's widow in 1509, but the matter remained controversial. When consulted by Wolsey at the end of May, John Fisher favoured this compromise, and affirmed the Pope's right to dispense in this case, stating that 'Otherwise it is in vain that Christ has said, "Whatever you loose on earth shall be loosed in heaven"' (Matthew 16: 19).[28] On 2 June 1527 Wolsey forwarded Fisher's opinion to the King, with a covering letter in which he tried to soften the blow by suggesting that the bishop of Rochester's judgement had been warped by his support for Catherine.[29] At this stage, Wolsey had still not told Fisher that Anne Boleyn was the other party involved, though the bishop must surely have guessed this, but

---

[27] G. Bedouelle and P. Le Gal, eds, *Le Divorce du roi Henri VIII* (Geneva: Librairie Droz, 1987), pp. 60–72; Kelly, *Matrimonial Trials*, pp. 139–40; *CSP Span* IV, i, p. 352 (no. 224); *CSP Span* IV, i, p. 786; *LP* V, 401; Bernard, *King's Reformation*, pp. 19–22.

[28] *LP* IV, iii, p. 1434 (no. 3148); M. Dowling, *Fisher of Men: A Life of John Fisher* (Basingstoke: Macmillan, 1999), p. 133.

[29] I, pp. 189–90 [*LP*, IV], ii, p. 1433 (no. 3147); Starkey, *Six Wives*, pp. 207–8.

in early July he finally revealed the name of the woman concerned. Already, by 2 June, news had reached England of the violent sack of Rome by Imperial troops, which had taken place in the previous month. This was a blow for Henry as it considerably reduced his and Anne's chances of securing a rapid verdict, which they still assumed would be in their favour, and it is surely wrong to suggest the contrary.[30] It was at this stage that the King and his advisers were forced to refine their argument against the marriage.

Henry was acutely aware of the importance of securing international support for his position. Not before time, in the summer of 1527 the issue was raised of the meaning of 'heirs' in the Leviticus text. Mary's supporters, Fisher being notable among them, argued that her birth could not be discounted for this purpose, as Henry (and Anne) wished. The relevant Hebrew text refers to 'barrenness' in general and not to the failure to produce sons. If this text had been adopted in the debate, it would have been clear that the birth of Mary negated the main foundation of Henry's 'scruple' about being married to Catherine, which was the supposition that God had punished the couple with childlessness. Throughout the whole episode, poor Mary was not counted at all, and her father declared to anyone who would listen that the fact that 'all' his children, i.e. sons, were dead demonstrated conclusively that he was being punished by God, though he expressed no concern for Catherine's loss.[31]

By the end of 1527, it appeared to many that Henry's best course would be to join the League of Cognac and help Clement to avenge himself on Charles V for the humiliation which he had suffered in the sack of Rome by Imperial troops in May of that year. Henry, though, remained fixated on what, according to the Emperor's ambassador Iñigo de Mendoza, he had told Catherine at Hunsdon on 22 June 1527 concerning the 'mortal sin' in which they found themselves as a result of their marriage. They must immediately separate, he told her, and she should choose where she should 'retire' to. Catherine is said to have burst into tears at this, and thus to have undermined her husband's resolve, so that he failed at that time to secure the immediate separation which he now desired. According to the Spanish diplomat, the King simply told Catherine to keep quiet about the matter, and shuffled away defeated. According to Wolsey, whose source, Richard Sampson, bishop of Chichester, was then at Court, the Queen stated firmly, on this occasion, that she and Arthur had *not* consummated their marriage and that she now wanted legal advice from foreign lawyers as she no longer trusted the English legal profession. Wolsey assumed that someone, probably Mendoza, had put her up to this, and feared that the presence of continental counsel would create problems for Henry's action.

---

[30] Bernard, *King's Reformation*, p. 9.

[31] Virginia Murphy, 'The Literature and Propaganda of Henry VIII's First Divorce', in *The Reign of Henry VIII: Politics, Policy and Piety*, ed. Diarmaid MacCulloch (Basingstoke: Macmillan, 1995), pp. 138–40.

Despite all this, on 25 July of that year, the feast of Spain's patron, St James the Greater, the King, Catherine and Mary were together at New Hall (also known as Beaulieu) in Essex.[32] Nonetheless, realizing how desperate her situation was, Catherine decided that she personally must inform her nephew Charles of her predicament. To convey her message effectively to him in Spain, she chose one of her Spanish servants, Felipe Felípez, so as to avoid compromising the Imperial ambassador in London. Felípez had served her for many years, having been with her in Ludlow in 1501–2, and was now one of her 'sewers', or waiters at table. Catherine was sure that Henry would try to have any messenger of hers intercepted, and it was decided that the Spaniard should openly ask Henry for permission to return home for the traditional 'family reasons', in this case a sick mother. After much subterfuge, Felípez reached Valladolid towards the end of July 1527, and Charles reacted as forcefully as his aunt had expected, writing to urge Henry to think again about the divorce plan. At the same time he despatched the general of the Observant Franciscan order, Francisco de Quiñones, to see the imprisoned Pope in Rome. Henry's 'Great Matter' was now international.[33]

Mary's role in all this, though absolutely central in the sense that the underlying issue was the succession to the English throne rather than the King's marriage to Catherine, appeared on the surface to be peripheral.[34] In September 1527, Juan Luis Vives returned to England to teach more Latin to the princess, but found himself, in addition, converted into a precious adviser to her mother.[35] On 26 October, ambassador Mendoza wrote to Charles V urging him to obtain a ruling from Clement as soon as possible, on the assumption that the Pope was bound to find in Catherine's favour. Later, the Queen told Charles that, on 15 November, a meeting of lawyers, convened by Henry and Wolsey, was due to 'decide' whether she was indeed the King's lawful wife, and that the result of these deliberations would be forwarded to Clement VII. There had already been a meeting at Hampton Court, in October, in which soundings had been taken from experts on the material to be included in the 'King's Book' on the divorce. Catherine was not meant to hear about these gatherings, but was the recipient of regular 'leaks'. In the autumn of 1527, a climate of paranoia seems to have affected the King and Court, this being demonstrated by the despatch to the Tower of London, on 25 October, of Richard Pace, who had been one of Henry's most loyal and active advisers on the divorce, and was now accused of leaking confidential information. In January 1528, a phoney war was begun by France and England against Charles V

[32] *LP* IV, ii, pp. 1466–7 (no. 3217); Starkey, *Six Wives*, pp. 208–10; Loades, *Mary Tudor*, p. 51.

[33] Starkey, *Six Wives*, pp. 210–11; Loades, *Mary Tudor*, p. 51.

[34] David Loades, *Henry VIII. Court, Church and Conflict* (Kew: The National Archives, 2007), p. 78.

[35] Starkey, *Six Wives*, pp. 210–12.

and, unsurprisingly, when Felípez somewhat rashly returned to England, the King sacked him from Catherine's household.[36]

Meanwhile, in Orvieto over Christmas and the New Year of 1528, Clement VII, who still felt unable to return to Rome, somehow fitted the English annulment case, as it was termed in canon law, into his considerable list of unappealing and intractable problems. The Pope had two options before him. He could establish what was known as a 'general legatine commission', with power to hear all the evidence, come to a judgment, and take any necessary action. Such a commission might explore all relevant issues, and was opposed by Henry and his advisers on the grounds that its remit was too broad, and that it might raise matters which they did not wish to be explored in what was effectively an international tribunal. The English also feared that Clement might use his power to revoke the case to Rome even before the legates on the ground, who might or might not include Wolsey, came to a decision. The second option was a 'decretal commission', which would have a much more restricted remit. In this procedure, the legate or legates would simply set out the relevant canon law, discover the facts, as far as they could, and give a verdict, without necessarily referring back to Rome.[37] Clement took the obvious step of appointing the 'cardinal protector' of England, Lorenzo Campeggio, to hear the case alongside Wolsey. With the usual caution of the Curia, Campeggio was openly appointed under a general commission, but secretly carried with him a decretal commission, which might be deployed if circumstances demanded it. The cardinal protector, a successful Bolognese merchant who had had a legitimate family and joined the papal clergy late in life, after the death of his wife, set out in August 1528 on what would prove to be a long, slow and gout-ridden journey to England. Meanwhile, in a conversation with Catherine's almoner, Robert Shotton, Wolsey mentioned the highly controversial issue of 'bloody sheets' from the night of her wedding to Arthur, and was shocked to learn that there was a 'Spanish' bull of dispensation for that marriage, now known to Catherine, in addition to the 1503 document which was being attacked by Henry and his supporters.[38]

Eventually, after much personal struggling, and some prodding by Henry's agents, Campeggio reached England, and was formally received by the King on 22 October 1528. Two days later, the cardinal met Catherine herself and famously put to her the proposal that she should retire to a convent as a nun, thus renouncing her role as queen consort of England, marginalizing her daughter, and leaving the coast clear for Anne Boleyn.[39] Although no contemporary source notes a connection,

[36] Ibid., pp. 213–16.
[37] Ibid., p. 217.
[38] *LP* IV, ii, p. 4625; Starkey, *Six Wives* pp. 214–21.
[39] Starkey, *Six Wives*, pp. 224–5.

Catherine may have been influenced, in her vehemence against this proposal, by the fact that her mother's hated rival for the Castilian throne, Juana de Castilla, was still living at this time in a convent in Lisbon, where she insisted, until her dying day, which would come on 28 July 1530, on signing herself *Yo la reina* ('I, the queen'). Born in 1462, Juana was involved, from infancy, in the complex politics of Castile. Although publicly declared to be the daughter of King Henry IV and his second wife, Juana de Portugal, the child was said by Henry's enemies, including supporters of Catherine's mother Isabella, to be in fact the product of an illicit liaison between the queen and a nobleman at court, Beltrán de la Cueva, who was one of the king's favourites. Those who believed this nicknamed Juana 'la Beltraneja', and the subsequent triumph of Isabella and Ferdinand ensured that the name would stick, even among supposedly impartial historians. In fact, Juana was almost certainly legitimate, and should therefore have succeeded to the Castilian throne.[40] It is most unlikely that Catherine was unaware of this earlier case, in which the combination of failed queenship and convents was not a happy one. In any case, both Campeggio and Wolsey seem to have been startled by the vehemence of the Queen's reaction, and by the professionalism with which she explored the legal aspects of her predicament. Thus on 28 October she was granted the foreign counsel which she had requested. Her team would now consist of her beloved Vives and two Flemish lawyers, in addition to seven Englishmen. By this time, though, Catherine had dropped her bombshell.

In early November 1528, the Queen appeared to be in a desperate situation. Her legal team informed her that their opposite numbers, acting on her husband's behalf, had come to them with serious accusations, which threatened to involve her personally. The King had apparently been told of a conspiracy to kill him, and Wolsey too. The deeds were supposed to be done by Imperial agents, on Catherine's behalf. Henry was said to be inclined to absolve her from responsibility, but she was not behaving to him as a wife should (in bed, that is), and was fomenting public demonstrations in her own favour and against the King. However, the main charge against her was that, in an unwifely manner, she had concealed from her husband a papal brief (letter) which she had in her possession. Contemptuously denying all the other accusations, concerning murder attempts and rabble-rousing, she stated that she had received the 'Spanish' brief, which had been sent by Julius II to her dying mother in November 1504, six months earlier, from Charles's ambassador, Mendoza. In fact, the document, which appeared, by using the crucial Latin word *forsan* ('perhaps', or 'possibly'), to admit the possibility that Arthur and Catherine had not had intercourse, which was what she stoutly maintained, had only just arrived in England. At this point, legal battle was joined in earnest.[41] It has been suggested that,

[40] Tarsicio de Azcona, *Juana de Castilla, mal llamada La Beltraneja* (Madrid: Fundación Universitaria Española, 1998).

[41] Starkey, *Six Wives*, pp. 221–32.

as her conflict with Henry continued in the last part of 1528, Catherine was not particularly interested in protecting the rights of her daughter Mary, preferring to concentrate on her own good faith and the validity of her marriage. This seems unlikely, since it is clear that both parents, whatever the strife between them, continued to love Mary.[42] As 1529 began, the annulment case remained in stalemate, however, and on 27 April Charles wrote to the Pope, demanding that he produce a verdict. The result was the revocation of the case to Rome on 16 July 1529.[43]

Mary was twelve years old when the legatine trial began, well able to comprehend that there was serious trouble between her parents, but still marginal to events, despite her supposedly continuing role in Wales and the Marches. In May 1528, it was reported that she and some of the Queen's ladies were suffering from smallpox, a common enough ailment at the time, but she seems to have escaped serious consequences, and also to have avoided entirely the major outbreak, in the summer of 1528, of 'sweating sickness', apparently a severe form of influenza which was then common in England, though Anne Boleyn did not thus escape.[44] In August 1531, Henry finally took the drastic action of separating mother and daughter. Catherine was sent to the More, near Rickmansworth, while Mary was despatched to Richmond Palace.[45] Before that, though, Mary seems to have been welcome in the *ménage à trois* at Court – Henry, Anne and Catherine. In 1529, 1530 and 1531, the Princess duly received her New Year's gift from her father, and he gave her other presents, too, from time to time. At this stage, no doubt because of other distractions including the acutely uncertain political situation on the Continent, there seems to have been no serious talk of marriage for Mary. Henri, duke of Orléans, would not reach the required canonical age for consummated matrimony until 1533, though the contract for this alliance was still in place. During the autumn of 1529, the Savoyard Eustace Chapuys, who was now Charles V's ambassador in London, heard a rumour that Mary would be married instead to her illegitimate half-brother, Henry, duke of Richmond. If there were problems with Henry VIII's marriage to Catherine, and Pope Clement VII was once again effectively in thrall to the Emperor, this grotesque idea, which possibly originated with Anne Boleyn, would hardly be feasible and, if it ever in fact existed, it was quickly abandoned. In the meantime, although she was forcibly separated from her mother, Mary's relations with her father continued intermittently. In the summer of 1530, for example, it is recorded that she sent him a buck deer as a gift, and by the end of that year she seems to have been set up more permanently with her own household, now in England not Wales. Indeed, in the first few months of 1531 relations, however strained, between father and daughter

[42] Loades, *Mary Tudor*, p. 54; Starkey, *Six Wives*, p. 232.
[43] Starkey, *Six Wives*, pp. 234, 236–7, 242, 246; *CSP Span* III, ii, pp. 861, 989–91.
[44] Starkey, *Six Wives*, pp. 325, 330–2.
[45] Ibid., p. 443.

were probably as good as they would ever be again. In March, Mary was at last given permission to visit her mother, supposedly for five or six days but in fact for a month, while in June Henry came to see her at Richmond, and the visit is said to have been a joyous success. However, by then Mary had once again begun to experience health problems.

After leaving her mother in March, she is said to have had severe stomach pains, inevitably put down to 'hysteria' at the time, and after three weeks the problem had still not cleared up and she appeared to be suffering from some kind of nervous disorder, of which more would be heard in her later life. On 12 July 1531 Henry paid Dr Bartelot £20 for providing a medical opinion, in addition to that of her own doctor. Yet, despite this display of fatherly concern, nothing can conceal the fact that by now Mary had become a token in Henry's battle with Catherine which was about to enter a new and more acute phase. In May 1531, it was still possible for the King and Queen to be together in Greenwich, and for their daughter to visit them, but the true situation was revealed in June, when Henry went on his own to see the Princess at Richmond.[46]

By then, Henry and Anne seem to have fallen out over what to do with her. At about this time, according to Chapuys, the King complained to the duke of Norfolk about his fifteen-year-old daughter's 'arrogance and her domineering attitude', saying that she was not like her mother, whom he now chose to portray somewhat idealistically as having never spoken 'boldly' to him – an unlikely scenario in the case of a daughter of Isabella of Castile.[47] By this time it was clear to most, at home and abroad, that Henry was absolutely determined to replace Catherine with Anne, and Mary had to await the outcome on the sidelines. She remained a public figure, however, and on 25 August 1531 she was visited at Richmond by a Venetian military commander, Mario Savorgnano. The visitor reported to the Signoria in Venice that she was full of life, 'beautiful', and accomplished in languages. Evidently he saw Mary before the full effect of her situation had worn her down.[48] But as the earlier intervention of physicians shows, she was in fact putting up a brave front while under considerable strain, as any royal daughter should. Between 1531 and 1533, Anne habitually ill-treated both Catherine and her daughter, whom she commonly referred to as a 'bastard', which hardly helped a teenager develop into a woman, and evidently was not meant to. At Christmas 1531 Mary received her father's usual gift but she was not invited to Court. It seems that she was effectively being pushed into taking her mother's side in the dispute over the divorce, though surviving accounts indicate that, in early 1532, her household was still being financed and supplied by the Crown as normal. In addition, Mary was now back on the marriage

[46] Loades, *Mary Tudor*, pp. 60–2.

[47] Ives, *Anne Boleyn* (Oxford: Oxford University Press, 1986), pp. 145–6; *LP* V, p. 216; *CSP Span* IV, ii, p. 23.

[48] *CSP Ven* IV, pp. 287–8; Starkey, *Six Wives*, pp. 443–5.

market, having been jilted once again, this time by Henri of Orléans, in
favour of Pope Clement's niece, Catarina de'Medici. After this, new
foreign suitors began to appear on the scene, among them the German
duke of Cleves, who sent across his chamberlain on an unsuccessful visit.
In reality, despite Savorgnano's glowing report, Mary must by now have
seemed a somewhat dubious prospect in the eyes of European royal families. She had been a late developer physically, and her legitimacy was, to
say the very least, in doubt, as her father's divorce case continued to be
stalled in Rome. In these circumstances, it is natural that she should have
regarded Catherine as virtually her only emotional lifeline. Although they
were not allowed to meet, according to Chapuys, mother and daughter
wrote regularly to each other with the help of loyal servants, none of these
letters apparently surviving. If Henry was trying to reduce Catherine's
influence on Mary, he was clearly failing.[49] The rise of Anne and the
eclipse of Catherine and Mary were demonstrated to all on 1 September
1532, when Henry publicly created Anne 'marquis' of Pembroke, with the
rank of a peer of the realm and a landed income of no less than £1,000
a year.[50] The Queen had to observe these proceedings in impotent fury, yet
Henry and Anne apparently felt insecure enough to have it falsely stated,
in subsequent accounts, that Mary had accompanied them to Calais,
shortly after Anne's investiture, to meet Francis I.[51]

    Although the events of the summer of 1532 seemed both irritating and
worrying to Charles V, he and his advisers still opted for caution when
dealing with Henry, despite their deep sympathy for Catherine and her
daughter. At the end of May 1532, the divorce was still officially regarded
as a private matter, even though, as a result of his desperate need to
counteract the power of Charles in Rome, Henry was once again making
overtures to the French, his September visit with Anne to Calais and
Boulogne being a symbol of this attempt. Francis was willing to receive
such an approach at the time because of his resentment at having been
forced, under the terms of the treaty of Madrid, to marry Charles V's sister
Leonor. It was not until the following year, however, that Catherine was
confronted with significant degradation from her position as queen consort
of England, with inevitable consequences for Mary. On 9 April 1533, a
delegation of royal councillors came to inform Catherine that her husband
and Anne Boleyn were now 'married', and that she should henceforth be
known not as 'queen of England', but as 'dowager princess of Wales',
being Arthur's widow.[52] A mere three days later, on Easter Sunday, Anne
made her first public appearance as 'queen'.[53] These moves were followed
by a third 'inquisition' into Catherine's marriages, this time conducted, at

[49] Loades, *Mary Tudor*, pp. 63–4.
[50] *LP* V, p. 508.
[51] Loades, *Mary Tudor*, pp. 64–7; Starkey, *Six Wives*, pp. 459–61.
[52] *CSP Span* IV, ii, p. 625; *LP* VI, p. 296.
[53] *LP* VI, p. 351.

a safe distance from the 'media' of London, in Dunstable Priory, by Thomas Cranmer, who had received papal bulls of appointment as archbishop of Canterbury, in succession to William Warham, on 23 May 1533. At that time, Catherine was living, on her husband's orders, at Ampthill in Bedfordshire, just twelve miles from Dunstable, but she refused to accept a summons to appear before Cranmer and, despite many legal defects in the case papers, the archbishop duly produced the verdict that his royal master required. All was 'done and dusted' in time for Anne's coronation, which was lavishly staged in London on 1 June 1533.[54] Although his marriage to his first wife had now been annulled, at least to his own satisfaction, Henry quickly discovered that his problems were about to become even more acute. He was forty-two years old, and his daughter Mary was seventeen, an age by which most princesses were already married and had normally produced heirs. Yet he had no son, and his new wife, as she was in the eyes of his appointees in the English Church if not elsewhere, was already in her thirties, and thus rapidly approaching the age at which Catherine herself had ceased to be able to conceive. Thus it was extremely fortunate, and in Henry's eyes divine approbation of his interpretation of Leviticus, that Anne went into confinement at Greenwich on 27 August 1533. All advance publicity, in England and on the Continent, had announced the imminent arrival of a son, but on 7 September a daughter was born and named Elizabeth, apparently after Henry's mother, Elizabeth of York, though the name of Catherine's mother, Isabella, was of course the same.[55] Her baptism took place in the Observant Franciscan church at Greenwich, on 11 September, and the infant was proclaimed 'the high and mighty Princess of England' thus displacing Mary as heir to the throne, as well as taking her title. But Catherine's half-Trastamaran daughter would fight back. Unprotected by her mother, and apparently abandoned by Charles, her first betrothed, she was, however, well and truly in the sights of Anne, who by the end of 1533 appeared to be victorious on all counts except the most vital one, that is, producing a son.

According to Chapuys, Anne was already boasting, in April 1533, that she would have Mary as her 'lady's maid', but now the fate of Catherine's daughter was to be even worse. She was to be forcibly incorporated into baby Elizabeth's household, so that her humiliation might be complete, and ceaselessly demonstrated. Mary was, of course, a daily reminder, both to her father and to Anne, of their failure to have the son whom they had proclaimed to Europe. On 5 July 1533, Catherine's 'demotion', and hence that of her daughter, was publicly announced, and although Mary was not directly attacked at that time, once Elizabeth was born, she was duly redesignated as 'the Lady Mary', the relevant order being given to her household

---

[54] Starkey, *Six Wives*, pp. 457, 484–503; Diarmaid MacCulloch, *Thomas Cranmer: A Life* (New Haven, CT and London: Yale University Press, 1996), pp. 92–4.

[55] Starkey, *Six Wives*, pp. 503–9; *CSP Span* IV, ii, p. 788.

chamberlain on the Feast of the Exaltation of the Holy Cross, 14 September. In a display worthy of her father and of her fiery Trastamaran ancestors, Mary summarily dismissed the instruction and, in early December 1533, the duke of Norfolk and a delegation of his fellow councillors arrived at New Hall/Beaulieu, Essex, to present her with a written version of the order, as she had requested. She refused to accept that she was no longer a princess, and defied her father's order that she should move into Elizabeth's household. The session was tense, and she withdrew to her room for about half an hour, apparently in an attempt to release her stress and compose herself. When she emerged, she produced a 'protestation' against her current situation, which seems to have been drafted by Chapuys. Finally, though, she was forced to leave for Hatfield, accompanied by a mere fraction of her existing household.[56] Not unnaturally, though perhaps not quite accurately, Chapuys blamed Anne for all this, on the grounds that she had 'bewitched' Henry. On the other hand, the King had ample motives of his own for behaving as he did. Even as queen and princess, Catherine and Mary were, after all, his subjects, and had to do what they were told, but Anne no doubt supplied much emotional energy to urge him on.

When she arrived at Hatfield, Mary refused to address Elizabeth as 'princess', though she was prepared, out of courtesy, to call her 'sister', as she was accustomed to calling the definitely illegitimate Henry Fitzroy 'brother'. For her, the two semi-siblings were in the same category. It is reported that when the duke of Norfolk refused to take a message from her to her father, in which she described herself as 'the princess', she once again retired to her room, in great distress. Thereafter, Mary tried to take as little part as possible in the life of the household, refusing to eat in hall, where she would have to show deference to the baby Elizabeth. Citing ill-health, no doubt with some justification, she ate early in her chamber, and tried to have her other meals brought there. Anne Boleyn wanted all this stopped, but some at least of Mary's servants seem to have been sympathetic to her, and when the new 'queen' came to Hatfield in February 1534, supposedly to conciliate her and restore order, her stepdaughter, as Mary was in the eyes of the English Church, refused the overture. Anne had put her aunt, Lady Anne Shelton, in charge of her, with instructions to box the girl's ears if she called herself 'princess', but little or no action was taken. Anne Boleyn feared that Mary could get round her father, who was prone to sentimentality and seems not to have shared his second wife's vindictiveness towards her. For this reason she managed to prevent Henry from seeing his elder daughter when he visited Hatfield in January 1534. He now proclaimed that he blamed Mary for her hot Spanish blood, yet he still praised her, at this time, to the French ambassador.[57] Anne, too,

---

[56] Starkey, *Six Wives*, pp. 513–15; *LP* VI, p. 617 (no. 1528).
[57] Starkey, *Six Wives*, pp. 516–18; *LP* VI, p. 809 (no. 1558); *LP* VIII, p. 68 (no. 171).

put national origin forward as an explanation for her failure to conciliate Catherine's daughter.[58]

By late 1533, Catherine seems to have believed that both she and her daughter were destined to have their faith in God tested by virtual or actual martyrdom. More immediately, on 17 December 1533, the duke of Norfolk appeared at Buckden in Huntingdonshire, where Catherine was now resident, in an attempt to enforce Henry's instruction to her servants to call her 'Princess Dowager' and not 'queen'. A few did take the required oath to do this, after bullying, but the duke failed in his second purpose, which was to persuade Catherine to move to nearby Somersham. She refused, on the grounds that she would suffer harm from the damp that abounded in that fenland site. Being unwilling to use violence, Norfolk withdrew to consult his master. After that, Catherine retired to her room, except when hearing Mass in the gallery, and her physical and psychological state went into a decline. In early 1534, the faithful Chapuys found such hostility at court towards Catherine and Mary that he decided not even to mention them unless he was commanded to do so. Finally, on 23 March 1534, Pope Clement gave sentence in consistory on the annulment, rejecting Cranmer's sentence at Dunstable, but not ruling on the crucial question of Catherine's virginity. It was a pyrrhic victory for the long-suffering Queen. On the very same day, parliament passed the Act of Succession, which cited Cranmer's verdict, and declared Catherine to be 'Princess Dowager'. The succession should pass to Anne's issue and then to that of any wife of Henry subsequent to her. If there was no male heir, Elizabeth would succeed and Mary would be cut out. However, legal wriggling room for the future was provided by the omission of Mary's name from the final draft, which became statute, and although this was not intended to be an act of kindness towards her, it would be useful later.

Nevertheless, that Act was a crushing blow to both mother and daughter, and it had large-scale consequences, as all the King's subjects were to be made to swear to accept and obey its terms.[59] In April, a further delegation of the Council arrived at Buckden to obtain Catherine's assent to the Act of Succession, but it had no more success than its predecessors in persuading her to accept her situation. However, in the following month Catherine was transferred to Kimbolton, also in Huntingdonshire, where she would spend the rest of her life. In July, on the transparent pretext of a pilgrimage to Our Lady of Walsingham in Norfolk, Chapuys passed near Kimbolton castle, a less damp spot than Somersham, and some of his entourage made contact with members of her household.[60] But Isabella and Ferdinand's youngest daughter had now become largely irrelevant to her former kingdom's life.

---

[58] Starkey, *Six Wives*, p. 296; *LP* VIII, p. 123 (no. 296).

[59] Loades, *Mary Tudor*, pp. 88–90; Statute 25 Henry VIII c. 2; *Statutes of the Realm*, ed. A. Luders and others, 11 vols (1810–28; Dobbs Ferry: Transmedia Publishing, 1972), iii, pp. 47–9.

[60] Starkey, *Six Wives*, pp. 519–22, 543.

Chapter 3

MARY BEREAVED, 1536–1547

In the last eleven years of her father's reign, Mary was to endure a series of ordeals which at times threatened her health and even her very life. But before that, by November 1535, her mother Catherine was suffering from pain and attacks of nausea, of a kind which had periodically affected her for more than a year. In early December she wrote to her nephew's ambassador, Eustace Chapuys, asking him for money to give as Christmas and New Year presents to her servants, and was then still hoping that Henry would allow her to move to a more salubrious spot than Kimbolton. She wanted to see the faithful Chapuys before too long and give him a proper reward for his service. On 29 December, though, Chapuys received a letter from Catherine's doctor, Miguel de la Sá, telling him that if he wished to see the Queen alive he should come to Kimbolton with all speed. The diplomat duly arrived there on 2 January 1536 and Catherine received him formally, but from her bed. Having apparently forgotten that the order had been driven from England by her husband, she asked to be buried in a house of Observant Franciscans and that 500 Masses should be said for her soul. Perhaps because of Chapuys's presence, between 3 and 5 January Catherine seemed to revive somewhat, and de la Sá even thought that she was out of danger. In addition, on the night before the Feast of the Epiphany (6 January), she received the boost of the arrival, against royal orders, of her former lady-in-waiting and companion María de Salinas, who was now countess of Willoughby. Thinking that the Queen was indeed past the worst, Chapuys left Kimbolton, but on the night of 6–7 January she had a sharp relapse, and began to prepare for the end. She made her final confession to God through Bishop Jorge de Athequa of Llandaff and received the sacrament of the Eucharist, after a characteristic argument with her confessor over whether, under canon law, Mass might be celebrated before dawn. Catherine dictated two last letters, one to Charles V and one to Henry, to whom she affirmed her love and loyalty, asking him to take particular care of Mary. At 10 a.m. she received extreme unction, and after this she prayed for a few hours, then appears to have drifted away, and died at 2 p.m. on 7 January 1536. In default of Observant Franciscans, the Benedictines took care of her obsequies, which were wholly traditional, and she was buried in the north choir aisle of Peterborough Abbey (subsequently Cathedral), on 29 January. Although the Office for the Dead and three High Masses of Requiem were celebrated, she received the ceremonial honours due not to a queen of England but to a dowager princess of Wales. John Fisher's successor as bishop of Rochester, John Hilsey, preached against rather than for Catherine, on the orders of the 'Supreme Head in Earth of the Church of England'. In his sermon the bishop claimed, implausibly, that on her deathbed Catherine had admitted that she was not the Queen of England.[1] There was no hesitation, on this occasion, in speaking ill of the dead.[2] Mary's mother had been steadfast to the end, but the cause or causes of her death were controversial at the time and have remained so since. At this distance, it seems most probable that she was not poisoned, as many of her supporters supposed at the time, but came to her end through a combination of stress, caused by grief and ill-treatment, with some physical problem, such as thrombosis. In the circumstances of remoteness and government nervousness which surrounded her death, it was natural, though, that some should have been suspicious.[3] It remained to be seen what would happen to the now motherless Mary.

Most foreign observers thought, or assumed, that, at the time of Catherine's death, her daughter was in mortal danger as well. This view was held in both Rome and Wittenberg, while Charles V thought that Mary was now certain to be poisoned, as he believed her mother had been. In the event, the treatment of the Princess Mary improved somewhat, after the difficult years of 1534 and 1535, apparently thanks to the fact that she had not supported any plan for rebellion in that period. Whatever the reason, Henry did not make his elder daughter take the oath required under the 1534 Act of Succession. Nevertheless, after this measure received the royal assent, on 30 March 1534, Thomas Cromwell had noted that copies should be sent to both Catherine and Mary. The Act should be read to them and an answer demanded, but in Mary's case, when Sir William Paulet and Anne Boleyn's father, the earl of Wiltshire, waited upon her on 21 April 1534, she does not seem to have been asked to swear the statutory oath. Nonetheless, Chapuys had not unreasonably supposed that both the Queen and the Princess, as he still regarded them, whatever changes of title had been ordered by Henry, were threatened with death if they did not swear the prescribed oath, just as Bishop John Fisher and Sir Thomas More had been executed on this pretext in the previous year. In 1536, Catherine escaped by another route, but this only made her daughter even more vulnerable. Before Catherine's death, both seemed to be protected by their royal blood, but their servants were not given similar immunity. By mid-May 1534, Catherine's household and Mary's servants had indeed been forced to take the oath, but Henry never went beyond intemperate threats to the ladies themselves, and it appears that the King had no wish to make a martyr of his first wife, while Mary retained her value as a marriage prospect until Anne bore him a child.[4]

[1] *LP* X, pp. 47–54, 104–6 (nos 141, 284); Starkey, *Six Wives*, p. 553.
[2] Mattingly, *Catherine of Aragon*, pp. 340–5.
[3] 1783 fol. 96; *LP* VII, p. 201 (no. 497); Loades, *Mary Tudor*, p. 93.
[4] Loades, *Mary Tudor*, pp. 89–90.

Chapuys reported that, in January 1536, the King and Anne Boleyn celebrated the news of Catherine's death, insulting the Emperor in the process, and it is evident that both were deeply relieved to hear of the former queen's departure.[5] Anne herself gave a large present to the messenger who brought her the news of Catherine's death, while her father Thomas Boleyn and brother George were now heard freely expressing the view that Mary, too, should be eliminated. According to the Imperial ambassador, Henry dressed in yellow from head to toe, which may simply have been in honour of the 'royal' Feast of Epiphany, or Three Kings, but certainly did not demonstrate any sense of mourning. On the following day, a Sunday, the King and his new queen attended Mass in triumphant, not to say gloating, style, and Princess Elizabeth was accompanied to church by trumpets and shown off proudly to the public.[6] Henry not only celebrated his first wife's death but worked hard, and successfully as it turned out, to use her funeral, despite its traditional liturgical pomp, to demonstrate that she had never in fact *or in law* been queen. He also wanted to make sure that he gained possession of all Catherine's remaining property, and this caused a potential problem. If she had really never been married to Henry, as he and his supporters claimed, then she died as a 'woman sole' who, as the widow of Prince Arthur, was fully entitled to dispose of her goods. She did indeed leave a will, and it was later estimated that her estate was worth more than £3,000, which was to be divided between her servants and her daughter Mary. However, with his customary skill and lack of scruple, the solicitor-general, Richard Rich, managed to divert Catherine's property into the royal coffers, treating her like any other aristocratic woman in England.[7] Over the succeeding weeks, Anne seems to have reacted to her rival's death in an ambiguous manner, rejoicing at her removal from the scene but also, and perhaps inevitably, wondering whether she herself might suffer a similar fate, if she failed to produce the male heir that her husband obsessively desired. Again, the source is Chapuys and, whether rightly or wrongly, the ambassador felt able to urge Lady Anne Shelton to treat Mary better, as her fortunes might soon improve.[8] Support for Chapuys's interpretation of these events may be found in the fact that Anne herself wrote to Lady Shelton at this time, urging her to relax the conditions in which her charge was being kept. She should now follow Gospel precept and show love to her enemy. Mary, on the other hand, should submit to her father before it was too late and he withdrew his favour from her once again. The fact that

---

[5] *LP* X, p. 51 (no. 141); Scarisbrick, *Henry VIII*, p. 335.

[6] Ives, *Anne Boleyn*, p. 295; Starkey, *Six Wives*, p. 549.

[7] *LP* X, pp. 15, 47–54, 154 (nos 40, 141, 384); Starkey, *Six Wives*, p. 550; Timothy G. Elston, 'Widow Princess or Neglected Queen? Catherine of Aragon, Henry VIII and English Public Opinion, 1533–1536', in *Queens and Power in Medieval and Early Modern England*, ed. Carole Levin and Robert Bucholz (Lincoln, NB and London: University of Nebraska Press, 2009), pp. 16–30, at p. 19.

[8] *LP* X, pp. 69–70 (no. 199).

Anne was pregnant again only added to the precariousness of Mary's position. Henry's new Queen was now openly threatening her: 'If I have a son, as I hope shortly, I know what will happen to her'.[9]

In the months following Catherine's death, Henry appeared, in public at least, to go on his joyous way, with a round of riding, hunting and other amusements, in the company of his 'laddish' friends. However, on 24 January 1536 he suffered a dangerous riding accident in the tiltyard, falling heavily from his horse. Had anyone by then begun to worry less about the possibility of Mary's succession to the throne, because of Anne's condition, this ominous event brought the matter back to mind, even though the King appeared to recover quite quickly.[10] A second omen was Anne's miscarriage of her second child, which took place on the very day of Catherine's funeral at Peterborough. Despite her efforts to respond bravely, even suggesting that her child had died because it had been conceived during Catherine's lifetime, Anne quickly found that her relations with her husband had deteriorated.[11] In these tricky circumstances, up to the end of February 1536, Henry still seemed to be trying more to placate his elder daughter than to bully her. On 10 February, Chapuys reported to his master that no further mention was being made of the oath under the 1534 Succession Act, but this approach seems to have had little effect on the deeply mourning Mary. She was still urging Chapuys to arrange for Imperial agents to remove her from her torment in England. Charles, though, in a development which would have great significance when she eventually came to the throne, demonstrated that, despite having been betrothed to Mary, he did not feel the same emotional attachment to her as he had felt towards her mother. For him, England was now a political rather than a personal problem and, indeed, at the end of February 1536 he asked Chapuys to try and negotiate a new alliance with Henry against France.[12] A kind of thaw duly developed in Anglo-Imperial relations after Catherine's death, and its main victim would prove to be Anne Boleyn.[13] In particular, it was at this point that Henry seems to have begun to pay more attention to Jane Seymour.

The future Queen Jane was the daughter of Sir Thomas Seymour of Wolf Hall, near Marlborough, Wiltshire. By early 1536, Henry was already becoming restless in his marriage to Anne Boleyn, and his eye was beginning to rove with serious intent. He was now free to seek a third wife without being put under pressure any more, at home or abroad, to take Catherine back, and a new marriage might also provide a solution to the intractable problem of Mary.[14] As Henry had once intended, Mary might even be declared legitimate again on the basis of her parents' 'good faith', despite their supposed

[9] *LP* X, pp. 47–54, 116–18 (nos 141, 307).
[10] *LP* X, p. 35 (no. 100).
[11] *LP* X, p. 35 (no. 102).
[12] *LP* X pp. 148–9 (no. 373); Loades, *Mary Tudor*, pp. 93–4.
[13] Loades, *Mary Tudor*, p. 94.
[14] Ibid., p. 95.

sin against God. In the eyes of most of Europe, though, Henry would be seen as acting under coercion from Charles V or the Pope. Also, without Anne Boleyn, there would no longer be any reason for Elizabeth to be preferred to Mary as heir to the throne. By April 1536, Henry was battling with his conscience over this subject, while debate continued among the courtiers. In this context, Mary's main supporters were the marquis of Exeter, Lord Montague, Sir Thomas Elyot, and Sir Nicholas Carew, with the inevitable involvement of Eustace Chapuys, as Imperial ambassador. Anne Boleyn's fate seems to have been effectively sealed in Council, and on 2 May she was arrested, on lurid charges of incest and adultery. Many, at home and abroad, assumed that the execution of Anne made Mary heir to the throne, at least for the time being, but with Henry such things, especially when they were so vital to him, were never straightforward.[15]

It is not entirely clear when exactly Henry VIII began to pursue Jane Seymour seriously. This may have happened by April 1536, when accusations of adultery began to be made against Anne Boleyn, and indeed his infatuation with Jane was already notorious at court even earlier, by March of that year.[16] It is even possible that this attraction had begun in the middle of 1534, in the form of a secret flirtation which grew out of the conventional techniques of courtly love to which Henry was so devoted. On the other hand, it may be that the King only became seriously interested in Jane early in 1536, since, according to his despatches, the phenomenon was first noticed by Chapuys on 10 February of that year.[17] By April 1536, though, the Seymours, and in particular Jane's brothers Edward and Thomas, were gaining influence. Also on the very day of Anne's execution, 19 May 1536, Archbishop Thomas Cranmer issued, as metropolitan of Canterbury and without reference to Pope Paul III, dispensations for affinity in the third degree between Henry and Jane, and hence for their marriage.[18] In his customary extravagant and, to some, highly insensitive manner, as soon as he heard that his second wife's head had rolled on Tower Hill, Henry boarded a barge and went to visit Jane. The very next day, they were betrothed, and on 30 May they were married quietly at Cardinal Wolsey's former London residence, York Place (Whitehall Palace). Earlier, Jane had been a lady's maid both to Catherine and to Anne, but now she herself was Queen, and parliament was recalled to ratify a new Act of Succession, which put first any future heirs of her body, and dashed Mary and Elizabeth's hopes of greater legal recognition.[19] A few weeks later, Henry's illegitimate son by Elizabeth Blount, Henry Fitzroy, duke of Richmond, died after a short illness. He received a more or less secret

[15] Ibid., pp. 95–7; Ives, *Anne Boleyn*, pp. 295–300; Loades, *Mary Tudor: The Tragical History of the First Queen of England* (Kew: The National Archives, 2006), pp. 43–5.

[16] Rex, *The Tudors*, pp. 74, 76.

[17] Ives, *Anne Boleyn*, pp. 194–5, 291–3.

[18] *LP* X, p. 384 (no. 915); Scarisbrick, *Henry VIII*, pp. 348–9.

[19] Scarisbrick, *Henry VIII*, p. 380.

funeral at Thetford Priory, which was organized on the King's orders by the duke of Norfolk.[20] Henry's marriage to Jane seems to have had considerable public support, and Jane's close relatives began to receive conspicuous honours. Thus in March 1536, even before the marriage, her older brother Edward was made a member of the privy chamber. His influence grew steadily there as Henry became ever more involved with Jane.[21] In the summer of 1536, however, the question was whether the advance of Jane and her family would also be to the benefit of Mary.

That year was to be perhaps the most traumatic in Mary's life. For the last three years, she had been living in difficult conditions, for one who was so inwardly assured of her true status in the kingdom. She had been bullied by many of her servants, chosen for the purpose by Henry and Anne, and she had been forced to subordinate herself, in a manner which was meant to be as humiliating as possible, to her baby sister Elizabeth. Yet she was still popular in the country. She was prevented from going to Mass in public, rather than in her household chapel, not because that form of service was forbidden at this stage, but because it was feared that, if she did, there would be demonstrations on her behalf, and in memory of her mother, by members of the public. Many thought that she had been cruelly separated from Catherine in her last days, and badly treated since. Nonetheless, in her enforced isolation from Court, Mary seems to have retained her determination, which had been evident since 1531, to seek a reconciliation with her father. She apparently saw his third wife, Jane Seymour, as a suitable intercessor, and imagined that the Royal Secretary, Thomas Cromwell, was her friend and advocate in this process. After Anne's execution, on 19 May, Mary waited, at Hunsdon in Hertfordshire, for a summons back to Court, and to begin with she was hopeful. Soon after Anne's death, Mary's former governess, Margaret Pole, countess of Salisbury, was called back to serve her, and many observers thought this to be a sign that Mary's rehabilitation would not be long delayed. Even Henry himself was heard to hint at such a possibility, but the Imperial ambassador, Eustace Chapuys, was rightly cautious. When some of Mary's former servants, filled with a new optimism, went out to Hertfordshire to offer her their services once more, she took his advice and sent them away again, saying that she could not receive them back without her father's approval. Yet it was possible for her to believe, as May went on, that Henry was indeed coming round, and there seems to have been some public expectation of a change. Even a French ballad, apparently produced at the beginning of June, declared that

> There is no heart so sad that it does not laugh
> While awaiting the Princess Mary.[22]

[20] Ibid., p. 381.
[21] Ives, *Anne Boleyn*, pp. 303–5.
[22] Pérez Martín, *María Tudor*, p. 272: 'Il n'y a cueur si triste qui ne rye/ en attendant la Princesse Marie'.

As she continued to mourn her mother, Mary received further visits from the wise and cautious Chapuys, but any warnings from him did not shift her from her conviction that Thomas Cromwell would help her back into her father's love and favour. Although he was far from sharing her optimism in this respect, Chapuys nonetheless agreed to relay communications from her to Cromwell. Thus on 26 May, Mary wrote to the Secretary, telling him that she would have approached him before in this matter, had she not thought it useless to do so, 'as long as that woman [Anne] lived, which now is gone, whom I pray our Lord of his great mercy to forgive'. Now that Anne was dead, Mary felt able to approach a man whom she remarkably described as 'one of my chief friends'. She now asked Cromwell to be a suitor to the King, and signed herself 'By your loving friend, Marye'. Her humility, or perhaps sensible caution, in not adding 'the Princesse' may also have led her to apologize for her 'evil' handwriting, caused by lack of writing materials for a long period before Lady Elizabeth Kingston brought her supplies, but the remark concerned was no doubt a not-so-subtle complaint as well. The main purpose of Lady Kingston's visit to Hunsdon was to fulfil a promise which she had made to Anne Boleyn, who was then on the point of death, to take to Mary an appeal to pardon her for the way in which she had treated her stepdaughter, something readily granted.[23]

Perhaps inevitably, given her distance from Court, Mary seems to have seen her desperate effort to regain her father's love as an entirely personal matter, outside the context of political events. Cromwell was of course only too aware that his royal master was absolutely determined to hold on to the ecclesiastical supremacy, and would demand complete and unconditional submission from Mary. The Secretary replied quickly to her letter of 26 May, clearly indicating to her that she would have to obey her father absolutely, if she wanted to be reconciled with him. The question was, how far would she have to go to prove that obedience? Cromwell showed a draft of this reply to Chapuys, and bluntly told him that Mary would have to obey his instructions in every particular, if Henry was to be won over. He also informed Chapuys that he had sent a lady whom Mary trusted to Hunsdon to try to convince her that she must do what was expected of her, and then asked him to help. Cromwell wanted Chapuys to write to the 'Lady Mary', send trustworthy servants to speak to her personally, and persuade her to write to her father in the required terms. Cromwell's letter does not survive, but Chapuys reported to Brussels that the Secretary had offered to translate the draft from English into Latin, so that the ambassador would know what Mary had to do. At this stage, Chapuys does seem to have believed that a reconciliation was possible. No doubt having heard from him or one of his agents that she now had permission to approach her father directly, on 30 May Mary wrote again to Cromwell, thanking him for

---

[23] Thomas Hearne, *Sylloge epistolarum*, in Titus Livius, *Vita Henrici Quinti* (Oxford: Sheldonian Theatre, 1716), p. 140; a fragment remains as BL Cotton MS Otho C.X fol. 283r; *LP* X, p. 968.

this and assuring him, effusively but also cautiously, that 'you shall find me as obedient to the King's Grace as you can reasonably require of me'. She trusted that this would be enough to readmit her to the royal presence.[24]

Thus, on 1 June, Mary for the first time wrote directly to her father in a humiliatingly submissive manner which must have cost her a great deal emotionally:

> I beseech your Grace of your daily blessing, which is my chief desire in the world. And in the same humble ways [ac]knowledging all the offences that I have done, . . . I pray your Grace, in the honour of God, and for your fatherly pity, to forgive me them for the which I am sorry, as any creature living, and near unto God, I do and will submit me in all things to your goodness and pleasure to do with me whatsoever shall please your Grace.

Telling her father that she was praying for him and Queen Jane to have a son, she signed herself 'your Grace's most humble and obedient daughter and handmaid, Mary'.[25] By this time, though, Henry was no longer prepared to take second place to God, and the letter was unsuccessful, as was another which Mary sent to him soon afterwards.[26] She received no reply to either. Things were looking desperate, and on 10 June Mary went even beyond her former limits in yet another letter to the King. This time, she declared that she was 'most humbly prostrate befor[sic] your most noble feet, your most obedient subject and humble child', but she still put her obedience to her father 'next to Almighty God'. At the same time, she wrote again to Cromwell, saying that she hoped she had followed his instructions to the letter, but adding that her duty to her father was complete, 'God and my conscience not offended', and putting her trust in the Secretary, 'as one of my chief friends, next unto his Grace and the Queen',

> Wherefore I desire you, for the Passion which Christ suffered for you and me, and as my very trust is in you, that you will find such means through your great wisdom, that I be not moved to agree to any further entry in this matter than I have done. But if I be put to any more, I am plain with you as with my great friends, my said conscience will in no ways suffer me to consent thereunto.[27]

This was the language of Mary's mother Catherine and of Thomas More, and it inevitably went down badly with Cromwell, who knew exactly how his master would react to such sentiments. His reply does not survive, but

[24] BL Cotton MS Otho C.X fol. 267v; Hearne, *Sylloge epistolarum*, p. 147.

[25] Hearne, *Sylloge epistolarum*, p. 146; BL Cotton MS Otho C.X fol. 268r (damaged by fire).

[26] BL Cotton MS C.X fol. 287r; Hearne, *Sylloge epistolarum*, p. 149.

[27] Hearne, *Sylloge epistolarum*, pp. 124–5; BL MS Cotton Otho C.X fol. 269v (damaged).

his disapproval is evident from Mary's response to it, which indicates that
he had provided her with a set form for her to use in order to regain her
father's favour. Thanking Cromwell for his latest epistle, she tried to deal
with his objection to her putting God before Henry:

> For I do not mistrust that the King's goodness will move me [to that]
> which should offend God and my conscience . . . For I have always
> used, both in writing and speaking, to except God in all things.

In this letter, Mary revealed that she was now suffering once more from ill
health, giving this as a reason why she now proposed to write to her father
using the exact words which had been drafted by 'Master Secretary'.

> Nevertheless, because you have exhorted me to write to his Grace
> again, and I cannot devise what I should write more but your own last
> copy, without adding or [d]iminishing, therefore I do send you by this
> bearer, my servant, the same, word for word, and it is unsealed, because
> I cannot endure to write another copy. For the pain in my head and
> teeth hath troubled me so sore these two or three days and doth yet so
> continue, that I have very small rest day or night.[28]

In Mary's resulting letter to Henry, the true author, Cromwell, seems to
represent very effectively her growing grief and pain, both physical and
mental. In it, they/she remind/s the King that she has written to him
twice before without acknowledgement, adding that, since

> I have not obtained my said fervent and hearty desire [to be in the
> King's presence and regain his love], ne any piece of the same, to my
> great and intolerable discomfort, I am enforced by the compulsion of
> nature, eftsones to cry unto your merciful ears, and most humbly pros-
> trate before your feet.[29]

This time, there was a response from Henry, but it was far from being the
one that Mary wanted.

On 15 June, the duke of Norfolk and Richard Sampson, bishop of
Chichester, went to Hunsdon on a royal commission. They had two questions to put to 'the Lady Mary'. Would she accept her father's 'headship'
of the Church of England, hence repudiating the bishop of Rome's
authority, and would she accept that her mother's marriage to the King
had been null and void, and hence that she was indeed, as Anne Boleyn
had said, a bastard? Once again, Mary vehemently refused to agree. She
steadfastly reaffirmed that she would, as she had always done, obey her
father in all things except three. She would accept nothing that went

<hr/>

[28] BL Cotton MS Otho C.X fol. 263b.
[29] Hearne, *Sylloge epistolarum*, p. 127.

against her mother's reputation, her own honour, and her religious faith. Never a gentle man, Norfolk's reply was brutal. He and Bishop Sampson had already told her that her 'disobedience' up to that point had been 'a monster in nature', compared with the way in which a daughter should behave towards her father. Now the duke lost his temper, as he was very prone to do. So 'unnatural' was her continued opposition to the King's will that he and the bishop 'could scarcely believe she was [Henry's] bastard, and if she were their daughter they would beat her and knock her head so hard against the wall that it made it as soft as a baked apple'. Mary was a traitress and should be punished. The commissioners then departed, instructing Lady Shelton to keep her charge under constant surveillance, and *incomunicada*.[30] It was indeed confirmed subsequently by judges that she was guilty of treason, and hence liable to the death penalty. Legal proceedings were opened against her, and the Council then met in a series of emergency sessions, from which the marquis of Exeter and Sir William Fitzwilliam were excluded, since they were regarded as Mary's supporters. In late June and early July, correspondence continued between Mary and Cromwell, in which the latter described her as 'the most obstinate woman that ever was', though he continued to seek reconciliation between her and her father, despite the fact that others regarded her as the figurehead for those who opposed the new religious settlement. In reality, the Secretary had so committed himself to the reconciliation that he began to feel, as he told Chapuys, that his own life, as well as Mary's, now depended on this initiative's success.[31] In his desperation, Cromwell began to put even greater pressure on the beleaguered 'princess', as she obstinately continued to see herself.

After the commissioners' return to London from their fruitless journey to Hunsdon, 'Master Secretary' wrote to Mary again, employing a mixture of unsubtle threats and moral blackmail. He accused her of having behaved 'diversely and contrarily' towards the duke and bishop, adding:

> Thus with your folly you undo yourself, and all that hath wished you good . . . Wherefore, Madam, to be plain, as God is my witness . . . I think you the most obdurate and obstinate woman, all things considered, that ever was, and one that so persevering, so well deserveth the reward of malice in extremity of mischief, or at least that you be both repentant for your ingrattitude and miserable unkindness, and ready to do all things that you be bound unto by your duty of allegiance.

With a belief in his own power and authority remarkably resembling that of his master, Cromwell then ordered Mary to sign the articles which he had drafted for her. If she refused, he would wash his hands of her

[30] *LP* XI, pp. 7–8 (no. 7).
[31] *CSP Span* V, ii, pp. 183–4 (no. 70).

entirely, since she would be showing obstinacy not only to her father but to God as well.[32] Perhaps precisely because she felt that Cromwell, as a mere subject, had overreached himself in addressing her in this way, and perhaps because of his apparent slur on her personal religious faith, Mary dug her heels in and refused to sign. Possibly she would have reacted differently if her father had written to her himself, but instead he showed his anger at her resistance by lashing out at her friends and allies. Not long after the departure from Court of Exeter and Fitzwilliam, two gentlemen of the privy chamber, Sir Anthony Browne and Sir Francis Bryan, were arrested and interrogated. Henry thought that they were encouraging Mary to defy him, and their evidence appeared to implicate one of her close friends, Sir Nicholas Carew. He had indeed exchanged letters with Mary, as well as with two other gentlemen of the privy chamber, Thomas Cheney and John Russell. Sir Francis Bryan was particularly talkative. He claimed that others, as well as those whom he accused by name, had been delighted at the downfall of Anne Boleyn, and were of the view that, if Jane Seymour did not bear Henry a son, Mary should be reinstated as heir presumptive. Not only that, but even before Catherine's death and Anne's arrest, these men had been conspiring against Anne with the aim of securing Imperial intervention and the restoration of religious obedience to Rome.[33] Also sent to the Tower of London was Lady Anne Hussey, wife of Mary's chamberlain, John, Lord Hussey, who was removed from his post at this time. Lady Anne's 'crime' had been to continue addressing Mary as 'princess', instead of 'lady', showing a disregard for royal orders which added the couple to the King's ever-lengthening list of 'Marian' suspects.

Given these actions on the part of her father, it became evident to his elder daughter, as June went on, that she herself was indeed, as much of Europe already feared, in mortal danger. Although his agents failed to uncover any substantive plot among those who were interrogated in the Tower, or among their connections, the King now decided that he would charge Mary with treason anyway. She was to be tried in her absence and pronounced 'contumacious' for not appearing in court. As was customary in the reign of 'Good King Henry', the judges were threatened with the severest penalties if they did not carry out his orders in the case, but they feared popular fury, if Mary was treated in this way, even more than their increasingly violent and unpredictable master. In desperation, they came up with a last-ditch suggestion. Could the Lady Mary not be required to sign a written document in which she would submit to the King's demands and thus fully recognize his authority? The King took this idea up, and Cromwell was instructed to write yet again to Mary, very much on the lines 'suggested' by the judges. This was the crisis, and Chapuys, naturally, was consulted again. He was fully aware, of course, that it was a matter of

---

[32] Hearne, *Sylloge epistolarum*, pp. 137–8.
[33] *LP* X, pp. 243–5 (no. 601), 377 (no. 908).

life and death, not only for Catherine's daughter but also for those who remained incarcerated under suspicion. As he subsequently explained to his master Charles V, he advised her not to sacrifice herself. To save her own life and also prevent further conflict in England, she should sign whatever was presented to her, and make any necessary pretence to the Crown, since, in such dire circumstances, God paid regard to the intention rather than the act itself. Chapuys told the Emperor that, as far as he could see, things were heading towards the restoration of Mary's legitimacy in English law, together with the bastardization of Elizabeth, as long as Henry got his way over her submission. The ambassador expressed optimism that, if Mary returned to Court in favour, she would be able to steer her father towards policies which better suited the Empire and the Papacy. The latter was a concern, given that Paul III had threatened a crusade against schismatical England. Chapuys's suggested remedy was that Charles's ambassador in Rome, the count of Cifuentes, should at the same time ask the Holy Father to grant a blanket absolution to Mary for anything that she was forced by her father to sign.[34] This spiritual loophole cannot have given much consolation to Mary, if any, in the agony in which she found herself in the second half of June 1536. She was ground between Cromwell's pressure on one hand, and Chapuys's on the other, with God her only refuge, except possibly for her distant cousin, Cardinal Reginald Pole, of whom much more will be heard.

Cromwell's letter, in reply to yet another written plea from Mary, was flatly uncompromising. In it he claimed to have been upset by her latest letter to him, which may well be true since by now he needed her submission to save his own skin. He stated unambiguously that her 'stupidity' was threatening her dearest friends as well as herself, and he predicted an exemplary punishment for her if she did not change her mind rapidly. He enclosed the formulations which she had to sign, and on 22 June 1536, a day which would haunt her for the rest of her life, she did so. She put her name, 'Marye', separately to three articles. The first was a complete submission to Henry as king, and the second fully acknowledged him as the 'supreme head in earth under Christ of the Church of England', rejecting 'the Bishop of Rome's pretended authority, power and jurisdiction within this realm, heretofore usurped'. The third recognized and acknowledged that her parents' marriage was 'by God's law and Man's law incestuous and unlawful'. Inevitably, in these circumstances, she had to accept that her beloved mother Queen Catherine, whom she had been mourning for just six months, was 'the late Princess Dowager', just Prince Arthur's widow.[35]

Chapuys, putting the Imperial interest first as always, reported to Charles that Mary's surrender was the best thing that she had ever done, since no one in the world could have saved her if she had not signed. However, he had to say that she was utterly crushed afterwards, and that he had tried to

[34] *LP* XI, p. 7.
[35] Hearne, *Sylloge epistolarum*, p. 142; *LP* X, p. 478.

console her by assuring her that the Pope would not censure her and would even praise her for what she had done, in the circumstances. In the event, though, Paul III did anything but help her. She learned, no doubt to her horror and despair, that he was sticking to the letter of canon law and would not give her licence to renounce secretly her submission to her father, and hence continue to be regarded as a Catholic in the eyes of the Church, on the grounds that she had succumbed externally to schism but not inwardly to heresy. Instead, because she had publicly assented to the royal supremacy over the English Church, she would have to reverse this action in the same way, which would be catastrophic for her in current circumstances. During the ever deepening religious conflicts of the mid-sixteenth century, the practice of 'Nicodemism', named after the Jewish leader who came secretly to see Jesus by night and thus received his teaching (John 3), was understood to refer to any Christian who concealed his or her true beliefs in the face of governmental restriction and persecution. This was highly controversial in both Catholic and reformed circles. In the very same year that Mary submitted to her father, the French reformer John Calvin condemned Nicodemism in letters, which he subsequently published, to Nicolas Duchemin, who had studied law with him at Orléans, and to Gérard Rousel, who, in the early 1520s, had been a member of a reforming Catholic circle at Meaux. As a basis for his opposition to those who kept their true beliefs secret, but outwardly conformed to the Catholic Church, Calvin used some words from the prophet Elijah to the people of Israel concerning their flirtation with paganism: 'How long will you go limping with two different opinions? If the Lord is God, follow him; but if Baal, then follow him' (I Kings 18: 21).[36] What made Pope Paul apply similar pressure to Mary is not clear, though the inflexible Reginald Pole was obviously influential in English matters, but such meticulous legalism took no account either of her own psychological state or of her father's violent intransigence. Paul did, however, allow her confessors to absolve her, in secret of course, like Nicodemus, along with others who inwardly rejected Henry's reforms but could not show their true beliefs. Charles V, not the Pope, would be Mary's emotional prop in the succeeding years.

It quickly became clear that her abject submission would not be enough for Henry, and that she herself would have to become, in some respects, a 'Nicodemite', even though the English schism had not yet fully become heresy from the Roman point of view. Mary's twice-widowed and increasingly unhealthy father still did not believe that her submission was genuine, and his continuing suspicion led him to demand yet more declarations from her. Finally, after so much steadfast resistance, she was required to recognize Anne Boleyn's daughter Elizabeth as heir to the throne. Also, she was interrogated about her views on the doctrinal changes which Henry had introduced to the English Church. At this point, it was as though the Pope and the

---

[36] Pérez Martín, *María Tudor*, p. 285; Bruce Gordon, *Calvin* (New Haven, CT and London: Yale University Press, 2009), pp. 190–5.

King were fighting inside her mind, and under these highly stressful conditions her views were demanded on such contentious matters as Purgatory and religious pilgrimages. After she had signed the three articles of submission, Mary received, by the hand of Thomas Wriothesley, a further document from Cromwell, on the King's behalf. In her reply, she accepted that Elizabeth was indeed the 'princess', though she asked to be allowed to continue calling her 'sister'. Cromwell had evidently indicated that some changes were going to be made to her household, and she said that she would accept whomever was sent, though she suggested three of her former retainers, Margaret Baynton, Susan Clarencius and Mary Brown. On the subjects of Purgatory, pilgrimages, saints' relics, and other traditional religious beliefs and practices, she very diplomatically, if not entirely convincingly, answered that she believed with her whole heart whatever her father believed.

Perhaps not surprisingly, the battle of wills between father and daughter, equally proud and certain of the absolute rightness of their views, would continue. Initially, though, all seemed to be sweetness and light. Some rejoicing over her capitulation was permitted at Court, she was officially recognized once again as the King's daughter, hence his anxiety over her attitude to Elizabeth, and she received a fine new wardrobe of clothes, as well as some of her old and trusted servants. Above all, though, Mary wanted to see her father again, and he now seemed to share the desire for a meeting, being encouraged in this direction by his current wife. Thus on Thursday, 6 July 1536, Mary travelled with a small escort from Hunsdon to Hackney, north of London, for a private meeting with her father and Queen Jane. Even if the atmosphere was strained, all three seem to have tried their best. Henry and Mary had not seen each other for five years, but now the King was as effusive as he could be, claiming that he was sorry they had been apart for so long. The Queen gave her a diamond ring, and Henry supplied a fairly lavish thousand crowns (£250) of pocket money. The next day, Mary returned to Hunsdon, and her father and stepmother to London.[37] It looked as though a return to Court was now on the cards, but Chapuys still saw ominous signs in Henry's attitude. Before she was readmitted, Mary had to endure another harrowing ordeal. She was made to write to Charles V and his sister, Mary of Hungary, formally confirming her submission to her father in every particular. Henry told Chapuys that he blamed the Emperor for his daughter's obstinacy, and implied that he expected the Habsburgs to go on causing him trouble, though he asserted that they would never succeed as long as he lived.[38] To ram the message home, including his own status next (just) to God, the King gave Mary a 'celebratory' ring, bearing his and Jane's images and an inscription which sententiously read:

[37] *LP* XI, p. 24 (no. 40); *CSP Ven* V, II, p. 195 (no. 71).
[38] *LP* XI, p. 229 (no. 576), pp. 241–2 (no. 597); *CSP Ven* II, p. 220 (no. 85).

Obedience leads to unity, unity to constancy and a quiet mind, and these are treasures of inestimable worth. For God so valued humility that he gave His only Son, a perfect exemplar of modesty, who in His obedience to His Divine Father, taught lessons of obedience and devotion.[39]

Henry knew exactly how to hit his first child at her most vulnerable point, the heart of her religious faith, and the words of this inscription must have been painful, when her mind was filled with memories of her but recently deceased mother, and uncertainty, thanks to Pope Paul, about the standing of her soul in the eyes of the Church and of God. Things were not getting any easier. While she awaited the summons to Court, Mary stayed at Hunsdon, still somewhat short of money but at least in the company of more congenial servants, many of whom she knew and had chosen. The infant Elizabeth seemed less of a threat since the execution of her mother, and Mary passed her time in the customary manner of the learned and cultured Tudors, studying a wide range of academic subjects and working on her keyboard and lute playing with court musicians, Master Pastor and Philip van Wilder respectively, the lessons being paid for by the King. Nonetheless, he was still nursing his suspicions about the sincerity of Mary's surrender. He demanded to know whether she continued to correspond with her cousin the Emperor. A search was made at Hunsdon and the drafts of two letters addressed to Charles were duly found and confiscated. Henry greatly feared Imperial influence over his daughter and ordered her to write again to Charles and Mary of Hungary, confirming her submission to her father in every particular. In Brussels as in Rome, her supporters prayed that she would be able to survive, if only as a 'Nicodemite'.

Inevitably, the five years of her separation from her parents, together with all the other pressures to which she was subjected and the death of her mother, did considerable damage to Mary's health. Back in 1534, when she was eighteen, John Heywood, who had written plays to entertain her as a child, addressed to her 'A description of a most noble lady, . . . who advertising her y[e]ars as face, saith of her thus in much eloquent phrase . . .':

In each of her eyes
Ther smiles a naked boye,
It would you all suffice
To see those lamps of ioye [. . .]
Her colour comes and goes
With such a goodly grace,
More ruddye than the rose
Within her lively face.[40]

[39] *LP* XI, p. 65 (no. 148).
[40] BL Harleian MS 1703, fols 108r–109r.

With its fashionable reference to Renaissance putti (the 'naked boye[s]'), this may be one of the last images, crafted by a literary master, of Mary as she was just before her long years of rejection, isolation and waiting began.

Even when Heywood wrote these lines, this view of Mary was either over-optimistic or harked back to better days. By August 1534, the medical, and perhaps psychological, problems from which she had been suffering since about 1530 had become so severe that the Imperial ambassador demanded that Henry take action. The King responded by sending his own physician, William Butt, who visited her on 2 September 1534, reporting back on the same day that she was in 'a mean state of health', at the beginning of a new bout of her 'old disease'. No doubt thinking like a professional medical man, and not a Tudor politician, Butt told the King that he had given instructions for Catherine's physician and pharmacist, Dr de la Sá and her other pharmacist, Juan de Soto, to attend to Mary. Possibly she was suffering from strong period pains in the form of bad headaches and stomach cramps, and Lady Shelton, who was running her household, was so concerned that she had sent for another pharmacist, Mr Michael, who had given her pills. These had provoked a severe reaction, with the result that the English pharmacist, no doubt fearing for his future, had firmly told Chapuys that he would not intervene further in the case. The Spaniards were allowed to treat Mary, but told that everything had to be done in English, not Spanish, to avoid accusations of political intrigue.[41] After her mother Catherine's death, in January 1536, such symptoms recurred, and seem to have been accompanied by a depression, or 'melancholy', which would haunt Mary for the rest of her life. Even after her partial, and for her traumatic, reconciliation with her father in the summer of that year, a further threat and torment appeared for Mary in the autumn, arising out of the actions of some who declared themselves to be her supporters.

What proved to be the greatest military and political threat to Henry throughout his entire reign started on 1 October 1536, with protests after the Sunday services – solemn procession, mass and evensong – in Louth parish church in Lincolnshire. The next day, the church was due to be visited on routine business by two commissioners from the King and the chancellor of the diocese of Lincoln. As the day went on, many of the congregation became convinced that much of the parish's liturgical apparatus, including processional crosses, incense thuribles and Eucharistic chalices made of silver, were to be confiscated and replaced with base metal objects. Many also believed that there were to be mergers of parishes and that the abandoned buildings would be torn down, like some of the smaller monasteries which had been dissolved earlier in the year. The confrontation between parishioners and officialdom, which took

[41] *LP* VII, p. 1129; Linda Porter, *Mary Tudor: The First Queen* (London: Portrait, 2007), pp. 102–3.

place in Louth on Monday, 2 October, quickly developed into an uprising, first in central and northern Lincolnshire and then in Yorkshire. The precise aims of the rebels, who severely frightened Henry and his government, are still a matter of controversy, some preferring to stress economic and social explanations to do with the extortionate financial demands of the government while others have emphasized the specifically religious issues with which the trouble apparently started.[42] It seems clear that the defence of traditional religion against attack from those perceived as heretics, in particular Secretary Thomas Cromwell and Archbishop Thomas Cranmer, as well as other bishops and officials who were held to be central to the reform, was a main motive. The primacy of religion in the uprising is demonstrated by the adoption, once it spread to Yorkshire, of the name 'Pilgrimage of Grace', together with the badge and banner of the five wounds of Christ crucified – the crown of thorns on the head, the nails through the hands and the two feet together, and the spear with which Jesus's side was pierced (Matthew 27: 29, 35; Mark 15: 17, 25; Luke 23: 35; John 19: 12, 18, 34).

Given the high state of alert and even fear which understandably gripped the King and his advisers in the autumn and winter of 1536–7, as rebellion appeared to spread like wildfire in the north, together with the traditionalist religious demands of the rebels, it seemed inevitable that Mary would be suspected of involvement. It is true that in the earlier 1530s she had followed her mother's example in refusing to have any contact with Elizabeth Barton, the 'Nun of Kent', whose prophecies against Henry's divorce and the Royal Supremacy led to her execution as a traitor in 1534.[43] The Nun did, however, speak up for Mary's rights as princess and heir to the throne, and the Act of Attainder drawn up against her and her clerical supporter Edward Bocking explicitly referred to her speaking of the possibility of rebellion in the country on Mary's behalf.[44] Now, two years later, Mary's recent reconciliation with her father was shaky in the extreme and Henry was convinced that she still had seditious links with Brussels and Rome; to cap it all, she was named in the rebel 'articles', drawn up in Pontefract castle in December 1536: 'Art. 3: Item, we humbly beseech our

[42] C. S. L. Davies, 'The Pilgrimage of Grace Reconsidered', *Past and Present*, xli (1968), pp. 54–76, reprinted in *Popular Protest and the Social Order in Early Modern England*, ed. Paul Slack (Cambridge: Cambridge University Press, 1984), pp. 16–36; M. L. Bush, *The Pilgrimage of Grace* (Manchester: Manchester University Press, 1996); R. W. Hoyle, *The Pilgrimage of Grace and the Politics of the 1530s* (Oxford: Oxford University Press, 2001); Geoffrey Moorhouse, *The Pilgrimage of Grace: The Rebellion that Shook Henry VIII's Reign* (London: Weidenfeld & Nicolson, 2002); Ethan H. Shagan, *Popular Politics and the English Reformation* (Cambridge: Cambridge University Press, 2003), pp. 89–128; Bernard, *King's Reformation*, pp. 293–404.

[43] 1/127, fols 63–7; *LP* XII, ii, pp. 121–2; Sharon L. Jansen, *Dangerous Talk and Strange Behaviour: Women and Popular Resistance to the Reforms of Henry VIII* (Basingstoke: Macmillan, 1996), pp. 51, 70.

[44] 1/82, fols 69–70; Bernard, *King's Reformation*, pp. 100–1.

most dread sovereign Lord that the Lady Mary may be made legitimate and the former statutes therein annulled . . .'[45] Also, John, Lord Hussey and his wife Lady Anne had served in Mary's household, the former as her chamberlain, until it was dissolved on the birth of Elizabeth in September 1533. When the trouble in Lincolnshire started, the Husseys were on their estates at Sleaford, in the south of the county, and appeared to give some support to rebels there, including a cart of food and drink from Lady Anne. They would never have been appointed to Mary's household if Henry had seen them as dissidents, and indeed they soon tried to dissociate themselves from the rebellion, yet they do seem to have shared the religious views of the 'pilgrims'. Although it used to be argued that the uprising was manip-ulated by the gentry and nobility, it now seems clear that Hussey and his social equals were put under heavy, and sometimes violent, pressure to support the protest. Hussey later died as a traitor for his pains, and Lady Anne remained in retirement after the revolt had been crushed, but even so no link was ever made between them and Mary.[46] Even more tellingly, when one of the main leaders of the Pilgrimage, the Yorkshire lawyer Robert Aske, was eventually interrogated, in April 1537, and made fulsome statements about her, still no one seems to have suggested that she was in any way involved in what had happened. Nonetheless, Aske's comments on the third Pontefract article are revealing and intriguing. He declared that Mary was 'marvellously beloved for her virtue in the hearts of the people', and added that

all the wise men of these parts much grudged she should so be made [illegitimate] by the laws of this realm, seeing she on the mother side was comen of the greatest blood and parage [descent] of Christendom . . . whose aunsitores [ancestors] were always, as of long time have been, great friends and favourers of the commonwealth of this realm.

This warm allusion to Mary's Spanish ancestry gives an interesting perspective on the supposed anti-Spanish fixation of the Tudor English, though there was of course a great difference between being ruled by rela-tives of a Spanish royal house and actually being subject to a reigning king of Spain. Aske added that he and others also 'grudged' the statute whereby parliament had granted the King absolute power to choose his successor, as well as declaring Mary to be a bastard. He did not, however, suggest that she was in any way connected with the Pilgrimage of Grace, and no such suggestion seems to have been made to him.[47]

---

[45] Hoyle, *Pilgrimage of Grace*, p. 461.

[46] Ibid., pp. 67, 159; Moorhouse, *Pilgrimage of Grace*, pp. 58–9, 85, 182, 194, 208, 300–1; Starkey, *Six Wives*, pp. 515, 598, 602; Bernard, *King's Reformation*, pp. 300–2, 319, 322, 324, 401.

[47] E36/119/fol. 96, in Bernard, *King's Reformation*, p. 342.

Henry and his supporters may also have thought that Mary would seek
support from the Papacy, and that the major rebellion in the north against
his religious reforms might bring intervention from Rome as well as from
the Habsburgs in Brussels. In the autumn of 1536, it must have looked
increasingly likely that such action, if it occurred, would be led by Reginald
Pole, who had his own claim to the English throne and was also talked of
as a likely husband for Mary, since Paul III had carefully kept him as a
deacon, and thus free from the normally irrevocable clerical orders of
priest and bishop. Not only was Pole now a cardinal, but he was also
appointed as papal legate to England, and despatched to Flanders to
monitor the events which seemed to be threatening to topple Henry's schismatical regime. Given her undoubted popularity in the country, and not
just in the north, as well as the evident popular support for her notions on
religion, Mary's response to unfolding events must have been watched with
almost morbid fascination by the regime and its loyal agents. The nightmare scenario was that a crusade would be sent to England, with Imperial
generalship and Pole as papal representative, leading to an uprising in
support of Mary as Catholic queen, like her Spanish grandmother. In the
event, despite great provocation, and whatever her personal views may
have been on what the government was doing, she seems to have avoided
any action which could be construed as treasonable even under her father's
increasingly draconian and comprehensive laws on the subject. Mary also
seems to have made no direct contact with Pole, no doubt on the advice
and with the active support of Chapuys, who represented to her the
sympathy but also the caution of her other cousin, the Emperor Charles. It
was no doubt politically wise, as well as humane, that, when Mary was
given the chance to choose servants for her reconstituted household, she
did not recall her former governess and mentor, Margaret Pole, countess of
Salisbury. In the succeeding years, Mary also avoided involvement in the
dissidence and supposed conspiracy, most if not all of it a fabrication of the
King and his inner circle, which would lead to the execution, in January
1539, of Reginald's older brother Henry, Lord Montague, along with other
relatives and servants of the Pole family – Edward Courtenay, marquis of
Exeter, Sir Edward Neville, George Crofts, John Collins and Hugh
Holland. The youngest Pole, Sir Geoffrey, was pardoned for the sake of the
evidence that he had blurted out, but none of the material gathered by the
government ever really amounted to a plot.[48] But, by then, Mary was
facing a new problem in the shape of a male heir to the English throne.

At the time when they had their meeting with Henry's older daughter,
at Hackney in early July 1536, he and Jane were not expecting a child, but
the prospect of the eventual arrival of the longed-for son at last persuaded
the King to summon Mary back to Court. Inevitably, although many were
delighted to see her back, she was paraded as a symbol of her father's

[48] Pierce, *Margaret Pole*, pp. 108–9, 115–40, 152–4; Bernard, *King's Reformation*, pp. 404–32.

victory.[49] The smallness of the reward which she received in return for her costly sacrifice was illustrated dramatically in the new Act of Succession. Despite her surrender, this statute did not recognize her as legal heir to the kingdom, as the ambassador Chapuys, for one, had hoped and even expected. Nevertheless, it did strip Elizabeth of the title 'princess' and her status as heir, but instead of Mary being restored to her initial position, it was declared that the succession would pass through the heirs of Henry and Jane, who were, of course, yet to be born, or else, interestingly and perhaps ominously for Jane, in default of such, through the children of any future queen. To add to the confusion, the 1536 Act of Succession also gave Henry the legal power to amend the succession further in any future will that he might make.[50] By the autumn of 1536, Jane had still not conceived, so her coronation was postponed, while Mary remained sufficiently in favour to be invited to ride through London with the King and Queen at Christmas that year.[51] Finally, on or about 23 May 1537, Jane's pregnancy became known at Court and the hymn of praise *Te Deum* was sung on this account at St Paul's Cathedral on the 27th. The Queen went into confinement at Hampton Court during September. After a long and difficult labour, she finally gave birth to her son Edward early on Friday, 12 October 1537, and he was baptized by Archbishop Cranmer in the palace chapel on the following Monday, with Mary as the prince's godmother. Within a week of the birth, public prayers were being offered for the Queen's health, and on 23 October her apparent recovery encouraged Henry to leave for his hunting-lodge at nearby Esher, but in fact she died at about midnight on 24–25 October, probably of puerperal fever, or some other infection associated with childbirth, which could not then be treated.[52] During that time, with the infant Edward heir to the throne under the terms of the 1536 Act, Mary remained at Court, no doubt giving her father some support in the great grief which he very publicly felt at the death of Jane.

In the autumn of 1537, Francis I and Charles V declared a truce in their long-standing conflict and started peace talks. This was a worrying development for Henry as it threatened to leave England an isolated minor power in European politics. The rapprochement did, however, have the interesting consequence of launching father and daughter on the royal marriage market at the same time, though with very different personal specifications. Given that it was likely to become more difficult for the English, at least for the time being, to foment conflict between France and the Empire, the attraction of alliances with other countries which were not aligned with either of these major powers became greater. On the other hand, a suitable

---

[49] *LP* XI, pp. 20–4 (no. 40).

[50] Statute 28 Hen. VIII, c. 7; Starkey, *Six Wives*, p. 600.

[51] Starkey, *Six Wives*, pp. 601–3.

[52] Ibid., pp. 605–8; Loades, *Mary Tudor*, pp. 103–16; Chris Skidmore, *Edward VI: The Lost King of England* (London: Weidenfeld & Nicolson, 2007), pp. 14–19.

fourth wife for Henry, to be queen consort of England, could only be found among European royalty or the English aristocracy. Given Henry's fear of intrigue among those with English royal blood, as witnessed by his suspicion of and violence towards the Poles and Courtenays, it was necessary to look abroad. Thus despite his mourning for Jane, which seems to have been genuine enough, encouragement from the Council, and particularly from Thomas Cromwell, very soon led him to begin looking for a wife abroad. The search would last two years, and Henry began with France and the Empire in the hope that a marriage alliance might be made before the two powers formally agreed peace, which carried the danger that they might together turn on schismatical England. Numerous women were mentioned but all escaped Henry's clutches. In France, the main candidates were King Francis's daughter Margaret, and Marie, the youngest sister of the duke of Guise and the cardinal of Lorraine. Marie de Guise was the favourite until, in May 1538, she married James V of Scotland and became the mother of Mary, 'Queen of Scots'. Well before that, in December 1537, Henry had, however, set his heart on marrying Christina, second daughter of the deposed King Christian II of Denmark, but also a niece of Charles V and Mary of Hungary. Christina had returned to the Habsburg Court in the Netherlands, having been widowed as duchess of Milan, and being assured of her great beauty and good temperament, Henry entered into a vain quest for her hand.[53]

While Mary's father mobilized the diplomatic corps on his own matrimonial business, he did not fail to notice that she, too, was a potential political asset for England. In the months following Queen Jane's death, Mary's duties as Edward's godmother became more important. Living most of the time at Hampton Court, she travelled on occasions, though not frequently, to the now motherless prince's nursery at Richmond Palace, seeing him in November 1537 and in March, April and May 1538.[54] By the standards of contemporary royalty this was a major effort and it does seem to have created an emotional bond between Mary and her stepbrother, which would be significant when he reached the throne. One project, that Mary should marry Luis, the widowed younger brother of John III of Portugal, was revived from 1536. His name had first been raised in connection with her a few months after her mother's death, and when she had already been declared illegitimate. Charles V had then proposed Luis as her husband, provided that her bastardization was first revoked. On 25 April 1536, Henry instructed his ambassador to the Imperial court, Richard Pate, to reject this proposal on the grounds that the marriage abroad of the now marginalized Mary would constitute foreign interference in the affairs of England. In his orders to Pate, Henry chose to ignore the suggestion that his elder daughter

[53] *LP* XII, ii, pp. 1004, 1285; *LP* XIII, i, pp. 56, 203; *LP* XII, ii, pp. 1172, 1187; *LP* XIII, i, pp. 123.

[54] F. Madden, ed., *The Privy Purse expenses of Princess Mary, daughter of King Henry VIII* (London: William Pickering, 1831), pp. 61, 67, 69.

should be legitimized again.[55] Nonetheless, by November 1536 it appeared that Luis was generally being seen as the most likely husband for Mary and, although her father was against the idea, he felt it necessary to put up a diplomatic smokescreen. Negotiations with Charles were allowed to continue with the hope, on the Imperial side, that marriage to Luis might provide Mary with an escape route from her now intolerable situation in England. Nevertheless, her father was attending at this time to overtures from the French king, who suggested that Lady Mary might marry his eldest son, the dauphin François and, when he died later in 1536, Francis I proposed instead the duke of Angoulême. Naturally, the French were also anxious that Mary should be legitimized once more, but Henry was still opposed to this and generally against her having a foreign husband. The possibility of her marrying Luis of Portugal did not however fade away entirely. In January 1538, in the new circumstances which followed the birth of Edward, Charles V revived the project. This marriage was now seen in Brussels as a way of binding Henry VIII into a new league of powers directed against France, despite the peace negotiations with Francis which were continuing on a parallel track. As bait, and to honour his late aunt's daughter, Charles was now prepared to grant the duchy of Milan to Luis, thus setting Mary up as consort of the ruler of one of the most important Italian states, though a Habsburg satellite. Henry, fearing diplomatic isolation if he refused, responded positively to the suggestion. He also needed Charles's support for a general council of the Church, which he hoped would curb the Papacy and usher in general reform, as well as legitimizing the divorce of Catherine. At the same time, his own desire to marry the dowager duchess Christina was in danger of further complicating diplomatic ties.

Nevertheless, by the end of February 1538, agreement on the betrothal of Mary and Luis seemed to be near, and with it the intriguing prospect of a Tudor presence in a strategically important part of northern Italy. At this stage, Henry believed that he had persuaded the Imperial ambassador in London, at least, that Mary should remain illegitimate, and succeed to the English throne only in default of all other lawful issue, male or female. Henry's bastard son, the duke of Richmond, had died in 1536, and his claims would in any case have been trumped by the arrival of Edward in the following year. A dowry of 100,000 crowns was offered to the Milanese for Mary, and such was the confidence on the Continent of the likelihood of an agreement by the end of March that it was believed, even in Rome, that Luis and Mary would shortly become duke and duchess of Milan. At this point, though, Henry started haggling over the dowry, because the French, who were desperately anxious to remove Habsburg – let alone Tudor – influence from Milan, proposed at the last minute that Mary should instead marry Henri, duke of Orléans, the future Henry II of

[55] *LP* X, p. 726.

France. Francis I seems genuinely to have feared that his old sparring partner Henry of England would instead marry the dowager Christina, and himself become duke of Milan, the political consequences of such a development being incalculable. Such were the problems caused by father and daughter seeking marriage at the same time. Francis hoped that, if his son Henri married Mary, he would achieve a bloodless victory in Milan, an outcome long desired by himself and his predecessors on the French throne. In the event, in May 1538, the English King withdrew from plans to marry Mary to Luis of Portugal and turned towards the French, while Christina definitively rejected him as a husband, sharply remarking that if she had two heads, she might have been able to spare him one. In appearance at least, Charles continued to back the Portuguese marriage for Mary, by October 1538 offering to make the grant of Milan to Luis a fact and declaring, apparently without consultation with Lisbon, in the cavalier manner so often adopted by Spanish kings towards Portugal, that if Mary should ever succeed to the Crown of England, Luis would fully abide by the laws of that kingdom. Yet at this stage the plan did not rate particularly highly among the strategic aims and needs of the Habsburgs, and it fell into abeyance.[56]

The next target of Henry's search for marriage, for himself and Mary, was Germany. The strategic attraction of this scheme was the avoidance of entanglements with the great powers, France and the Empire; the practical reason was a failure to achieve any success with either. Another factor was the manoeuvring in religion which Henry was undertaking in his newfound role as 'supreme head' of the English Church. If one wished to avoid being pro-French or pro-Habsburg, Roman Catholic or explicitly 'Protestant', then the muddled German situation might provide opportunities. Although Thomas Cromwell doubtless did not bear the sole responsibility for what followed, with which he was later saddled at the cost of his life, in the prevailing circumstances he saw the possibilities of such a move. In January 1539, Henry was convinced that the newly reconciled Francis and Charles might attack him, and thus agreed to send Christopher Mont as his ambassador to Duke Johann Friedrich of Saxony, a devout Lutheran and leading member of the Schmalkaldic League of Protestant German princes, who were engaged in a life-or-death struggle with Charles, as Emperor. The duke was married to Sybilla, eldest sister of Duke Wilhelm of Cleves, who was intended by the English to help secure an arrangement by which King Henry would marry the next sister in line, Anne of Cleves, while the Lady Mary was to marry the duke of Cleves, Jülich and Berg himself. As in the earlier negotiations with France and the Empire, Mary's illegitimacy was bound to be an issue, but Cromwell instructed Mont to tell the Germans that although she was only a 'natural' daughter of the King, she nonetheless had great beauty and moral qualities which would more

---

[56] *LP* X, p. 726; H. F. M. Prescott, *Mary Tudor: The Spanish Tudor* (London: Phoenix, [1940] 2003), pp. 91, 116–17.

than compensate for all the rest.[57] After months of negotiation and delay, it was agreed, in October 1539, that Anne would indeed become Henry of England's fourth wife. Her 'reformed' religious affiliation was sufficiently ambiguous to match that of Cranmer's England, given that her brother's territories were uncomfortably sandwiched between the Habsburg Netherlands and various Catholic German states. Another German prince, instead of the duke of Cleves, was lined up for Mary's hand.

Philip, duke of Bavaria, was a nephew of the count-elector of the Rhineland Palatinate. Although he had not formally joined the evangelical camp, he was no friend of the Habsburgs or of Rome, and his appearance, in the autumn of 1539, as a prospective husband caused another crisis for Mary, who was evidently still very disturbed by her forced submission to her father three years before. Perhaps Henry or Cromwell realized that the brutal tactics they had used in 1536 would not do now. In December 1539, Thomas Wriothesley, who was in any case close to Master Secretary, was chosen to communicate the duke of Bavaria's candidacy to Mary, who was then living in Hertford castle. Very unusually for a foreign royal suitor, Duke Philip was then in England, in advance of Anne of Cleves's arrival to marry the King. Mary wrote back to Wriothesley, in what must have seemed like something of a rerun of her harrowing time in the summer of 1536, saying that while she would of course obey her father in all things, she would rather remain single than marry someone who was not a full adherent of traditional Catholic religion. Nonetheless, just before Christmas 1539, she agreed to come to London and meet Philip, which she did on 26 December with an interpreter who could no doubt act as chaperon as well as helping if the pair's Latin proved inadequate, which was unlikely in Mary's case. The meeting took place in the abbot of Westminster's garden and, in a notable breach of protocol for which the lady did not apparently rebuke him at the time, the enthusiastic duke kissed Mary, as well as giving her a bejewelled cross. He had perhaps been emboldened by the seriousness with which her father and the government were treating his suit. Philip had offered to serve Henry in battle, and a formal treaty was drafted whereby Mary would waive all her rights to the English throne and go to Germany with a substantial dowry of £7,000. These moves, which seem to represent Cromwell's ambition as well as Henry's desperation, caught both the French and the Habsburgs on the hop. When he heard of it, the French ambassador in London thought the wedding would take place in mid-January 1540, and the news of these events, which as far as possible had been kept from Charles's ambassador, caused consternation in Brussels and also in Rome, where it was believed initially that the deed had already been done.[58] Duke Philip, too, seems to have thought that the deal was on. He left for Germany after Christmas, but returned in the New Year, was created a knight of the

[57] *LP* XIV, i, p. 41 (no. 103).
[58] Hearne, *Sylloge epistolarum*, pp. 149–51; *LP* XIV, ii, pp. 269–71 (no. 733).

Garter by Henry and even met Mary again. It seems that the eventual collapse of the Bavarian scheme was a collateral consequence of Henry's own marital failure with Anne of Cleves.

At Greenwich on 6 January 1540, the Feast of the Epiphany, Mary attended her father's fourth wedding, to Anne. Henry's rejection of this unfortunate lady, who at twenty-four was just a year older than Mary, has been much discussed but never fully explained. She and Mary seem nonetheless to have developed a friendship which survived the annulment by Cranmer of the King's fourth marriage, and continued into Mary's own reign. Before that Mary avoided any public reaction to the downfall of Thomas Cromwell and his execution on 29 July 1540, and her relationship with her father between then and his death remained as variable as his own mood and temperament. Any satisfaction which Mary may have drawn from the death of her former tormentor, Cromwell, was cruelly balanced by the burning shortly afterwards, at Henry's order and supposedly for 'papism', of her old schoolmaster Richard Fetherstone. The brief reign of Catherine Howard, from July 1540 until November 1541, saw Mary remain on 'the queen's side' at Court, but in the strange situation of having a stepmother who was five years younger than herself, and also a cousin of the hated Anne Boleyn. There seems to have been a wide temperamental gap between the two women despite their common taste for fine clothes and jewellery. Catherine complained to Henry that Mary was much less respectful towards her than she had been to any of her predecessors as queen, with the result that the two avoided each other as far as possible. But the discrediting and death of the young Catherine, for serial promiscuity and adultery, at least left Mary in a kind of stability.

Things would, however, be different when, on 12 July 1543, Henry married his sixth and last wife, Catherine Parr, also known by her former surnames Green and Latimer. At the time, although Mary seems to have had no separate household of her own, she appears to have been close to her father once more as he tried to recover from his depression over Catherine Howard's behaviour, and she was one of the few who attended the wedding. Catherine Parr had served in Mary's household years before and the two were already friends before the latter became queen, on 12 July 1543. When she did, Catherine seems to have enjoyed ordering in the best foreign fashions and looking at them with Mary. They also seemed to share cultural and religious tastes. Catherine profited from Mary's high level of education. There is an understandable but misleading tendency to project back on to the religious and spiritual life of the 1540s the confessional or denominational divisions which would crystallize later in the century. In particular, it sometimes seems to be assumed that personal devotion to Christ as Saviour was unique to those with evangelical or reformist views, but this is to ignore the deep devotional currents of the late Middle Ages, exemplified by the Netherlandish *Devotio moderna*, which strongly influenced all of western Europe well into the sixteenth century. In this context, it was quite natural for Catherine Parr to translate works by John Fisher and by the Florentine Dominican reformer Girolamo Savonarola. This was possible even though Fisher had been executed by her husband as a traitor for his traditional religious beliefs and Savonarola had been burned as a heretic. To stress this devotional core is not of course to suggest that Catherine and Mary saw eye to eye on all religious matters, but it indicates a serious basis for their friendship in the last days of Henry VIII.[59] What seemed like a new lease of life, intense, personal and Christ-centred, begun with the arrival of Henry's sixth queen, did not however enable Mary to escape from the health problems which had beset her for many years, and there is evidence of doctors' visits in 1543 and 1544. Her ailing father's vindictiveness, combined with indecision, added further to both his daughters' difficulties.

In late 1543 and the first months of 1544, what proved to be a final attempt to establish the succession was made by Henry. The problem was what to do if Edward, the 'natural' heir, had no children, since according to the 1536 Act, Mary and Elizabeth were both bastards. Under the terms of the new 1544 Act, the order of succession was established as Edward and his heirs, followed by Mary and her heirs, followed by Elizabeth and her heirs. If none of these plans was successful, there should be resort to the heirs of Henry's sister Mary, no mention being made of his other sister, Margaret, or her granddaughter Mary, queen of Scots. The surviving heir of the 'other' Mary Tudor, Henry's sister, and her second husband, Charles Brandon, duke of Suffolk, was Frances, wife of Henry Grey, marquis of Dorset. Once again, then, the future Mary I was left in second place with the strong possibility that she would be definitively excluded from the succession if her half-brother married and produced children. However, there was one provision in the Act which would later prove to be crucial. This was that, as in the 1536 Act, the right was reserved to the sovereign to amend the order of succession further in any subsequent will and testament. This was a move of great constitutional significance since it meant that the succession was now in effect to be determined not by legitimacy of birth or by hereditary right, but by the will of the sovereign acting under parliamentary statute, a paradoxical consequence of the actions of a monarch who was evidently absolutist by temperament. More immediately, the 1544 Act was of great personal importance to Mary and Elizabeth since it said nothing about their legitimacy even though they were now to be included, however marginally, in the succession. This would clearly affect the marriage prospects of both of them. Yet, despite these difficulties, Mary seems to have spent the last years of her father's reign in comparative peace, probably because she was not expected to become queen.[60] Things would, of course, change drastically when Henry died.

[59] Susan James, *Catherine Parr: Henry VIII's Last Queen* (Stroud: The History Press, 2008), pp. 157–68, 188–204.
[60] Ibid., pp. 77, 94, 106–7.

Chapter 4

STRUGGLING WITH THE YOUNGER BROTHER, 1547–1553

In the aftermath of their father's death, in the early hours of 28 January 1547, the new King Edward wrote to his stepsister Mary in a sententious manner, very probably with the guidance of his tutors:

> We ought not to mourn our father's death, since it is His will, who works all things for good . . . So far as lies in me, I will be to you a devout brother, and overflowing with all kindness.[1]

Mary, separated from Edward by an age gap of over twenty-one years, was still personally close to Henry's last wife, Catherine Parr, but she was nevertheless about to lose her recognized royal position.[2] Neither Mary nor Catherine was apparently present when the King died, and although Edward and Elizabeth were quickly brought to Court thereafter, Mary was not.[3] Worse, it seems that Mary had not even been made aware, in January 1547, that Henry was *in extremis*, since she later complained of having been kept in the dark.[4]

At the time of her father's death, Mary and those who supported and cared for her were naturally frustrated that she remained unmarried, and she was still feeling the loss of her friend and support, the Imperial ambassador Eustace Chapuys, who had left England for good in March 1545. 'The Lady Mary' might feel buoyed up by her apparent popularity with the great bulk of the English public, but Henry's last will and testament did not alter her status as illegitimate, thus leaving in place the ambiguity involved in the possible, though seemingly unlikely, accession to the throne of a bastard queen, which was entailed by the 1544 Act of Succession. Apparent anomalies in the completion, authentication and subsequent handling of Henry's will have led some to suggest that it was tampered with after his death. It is not doubted that it was signed and sealed in the King's presence, and that of various councillors, including the future duke of Somerset, Chief Secretary William Paget, and Sir Anthony Denny, on 30 December 1546. However, Henry's signature seems to have been added ⸻ means of the 'dry stamp', which enabled it to be traced by the clerk of

5087, fol. 35, printed as *LP* I, pp. 39–40; Skidmore, *Edward VI*, p. 51.
, pp. 690–720.
p. 107.
III, p. 211.

the privy seal, William Clerk. This was a common procedure even before the King became seriously ill, not least because of his notorious impatience with routine government business, but the oddity is that the will is not listed by Clerk as having been dry-stamped until the end of January 1547, on or after the 27th, and therefore immediately before or after the King's death. Suspicion has been aroused both by this delay and by a clause in the will concerning 'unfulfilled gifts', supposedly intended but not made by Henry, which afterwards allowed Lord Protector Somerset and his fellow executors and councillors to award themselves various honours and financial privileges.[5] Whatever the truth of the case, her father's will, which was accepted as genuine and legal by Edward VI's government, stipulated that Mary might not marry without the signed and sealed consent of a majority of Edward's new Council. In early 1547, it looked as though the taint of her illegitimacy might never be removed if the new king grew up to marry and produce heirs, since the succession would automatically pass through them before it would ever reach the much older Mary. In these circumstances, the marriage portion of £10,000, granted to her in Henry's will, may have seemed a remote prospect. Nevertheless, although the will failed to resolve questions surrounding her legitimacy and marriage, it did appear that the new reign would at least see an improvement in her economic state and personal prospects. Up to this point, Mary had lived under the direct financial control of the royal household. For the last three and a half years she had therefore had no household of her own, apart from a small staff of chamber servants. From now on, she would have an independent income of £3,000 a year. Even if she could still not legally be known as 'princess', she was now one of the richest women in England. In these circumstances she might have hoped for greater political and religious freedom, too. Meanwhile, Henry's third Queen Catherine was of course free to marry again, while Mary was not, but there was nonetheless much to be said for a significant measure of economic independence. Yet the thought of this may have been as daunting as it was exhilarating.[6] It also definitively revealed Henry VIII's inability or refusal to make important decisions concerning anyone other than himself.

Within a few days of the old king's death, Mary was joined by Elizabeth in the dowager queen's entourage at Court, but this was clearly a temporary arrangement. Elizabeth, too, benefited from a fairly generous financial settlement in Henry's will. Now thirteen years old, she remained at Court

---

[5] Skidmore (*Edward VI*, p. 47) appears to believe that Henry's last will and testament was indeed tampered with, but most other specialists have tended towards the opposite view (Scarisbrick, *Henry VIII*, pp. 488–94; Jennifer Loach, *Edward VI*, ed. George Bernard and Penry Williams (New Haven, CT and London: Yale University Press, 1999), pp. 20–2; Loades, *Henry VIII*, pp. 207–10; Lucy Wooding, *Henry VIII* (London and New York: Routledge, 2009), p. 275). The original will is 1/227; see also *LP* XXI, ii, p. 654.

[6] Loades, *Mary Tudor: The Tragical History*, pp. 67–8.

for the time being, but would soon have her own estates to run. According to François van der Delft, who succeeded Chapuys as Imperial ambassador in England, Mary was initially annoyed with Edward Seymour, earl of Hertford and soon to be duke of Somerset, because he did not visit her during her period of mourning for her father. In the first two weeks of February 1547, while Henry was still unburied, Seymour was far too busy securing his own political position as the new lord protector of the nine-year-old Edward and his kingdom. While this process was under way, Mary had to be kept in the dark for this reason and also because the fundamental legitimacy of Edward VI and his new regime was being seriously questioned by Catholic rulers on the Continent.[7] Not only did they regard Catherine as having been Henry's only legitimate wife, meaning that between her death and his own he was a widower, but he was also a heretic and a schismatic. By this interpretation, Edward was illegitimate as well and only Mary could legitimately succeed to the English throne. Yet the most important point to notice is that, whatever may have been thought in the Imperial Court and the Roman Curia, there is no evidence that Mary failed to accept her father's will, which placed her half-brother on the throne and ordered the continuance of the Royal Supremacy over the Church of England. Edward's succession and the continuation of that supremacy seem to have been generally accepted in England, and Pope Paul III's support for Mary as the legitimate successor to her father was ignored. Nevertheless, when Mary was not mentioned in the proclamation of Edward as king, on 31 January 1547, van der Delft professed himself to be surprised. Perhaps misinformed or uninformed by the Imperial ambassador, Charles's sister Mary of Hungary could still write to van der Delft, on 6 February:

> We make no mention at present of the young prince as we are ignorant as yet whether or not he will be recognised as King . . . We likewise refrain from sending you any letters for our cousin Mary, as we do not yet know how she will be treated.[8]

Charles V himself was equally cautious, telling van der Delft, in mid-February 1547, that he had duly reciprocated Edward's official greetings, as one crowned head to another, but without offering formal recognition of the boy's title. Naturally, the Emperor wanted to use Mary as a tool to control or destabilize the new English regime, but Protector Somerset shrewdly guessed that he would not do so until or unless it was clearly demonstrated to him that the political situation in England was favourable to such an enterprise.[9] This did not seem to be so in the first few months of 1547, and indeed by April of that year all the courts of Europe, apart from the Pope's,

[7] Loades, *Mary Tudor*, p. 135.
[8] *CSP Span* IX, pp. 7, 15: Loades, *Mary Tudor*, pp. 135–6.
[9] *CSP Span* IX, p. 30; Loades, *Mary Tudor*, p. 136.

had recognized Edward as king. Charles V was in any case preoccupied with his battle against the German Protestant princes.

On a personal level, Mary's reaction to her father's death is not precisely known. Later on, and particularly when she was queen herself, she would show respect for him but never affection. In the meantime, she lived quietly in the dowager queen's household, until Catherine defied the Council by marrying the protector's brother, Thomas Seymour. As a result of this development, at the end of April 1547 Mary duly received her portion in accordance with Henry's final will and at last acquired some measure of independence. Even now, Mary did not see the will itself, the evidence for this being that she was unable to tell van der Delft precisely what her marriage portion was. Thus the ambassador was able to suppose that it was not adequate for one of her rank, who might have been queen if the Catholic view of Henry's first marriage had been applied. In fact, it appears that the value of Mary's share was £3,819 18s 6d, this being a fifth more than the sum stipulated in the will and making her wealth equivalent to that of the fifth or sixth richest peer in England.[10] Most of the lands, advowsons (rights to present to clerical livings) and other perquisites involved were situated in Norfolk, Suffolk and Essex, and among them was Kenninghall, a fine Norfolk house which had then been in the Crown's possession for only a few weeks, since the attainder of the third duke of Norfolk, who had intended it to outdo Hampton Court in splendour. Also notable among Mary's new estates were her familiar haunts of Hunsdon in Hertfordshire and New Hall (Beaulieu) in Essex.[11] These and all the other properties involved were formally granted to their new possessor on 17 May 1547, but Mary remained initially in Havering, which was not to be included among her estates, before moving to Norfolk in July. She seems to have formed her new establishment gradually, between mid-April and mid-September 1547, and to have received a royal pension to tide her over until income started to come in from the estates. These properties were granted to her for life, or until she married, in accordance with the terms laid down in her father's will. If she ever succeeded to the throne, an event which in 1547 seemed highly unlikely, all these goods would naturally revert to the Crown.[12]

In the early months of Edward's reign, it is not clear whether Mary's 'well-willers' (supporters) could have been called an 'affinity', that is, a coherent group in the political terminology of the period. At this time, she had an entourage of about a hundred people, and van der Delft was quite wrong to suppose that she had been shabbily treated by Henry and by Edward's Council since the grants of 1547 made her a territorial, and potentially a political, magnate in East Anglia where she effectively

[10] *CPR* Edward VI, II, p. 20; Loades, *Mary Tudor*, p. 137.
[11] Eric Ives, *Lady Jane Grey: A Tudor Mystery* (Malden, MA and Oxford: Wiley-Blackwell, 2009), p. 86.
[12] Loades, *Mary Tudor*, p. 139.

replaced the Howard dukes of Norfolk in that role. By now, her support network of the 1530s, led by the Courtenays and the Poles, had disintegrated, largely because of judicial violence on the part of the Crown, and Mary was not close to the Howards and Bishop Gardiner after 1540. Once her half-brother and his advisers began to move ever more energetically towards further reform of the 'Church of England', religion, rather than personal political following, increasingly became the main focus of her existence.[13] There is no discernible sign before 1547 of her rejecting her father's religious manoeuvres, even when they appeared to head in an evangelical direction. However when, during 1548, the Mass itself became an issue, van der Delft began to notice that Mary was attending the service more frequently, hearing up to four celebrations a day, which was quite exceptional for a layperson.[14] She also protested to Lord Protector Somerset about Edward's first set of religious injunctions, issued in 1548, which banned the use of the rosary as well as parish processions before Mass on Sundays and major festivals and the ringing of the Sanctus bell at the consecration of the bread and wine of the Eucharist. The bell was instead to be rung at the beginning of the sermon, presumably to attract stragglers to the word rather than the sacrament.[15] By the end of that year, Edward's Council was becoming increasingly concerned at Mary's apparent use of the Sacrament of the Altar to rally support and cause dissidence for the government. A clash appeared inevitable as the draft Act of Uniformity, which would introduce the first English Prayer Book, headed towards parliament. By early 1549, it seemed to some observers that the very survival of Somerset's government was threatened by Mary's becoming a symbol and focus for supporters of the traditional Latin liturgy in its late Henrician form. Like Nicodemus, who followed up his secret visit to Jesus by publicly defending Him and His disciples to his fellow Pharisees (John 7: 50–2), Mary was about to come out into the open. Her relationship with her cousin the Emperor, one-sided as it may have been in personal terms, added an important international dimension to her potential for resistance and even rebellion.

It seems that at some point in the autumn of 1547 Mary had written to Protector Somerset, with whom she had previously got on fairly well, to protest formally against his religious policy on the grounds that, by not waiting for Edward to come of age before acting, he and the Council were defying the provisions of Henry's last will. Somerset professed amazement at Mary's words, blaming traditionalists such as Gardiner for leading her on. Her letter, which has to be reconstituted from Somerset's reply, appears to have urged that Henry's traditionalist Act of Six Articles (1539) should remain in force for the time being. It is particularly important to

[13] Ibid., p. 141.
[14] *CSP Span* IX, p. 100.
[15] *CSP Ven* V, p. 532 (no. 934); *CSP Ven* VI, pp. 1053–4 (no. 884).

note that Mary seems at this time to have accepted the state and nature of the Church as Henry left it. The changes which Somerset, Cranmer and others proposed would only serve to support the argument of the Papacy, which was that once the authority of the bishop of Rome was removed from England, every new government was likely to introduce a further change of religion. Against this, the Lord Protector argued that the old king had not bequeathed a permanent settlement of the Church, but rather an incomplete reformation. Thus it was only possible to consolidate the abolition of papal authority in England if 'popish doctrine' went as well. Somerset apparently asked Mary to 'call to your remembrance what great Labours, Travels [travails] and Pains his Grace [Henry VIII] had, before he could reform some of those stiff-necked Romanists or Papists, yea, and did they not cause his Subjects to rise and rebel against him [for example in the Pilgrimage of Grace in 1536]?'[16] The Protector hoped that Mary would amend her views on what he termed 'popery' in religion in the same way as she had earlier submitted to her father's 'headship' of the English Church.

In fact, when the new Prayer Book was enacted by statute, Mary moved to challenge the King's authority and even the validity of his laws, at least in so far as they touched the Catholic religion. On Whit Sunday, 9 June 1549, when the new book was supposed to be used for the first time in all churches, Mary organized a particularly splendid mass of Pentecost, according to the old, Latin rite, in her chapel at Kenninghall. This news reached the King's Council with great rapidity, and on 16 June that body wrote advising her to obey the Act of Uniformity and all other royal laws. She was to cease altogether the celebration of the old Mass in her household and use instead the new English service.[17] This time, though, Mary would not surrender abjectly, as she had done in 1536. She was now thirty-three years old, not twenty, and had been toughened by her largely bitter experience in the intervening years. It remained to be seen what the international Catholic reaction would be to the new liturgical and political order in England.

As early as January 1549, Charles V protested in writing to the English Council, which he regarded as weak and subject to his influence, that it should not interfere with Princess Mary's religious observance, while van der Delft gave her the verbal support that she craved. Later, on 10 May, Charles instructed his ambassador to demand a written assurance to this effect, a request which Protector Somerset naturally rejected, arguing, reasonably enough, that her current, and now illegal, religious practice was a matter of public interest as well as private conscience, and might

---

[16] See the reconstitution of this correpondence in a letter from Gardiner to Somerset, 21 May 1548, cited in Loades, *Mary Tudor*, pp. 143–5.

[17] *APC* II, 291; Loades, *Mary Tudor*, p. 143; Loades, *Mary Tudor: The Tragical History*, pp. 74–5.

cause disorder.[18] Even so, as a concession, Edward Seymour was willing to allow Mary to have the Latin Mass celebrated in private, for the sake of her royal rank and her tender conscience, until King Edward came of age and could decide the question for himself. In his disgust at this response, van der Delft rashly blurted out that even if Mary wanted to change her religion, his master Charles would not allow it. She would not be permitted by the Emperor to give way in this matter, as she had done when she accepted the royal supremacy, as well as her own illegitimacy, in 1536. This utterance of course confirmed in the minds of Protector and Council the notion that Mary was the pawn of a foreign power, who must be closely observed as a likely source of internal dissidence and even a pretext for invasion from abroad.[19] Initially, Mary's defiance seems to have been taken more seriously by Edward's government than the actual rebellions which developed in Devon and Cornwall, and later in Norfolk, in the summer of 1549.[20] In reality, it is notable that, once again, as in the 1530s, no direct and incontrovertible evidence has been found to implicate Mary in either of these major social and political upheavals, though detailed accusations were made against her by Edward's Council.[21] The emegency caused by the West Country revolt against the English Prayer Book does however seem to have had the immediate, if paradoxical, consequence that Somerset reduced his pressure on her to curtail or end the celebration of the Latin rite in her household. Even so, a few of her current or former servants were indeed found to have been involved in the western rebellion, though not in Kett's uprising in Norfolk, which had a strongly evangelical emphasis in its religious attitudes and led at first to material damage to some of Mary's East Anglian estates.[22]

While she may have taken no direct political action at this time, attempts were made to involve the Lady Mary in plans to undermine the government of Lord Protector Somerset and make her regent for Edward in a conservative 'revolution'. It seems that, in the summer and early autumn of 1549, there was a 'Catholic party' led by the earls of Arundel and Southampton, and also involving John Dudley, earl of Warwick and future duke of Northumberland, despite the fact that he appears not to have shared the religious views of Mary's more fervent supporters. Evidence that there was indeed a conspiracy emerges from the correspondence of the Imperial ambassador, van der Delft, with Charles V's government. A reply from Brussels, dated 17 September 1549, indicates that Mary had received information in the previous month about the plans of this

---

[18] *CSP Span* IX, p. 375; W. K. Jordan, *Edward VI: The Young King: The Protectorship of the Duke of Somerset* (London: Allen & Unwin, 1968), pp. 206–9.

[19] Loades, *Mary Tudor*, p. 148; Loades, *Mary Tudor: The Tragical History*, pp. 74–5.

[20] Loades, *Mary Tudor: The Tragical History*, pp. 76–7.

[21] Ian W. Archer and others, eds, *Religion, Politics and Society in Sixteenth Century England*, Camden Society, 5th series, xxii (2003).

[22] Loades, *Mary Tudor*, p. 149; Loades, *Mary Tudor: The Tragical History*, pp. 77–8.

group, which also included William Paulet, Lord St John and future marquis of Winchester. She had been asked if she would be willing to take part in an attempt to overthrow Somerset and, as was her custom, had sought, through his ambassador, the Emperor's advice. Charles's response had been to throw cold water over the whole scheme, and Mary took no action.[23] In fact, a specific plot against Somerset, with the earl of Southampton's residence at Titchfield as a centre of dissident activity, may have been hatching since May or June, but it took a while for Somerset to become aware of the real danger to his person. At the beginning of October, though, he discovered while with the King at Hampton Court that various 'lords of the Council' in London were planning to overthrow him. On 5 October, he announced in a royal proclamation that Dudley and his co-conspirators wanted to end the protectorate and make Mary regent. On the verge of their victory over Somerset, which would be plain by the end of October, the dissident lords issued a denial that they had offered the regency to Mary in a letter addressed to her as early as the 9th.[24] They also wrote about this to various individuals, including one of her strongest supporters, Henry Parker, Lord Morley. Although he responded by protesting his loyalty to the Lord Protector, the fact that he was approached by the conspirators seems to indicate that involvement in Dudley's scheme may have spread more widely among the political class than just the inner core. In November 1549, with Somerset deposed, Arundel seems still to have been trying to involve Mary in the government, but she refused.[25]

After her failure to act in 1549, perhaps the most crucial event in Mary's life during Edward's reign was her near-escape from England at the beginning of July 1550. She had become increasingly concerned about her future in the kingdom after Somerset was replaced as head of government by Dudley, by November 1549. Specifically, she feared that her concession for private celebrations of mass in Latin would be withdrawn, as she knew the Council was aware that these services were not entirely 'private' in that visitors to her residence were still attending them, despite orders to the contrary. In mid-April 1550, the Council duly warned Mary that she should allow only her chamber servants to attend such celebrations, and by the end of the month she had summoned van der Delft to Woodham Walter, near Maldon in Essex, to tell him that she now wished to flee to the Netherlands, under the Emperor's protection.[26] The ambassador argued against such a plan, asking what Edward would do once she was out of the country. She

---

[23] *CSP Span* IX, pp. 445–6, 449.

[24] 10/9/33; Tyler, *England under the Reigns of Edward VI and Mary*, 2 vols (London: Richard Bentley, 1839), i, pp. 248–51.

[25] For the 1549 regency episode, see D. E. Hoak, *The King's Council in the Reign of Edward VI* (Cambridge: Cambridge University Press, 1976), p. 241, Prescott, *Mary Tudor*, p. 159, Loades, *Mary Tudor*, p. 149, Porter, *Mary Tudor*, pp. 163–6, Skidmore, *Edward VI*, pp. 137–9.

[26] *CSP Span* X, pp. 82–3; Skidmore, *Edward VI*, p. 171.

apparently answered that if she stayed, and her half-brother died, she would probably be executed, whatever the stipulations of Henry's will. To begin with, Mary said, she would be forced to move away from the coast and be cut off from her loyal servants and other supporters. Her arguments at this time have been described as 'confused', but this seems somewhat harsh, given the uncertainty of her situation, not least because of the disagreements on the subject within the Council itself. In the end, she rejected the idea of escape, now attributing it, according to the record, to van der Delft rather than herself.[27] In reality, the ambassador told Charles V that he had tried to dissuade Mary from fleeing, but that she now seemed determined to do so, partly because of Lord President Dudley's growing hostility towards her and her religious practice. In these circumstances, he thought that she had better leave England as soon as possible, just as he himself was due to be recalled shortly in any case because of ill-health. He suggested two possible schemes to his master. One was that Mary should join him, in disguise, when he sailed legitimately for the Netherlands. A second plan was more elaborate: a grain-trading boat should dock at Maldon, on the Blackwater estuary, pick her up secretly and take her to an Imperial warship, which would be waiting out to sea. During May, Charles finally became convinced that his Tudor cousin should leave England, and he seems to have been encouraged in this change of heart by his more decisive and interventionist sister, Mary of Hungary.[28]

It was agreed that the attempt would be made in early June, at the time of van der Delft's recall. His replacement as ambassador in London, Jehan Scheyfve, was to know nothing of the plan so as not to be compromised at the start of his diplomatic work. Instead, the carrying out of the operation was to be entrusted to van der Delft's secretary, Jehan Dubois. At this time, Mary was living further inland, at New Hall/Beaulieu, but she now moved back to Woodham Walter, which was about two miles from the shore, on the pretext of repair work at her former residence. Two Imperial warships, under the command of Cornelius Schepperus, finally arrived off Maldon on 30 June 1550, while on the same day Dubois, pretending to be a corn merchant, went to Harwich, where he waited overnight because the coastal passage to Maldon was reckoned to be difficult after dark. On 1 July he duly set sail, on a calm sea which seemed ideal for the enterprise. Dubois arrived in Maldon the next day, his ship was moored away from the shore, and he then wrote to the head of Mary's household, Robert Rochester, in 'simple Latin'. However, when his men unloaded their grain on the jetty, none of The Lady Mary's men was there to meet them. Dubois wrote again, urging Rochester and Mary to move fast, since Schepperus was about to appear with a small fleet off nearby Stansgate. The tide was in the plotters' favour, but there was a danger that Dubois's ship might be beached if they delayed until the waters receded. The secretary now said that he would dispose of

[27] *CSP Span* X pp. 127–8; Skidmore, *Edward VI*, p. 171.
[28] *CSP Span*, X, pp. 47, 94, 111, 124–35.

his load of corn in Maldon, and be ready to leave that night (2 July). He urged that Mary should not bring too many of her female servants with her, since he feared that they might disrupt the operation. After this, news reached Dubois that Rochester was dithering at Woodham, so he continued writing another letter for despatch to Mary's household. Meanwhile, though, a messenger arrived from Woodham saying that Rochester would come to Maldon to meet Dubois in the shelter of St Mary's church, where they would pretend to bargain over corn in case of hostile witnesses. This meeting duly took place just an hour later, and in it Rochester raised a series of difficulties with the operation. Firstly, he told Dubois that it would be very hard for Mary and her servants to get to Maldon as they were already under surveillance by local inhabitants acting on behalf of the government. In addition, Edward and his Council had spies within the household itself, something he suggested, Mary was unaware of. In any case, Rochester was opposed to his mistress's escape on the grounds that she might live comparatively freely if she remained in England but would lose her right to the throne if she did leave and Edward subsequently died. Irritated by this prevarication, Dubois insisted on an immediate decision, one way or the other. They parted in angry disagreement, and pressure subsequently increased on the Emperor's agents when they came into conflict with local officials while attempting to continue the sale of their corn at this 'unsocial' hour. Desperate for action, the Imperial secretary and his men set out at one in the morning for Woodham Walter, where they found Mary packing heaps of possessions into hop-sacks, apparently for the voyage. Fearing that this would disrupt the enterprise further, Dubois attempted to assure Mary that she would be amply provided for when she reached the Netherlands.

It is impossible to say whether Mary knew, or remembered at this hour of emergency, how her aunt Juana had been deceived in this way when she married Charles's father Philip in 1496 and had been deprived of what had been promised in the Netherlands, but she insisted on having up to two extra days to pack. By this time, Schepperus had been warned not to put in to shore that night, but this meant that Dubois would need a new 'cover story', as his disguise as a corn merchant was wearing thin. Having seen the Imperial ships offshore, Maldon locals had become increasingly suspicious, and were now threatening to seize Dubois's ship on behalf of King Edward. It might appear from all this that Comptroller Rochester acted throughout with the aim of keeping Mary in England. He knew that Edward was ill, and that Mary was showing signs of uncharacteristic panic. Dubois reported that she spent the night of 2–3 July running about Woodham Walter crying out, 'What shall I do? What is to become of me?' At 2 a.m., having finally lost patience and fearing for his own safety, Dubois left for Maldon and sailed out to embark with Schepperus. His stated intention was to return to the Netherlands and make another voyage to England in ten days' time, when the fuss had died down, but this never happened. News of the plot finally reached Edward's Council on

13 July and the response was robust. Sir John Gates was despatched to Essex with a contingent of cavalry, as Edward later recalled in his diary, 'to stop the going away of the Lady Mary', to Antwerp, it was thought. After this, 500 troops were sent to garrison the ports in this part of the county and the duke of Somerset and Lord Russell were ordered to raise a further 800 men for service in Essex. The Maldon episode proved, perhaps fortunately as it turned out, to be Mary's last chance to escape abroad.[29]

The idea of flight did not die immediately and completely. On 24 July 1550, the provost of Flanders reported to Mary of Hungary that the expedition to England earlier in the month was still being widely discussed, and some even believed that Mary was already in Flanders. Two days later, the French ambassador to the Imperial court, Bassefontaine, interestingly reported a rumour that Mary would marry Prince Philip of Spain, this probably being the first inkling of what would happen in July 1554.[30] Though the whole escape plan might be regarded as too decisive and risky for the ailing and hyper-cautious Charles to undertake, Mary of Hungary and Chancellor Granvelle were obviously keen on it. Mary subsequently felt it necessary to protect her position, persuading Scheyfve, when he took up his post as ambassador in London soon afterwards, to stress to Edward's councillors that Schepperus had never landed on English soil, though the rest of the story could hardly be denied.[31] Charles, like Dudley, probably never wanted Mary to leave England, and in the spring of 1550 slow negotiations were going on for a Portuguese marriage for her to Dom Luis, but Mary was not consulted about this so she continued to imagine an escape for herself. It is by no means certain, however, that she was acquiring this early a feeling that she was likely to become a martyr. She was in fact defending the Mass, which had been the non-negotiable heart of her father's religion, as well as hers, but it need not be assumed from this that she expected to die for it, even under Dudley's rule, and her hesitation at Woodham Walter at the beginning of July 1550 seems to suggest a divided rather than a confused mind, which was totally understandable in the circumstances.[32]

In the three years between the abortive escape effort in Essex and Edward's death, in July 1553, the Council became ever more aggressive towards Mary. Her chaplains were now told to stop celebrating the old rite and to adopt the successive English Prayer Books of 1549 and 1552. Their mistress was naturally furious, and immediately enlisted the support of Scheyfve, but it may well be that she thus fell into a trap which Edward's advisers had set. This was to use pressure on her household devotions to

---

[29] *CSP Span* X, pp. 124–5; Skidmore, *Edward VI*, pp. 172–5; *England's Boy King: The Diary of Edward VI, 1547–1553*, ed. Jonathan North (Welwyn Garden City: Ravenhall Books, 2005), p. 62; Loades, *Mary Tudor*, pp. 153–7.

[30] *CSP Span* X, p. 142; Loades, *Mary Tudor*, p. 157 and note.

[31] Loades, *Mary Tudor: The Tragical History*, pp. 84–5.

[32] Ibid., pp. 81–5.

make her demonstrate to the English public that she was attached to a foreign power, rather than the English Crown and people. On 22 July 1550, Sir William Petre and Richard, Lord Rich were nominated by the Council to go to Mary, probably to discuss the issue of the mass. She would not come to Court for fear, she said, of being forced to conform to the new liturgy, but she was prepared to meet the two delegates at Leigh Priory. There was, of course, no progress on the central point. The Council's view that she was now compromised because of the Habsburg connection appeared to be confirmed on 4 September 1550 when Charles V wrote to Scheyfve telling him to demand an unconditional assurance from Edward and his government that Mary could keep the Latin Mass. Nothing seems to have resulted from this, and, indeed, a kind of phoney war ensued until December of that year. One of her servants, named Kempe, was even allowed to visit Flanders and return to England without retribution being exacted. On 1 December, though, the Council wrote once again to Mary, instructing her to allow the sheriff of Essex to serve writs on her, ordering the celebration of the new English services by her chaplains. This was, of course, a long-standing demand, but the crucial change appears to have been that this time, totally against his much older half-sister's expectation, Edward himself intervened personally in favour of the enforcement, in her case, of the 1549 Act of Uniformity. On 4 December 1550, Mary answered the Council that her chaplains were covered by household immunity in accordance with her earlier agreement with Protector Somerset, and she also asserted that, in any case, some of the chaplains named in the writs were no longer members of her household. On Christmas Day 1550 the Council replied, stating that the agreement to which she referred, which had been made on the King's behalf, never went beyond her most immediate servants, and had certainly never allowed the Mass to be celebrated in her house in her absence.[33] It was on 24 January 1551 that Edward directly intervened in the matter, part of the relevant letter to Mary being in his own, distinctive hand. In it he upbraided her for her defiance, which in his view was all the more significant because of her high rank in the kingdom, as well as the fact that she was his close relative.[34] This rebuke seems to have hurt Mary deeply, with its implied threat and in particular the new and horrifying realization that she could no longer imagine, as she had previously done despite all advice to the contrary, that Edward was simply being led astray by her advisers, including Dudley and Cranmer. Now it was clear that 'King Josiah' himself had a fuller reformation in mind, and that he had his elder sister in his sights. It seemed as though she might be heading, emotionally, for the kind of surrender which she had made to Henry in 1536, but this did not happen. Instead, the foundations began to be laid for her own reign, which would begin so unexpectedly in 1553.[35]

[33] Loades, *Mary Tudor*, pp. 157–9.
[34] *CSP Span* X, pp. 309–12.
[35] Loades, *Mary Tudor*, p. 159.

Yet until July, it seemed that such an outcome was becoming ever more unlikely, at least in the eyes of those at the centre of English political activity. This was because, in his last years, the King worked to exclude both his half-sisters from the succession. Scholars continue to differ in their attribution of the authorship of the manuscript, in Edward's hand, which is entitled *Devise for the Succession*, and a totally secure narrative of its composition cannot be established.[36] Nevertheless there seems now to be no doubt that the document, with later corrections, was written by the King himself, even if it is not entirely clear where the ideas came from. Fortunately, what appears to be its first version, with amendments, survives.[37] Its original text, like Henry VIII's will, completely excluded from the succession the Scottish line which descended from Henry VIII's sister Margaret, the wife of James IV, through their granddaughter Mary Stuart, Queen of Scots, but went further by also ruling out Mary and Elizabeth in favour of the descendants of Henry's other sister, Mary Tudor, the duchess of Suffolk. The 'Devise' was, however, subsequently altered by the addition of two words, leading to other textual adjustments, which together had the effect of outlining a succession, in the case that Edward himself had no heirs, first through the non-existent heirs of the older Mary Tudor's daughter Francis Grey, duchess of Suffolk, then through Frances's daughter Jane, and subsequently through Jane's male heirs, if any. In current historical writing there are alternative versions of the origins of this highly controversial document. The first of these, which was generally held at the time, both in England and on the Continent, is that the duke of Northumberland and perhaps other councillors were responsible for the 'Devise'.[38] In this narrative, by the beginning of 1553, with the King's health in decline, leading members of Edward's government came to the view that Mary, though the most obvious heir, under the terms of the 1544 Succession Act, should somehow be excluded. The results of their deliberations were communicated to Edward by the vice-chamberlain, Sir John Gates, and he drew up the appropriate document.[39] Whatever the details of the operation, if such there was, in June 1553 the Imperial ambassador Scheyfve told Charles V that he thought Northumberland wanted the throne for himself.[40] On 21 May, the duke's son, Lord Guildford Dudley, had married Lady Jane Grey, and this would certainly fit in well with the amended 'Devise', at least, if not the grandest ambition on the part of Guildford's father, which would indeed have been to take the throne for himself. In reality, it seems that Edward and Northumberland, together with some other councillors, shared responsibility for what happened, though they may well have been in conflict over how exactly to proceed. In what proved to be his last few months of life,

---

[36] The original is in the Inner Temple Library, Petyt MS 538/47, fol. 317. On the chronology of the 'Devise', see Ives, *Lady Jane Grey*, pp. 137–58.

[37] Inner Temple, Petyt MS 538/47, fol. 317

[38] S. T. Bindoff, 'A kingdom at stake, 1553', *History Today*, iii (1953), 642–8.

[39] Guy, *Tudor England*, p. 226.

[40] *CSP Span* XI, p. 49.

Edward was just beginning to be more directly involved in the government of the country, yet he remained dependent on Northumberland to a considerable degree.[41] The duke, as lord president of the Council, seems to have thought that, if Mary succeeded, not only would the current reformation of the English Church come to an end, but he himself would lose power. Thus it was Northumberland who played the main role in ensuring the change from Mary to Lady Jane Grey, and he was not above exploiting for this purpose the ailing Edward's increasing disapproval of his elder sister's love of lavish court life and traditional religion. Yet it may be that the religious conflict was not the main reason why the fifteen-year-old king wanted Mary excluded from the succession. Rather, it was her illegitimacy, never explicitly ended by Henry, which provided a pretext for the setting aside of the 1544 Act of Succession and of the late King's will. Under the canon law of the Roman Church, which still applied in England despite Archbishop Cranmer's strong desire to revise and reform it, a bastard in law might not inherit the throne, and thus both Mary and Elizabeth were excluded, the latter probably because she had never got on with Northumberland. It would thus be necessary to look elsewhere for the next monarch.[42] If this analysis is correct, the crucial alterations to the 'Devise', which appear to be in Edward's hand and settled the succession on Jane, may well have been suggested by Northumberland, even if the King was responsible for the original version.

The alternative view ascribes both initiative and authorship to Edward himself. From this viewpoint, it has been argued that the original document was composed by Edward, perhaps in late 1552 or early 1553. At this time, his tutors were schooling him in politics as well as academic subjects, and, according to this theory, the 'Devise' may well have begun its life as a schoolroom exercise, and not as an answer to a current and pressing question. If this dating is correct, Edward would have produced the original text when there were no particular concerns about his overall health and he had every expectation, as did his subjects, that he would grow to manhood, marry and have children. Possibly one of his tutors, for instance the secretary to the Privy Council, William Thomas, gave him a hypothetical question to answer in an essay, perhaps on the lines of asking what would have happened if the 1544 Act of Succession had never been passed. It is impossible to know whether or not the royal tutors desired a change to be made to the succession as Henry had ordained it, but it seems reasonable to assume that the matter was being considered, by some at least, well before an urgent need arose, even though the general public apparently assumed that Henry's will would be carried out, thus placing Mary on the throne after her brother's death. It is also possible that Northumberland himself was not in fact looking, in the first part of 1553, to cut Mary out; and at that stage he did

[41] Rex, *The Tudors*, p. 126.
[42] Ibid., pp. 126–8.

seem fairly well disposed towards her, at least in public. However, this generosity, if such it was, concerned lands and revenues, but certainly not her views on religion. Yet it is also possible that Northumberland's invitation to Mary to come to Court, in February 1553, may have indicated that he still indeed expected her to become queen, and this may have meant that the initiative for the 'Devise', and in particular its late modification, should in fact be largely, if not totally, ascribed to Edward himself. In this case, again, theory has to take over from evidence, but it is certainly true that the March 1553 parliament did not formally discuss the issue of the succession. This does not, of course, mean that the matter was not considered behind the scenes, but if that did happen, no stir on the subject was created in the country at the time. It is also possible that the Dudley marriages in May 1553, including that of Jane and Guildford, were not then seen as part of any kind of plot: certainly Scheyfve gives no evidence of having viewed them in such a light. Nevertheless, as has already been noted, the Imperial ambassador certainly did believe that Northumberland was plotting with the general aim of excluding Mary. If his analysis was correct, which cannot be assumed, it would appear that the collapse of Edward's health in June 1553 forced Dudley to change his plans, hence the amendments to the 'Devise' in favour of Jane, a development which now suited both the King and the lord president. A female successor was clearly distasteful to Edward, but if there had to be one, Jane's accession was at least likely to conserve the religious reforms to which he seems by now to have been personally devoted, something that he was sure Mary would not do.[43]

Whether or not the main initiative was his, Northumberland could not have achieved the planned change of royal succession to Jane Grey on his own, and the highly reluctant privy councillors and crown officers were only persuaded to suppress their misgivings by a clear demonstration that Edward was passionate in demanding such a change. These objections were substantial. There was a question over whether the King, as a minor, could legally take such an action in any case, while the lord chief justice, Sir Edward Montague, held that no letters patent could overthrow an existing statute, such as the 1544 Act of Succession, without the latter being repealed by parliament. Indeed, it would be treasonable, under the terms of this Act, to put Edward's 'Devise' into effect. However, after Northumberland had failed to persuade the councillors and judges, Montague was summoned, along with other senior judges, before a sick and angry King on 15 June 1553, with the Lord President and his henchmen also present. The lawyers were told by their sovereign that Mary must be excluded because she would threaten religion, while Elizabeth was the daughter of the adulteress Anne Boleyn and therefore ineligible. Faced with this pressure, Montague perhaps inevitably succumbed and accepted Edward's wishes, though only on condition that the relevant letters patent were duly ratified by parliament, which

---

[43] Loades, *Mary Tudor: The Tragical History*, pp. 94–97; Skidmore, *Edward VI*, pp. 247–9.

would be summoned for 18 September of that year. Even so, according to Robert Wingfield's account, completed in 1555 with Mary as Queen and written by one of her most fervent supporters, Lord Chief Justice Montague only accepted Edward's will in return for a personal pardon, to be given under the Great Seal of England.[44] Naturally, Montague subsequently needed to justify his action to Mary once she was on the throne, and duly did so. But, in the conditions of the sixteenth century, it was inevitable, in any case, that he would have had to obey his then sovereign's direct command. It was also possible to argue, in common law, that an English king was entitled in any case to make law personally, if no parliament was in session. Whatever the legal issues, it seems that Montague's submission in June 1553 allowed others to square their consciences, notably Cranmer, who now felt absolved from his perjury, at least in this respect, when he accepted Jane as his new sovereign having earlier sworn to give allegiance to Mary as his future Queen.[45]

On 19 June, chancery began to draft the writs for a new parliament, which was to convene on 18 September. Two days later, the relevant letters patent were duly issued, declaring Jane Grey to be the primary heir to the throne and arguing that the 1544 Act of Succession should be put aside on the grounds that there were various other acts on the statute book which contradicted it. Mary and Elizabeth, since they were illegitimate, were 'to all intents and purposes . . . clearly disabled to ask, claim or challenge the said Imperial Crown of England'. The document, which, in the peculiar circumstances of its issue, had some of the characteristics of both a will and a royal proclamation, also warned of the risk that, if either of Henry's daughters succeeded and then married a foreign prince, he might 'practise to have the laws and customs of his . . . native country . . . practised . . . within this realm . . ., to the utter subversion of this commonwealth'.[46] This question would indeed arise soon afterwards. Having been drawn up in his presence, the letters patent of the succession were signed by Edward in six places, and in addition, between 15 June and the issue date of the 21st, the document was signed by just over a hundred others, who included the leading members of his Privy Council, nobles, judges and prominent members of the City of London Corporation. Apparently as a reward for his consent, the earl of Arundel was pardoned for his earlier plotting against Northumberland, and members of Edward's privy chamber also received gifts at this time. The whole procedure still seems to have been generally regarded as somewhat dubious, however, since an additional document was drawn up whereby the same signatories were required to swear that they would support and fulfil the terms of the letters patent of the succession, even to death. Now everything centred on a young king who hovered between life and death.

[44] Loach, *Edward VI*, pp. 164–5.
[45] Rex, *The Tudors*, p. 128.
[46] Inner Temple, Petyt MS 538/47, fol. 317.

Contrary to what is sometimes asserted, despite the incidence of normal illnesses of childhood, Edward's health seems to have been generally robust until February 1553, when he caught a feverish cold, which this time he failed to shake off as he usually did. He was unable to go to the Palace of Westminster in the customary way to open parliament on 1 March, instead performing the ceremony in the Great Chamber of Whitehall Palace, nearby.[47] On the 17th of that month he was still 'weak and thin' and restricted to his chamber in Whitehall, and he did not undertake his planned move to Greenwich for Easter because, according to the Imperial ambassadors, he was still suffering from catarrh and a cough. He did, however, begin to walk in the gardens of Westminster after this, though still under close medical supervision.[48] On 11 April he finally moved out of London to Greenwich, but he appeared only once in public during the rest of the month and that was on the day after his arrival there. At this time, Scheyfve claimed to have heard from 'a trustworthy source' that Edward was wasting away, and that fluids in alarming colours – greenish yellow, black, pink – were being discharged from his mouth. The informant, a medical student called John Banister, said that the doctors were baffled by the King's illness.[49] Again according to Scheyfve, there was a medical case conference a week later, since it was now clear that Edward was unlikely to live much longer.[50] On 7 May, both Secretary William Petre and Northumberland wrote letters which implied that the King's health was improving, but this was clearly not so, though the reality was kept from the English public and it is not known whether Mary and Elizabeth were aware of the situation at this stage. The Imperial ambassador continued to be a useful, and probably quite reliable, source during May and June, though the medical information which he picked up is difficult to interpret from the terminology then used. According to Scheyfve, Edward's doctors had by now concluded that he was suffering from an *aposthème* (suppurating tumour) on the lung, or from some other biological attack on that organ. Ulcers were breaking out on his body and he was suffering from a persistent, racking cough. His skin was dry and overheated, his belly was swollen, and he now suffered permanently from fever.[51] On 17 May, he was just about well enough to receive French ambassadors, but they found him weak and coughing, and by the end of the month he was in an even worse state. It was said that his head was going to be shaved and have plasters placed upon it.[52]

In sixteenth-century Europe, the severe illness or death of a member of a ruling family commonly led to rumours of nefarious activity, usually

[47] *CSP Span* XI, p. 9; *The diary of Henry Machyn, citizen and Merchant-Taylor of London, from A.D. 1550 to A.D. 1563*, ed. J. G. Nicholls (London: Camden Society 1st series, xiii, 1848), p. 32.

[48] *CSP Span* XI, pp. 17, 22.

[49] *CSP Span* XI, p. 35.

[50] *CSP Span* XI, p. 37.

[51] *CSP Span* XI, p. 40.

[52] *CSP Span* XI, pp. 44–5; Loach, *Edward VI*, pp. 159–60.

poisoning. In Edward's case, Scheyfve made a comparison, presumably based on what the English doctors were saying, with the disease which had killed Henry VIII's illegitimate son in 1536.[53] It is not now known how Henry Fitzroy died, and in Edward's case it is possible to come to differing conclusions concerning the nature of the young King's fatal illness. A Venetian ambassador reported, early in Mary's reign, that Edward died of 'consumption', that is, tuberculosis, and this statement may at least serve as a starting point.[54] Yet this is unlikely, for several reasons. Firstly, while tuberculosis lives in the body for a long time before becoming fatal, Edward had not, suffered from ill-health throughout his young life. In Jennifer Loach's words, '[W]hatever it was that afflicted Edward, it was not in evidence before early 1553'.[55] The timing and length of the young king's terminal ill-health are clearly crucial in helping to account for the behaviour of the duke of Northumberland and his allies in the months before July of that year. According to Loach, who took professional medical advice on the subject, Edward's symptoms, as recorded in the limited and unhelpful contemporary sources, do not indicate that he had been suffering from tuberculosis for a long time. Also, although the sources refer frequently to his coughing and to the lurid colours of the sputum he discharged, there is little or no reference to his coughing up blood, which is a classic symptom of tuberculosis. To Loach, reports by Scheyfve and others in June 1553, which refer to fever and the coughing up of foul-smelling infected matter, suggest that Edward suffered from a severe pulmonary infection. This would have begun as a feverish cold and developed into severe bronchopneumonia, which was untreatable at the time. Without modern antibiotics, the disease would, over time, have damaged the bronchi and lungs. As a result, the bronchi would have dilated, becoming filled with pus and other secretions, resulting in a condition known as bronchiectasis. Inflammation of the lungs would have led to the development of abcesses, and Edward would have coughed up the foul sputum which emerged from these. The infection would have spread into the pleural cavity, causing empyemia, which would result in some of the symptoms which are reported in this case – a fluctuating fever, weight loss and more thick and foul-smelling sputum. After a while, the pus and other toxins would have begun to attack other vital organs, leading to septicaemia, and death. On advice, Loach suggests that reported swelling of Edward's lower body, in June 1553, may indicate kidney failure. The whole process would have taken about five months, which in general terms corresponds with what was recorded at the time.[56] If this is indeed what happened, more or less, Edward's Council could reasonably have felt the need to act, but not urgently until the latter part of June.

[53] *CSP Span* XI, p. 49.
[54] *CSP Ven* V, p. 536.
[55] Loach, *Edward VI*, p. 161.
[56] Ibid, p. 162, with advice from Paul Beeson and Trevor Hughes.

An alternative theory, dating the King's serious health problems back
to the previous year, is offered by Chris Skidmore. Like Loach, he refers to
the theory, current at the time, that Edward had been poisoned, suggesting
that its power derived from his long period of seclusion, the delay in
proclaiming his death, and the general air of mystery and secrecy which
surrounded his last months. Not surprisingly, given the state of medical
knowledge at the time, the royal doctors George Owen and Thomas
Wendy felt out of their depth and called in Northumberland's personal
physician, as well as a dozen other London practitioners, all of whom were
sworn to secrecy concerning the King's medical condition. Ambassador
Scheyfve reported that the King was also attended by an unknown
female healer, who was allowed to administer her medicines to him under
professional supervision.[57] Her remedies appeared not only to have failed,
but to have made the patient's health worse. The surgeon who subsequently opened up the King's chest declared that he had died of a disease
of the lungs, while others observed the cough and cold which have
already been mentioned. In April 1552 Edward himself recorded that he
had fallen ill with measles and smallpox, and that short illness may in fact
have been significant, even though his recovery was rapid and apparently
normal.[58] According to modern research, measles can suppress immunity
to tuberculosis. Not only that, but its bacteria can survive within cells and
be reactivated by the arrival of a later disease. After the King's death, the
dissecting surgeons reported finding his lungs ulcerated and putrefied,
and these symptoms, along with the cavities in the lungs which were also
reported, seem to support the measles theory. Possibly, Edward had already
been in contact with a tuberculosis sufferer before he contracted measles
in 1552 and, if so, when he himself succumbed to tuberculosis the outcome
would have been rapid. The reported symptoms which suggested poisoning
to his contemporaries – swelling legs, falling pulse rate, loosening of finger-
and toenails, discoloration of the skin – would thus have been secondary
effects of tuberculosis, aggravated by the earlier attack of measles, and
of the subsequent onset of septicaemia and cyanosis, the latter depriving
the blood of oxygen and thus turning skin and membranes purple. This
seems to be the best explanation of the young King's death. Although, in a
note, Skidmore suggests that his account contradicts that of Loach,
outlined above, it seems perfectly possible to combine the two versions if
one accepts that Edward's medical history in 1553 did not arise out of
nothing. The theory of still earlier contact with tuberculosis, which was
activated by the incidence of measles in the previous year, would still
allow for many of the details which are provided in contemporary
sources.[59] This second version of events does not materially affect analysis

[57] *CSP Span*, XI, pp. 37, 70; Skidmore, *Edward VI*, pp. 260–2.
[58] Skidmore, *Edward VI*, p. 260.
[59] Ibid., p. 328, n. 51.

of the Council's handling of the succession question in Edward's last months of life.

The obsessive secrecy which surrounded his last illness inevitably created problems for both Mary and Elizabeth, as well as for their advisers and supporters, including those at Court, in assessing their political situation and deciding on future action. The duke of Northumberland, who was fully aware of the state of play, pursued ever more actively his long-standing desire for a French alliance in order to stave off Mary and the Habsburgs and to protect the Protestant succession as it had been set out in the 'Devise'. In this course, he knew that he had his sovereign's full support. Edward was already betrothed to Isabelle, daughter of Henry II of France, but as any marriage was now likely to be impossible, it seemed to Northumberland that his only hope of success was to secure the direct help of French troops. On 30 April 1553, before the full seriousness of the King's medical condition was known, Antoine de Noailles had arrived in London to replace René de Laval de Boisdauphin as French ambassador, and the two initially worked together. On 4 May they approached the Council to ask for an audience with Edward, so that Noailles could present his credentials. They were told that the King was too unwell to receive them, but a fake 'audience' was arranged for the sake of appearances. The Frenchmen sensed deep unease in the English Council about the succession.[60] All this took place on 7 May, and according to the ambassadors' subsequent report to King Henry II, the meeting in fact took the form of a conversation with Northumberland, during which he asked them how they thought he should proceed.[61] So just as Mary would do nothing without consulting the Imperial ambassador, Scheyfve, it now appeared that the Lord President was using the French diplomats in the same way. The accuracy of their advice was however limited by the fact that they knew nothing at this stage about Edward's 'Devise', and probably had less information than Scheyfve about the King's true medical condition, though they no doubt suspected the worst. Their conversation with Northumberland on 7 May injected extreme urgency into their report and galvanized the French King into action. Seeing that the future European role of the English Crown, contested as it was by France and the Habsburgs, was likely to be thrown into question very soon, even if the plan for Lady Jane Grey's succession was still unknown in Paris, Henry II responded to the news from his ambassadors in London by sending his diplomatic secretary and close confidant, Claude de l'Aubespine, to join them. This mission was secret enough to be concealed from the English embassy in Paris. According to the ever vigilant Scheyfve's despatch to Brussels on 30 May, L'Aubespine reached the English capital in time for the second day of Lady Jane and Guildford Dudley's wedding

---

[60] René Aubert de Vertot, *Ambassades de Messieurs de Noailles en Angleterre*, 5 vols (Leiden: Chez Dessaint et Saillant, Durand and others, 1763), ii, p. 4.

[61] Ibid., p. 6.

celebrations. No instructions to Henry's special envoy or report on his mission survive in French diplomatic correspondence, which means that the only source is Scheyfve. He reported that L'Aubespine went to Greenwich Palace on 28 May, with Noailles and Boisdauphin, for a very well attended meeting of Edward's Council. This too was highly secret, to the extent that it does not appear in the register of Privy Council acts. According to Scheyfve, Northumberland had been away from London but returned for this session, at which a request was made that the Lady Elizabeth should be godmother to the French king's infant daughter, and French help was indeed offered, in case of Edward's death, but in return for the cession to France of the lordship of Ireland, which had been designated a kingdom under the English Crown by Henry VIII in 1541.[62]

The Court and the general public were led to believe that Edward had received Noailles and Boisdauphin on 7 May and, indeed, even in early June he continued to receive some visitors and tried to carry on his studies with Sir John Cheke, but after the letters patent on the succession had been issued he appears to have lost all hope of recovery from his ever more debilitating illness. By now, the Council was meeting away from the privy chamber, in a secret room to which even secretaries were not admitted. By mid-June, divergent rumours concerning the King's health were circulating, and on 19 June 1553 the Council ordered a prayer for his recovery to be said daily in his chapel.[63] The surprise with which this prayer was greeted when it was posted in the City of London indicates how effectively the true medical situation had previously been concealed. Scheyfve thought that news of Edward's decline had been made public at this time in order to test the political water.[64] On 18 June, though, Antoine de Noailles, who had by now fully taken over as French ambassador, was assured by the Council that the King's health was improving. To reinforce the point, ceremonies such as the playing of trumpets to announce courses at dinner were reintroduced as though the sovereign were present, but Noailles was not fooled and neither, very probably, were Londoners, who could not have missed the extra night watches which were now set, the new restrictions on the opening hours of the city gates, the increase in the number of guards in the Tower of London, and the stricter confinement of its prisoners. Nobles and their retinues began to reappear in the capital having been summoned by the Council, while few could have failed to notice the sudden arrival of twenty armed ships in the Thames.[65]

It seems that Northumberland was still hoping, as the end of June 1553 approached, that Edward could hang on for a few months so that French support might be secured and the 'Devise' put into effect. If the King was still alive when parliament assembled on 18 September, this document

<hr>

[62] *CSP Span* XI, p. 55; Ives, *Lady Jane Grey*, pp. 154–7.
[63] The text of this prayer is partially reproduced in Skidmore, *Edward VI*, p. 327 n. 28.
[64] *CSP Span* XI, p. 53.
[65] Vertot, *Ambassades*, ii, pp. 33–4, 48.

would be given the force of statute. Nature and politics combined to enforce a different outcome, however. On 25 June, it seemed certain that Edward would die very soon, but he then appeared to rally, although his fundamental condition did not, of course, improve.[66] The French took the opportunity to press for a closer alliance with England and tried to draw Northumberland further away from Charles V, the bait being political and military support for Jane's accession to the throne. The French ambassador could not, however, tempt the Lord President, Northumberland, into divulging the existence of the 'Devise', or what had been done with it. At this stage Henry II and his advisers seem to have thought that Northumberland himself might be the next king, and professed themselves not to be opposed to the idea.[67] In Brussels, too, rumours were rife by the end of June that Edward was dying, or even already dead. The English ambassador to the Imperial Court, Sir Philip Hoby, was told, in a letter from William Cecil, to fear the worst for his King's future health. Significantly, Hoby reported in return to London that Charles had sent three new ambassadors there, to act as advisers to Mary if she were to make a bid for the throne. If she succeeded, he told Cecil, the supporters of 'God's Word' would be lost, and England would be in a worse case than the biblical Sodom and Gomorrah (Genesis 18: 22–19: 26), filled with immorality and homosexuality.[68] In the event, of course, Edward's 'Devise' was put into effect, and Lady Jane Dudley, as she had been known since her marriage to Lord Guildford, was proclaimed queen on 10 July, that is, three days after her predecessor's death.[69]

Known later as a 'nine-day wonder', though it could be said that her 'reign' in fact lasted from 6 to 19 July, Jane normally appears in the indexes of modern historical works under her surnames, Grey or occasionally Dudley, rather than her regnal name. Although she has achieved some fame, not least in cyberspace, as a wronged victim of Tudor power politics, and even as a Protestant martyr because of her execution in 1554, Lady Jane Grey (b. 1536/7) seems to have made little personal impact on the events of her short life, and one modern historian has felt impelled to adopt a 'novelistic', semi-fictional approach in order to write her biography, though Eric Ives has since achieved a comprehensive account by using conventional historical methods.[70]

According to her own subsequent and apparently authentic testimony, in a letter to Mary which was collected by the papal representative Gianfrancesco Commendone, on 10 July Jane, was brought from the duke

[66] *CSP Span* XI, pp. 66, 67.

[67] Vertot, *Ambassades*, ii, pp. 35–8; E. H. Harbison, *Rival Ambassadors at the Court of Queen Mary* (Princeton, NJ: Princeton University Press, 1940), p. 43.

[68] Samuel Haynes, ed., *A collection of State Papers left by William Cecil, Lord Burghley* (London: William Bowyer, 1740), pp. 153–4.

[69] Guy, *Tudor England*, p. 226.

[70] Alison Weir, *Innocent Traitor* (London: Hutchinson, 2006); Ives, *Lady Jane Grey*.

of Northumberland's residence at Syon to the Tower of London by her
sister-in-law, Mary Sidney. Although no councillors initially appeared to
meet her, a ceremony was quickly organized in which she was formally
received there by a gathering of nobles.[71] Her mother, Henry VIII's great-
niece Frances Grey, duchess of Suffolk, carried her train. There was
artillery fire, and she was subsequently proclaimed by two heralds as queen,
in four districts of the City of London. The proclamation stated that the
Lady Mary was illegitimate, and therefore ineligible for the throne, and the
procedures involved in a normal monarchical succession were followed.[72]
The mayor and aldermen of London swore allegiance to Jane, and letters
were sent by what was now her Council to sheriffs and justices of the peace
throughout the kingdom, announcing the accession to the throne of
England's first reigning queen and ordering them to prevent disturbances
which might arise from the exclusion of Mary, who, the letters declared,
was either in flight to Flanders or awaiting Imperial intervention in East
Anglia. In London itself, Bishop Nicholas Ridley had already, on Sunday 9
July, preached a sermon at Paul's Cross, outside his cathedral, denouncing
Mary and Elizabeth as bastards, accusing both of opening the way to
foreign domination by marriage, and attacking Mary as a 'papist'. Jane
would remain in the Tower for the rest of her reign, and while Mary of
course took no part in these events in London, her activities elsewhere
would soon come to the attention of Northumberland and the rest of the
Council. On 10 July, it still seemed to Jane's supporters that she was in a
strong position. She and her allies were in possession of the Tower of
London, the royal treasury, ships and troops. Mary was being hunted by
Jane's cavalry, and it was expected that more troops would join them, to cut
off her likely retreat to the Continent. The duke of Northumberland had
already sent half a dozen ships to lie off East Anglia for this purpose. All
looked sweet for the new Protestant queen. But by that time, the second
royal coup of 1553 was already under way.

---

[71] Commendone, *Accession*, pp. 45–48; Ives, *Lady Jane Grey*, pp. 18–19, 187.
[72] C. Wriothesley, *A Chronicle during the Reigns of the Tudors from 1485 to 1559, by Charles
Wriothesley, Windsor Herald*, ed. W. D. Hamilton, 2 vols (London: Camden Society, 2nd
or new series, XI, 1875–7), ii, p. 86; *CSP Span* XI, p. 106; *Chronicle of Queen Jane*, p. 3; Eric
Ives, *Lady Jane Grey: A Tudor Mystery* (Malden, MA and Oxford: Wiley-Blackwell, 2009),
pp. 187–8, 321 nn. 25–6.

Chapter 5

A YEAR OF TWO COUPS, 1553

As King Edward prepared to meet his Maker, Mary was about to take action which had precedent in her Spanish family. During the night of 11–12 December 1474, Henry (Enrique), king of Castile and León, died in the Alcázar (castle) of Madrid. Henry had been ill for some time, but he nonetheless seems to have died suddenly, and the exact cause of his death is not known. Setting out early on Sunday the 12th, one of the late King's servants, Rodrigo de Ulloa, travelled north-west, through the snow-covered Guadarrama mountains, and by the time the short December day came to an end he was in the Alcázar of the Castilian cathedral city of Segovia and had told the Princess Isabella that her half-brother was dead. The reaction of the future Mary I of England's maternal grandmother was swift and decisive. Apparently not expecting death at that particular time, Henry seems to have made no will, either written or oral. He had been using the Madrid Alcázar as a hunting-lodge in an attempt to find solace from his mental and physical affliction in the mountains and heathland which surrounded the then insignificant Madrid, future capital of Castile and Spain; his Council was not with him. In the circumstances, Ulloa gave Isabella the wise and conventional advice that she should await the assembly and decision of the Castilian royal council, which had been running the kingdom's affairs during Henry's illness and would have to choose between her and Henry's supposed daughter Joanna (Juana), whose legitimacy was disputed. Both women had at different times been recognized by the Castilian cortes (parliament) as the King's successor. Isabella took no notice at all of this counsel and, immediately, on that Segovian December Sunday, began to prepare what may justly be described as a partly constitutional coup. On the Monday morning, 13 December 1474, the feast day of the virgin martyr St Lucy, without informing her husband Prince Ferdinand, who was then with his father, King John II, in Zaragoza, the capital of Aragon, the princess had herself proclaimed Queen with the simple ceremony which was customary in Castile. In the Plaza Mayor (main square) of Segovia, Isabella swore to obey the commandments of the One, Holy, Catholic Church, to seek the commonweal of the Castilian people, and never to give away any of the territories of the Crown of Castile, but rather to respect all the privileges, franchises and exemptions of its cities, towns and villages. This done, the ad hoc assembly accepted her as Queen, and her heralds cried, in the traditional manner, 'Castile, Castile, Castile, for the Queen and our Lady, Queen Doña Isabella, and for the

King Don Ferdinand *as her legitimate husband* [author's italics]'. The royal party then entered the nearby cathedral for Mass.

Conventional as they may have been in their basic outline (there was no tradition of anointing and crowning in Castile), the events of the day had some novel or unusual features. Unlike England and France, Isabella's new realm had been governed by a queen before, on more than one occasion, but there had not been a male monarchical consort before, and the absent Ferdinand's role remained to be defined. As things then stood, he would inherit in his own right only the neighbouring 'Crown of Aragon', which included the kingdom of Aragon itself, Catalonia, Valencia and the Balearic islands, as well as claims to some other Mediterranean territories. Also, the Segovia ceremonies conspicuously lacked the presence of nobles and prelates. No leading magnates attended, and the only bishop on hand was the local diocesan, Juan Arias Dávila. The response of the great and the good of Castile was thus highly uncertain, and two vital tasks faced the new 'queen' at once. Her husband had to be informed of his change of situation, and something would have to be done about Princess Joanna. Eventually, Isabella and Ferdinand would establish an awe-inspiring regime over most of Spain and part of the Americas, but in the meantime they would have to win a civil war and beat off a Portuguese invasion of Castile, before Isabella's Segovia coup could be regarded as effective.[1] Compared with this generally unacknowledged precedent, how would their granddaughter Mary fare in the England of 1553?

Despite the attention which has been lavished upon it by historians, the sequence of events that brought Mary from Hunsdon in Hertfordshire to Kenninghall, Norfolk, then Framlingham, Suffolk, and eventually to London, between 4 July and 3 August 1553, has still not been established with completeness and certainty. Such has been the effectiveness of those involved at the time in concealing or distorting their actions and intentions. Nonetheless, things seem to have happened more or less as follows. Both Mary and Elizabeth were summoned to London by the Council before the King died, and probably at the end of June or the beginning of July. Earlier accounts, including that of H.F.M. William Prescott, suggested that, while Elizabeth stayed put in Hatfield House, Mary initially obeyed the royal summons and headed towards London, having reached Hoddesdon by the time of Edward's death at Greenwich on 6 July.[2] The general view now is that Mary did indeed leave Hunsdon on 4 July, but headed northwards. By that time the Imperial ambassadors were aware of the dying King's 'Devise', but it is not known whether Mary had heard of it too, either from these diplomats or from others.[3] Travelling in the short summer night with a small contingent of her household – two ladies and six gentlemen – as

---

[1] Azcona, *Isabel la Católica*, pp. 237–8; Azcona, *Juana de Castilla*, pp. 48–56; Edwards, *Ferdinand and Isabella*, pp. 1–3.

[2] Rex, *The Tudors*, p. 131; Prescott, *Mary Tudor*, p. 209.

[3] *CSP Span* XI, p. 71.

well as servants, she avoided the most direct route to her Suffolk and Norfolk estates for fear of interception by agents of Northumberland and the Council. Thus she did not go via Bishop's Stortford and Dunmow, but instead headed, via Royston, for Newmarket and Thetford. After about twenty miles she stopped for what remained of the night and for early morning Mass, at Sawston Hall in Cambridgeshire, the home of a sympathizer, Sir John Huddlestone. The next day, the 5th, she proceeded, according to some accounts disguised as a servant of one of Huddlestone's retainers, after about sixty miles reaching Hengrave Hall, just north of Bury St Edmunds, where she stayed the night with Lady Burgh.[4] When leaving Hunsdon, Mary had apparently given herself cover by announcing that the illness of three or four of her servants had forced her to evacuate the house, and the precaution was necessary since news of her departure soon reached London. The fact that she was heading towards Thetford, on a road which led eventually to Great Yarmouth, seems to have suggested to Northumberland and his allies that Mary was planning, this time in earnest, to flee to the Netherlands.[5]

There is still some dispute over exactly how Mary received the news that her half-brother had died. According to one interpretation, she travelled to the seventy-room manor house of Kenninghall without knowing that the King was dead, and was given the news there on 8 July. After she was safely on the throne, a claim to have sent this initial information was made by Sir Nicholas Throckmorton (Throgmorton). He had been acquitted of treason in 1546 as a result of the trial, ordered by Henry VIII, in which Henry Howard, earl of Surrey and son of the duke of Norfolk, was executed for that offence, and he had subsequently become a gentleman of Edward VI's privy chamber.[6] According to the version of events given by Robert Wingfield, who was personally involved in Mary's venture, the fateful message, whoever had sent it, was delivered to her by her goldsmith, a citizen of London who is thought to have been one Robert Raynes, at Euston Hall near Thetford, on 8 July.[7] Mary may have been reluctant to believe this message because it came from Throckmorton, who was not known as her supporter, but in any case it was necessary for her to be absolutely certain of the truth as a self-proclamation while the King was still alive would clearly have been treasonable and would almost inevitably have led to her death.[8] But by the time she was in her own house of Kenninghall, on 9 July, her doubts had been overcome and she was ready to have herself proclaimed queen.

---

[4] Prescott, *Mary Tudor*, pp. 209–10; Guaras, *Accession*, pp. 42, 89–90.

[5] Prescott, *Mary Tudor*, p. 210.

[6] *Chronicle of Queen Jane*, pp. 1–2.

[7] Robert Wingfield, 'The *Vita Mariae Angliae* of Robert Wingfield of Brantham', ed. Diarmaid MacCulloch, Camden Miscellany, 4th series, xviii (London: Royal Historical Society, 1984), pp. 181–301.

[8] Loades, *Mary Tudor*, pp. 174, 176 and n.

The relevant messenger seems to have been a physician, John Hughes, who was able to confirm what the goldsmith had told her. This seems to have happened during the evening of 8 July, as Mary later informed the Imperial ambassadors.[9] On the following day, which was a Sunday and the day before Jane was proclaimed in London, she assembled her household at Kenninghall and proclaimed herself queen. According to her faithful servant Robert Wingfield, who was present, the reaction was strong and joyful:

> Roused by their mistress's words, everyone, both gently-born and the humbler servants, cheered her to the rafters and hailed and proclaimed their dearest princess Mary as Queen of England.[10]

On the same day, Mary wrote to the Council in London, demanding its allegiance.[11] Meanwhile she told her household that Edward's death had caused the Crown to pass to her, by both divine and human law, while, many miles away, Lady Jane Grey was brought from Syon to Chelsea, and from there to the Tower of London in order to be proclaimed queen in accordance with the late King's 'Devise'. Mary's letter was technically not addressed to a council as such, but to a group of individual former councillors, who since 6 July had pretended that Edward was still alive and, as she wrote it on the 9th, were planning to install Jane as Queen. Having carefully stated that she had 'sure advertisement' of Edward's death, she reproached the 'councillors' for not having informed her of the fact themselves, and rested her claim to the throne on the relevant parliamentary statute, on her father's last will and testament, and on unspecified 'other circumstaunces advancing our right'. She also said that she was aware of 'your consultations, to undo the provisions made for our preferment', though she assured the recipients that she was willing fully to pardon all those who would abandon their 'great bandes and provisions forcible' and acknowledge her as queen. In conclusion, Mary ordered 'her' Council to have her proclaimed in London and throughout the kingdom and, in a flurry of decisive administrative activity which spoke of earlier planning, she prepared and despatched numerous other letters, similar in content, to gentlemen in neighbouring counties and to various other parts of England.[12] She was clearly prepared with a secretarial staff at Kenninghall, and thus was able to call in the loyalty of her entire 'affinity', including her household, her immediate tenants and local and more distant 'well-wishers'.[13] In particular, Mary sent a letter to

---

[9] *CSP Span* XI, pp. 72–6; Loades, *Mary Tudor: The Tragical History* pp. 99–100; Rex, *The Tudors*, p. 132.

[10] Wingfield, *Vita*, pp. 203, 252.

[11] Loades, *Mary Tudor*, p. 100.

[12] Wingfield, *Vita*, pp. 203–4, 252–3; Foxe, 1570, pp. 1567–8; Porter, *Mary Tudor*, pp. 195–6; Alexander Samson, 'The Marriage of Philip of Habsburg and Mary Tudor and anti-Spanish Sentiment in England', Ph.D. thesis, University of London, [1999] 2009, pp. 40–1.

[13] BL Lansdowne MS 1236, fol. 29 (letter from Mary to gentlemen of the liberty of [Bury] St Edmund[s]); Ives, *Lady Jane Grey*, p. 230.

Sir Edward Hastings, absolving him of his allegiance to Jane and urging him to raise Buckinghamshire and Middlesex in her support.[14] Sir Edward duly responded, along with Lord Windsor, while Sir John Williams produced a similar result in Oxfordshire. Indeed, Mary rapidly acquired a strategically significant block of support among Catholic gentry in the Thames Valley and as far north as Northamptonshire. In northern England, Lord Dacre quickly pledged allegiance to Mary, while in Wales an initial declaration in Jane's favour by two of the duke of Northumberland's supporters, Ellis Price and Richard Bulkeley, was soon reversed.[15] Also on the 9th, Mary finally contacted the Imperial ambassadors, who had up to then remained entirely on the margin of affairs. In her message, she asked them to send her a messenger by return so that they might exchange information. Already Mary seems to have felt that a conspiratorial silence was no longer necessary.[16]

Mary's letter reached the Council – which was now Jane's, according to Edward VI's version of the law – at the Tower of London on Monday, 10 July. Its contents certainly seem to have spoiled the dinner of Northumberland and his allies and, no doubt because they feared that their personal ambitions would be frustrated by the fall of Jane, the duchesses of Suffolk and Northumberland are said to have burst into tears when they heard the news. The Council's initial reaction, under Northumberland's forceful direction, was defiance of the excluded 'queen'. Mary's messenger, her elderly retainer Thomas Hungate, was immediately sent to cool his heels in one of the less salubrious apartments of the Tower, even though some councillors very probably had more than a little sympathy with her claim.[17] At this stage, it appears that the Council still assumed that Mary would flee to the Netherlands, since one of the Lord President's sons, Robert Dudley, who would later be Elizabeth's favourite, was despatched into East Anglia with troops to intercept and arrest her.[18] On Tuesday the 11th, the news reached London that the earl of Bath had joined Mary, while the earl of Sussex was on his way to Kenninghall. Several East Anglian gentlemen had by now come to join her inner core of supporters, and they included Sir Thomas Wharton, Sir John Mordaunt, Sir Richard Southwell, Sir William Drury, Sir Edmund Peckham and Sir Henry Bedingfield with his two brothers.[19] The earliest known list of Mary's declared and active supporters,

---

[14] Reproduced in Mortimer Levine, *Tudor Dynastic Problems, 1460–1571* (London: George Allen & Unwin, 1973), p. 170.

[15] Wingfield, *Vita*, p. 260; Glanmor Williams, 'Wales and the Reign of Queen Mary I', *Welsh History Review*, x (1981), 334–58, at p. 336.

[16] *CSP Span* XI, pp. 82–3.

[17] Ibid.

[18] Wingfield, *Vita*, pp. 206–53; *CSP Span* XI, p. 73.

[19] *Chronicle of Queen Jane*, p. 5; Wriothesley, *Chronicle*, 2, p. 87; Wingfield, *Vita*, pp. 4–5; Jennifer Loach, *Parliament and the Crown in the Reign of Mary Tudor* (Oxford: Clarendon Press, 1986), pp. 2–3.

dated 14 July, contains forty names, thirty-two of them being gentlemen or of higher rank.[20] At the time, commentators, including the Imperial ambassadors in London, perceived some kind of 'popular' uprising in East Anglia and elsewhere.[21] It is true that Robert Wingfield, an eyewitness to many of the crucial events of July 1553, commonly mentioned in his Latin 'Life of Mary' the involvement of the *plebs*, *populus* and *vulgus*, but these terms seem to have referred only in a general way to those who were neither nobles nor gentlemen, and not to a 'lower-class' movement of the kind so deeply feared by sixteenth-century governments.[22] Thus there is no doubt that Mary's success depended on the attitude taken by leading men in the shires. When the surprising news of Jane's succession finally penetrated outside London, it presented many aristocrats and justices of the peace with a dilemma. There was evidently a general feeling among members of all social classes that Mary had been wrongly excluded, but this certainly did not mean that all would rise to defend her. Due allowance must, of course, be made for the fact that most evidence about individual attitudes and loyalties during the crisis was given and collected after Mary had won. Nevertheless, it does appear that, for example in East Anglia and Lincolnshire, where Jane's government made its most serious effort to repress Mary's supporters, local authorities in town and countryside at first accepted without demur the implementation of the 'Devise'. When it became clear that Henry VIII's daughter was prepared to fight for the throne, justices ordered local musters on Queen Jane's behalf and tried to silence opposition to her rule by bailing those spreading contrary rumours to appear for trial at quarter sessions.[23] Many, quite naturally, kept their heads down and awaited developments, but open opposition to Mary was expressed in west Norfolk, and particularly in King's Lynn, quite close to the geographical centre of her support.[24]

Despite the bluster with which Mary's letter was initially greeted, and the strength and defiance of the reply which the Council despatched to her, it seems in fact to have dawned on at least some members of Jane's entourage that her rival's cause was rapidly gaining momentum. As a result, the Council agreed that a second military expedition should be mounted, in order to arrest Mary and her leading supporters. The proposal was that the duke of Suffolk should command the troops, but it is said that either Jane herself or her mother objected to this and, whatever the precise course of events, Northumberland finally agreed to lead the army himself.[25] On Wednesday, 12 July a muster was called on Tothill fields.

---

[20] *APC* IV, pp. 429–30.

[21] *CSP Span* XI, p. 96.

[22] Wingfield, *Vita*, introduction by MacCulloch, p. 188; R. Tittler and S. L. Battley, 'The Local Community and the Crown in 1553: the accession of Mary Tudor Revisited', *Bulletin of the Institute of Historical Research*, lvii (1984), pp. 131–9.

[23] F. Madden, ed., 'The petition of Richard Troughton', *Archaeologia*, xxiii (1831), pp. 18–49, text, pp. 23–46; Ives, *Lady Jane Grey*, p. 194.

[24] *APC* IV, pp. 297, 304, 305, 315, 415; Tittler and Battley, 'Local community', pp. 132–7.

[25] *Chronicle of Queen Jane*, p. 5.

Northumberland's men were to be paid 10d a day, 'to fetch the Lady Mary', and the levy was proclaimed all over London. That night, three wagons arrived at the Tower containing both large and small guns, billhooks, bows and spears for the use of this army, which was intended to head first of all towards Cambridge. Meanwhile, in the most important city of East Anglia, Norwich, uncertainty had prevailed earlier over whether or not King Edward was dead, with the result that Mary's messengers were not initially admitted, but the uncertainty had now been ended and Henry's originally designated heir was duly proclaimed there on 12 July. Equally significantly, on this day Mary moved her headquarters, which was receiving ever greater quantities of supplies, from Kenninghall to the much more defensible former Howard castle of Framlingham in Suffolk.[26] There had been similar doubts in the other major East Anglian town, Ipswich. There, on 11 July, now sure that Edward was dead, the sheriff of Norfolk and Suffolk, Sir Thomas Cornwallis, together with Lord Thomas Wentworth and other Suffolk gentlemen, declared for Jane. Soon afterwards, though, one of Mary's servants, her receiver Thomas Poley, came to Ipswich marketplace and proclaimed her queen instead. Such was the apparent enthusiasm there in Mary's support that Cornwallis and his friends rapidly changed their minds.[27]

Early in the morning of 13 July, the duke of Northumberland had military harness prepared for his men. Horses and carts were requisitioned in the city of London, ready for the expedition to arrest Mary which left London, first of all for Ware in Hertfordshire, early on 14 July. Although, a week earlier, he had sent 300 of his retainers with his son Robert in pursuit of Mary, he still had 200 of them, and 400 other troops, to put in the field, along with up to 300 of the duke of Suffolk's men. His force also contained infantry and artillery, and among his staff were distinguished soldiers, such as Lord Grey of Wilton, the earl of Westmorland, Sir Peter Mewtes, Thomas Dacre, Edward Fortescue, and the captains of Bowcastle and Carlisle castle. The army's auditor and treasurer was the experienced Sir Thomas Mildmay.[28] Sources indicate that the duke, rightly as it turned out, mistrusted his fellow councillors, and attempted to secure a commitment of loyalty from them before he set out for Cambridge. The arrangement supposedly made at this time was that the Council would subsequently send more troops to Newmarket to reinforce Northumberland before he took Mary on directly. Despite all this it seems clear that there was no unity in Jane's Council, and, in a sombre speech to that assembly before he departed, the duke stated unambiguously that he feared betrayal. Needless to say, members of the Council vehemently denied any such intention and the earl of Arundel,

---

[26] Ibid., pp.8–9; Wingfield, *Vita*, pp. 209, 257.
[27] Anna Whitelock, *Mary Tudor: England's First Queen* (London: Bloomsbury, 2009), p. 171.
[28] *CSP Span* XI, pp. 94, 103, 253, 261; Guaras, *Accession*, p. 91; Wingfield, *Vita*, p. 262; P. L. Hughes and J. F. Larkin, *Tudor Royal Proclamations*, 2 vols (New Haven, CT and London: Yale University Press, 1964–9), ii, pp. 16–17.

who had previously been much ill treated by Northumberland, went so far as to declare that he would accompany him, 'to spend his blood, even at his feet'.[29]

While preparations for Northumberland's departure were going on in London, and apparently just before Mary's move from Kenninghall to Framlingham, one of her main supporters, Sir Henry Jerningham, travelled to Ipswich with the aim of recruiting more men for her army. He was to receive a pleasant surprise. On 4 July, with Edward still hanging on to life, the Imperial ambassadors had reported to Brussels that there were naval ships in the Thames, from Limehouse to Greenwich, though still without their full crews.[30] It is not known when exactly the fleet sailed, but it seems to have consisted of three warships of between 200 and 300 tons and three somewhat smaller pinnaces. The Council had sent them to patrol the East Anglian coast in order to prevent Mary's being spirited away by Charles V's agents, and by 13/14 July they were off the Orwell estuary, under the command of Sir Richard Brooke, who had served in action against France and Scotland, in 1544 and 1545.[31] The intention was evidently to catch Mary in a pincer movement between the Dudleys on land and Brooke's fleet at sea. Wingfield's account of what followed, which was no doubt based on what he was told by Jerningham himself, has a delightfully operatic air. On 14 July, two gentlemen who were now in Mary's service, John Tyrrell and Edward Gleham, had successfully recruited Thomas, Lord Wentworth, a leading East Anglian magnate, to the cause. That same night, Henry Jerningham stayed with a Welsh innkeeper, Philip Williams, who was a strong supporter of Mary. Williams told him that five of the late King's ships had been forced by the weather to take refuge in the Orwell estuary. He said that the crews had already mutinied, 'because of the disowning of Princess Mary', and that they were keeping their officers on the Orwell against their will. The two men then sat up through the night, discussing the need to secure Ipswich, since the Welshman had heard of the duke of Northumberland's move on Cambridge. Williams then told Jerningham that among his guests that night were the negotiators with Wentworth, Tyrrell and Gleham, and the delighted Jerningham asked his host to wake them all at dawn, so that they could go to nearby Landguard point and inspect the beached squadron. The three duly arrived on the coast next morning (15 July), summoned the commander of the squadron, Richard Brooke, and took him back to Framlingham to report to their queen. In the event, the ships themselves were not used by Mary in her bid for the throne, but the episode was one of the most important in her campaign, since both the crews and the

---

[29] *Chronicle of Queen Jane*, pp. 6–8; Wriothesley, *Chronicle*, 2, p. 83; Prescott, *Mary Tudor*, pp. 214–15; Porter, *Mary Tudor*, p. 207.

[30] *CSP Span* XI, p. 71.

[31] Guaras, *Accession*, pp. 92–4; *LP* XX, ii, p. 88; J. D. Alsop, 'A Regime at Sea: The Navy and the 1553 Succession Crisis', *Albion*, xxiv (1992), pp. 577–90, at p. 579.

ships' guns added to her forces, the latter crucially increasing the threat which she posed to Jane's regime.[32]

Meanwhile, just as Philip Williams had been told, Northumberland left London on the morning of Friday, 14 July. He rode out through Shoreditch, and afterwards remarked that although large crowds watched his departure, no one wished him 'God-speed'. Sullen acquiescence seems to have been the order of the day among the citizenry of London. He had promised the Council that he would bring Mary back within a few days, 'like a rebel as she was', and the Spanish merchant and chronicler in London Antonio de Guaras says that he took with him 'almost all the [late] King's regular guard' ('casi toda la guarda ordinaria del Rey').[33] Guaras appears to be referring here to a contingent of the small elite guard known as the 'gentlemen pensioners', which had been set up by Henry VIII in 1539. Investigation after Mary's victory indicates that 29 of the 49 Gentlemen accompanied Northumberland on this campaign, probably being the contingent on duty by rota at the time.[34] While the duke and his army were marching north in the direction of Cambridge, Mary made another appeal from Framlingham to the Imperial ambassadors in London. They duly reported this to Charles, but offered no assistance, although at this stage Mary told them that she was still in desperate straits, even though men and supplies were steadily flowing into her camp.[35]

At Ware, Northumberland was joined by his sons, except for Robert, with reinforcements from their estates in the Midlands. Having stayed there overnight, the duke and his army left on the morning of 15 July for Cambridge, where they would arrive that evening. Before that, though, he began a violent, and ultimately counter-productive, campaign of vengeful destruction against those who had immediately supported Mary's claim to the throne. In particular, he sent Lord George Howard to sack and burn Sawston Hall, where Mary had stayed on her way to Kenninghall, and it is said that, in a special piece of vindictiveness, Howard returned to Cambridge with a missal and a chalice which had been used for the Mass which she had attended on 6 July in Sir John Huddlestone's chapel there. Once in Cambridge, Northumberland stayed with the provost of King's College, Sir John Cheke, who had recently worked for Jane's government, as for Edward's before her. On Sunday, 16 July, apparently under heavy pressure, the vice-chancellor of the university, Edwin Sandys, preached in Great St Mary's Church on a text from Joshua (1:16–18), in which those Israelites who rebelled against Joshua, the successor of Moses, were

[32] Wingfeld, *Vita*, pp. 210, 259; Loades, *Mary Tudor: A Tragical History*, pp. 101–2.

[33] Guaras, *Accession*, pp. 44, 91.

[34] R. C. Braddock, 'The Character and Composition of the Duke of Northumberland's Army', *Albion*, vi (1974), pp. 13–17, and 'The Duke of Northumberland's Army Reconsidered', *Albion*, xix (1987), pp. 13–17; W. J. Tighe, 'The Gentlemen Pensioners: The Duke of Northumberland and the Attempted Coup of 1553', *Albion*, xix (1987), pp. 1–11.

[35] *CSP Span* XI, pp. 88–9.

roundly condemned. Sandys is also said to have brandished the chalice and missal which had been stolen from Sawston.[36] By then, though, dissension seems to have broken out among Northumberland's forces. George, Lord Howard, for example, was becoming increasingly unhappy with the Lord President's scorched-earth policy. The two men quarrelled violently, and the result was that Howard changed sides and left to join Mary in Framlingham. This turned out to be the beginning of the end for Northumberland's bid to arrest Mary, and by now Sandys's sermon, in which he had lambasted Mary as a bastard and a traitor, looked hopelessly out of place. The planned rendezvous at Newmarket, which took place on 18 July, produced no extra troops but only bad news from the Council, in letter form. Success for Mary was looking ever more likely. Nonetheless, despite losing the services of Howard, Northumberland carried on with the pillage, advancing destructively towards Bury St Edmunds, but the promised reinforcements never arrived from London, and neither did troops from William Cecil's bases in Stamford and Burghley.[37] Far from rallying to Jane and Northumberland's cause, Cecil, who had been a highly influential royal secretary under Edward and was active early in Jane's regime, abandoned her cause and fled from London, with the assistance of his servant Richard Troughton, to his home area in south Lincolnshire.[38]

From the fringe of the action, whether in East Anglia or London, where they had been placed by the Emperor's order as well as local circumstances, ambassador Simon Renard and his colleagues seem still to have thought, on Sunday the 16th, that Jane would succeed in holding on to the throne. Yet it is reasonable to suppose, as various historians and biographers have done, that the very pessimism and inaction of the Imperial representatives in England helped to ensure Mary's eventual, and now imminent, success. There was always a risk that overt aid to her from Charles V and his agents would turn away potential English supporters. Things were about to change drastically, however. On that Sunday, dissension among Jane's supporters in the Tower became impossible to hide. According to the resident 'Tower' chronicler, not only were there disturbances within, which led to the gates being checked and locked, and the keys handed to Queen Jane in person at seven o'clock in the evening, but it was discovered during the rounds that the Lord Treasurer, William Paulet, marquis of Winchester, was missing. Such was the state of anxiety which prevailed that evening that the Treasurer was fetched back from his house on the pretext that a royal seal had gone missing from the Tower. This was not a good omen, and Renard and his companions, who quickly heard of these goings-on, began to believe that Mary might win after all

[36] Foxe 1583, pp. 2086–7.
[37] *Chronicle of Queen Jane*, p. 9.
[38] Stephen Alford, *Burghley: William Cecil at the Court of Elizabeth I* (New Haven, CT and London: Yale University Press, 2008), pp. 42, 50–64.

as long as she could withstand Northumberland's assault in Suffolk.[39] The disintegration of Jane's regime was now rapid. On Monday, 17 July it was revealed that the Treasurer of the Mint, Sir Edward Peckham, had gone to join Mary, taking some of the Crown's money with him. The guard on the Queen in the Tower was increased but Jane's regime was now tottering, and on 18 July her Council disintegrated.[40]

Indeed, on that day, the Council announced rewards, carefully calibrated according to social rank – £1,000 worth of land in fee for a nobleman, £500 worth for a knight, and £100 worth for a yeoman – for anyone who apprehended the duke of Northumberland.[41] Also that day, John de Vere, earl of Oxford, not a strong political figure but nevertheless the second most senior earl in England, joined Mary's cause, bringing with him influence over much of Essex. At this time, on the brink of victory but not knowing it, she issued a new proclamation to the English. The document in question remains in the possession of the Bedingfield family, which supported Mary from the start, and it begins thus:

> By the Queen. Know ye all good people that the most excellent princess Mary, elder daughter of King Henry VIII and sister to King Edward VI, your late sovereign Lord, is now by the grace of God Queen of England, France and Ireland, Defender of the Faith, and very true owner of the Crown and government of the realm of England and Ireland and all things thereto justly belonging, and to her and no other ye owe to be her true liege men.

Mary adds that she is 'nobly and strongly furnished of an army royal under Lord Henry, earl of Sussex, her Lieutenant General, accompanied with the earl of Bath, the Lord Wentworth, and a multitude of other noble gentlemen'. Without even naming her cousin Jane Grey or her claiming of the throne, Mary goes on to denounce 'her most false traitor, John duke of Northumberland, and his complices who, upon most false and most shameful grounds, minding to make his own son [Guildford] king by marriage of a newfound lady's title, or rather to be King himself, hath most traitorously by long continued treason sought, and seeketh, the destruction of her royal person, the nobility and common weal of this realm'. The proclamation ends with the rallying cry:

> Wherefore good people, as ye mindeth the surety of her said person, the honour and surety of your country being good Englishmen,[42] prepare yourselves in all haste with all your power to repair unto her said armies,

---

[39] *Chronicle of Queen Jane*, p. 9; *CSP Span* XI, pp. 91–3.
[40] Prescott, *Mary Tudor*, p. 219; Loades, *Mary Tudor: The Tragical History*, p. 102.
[41] *APC*, IV fol. 296.
[42] The stress on English patriotism, while natural enough in such a context, may also imply criticism of Northumberland's political flirtation with the French in that year.

yet being in Suffolk, making your prayers to God for her success . . .
upon the said causes she utterly defyeth the said Duke for her most
errant traitor to God and this realm.

Intriguingly, the 'Bedingfield' proclamation goes on to specify almost
precisely the same rewards for anyone who detained Northumberland as
were set out at this time by the Council in London:

> Anyone taking him, if a noble and peer of the realm, to have one thou-
> sand pounds of land in fee; if a knight five hundred pounds in lands, with
> honour and advancement to nobilitie if a gentleman under the degree of
> knight, five hundred marks of land in fee and the degree of knight; if a
> yeoman, 100 pounds of land in fee and the degree of a squire.[43]

It would be fascinating to know whether there was already collusion
between at least some of Jane's collapsing Council in London and Mary's
government-in-waiting in Framlingham, but such a link cannot as yet be
established.

By now, the rumour mill was suggesting the grossly inflated figure of
30,000 for Mary's army, and a collapse of morale seems to have been wide-
spread among what remained of the Grey–Dudley axis. The man who
stepped forward at this point to finish Jane's 'reign' and officially recognize
Mary as rightful queen, was one who certainly had no need of the social
and economic baits that were offered by the Privy Council and the
Bedingfield proclamation. He was none other than one of England's
most senior noblemen, Henry Fitzalan, earl of Arundel. In the duke of
Northumberland's absence, he convened a meeting of the Council for
Wednesday 19 July, and it took place in highly unusual circumstances. Even
at this stage, and with news of the loss of the five royal ships, not all were
prepared to accept Mary as legitimate queen. However, a group of councillors, including the earls of Arundel, Bedford, Pembroke, Shrewsbury and
Worcester, and Lords Paget, Darcy and Cobham, had abandoned Jane in
the Tower and convened at Baynard's Castle, which was Pembroke's
London residence. Although the meeting began in the morning of the 19th,
the decision to change allegiance was not made until the afternoon. Then,
while out riding in London, the lord mayor met the earl of Shrewsbury and
Sir John Mason at Paul's Wharf, on the Thames. After a brief conversation, the mayor left to summon his aldermen to St Paul's Cathedral, then
joined the dissident councillors in Baynard's Castle.[44] Between five and six
o'clock in the evening, a small group of horsemen set out from there with
two heralds, some mace-bearers and three trumpeters in the direction of
the Cross at Cheap. As they went up the hill from the riverside to St Paul's
Churchyard, crowds of people, who had evidently heard rumours of what

---

[43] Oxburgh Hall, Bedingfield MS, in Porter, *Mary Tudor*, pp. 208–9.
[44] Wriothesley, *Chronicle*, 2, pp. 88–9; Prescott, *Mary Tudor*, pp. 219–20.

was afoot, began to gather, and the officials' way was blocked. At Cheap Cross, though, they were eventually able to form up, and the trumpets were sounded. Before a crowd of Londoners, of all social ranks, Garter King of Arms read out a new proclamation. According to contemporary accounts, the reading took place in complete silence until Mary's name was mentioned, then, as Guaras wrote,

> the content and joy of all were such that almost all cast up their caps into the air without caring to recover them, and all who had money in their purses threw it to the people. Others, being men of authority and years, could not refrain from casting away their garments, leaping and dancing as though beside themselves . . . And so great were the cries and acclamations when they drank for love of the Queen, as is the custom here, that it seemed as if all had escaped from this evil world, and had been transported to [heavenly] glory (*aportado ala gloria*).[45]

It appears, not surprisingly, that the reading of Mary's titles ('style') was drowned out, but this was only the beginning of the celebrations. From Cheap Cross, the councillors proceeded to St Paul's Cathedral, where the choir was waiting, and the triumphant canticle *Te Deum laudamus* ('We praise Thee, O God'), was sung with organ accompaniment, which had become a rare or unknown thing under Edward.

By this time the bells of the City churches were ringing and the revels continued all night, while messengers left to carry the news to the rest of the kingdom. Meanwhile, the Imperial ambassadors found that their situation had suddenly been transformed. Earlier on that Wednesday, 19 July, the Secretary to the Council, Sir John Mason, and the earl of Shrewsbury waited upon Simon Renard and his team at their lodgings. Their message was in total contrast to the dismissal which they had attempted to deliver soon after Edward VI's death. Now, they claimed that only three or four councillors had ever really supported Edward's 'Devise', and gave the ambassadors the amazing news that Mary was about to be proclaimed queen.[46] In reality, Mason and Shrewsbury were but recent converts to the new sovereign's cause. Those who took part in the Baynard's Castle meeting had had, after all, to abscond from the Tower. Now things were very different and, at around nine o'clock in the evening of the 19th, the earl of Arundel and Lord Paget, with an escort of about thirty horsemen, left London to go to Mary at Framlingham.[47] While the noisy celebrations continued in the city, 'Queen' Jane's father, the duke of Suffolk, who had witnessed the scene, returned to the Tower with a small contingent of troops, and himself proclaimed Mary on Tower Hill. By the

[45] Guaras, *Accession*, pp. 48–9, 96; see also Machyn, *Diary*, p. 37, *Chronicle of Queen Jane*, pp. 11–13, Wriothesley, *Chronicle*, 2, pp. 88–9.
[46] *CSP Span* XI, pp. 94–7.
[47] Guaras, *Accession*, pp. 49, 96–7; Wriothesley *Chronicle*, 2, pp. 88–9.

time he got inside, his daughter was having supper, and it is said that in a display of that brutality which her parents, and especially her mother, had so often inflicted on the unfortunate young woman, himself tore down the royal canopy from above her head, saying, somewhat belatedly, it might be thought, that such things were not for her. That afternoon, Lady Throckmorton had gone to act as proxy for Jane as godmother to the child of a member of the Royal Guard. By the time she returned in the evening, all signs of royalty had been removed from Jane's chambers and she was told that the former 'Queen' and her husband Guildford were now prisoners, awaiting Mary's will.[48]

At this stage, of course, Mary knew nothing of recent events in London, and it is clear that as Thursday 20 July dawned she still believed that she would have to defeat Northumberland in battle if she was to become queen. Thus she decided to review her troops that afternoon, in preparation for action. According to Wingfield, who was in an ideal position to know, the inspection was announced with a royal trumpeter:

> On this day all ranks of soldiers were ordered through those chosen for that duty to go down to the appointed place [below Framlingham Castle], the standards were unfurled and the military colours set up; everyone armed themselves fully, as if about to meet the enemy.[49]

The army consisted of pikemen, harquebusiers, archers and cavalry, and during the afternoon of the 20th it was divided into two sections, one led by the lord marshal, Lord Wentworth and the other by the supreme commander, the earl of Sussex. At about four o'clock, Mary emerged from the castle to carry out the inspection, but she quickly became concerned that her white horse would not cope with the noisy military display and dismounted. According to Wingfield, she then spent three hours among her men, thus not only imitating her mother Catherine and her grandmother Isabella, but also anticipating William Shakespeare's account of Henry V's behaviour the night before the battle of Agincourt in 1415.[50] That evening, Arundel and Paget, who had marshalled the 'repentant' royal Council back in London, arrived in Framlingham and informed Mary that she had been proclaimed Queen. These two men were good choices to represent the Council in this delicate situation. Arundel, though not apparently Paget, had openly opposed the religious reforms of Edward's reign, and both had strong political reasons to dislike Northumberland and reject his dynastic schemes.[51] In 1552, Paget had been stripped of the order

---

[48] *CSP Span* XI, pp. 111–16.
[49] Wingfield, *Vita*, pp. 216, 264.
[50] Ibid., pp. 216–17, 264–5.
[51] Loach, *Edward VI*, pp. 92, 93, 165; Skidmore, *Edward VI*, pp. 177, 191; *CSP Span* X, pp. 166–8; Andrew Boyle, 'Hans Eworth's portrait of the earl of Arundel and the politics of 1549–50', *English Historical Review*, cxvii (2002), pp. 25–47.

of the Garter for supposed financial corruption and briefly imprisoned in the Tower, while Arundel had also been fined and exiled from Court for a while. Although both had subsequently been restored to the Council board, the hurt no doubt rankled still. Meanwhile, matters were coming to a crisis for their old enemy, too, but Northumberland's fate would be less agreeable.

The now ex-lord president seems to have heard news of Mary's proclamation the same day. On Thursday 20 July, now back in Cambridge, he evidently decided that he had no choice but to follow the example of his former colleagues. He asked for a herald and four trumpeters in order to carry out the ceremony properly, but none were to be found so that he had to proclaim Mary himself, apparently throwing his cap in the air in what must have been an utterly insincere and unconvincing gesture. On Sunday 23 July, the earl of Arundel left Framlingham for Cambridge, where he effected the arrest of Northumberland, who had refused to submit to the indignity of being taken into custody by the mayor of Cambridge. Whether Arundel claimed the reward offered by the Council is not recorded. Having submitted to the premier earl of England, the duke asked for mercy, but was given no encouragement. Thereafter, Mary's progress towards London and to control of the government was steady, though not particularly rapid. On Monday, 24 July she disbanded the bulk of her army at Framlingham, though some of her commanders thought this unwise, and headed first for Ipswich, which was the base of Thomas, Lord Wentworth. According to the chronicle, she was met by the bailiffs and some of the people of Ipswich on the heath above the town and given the not insubstantial sum of £11 sterling. Once within the town itself, she was offered by some small boys a golden heart, inscribed 'the heart of the people'. Finally, at sunset on the 24th, she reached Robert Wingfield's house. On 26 July, Mary left Ipswich for Colchester, where she arrived late the same evening, lodging with one Muriel Christmas, who had once been a household servant of her mother Catherine. She then spent a few days at New Hall/Beaulieu, in Essex. On 31 July, she arrived at Ingatestone Hall, the Essex home of royal secretary Sir William Petre, where she spent the night, before moving on to the village of Pingoe, which was just a short distance away, and then to Havering and finally Wanstead, whence she would make her entry into the capital.[52]

During her progress from Framlingham to the outskirts of London, when she showed herself to her subjects as she would rarely do subsequently, Mary perhaps inevitably received a series of supporters and supplicants, the latter naturally desperate to compensate for their 'error' in having offered allegiance to 'Jana Regina'. In the midst of her sudden success, the new queen had to make rapid decisions as to the reliability of those who now prostrated themselves before her, metaphorically or even literally. Leaving aside those who had not wavered in their support, in particular the East Anglians who

[52] Wingfield, *Vita*, pp. 220–3, 269–71.

would form the backbone of her household and government from August 1553, some others had made the transition rapidly from Northumberland to Mary, notable among them being Lord Grey, who had quarrelled with the Lord President in Cambridge, and the earl of Arundel and Lord Paget, who brought the submission of much of Jane's Council to Framlingham.[53] While these men were admitted to Mary's service despite their dubious record, the marquis of Northampton, who belatedly proclaimed her as queen at Cambridge when Northumberland threw in the towel, was not trusted, and spent some time in prison.[54]

Since he was close to Mary during this period, Robert Wingfield's account of the series of nervous supplicants who greeted her on her journey to London can probably be largely relied on. On or about 24 July when she left Framlingham, she was joined by Anthony Browne, son of his namesake, who had been master of the horse to both Henry VIII and Edward VI, and also by Francis Englefield, the son of a judge. While at Robert Wingfield's house in Ipswich, on 24–25 July, Mary received Elizabeth Mary Howard, duchess of Richmond, the widow of Henry VIII's bastard son Henry Fitzroy. Apparently this was not an easy encounter. The duchess had earlier insulted Mary, in a letter to Edward VI's Council, and the new queen made her cool her heels overnight, never subsequently admitting her to full favour. Very different treatment was given, during this stay in Ipswich, to Thomas Heneage, who had formerly been a chief gentleman of Henry VIII's privy chamber. Heneage had not, according to Wingfield, been unequivocal in his support for Mary during Jane's brief reign, but he was none the less well received, though he died a few days later of a stroke, which Wingfield ascribed to his joy, comparable to that of the biblical Simeon, who passed away after seeing another Mary's son, Jesus, in the Temple at Jerusalem.[55] Wingfield also records at this time the submissions of Sir William Cecil and Nicholas Bacon, who had been central to the plans of both Edward and Northumberland, as Secretary to the Council and Attorney of the Court of Wards, respectively. As Wingfield delicately puts it, both men 'were not strangers to this factious conspiracy'. Cecil, in particular, had been playing a double game ever since Jane became Queen.[56] On 26 July, while Mary was en route from Ipswich to Colchester, she was approached by Henry Neville, Lord Abergavenny, who had raised what Wingfield perhaps optimistically describes as a substantial force for her in Kent. The chronicler comments that, by the time the Queen arrived in New Hall/Beaulieu, so many

[53] *CSP Span* XI, pp. 106–9; H. Ellis, *Original letters illustrative of English history*, 3 vols (London: Harking, Tiphook and Lepard, 1824–46), ii, 2, p. 243.
[54] Guaras, *Accession*, pp. 97–8; Wriothesley, *Chronicle*, 2, p. 90.
[55] In the canticle *Nunc Dimittis*, 'Master, now you are dismissing your servant in peace, according to your word', Simeon said of Jesus: 'for my eyes have seen your [God's] salvation, which you have prepared in the presence of all peoples' (Luke 2: 29–30); Wingfield, *Vita*, pp. 220–1, 269–70.
[56] Wingfield, *Vita*, pp. 221, 270; Alford, *Burghley*, pp. 48–64.

people had come to her support that there were no spare lodgings within a three-mile radius of the house. Conspicuous among those who attended Mary at Beaulieu was Jane's mother, Frances Grey, duchess of Suffolk. This must have been a tense interview, but a combination of blood relationship and royal mercy allowed the duchess to be reconciled to the sovereign who had been designated by Henry VIII and by parliament, and whom she had been happy to set aside for the benefit of her daughter Jane. When Mary reached Havering, on 31 July, she received several of the former pillars of the Edwardian and Northumberland regimes: William Paulet, marquis of Winchester and Lord Treasurer, John Russell, earl of Bedford and Keeper of the Privy Seal, Francis Talbot, earl of Shrewsbury, Henry Somerset, earl of Worcester, and William Herbert, earl of Pembroke.[57] The time was rapidly approaching when Mary would have to make some tough political decisions, since a government had to be formed. First, though, she had to meet her half-sister.

On the face of it, Elizabeth made a straightforward, if spectacular, gesture of welcome to the new Queen. According to contemporary accounts, she rode with an armed escort of about a thousand horsemen, including her gentlemen arrayed in the green-and-white Tudor livery, to meet Mary. Thus the two entered London together, on 3 August 1553, with more or less equivalent forces, since Mary was accompanied by her gentlemen preceding her and her ladies following, and a cavalry escort of 700.[58] But many people knew at the time that Elizabeth's behaviour was not straightforward at all. She had, after all, stolen Mary's thunder by entering London before her, with her massive escort, on 29 July, to stay at Somerset House, which had previously been the town residence built by the late duke and lord protector, Edward Seymour, but was now her own. She had apparently brought about 2,000 armed men with her to London, though she took only about half that number to meet Mary at Wanstead on 3 August. Soon after these events, the future cardinal Gianfrancesco Commendone, who had been sent incognito to England as the envoy of the papal legate to Charles V, Cardinal Girolamo Dandino, showed his awareness of the tension between the Queen and the Princess. Commenting on the events of 29 July–3 August, he wrote:

> And it can be gathered therefrom in which way the Almighty takes care of the Queen and rewards her endurance; namely by having reverence paid to her by [Elizabeth], for whom in times gone by she had carried the train of the robe. She had to do that, under threat of heavy punishment, by order of her father, who favoured My Lady Elizabeth no less in consideration of her mother [Anne Boleyn], whom he loved as his own eyes, than because she was a Protestant.[59]

[57] Wingfield, *Vita*, pp. 222, 271.
[58] Machyn, *Diary*, pp. 37–8; *Chronicle of Queen Jane*, p. 13; Wriothesley, *Chronicle*, 2, ii, p. 32; Wingfield, *Vita*, pp. 222, 271.
[59] Commendone, *Accession*, pp. 3–61, 99–131, at pp. 22–4, 110.

Elizabeth had carefully kept aside and apart during the previous month when her troops would have been of great value to her half-sister, not least in propaganda terms. Once she knew of Mary's success, she had written to congratulate her, but Commendone, as an experienced diplomat trained in Italian politics, immediately spotted the underlying tension between Henry VIII's daughters.

Mary's faithful supporter Robert Wingfield naturally offers a glowing account of the events of 3 August 1553:

> On her arrival, the Queen was received by all ranks of society, lords and commons alike, with incredible honour and boundless love. First, nothing was left or neglected which might possibly be contrived to decorate the gates, roads and all places on the Queen's route to wish her joy for her victory. Every crowd met her accompanied by children, and caused celebrations everywhere, so that the joy of that most wished-for and happy triumphal procession might easily be observed, such were the magnificent preparations made by the wealthier sort and such was the anxiety of the ordinary people to show their goodwill to their sovereign.[60]

Lest it should be thought that Wingfield viewed these events through rose-tinted spectacles, even John Stowe, writing in the following reign and from a very different pespective, had to admit that Mary went to the Tower of London on that day 'with a goodly band of noble men, gentlemen, and commoners', though he artfully implied that they were all outsiders, 'gathered out of all partes of the realme', who 'came to London'.[61] Whatever the relative accuracy of these contrasting interpretations, as Mary and her company of about a hundred ladies rested in the Tower that night she must have known that immense challenges faced her immediately.[62] How well prepared was she to confront them?

On the subject of Mary's political instincts and ability, it is hard for the reader who wishes to retain as far as possible a lack of prejudice to penetrate the powerful opinions of modern historians who have offered accounts of her character and life. In the 1940s, H. F. M. Prescott referred to Mary's 'utter simplicitly', asserting that

> Had she been a citizen's wife, she might have been described as an active little body . . . If this was the Queen, what were the men who were to be her instruments and ministers? . . . From these men Mary was divided by a gulf as wide as the miles between Rome and Geneva.

---

[60] Wingfield, *Vita*, pp. 222, 271.

[61] *A summarie of our Englysshe chronicles, diligently collected by John Stowe, citizen of London, in the yeare of our Lorde 1566*, fol. 246v, in Loades, *The Chronicles of the Tudor Queens* (Stroud: Sutton Publishing, 2002), p. 13.

[62] Guaras, *Accession*, pp. 51, 99–100.

Yet she was forced to use them . . ., the new Queen dared not alienate such a large band, but she could never really trust them.[63]

These statements contain in essence much of the discussion which has occurred subsequently concerning Mary's possession or lack of strength of character and political acumen, and hence her ability or otherwise to choose a good government and control it. The 'little woman' approach is still maintained by David Loades in his first major contribution to modern scholarship concerning the Queen and her reign. In words which already seemed old-fashioned in the midst of the 'swinging [Nineteen-]Sixties', he administered a severe 'patriarchal' put-down to a queen who gained the throne at the age of thirty-seven after more than twenty years of often harrowing life:

> Mary inherited no strong minister and lacked the discrimination to appoint one, so that her own limitations were ruthlessly exposed. She was permanently conscious of her inadequacy, and this consciousness added to the unhappiness of her singularly unfortunate life. A woman of exemplary piety and domestic instincts, who would have made an excellent housewife, she was compelled to wrestle with problems which would have baffled much wiser heads. She was frequently ill with worry, sometimes prostrate with grief and frustration, and ever and anon gave way to ill-considered bursts of rage.[64]

Had her father coped any better with the responsibilities and dilemmas of government?

In his first biography of Mary, published in 1989, Loades uses more moderate language on this subject, but still suggests that her inexperience led her to entertain 'excessively high' expectations of her councillors, resulting in part from her 'inability to cope with a normal level of dispute and disagreement', so that his subject still appears a weak, silly and petulant woman.[65] In his second biography, which appeared in 2006, Loades describes Mary, when she took up the reins of power in August 1553, as being 'in the position of the leader of a hopeless opposition party who suddenly finds herself prime minister'.[66] Although he does not mention the name, no doubt because the allusion will be obscure to many, he appears to be referring to a bittersweet comedy series, produced by the BBC and entitled *The Amazing Mrs Pritchard*, in which the woman in question did precisely that and was forced to take on corrupt and failed members of the existing political establishment in order to form a government. Since Mrs Pritchard was eventually brought down by a mixture of

[63] Prescott, *Mary Tudor*, pp. 226, 229–30.
[64] Loades, *Two Tudor Conspiracies* (Cambridge: Cambridge University Press, 1965), p. 10.
[65] Loades, *Mary Tudor*, p. 188.
[66] Loades, *Mary Tudor: A Tragical History*, p. 204.

cynicism at home and uncontrollable events abroad, her fictional fate may indeed provide quite a good analogy to Mary's short reign. To be fair, Loades more or less indicates this in his earlier biography:

> Given her own lack of political experience, what Mary needed was an established regime in working order, such as her father had inherited. The circumstances of her accession made this impossible, and what she assembled was a difficult, nervous, cross-grained bunch of men, who needed a lot of driving and coaxing.[67]

More recently, scholars of Mary and her reign have continued on this more sympathetic line. Anna Whitelock has referred to the Queen as 'a woman in a man's world', who showed both resolution and leadership.[68] In her biography, Linda Porter also takes a very positive attitude to Mary's assumption of power in 1553. She states her own position unequivocally:

> The picture of Mary as a woman who had little grasp of what was going on, who could not work with her politicians and was essentially run by her cousin, Charles V, is entirely false. From the very beginning, the queen had a clear idea of what she wanted to do and the utter determination to achieve it. She never, even when unwell, shrank from the business of government, and she knew that she must draw on the experience of the men who had tried to deprive her of her throne.[69]

Mary's first test was indeed how she dealt with those who had defied the 1544 Act of Succession and Henry VIII's will and, in her eyes and those of many others, rebelled and thereby committed treason against her. Both Linda Porter and Judith Richards take the formation of Mary's first government as an example of her political acumen and decisiveness. In this kind of situation, virtue and vice are very much in the eye of the historian who beholds, so that one man's 'feminine' weakness and indecisiveness is another woman's wisdom, skill and pragmatism. This is a highly subjective and inexact science and, just as it was in the summer of 1553, each case must be judged on its merits in the hope of arriving at a fair overall impression.

In the sense that their sin was as scarlet in Mary's eyes, it is relatively easy to understand the fate of those whom she regarded as rebels and traitors. In examining her actions, it should never be forgotten that she had very little time in which to move. On 18 July, the day before her proclamation as queen in London, the marquis of Northampton, the earls of Huntingdon and Warwick, Lord Grey of Wilton and Admiral Lord

---

[67] Loades, *Mary Tudor*, p. 190.
[68] Anna Whitelock, 'A Woman in a Man's World: Mary I and Political Intimacy, 1553–1558', *Women's History Review*, xvi, no. 3 (2007), 323–34.
[69] Porter, *Mary Tudor*, p. 231.

Clinton, among other prominent personages, were still with the duke of Northumberland at Cambridge, and hence were supposedly loyal subjects of Queen Jane. By 25 July, Northumberland, his sons and the marquis of Northampton were in prison, replacing the duke of Norfolk, Edward Courtenay, and Bishops Gardiner, Bonner and Tunstall, who had been released. Yet when it came to forming a government, Mary's dilemma was clear. Those who had unequivocally shown themselves as loyal to her were easy to identify, but things were not so simple in the case of those who came to her once her victory was complete. After the turmoil of July, Mary had to re-establish orderly government as soon as possible, and so it was inevitable that risks would be taken in choosing office-holders. Between mid-July and the end of August, men – and it had to be men in such cases – were chosen by the Queen to occupy posts in two distinct categories, the Privy Council, and the Court in its various departments. She inherited a complex organization, including several activities which were separately supervised and run, rather like the 'agencies' which have been devolved from the late twentieth- and early twenty-first-century British government. Cases in point were the royal stables, which were accounted for separately from the household and the chamber, and were not even directly run by the master of the horse, and the Chapel Royal, which was run independently by its dean. There were similar arrangements for the department of Tents and Revels, and the Great Wardrobe, as well as the Jewel House, the Works, the Ordnance and the Royal Barge.

When, in the spring and summer of 1547, Mary was set up separately from Edward VI's Court, under the terms of their father's will she had automatically acquired a household of her own, while in July and August 1553 she had rapidly to acquire a Council as well. As far as the household was concerned, when she first heard the rumour of her half-brother's death, at Hunsdon on 4 July 1553, her three 'head officers' were Sir Francis Englefield, Edward Waldegrave and Robert Rochester, and her household staff had a predominance of members from Hertfordshire, Essex, Suffolk and Norfolk. In early 1553, Mary probably had a household of about a hundred, including twenty-three gentlemen and six ladies, as well as four chaplains and a range of other servants.[70] Once in Kenninghall, of course, and especially after her move to Framlingham, she was joined by many more people of all ranks. On 19 July, she had already assembled a Council of twenty-one men, including her household officers, and East Anglian gentlemen with a traditional approach to religion, who had rallied to her cause in the early days. Yet although they had been successful in putting Mary on the throne, these men were unproven at the national level.[71] Thus, by mid-August 1553, she had felt it necessary to appoint more than a dozen

---

[70] Loades, *Mary Tudor*, pp. 140–1.
[71] D. E. Hoak, 'Two Revolutions in Tudor Government: The Formation and Organisation of Mary I's Privy Council', in C. Coleman and D. Starkey, eds, *Revolution Reassessed* (Cambridge: Cambridge University Press, 1986), pp. 87–115.

of Edward's councillors, though none of the Kenninghall–Framlingham group was removed. With the addition of former opponents of Edward and his governments' policies, including those whom she had released from imprisonment such as Bishop Stephen Gardiner and the duke of Norfolk, her Council had swollen to forty-four. It has frequently been argued that not only were there too many people in this body to formulate policy coherently, but that many of these men were not in any case up to the job. Before considering individuals, though, two general points may usefully be made. Firstly, all over western Europe, in the late fifteenth and sixteenth centuries, it was common, if not universal, for monarchs to be advised by two categories of people – hereditary noble officers on the one hand, who offered 'counsel' in their capacity as 'feudal' vassals and, on the other hand, a combination of 'service' nobles and bourgeois of 'lower' birth, some of them in clerical orders, who used their intellectual skills for their sovereign in return for financial and social rewards. In such a system, it was common for many councillors, especially those who were not well-qualified as bureaucrats, to be frequently absent from council meetings, leaving a small group of well-qualified men to run the administration on a day-to-day basis. Thus the large size of Mary's Council was not necessarily an impediment in itself to coherent and efficient government. It is also commonly asserted that public service in the shires did not fit a man for a role in national government. Yet even today cabinet members are frequently recruited from local government via a seat in the House of Commons, and in the vastly more decentralized political system which the Tudors inherited, government at the centre was 'small' in size and scope. Its members, whether nobles or gentlemen, commonly drew their support from their native towns and counties, and the great bulk of local government and the administration of justice was in their hands and those of their relatives and affinity, for example as regional magnates or justices of the peace.[72] In particular, Mary's main base for her bid for the throne, East Anglia, not only contained, in Norwich, one of England's largest cities, but was also one of the kingdom's main conduits for political and economic relations with the prosperous and strategically significant Habsburg Netherlands. It is hard to imagine that leading figures from that region were totally devoid of business and governmental skills. Nevertheless, it is undeniable that Mary faced formidable political challenges when she began to establish herself in London in August 1553.

Very quickly it became clear that, in accordance with the custom in other reigns and other countries, the new Council effectively split into two groups. One, consisting of about twenty people, attended meetings regularly and acted professionally with the Queen, while the rest largely abandoned the centre of power. Tension was inevitably created by the fact that Marian loyalists now had to work on a daily basis with men who had

---

[72] S. J. Gunn, *Early Tudor Government, 1485–1558* (Basingstoke: Macmillan, 1995), p. 13.

explicitly acted to exclude their beloved mistress from the throne which they regarded as her right. The earl of Derby reported to the Imperial ambassadors that some of her loyal councillors were complaining about the inclusion among them of people who had even wanted Mary dead, and they strongly, and in many cases with justice, expressed resentment at accusations of incompetence from those whom they not unreasonably regarded as the corrupt remnants of a failed regime.[73] Simon Renard and his colleagues seem to have been all too ready recipients of this kind of gossip, but, given the often embittered character of their sources, their view of the inner workings and efficiency of Mary's government should not be totally relied upon.[74]

In any case, it does appear that Renard, like so many much more recent historians, misunderstood the relationship between the Privy Council and the Court, and particularly between the Council and the royal household. It is true that Mary began with her existing household when choosing those who would surround her in government, but she had been away from the heart of government for many years and could not have accumulated sufficient expertise among her servants to fill all the offices of state. It was natural that she should have kept on those who had been loyal to her in the time of mortal danger, and it is arbitrary and unfair to describe them as 'devotees rather than advisers'.[75] Moreover, by no means all of Mary's new team came from the East Anglian gentry or from that region's nobility. The earl of Arundel, who had played such a crucial role in the transition from Jane and Northumberland's regime, became 'Great Master' of the Court and lord steward, while the earl of Oxford, who had rallied fairly quickly to her cause, bringing much of Essex with him, regained his ancient family's hereditary office of lord great chamberlain. Crucially, though, members of Mary's inner circle took senior offices in her now greatly expanded household: Robert Rochester became comptroller, Edward Waldegrave keeper of the wardrobe, and Sir Henry Jerningham vice-chamberlain and captain of the guard. However, she left in place financial officers from Edward's household: Sir William Cavendish as treasurer of the chamber and Sir Thomas Cheney as treasurer of the household. Sir Thomas Cawarden remained as master of the revels, and the relatively conservative Thomas Thirlby stayed on as dean of the Chapel Royal until 1554, when he became a bishop. Sir Edward Hastings, who had, crucially, raised troops in Buckinghamshire and Oxfordshire when Mary declared her claim at Kenninghall, became master of the horse.[76] So when she finally gained full freedom to choose her own household, Mary picked long-standing retainers with the addition of some East Anglian gentlemen who had not before been closely associated

[73] *CSP Span* XI, p. 172.
[74] Porter, *Mary Tudor*, pp. 233–4.
[75] Guy, *Tudor England*, p. 228.
[76] Loades, *Intrigue and Treason: The Tudor Court, 1547–1558* (Harlow: Pearson Longman, 2004), pp. 309–11.

with her. Robert Rochester, bailiff of Lavenham in Suffolk, had been in her service since about 1550, and his brother John Rochester had been a Carthusian monk – both were firm traditionalists in religion; while Edward Waldegrave had estates among Mary's lands in Botley, Essex, and Sudbury, Suffolk. He was Robert Rochester's nephew, and this may well have been his route into her service.[77]

Whatever appointments the new Queen made to the traditional offices which were occupied by men, she quickly indicated that women were now to be at the centre of her household and entourage, though it remained to be seen whether or not this change would have a significant effect on the government of England. According to her confidant Simon Renard, the answer to this question was not long in coming. First, she installed her initial escort of a hundred ladies in the Tower of London, a move which in itself may have been seen by some as a significant gesture and must have caused quite a change of atmosphere after the male-dominated Court of Edward VI and the sombre and beleaguered reign of Jane. No doubt in reaction to his ambassadors' reports, as early as 23 August, Charles V wrote to his London embassy, expressing concern that Mary's ladies were having too much influence on public affairs.[78] In view of this attitude it is appropriate at this stage to examine the role of women in her Court and administration. Earlier scholars tended to assume that everything important happened in the all-male Council. In the 1940s, Prescott gave little attention to the importance of women in Mary's regime, describing her as a 'private lady' (as with David Loades's 'good housewife') and adding that 'her women loved her and respected her, and yet they sometimes treated her as one who needed instruction in the ways of the world'.[79] Recently, scholars have begun to examine the question of Mary's female servants and supporters more carefully and more positively. No longer is her privy chamber described as a 'glorified boudoir'.[80]

In the fifteenth century, such disparaging male comments had been made about Mary's grandmother. Considering the irregular circumstances in which Isabella seized the throne of Castile in December 1474, it is perhaps not surprising that criticism of her and her rule, despite the presence beside her of her husband Ferdinand, was strong in some quarters, but there is no denying the existence, during her thirty-year reign, of personal and generically anti-female attacks. Perhaps the most distinguished, in literary terms, of the Castilian Queen's opponents was Alfonso de Palencia, who composed a history, in humanist Latin, of the reigns of

[77] Anna Whitelock and Diarmaid MacCulloch, 'Princess Mary's Household and the Succession Crisis, July 1553', *Historical Journal*, 1 (2007), pp. 265–87, at p. 270.

[78] *CSP Span* XII, p. 186.

[79] Prescott, *Mary Tudor*, pp. 226–32.

[80] Loades, *Mary Tudor*, p. 192.

Henry IV and Isabella and Ferdinand, up to the capture of Granada in 1492. In this substantial and learned work, originally entitled *Gesta Hispaniensia* ('Spanish Deeds'), but commonly known as the 'Decades' because it was modelled on the magnum opus with that title by the Roman historian Livy (Titus Livius, *c.* 64-59BC–AD17), Palencia frequently stresses the importance of sex and gender in government and politics.[81] The chronicler's trail of criticism and accusation led through attacks on her female advisers and collaborators directly to the Queen herself, whom he startlingly described in his 'Decades' as 'a mistress of dissimulations and impostures (*magistra dissimulationum simulationumque*)'.[82] He saw Isabella not as a usurper of the throne (he was not a supporter of her rival, Joanna), but as having usurped a masculine role by attempting to exercise rule personally and directly. Thus she 'unnaturally' combined the power of a male ruler with her 'feminine' wiles, making a deadly and unfair combination which was doubly dangerous. The relevant passage of Palencia's 'Decades' reads more like a vitriolic private memorandum than the published or, in today's conditions, publishable work of a historian. He never succeeded in reconciling the fact of a female monarch with the profoundly masculine values of late medieval society and politics. In August 1553, it remained to be seen how Isabella's granddaughter Mary would fare in the face of comparable problems and similar values.

Until quite recently, such has been the concentration by most historians of the Tudors on male courtiers and councillors that little attention has been paid to Mary's female staff and advisers. Yet the basic facts have long been clear enough. In the crucial privy chamber, the four principal gentlemen and the eighteen other gentlemen who had served Edward in his last days were quickly replaced by seven ladies, thirteen gentlewomen and three chamberers. The only remaining males in the chamber were two gentlemen and seven grooms, who lost their role as intimates of the ruler and found themselves reduced to running errands and guarding the door. Only two of these men, John Norris as chief usher and George Brodyman as keeper of the privy purse, retained significant roles in this heart of government. Perhaps slightly more than half of the women who were now to serve Mary had been close to her, in one capacity or another, in her earlier years, and no doubt their constant presence gave her some comfort in new and often difficult circumstances.[83]

If the influence of Mary's predominantly female household is to be adequately assessed, the starting point should be the question of what the political relationship between that group and the Council was in fact. There

---

[81] Alfonso de Palencia, *Crónica de Enrique IV*, and *Guerra de Granada*, ed. and Spanish trans. Antonio Paz y Melia, *Biblioteca de Autores Españoles*, cclvii, cclviii, cclxvii (Madrid: Editorial Atlas, 1973–5).

[82] Alfonso de Palencia, *Cuarta década de Alonso de Palencia*, ed. and trans. José López de Toro (Madrid: Real Academia de la Historia, 1970–4), ii, 167, 196.

[83] Loades, *Mary Tudor*, p. 192.

are obvious problems in interpreting Mary and her government on the basis
of the traditional, male-dominated sources, and one can certainly detect in
her reign the attitudes and resentments which Alfonso de Palencia so strongly
and bitterly represented in the case of her grandmother Isabella. Given the
views prevailing at the time, which largely denied a political role to women,
it is not surprising that it is hard to adopt the biographical approach to
Mary's leading female courtiers which is conventionally used for their male
counterparts, even though many of them were married to equally prominent
men. Even so, the attempt must be made. Highest in rank in Mary's household were the ladies of the privy chamber, notable among them being Lady
Anne Petre, wife of Secretary Sir William Petre, with whom Mary had
stayed, at Ingatestone Hall, on her way to London, Sir Henry Jerningham's
wife Lady Frances, Lady Frances Waldegrave, wife of Sir Edward, and Lady
Eleanor Kempe. Only two among Mary's eleven gentlewomen have any
documented historical personality – Susan Clarencius and Jane Dormer.

Born in Essex, probably just after 1500, Susan White married Thomas
Tonge, who was Clarence (or Clarenceux) King of Arms for just two years
before his death in 1536, and although she was probably a widow by the
time she entered Mary's service, he nonetheless bequeathed to her the
nickname, or 'surname', 'Clarencius'. So close to Mary was Susan that she
demanded consideration as a political figure, in the sense that she largely
controlled the access of others to her mistress. From 1553, her official title
was 'mistress of the robes', a new post which seems to have combined
those of yeoman of the wardrobe and groom of the stool, the latter supervising the most intimate excretory functions of the ruler in a male privy
chamber. However, foreign diplomats, such as the Venetian ambassador
Michieli, soon recognised Susan's importance as a conduit, for example, to
annuities, pensions and wardships.[84] Jane Dormer, who subsequently
became famous by marrying one of Philip I and II's most prominent
courtiers and diplomats, Gómez Suárez de Figueroa, count of Feria, came
from a Buckinghamshire family and seems to have joined Mary's East
Anglian household in 1548. Even in her case, though, little personal information exists concerning her role in government.[85] This in itself speaks
volumes for the prevailing values of the 1550s.

While Mary had been able to constitute her Council and household by
mid-August 1553, the most prominent of ex-Queen Jane's supporters
remained to be dealt with. Imperial correspondence in July of that year indicates that Charles V, whose support had been lukewarm to non-existent
during Mary's bid for the throne, was very anxious that she should be
merciful in victory. In fact, the new Queen needed no such urging. To most,
it seemed that the primary source of her recent troubles, the duke of
Northumberland, was bound to die a traitor's death along with his sons.

[84] *CSP Ven* VI, ii, p. 1084; Porter, *Mary Tudor*, p. 249.
[85] S. J. Gunn, 'A Letter of Jane, Duchess of Northumberland, in 1553', *English Historical Review*, cxiv (1999), p. 1270.

Many thought that other more or less automatic candidates for execution were the duke of Suffolk and his daughter 'Queen' Jane. If she were executed, it seemed to them inevitable that her husband Guildford Dudley would die too, even though, during her brief reign, his wife had refused him a crown. Yet by 31 July, the duke of Suffolk had been pardoned and released from the Tower, probably at the intercession of his wife, but that did not save Jane. After that Dudley's sons, apart from Guildford, were tried but pardoned, as were the marquis of Northampton, the earl of Huntingdon, Sir Andrew Dudley, brother of the duke of Northumberland, and even their relative Henry Dudley, who had gone to France in an attempt to obtain help to prop up the regime of Jane Grey. Both then and later, there was particular amazement that Mary spared Jane. This was in almost total contrast to her father's behaviour, and needs to be borne in mind when considering Mary's later 'bloody' reputation. In mid-August, she told Renard that she was determined to pardon Jane. She had received a long and dignified confession from her predecessor, and seems to have treated it in accordance with the traditional Christian practice of the Sacrament of Penance and Reconciliation. She told Renard: 'My conscience will not permit me to have her put to death.'[86] Evidently, Northumberland was being blamed for everything and would be punished, but Renard thought this generosity with others was risky. According to his report to the anxious Charles, in his discussion on this subject with her Mary indicated that she might eventually set Jane Grey free, though only if she felt confident it was safe to do so. In her eyes, Northumberland was a totally different case, though he was treated honourably while imprisoned in the Tower of London. Eventually, on 18 August 1553, he was brought to trial by his peers in Westminster Hall, and it soon became clear that, during his weeks in captivity, he had decided not to go down without a fight. He did his very best to keep his composure, and his defence was that he had simply carried out the orders of the late King, with the agreement of the Council.[87] He pointed out that his noble judges had been as involved as he with Edward's 'Devise' and Jane's succession, but of course this did him no good. In what was no doubt, as Renard thought at the time, a proper gesture of Christian compassion, and also turned out to be an astute political move, Mary sent to the former lord president a priest who was of her mind in religion. Surprisingly to most, this seems to have been requested by Northumberland himself, and the priest in question was none other than his old sparring partner Stephen Gardiner. Even more amazingly, the result of this intervention was a full recantation of reformed views by Northumberland, which caused a sensation not only in England but throughout Europe. The trials of Sir Thomas Palmer and Sir John Gates quickly followed and also resulted in guilty verdicts, though Palmer cried out in desperation that his judges were traitors too, 'and have deserved

[86] *CSP Span* XI, pp. 166–73.
[87] Ives, *Lady Jane Grey*, pp. 248–9.

punishment as much as me and more'.[88] Whatever their personal views, Gates and Palmer were brought along with Northumberland's sudden professed return to the traditional faith and, on 21 August, in the presence of the Common Council of the City, all three were present at a celebration of mass and confessed that 'they had erred from the true Catholic Faith fifteen years'.[89] This confession did not save them from their execution as traitors, which took place the next day, a large crowd assembling on Tower Hill to witness in particular the death of the awesome Northumberland.

Contemporary accounts of Northumberland's last days and late recantation can only go so far in trying to explain both his behaviour and Mary's attitude towards him. Writing to Don Beltrán de la Cueva, duke of Alburquerque, Antonio de Guaras, who was present in London to witness events, described the setting of the trial in Westminster Hall, and was evidently impressed by the dignified nature (*autoridad*) of the proceedings. The Queen was represented as president of the Court by the duke of Norfolk, who held his wand of office and sat with other peers of the realm on either side to act as judges. Guaras wryly comments: 'And these same judges, or most of them, were those whom Northumberland had left in the Tower with [Lady] Jane (*la Joanna*)' (when he departed for Cambridge). According to Guaras, who was evidently an eyewitness, when Northumberland was brought in, he bowed three times to the floor before reaching his place. To Guaras, Northumberland looked 'good and brave, full of humility and gravity'. Norfolk, who had earlier been imprisoned for some years by Northumberland, looked at him severely, and the duke's extravagant obeisance was acknowledged only with the perfunctory touch of a cap. Three charges were brought against the prisoner. Firstly, he was accused of raising troops and leading them in the field, on and after 18 July, against the Queen, even though she had already been proclaimed in London and in the kingdom. Secondly, he was charged with having himself proclaimed captain-general of England, and thirdly, he was accused, while in the field, of having proclaimed Jane as queen and Mary as a rebel and a bastard. According to Guaras, the twelve peers who acted as judges were moved by his open and instant admission of guilt in relation to all three charges and could not prevent themselves from weeping. As Northumberland had pleaded guilty, the judges did not have to give a verdict. He asked that two or three peers should subsequently visit him in prison so that he could inform them of some important matters in the Queen's service. He begged the Queen for mercy, and petitioned her to allow him four or five days more in which to regulate his spiritual affairs, and this was granted. He was sentenced to a traitor's death, by hanging, drawing and quartering, with his heart and entrails to be burned. Also on 18 August, Northumberland's son John Dudley, earl of Warwick, was condemned to death, as was the marquis of Northampton. According to Commendone, Northampton told the judges that he had never

---

[88] *CSP Span* XI, pp. 183–93.
[89] Wriothesley, *Chronicle*, 2, p. 100.

been part of the government, had spent much of his time hunting, and had therefore not been involved in Northumberland's plots, but this somewhat feeble defence was rejected. On the next day, Northumberland's brother, Sir Andrew Dudley, and also Sir John Gates, Sir Thomas Palmer and Sir Harry Gates were tried and condemned in the same way.[90] Not all suffered the death penalty. As the highly unsympathetic Robert Wingfield succinctly put it: 'Meanwhile the most generous princess, extravagant, if I may say so, in bestowing her mercy, gave a capital sentence to no more than three of this crowd of wretched scoundrels (*ex anta caterva pessimorum hominum*): Northumberland, the seed-bed of the whole business, Sir John Gates and Sir Thomas Palmer; in this she greatly outdid the praises of her ancestors.'[91]

Ever since the day of his execution, Northumberland's return to the traditional Christian religion, which he had done so much to undermine and transform under Edward VI, has been debated by commentators and historians. There is no surviving record of what passed between John Dudley and Bishop Gardiner, and it is impossible to determine whether he was sincerely converted or merely believed that he could avoid death by once more affirming Catholicism. It is not certain that a letter which he apparently wrote to the earl of Arundel during his last night alive is genuine, but in it he seemed to acknowledge that he had underestimated Mary, and purported not to be able to see why, now that he had repented of his treachery and his 'heresy', he should not remain alive and serve her faithfully. He asked:

> . . . is my crime so heinous as no redemption but my blood can wash away the spots thereof? An old proverb there is and true that a living dog is better than a dead lion. O that it would please her good grace to give me life, yea, the life of a dog, that I might live and kiss her feet, and spend both life and all I have in her honourable service, as I have the best part already under her worthy brother and her most glorious father.[92]

In total contrast is Jane Grey's indignant outburst, reportedly spoken to Mary on hearing that Northumberland was suing for pardon, which puts him in a very different, and piercing, light:

> Woe worth him! He has brought me and my stock in most miserable calamity and misery by his exceeding ambition. But for the answering that he hoped for his life by his turning, though other men be of that opinion, I utterly am not; for what man is there living, I pray you, although he had been innocent, that would hope of life in that case, being in the field against the Queen in person as general, and after his

[90] Guaras, *Accession*, pp. 53–5, 101–4; Commendone, *Accession*, pp. 26–7, 112.
[91] Wingfield, *Vita*, pp. 225, 274.
[92] BL Harleian MS 787, fol. 61.

taking, so hated and evil spoken of by the commons? . . . Who was judge that he should hope for pardon, whose life was odious to all men? But what will ye more? Like as his life was wicked and full of dissimulation, so was his end thereafter . . . Should I, who am young and in my few years, forsake my faith for the love of life? . . . But life was sweet, it appeared, so he might have lived, you will say, he did not care how.[93]

Jane evidently denies the authenticity of Northumberland's conversion, and hence of the speech which he made to the crowd before his execution and which survives in versions by more than one commentator.

According to Guaras's account, which may well be, as with his version of the trial, that of an eyewitness, Northumberland admitted that he had offended God, and asked for the forgiveness of any whom he had offended, whether present or absent. To this the people all answered: 'God forgive you.' Continuing in this penitent and self-deprecating mode, the duke went on to refer to the religious changes which had been taking place in England since the reign of Henry VIII. He blamed its departure from the 'true Catholic Church' for the troubles which had since befallen the kingdom. He asserted that he had returned to Catholic Christianity of his own volition, and not because of anything the Queen had done or at the urging of friends or because of the intervention of Bishop Gardiner of Winchester. He urged his listeners to ignore the preachers of 'false doctrine' and to stick with the clause of the Apostles' Creed: 'I believe in the Holy Ghost, the Holy Catholic Church, the Communion of Saints'. He concluded by urging the crowd to avoid violence and divisions like those which were then occurring in Germany because of religion, and to live peaceably in obedience to the Catholic Church and to the Queen.[94] According to Commendone, after finishing his speech, Northumberland knelt down and asked the crowd to witness that he was dying as a Catholic. He recited several psalms and the Lord's Prayer in Latin, granted the customary request from the executioner for forgiveness, made the sign of the cross, put his head on the block and was beheaded.[95] But the fact that Northumberland, in his last speech, concentrated on religion was an indication of one of the main problems that faced Mary at the beginning of her reign.

An immediate issue, though not apparently as urgent as might have been expected, was the funeral and burial of the late King Edward. When Henry VIII had died it was possible to use the traditional rite in the Sarum use, which was still the legal liturgy of the English Church despite the reforms that had taken place in other respects. However Edward VI's

---

[93] *Chronicle of Queen Jane*, pp. 25–6.
[94] Guaras, *Accession*, pp. 57–9, 106–8. A lengthier version of Northumberland's speech, but on the same lines as Guaras's account, is included in Commendone, *Accession*, pp. 27–30, 113–14.
[95] Commendone, *Accession*, pp. 30, 114.

reign had radically changed the situation and, for the first time in English history, the form of service to be used for the consignment of a deceased monarch to the earth was controversial. When she arrived in London as Queen, Mary was, of course, still head and governor of the Church of England, and the only legal form of public worship in the kingdom was the Book of Common Prayer of 1552. Equally clearly, in Edward's reign Mary had struggled against the Privy Council and, though she could scarcely admit it, against her young half-brother, to preserve the traditional liturgy, and in particular the Mass, in her own private country house chapels. Her views were well enough known, and it is therefore understandable that Charles V's ambassadors in London, and the Emperor himself, should have been nervous that Edward's funeral might become a focus for the religious conflict which their policy of moderation was aimed at suppressing or even removing. Before the end of July 1553, the Queen told the Imperial ambassadors that she was unhappy about letting Edward go to his grave without the support of the traditional liturgy and ritual, and asked their advice, no doubt expecting a 'Catholic' answer. They, however, being aware of their master's desperate concern that no unnecessary provocation should be offered to those of the 'reformed' persuasion, replied in writing, praising her religious correctness but warning that a traditional funeral might stir up resentment among supporters of the Edwardian reforms, especially in London, and even precipitate a violent reaction. Not only that, but, since Edward had lived and died as a heretic and schismatic in Catholic eyes, it would not be appropriate to use the old liturgy for his funeral and burial.[96] In the end, Mary accepted a compromise that Renard had suggested in a secret memorandum dated 2 August. Edward should be buried according to the Prayer Book rite, but since protocol did not require a dead monarch's successor to be present at his funeral, Mary need not risk damnation by attending this heretical service. Instead she was free to arrange a traditional requiem Mass elsewhere. On 8 August the ambassadors reported to Charles that Mary was going to follow their advice, 'with the consent of her whole Council', and this arrangement was duly implemented that day. At this time, not only was the 1552 Prayer Book the only legal service-book in England, but its main composer, Archbishop Thomas Cranmer, was still in office, and apparently carrying out his normal duties. It was of course expected that the archbishop of Canterbury would conduct the funeral of a monarch and, as a result of Mary's agreement to compromise, Cranmer duly did so.

The traditional funeral liturgy contained the Office for the Dead, consisting of the 'hours' of vespers, matins and lauds, said or sung, commonly known as the *Dirige* or 'Dirge', as well as one or more Masses of requiem, offered for the soul of the departed.[97] In the first English Prayer

---

[96] *CSP Span* XI, pp. 117–19, 134; Loades, *Mary Tudor*, p. 193.
[97] Eamon Duffy, *The Stripping of the Altars: Traditional Religion in England, 1400–1580*, 2nd edn (New Haven, CT and London: Yale University Press, 2005), p. 210.

Book of 1549, 'The Order for the Burial of the Dead' contained, after a
service of prayers and scriptural readings and quotations which appeared to
substitute for the 'Dirge', a proper psalm, a very lengthy gathering prayer
(collect), and epistle and Gospel readings for 'The Celebracion of the holy
communion when there is a burial of the dead'.[98] On the other hand, the
1552 Prayer Book made no explicit provision for the celebration of the Holy
Communion at a funeral, and reduced the set text of the service to less than
half of its previous length.[99] In the case of Edward VI, though, all available
accounts indicate that the funeral rites, even though centred on the Prayer
Book which he authorized and appears genuinely to have believed in, were
much more elaborate than the sparse treatment prescribed for his former
subjects. Renard reported to Charles V that the late King was buried in
Westminster Abbey 'with little ceremony', but against this he referred to
choirboys and banners.[100] The King's body had been embalmed and placed
in a lead coffin at Greenwich, where he died, and had thus been preserved
from 6 July until his burial over four weeks later. The coffin was transported
by river to Whitehall Palace and the night before the funeral it was carried
from there to Westminster Abbey in a traditional procession which included
'a great company' of choirboys in surplices, 'singing clerks' and, poignantly,
twelve 'bedesmen' of his father from the former Observant Franciscan
('Greyfriars') church at Greenwich, which had played such a crucial part in
the religious life of the Tudors. The late King's servants, dressed in black,
carried banners which displayed heraldic emblems of his ancestry, including
the red Welsh dragon of Cadwallader and Owen Tudor, the Lancastrian
greyhound, and Henry VIII's lion. Three heralds followed, respectively
carrying Edward's helmet and crest, his shield, sword and Garter, and his
armour. Nine of his former retinue, dressed in black and each carrying a
banner, followed on a 'chariot', with horses draped down to the ground in
black velvet. After all these men came the coffin itself, draped in blue velvet,
on a chariot covered in cloth of gold, and on the coffin, in accordance with
tradition, was an effigy of Edward in full royal life, carved by the Italian
sculptor Niccolò Bellini. The effigy wore a crown and the collar of the order
of the Garter, and held a sceptre; the coffin was surrounded by the standards of the Garter, the Tudors and the Seymours, and it is said that
onlookers wept and moaned, as in royal funerals all over Europe in that
period and for centuries before. Once in the Abbey, Edward was laid on a
hearse draped with black velvet and surrounded by lit tapers on stone
candlesticks, forming the traditional *chapelle ardente* ('burning chapel') of
medieval and early modern Catholic royal exequies. According to Henry
Machyn, who seems to have been an eyewitness and who provides this

[98] *The First and Second Prayer Books of Edward VI* (London: The Prayer Book Society, 1999),
p. 276.
[99] *First and Second Prayer Books*, pp. 424–7.
[100] *CSP Span* XI, pp. 155–7.

account, on the following day, 8 August, Archbishop Cranmer reverted to the practice allowed by his first English Prayer Book and celebrated the Holy Communion during the funeral. Sixteenth-century chroniclers are notoriously, and often maddeningly, vague about the details of liturgy and church music, but if this did happen, it does appear that, when it came to his beloved 'King Josiah', Cranmer felt that a Eucharistic celebration was needed, whatever his theological mind now told him. Many of those who attended Edward's funeral had been present at his baptism in Hampton Court chapel. They included his former tutor, royal almoner and dean of Westminster, Richard Cox, who was apparently released from prison to attend, though the duke of Northumberland was not. Apart from Cranmer, the only reforming bishop present was Hugh Latimer, and a sermon unsympathetic to the late King's achievements was preached by Mary's choice, George Day, who had just been restored to the see of Chichester. Edward was buried beneath the altar which had been constructed for the tomb of his grandfather Henry VII.[101] Meanwhile, Mary, in accordance with her agreement with Renard, remained in the Tower of London, where she had a requiem Mass celebrated for her godson's soul by Bishop Stephen Gardiner. According to Guaras, this action amazed some Londoners and gave new heart to religious traditionalists.[102]

Possibly the events surrounding Edward's funeral, when combined with uncertainty about the new Queen's religious policies, helped to foment religious conflict, especially in London where, then as now, the slightest happening tended to acquire disproportionate importance in comparison with the doings of the rest of the country. Contemporary commentators, both English and foreign, record one violent incident, which took place on the Sunday after the late King's funeral. On 8 August Mary moved upriver from the Tower of London to Richmond Palace, having, according to Robert Wingfield, caused great scandal to those whom he describes as 'sectaries' (*sectarii*) by having a requiem celebrated for her godson. According to Wingfield, a sermon preached at St Paul's Cross on the following Sunday by one of Mary's chaplains, Gilbert Bourne, took a traditionalist turn, praising the now restored Bishop Bonner of London and asserting Catholic teaching on the sacraments. When he attacked the preachers of reform, and in particular John Rogers, who on 6 August had preached a violently anti-Catholic sermon from that same pulpit, someone in the congregation, described by Wingfield as a member of the *novi collegii* (new 'college', perhaps meaning Protestants) threw a dagger at him and forced him to leave the pulpit hastily.[103] According to Antonio de Guaras,

---

[101] *Chronicle of the Greyfriars of London*, ed. J. G. Nichols (London: Camden Society, 1st or old series, 1851), pp. 82–3; Machyn, *Diary*, pp. 39–40; MacCulloch, *Cranmer*, p. 547; Skidmore, *Edward VI*, pp. 283–4.

[102] Guaras, *Accession*, pp. 52, 101.

[103] Wingfield, *Vita*, pp. 223–4, 272.

a large number of people went to hear the preacher at St Paul's that Sunday, 'because good men [i.e. traditionalists] had not been permitted to preach for several years . . .'; 'the good [went] for their comfort and the heretics out of curiosity'. Guaras gives a much more detailed account of the sermon than Wingfield. According to him, the preacher said that Bishop Bonner had been imprisoned for four years for preaching the truth about the 'Holy Sacrament of the Altar', and other religious matters. At this point, those of a Protestant persuasion began to create a disturbance, being upset, according to Guaras, at the Mass which had been celebrated for Edward in the Tower. He states that a number of people in the congregation drew their daggers and brandished them, shouting at the preacher that he was a liar, and that all the things he was praising were no more than idolatry. Members of the corporation of London were present, but were unable to control what had now become a riotous crowd. As Wingfield also noted, the preacher had to abandon the pulpit. Guaras does not mention a dagger actually being thrown, but says that Bourne came again to preach on another day, this time guarded by members of Mary's Privy Council and three or four hundred halberdiers. Evidently seeing the requiem for Edward as a catalyst for religious conflict, Guaras adds that when a different priest, 'following the Queen's example', celebrated Mass in his unnamed London parish church, he was stoned and had his vestments torn from him.[104] Mary could no longer be in any doubt that the public expression of the old religion would not be restored without controversy and disturbance.

Much of the energy of Mary and her government in the early months of her reign was devoted to the question of religion, but they had inherited a lengthy list of problems along with the downfall of Edward, Northumberland and Jane. The treasury was virtually empty and the Antwerp bankers were unfriendly because the repayment of existing loans was overdue. Scotland was still seething after the violence which had been done to its population in Edward's reign, particularly under the command of the duke of Somerset, and Ireland was highly unstable. The most immediate issue, however, was the threat from France, which focused particularly on the English enclave, or Pale, which contained Calais and Guisnes. Mary had had to tackle relations with France even before she arrived in London to take the throne. At New Hall/Beaulieu in Essex on 29 July 1553 she had met the Imperial ambassadors, and the main item for discussion was France. The recent arrest at Calais of Henry Dudley, on his way back from seeking French military aid for Northumberland, had concentrated minds. Henry II and his advisers, notably the Constable Anne de Montmorency and the Guise family, had always opposed Mary's succession to the English throne, and now Calais and its Pale looked vulnerable. In an example of her

104 Guaras, *Accession*, pp. 55–7, 105.

decisive action from the start, and of her pragmatic willingness to overlook, when necessary, the misdemeanours of her noble subjects, Mary appointed the rehabilitated Lord Grey, on 31 July, to raise troops for service in France.[105] Before this, on 24 July, the prickly Lord William Howard, as governor of Calais, had rebuffed the Constable Montmorency, who, not yet knowing that Northumberland had been defeated, had written to offer French military aid in the case of attack by Charles V's forces, which were already engaged against France in adjoining Picardy. Although some of her advisers thought Howard had been too undiplomatic, Mary herself wholly supported his attitude and action.[106] Even so, for the next couple of months, with the Empire and France at war, Mary was able to concentrate largely on what seems to have been her main preoccupation now that she had gained the throne: religion.

All available sources indicate that the Queen was genuinely surprised and upset by the hostile reaction of some Londoners to what she regarded as a necessary piece of spiritual care and honour for her deceased godson in having requiem Masses offered for his soul. When, on 8 August, Mary moved to Richmond, she may well have feared that the Tower of London would otherwise become her own prison, as it still was then for Jane Grey and for the duke of Northumberland. In any case, the Queen's immediate reaction was to indicate that she was prepared to tolerate the use of the Prayer Book. This eirenic approach, highly unusual in official circles in Europe in the 1550s, is best represented by the proclamation on religion which Mary issued from Richmond on 18 August 1553.[107] Given that the document begins by complaining of the 'great inconveniences and dangers [which] have grown to this her Highness's realm in time past through the diversity of opinions in questions of religion', it hardly seems entirely appropriate to see it as advocating, or even permitting, religious tolerance. Mary says that the trouble in the early days of her reign was caused by 'certain false and untrue reports and rumours spread by some light and evil disposed persons'. She goes on to profess openly her traditional Catholic faith, but affirms that she 'mindeth not to compel any her said subjects thereunto unto such time as further order by common assent may be taken therein'. Thus it is clearly indicated that any freedom in religion will be temporary, but while this period lasts no subject should stir up trouble over religion and, in particular, the Queen 'willeth and straightly chargeth and commandeth all her said good loving subjects to live together in quiet sort and Christian charity, leaving those new fangled and devilish terms of papist or heretic, and such like'. After making such pious exhortations, the

[105] Loades, *Mary Tudor*, p. 186; A. Grey, *A Commentary on the Services and Charges of Lord Grey of Wilton* (London: Camden Society, xl, 1840), appendix, p. 40.

[106] Vertot, *Ambassades*, ii, pp. 85–8, 105–7; *CSP Span* XI, pp. 129–35; Prescott, *Mary Tudor*, pp. 222–33.

[107] 11/1/7 in Hughes and Larkin, *Tudor Royal Proclamations*, ii, no. 390, and Loades, *Chronicles*, pp. 17–19.

Queen expresses concern about the divisive effect of 'fond books, ballades, rhymes and other lewd treatises in the English tongue concerning doctrine in matters now in question', and goes on to charge her subjects, of whatever rank, except in the universities, not to 'interpret or teach any Scriptures or any manner points of doctrine concerning religion, neither also to print any books, matter, balad rhyme, interlude process or treatise, nor play any interlude except they have her Grace's special licence in writing for the same; upon pain to incur her Highness's indignation and displeasure'. The rest of the proclamation orders the pursuit of any who were involved in the duke of Northumberland's 'rebellion', but the notable point here is that the censorship proposed in the Richmond proclamation of 18 August went at least as far as the measures that the Spanish Inquisition was attempting to enforce at the time, and thus the document hardly betokens the kind of openness that a superficial reading might initially suggest: it was more a 'gagging' than a 'toleration' measure.[108] Indeed, at the time of its issue, Guaras was under no illusion concerning Mary's true attitude and intention, telling the duke of Alburquerque that 'although in this matter of the Pope the heretics are very stubborn, the Queen is so Catholic that it is held for certain that her Highness will have no regard to heretical knaves (*vellacos hereges*), but [rather] to her conscience which is the truth'.[109] Guaras would soon be proved right.[110] In the meantime, though, a coronation had to be planned.

[108] John Edwards, *The Inquisitors: The Story of the Grand Inquisitors of the Spanish Inquisition* (Stroud: Tempus, 2007), pp. 177–84; Stuart B. Schwartz, *All Can be Saved: Religious Toleration and Subversion in the Iberian Atlantic World* (New Haven, CT and London: Yale University Press, 2008), pp. 1–15.

[109] Guaras, *Accession*, pp. 61–3, 108–11.

[110] Loades, *Mary Tudor*, p. 196.

Chapter 6

A CROWN AND A HUSBAND, 1553–1554

As soon as Mary was established on the throne, her coronation became an issue. Although the people had warmly welcomed the victorious Queen into London at the beginning of August, very soon there were disagreements among her councillors and within her household, not least because of her merciful treatment of some former opponents, whose presence at court and in government greatly offended 'loyalists'. Also, while the use of fines from these enemies helped to replenish the almost empty exchequer which Edward and Jane had bequeathed, there was a feeling, among both the native English and foreign ambassadors, that trouble was being stored up for the future. In addition, some of her Council proposed that parliament should be summoned before the coronation took place, so that, as Mary's own lord chancellor, Bishop Stephen Gardiner, argued, her title might be made fully secure in law by means of the repeal of the statutes which 'bastardized' her and her half-sister Elizabeth, and the overruling by Act of Parliament of Edward VI's will. Mary successfully objected to the summoning of her first parliament before Coronation Day, which proved to be 1 October 1553, even though writs of summons to it had been sent out as early as 14 August.[1] She was concerned that the suggestion of a pre-coronation parliament came from the more Protestant councillors, as well as the traditionalist Gardiner, and therefore might lead to legal challenges to her possession of the crown, even before she had been formally given it.[2] Also, in the background lay the precedent, which would inevitably occur to some members of the new parliament, of their predecessors' ratification, on 15 October 1399, of Henry IV's usurpation of the throne of Richard II.[3] This was not an example that Mary would have wished to see recalled in the late summer and autumn of 1553.

It appears that preparations for the coronation began in London on or about 12 September.[4] Until the last week of that month, Mary was at Richmond Palace, but then she moved to what Robert Wingfield describes as a 'hunting-lodge', this apparently being St James's Palace. From there,

---

[1] MacCulloch, *Cranmer*, p. 547.

[2] *CSP Span* XI, pp. 239–42; Prescott, *Mary Tudor*, pp. 247–9.

[3] Loades, *Mary Tudor*, p. 20; *Rotuli Parliamentorum*, iii, 426, in S. B. Chrimes and A. L. Brown, eds, *Select Documents of English Constitutional History, 1307–1485* (London: A & C Black, 1961), pp. 197–8.

[4] Loades, *Intrigue and Treason*, p. 138.

she moved by barge, apparently on 27 or 28 September, to the Tower of London. On this occasion, she was accompanied by, among others, Elizabeth and the mayor and aldermen of London in a splendid river procession, and the conflicting sounds of gunfire and music.[5] On 29 September, the Feast of St Michael and All Angels (Michaelmas), Mary restored traditional practice, which had been altered on religious grounds by Edward, when she conferred knighthood of the Bath on fifteen men. Among those honoured in this way were some of her faithful retainers, notably Robert Rochester, Henry Jerningham and William Dormer, as well as various sons of the nobility, including Edward Courtenay, newly created earl of Devon, and of important councillors. However, she handed over to the earl of Arundel the perhaps unfitting duty, for a royal lady, of spending part of the new knights' vigil with them. Wingfield, who boasted of having obtained the complete list of new knights of the Bath from 'the lord of the apparitors (heralds)' of the order, comments that 'Although this Order is inferior to that of the Garter, it is in fact much older'.[6] Then, on Saturday, 30 September, Mary processed in splendour from the city of London along the Strand to Westminster in preparation for her coronation in the Abbey on the following day.

Various sources, English and foreign, combine to provide an adequate, though not complete account of the events of the day and while the details of what happened may seem somewhat excessive at this distance, it was one of Mary's greatest days, and the actions and symbolism it involved were of immense importance in establishing the nature and success of her regime. During the previous two or three weeks, the city authorities, as well as individual institutions and citizens of London, had worked to prepare the route and organize displays and events along it to welcome and entertain the Queen. The conduits were repaired and decorated, the streets were gravelled to prevent horses and men from slipping, and, on the morning of the procession, carpets and tapestries were festively hung as decorations from windows and balconies.[7] On the 'big day', while children and adults were no doubt involved in last-minute rehearsals of songs and speeches, and the finishing touches were put to 'pageant' displays and triumphal arches, Mary prepared herself to enter the carriage which would bear her first to Whitehall Palace, departing at one in the afternoon. According to the 'Tower' chronicler:

[5] Wingfield, *Vita*, pp. 226, 275; Judith Richards, *Mary Tudor* (London and New York: Routledge, 2008), p. 135; Loades, *Mary Tudor*, p. 205; Porter, *Mary Tudor*, p. 255.

[6] Wingfield, *Vita*, pp. 226, 275; Machyn, *Diary*, pp. 45, 334n; College of Arms MS I, 7, fol. 65v. Those knighted for Mary's coronation were the earls of Devon and Surrey, Lord Berkeley, Lord Abergavenny, Lord Lumley, Lord Mountjoy, Lord Herbert of Cardiff, Sir William Paulet (soon to be marquis of Winchester), Sir Hugh Rich, Sir Henry Clinton, Sir Henry Paget, Sir Robert Rochester, Sir Henry Jerningham, Sir Henry Parker and Sir William Dormer, father of Jane.

[7] *Chronicle of Queen Jane*, pp. 27–31; Machyn, *Diary*, pp. 45–6; Loades, *Mary Tudor*, pp. 205–6.

The last daie of September 1553, the quene came throughe London towardes her coronation, sytting on a charret of tyssue [rich cloth], drawne with vi horses, all betrapped with redd velvett. She sytt in a gown of blue velvet furred with powdered armyen [ermine] hangyng on hir heade a call [cap] of clothe of tynsell besett with perl and ston[e], and about the same upon he[r] hed a rond circlet of gold, moche like a hooped garlande, besett so netely with many precyouse stones that the value therof was inestymable, the said call and circle being so massy and ponderose that she was fayn to beare uppe hir hedde with her hands.[8]

The questioning and soul-searching which surrounded the issue of how to treat England's first accepted queen regnant at her coronation even permeate the details of the event which are provided by contemporary chroniclers. To begin with the procession, the Tower chronicler, who was presumably an eyewitness, refers to Mary's having been borne in a 'carret', or carriage, ás does Antonio de Guaras, who seems also to have witnessed events personally.[9] On the other hand, Cardinal Dandino's envoy Gian Francesco Commendone, who may also have been an eyewitness, has the Queen riding in a litter (*lettica*), open on all sides and with a canopy of cloth of gold (*baldacchino d'oro*), and drawn not by six horses but by two mules.[10] Whether or not Commendone was present at all or some of the events in and surrounding Mary's coronation, there is an inevitable suspicion that the Venetian was influenced, consciously or otherwise, by traditional ceremonies from the *R[o]yalle Booke*, associated with the crowning of English queens consort, who would normally be transported in a litter, lying on a couch.[11] To add further to the doubt, Wingfield describes the vehicles used in the procession as 'carriages or litters' (*in carribus vel lecticis*), which hardly helps. None of the contemporary sources record whether Mary had her hair up or flowing long during the procession and coronation, so that it is impossible to say for certain whether she adopted the traditional, 'maternal' role in this respect, with her hair down, or launched herself as a 'king', with it up. However, on the charters that were issued in her name before her marriage, as well as on her early coins as sole ruler, Mary was represented in the closed Imperial crown, with her hair hanging down loose, an image which was later copied, like so much of Mary's practice, by Elizabeth, who appeared thus at her own coronation, and indeed suggested at the time that she was following her sister's precedent.[12]

There is less controversy concerning the composition of the coronation procession, though the continental commentators provide more details of

[8] *Chronicle of Queen Jane*, p. 27, also in Loades, *Chronicles*, pp. 14–15.
[9] Guaras, *Accession*, pp. 70, 118.
[10] Commendone, *Accession*, pp. 31, 114–15.
[11] Laynesmith, *The Last Medieval Queens*, pp. 92–4.
[12] Richards, *Mary Tudor*, p. 138.

the foreign contingents than do their English equivalents. The Tower chronicler says that the Queen was preceded by 'a number of gentlemen and
knights', then some judges, followed by 'diverse doctors of dyvynity',
'certayn bishops' (i.e. those who were not in prison or otherwise out of circulation), 'certayne lordes', then 'followed moste parte of her Counsaille'. The
Queen's carriage (or perhaps litter) was immediately preceded by the Lord
Chancellor, Stephen Gardiner, bishop of Winchester, and the Lord
Treasurer, William Paulet, marquis of Winchester, who held the Great Seal
of England and the ceremonial mace respectively. The earl of Oxford
carried the sword of state in front of the Queen, and Sir Edward Hastings
led the first horse drawing her carriage. After Mary herself came a closed
carriage ('chariot') bearing Elizabeth, facing forward, and the former Queen
Anne of Cleves, facing towards the rear. After these two ladies rode Sir
Thomas Stradling, and then came two other 'chariots' containing other
peeresses and gentlewomen. They were followed, according to this source,
by the probably quite startling display of forty-six gentlewomen (other
sources say up to seventy), as a female cavalry escort, dressed in red velvet
cloaks provided and paid for by the Queen.[13] Wingfield remarks that such a
'flock' (*grex*) of peeresses, gentlewomen and ladies-in-waiting had never
before been seen on such an occasion.[14] The people of London could be in
no further doubt that they now had a woman as their reigning monarch.
The dress of those processing is described in much greater detail by Guaras.
He states that the preceding English gentlemen wore beautiful lined silk,
with their horses similarly covered down to the ground. The barons and
peers, who followed this advance guard, were dressed in cloth either of gold
or of silver and their horses were caparisoned in the same way. Unlike his
English equivalent, Guaras particularly notes four Italian merchants, riding,
as he says pointedly, among the English barons and nobles, and just as well
turned out as the others: Micer (Master) Jacobo Foscarino, Micer Marco
Antonio Feico, Micer Marco Bernardo and Micer Jacobo Ragazoni. After
these Italians came four other (apparently foreign) merchants, dressed
magnificently in black, richly lined velvet, with their grooms and horses
clothed in the same high-quality material. After these came four Spanish
knights, dressed in purple cloaks lined with silver cloth, whom Guaras, a
long-term resident in England but still a Spanish patriot, praised highly. In
the group that preceded the Queen's carriage, Guaras mentions next 'other
leading lords' and four foreign ambassadors, representing Charles V, the
kings of France and Poland, and the Most Serene Republic of Venice, who
demonstrated the strength and variety of England's international links.
Then, intriguingly, came two men dressed in ducal robes, who were meant
to represent the English claims to the duchies of Normandy and Gascony.
Guaras adds the details that Mary herself was escorted by the duchess of
Norfolk, the marchioness of Winchester and the countess of Arundel, while

[13] Loades, *Chronicles*, p. 15.
[14] Wingfield, *Vita*, pp. 226–7, 275–6.

his editor, Garnett, completes the list with the marchioness of Exeter.[15] The procession was escorted by about three hundred royal foot guards, 'gentlemen of the axe [gentlemen pensioners] as well as bowmen [Yeomen of the Guard]'.[16]

Entertainments along the processional route, mentioned by various writers, were provided by both English subjects and foreigners. At the conduit on Cornhill, in the City, were three children, dressed up as Grace, Virtue and Nature, while a small fountain in Gracechurch Street flowed with wine on the day. John Heywood of the Chapel Royal, an old friend of Mary, who had written plays for her when she was a child and who was a relative by marriage of Sir Thomas More, brought his 'playing [acting] children', and himself recited an oration to the Queen in Latin and English while seated under a 'Vine of Plenty'. Boys of St Paul's School 'sang diverse staves in gratifying the Queen', while representatives of the city, no doubt anxious to keep or gain favour with the new regime, gave her a present of £1,000 sterling.[17] Perhaps the most spectacular live entertainment, which paralleled the tightrope walker at Edward's coronation procession, was provided by Piet, a Dutch acrobat, who perched on the weather vane of St Paul's Cathedral

> holding a streamer in his hand five yards long, and waving thereof stood for some time on one foot, shaking the other, and then kneeled on his knees, to the great marvel of the people. He had two scaffolds under him, one above the cross [on the cathedral tower], having torches and streamers set on it, and another over the ball of the cross, likewise set with streamers and torches, which could not burn, the wind was so great.

Piet was paid handsomely by the city for his spectacular exploits.[18] There were also fixed entertainments in the form of pageants (tableaux) or triumphal arches, and some evidence survives of their design and composition, by which the people living in Mary's London, both English and foreign, followed in the tradition of the previous century. Like others, Guaras reports that Mary's procession passed under triumphal arches, most of which were English in design and manufacture, while others were offered by the main foreign mercantile communities of London. Both Guaras and Commendone mention the efforts of the German Hanseatic merchants, but agree in regarding the Genoese and Florentine arches as the stars of the show in this respect. Although their transcriptions vary, the Spanish and Venetian chroniclers record the Latin inscriptions that adorned the Genoese arch, which Guaras thought to be the best piece of work in all. The upper text on the front, as the procession met it, credited

[15] Guaras, *Accession*, pp. 69–72, 117–20.
[16] Commendone, *Accession*, pp. 31, 115.
[17] Loades, *Mary Tudor*, pp. 205–20; Loades, *Intrigue and Treason*, p. 139.
[18] Skidmore, *Edward VI*, p. 59; Porter, *Mary Tudor*, p. 257.

Mary with 'the palm of virtue', while the inscription on the frieze below
read: 'Virtue overcame [in Mary's arrival on the throne], justice achieved
supremacy, virtue triumphs, mercy (*pietas*) is crowned, the safety of the
commonwealth (*respublica*) is restored.'[19] The greatest attention is paid by
commentators, and probably was by general onlookers on the day itself, to
the Florentine arch. The learned will have appreciated, as do Guaras and
Commendone, the Latin inscriptions in which the Florentines praised
Mary as a Renaissance ruler. Commendone provides much more detail
than the Spaniard, whose Latin may have been less good. He says that
there were four statues on this arch, representing the cardinal virtues –
prudence, temperance, fortitude and justice – together with a statue of
Fame, with lines written below it in praise of Mary. In addition, a statue
of the Queen was accompanied by those of three other women – the
Greek goddess of wisdom, Pallas Athene, inscribed 'Unconquered Virtue'
(*Invicta virtus*), the biblical Judith, slayer of Holofernes (Judith 10–13),
labelled 'Liberator of the Fatherland' (*Patriae liberatrici*) and, perhaps most
intriguingly of all, Tomyris, labelled 'Avenger of Liberty'. The image of
the Jewish heroine Judith, who murdered the Assyrian Nebuchadnezzar's
General Holofernes and thus saved her people from extinction, is striking
as a representation of female monarchy. This is especially so if the recently
executed duke of Northumberland is seen as the beheaded Holofernes,
the deed in the Biblical story being done by the woman's own hand, not
the judicial system. Yet the allusion to Tomyris is perhaps even more
extraordinary in its symbolism. She is said to have been a queen of Scythia
(in the northern Black Sea region) who in the sixth century BC slew the
elder Cyrus of Persia. No doubt the Florentines were referring to their
fifteenth-century compatriot Poggio Bracciolini's Latin translation of
Diodorus Siculus' Greek account of this episode, but Tomyris's story had
also arrived in England, in John Skelton's translation, *c.* 1485.[20] In 1553,
there was certainly no shortage of female rulers or regents in Italy, but the
London Florentines' choice of figures for Mary's coronation is nonetheless
striking.[21] Having completed the journey from the City of London to
Westminster, Mary and her immediate entourage entered Whitehall
Palace, to rest and to await Coronation Day itself.

On the morning of Sunday, 1 October the Queen undertook the short
journey by barge to the Palace of Westminster, where she and her
entourage made their final preparations. At about eleven o'clock she left
the palace in procession for the short walk to Westminster Abbey. Mary
was dressed in a gown of blue velvet, trimmed with miniver and powdered

[19] This is a combination of the wording in Guaras, *Accession*, pp. 71, 119 and
Commendone, *Accession*, pp. 31, 115.
[20] Guaras, *Accession*, pp. 72, 120; Commendone, *Accession*, pp. 32, 115; Samson, 'The
Marriage', p. 53.
[21] S. L. Jansen, *The Monstrous Regiment of Women: Female Rulers in Early Modern Europe* (New
York and Basingstoke: Palgrave Macmillan, 2002), pp. 155–79.

ermine, and the same jewelled 'cyrclet' as she had worn on her head the previous day. The regalia, or crown jewels, were carried into the abbey by peers, as part of the procession, and over her gown the Queen wore, in the traditional manner of a sovereign king, a crimson velvet robe with its train carried by her great chamberlain, the earl of Oxford, and the duchess of Norfolk. She was 'supported' on her right side by the elderly, and newly restored, bishop of Durham, Cuthbert Tunstall, and on the left by the earl of Shrewsbury. After her came Elizabeth and Anne of Cleves, and numerous peeresses and other ladies. The procession passed from palace to abbey over a blue carpet, which was later 'distributed', in some disorder, among the citizenry, who traditionally regarded a coronation as an opportunity to be given, or to appropriate, royal largesse. Mary was met at the west door of the abbey, under a gold canopy, by the bishop of Winchester, who was to perform the coronation ceremony, and by a total of seven other bishops, this number probably including her escort, Tunstall. Several canons of the abbey also welcomed her.[22] According to Guaras, the foreign ambassadors were, at the Queen's command, already in the Abbey when she arrived. A platform had been constructed at the crossing of the Abbey, and when Mary reached it in procession she mounted twenty steps, and then a further ten to reach her throne, which had been placed on a dais resting on the platform. After she had sat momentarily on the throne, Bishop Gardiner, in his capacity as Lord Chancellor, led her to the four edges of the platform in turn so that she might be shown to the people. Four times, the bishop asked those assembled, first whether they believed Mary to be the true heir to the throne, and secondly whether they would receive her as queen. In each case, there was universal assent, and after this Mary went up into the abbey choir and to the high altar. The liturgy which followed was that adopted by Mary's grandfather, Henry VII, though with minor modifications. Edward, as a child of nine at the time of his coronation in 1547, and Mary, as an adult but female, were not expected easily to fulfil every demand of a ceremony which lasted several hours in its traditional late-medieval form. The first problem for the new Queen in the heavy and elaborate clothing she was required to wear was that, on her arrival before the high altar at the east end of Westminster Abbey, she had to prostrate herself before the divine presence, specially concentrated there in the previously consecrated bread of the Eucharist. A velvet cushion was provided to soften the effect, but still this cannot have been an easy manoeuvre. While Mary remained in that position, Bishop Gardiner intoned the collect, or gathering prayer, *Deus humilium*, which represented her humility, even as a monarch, before God, and which Archbishop Cranmer had recited at her brother's coronation

[22] *Chronicle of Queen Jane*, p. 28; also in Loades, *Chronicles*, p. 15; Commendone, *Accession*, pp. 32-3, 116; Wingfield, *Vita*, pp. 227, 276; Guaras, *Accession*, pp. 72, 120.
[23] Guaras, *Accession*, pp. 72-3, 120-1; *Chronicle of Queen Jane*, p. 28; also in Loades, *Chronicles*, p. 15; *APC* new series, II (1546-7), p. 30.

six years earlier.[23] Her prostration, as well as demonstrating publicly the humility which she had no doubt shown on many occasions in the more intimate setting of country house chapels, also re-enacted the abasement of a candidate for ordination to the priesthood of the Catholic Church, and that of the sacred ministers at the beginning of the liturgy of the cross on Good Friday.

It is impossible to know whether at any stage during the proceedings of this day Mary remembered her earlier religious scruples about the whole ceremony. On 1 October 1553, England was of course still in schism from the Roman See, and the only legal liturgy in her kingdom was the 1552 Book of Common Prayer, since no parliament had met to repeal the relevant legislation before the coronation. During August and September, Mary had agonized over the question of whether a faithful Catholic, as she regarded herself, could be validly crowned in these circumstances. In a letter written at Rome on 20 September, Pope Julius III reported to Cardinal Pole, who was then staying in a Franciscan house on an island in Lake Garda, on the account which he had received from Commendone of the situation·in England in this and other matters. The question of the coronation was delicate, and Julius told Pole that he had not shared even with the cardinals in consistory the upshot of Commendone's interview with Mary in which she had sought papal absolution for proceeding with her coronation in such ecclesiastically irregular circumstances. In response, Julius said that he was remitting to Pole the job of administering such absolution on his behalf, according to the English cardinal's discretion, so that Mary would be consoled, and 'nothing illicit will be done'.[24] As early as 19 September, Henry Pyning had reported to Pole, having first spoken personally to the Queen, that she had indeed already asked Commendone about this absolution, but only now did Pole hear about it.[25] Later, in a letter to the Pope from Trent, dated 30 September, Pole reported that he had carried out his instruction, commenting that, absolved thus, Mary could be 'most secure in conscience, because the Lord God sees into her heart'. Pole asked for written confirmation of the absolution to be sent to her as soon as possible.[26] Thus Mary was readily given the assurance of the Roman Church that she might be crowned as a Catholic monarch, but earlier, while she was still in what she regarded as ecclesiastical limbo, she had also become concerned about the chrism, or holy oil, which would be used to anoint her during the coronation ceremony. Regarding the oil that had been used by Archbishop Cranmer to anoint Edward as tainted by schism and heresy, she had consulted Bishop Gardiner, who would perform this rite for her. As a result, consecrated

[24] ASV Fondo Borghese serie Y, 8, fols 111r–113v, in J. Ignacio Tellechea Idígoras, *La legación del Cardenal R. Pole (1553–54): Cuando Inglaterra volvió a ser católica* (Salamanca: Centro de Estudios Orientales y Ecuménicos 'Juan XXIII', 2002), app. 2 doc. 3, p. 182.

[25] *CRP*, 2, pp. 193–4 (no. 689).

[26] BAV Vat. Lat. 6754, fols 69v–74r; *CRP*, 2, pp. 207–8.

oil from Catholic Flanders, sent by Charles V's chancellor, Cardinal Antoine Perrenot de Granvelle, bishop of Arras, was used in the Abbey on 1 October.[27]

After the prostration and collect, Mary sat in the abbey choir to hear Gardiner's sermon, which according to Commendone concerned obedience to the King, on which, in the tract *De vera obedientia* of 1534, the bishop of Winchester had famously written, nearly twenty years earlier, to justify the Royal Supremacy of Mary's father. Then she took the coronation oath.[28] Before the ceremony, Gardiner had worked with Mary on the exact wording which should be used. To the formal question which would first be asked by the bishop, 'Will ye grawnte to kepe to the people of Englande and others your realms and dominions the lawes and liberties of this realme and other your realmes and domynions?' was added the phrase, 'the just and licit laws of England'.[29] Not surprisingly given her views, and unlike Edward, who had touched a copy of the Gospels on the altar, Mary reverted to the former practice of swearing the coronation oath on the Sacrament of the Lord's Body.[30] Significantly, some of the wording which had been added to the oath at Edward's coronation was retained for Mary. Thus she was required to 'graunt and promitte' to make no newe lawes but such as shalbe to t[h]'honour and glory of God, and to the good of the Common Wealth, and that the same shalbe made by the consent of your people as hath been accustumed'.[31] Here, some of the constitutional theory associated with the Royal Supremacy over the Church was effectively retained in that the sovereign was seen as the maker of new laws as well as the custodian of old ones, though all within the traditional constitutional safeguards. In a letter dated 19 September, Cardinal Pole's servant Henry Pyning had reported that she intended to swear the oath that her father had sworn, but this is not quite what happened.[32] Unspecified litanies, though very probably those of the Virgin Mary and the saints, were sung and then the truly exceptional character of the crowning of a queen regnant became fully apparent.

After these petitionary prayers had been concluded, the traditional rite of coronation began. Mary sat down in front of the altar in her underdress, which was a kind of formal petticoat, and then Bishop Gardiner used the oil from Flanders to anoint her shoulders, breast, forehead and temples. She was then dressed in a type of long, white surplice known as a rochet, such as was worn by bishops and mitred abbots. Thus the notion of the monarch as 'priest-king', on the ancient Jewish model of David and

[27] Loades, *Mary Tudor*, p. 206.
[28] Shagan, *Popular Politics*, pp. 47–8.
[29] *APC* n. s. II, pp. 30–1, also in *English Historical Documents*, v, *1485–1558*, ed. C. H. Williams (London: Eyre & Spottiswoode, 1967), p. 467 (no. 45, i).
[30] College of Arms MS 1, 7, fol. 69R; *APC* n. s. II, p. 31.
[31] *English Historical Documents*, ed. Williams, v, p. 467 (no. 45, i).
[32] *CRP*, 2, pp. 193–214 (no. 689).

Solomon, was applied in England for the first time to a woman. Peers brought the regalia, which had been specially consecrated beforehand. In a ceremonial affirmation that she possessed the full powers of a male ruler, the Queen was briefly spurred and girt with a sword, as Guaras comments, 'like those who are armed as knights'. The sceptre of a king was then placed in one of her hands, and the Queen's sceptre, topped by the dove of peace, was placed in the other. Finally, in an arrangement which the contemporary writers do not specify precisely, she was given the royal orb of gold, surmounted by a cross. Wearing the crimson velvet robe of a king, trimmed with ermine, Mary was led from the dais to the high altar, where she made a symbolic offering of the sword with which she had been girded by Bishop Gardiner during the 'knighting' ceremony. The sword was then given to the earl of Arundel, who, as lord steward, thereafter carried it before the Queen.[33] After this, three crowns were brought by Gardiner and the duke of Norfolk and successively placed upon her head. The first was the crown traditionally associated with Edward the Confessor, whose shrine in Westminster Abbey would be restored, on Mary's orders, in 1556–7.[34] According to a manuscript in the College of Arms, the second was 'the Imperial crowne of this realme of Englande', this apparently being the one commissioned by Henry VIII some years into his reign.[35] The third crown had been made for Mary, to fit her and be worn for the rest of the ceremonies of the day. When the closed Imperial crown was placed on her head, the ancient canticle of praise, *Te Deum laudamus* ('We praise thee, O God'), was sung. Gardiner, in his role as Lord Chancellor, read out the Queen's coronation pardon, which excluded many who had supported Edward's 'Devise' and the regime of Jane. Then, in his role as bishop of Winchester, Gardiner did homage to Mary, in her regalia and on her throne, on behalf of all the bishops, afterwards kissing her left cheek. The Queen then received the homage of the duke of Norfolk in the same manner, on behalf of the dukes, the marquis of Winchester for the marquises and the earl of Arundel for the earls. After this all the other lords made obeisance. This part of the ceremony, which must have taken some time, was followed by the celebration of Mass by the bishop of Winchester. Neither English nor continental commentators provide details of the form of service used, but there is evidence that the service was sung, and it is therefore likely to have been a solemn nuptial Mass according to the Sarum rite, in which Gardiner was no doubt assisted at the high altar by some of his episcopal colleagues. Guaras notes that the Queen knelt devoutly throughout the celebration, but there is no record of her receiving communion. If she did not, this may owe as much to the liturgical and pastoral custom of the period as to

---

[33] College of Arms MS 1, 7, fol. 70v.
[34] Thomas Cocke and Donald Buttress, *900 Years: The Restoration of Westminster Abbey* (London: Harvey Miller, 1995), pp. 29–31.
[35] College of Arms MS 1, 7, fol. 71r.

any lingering doubt in the minds of Queen or clergy concerning the validity of the sacrament, in the irregular situation which still prevailed in England. Once the Eucharist had been completed, Mary retired to a side room, to compose her regal attire for the recession from the Abbey to Westminster Hall. She soon emerged from it in her crimson, ermine-trimmed royal robe, and carrying the king's sceptre in one hand and the orb in the other. She wore her own jewelled crown on her head.[36].

According to the Tower chronicler, when the Queen left Westminster Abbey, three swords were carried before her, two sheathed and one naked, the last representing her sovereign power, as had been done for her grandmother Isabella in Segovia in 1474. Once again, the procession passed over rich material, which would not remain whole for long. On entering Westminster Hall, she was met by the duke of Norfolk in his capacity as hereditary high marshal of England, and the earl of Arundel, for the occasion in his equally traditional role as lord constable of England, and as officer in charge of the chest (coffer) of gold cups and other plate which were used at the coronation banquet. By now it was about five o'clock in the afternoon and this suggests that the somewhat abbreviated form of ceremony, which had been devised for the boy-king Edward VI, was used again on this occasion. Even so, and unsurprisingly, once in the hall Mary retired for some time to rest in a private chamber before taking her place at the centre of the high table with her sister Elizabeth and Anne of Cleves seated some distance away on her right, and Bishop Gardiner at a diplomatically similar distance on her left. Norfolk and Arundel were on horseback for this occasion, and rode continually round the spacious hall during the lavish banquet, at which it is said that no fewer than 312 dishes of food were presented to the Queen, and over 7,000 produced in total for the assembled company. It must not be imagined that this lavish meal proceeded in the sedate manner of modern state banquets. One sensation was planned: in the middle of the proceedings, a knight on horseback, in shining armour, entered the hall, and, in true Arthurian fashion, threw down his gauntlet, challenging to combat any man who still questioned Mary's right to be sovereign queen of England. He was Sir Edward Dymoke, who, as Wingfield wryly pointed out, had inherited this practice from the coronation of Henry IV, who had in fact usurped Richard II's throne, though the chronicler carefully added that the ceremony was 'nevertheless a duty of great honour and fame'.[37] Having read out his challenge without response, even in the tense political conditions then prevailing, Dymoke picked up his gauntlet again and headed for the Queen. She thanked him, and gave him the gold cup of wine from which she had been drinking. He drank from it too, then took it away as a present. Afterwards, the foreign ambassadors came to kiss hands and congratulate Mary. Soon afterwards, by now some way into the evening, the banquet ended. The Queen thanked everyone for

[36] Guaras, *Accession*, pp. 72–4, 120–2; Commendone, *Accession*, pp. 32–4, 116.
[37] Wingfield, *Vita*, pp. 228, 277.

taking the trouble to come, and then retired to her private chamber before returning by barge to her palace, where the rest of the night was spent in music, dancing and other entertainments. However, while, unlike in the case of Jesus's parable, the invited guests did indeed accept her invitation to the feast, those in the highways and byways came in nevertheless, without being in any way compelled (Matthew 22: 1–10; Luke 14: 16–24). One account suggests that nearly 5,000 of the dishes which had been prepared were taken away by the general public, and the Tower chronicler gives a vivid account of what happened:

> there was ill scramble for the cloth and rails [on the processional route], then ther was the wast meat cut out of the kitchen made under the pallaice with bordes, which was very much of all kinde of meat. And when they had don casting out meat ther was no less scrambling for the kitchyn it self, every man that wolde plucking down the bordes therof, and carrying it away, that yt might welbe callyd a wast [sack] indedde.[38]

Redistribution of wealth and possessions took its own particular form in mid-Tudor England.[39]

Parliament assembled a few days after the coronation ceremony had been held. Then, as so often thereafter, as well as listening to her English political advisers, Mary had, in the other ear as it were, equally strident and insistent voices from abroad: Charles V and his chief minister, Cardinal Granvelle, Pope Julius III and his legate to England, Cardinal Reginald Pole, as well as various subordinate agents of both Empire and Papacy. For the Roman Church, the prime aim was, of course, to regain the obedience of England, but senior churchmen quickly became aware of the political difficulties that Mary and her advisers were facing, thus showing consider-able understanding of the realities of the English scene. As early as 19 August, when Mary had been barely a fortnight in possession of London, Vincenzo Parpaglia, a curial official, wrote from Rome to his friend Pole, who was then at Maguzzano in Italy, concerning the current situation in England. He indicates that the Pope and his advisers were by then aware that Pole believed Mary would follow the example of her father in consulting parliament about everything important, including of course the reconciliation of England and Rome.[40] Shortly afterwards, Pole himself, who was desperately anxious to go to England as soon as possible but was being restrained both by Charles V and by Julius III, sent a representative, his secretary Antonio Fiordibello, to the Emperor, among his instructions being to make the suggestion that Mary might apply what Pole claimed to be the English custom of using the first parliament of a

---

[38] Loades, *Chronicles*, p. 16.

[39] Guaras, *Accession*, pp. 7–75, 122–3; Wingfield, *Vita*, pp. 228, 277; Commendone, *Accession*, pp. 34, 117; BL Additional MS 34320, fol. 97.

[40] *CRP*, 2, pp. 164–5 (no. 651).

reign to put the kingdom in order and satisfy grievances.[41] A week later, on 26 August, Parpaglia wrote to Pole with the latest thinking in Rome: Mary should 'reform' her Council, presumably to remove Protestant sympathizers, and use parliament as a first step towards putting the English religious situation back to where it had been at the end of Henry VIII's reign. Correcting doctrine might come before ending the schism, if both could not be done at once. Pole was advised to proceed calmly and steadily, without making things any more difficult than necessary for Mary.[42] Particularly revealing of the views of Mary's main foreign supporters at this time is a long and detailed letter sent by Charles V's chancellor Granvelle to Pole on 6 September. In this text, which explicitly represented the Emperor's views, it appears that while Charles and his relations and friends believed that the defeat of the duke of Northumberland's plans and the fall of Queen Jane were divinely inspired, and Mary's accession 'miraculous', they did not think it would be wise for Pole, being a representative of the Pope, to go immediately to England. The restoration of Roman Christianity to Mary's kingdom had to have popular support, and Julius's legate was firmly informed that, in the view of the Emperor and his advisers, including the author of this letter, the Queen would have to go through parliament in order to reverse what they saw as the heretical and schismatic religious policies of her father and brother.[43]

During September, Mary had continued to be subjected to advice at home and from abroad. On the 8th of that month, Fiordibello reported to Pole from Brussels that she had been persuaded to wait for parliament to remove her 'headship' of the Church in England.[44] On the same day, Pole wrote to his friend Girolamo Muzzarelli, showing his impatience to get back to England. If that was not possible, he still thought that Mary's first parliament should tackle the question of restoring papal authority.[45] Given the history of legal relations between England and the Papacy since the mid-fourteenth century, it was natural that parliament should be involved in the implementation of the new Queen's religious policy.[46] On 19 September, Pole's messenger, Henry Pyning, had a secret audience with the Queen in London, and reported immediately to his master that Mary wanted her first parliament to repeal all the statutes that separated the English Church from Rome. She also advised Pyning, who was staying in London with the well-established Italian merchant Antonio Buonvisi, to keep his errand secret and pretend that he too was an Italian.[47] This indicates the atmosphere in which

[41] *CRP*, 2, p. 166 (no. 6550).

[42] *CRP*, 2, pp. 169–70 (no. 661).

[43] BAV Vat. Lat. 6754, fols 46v–48r, transcribed in Tellechea, *Legación*, pp. 68–70, calendared in *CSP Span* II, pp. 176–7 and *CRP*, 2, pp. 184–5 (no. 677).

[44] *CRP*, 2, p. 187 (no. 681).

[45] *CRP*, 2, p. 188 (no. 682).

[46] Chrimes and Brown, *Select Documents*, pp. 72–5, 80–1, 140–1, 155–7, 184–5.

[47] *CRP*, 2, pp. 193–4 (no. 689).

Mary was operating, as far as her relations with the Roman Church were concerned, in the days leading up to her coronation. In his lengthy letter to Pole, dated in Rome on 20 September, Julius III reported on the discussion of Commendone's reports from London which had taken place in the consistory of cardinals. He told the legate that they rejoiced in Mary's desire to restore England to the Roman obedience, but felt that it would be 'prejudicial' if this matter were not even mentioned at the forthcoming parliament. There now seemed to be a greater sense of urgency in Rome than had earlier been the case, since in this letter Julius pressed Pole to stay as close to England as possible. Even if he could not yet enter the kingdom, he should press matters forward as much as he could, although Mary's problems with 'heretics' were fully recognized.[48] On the day of the coronation procession in London, Pole wrote to the Pope, telling him that, in the forthcoming parliament, the Queen intended 'to lift all the iniquitous laws [on religion, which had been] introduced in that kingdom', including that against papal primacy.[49] By then, though, the English parliamentary process was beginning to take its course.

The constitutional role and status of parliament in Tudor England in general, and not just in ecclesiastical matters, are as controversial among historians today as they were at the time. While the lay peers continued to be summoned individually – as did the bishops who sat with them – and the Church Convocation of Canterbury continued to meet in parallel, between Henry's accession in 1509 and Mary's death in 1558, the number of members sitting in the Commons, whether for boroughs or shires, rose from 296 to 376. Meanwhile by April 1554, when the episcopal bench had been reinforced, the Upper House consisted of forty-nine temporal and twenty-one spiritual peers. In the case of the Lower House, writs of election had been sent out, as usual, in August, and in the heated political atmosphere of the first weeks of Mary's reign the ability of the government to control elections was a crucial matter, especially as it concerned religion. The writs were sent to sheriffs in the counties, to the warden of the Cinque Ports, and the office of the duchy of Lancaster. In the counties, sheriffs, as the representatives of the sovereign, had considerable influence over the electoral process. Contests were rare, and the Crown directly controlled the great bulk of the county seats through royal manors within them or else through such crown enclaves as the towns within the duchy of Cornwall, and the West Country 'stannary' (tin-mining) towns. Borough constituencies were frequently used as routes into parliament for royal officials and crown servants, who would be expected to support the government in the chamber, though others were controlled or influenced by noble or episcopal patrons. In addition, sheriffs were given control over the timing of the issue of election writs, and were not above releasing or withholding them, as well as control over circular letters sent out by the government to

[48] Tellechea, *Legación*, pp. 180–1 (ASV Fondo Borghese, serie Y, 8, fols 111r–113v).
[49] Tellechea, *Legación*, p. 74 (ASV Segr. Stato. Ingh., 3, fols 50r–51r); *CRP*, 2, p. 202.

disadvantage candidates of whom they, or the Crown, disapproved. In addition, the Crown had the power to enfranchise new boroughs, which it might naturally expect to control. By the time of Mary's first parliament, eight new boroughs with seats in the Commons had been created since 1500. Also, although the Speaker was supposedly elected freely by the Commons, holders of this office in fact played an active part in exercising royal influence. A typical example was the Speaker of Mary's first parliament, Sir John Pollard, who was a lawyer and also deputy chief steward of 'the South' (its southern properties) for the duchy of Lancaster, which had been integral to the Crown itself since the reign of Henry IV.[50]

Questions such as the degree of priority of statutory acts of parliament over the common law were still a matter for debate, and in Mary's reign the power of the monarch to amend enacted statutes was also controversial, but by the time the members of Mary's first parliament assembled at the beginning of October 1553 it seems to have been generally understood, abroad as well as at home, that any change in the ecclesiastical order would require parliamentary action in the form of the repeal of old statutes and the enactment of new ones.[51] According to the tradition, which Mary revived, proceedings began with the celebration, in St Margaret's church, Westminster, of a mass of the Holy Spirit, with the particular intention of asking for God's guidance. Indeed, the entire parliament, which lasted, with intervals, from 5/6 October until 5 December 1553, was retrospective in tone. Robert Wingfield declared that the purpose of the session was that 'by [its] authority religious dissension might be brought to an end'. He noted that the parallel Convocation of Canterbury, held at St Paul's, led to fierce and, in his view unseemly, debate between reformers and traditionalists, and was quickly dissolved.[52] Commendone, who, as a papal representative, was clearly an interested party in religious and ecclesiastical matters, summarized the main achievements of this parliament as twofold. Firstly, the marriage of Henry VIII and Catherine of Aragon was confirmed as lawful, while the offspring of all his other wives or concubines, which could only mean Elizabeth, were declared illegitimate. Secondly, all Edward VI's laws on religious matters were repealed. These concerned church liturgy and ceremonies, the marriage of priests, and the royal headship of the Church of England.[53] In fact, other business was also transacted, though the Journal of the Lords for this parliament does not survive.

The parliament which assembled in October 1553 was likely to be favourable to Mary's policies since it came together in a climate of strong support for her, but the Queen's major aims in the religious sphere were not revealed to those outside her inner circle, at home or abroad, until the session had begun. It seems likely that most if not all those elected to the

[50] Loach, *Parliament and the Crown*, pp. 23–34.
[51] Gunn, *Early Tudor Government*, pp. 183–7.
[52] Wingfield, *Vita*, pp. 228, 277.
[53] Commendone, *Accession*, pp. 36–7, 117–18.

Commons, as they headed for Westminster, imagined, in their ignorance of the letters that were criss-crossing Europe between London, Brussels, Rome, and Pole in his various residences, that they would do no more than restore the Church to its condition at the time of Henry VIII's death, in the belief that one could be a true Catholic Christian without having to submit to the authority and jurisdiction of the Pope in Rome. Despite being, of course, keen to return to Catholic doctrine and practice, even the restored traditionalist bishops did not show any sign of wanting a return to papal jurisdiction, although they would do the necessary when the time came. In addition, those among the MPs who were the proud 'possessioners', as contemporary language had it, of former ecclesiastical property, including lands and abandoned monastic buildings which had been converted into country houses, probably did not imagine that anything the Queen did would threaten these delightful trophies of their wealth and status. Their illusions would quickly be shattered.

In this period, it was not customary for the monarch to attend the opening of parliament and personally outline the government's programme. Instead, the Lord Chancellor made the 'gracious speech', and on this occasion Stephen Gardiner probably shocked many when he alluded to the restoration of England to the Roman obedience. It seems that even Simon Renard, the Imperial ambassador who was Mary's close confidant in these matters, had only known for about a month that this was her intention, and was extremely concerned that her regime might be destabilized by the fears of the 'possessioners'.[54] Perhaps in response to this concern, Gardiner made no specific allusion to former church property in his opening speech, and the first item of parliamentary business in fact concerned treason and felony. Over the summer, a review had apparently taken place of the various laws on these subjects which had been passed under Henry VIII and Edward VI, and the result was that a bill (or 'book' in contemporary parlance) was brought forward, and duly enacted, which returned English statute law on treason to its state under the 1352 Act of Edward III, while the law of felony was restored to its condition at the time of Henry VIII's death. The Treason Bill was handed down by the Lords just a week into the session, on 12 October, and the measure was enacted without difficulty. The fourteenth-century Statute of Praemunire, whch forbade the submission of English subjects to foreign jurisdiction, had been tightened in the previous reign. Now, though, it too was returned to its original state, thus opening the way to a renewal of legal and financial contact between England and the Roman See, though not without reservations.[55] The overall purpose of these changes seems to have been to remove, as far as possible, any innovations which had occurred in Edward's reign, and perhaps increase the popularity of the current regime.

[54] *CSP Span* XI, pp. 214–21.
[55] Prescott, *Mary Tudor*, pp. 251–2; Loades, *Mary Tudor*, p. 207.

Mary gave parliament a short break, starting on 21 October, but in the second session the question of her title to the throne was dealt with. The interval may have been intended to secure a propitious political climate. Given the general, if not universal, public support that Mary had had ever since the death of Edward, it is not surprising that the relevant bill quickly passed through parliament when the second session began on 24 October. The resulting Act repealed all the legislation of Henry VIII concerning his marriage to Catherine of Aragon, and also the 1544 Act of Succession, in which 'yor Highnes is named or declared to bee Illegitimate, or the said marriage between the said King, yor Father and the said Quene yor Mother is declared to be against the woorde of God or by any means unlawful'. The new Act instead declared the marriage of Mary's parents 'to bee and stande within Goddes Lawe and His most Holy woorde, and be accepted, reported and taken of goode effecte and validitee to all intentes and pourposes'.[56] The form of this Act gives a clear indication of the manner in which parliamentary legislation might be organized in this period, with a flexibility which allowed major changes to be made to statute law in a single, relatively simple, measure. It is also notable that, in October 1553, Mary, whatever the deepest concerns of her heart, allowed her political managers to ensure the passage of less controversial measures, before more difficult religious issues were tackled. Evidently, she was far from lacking political skills of her own, and had no wish to be a helpless woman on the margins of government. The next act passed in this parliament is headed: 'An Acte declaring that the Royall Power of the Realme is in the Queenes Ma[jes]tie as fully and absolutely as ever it was in any of her moste noble Progenitours Kinges of this Realme'. The first chapter of this statute notes that the royal prerogative in England included 'the Correccion and Punishment of all Offendours agaynst the Regalitie and Dignitie of the Crowne and the Lawes of the Realme unto the Kinge'. This text suggests that, if these powers are fully given to a woman, 'the malitious and ignorant persones may bee hereafter induced and perswaded into this errour and folly, to thinck that her Highnes coulde ne shoulde have, enjoye and use such lyke Royall Authoritie, Power, Preheminence, Prerogative and Jurisdiction, nor doo ne execute and use all thinges concerning the sayd Statutes'. Of course the new statute attempted to refute such views and arguments completely, stating that Mary should have all this power and authority 'without Doubte, Ambiguitie, Scruple or Question: any Custome, Use or Scruple, or any other thing whatsoever to be made to the contrary not withstanding'.[57] Nevertheless, there is a certain degree of anxiety in this formulation, which more than suggests that there were some in the England of 1553 who shared the views on this question of those who had earlier disputed the right to rule of Mary's grandmother Isabella, in Spain. On top of this, pressures from the

---

[56] *Statutes of the Realm*, 4, i, p. 201 (1 Mary, st 2, c. 1); also in Loades, *Chronicles*, p. 22.
[57] *Statutes of the Realm*, 4, i, p. 222 (1 Mary, st. 3, c. 1); also in Loades, *Chronicles*, pp. 22–4.

Continent only added to the strain that the Queen was suffering at home as she struggled to reorder her kingdom in what she regarded as a true and godly manner.

On 30 September, when the coronation celebrations had already begun, Cardinal Pole had written to Julius III from Trent giving his views on what Mary would do in her first parliament.[58] Later, after the session had begun at Westminster, on 8 October, the Queen herself wrote to Pole. Addressing him as 'Good cousin and Reverend Father in Christ', Mary thanked Pole for his various letters, and strongly affirmed her complete obedience to 'the spouse of Christ and my spiritual mother, the Church of Rome'. Two days into the new parliament, she professed herself still to be completely confident that it would remove 'all those statutes which have been the origin of our suffering in this kingdom', and at this early stage hoped to obtain, in addition to the personal absolution which had enabled her to proceed with her coronation a week earlier, 'a general pardon [for the kingdom] from the Pope's Holiness'. While her parliamentary managers struggled to pilot controversial legislation through the two houses, Mary optimistically told Pole that, 'having complete faith in the miraculous mercy of God, this Parliament will abolish all these statutes'. This letter, in Mary's own hand, was brought to Pole by Henry Pyning, who showed it first to the nuncio in the Low Countries, Cardinal Dandino, no doubt in the expectation that he would divulge its contents to Charles V and his advisers before it reached the Pope.[59] On 21 October, when religious questions had still not come up before the parliament in Westminster, Pole, who was now at Dillingen near Augsburg, wrote again to Julius III, enclosing letters which Mary had written to her 'good cousin' in her own hand and urging the Pope to give all possible support to her enterprise in England, since it was 'to the glory of God's divine majesty, to the benefit (*beneficio*) of the Church, and to the singular favour of the Pontificate of Your Holiness'.[60] The Queen had substantial reason to believe that many or most of her subjects were happy to support her efforts, given that August and September had brought spontaneous efforts, from London to Yorkshire, to restore Catholic worship and church ornaments, even without any legislative change. The restoration of papal authority might not, however, receive the same degree of support.[61] This was Mary's personal world during her first parliament: on 28 October, she sent a letter to Pole at Dillingen which on the way was seen by Charles V in Brussels. In what seems to have been her first personal contact with the

[58] Tellechea, *Legación*, p. 74.

[59] Ibid., pp. 23, 78–9 (ASV Segr. Stato. Ingh., 3, fol. 56 r–v).

[60] Tellechea, *Legación*, pp. 22–3, 77–8 (ASV Segr. Stato. Ingh., 3, fol. 55 r–v).

[61] Michelangelo Florio, *Historia de la vita e de la morte de l'Illustrissima Signora Giovanna Graia [. . .]* (Middelburg, 1607), p. 38: *CSP Span* XI, p. 188; Scarisbrick, *The Reformation and the English People* (Oxford: Basil Blackwell, [1984] 1989), p. 104; A. G. Dickens, 'Robert Parkyn's Narrative of the Reformation', *English Historical Review*, lxii (1947), pp. 58–83, reprinted in Dickens, *Reformation Studies* (London: Hambledon, 1982), pp. 287–312, at p. 309.

Cardinal, she explained, clearly with considerable embarrassment and discomfort, that she had been advised by her Council to have parliament 'annul' by statute her father's divorce of her mother. She then goes on to report that there was trouble in the Lords over the bill to abolish the 'supreme headship' of the Church in England. In the event, this had been passed as an act by the Upper House on 26 October, and went through the Commons, apparently without conspicuous dissent, three days later.[62] Thomas Mayer suggests, in the context of this letter to Pole, that Mary had got herself in a muddle over the doings in parliament at the end of October, but in fact she was simply having to admit to her Catholic friends and allies abroad that political reality did not correspond with their shared religious ideals.[63]

In the Act of this parliament which declared the marriage of Mary's parents valid, no reference was made to the judgment of the Roman consistory to that effect, issued on 23 March 1534.[64] The omission was politically necessary since, as she told Pole, Mary found herself forced to remain for the time being the supreme head of the Church in England. In late October 1553, the Lords had expressed a willingness to repeal all legislation concerning the Church which had been enacted by parliament, back to the year before the 1534 law which had first bastardized her, and this would implicitly have restored papal authority and ended Mary's 'headship'. However, it quickly became clear that even such an arrangement as this would not pass through the Commons, so Mary had to accept that this matter should be deferred. Even so, having secured the status quo in the question of headship, the parliamentarians were willing, in compensation as it were, to oblige the Queen in other religious matters, though not without some heated debate. Thus, by the time the parliament came to an end, on 5 December 1553, Edward's statutes enforcing the use of the 1552 Book of Common Prayer, permitting the marriage of priests and reducing the number of sacraments from the seven which had been definitively declared in 1439 by the Council of Florence, to two – baptism and Holy Communion – had all been repealed.[65] Of course, Mary had to justify her apparent surrender on headship to her continental advisers. Present on the spot was Simon Renard, who, since he appreciated the political bind that she was in, advised her to cede the point at this stage and raise the subject again in her second parliament.

Apparently feeling herself inadequate to tackle this fundamental issue against the grain of most of the English political class, the Queen turned to Renard, asking him to draw up a list of arguments which she could deploy against those who opposed her on the question of papal authority.

[62] *CRP*, 2, pp. 222–3 (no. 746); Loach, *Parliament and the Crown*, p. 79; Loades, *Mary Tudor*, p. 207.
[63] *CRP*, 2, p. 223 n. 244.
[64] *LP* vii, pp. 363, 368, 370; *CSP Span*, V, p. 29; Scarisbrick, *Henry VIII*, pp. 332–3 and n. 2.
[65] Prescott, *Mary Tudor*, p. 253.

Renard duly obliged, although he told Charles V that it was only the lack of theological expertise he perceived in the English establishment that persuaded him into this territory, in which he claimed no special skill.[66] The failure of the first parliament to tackle the question of restoring papal jurisdiction was, of course, intensely frustrating to Pole, who was not allowed to be present in London to bolster Mary's determination. Thus, in a letter written at Dillingen on 29 October, he told Charles that it was still his view that the question of papal obedience should have been tackled before and not after the coronation. Also, contrary to the 'deal' which produced the new statute declaring Henry and Catherine's marriage to have been valid, it was in fact essential that the Papacy should be involved in regularizing Mary's legal status in England.[67] For the moment, though, Pole had to attempt to possess his soul in patience, since the Emperor, having read both his letter of 29 October and letters from Mary, responded from Brussels on 8 November by ordering the legate not to proceed to England. The Queen had apparently told Charles that she did not want Pole back in his native land at this stage, but, given her deep religious concerns, it is hard to believe that this was her true will.[68] By early November 1553, she seems simply to have been overborne by events. Meanwhile, thinking in Rome on the English situation is probably well represented in a letter to Pole from his friend Cardinal Innocenzo del Monte, dated 28 October. In it del Monte states that, while Mary's good intentions were not doubted in the Curia, there was a danger that the whole situation of the English Church might suffer shipwreck (*naufragio*) if the issue of ecclesiastical property in lay hands was not tackled. Even so, Rome agreed with the Emperor that Pole should not go to England at this stage.[69]

His absence from the country did not, however, prevent the cardinal legate to England from offering his advice to the hard-pressed Queen. On 15 November, Mary wrote to Pole from London to express her regret that he could not return to her kingdom soon, but fearing that his life would be in danger if he did. Reporting on the doings of parliament up to that date, she confirmed that, although she had hoped that the Roman obedience would have been restored by then, there would now be a delay of three or four months. Significantly, she states that religion in England had now been put back into the state in which it was 'at the time of the death of King Henry, our father of most pious memory', and tells Pole that, although things in parliament had been difficult, she hoped that what had been done so far would act as food for the journey forward (*quasi viaticum*).[70] Mary was now hoping that Pole might at least come to Brussels, where he had a

---

[66] *CSP Span* XI, pp. 294–300.

[67] BAV MSS Vat. Lat. 6754, fols 85v–86v; *CRP*, 2, pp. 223–4 (no. 747).

[68] *CSP Span* XI, pp. 346–7 (copy to Renard); *CRP*, 2, p. 225 (no. 751).

[69] AGS E 879–71.

[70] Appropriately, given Mary's religious concerns, the word *viaticum* is traditionally used of the Eucharist, when the sacrament is given to those in danger of death.

second legation to attempt to secure peace between the Habsburgs and France, so that communication between them would be easier.[71] For the moment, the Cardinal remained in Dillingen, but on 18 November he both wrote again to Mary and gave a set of written instructions to his new envoy to the Imperial court, the Spanish Dominican theologian Pedro de Soto, who would later attempt to bring Archbishop Thomas Cranmer back to the Roman Church. In his memorandum to Friar de Soto, Pole repeated his opinion that Mary should have begun with the restoration of papal authority. Speaking theologically, as he so often did in such circumstances, he said that the situation of England was still dangerous because the kingdom risked damnation as long as it remained in schism. Although Mary had received her crown from God himself, Pole asserted, England's ecclesiastical situation could not be regularized until the matter of church goods was resolved. Perhaps too much influenced by his private correspondence with Mary, who opened her heart to him in a not over-diplomatic way, Pole asserted that resistance to the Pope in England was being exaggerated, and that even the nobles would be willing to hand over their formerly ecclesiastical possessions once they knew their Queen's firm will to return to the Roman obedience.[72] On the same day, in his letter to Mary herself, Pole expressed himself even more fiercely and frankly. He told his 'good cousin' that since her kingdom depended on God's favour, it would be destroyed if correct policies were not followed. Indeed, just as heresy and schism in Orthodox eastern Europe had opened the way to the Ottoman Turks, England itself would have been similarly lost if Mary had not gained the throne. Now, though, the Queen was facing 'heretics' in a parliament that could not properly discuss religious matters at all, except perhaps under direct divine inspiration. Pole was scathing about Mary's councillors, who appeared to him to be disregarding the Gospel, and hence presenting business in the wrong order, while they evaded the fundamental question of obedience to the Pope. The cardinal legate went on to treat Mary like a penitent who is receiving the Sacrament of Penance and Reconciliation. Piling on intense emotional pressure, he berated her for ingratitude in not putting the papal obedience first after she had been placed on the throne through God's grace. Up to then she had been brave, and she should not become timid now as queen. Pole, in an extraordinarily harsh examination of her personal religious faith, sternly urges her to act urgently to restore the link with Rome, asking God for His aid, as she had constantly done when she was 'the Lady Mary'.[73] In addition, while being subject, during October and early November 1553, to this emotional pressure, on top of political opposition and foot-dragging in her Council and parliament, Mary had two other vital and related questions weighing on her mind – whether or not to marry, and if so whom.

[71] *CRP*, 2, pp. 228–9 (no. 757).
[72] *CRP*, 2, pp. 229–31 (no. 759).
[73] *CRP*, 2, pp. 231–2 (no. 760).

Even if the notion of a ruling female monarch was becoming somewhat less unfamiliar in western Europe in the mid-sixteenth century, the overwhelming expectation, when Mary finally secured her throne, was that she should marry. It was almost universally assumed that she would need a husband to help her carry on government successfully, and perhaps to take on the entire responsibility in her name, and a husband would obviously be needed if an heir was to be produced to secure the dynasty. Given the highly dubious genetic record of the Tudors, this was a particularly important point. Everyone concerned was well aware that Mary was thirty-seven years old when she came to the throne and that in the circumstances of childbirth then prevailing, even for the wealthiest and most privileged and protected women, the risks were very great indeed, and would have been so even if she had been much younger. In the eyes of her loyal supporters, though, Mary simply had to make the effort, if only to prevent Elizabeth from succeeding her under the terms of their father's will. Marriage and religion were to be inextricably connected in the year following her self-declaration as queen at Kenninghall.

From early July 1553, Charles V had been crucial to Mary's plans in this respect. The two were cousins, and had twice been betrothed in earlier years. Thus the Emperor had a personal interest in the new Queen of England's fate, but he and his advisers had serious political concerns of their own. Dynastic, political and economic interests combined to recommend an alliance between Mary's kingdom and the Habsburgs and, according to the rules of European diplomacy in the period, the best way to seal an alliance was to use the traditional, and highly successful, Habsburg technique of marriage. The urgency for Charles of improving relations with England was underlined by the betrothal of Henry II of France's son, the Dauphin François, to Mary, Queen of Scots, the daughter of James V of Scotland and Mary of Guise, and granddaughter of Henry VIII's sister, Margaret Tudor. If the French gained control of England too, for example through just such a dynastic marriage, the threat to traffic of all kinds between the Habsburgs' northern and Spanish territories was obvious. In early August 1553, Charles and his advisers, notably the chancellor, Granvelle, bishop of Arras, were so concerned not to rock Mary on what they regarded as her shaky throne that they did not openly propose a foreign marriage to her, instead suggesting that she marry an English aristocrat. Once Renard and his colleagues in the London embassy were able to assure Brussels that Mary's regime was safely in charge, they began to suggest to her an alliance with a foreign prince instead. Given her persistent nature, and her childhood betrothals, she naturally expressed a desire to marry Charles himself, but although his age, fifty-three, was not an impediment, his health was bad and, while many abroad did not yet know it, he was already intending to take the unprecedented step, for an 'Emperor of the Romans', of abdicating from his various crowns and other titles as ruler of his many lands. It was at this point that the name of Charles's son Philip, Prince of Spain, began to be mentioned in this context. There was, however, a problem: Philip was already negotiating to marry a different Mary, Princess Maria of Portugal.[74]

The Prince of Spain had decided to take as his second wife his Portuguese cousin Maria, the only surviving child of King Manuel of Portugal (1469–1521) and Charles V's sister Leonor. The match had various attractions to offer. Alliances of this kind between the Spanish and Portuguese kingdoms were traditional, she was a cultured lady, and she would come with a handsome legacy from her parents, and a dowry of 200,000 ducats, offered by her half-brother, King John III of Portugal. When her mother Leonor died, Maria would also receive her lands and revenues as dowager queen of France. A further attraction to Philip was that, although she had no direct political experience, the Portuguese princess would be able to act as regent of Spain and its New World territories when, as planned, he headed north to the Netherlands to join and assist his father, and begin to take over some of his Habsburg inheritance. By the 1550s, relations between father and son were personally extremely bad, however, and Philip did not allow his marriage plans to be revealed in the Netherlands until they were already common knowledge in the Iberian Peninsula. When the scheme did finally become known in Brussels, Philip nonetheless decorously pretended in public that his father was entirely in charge of the search for a second wife for him, and in view of what happened subsequently he may have come to regret this generosity. In the meantime, both Philip and Charles had to give consideration to the Habsburg family compact, signed in March 1551 with Charles's brother Ferdinand, king of the Romans, in which the dynasty presumed to plan for the future of a large part of continental Europe. Owing to an ambiguity in the Spanish translation of the original French text of the treaty, Philip feared that, by its terms, which he was very anxious not to invalidate by any action of his, he was required to arrange quickly to marry one of Ferdinand's daughters, and he duly consulted his father and his aunt Mary of Hungary about this. In order to extricate Philip from a possible marriage alliance with Ferdinand's branch of the Habsburg family, Charles and Mary suggested that he should propose to marry one of the princesses immediately, and affirm that he would do so only if the 1551 family pact was published. This was something that Ferdinand, who was then engaged in the negotiations between the Catholic and Protestant princes of the German empire that would eventually lead to the compromise of the Augsburg 'Interim' of 1555, would almost certainly not do, since all the princes would probably object to the Habsburgs' deciding the Imperial succession without reference to the seven princely and archiepiscopal Electors. In these circumstances, the princes would almost certainly have broken off their talks with Ferdinand and he would have been discredited. There is no evidence that

[74] M. J. Rodríguez-Salgado, *The Changing Face of Empire: Charles V, Philip II and Habsburg Authority, 1551–1559* (Cambridge: Cambridge University Press, 1988), pp. 79–80.

Philip ever put this scheme into practice, but in any case nothing more was heard of any marriage between him and a Habsburg princess.[75]

In the meantime, in the late spring and summer of 1553, all seemed to be set fair for Philip's Portuguese marriage, but, much to his surprise, he discovered that there was opposition to the alliance in Brussels. First, he was ordered to hand over the negotiations to Maria's mother, Queen Leonor, ostensibly on the grounds that the Portuguese Crown would be more generous in the settlement offered if they were dealing with their Queen Dowager rather than a Spanish prince, even one of partly Portuguese descent. In reality, Charles V and Mary of Hungary expected to be able to dominate their sibling, the malleable Leonor, but the crucial point, in the context of Mary Tudor's new reign in England, is that Philip's father and aunt acted as they did before they knew for certain that Northumberland and Jane had been defeated, and did so because they had different ideas from Philip about the Portuguese Maria's future role. While Philip wanted to use her dowry to fund his journey to the Netherlands and the cost of campaigning there, leaving his new wife as regent in Spain, Charles and his advisers, whose 'world-view' centred increasingly on the Netherlands, had other strategic plans, which would soon be of vital interest to England as well. In 1548, after much pondering, Charles had decided that Philip should inherit the 'Burgundian' territories in the Netherlands, but he was determined that Don Carlos, the son of Philip and his first wife, should only rule over the Spanish Trastamaran inheritance. It was thus essential for Maria of Portugal to come to the Netherlands with Philip in order that she should give birth there to the heir who would rule these lands in future. Charles and Mary of Hungary also had secret fears of instability in Spain itself, but contented themselves with telling Philip that the Netherlands were in such an insecure condition that he must sacrifice everything else to come there.[76]

Philip's response to the instruction to hand negotiations over to Dowager Queen Leonor was on the contrary to despatch his faithful friend Ruy Gómez de Silva to Lisbon with full powers to complete the marriage agreement. John III of Portugal realized that Philip and his father were divided, and exploited the situation to drive a hard bargain. He reduced the dowry on offer with Maria to its basic level, without any French goods from Leonor, and demanded what Charles V still owed from the settlement of his own wife, Philip's sister Juana. Ruy Gómez managed to restore the dowry to 400,000 ducats, but it was clear by August 1553 that Philip was so determined to marry Maria that he was prepared to settle on inferior terms. Thus on 8 August 1553, he wrote to the Spanish ambassador in Lisbon, telling him to try to increase the dowry if possible, but to come to an agreement with the Portuguese in any case. In the event, though, the messenger with the relevant letter was recalled and it was never sent.[77] Mary of England was

[75] AGS E 98, fols 135–40; Rodríguez-Salgado, *Changing Face*, pp. 77–8.
[76] AGS E 98, fols 136–40; Rodríguez-Salgado, *Changing Face*, p. 78.
[77] AGS E 376, fol. 213; Rodríguez-Salgado, *Changing Face*, p. 79.

that close, unknowingly, to losing her future husband, but Philip had by then heard from his father that marriage with her was now a possibility. In Portugal, Maria was already being referred to as 'princess of Spain', and John III asked when she should depart for the neighbouring kingdom to be married, but Philip pursued his devious way in order to cover up the impending betrayal. On the one hand, he kept the negotiations with Portugal open in theory, while elsewhere maintaining that he was delighted to be marrying the much more prestigious Queen of England. After some delay, he wrote to Charles claiming that the good news of this change of plan had come at an opportune moment since he had just decided to break off negotiations with Portugal (!), and his conduct thereafter did nothing to improve relations between the two Iberian kingdoms.[78]

Although it has so far been stated, according to the relevant documents, that the Emperor took personal charge of the negotiations for the marriage of Philip and Mary, other evidence suggests that this was not in fact so. Charles was suffering from one of his increasingly severe bouts of ill health, which rendered him deeply depressed and unwilling to transact government business beyond reading the shortest of letters and documents. His faithful minister Granvelle later claimed that he himself had in fact handled the entire business, in conjunction with Mary of Hungary and with legal advice from the Dutch councillor Viglius, and Charles never contradicted this interpretation. Even so, the plan which evolved, in which Mary and Philip's heirs would rule a new Anglo-Netherlandish state, was certainly an extension of the ailing Emperor's devout hopes and wishes.[79]

It does indeed appear that Charles had taken the initiative personally, at least when the idea of the Anglo-Spanish marriage was first mooted. By the end of July, and before Mary had taken possession of London in person, Simon Renard had been told to raise such a possibility with her and her advisers, who at this stage were effectively her Kenninghall and Framlingham 'Council'. Also, in one of the many twists and turns of the duplicitous, and often acrimonious, relations between Charles and his son, he did in fact, as early as 30 July, write to tell Philip that, since things had turned out so well for her, Mary might recall her childhood betrothal to him. No doubt, the Emperor suggested, if the English were prepared to accept a foreign king at all, they would prefer him to any other, but he was too old and ill, so that the best course would be to try to persuade them to accept Philip instead, as long as the Portuguese negotiations had not gone too far.[80] It was probably more out of concern for the future of his dynasty than for that of the Catholic Church in England that Charles urged restraint on Mary in her religious policy once she took up the reins of power in early August. However, it was as early as 29 July that Renard,

[78] *CSP Span* XI, pp. 177–8.
[79] Charles Weiss, *Papiers d'État du Cardinal de Granvelle*, 9 vols (n. p. 1841–52), iv, pp. 78, 144, 149–51, 298–300; Rodríguez-Salgado, *Changing Face*, p. 81.
[80] *CSP Span* XI, pp. 126–7.

who, with his colleagues, had kept well out of the way during Jane Grey's brief reign, went to meet Mary at New Hall/Beaulieu in Essex. He raised the question of marriage, and the new Queen said that although her personal preference would be to remain single she was prepared to marry for the sake of the country.[81] In the second week of August, after Mary had entered London in triumph and then moved to Richmond Palace, Renard visited her again and returned to the subject. Not unreasonably, given the number of her supposed supporters who had seemed happy, not long before, to give their allegiance to Jane and Northumberland, Mary now told the ambassador that she regarded her subjects as 'variable, inconstant and treacherous' and thought that she was unlikely to marry one of them. Significantly, in early August, William Paget, who had had a prominent role in Somerset's administration, but along with Arundel had then apparently lost his political career and hence joined him in quickly submitting to Mary, mentioned in a private conversation with Renard the possibility of her marrying Philip. Paget does not appear to have been personally in favour of the restoration of England to the Roman obedience, but after this talk with Renard he came to be regarded by the Emperor's side as one of their main allies in the English Privy Council.[82] Paget's August intervention was thus important for the future, but during the rest of Mary's first month in power, despite what she said to Renard in private, many in the English political class thought that she would most probably marry Edward Courtenay, whose background and role in proceedings deserve further consideration.

Renard and his companions had reported to Charles as early as 22 July that rumours of a possible marriage between Mary and Edward were circulating, in London and elsewhere, and were proving popular.[83] Born in 1526, the son of Henry and Gertrude Courtenay, marquis and marchioness of Exeter, he was imprisoned without trial in the Tower of London as a result of the treason charges levied by Henry VIII's government against members of his family, as well as the mother and brother of Cardinal Reginald Pole. Incarcerated there with his parents on or about 4 November 1538, he was released by Mary in August 1553, having been tutored in prison by Bishop Stephen Gardiner, who seems to have come to regard him as a protégé.[84] Although some have been kind enough to excuse Courtenay on the grounds of his long imprisonment during the formative period between his twelfth and twenty-seventh years, most observers have treated Edward Courtenay's character harshly. It seems undeniable that, despite her close friendship with Edward's mother who escorted her at her coronation, Mary always had strong reservations about him because of his arrogance and dissipation once released from the Tower, and she never showed him any particular favour,

[81] *CSP Span* XI, pp. 129–34 (2 August).
[82] *CSP Span* XI, pp. 155–8; Skidmore, *Edward VI*, pp. 210, 225; *CRP*, 4, p. 399.
[83] *CSP Span* XI, p. 114.
[84] Pierce, *Margaret Pole*, pp. 131, 172–4, 181–3.

except the grant of the earldom of Devon. Unlike many of her subjects, including his patron Stephen Gardiner, she never seems to have regarded him as her potential husband.

While it was still not clear, in the autumn of 1553, that Philip of Spain had actually abandoned Maria of Portugal and was intended for Mary of England instead, it appeared to some in his native land that Dom Luis, son of King John III, might renew his suit for the Tudor Queen's hand, which had been offered in the previous reign. In this case too, the Portuguese royal house was destined to suffer disappointment. Once it became clear that Philip was the leading candidate and negotiations between Brussels and London were under way, Charles felt it necessary to assure Prince Luis, through the Imperial ambassador in Lisbon, Luis Sarmiento, and by personal letter that the choice was ultimately Mary's, though it is very likely that the Emperor and his advisers had indeed intervened to ensure a clear run for Philip.[85] The process whereby the Prince of Spain would eventually become King of England was very far from being smooth and uncomplicated.

By the autumn of 1553, the two remaining suitors, who had some reason to regard themselves as having a good chance of success in becoming consort to the English Queen, were Edward Courtenay, earl of Devon, and Philip, Prince of Spain. It should be noted, though, that even at this late stage there was also some following for Reginald Pole as a possible husband, despite the fact that he was a cardinal and papal legate, since he was still a deacon, not a priest, and it would have been possible for Pope Julius III to dispense him from the relevant vows and orders. Pole had Plantagenet blood in him through his descent from a brother of Edward IV – George, duke of Clarence – but he seems in fact to have been of the view that Mary should not marry at all, on the somewhat hazardous grounds that, if she remained single and did her duty to God, He would provide for the English succession.[86] To the Roman Curia, the Queen's rapid release of Edward Courtenay from the Tower of London suggested that he might well become her husband. Thus on 12 August 1553, Cardinal Alessandro Farnese wrote to Pole to congratulate him on the release of Courtenay, expressing confidence that the young man would marry Mary.[87] Meanwhile, though, Philip's chances of success grew ever greater.

Between 2 and 23 September 1553 Charles was away at war, and not in personal charge of negotiations. During that time, it still seemed likely that Mary would marry Luis, and Philip was still generally expected, especially in Iberia, to marry Maria of Portugal. In England, however, things looked very different. At the beginning of September there was a rumour, believed by the French ambassador, Antoine de Noailles, that Philip's

---

[85] *CSP Span* XI, pp. 374–5; *RMT*, p. 58; Loades, *Intrigue and Treason*, p. 147.
[86] Loades, *Intrigue and Treason*, p. 152.
[87] *CRP*, 2, p. 161 (no. 648).

name had been mentioned to Mary by Renard.[88] In reaction, on 19 September, Noailles wrote to his own king, asking for more funds to help promote the cause of Courtenay. He apparently hoped to lavish French favours on the Queen and thus persuade her not to marry Philip.[89] A day later, Renard reported to Brussels that Mary was being put under pressure to marry by the ladies of her chamber, who were ceaselessly gossiping about betrothals and weddings.[90] In addition, during the first half of September, Noailles was working to stir up the Venetian ambassador in London against the possibility of Mary's marrying Philip, and also suggesting prophetically to the Lord Chancellor, Stephen Gardiner, who in any case supported Courtenay rather than Philip, that the Prince would be almost totally absent from England, if he became Mary's husband, because of his other commitments.[91] By the beginning of that month, Mary had in fact come to two decisions – firstly that she would give marriage the highest priority, and secondly that the choice of a husband would be entirely hers, though in secret consultation with Charles V. Thus she asked the Emperor to tell Renard never to mention the subject of her marriage in public. In accordance with this policy, when Philip's own ambassador, Don Iñigo de Mendoza, arrived in London at the beginning of September, to congratulate the Queen on her accession, no mention was made to anyone outside her most intimate circle of the possibility of the two becomng spouses. Mary was apparently so anxious to avoid a leak that she had the Council come out from London to Richmond Palace to prevent any of them from meeting the Spanish delegation.[92] It appears to have been on 8 September that Mary and Renard explicitly mentioned Philip for the first time in conversation, and it was the Queen who first spoke his name. Renard alluded to the powerful rumour that she would marry Courtenay, but Mary denied having any feelings for him, having not even seen him more than once since she had freed him from the Tower. The ambassador reported that he had mentioned other possible foreign candidates in this conversation – Archduke Ferdinand of Austria, Emmanuel Philibert of Savoy, the heirs of Florence and Ferrara, and the Dauphin of France – and he and the Queen had a frank discussion about relative ages. Renard apparently remarked that all the likely candidates were about ten years younger than Mary, while the older ones were too old or else too infirm for matrimony, given the desperate need for an heir. Renard surmised that Mary had guessed that he was discreetly pushing Philip forward, but she initially replied that she understood him to be already betrothed to Maria of Portugal. Although the ambassador stated, correctly, that no contract had yet been signed between Philip and

[88] *CSP Span* XI, pp. 238–42.
[89] Vertot, *Ambassades*, ii, pp. 142–8.
[90] *CSP Span* XI, pp. 212–14.
[91] *CSP Span* XI, pp. 174–82.
[92] *CSP Span* XI, pp. 212–14.

Maria, the English Queen continued to talk as though they were already married, expressing regret that the Prince of Spain had married such a close relation. She added, not entirely accurately, that she herself was old enough to be the mother of all the younger candidates for her hand, including Philip. Mary also seems to have articulated some of the objections to the 'Spanish marriage' which were being made by Gardiner and others among her English advisers. For one thing, Philip would want to live in Spain, and her beloved Charles must surely know that the English would never accept a king who had foreign lands to look after as well. At this point Renard began to talk Philip up vigorously, saying that he had previous experience as a married man of six or seven years' standing, and was remarkably mature for his age. Crucially, Mary revealed to the ambassador that she had never harboured voluptuous thoughts for a man, and had not even considered marriage until she arrived on the throne. Equally importantly, she told Renard that she would not reveal her choice of Philip, if she made it, to her Council: Charles V himself must do this.[93] The next day, 9 September, Renard's colleague Scheyfve, possibly in an attempt to queer his fellow ambassador's pitch, wrote to Granvelle saying that the English would much prefer Archduke Ferdinand to Philip as a husband for their sovereign. This advice was, however, ignored.[94]

While these crucial secret discussions were going on between Mary and Charles's agents, Noailles, without full knowledge of what was happening, continued to work against the Spanish marriage. On the night of 6/7 September 1553, an English subject, probably Sir John Leigh, informed Noailles, just slightly prematurely it seems, that Mary would certainly marry Philip, though he only had circumstantial evidence to this effect. Even if this was an inspired guess, the French ambassador was right to believe it. On 7 September, he wrote to his master, urging him to inform Mary and her government that he would regard even Philip landing temporarily in England as an act of war. In reality, though, Henry II was not in a strong position to respond, since he had no plausible alternative husband to offer. There were no available adult French princes of the blood, the King's younger brother, the duke of Orléans, having died unmarried in 1545, and the French knew that it would be politically and militarily impossible to install Mary, Queen of Scots in her namesake's place. In the circumstances, the only practical French policy was to back Courtenay.[95]

It was, of course, inevitable that news of Mary's choice of spouse would leak out, given the intimacy of the Tudor Court, and it is equally unsurprising that the Council should react to the gossip in a hostile manner, seeing that it had not been consulted. By 14 September opposition was beginning to coalesce around Lord Chancellor Gardiner, who was backed

[93] *CSP Span* XI, pp. 212–14.
[94] *CSP Span XI*, pp. 227–8.
[95] Vertot, *Ambassades*, i, p. 1445; *RMT*, p. 65.

by some of Mary's most loyal servants – Rochester, Waldegrave and Englefield. Not only did she not inform, let alone consult, these faithful retainers who had brought her to London in triumph, but she actively misled them by stating that she would make no decision on matrimony until parliament met in early October.[96] Mary's political approach, at this early stage in her reign, was not without its problems.

On 20 September, Renard finally received instructions from Brussels on how to proceed, and these suggest that Charles V and/or his advisers were, very reasonably, still uncertain that Mary really intended to marry Philip. The ambassador was told to propose his suit only if he thought that the English would not object, or that any objections might safely be over-ruled. The expectation evidently was that Mary's subjects would indeed oppose a Spanish marriage. The message had reached the Imperial court that the Queen had consulted only foreigners about finding a husband, and the London embassy was clearly told that the sole purpose of the marriage would be to secure the Netherlands, and not to give priority to England.[97] In early October, even though Mary was happy to rely on foreign advice, Renard wisely decided that at least some of her Council should be told of her probable marriage to the Spanish prince. Given that he had, apparently spontaneously, mentioned Philip's name to the French ambassador in the previous month, it seemed reasonable now to approach William Paget first. Mary agreed to this, even proposing Paget's name. An unobtrusive meeting between him and Renard duly took place, and the Lord Privy Seal suggested that the ambassador should write personal letters to select councillors – Bishops Gardiner and Tunstall, the earls of Arundel and Shrewsbury, Sir William Petre, Sir Robert Rochester, and Paget himself. Paget rashly claimed to Renard that this group 'governed' the Council and would be able to 'guide' the Queen.[98] After this, Paget dined with the French ambassador and tried to convince him that the Council knew about the plan for a Spanish marriage – which it did not, at least as a body – but had abandoned such a scheme. On the following day, Paget assured Noailles that Courtenay, on the other hand, had spent some hours, the previous afternoon, in the chamber of his mother, the marchioness of Exeter, and had been visited during that time by Mary herself. This was, of course, pure fiction, but it provided a good smoke-screen for Imperial intrigues.[99] On the same day as Paget had his dinner with Noailles, Renard visited the Queen in her privy chamber and, under the cover of the singing of a young lady of the Court, accompanying herself on the lute, he managed to tell Mary that he had now received credentials from Charles V to begin negotiations for her marriage to

[96] *CSP Span* XI, pp. 233–7.

[97] *CSP Span* XI, pp. 230–1, 243–8.

[98] *CSP Span*, XI, pp. 265–72.

[99] Armand Bascher, 'List of the French Ambassadors in England', in *Report of the Deputy Keeper of the Public Records* (London: HMSO, 1876), app. 1, pp. 182–94.

Philip, but would not discuss them with her in a public audience. She told him to come to her the next day, secretly, at five or six in the evening. Thus it was in a riverside gallery at Westminster that Mary first heard the formal proposal that the Emperor made on behalf of his son.

Now it was the Queen's turn to show caution. She expressed doubts, both about the attitude of her subjects and about Philip himself. Significantly, she also put down a marker for the future, saying that she would obey him as her husband, but would not allow him to encroach on the government of England or interfere with parliament. She also continued to maintain her previous position that Charles V must inform her Council of the proposal, though at least this meant that she now admitted that the councillors must know about it. Diplomatically, Mary concluded that all outstanding issues should be settled in the marriage treaty.[100] On 13 October, Renard received a note from the Queen, scribbled in haste, which asked him to come to her urgently and privately that evening, in advance of the public audience which was planned for the following day. Renard obeyed the summons, and found Mary in an agony of doubt, mainly about Philip's character. In an un-regal manner, she gripped the ambassador's wrist and begged for reassurance about a much younger man whom she had never even seen. In her tossing and turning she had apparently dreamt, as she told Renard, that she could indeed see Philip in England, if only briefly, before she finally undertook to marry him.[101]

Mary's personal torment would continue for a further fortnight. By 28 October 1553, Renard had spoken to her again about Philip, and Gardiner, Waldegrave and Englefield had been to her to propose that she marry Courtenay. As she had anticipated in her conversations with Charles V's ambassador, Gardiner warned her that the English would never willingly accept a foreign king; Englefield, obviously unaware of Habsburg grand strategy, then chipped in to say that Philip would want to remain in Spain, and claimed to know that he was not popular with his subjects there. Waldegrave then added, not unreasonably, that if Mary married Philip, there would inevitably be renewed war between England and France. In reply, the Queen repeated some of Renard's arguments in favour of the marriage with Philip. Nonetheless, as he had still received only a tentative statement that she believed she would indeed wed the Prince of Spain, Renard was afraid that Mary would succumb to the heavy pressure applied by Gardiner and his supporters. Although she told him that she really did not like Courtenay, Dr Nicholas Wotton wrote from the French Court that Henry II was making every effort to prevent the Spanish marriage, and had the young earl of Devon in mind. Mary still wavered, and asked for more consultation with Charles. Renard, who seems to have had more of her confidence than anyone else, tried to goad her into making the decision

---

[100] *CSP Span* XI, pp. 288–93.
[101] *CSP Span* XI, pp. 293–300.

that he wanted, but still she hesitated.[102] Then finally, late in the night of 29 October 1553, Mary made up her mind. Dramatically, she summoned Renard to her chamber and there, in his company and that of her faithful Susan Clarencius, and in the presence of the consecrated Host of the Blessed Sacrament of the Eucharist, she announced that she would indeed marry Philip. In these circumstances, given the nature of her personal belief and devotional life, the decision was obviously irrevocable and, according to Renard, it was announced after she had said or sung Rabanus Maurus's great hymn of invocation of the Holy Spirit, *Veni Creator Spiritus*, in which her companions joined. That same night, Renard wrote to Prince Philip, informing him of this new development and suggesting that he had better brush up his French and Latin.[103] Despite the secrecy of the midnight session, the news spread rapidly in London, too, and the opponents of the Spanish alliance quickly decided to fight the Queen's decision in parliament.[104]

Mary's secretive approach to choosing a husband was probably not due to any positive desire to ignore the views of her subjects, but she undoubtedly regarded the matter as something to be decided by her sovereign will. After her decision of 29 October 1553, she waited until 8 November to tell the Council of it formally, in a select and supposedly confidential session, and no voice was raised in objection around the board. Gardiner argued with her in private, but said nothing in Council.[105] According to Renard's letter to Brussels, dated 6 November 1553, the Lord Chancellor told the ambassador that he thought the English would be very reluctant to accept a foreign king, and in particular a Spanish one, because of that nation's characteristics, which were already stirring up opposition in Flanders.[106] Two days later, Renard reported to the Emperor another conversation with Gardiner. This time the bishop used economic rather than nationalistic arguments against the marriage of Mary and Philip, saying that, if it resulted in the opening up of the English market to the Spanish and their allies, English merchants would suffer. This became an argument between protectionism and free trade, with Gardiner pointing to the recent restoration by Mary of the privileges of the north German Hanse merchants as an illustration of how liberalization damaged the English economy, while Renard urged that the removal of trade barriers would in fact enlarge the economic cake for everyone.[107] At this time, Renard unsurprisingly became convinced that Gardiner was the ringleader of parliamentary opposition to Mary's marrying Philip.[108] Afterwards, he also reported that

---

[102] *CSP Span* XI, pp. 312–15, 319–24.
[103] *CSP Span* XI, pp. 327–30.
[104] *CSP Span* XI, pp. 332–6.
[105] *CSP Span* XI, pp. 337–45.
[106] *CSP Span* XI, pp. 338–9.
[107] *CSP Span* XI, p. 340.
[108] *CSP Span* XI, p. 333.

there was great concern in London that the French might take direct action, as Noailles in fact wished, by conspiring with English Protestants against Mary, or else by attempting to install Mary, Queen of Scots on the English throne.[109] The nature of these threats might have been seen as an argument in favour of an English marriage, probably to Courtenay, on the grounds that the primary need was to defend the realm rather than become engaged in the continental entanglements that a nuptial alliance with the Habsburgs would inevitably bring. Mary was clearly aware of all these issues, and although she never openly asked for her Council's advice as a body, probably because she knew that she could not obtain the support of a majority in those circumstances, she had not gone beyond precedent in choosing a foreign husband without advice.[110] She may not have asked for formal counsel from her subjects, but she nonetheless felt that she had obtained their consent. As the Tower Chronicle indicates, by the middle of November, even though Court and Council were meant to keep it secret, the news about Philip was out, and 'heavily taken of sundry men'.[111] Meanwhile, the Queen, who was quickly aware of the organization of a parliamentary petition for her to marry an Englishman, pleaded ill-health as a means of delaying its presentation, at least until she had spoken to the Council. Finally, on 16 November 1553, she received a joint delegation of the Lords and Commons. The Lord Chancellor stood by her side, and the Speaker, Sir John Pollard, launched into a long disquisition in favour of her marrying an Englishman. This distinguished lawyer was apparently long-winded and rambled, some saying that he had lost his written text in the flurry of suddenly being summoned before the Queen. Because of the length of his speech, or perhaps because of her ill-health, Mary first broke with protocol by sitting down during his discourse, and then did so again, more spectacularly, by replying herself, instead of having Gardiner speak on her behalf. In a burst of what has variously been described by historians as feminine pique and Tudor rage, she told the assembled parliamentarians that she had as much right as any other Englishwoman to choose her own husband, and that it was therefore impertinent of them to seek to direct her, as a woman and a sovereign. Now apparently hurt and angry, she added, daringly and perhaps rashly, that if she was made to take a husband whom she did not want, she would have no children and would be dead within three months. The delegation left, bruised but now totally certain of the Queen's decision, while Mary herself, quite unfairly, rebuked a tearful Gardiner for inflicting Pollard and his henchmen on her, and unjustly accused him of conspiring against her.[112] Relations between the Queen and her Lord Chancellor would never be the same again, but the marriage plans proceeded apace.

[109] *CSP Span* XI, pp. 343, 372.
[110] *RMT*, p. 71.
[111] *Chronicle of Queen Jane*, p. 35.
[112] *CSP Span* XI, pp. 370-3.

Once they realized that Mary was not to be shifted from her plan to take Philip of Spain as her husband, her councillors devoted themselves to securing the best possible terms from Charles V. They also began to plan for Philip's coming to England as King, and on 21 November 1553, Renard wrote to tell Charles that the English were planning to have the Prince served entirely by Englishmen and Netherlanders when he was in England. On this point, which later proved to be contentious, Charles was vague in his response.[113] At the end of the month, Renard, clearly anxious that Philip should have a means of gaining personal influence in England, wrote to tell him to bring at least a million ducats when he came, but also, very importantly, that he was to play absolutely no part in the negotiation of the marriage treaty, which was to be done between Brussels and London.[114] In the last week of November 1553, a draft set of proposals for the treaty was drawn up in England, approved by the Council and used as the basis for future negotiation.[115] At the same time, preparations were going on in the Netherlands, in a climate of deep hostility to Philip which apparently paralleled that in England.[116] The Emperor was happy with most of the English proposals, which were drawn up by Paget and, ever preoccupied with his Burgundian inheritance, he asserted that he had taken measures to prevent any claim to it from his brother Ferdinand's branch of the family. In addition, if the marriage between Philip and Mary went ahead and they left no heirs, Ferdinand's second son, Maximilian, was to have no claim to the Crown of England.[117] Finally on 4 December, the Emperor appointed four commissioners, all of them from the Netherlands, to negotiate the marriage agreement. They were Lamoral, count of Egmont, Charles, count of Lalaing, Jehan de Montmorency, sieur de Courrières, and Philippe Negri, chancellor of the chivalric Order of the Golden Fleece (*Toison d'Or*).[118]

These negotiations in fact resulted in two treaties, one concerning Mary's dowry and the English succession, and the other setting out the conditions and safeguards which were demanded by the English Privy Council. As far as the succession was concerned, it was provided that, if Philip and Mary had a son, he should inherit England and the Netherlands, but have no claim over Spain and its overseas territories as long as Philip's son from his first marriage, Don Carlos, survived, and his line continued. If the only surviving child of Philip and Mary was a daughter, the same conditions applied, but she should seek the approval of Don Carlos before marrying. If Carlos's line failed, the entire inheritance would go to the heirs of Philip and Mary, but if Mary died before Philip, the latter would have no claim to the English Crown, which would be assigned according to the laws of that

[113] *CSP Span* XI, pp. 381, 391.
[114] *CSP Span* XI, p. 404.
[115] *CSP Span* XI, pp. 397–8.
[116] Harbison, *Rival Ambassadors*, pp. 99–100.
[117] *CSP Span* XI, pp. 387–92.
[118] *RMT*, p. 73 and notes.

kingdom alone. Thus there would be no possibility of Don Carlos or his descendants ever obtaining the throne of England. Philip was to receive the title of 'King of England' and exercise sovereignty jointly with his wife, though in a severely restricted way. He should uphold all the laws of England, grant no English office to an alien, and should not take Mary out of the kingdom without the consent of the nobility. Crucially, he was not to have or use executive authority in his own right. Also, although the existing treaties of friendship between England and the Empire, concluded in 1543 and 1546, under which the English were obliged to send 6,000 troops if Habsburg territory was attacked by the French, were to remain in force, Philip should now undertake not to involve Mary's kingdom in war against France.[119] It is clear from these terms that although Gardiner and his allies had been unable to prevent Mary from choosing Philip as her husband, they had done everything possible to make him as 'safe' to England as a native candidate would have been. These draft articles, dated 7 December 1553, were signed by Gardiner and twenty-three other councillors, while in the Netherlands, Granvelle was taking the main role on the Emperor's behalf in ensuring that matters went smoothly.[120] During the Christmas season, on 27 December 1553, the four Imperial commissioners arrived in England to conclude the treaty, and the result, which bore an almost total resemblance to the English Council's proposal, was quickly completed and was proclaimed in England on 14 January.[121] By then, though, Philip had had to be informed, at last, of what precisely awaited him. His reaction was strong.

At Valladolid, on 4 January 1554, the Prince of Spain had a notarial document drawn up before his high steward (*mayordomo mayor*), the duke of Alba, his accountant (*contador*) and favourite, Ruy Gómez de Silva, and a royal secretary, Juan Vázquez de Medina. Given the prominence of these witnesses, it was clear that the document in question was of very great importance. This was indeed so since, after citing the terms of the marriage treaty with Mary, it stated that Philip was now required to grant powers to commissioners of his own, to ratify the articles (*capitulaciones*) of the treaty, and swear on his behalf to uphold them. However, in this text Philip recorded that he had known nothing about the terms of the treaty until it had been completely drawn up, by others. In these circumstances, he was still willing to marry Queen Mary, and would give his representatives full power to agree this, but not 'in order to bind himself or his heirs to observe the articles [of the marriage treaty], especially any [unspecified] that might burden his conscience'. In this solemn document, he 'protested' this text once, twice, three times, or as many times as were necessary to make it fully valid in law, and stated that he did this only to achieve the aforesaid object, which was his

[119] Thomas Rymer and others, *Foedera* (Hagae Comites [The Hague], 1641–1713), p. 377.
[120] M. van Durme, *El cardenal Granvela (1517–1586): Imperio y revolución bajo Carlos V y Felipe II*, 2nd edn (Barcelona: Editorial Teide, 1957), p. 143.
[121] Hughes and Larkin, *Tudor Royal Proclamations*, ii, pp. 21–6.

marriage to Mary.[122] The motives and meaning of this precautionary document (*ad cautelam*), of which there are multiple copies in Philip's own archive
of Simancas but which seems never to have become known to Mary, have
naturally been much discussed. It might be regarded as a form of perjury, or
at least as an exercise in 'mental reservation'.[123] There is no doubt that
Philip's prospective marriage to Maria of Portugal was regarded in Spain at
that time as a 'done deal', and was extremely popular with the public. Thus
the prospect of their prince becoming King of distant England may well not
have appealed. More probably, Philip, who by now had very different ideas
on the future of the Habsburg Empire from those of his father, was piqued
by his exclusion from the treaty negotiations. He no doubt thought that far
too much had been given away to the English, but he would do his duty.
Unfortunately, by the beginning of January 1554, some Englishmen were not
prepared to accept him, and were ready to take action.

[122] AGS PR 7; *CSP Span* XI, XII, p. 6.
[123] *RMT*, p. 76.

Chapter 7

ENGLAND TRIES EUROPEAN INTEGRATION, 1554

It seems to have been Queen Mary's outburst when meeting a parliamentary delegation on 16 November 1553, together with indications emerging from her Council that she had indeed chosen Philip of Spain to be her husband, which suggested to some members of the English political class that it was time for 'regime change'. Probably, all those involved with government had some kind of crisis of conscience at the prospect of a foreign consort for their Queen. Many were no doubt well aware that, back in 1532, a book entitled *A Glasse of the Truthe* had appeared, which attempted to justify the annulment of Henry VIII's marriage to Mary's mother. It contained a crystal-clear statement of the problems that would face his elder daughter if she ever succeeded to the throne:

> If the female heir shall chance to rule, she cannot continue long without a husband, which by God's law, must then be her governor and head, and so finally must direct the realm.

Mary would have to obtain popular consent if the marriage was to be a political success. Also, there would inevitably be problems if the Queen's choice was a foreigner, though there was perhaps some consolation for Mary and her pro-Philip advisers in the fact that the book expressed even more concern about her marrying an English subject:

> And as touching any marriage within this realm, we think, it were hard to devise any condign [worthy] and able person, for so high an enterprise, much harder to find one with whom the whole world would and could be contented to have him ruler and governor.[1]

In the circumstances of November 1553, with the Queen's mind clearly made up, the leading opponents of Philip among her inner circle, including Lord Chancellor Gardiner and her faithful retainers Rochester, Englefield and Waldegrave, felt constrained to suppress their opposition and remain loyal to the Queen. At the same time, leading nobles such as the marquis of Northampton, the earl of Arundel and the earl of Pembroke seem to have felt that, having narrowly escaped punishment, and even death, for their earlier support of Northumberland and Jane Grey, they were now

---

[1] Anon., *A Glasse of the Truthe* (London: Thomas Berthelet, 1532), sigs A2v–A3v.

constrained to support their merciful Queen in her marriage, whatever
their personal misgivings. Those of lesser rank or involvement, however,
evidently felt no such inhibition. According to the indictment of participants in the subsequent rebellion, on 26 November 1553, a week after
Mary's outburst before Speaker Pollard and his delegation, a meeting
took place which involved at least a dozen men with conspiracy on their
minds. Four of them – Sir Peter Carew, Sir Edward Rogers, Sir Nicholas
Throckmorton and Sir Edward Warner (who was indicted later) – were
members of the Commons.[2] Others at the meeting included Sir James
Croftes, Sir Nicholas Arnold, Sir William Pickering, William Winter,
Sir Thomas Wyatt, Sir George Wyatt and William Thomas.[3] Many of
these men had served Edward VI, and some had been retained by Mary.
Thus Winter had been surveyor to the navy since 1549 and was still in post
in 1553, Rogers was principal gentleman of the privy chamber between
1549 and Edward's death, Thomas had been tutor to Edward VI and clerk
to his Privy Council, Pickering had been Northumberland's ambassador to
France, Croftes was lord deputy in Ireland in 1551–2, and Warner had
actually held the Tower of London for Queen Jane during the fraught
events of the previous July. Finally, Throckmorton was a gentleman of
Edward's privy chamber, though he claimed to have assisted Mary in her
bid for the throne by providing early news of the King's death. By
Christmas, the conspirators had been joined by the duke of Suffolk, despite
the merciful treatment that he too had received from the Queen.[4]

At this early stage, Edward Courtenay, whom some regarded as the ideal
man to fulfil the role of native husband, was evidently thought by the government to be a potential focus for conspiracy or rebellion, but according to
French sources he already had cold feet, though he was persuaded by the
conspirators to remain in the scheme, at least for the moment.[5] By the time
that Mary's first parliament was dissolved, on 6 December 1553, the conspirators had realized that they needed to address the question of aims and
methods. Although the very existence of a plot suggests a certain weakness in
Mary's personal and political authority, those involved in planning sedition
seem to have decided early on that there was no prospect of a successful court
intrigue, and that the route of regional rebellion should be tried instead. The
initial scheme was that Sir Peter Carew, a former sheriff of Devon, would
organize a rising in the West Country, while Sir Nicholas Arnold rose in
Gloucestershire and Sir Thomas Wyatt in Kent. As for the ultimate goal of
the rebels, it was felt, by the beginning of December 1553, that there was no
prospect that Mary would change her policies on religion and marriage, the
consequence of this being that she would have to be overthrown. Her obstinacy of character meant that she would never accept defeat in these matters

[2] Loach, *Parliament and the Crown*, p. 80.
[3] *KB* 27/1574 Rex V.
[4] Loades, *Two Tudor Conspiracies*, pp. 16–17.
[5] Vertot, *Ambassades*, ii, pp. 253–6.

which were so vital to her, and still remain Queen. According to the Tower chronicler, the most extreme proposal, made at this stage by William Thomas, was that she should be assassinated. It is said that Thomas went so far as to arrange for one John Fitzwilliam to do the deed, but this plan was vetoed by Arnold, Croftes and Thomas Wyatt. Thereafter, Thomas seems to have lost his leadership role to Croftes, but the aim of removing Mary was not abandoned. If she was to be replaced, Elizabeth should be Queen in a perverse fulfilment of the terms of their father's will and the 1544 Act of Succession, and then Courtenay might become her consort rather than Mary's.[6] This idea had been floating around since August, and seems to have been well established among the malcontents by Christmas 1553. Whatever efforts were made by the plotters to maintain secrecy, by 11 December Renard knew that something was afoot, accurately reporting to Brussels that trouble was expected in England by Easter 1554.[7]

By about the middle of December 1553, it was clear that the only representatives of the nobility in the conspiracy were to be the ungrateful duke of Suffolk and his brothers, Thomas and John. The rebel scheme had now crystallized as a supposedly popular uprising, with the hope and expectation of French support, though approaches to Noailles were furtive for fear that the rebels' exploitation of English xenophobia against the Spanish might, by extension, discredit help from Henry II of France as well. For his part, the French King naturally wanted to prevent Mary from marrying Philip, but he and his advisers doubted the capacity of the English conspirators. He was in any case being given conflicting advice at home by those whom he most trusted, since the Constable of France, Anne de Montmorency, favoured collaboration with Mary, while the Cardinal of Lorraine and the duke of Guise urged direct intervention against her. The result was that Noailles, in London, received contradictory instructions, and was not cleared to offer military help to the rebels until it was too late. By 23 December, Noailles had heard that Plymouth was preparing for a Spanish landing, and believed that a combination of the English rebels and French forces could block Philip's imminently expected passage from France to England. At about this time, an anonymous Englishman, probably one of the piratical Devonian brothers Killigrew, reached the French Court at Fontainebleau, offering to bring eight or nine English ships into Henry II's service by the end of January 1554, but the French King was suspicious of the whole plan.[8] By Christmas 1553, both Renard and Paget had been on the alert for plots for several weeks, and they were right to be so. The outline rebel plan now consisted of four risings in the shires, which were to converge on London. Croftes

---

[6] *Chronicle of Queen Jane*, p. 69.

[7] *CSP Span* XI, p. 472.

[8] Harbison, *Rival Ambassadors*, pp. 89–136; Frederic J. Baumgartner, *Henry II, King of France (1547–1559)* (Durham, NC and London: Duke University Press, 1988), pp. 165–6; Vertot, *Ambassades*, ii, p. 342.

was to raise Herefordshire, Wyatt to rise in Kent, Carew and Courtenay in Devon, and the duke of Suffolk in Leicestershire, the whole thing to start on the following Palm Sunday, 18 March 1554. It was initially thought that the main action would be in Devon. On 29 December, in the midst of the Christmas festivities, Renard told Charles V that he and Paget would act to ensure that the Queen received no nasty surprises, but they were still not aware of what exactly was being planned.[9]

Things soon became clearer, however. By early January 1554, Renard knew that there was indeed a plot, supported by Noailles, and involving both the earl of Devon and Elizabeth. He had no details, though, and did not at this stage inform the Queen so as not to alarm her with unsubstantiated rumours. The question of her younger sister's involvement was controversial at the time, and remains so. To date, no direct documentary or circumstantial link has been found, but it was natural that those who were unhappy with some of Mary's main policies should have at least imagined a scenario in which she was replaced by Elizabeth and Courtenay, who might be expected to maintain a reformed Christianity and avoid subordination to continental powers, including the Papacy. In any case, the intention of the conspirators was that the New Year would see the beginning of a process of careful preparation for co-ordinated uprisings nearly three months later. In the event, on 2 January, a totally unexpected hitch occurred, which had the effect of making the West Country alone the first focus of active rebellion. Mary's Council suddenly summoned one of the main plotters, Sir Peter Carew, from Devon to London. The relevant record suggests that this was in fact a second summons, but there is no detail concerning an earlier one, and it seems unlikely that Carew's subversive plans were known at this stage in London. It is true that Carew had spoken against the Spanish marriage in the recent parliament, but he had sworn allegiance to Mary early in her takeover of power and does not seem to have been regarded as suspect before the end of 1553. Sir Peter and his fellow conspirators were not to know this, however, and news of his summons caused panic in their ranks. They naturally feared that, once in the hands of the government, he would spill the beans, but if he stayed in the West Country he would probably be subject to even greater suspicion, and details of the plot might still leak out. The idea at once took root that the rebellions would have to be brought forward, even though things were far from ready. This was indeed the policy adopted by Carew, who did not respond to the Council's summons, instead remaining in Devon and soliciting the support of his uncle, Sir Gawain Carew, and another Devonian gentleman, William Gibbes of Sullerstone.

By 4 or 5 January, rumour was rife in south Devon that Philip was approaching the coast with a large fleet, and lurid atrocity stories were circulating. In these circumstances, Sir Peter Carew, his uncle Sir Gawain and Gibbes saw that they needed to consolidate their position before the

[9] *CSP Span* XI, p. 472.

Council took action against the recalcitrant Sir Peter. With increasing urgency, they sent their servants around the county to solicit support, apparently on an anti-Spanish basis rather than as an overt threat to the Queen herself.[10] By mid-January, the Council had heard that rumours were flying in Cornwall as well as Devon that a Spanish invasion was imminent, some even suggesting that there were already some 'outlandish' (foreign) men in Plymouth.[11] On 8 January, the Devon gentry assembled in the normal way for the assizes at Exeter, but, inevitably, the question of the supposed Spanish threat became a matter for discussion outside the formal session, which began on the following day. Initially the two Carews and Gibbes raised the matter but, crucially as things turned out, the sheriff, Sir Thomas Dennis, instantly reacted by seeing the three as malicious, and as traitors to the Queen. Thus when the Carews and Gibbes formally reported the rumoured Spanish threat to Dennis during the opening session on the 9th, having meanwhile been joined by Sir Arthur Champernoun, of Dartington Hall near Totnes, they received a dusty answer. On the 10th, John Ridgeway, acting on instruction from the sheriff after consultations, wrote a letter to Mary's Council, reporting the potential disturbance and assuring it of the loyalty of the city and county authorities in Exeter. Already, at this early stage, the dissident gentry started to cover their backs by loudly protesting their loyalty to the Queen. As so often during the crisis of 1553–4, the Council in London was slow to respond, only sending instructions to Exeter on 16 January, which did not arrive there until three days later. In the meantime, Dennis took his own measures, on 17 January garrisoning Exeter against possible attack, no doubt with a powerful memory of what had happened there during the Prayer Book rebellion, less than five years before. Such was the confusion and apprehension in government circles, though, that some actually thought Dennis was one of the rebels, and not the bastion of royal authority that he really was.

The level of fear in London was further ratcheted up by the supposed news, reported by Renard on 18 January, that a French fleet was in the process of assembling off Normandy. It was at this point that the Imperial ambassador decided to inform the Queen of the danger that she was in and urge her to take immediate measures to protect herself.[12] News of the relevant ambassadorial audience with Mary quickly reached the London-based conspirators, and it persuaded Thomas Wyatt and another plotter, Sir William Pickering, to depart for Kent on the 19th, while Croftes remained in London to monitor events.[13] By the time that the Council's orders arrived in Exeter that same day, things in Devon were deteriorating from the government's point of view. There were rumours in the city that

[10] *SP*, ii/2/ no. 15; *CSPDM*, p. 22.
[11] *SP* ii/2 no. 5; *CSPDM*, p. 15.
[12] *CSP Span* XII, p. 34.
[13] Harbison, *Rival Ambassadors*, p. 126 (Noailles to Montmorency, 21 January 1554).

a group of gentry and their retainers were about to arrive, with the aim of deposing the mayor and the corporation. Panic measures, including the hasty collection and manufacture of armour, were being implemented in Exeter, but what followed was a war of nerves. It was said that Edward Courtenay was 'secretly' residing in Sir Peter Carew's house at Mohun's Ottery, and also that some of Carew's men had paraded a cartload of armour through Exeter in broad daylight.[14] In fact, the rebels were much weaker than the rumour mill made them appear. Sir Peter Carew lacked a major 'affinity' of supporters in the county, and while Courtenay would have been able to appeal to the personal family loyalty of many, he was not in fact present in Devon to exert his influence directly.[15] Instead, the earl of Devon was about to change the course of the entire rebellion against Mary and her future husband. On 21 January, for whatever reason, Bishop Gardiner summoned his protégé for an interview, and found out about the conspiracy. It is not possible to know how much information the young earl handed over, but the fact that he had any involvement at all with the rebels was certainly bad news for the Lord Chancellor, who had already seriously fallen out with Mary over her determination to marry Philip. In a cleft stick, Gardiner tried to conceal Courtenay's involvement from the Queen and his fellow councillors, and urged them to adopt a conciliatory approach to the dissidents, no doubt in the fervent hope that the full truth would never emerge. Meanwhile, another part of the December plot was about to be put into premature action. The news that Gardiner had interrogated Courtenay reached the duke of Suffolk at Sheen, and caught him entirely unprepared to start his planned rising in the Midlands. Given that his daughter Jane Grey was still alive, the Council suspected that the duke's aim might be to replace Mary with her, rather than Elizabeth, and this naturally placed heavy suspicion on her father. Apparently as a test of loyalty, Suffolk was initially offered the command of the royal forces, and his refusal virtually proved to the Council that he was indeed a conspirator.

In Devon, also on 21 January, a nervous and fraught meeting took place at Mohun's Ottery between the host, Sir Peter Carew, and Sir Arthur Champernoun. Now fearing retribution from the Crown, such as had brutally crushed the Prayer Book rebellion of 1549, the Devon conspirators began to quarrel among themselves. Nonetheless, on 22 January, William Gibbes and Sir Gawain Carew also came to Mohun's Ottery, but even with their reinforcement, the rebel group seems to have amounted at this stage to no more than twenty or so. The game was up and, ever the realist and no fanatic, Peter Carew next day wrote a letter of submission to Sir Thomas Dennis. Unaware of this turn of events, at about this time Mary's Council despatched Sir Anthony to Devon with orders to secure Exeter and the county. At this time, it was still believed in London that

[14] *APC* IV, p. 385.
[15] Loades, *Two Tudor Conspiracies*, p. 39.

Sheriff Dennis had rebelled, and that there was an organized conspiracy among the Devon gentry to put up violent resistance to Philip's landing in England. Exeter itself was believed, wrongly of course, to be in rebel hands. At last galvanized into action, the Council still believed that the main danger to Mary's rule came from Devon, and that the rebels' anti-Spanish 'manifesto', against a marriage with Philip, was no more than a cover for an attempt to reverse the Queen's religious policies by force. Nevertheless, Mary was now urging that the marriage treaty with Philip should be concluded as soon as possible. Writing from St James's Palace on 22 January 1554, she told Sir Anthony, and also other supporters of hers, Sir Hugh Pollard and Sir Richard Edgecombe, that false rumours were being spread, particularly in the West Country, about the supposed imminent arrival of Prince Philip and other Spaniards. To pre-empt any trouble that might arise from this tale, she told the three knights that she had ordered the publication of the full terms of the marriage treaty, from which it would be seen that it did not compromise either her status as Queen or English independence.[16] On the same day, she addressed a letter to Nicholas Heath, lord president of the Council and bishop of Worcester, with copies for the earl of Shrewsbury, the Council of Wales and the Marches, the Council of the North, Bishop John Veysey of Exeter and Bishop John Capon of Salisbury. In this document she expressed concern about the disturbances which were being caused by anti-Spanish feeling in Devon and Cornwall, though she understood that most Devonians were still loyal to her. She regretted that some of her subjects had been led astray by false rumours since her projected marriage was being made entirely for the good of the realm.[17] The marriage treaty itself was indeed published that day while, on 23 January, Sir Peter Carew wrote to Sheriff Dennis from Mohun's Ottery to protest his innocence, and on 24 January Sir Gawain Carew wrote to the sheriff from Tiverton to assure him that there had never been any intention to cause disturbances in Exeter, so that Dennis's protective measures in the city were unnecessary.[18] On the same day John Ridgeway, in Torre, sent the sheriff a report on the current situation in Torbay and the South Hams. After he returned to Dartington from his meeting at Mohun's Ottery with Sir Peter Carew, Sir Arthur Champernoun had summoned the mayor of nearby Totnes to meet him; otherwise he would make the short trip into town to talk to the mayor and burgesses. Ridgeway had the apparently correct impression that, by this time, Peter Carew and Champernoun were not sure how to proceed. He had heard that Champernoun was now in favour of accepting Philip in England, since this was clearly the Queen's will. According to Ridgeway, on 23 January, the mayor and some burgesses of Totnes had indeed ridden out to Dartington and told Champernoun that this small but important tidal

---

[16] *SP* 11/2 no. 5; *CSPDM*, p. 15.
[17] *SP* 11/2 no. 6; *CSPDM*, p. 16.
[18] *SP* 11/2 nos 11, 12; *CSPDM*, pp. 18–19.

river-port was unwilling to rise against the Queen, even though a minority of Totnesians were in favour of doing so. Ridgeway estimated that there was equipment in the town for about 200 men, who would defend the Queen if required.[19] At about this time, John Blackaller, royal lieutenant of Exeter, reported to the Council that there had indeed at one time been a danger of rebellion in the city and that armed men had been sighted at nearby Fairmile on 22 January, so that a watch was still necessary, particularly as Exeter castle was in a poor state of repair.[20] On 25 January, Sir Thomas Dennis reported to Mary's Council that in response to its order of the 18th he had tried to summon Sir Peter Carew to Exeter, but Carew had announced that he would go straight to London to defend himself.[21] Meanwhile, just as things were calming down in the West Country, a new problem was emerging in the Midlands.

On 25 January, the duke of Suffolk was duly summoned to Court, though he claimed to be confident that he would escape punishment once again, as he had done after the fall of his daughter Jane's regime. Nonetheless, he also seems to have thought that the moment had come to fulfil his planned role in the rebel plot, so that when he left Sheen, he headed not for London but for his stronghold at Bradgate in Leicestershire. The earl of Shrewsbury reported this manoeuvre at once to the earl of Arundel. At his trial three weeks later, after the rebellion had been defeated, Suffolk claimed that he had disobeyed the Council on the advice of one of his brothers, preferring the safety of his Leicestershire estates to another visit to the Tower of London, which cannot have had happy associations for him.[22] In fact, Suffolk's two brothers were not with him at Sheen when he fled, but were asked to join him at St Albans as he headed north. Perhaps inevitably, Simon Renard blamed his French opposite number Noailles for involving Suffolk in the rebellion, and this may well have been true, at least in part.[23] The Council, now at long last on full alert, quickly guessed the duke of Suffolk's aim, and despatched the earl of Huntingdon to the Midlands to arrest all 'traitors', whose names were publicly proclaimed on that day. Circular letters were sent to the relevant counties with details of Suffolk's treason, and they suggest that Mary's Council was now receiving better intelligence of developments elsewhere in the kingdom. On 27 January, Gardiner reported to Sir William Petre that he had one John Harrington in his house as a suspect, sending him next day to the Tower. Meanwhile, Suffolk's brothers failed to rendezvous at St Albans, instead catching up with him at Lutterworth in Leicestershire. It is suggested that Suffolk and his henchmen may have proclaimed Jane as Queen once again, but it is equally probable that publicly they took the same anti-Spanish line as their fellow conspirators elsewhere in the country, while still accepting

---

[19] 11/2 no. 13; *CSPDM*, p. 19.
[20] 11/2 no. 14; *CSPDM*, pp. 19–20.
[21] 11/2 no. 16; *CSPDM*, p. 22.
[22] *Chronicle of Queen Jane*, pp. 37, 61.
[23] *CSP Span* XII, p. 34.

Mary as Queen.[24] On 28 January, apparently in anticipation of Suffolk's rebellion spreading more widely, the Council wrote to the sheriff and justices of Gloucestershire accusing the duke and his brothers, as well as Peter Carew and Thomas Wyatt, of stirring up sedition on a false manifesto of resisting the arrival of Philip and his Spaniards in England, while their true aim was claimed to be to restore Jane Grey to the throne, with Guildford Dudley as her consort. To counteract this propaganda, the Gloucestershire authorities were to ensure that the county's people were fully aware of the actual terms of the marriage treaty, and also to raise 300 men in case of trouble. At the same time, in the Midlands, the duke of Suffolk was beginning to assemble supporters at Bradgate.

On 29 January, the duke was joined by his kinsman George Medley, of Tilty, Essex, while his own secretary, John Bowyer, had arrived in Leicestershire with 100 marks in cash, which had been extracted from a debtor in London. Suffolk was short of troops, and it would be necessary to raise some more. Initially, Bowyer sent letters to the town councils in Leicester and Northampton and to the bailiff of Kegworth, urging them to support the duke's cause, at least with money and advice. On the night of the 29th, Suffolk wrote a personal letter to Mary justifying his actions before riding from Bradgate to Leicester, where he was received without opposition, the municipal authorities closing the gates with himself and his men inside. Ominously, though, by this time the disturbances in Devon, in so far as there had been any, were effectively over.[25] Suffolk went ahead nonetheless, and issued at Leicester his proclamation against the Spanish marriage. After this, the town's mayor said that he hoped the duke meant no harm to Queen Mary, and was assured by him, hand on sword, that he had no such intention. Very few joined his cause as a result of the proclamation, though, and he left Leicester that day for Coventry with only about 140 men. Once there, Suffolk received the good news that the bailiff of Kegworth, Robert Palmer, had contributed £500 to the cause, and also wrote to his servants back at Sheen, asking them to send his plate on to him. The duke had high hopes of Coventry, since the ground had been prepared for him by one of his secretaries, Thomas Rampton, who had been sent there to spy out the land. Rampton had managed to assemble a small group of sympathizers among the Coventry traders, who hoped to be able to extend the uprising to Warwick and Kenilworth, both towns with castles which would have given Suffolk a strong Midlands base. However, Rampton's recruits were not representative of the citizens of Coventry; some had only recently arrived there from London, and none of them held borough office, either then or later. Also, by 30 January, retribution was nearing the city in the form of the earl of Huntingdon and his men. The duke of Suffolk's 'treason' was proclaimed in the towns and villages surrounding Coventry, and Thomas Rampton quietly slipped away from

[24] Loades, *Two Tudor Conspiracies*, p. 27.
[25] 11/2 no. 26; *CSPDM*, p. 29 (report of Sir John St Leger to Council).

his side when the citizens declared against him. By the time one of Suffolk's retainers, William Burdet, and his men returned from nearby Warwick, Coventry's gates were closed against them, and when he heard this, the duke surrendered without a fight. He gave his money away to his retainers, and told them to shift for themselves. Thus the Midland revolt came to an abrupt end and Mary's regime survived. Her popularity proved to be greater than that of Jane Grey and her father, and Sir James Croftes's proposed rising in Herefordshire never happened at all. Nevertheless, the Queen was about to face the greatest threat of her reign, from Sir Thomas Wyatt and his men in Kent.

To understand what happened, and why it placed Mary in such danger, it is necessary to go back to Wyatt's departure from London for his castle at Allington, on Thursday, 19 January 1554. When he arrived there, he summoned his friends and supporters to a council of war. Mary and her advisers, among them Gardiner, Paget and Renard, were aware that trouble was brewing, but until 21–22 January they still believed that it was going to emerge in the south-west. By now, though, Mary had ordered the raising of more troops, and several individuals had been arrested in London. As a precaution, she made all members of her own household swear an oath of loyalty to Philip as King of England, even though he had not yet attained that dignity. Her inner circle remained divided on what to do, Renard urging that a direct appeal should be made to Charles V for military aid, while Gardiner, still mindful of the danger posed by his association with Edward Courtenay, again advised conciliation. William Paget, on the other hand, who favoured the Spanish alliance, urged a military response, to be commanded by Lord Clinton and the earl of Pembroke.[26] Closer to the action, on 23 January, the sheriff of Kent, Sir Robert Southwell, wrote to the Council, still not apparently aware of what Wyatt was plotting at Allington castle. He reported that on the previous day one William Isley had walked into Ightham, near Maidstone, and told anyone who would listen that the Spaniards were coming to England, threatening atrocities, that the Devonians had already risen against them, and that the men of Kent should do the same. The initial response seems to have been apathetic, but the incident was reported to the Council by William Colman, a blacksmith of Ightham.[27] On 24 January, news of the goings-on in Kent reached the Imperial embassy, where Renard assumed that the issue was religion, rather than the Spanish marriage. The Habsburgs had always urged caution in this area on Mary, and instantly blamed Gardiner, who was also, of course, opposed to her marriage to Philip, for having used too much vigour and ferocity in restoring the old religion. Nonetheless, Mary was militarily so weak that Gardiner's policy of conciliation towards the rebels seemed to be the only option. On the 22nd, she had instructed two of her faithful supporters, Sir Edward Hastings and Sir Thomas

---

[26] *CSP Span* XII, p. 31 (18 January).
[27] 11/2 no.10 (1); *CSPDM*, p. 18.

Cornwallis, to investigate Wyatt's activities, and on 23–24 January a herald, probably sent by them, arrived at Allington castle with a message in the Queen's name which he was not allowed to deliver. At this stage, the Council seems not to have been sure whether Wyatt was a rebel or a loyalist, but his treatment of the herald must have appeared ominous. At this stage his manifesto, as it was proclaimed to potential supporters, was explicitly anti-Spanish. He had not, up to then, been a conspicuous supporter of the Protestant cause, and he now tried to convince recruits that they would be part of a national uprising, aimed, in the traditional manner, at freeing the Queen from 'evil counsellors', and in particular at preventing her from marrying Philip of Spain. There was no clear indication at this stage that he intended to remove Mary from the throne, and he did not feel secure enough to be able to reject out of hand the Council's offer of negotiations, despite his high-handed treatment of the herald. In London, though, it had become painfully obvious, by the last week of January 1554, that Mary was living in something of a political vacuum, with little or no solid and unquestioning support, while in Kent itself, to the end of Wyatt's campaign, the 'loyalist' response was feeble and reluctant. About thirty gentlemen of the county actively supported Wyatt, while only about half that number came out to fight for the Queen.

On 24 January, Sheriff Southwell, with Henry Neville, Lord Abergavenny, started trying to raise a force to defend the regime, but initially with little success. Wyatt was still faced by an open door, but he would need to act quickly.[28] On the following day he made his move, raising his standard at Maidstone, with a proclamation that he would 'protect' the Queen against the Spanish 'threat'. Very similar proclamations were made by Sir George Harper at Rochester and Sir Henry Isley at Tonbridge. Such announcements were also made in other places in Kent, and some justices of the peace were illegally imprisoned for speaking against them. There was no further military action that day, but in the evening Sir Robert Southwell, in reporting his raising of troops to the Council, said that proclamations against the Spanish had also been made in Sussex and Essex. He suggested that the Queen should withdraw from London to a safer place.[29] Meanwhile, in the capital itself rumours were rife. The numbers who had risen in Kent were grossly exaggerated, and Lord Cobham, whose castle at Cooling was close to that of his nephew Wyatt, was initially suspected, as Sheriff Dennis of Exeter had been, of having joined the rebels. The lack of hard fact caused panic in London, and further false rumours arose of rebellion in Cornwall and Wales: some expected the nightmare of 1549 to recur in a new form. Affected by the London and Westminster gossip, as they so often were, the French, Imperial and Venetian ambassadors, each with his own axe to grind, enthusiastically spread around Europe the fear of some, that Mary's regime was facing imminent downfall. In a rare moment of decisiveness, amidst the impotent panic

[28] Proctor, *Historie*, p. 50.
[29] 11/2 no. 17; *CSPDM*, pp. 22–3.

shown by most of those who surrounded the Queen, Lord Treasurer Paulet then went to the London Guildhall to ask the city authorities for an initial force of 200 soldiers.[30] In addition, warrants were sent to the leading nobles, summoning them to ride to the Queen's defence with their retinues. The lord admiral, William Howard, was to be the overall commander, and the sheriffs of Surrey, Sussex and Kent were told to obey his orders. On Friday, 26 January, two suspects, the marquis of Northampton and Sir Edward Warner, were arrested and confined to the Tower. On Saturday the 27th, Sir Thomas Cawarden's large armoury at Bletchingley was confiscated to prevent it from falling into rebel hands, but, on a parallel track, a further unsuccessful attempt was made to open negotiations with Wyatt. By this time, open rows had broken out among Mary's councillors. In particular, Paget and Renard, who were naturally the main advocates of Philip's cause in England, accused Gardiner of trying to sabotage the Crown's military preparations, feeble as they were. To the delight of Noailles, the Lord Chancellor was even accused of being an ally of Wyatt himself.

Finally, on 26/27 January, the Council decided to send an army into the field against Wyatt. A motley force of 800 or so men had been assembled, and, amazingly, it was commanded by the eighty-year-old duke of Norfolk. By this time, Wyatt had moved his headquarters from Maidstone to the far more defensible Rochester, with its castle and famous bridge. On Saturday, 27 January, having assembled about 2,000 men, he proclaimed that the real traitors to the Queen were in fact Southwell and Abergavenny. In addition, Sir Thomas Isley had a small force in Tonbridge, and Henry Isley another, in Sevenoaks. Meanwhile, Southwell and Abergavenny, with about 600 men, were stationed at Malling in an attempt to prevent the Isleys from joining up with Wyatt at Rochester. Sheriff Southwell urged the men of Malling to take up arms for the Queen, but again the response was apathetic. As expected, on Sunday, 28 January Henry Isley and his men left Sevenoaks and, after some hestitation, Southwell confronted them at Wrotham in what turned out to be one of the few serious military actions during the rebellion. A few of Isley's men died, and about sixty were taken prisoner, thus demonstrating what the royal forces could do if they showed some determination. After the battle, Sir Henry Isley fled to Hampshire, and rebel prestige suffered a blow, which led Wyatt to see that he was unlikely to receive much more support than he already had in Kent, and should head for London soon. Meanwhile, news of events in the west of the county reached east Kent. The mayor of Canterbury ordered the town's defences to be strengthened, while his equivalent in Dover introduced measures to control 'strangers', but no one at all in that part of the county seems to have joined Wyatt. On 28 January, Lord Abergavenny was able to report to Sir Henry Jerningham, who was one of Mary's most faithful supporters, that the mayor of Rochester had come back to the loyalist side,

[30] *Chronicle of Queen Jane*, pp. 36–7.

along with some of Thomas Isley's men.[31] On the same day, the duke of Norfolk left London, not knowing that about 500 of his London troops had already agreed to defect to Wyatt. It appears that the French embassy had been involved in this treachery, and late that night the grand plan was discovered by Lord Cobham's steward. Cobham himself immediately passed this information on to the duke of Norfolk, urging him to advance no further into Kent, but he was Wyatt's uncle, and Norfolk did not trust him, quite reasonably, since at least one of his sons was in Wyatt's camp at the time. Thus, on the morning of Monday 29 January, the duke wrote to tell the Council that he intended to mount a frontal attack on Wyatt at Rochester bridge, though, in fairness, he did also enclose Cobham's warning letter for perusal by Mary's advisers.

Norfolk's plan to confront the rebels at Rochester would have been militarily suspect even without any defections from the royal army to Wyatt's side. Despite the addition of the contingents provided by Sir Henry Jerningham, Lord Cobham and Sir John Fogge, Norfolk was still heavily outnumbered, having about 1,200 men to Wyatt's 2,000. With the cathedral city at their back, the rebels had the more defensible position and, inexplicably, Norfolk did not even inform Southwell and Abergavenny that he was going to advance, so that they were unable to provide vital reinforcement. It seems that faulty intelligence, supplied by Sir George Harper, had convinced the duke that Wyatt's men were demoralized.[32] In the event, humiliation followed for the elderly Norfolk and the royal cause. As secretly prearranged, probably with the leader alone, a large proportion of the London trained bands ('Whitecoats') cried, 'We are all Englishmen! We are all Englishmen! A Wyatt! A Wyatt!' and marched over to join the rebels.[33] Norfolk had no option but to retreat towards London, with Jerningham, the earl of Ormonde, and the remnants of Mary's army. Ominously for her, the outcome was widely celebrated in the city itself, though it would soon emerge that Wyatt had not been greatly strengthened by the arrival of the defectors.[34] Lord Cobham meanwhile withdrew to his castle at Cooling, the next day writing to inform the Council that he would not be able to hold out if attacked, and that he had already received an overture from his nephew Wyatt.[35] At midnight on January the 30th, Lord Abergavenny finally heard the news of what had happened at Rochester. He went to see Sheriff Southwell, accompanied by a few of his men, but morale in his force was low, most of his troops either going home at this point, or defecting to Wyatt. Not unreasonably, Abergavenny was furious at Norfolk's failure, news of which spread rapidly through Kent and the neighbouring counties.[36] Even so, very few

[31] 11/2 no. 22 (1); CSPDM, pp. 25–6.
[32] 11/2 no. 30; CSPDM, p. 31; Chronicle of Queen Jane, pp. 37–9.
[33] Chronicle of Queen Jane, pp. 37–9.
[34] Ibid., p. 39; Proctor, Historie, p. 70.
[35] 11/2 no. 24; CSPDM, pp. 28–9.
[36] 11/2 no. 30.

joined Wyatt's army at this point. There was no general uprising, and no French military intervention. On the other hand, there was also now no royal army to resist Wyatt if he headed straight for London, but he was extraordinarily reluctant to do so. At the end of January 1554, there seemed to be no strong upsurge of support for Mary, and it rather looked as though many hoped Wyatt would succeed without their needing to act. The Council was conspicuously failing to give a lead, and the Queen's policies on religion and marriage continued to be divisive, even among those who wanted her to remain as queen. She gives every appearance of having been utterly bewildered by her situation at this stage, while Southwell and Abergavenny were paralysed in Kent, doing nothing until Wyatt finally began his leisurely march to London on 30 January.[37]

On the next day, the Council finally agreed that Renard should ask Charles V for a fleet to patrol the Channel and prevent French intervention.[38] Serious efforts were also made, at last, to raise more troops, an example being set by Lord Treasurer Paulet, who produced a force of 500 infantry and 200 cavalry.[39] Others did not follow, however, and when February began, Mary still had no effective army to field against Wyatt. Thus there appeared to be no alternatve to Gardiner's policy of appeasement and on 31 January a new attempt was made to open negotiations with Wyatt. The royal offer was to set up a special commission to discuss the rebel grievances concerning the Queen's marriage, and also to pardon all those who returned to their homes within twenty-four hours of agreement. Confident of success, Wyatt demanded securities for the keeping of these terms, and it appears that neither side was negotiating sincerely. Since 26 January, royal proclamations had claimed the rebellion to be heretical as well as seditious, while Wyatt insolently demanded custody of the Tower of London and even Mary herself as a hostage. The daughter of Henry VIII was not going to take lying down such a slur on a sovereign, and Gardiner's strategy now lost all credibility, especially when he made the mistake of advising the Queen to withdraw to Windsor. The Council now had to take practical action at once, beginning with a proclamation that day, in London and Southwark, that Wyatt and his men were all traitors. On the next day, having at last stopped listening to the prevaricating and conflicting advice of the councillors, Mary took her fate into her own hands.

At three o'clock in the afternoon on 1 February, she rode from Westminster to the City Guildhall, escorted by peers and armed guards. There, before the mayor, corporation and citizens, she first read out Wyatt's latest communication, in which he had demanded control over her and the Tower, and then launched into the speech of her life. This anticipated Elizabeth's famous Tilbury discourse of 1588, against Spain, with the

---

[37] *CSP Span* XII, p. 55.
[38] *CSP Span* XII, p. 64 (1 January 1554).
[39] *CSP Span* XII, p. 58.

advantage that it actually happened, and is recorded in several contemporary sources.[40] In the manner of her father, Mary seems to have produced a speech that was powerful, passionate, and not without a touch of expedient dissimulation, such as her grandmother's critic, Alfonso de Palencia, would have expected and disapproved of, at least when done by a woman. According to Proctor, she told the assembly that she had just sent two of her privy councillors to try to bring Wyatt round by peaceful argument, so as to avoid bloodshed if possible, even though he was an arrogant traitor. Daringly, she asserted that, as far as her marriage was concerned, she had done everything with the consent and advice of her whole Council, and in the interest of the entire kingdom. In a purple passage of characteristic Tudor and Trastamaran eloquence, she proclaimed that she was already 'married to the Common Weal', for which she wore a wedding ring, that of her coronation, which she would never take off. She promised that she would never desert her people, and would if necessary shed her blood to protect them.[41] By all accounts, this speech had the desired effect of galvanizing her subjects and, after she had delivered it, she returned to Whitehall to co-ordinate action against the rebels. Paget and his supporters now dominated the Council, and preparations were at last made to fight Wyatt's approaching army. The earl of Pembroke was appointed as chief captain, with the support of Lord Admiral Howard, while the lord mayor of London was charged with the security of the city. It was still not certain what kind of welcome Wyatt and his men would receive from ordinary people, but the outcome would soon be known.

In Kent, on 2 February, Southwell and Abergavenny finally made a move, agreeing to amalgamate their forces in Rochester on the 4th. The day before, after a slow journey which included a desultory 'siege' of Lord Cobham's Cooling castle, Wyatt arrived in the south bank suburb of Southwark, in the full expectation that he would be allowed to march straight across London Bridge into the city. Instead, he found the southern defences of the bridge closed against him, and armed citizens waiting on the north bank. Despite this, the rebels were civilly received in Southwark and allowed to stay there until, on 6 February, they set off westwards to cross the Thames at Kingston. While in Southwark, the troops were generally well behaved, though they did apparently find time to vandalize Bishop Gardiner's library at Winchester House, which was his London palace, thus conveniently destroying evidence of its owner's involvement with Edward Courtenay. There was also talk of freeing Gardiner's religious prisoners. Thus the situation in London remained nervous and unstable between 3 and 6 February. All river traffic was ordered to remain at moorings on the north bank, and military musters were held on

---

[40] Proctor, *Historie*, p. 77 [= Loades, *Chronicles*, pp. 35–6; Machyn, *Diary*, p. 53, Anon., *A Diary of events regarding* [. . .] *the rebellion of Thomas Wyatt* [. . .]], in *Accession*, ed. Malfatti, pp. 66–8, 133–4.

[41] Loades, *Chronicles*, p. 36.

St James's Fields, between London and Westminster, and also on Finsbury Fields. Citizens wore armour at work, since a surprise attack was feared. The London Court of Common Council was suspended, though the courts at Westminster continued, with lawyers wearing armour under their robes. However, good news came in the form of the collapse of the duke of Suffolk's attempt at a rising and his subsequent arrest. Buoyed up by this success, the Council offered a pardon to all Kentish rebels who surrendered, except for Robert Rudstone, Sir George Harper and Henry Isley, with the price of £100 being placed on Wyatt's head.[42]

At about four in the morning on Wednesday, 7 February, Londoners were awoken by news that the rebel forces were approaching from the west, having crossed the Thames at Kingston with some difficulty, thanks to a partly broken down bridge and a guard on the right bank. The planned military musters that day were brought forward from six o'clock, an emergency Council assembled in Mary's bedchamber and the more panicky urged her to flee, but once again she showed the spirit of her Tudor and Trastamaran ancestors. The Tower chronicler commented that 'many thought she wolde have ben in the felde in person'.[43] She sent assurance to her people that she would stay in Westminster until the trouble was over. In fact, had Mary been better protected, though Clinton and Pembroke now assured her that she would be safe in their hands, Wyatt's much weakened army would have posed no threat at all. He had had to abandon his artillery in the Thameside mud at Kingston, and by the time he reached London, Pembroke's forces were on parade to meet him. Wyatt's troops were so tired after their forced march that he waited until daybreak before sending them into action. The resulting skirmishes had a somewhat unreal, though nonetheless threatening air. The indecisiveness of commanders and men, on both sides, should perhaps not be too harshly judged. In the confused circumstances of Mary's first regnal year, it was extremely hard to know who was on whose side, and many Englishmen must have shared their Queen's natural inclination to avoid bloodshed where possible, a trait she had displayed the previous August towards Jane Grey's supporters and had publicly reaffirmed much more recently in the Guildhall. For much of the day, loyal and rebel forces manoeuvred round each other, between Westminster and Ludgate, and at one stage the porters felt it necessary to shut the gates of St James's Palace in order to protect the Queen. In the end, Wyatt was refused entry to the City, and immediately realized that he had lost. He and his retreating men were then attacked by royal troops at Temple Bar and chased back to Charing Cross. There had been no repeat of the defections at Rochester, and when a herald appeared and urged him to surrender, thus avoiding further bloodshed, Wyatt meekly complied, and was led to Court a pris-

[42] 11/ no. 28; *CSPDM*, pp. 30–1; *Chronicle of Queen Jane*, pp. 43–5.
[43] *Chronicle of Queen Jane*, p. 48.

1 Both regal and intimate, this portrait by Hans Eworth of Mary as Queen in 1554, wearing the jewel which Philip sent her, shows her gaze steady, with a touch of apprehension probably connected with her marriage and its implications.

2 This medallion, attributed to Lucas Horenbout, shows Mary at the age of about nine. Already looking serious and intense, even before the turmoil that would overwhelm her and her mother, she proclaims what would become a lifelong attachment to her betrothed, Charles V, by wearing round her neck a pendant inscribed ' Emperour'.

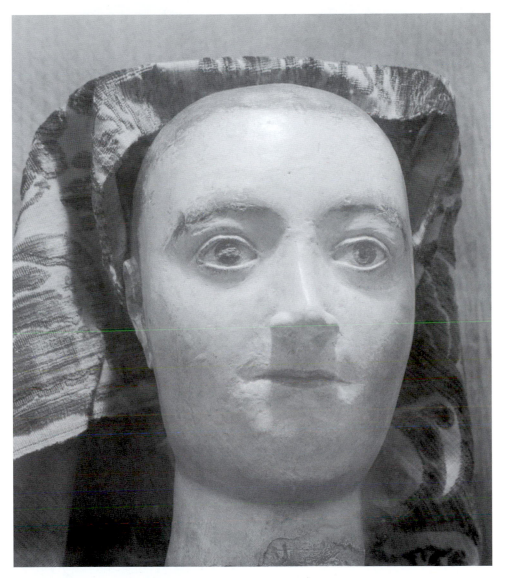

3 Mary's effigy, carried in full regalia to her funeral above the coffin containing her body, is stylized and ceremonial, but nevertheless manages to convey her steadfastness and determination in life, and perhaps beyond it.

4 This gold ryal of 1553, modelled on the Spanish *real*, shows Mary as sole sovereign, with her hair down, wearing the closed Imperial crown and holding the sword of state in her right hand. She is seated, greatly out of scale, in a ship with a banner bearing the letter 'M' in its prow, and a large Tudor rose beneath her feet. The obverse shows crowns, English heraldic lions and fleurs-de-lis, the whole design stressing the independent, sovereign status of the kingdom ruled by Henry VIII's daughter.

5 The silver sixpence of Philip and Mary (1554) shows how the new problem of a dual monarchy was solved in the coinage. The heads of the King and Queen, with some attempt at portraiture, face one another beneath a 'floating' Imperial crown, something that worried many English people who wanted no foreign ruler. On the reverse are the quartered arms of Philip and Mary, emphasizing their joint sovereignty.

6 The initial capital of Mary's first Queen's Bench plea roll, for Michaelmas term 1553, is a dramatic painting which emphasizes the belief that her arrival on the throne was divinely ordained. She sits, under a gold canopy of estate, her hair down and wearing the Imperial crown. She holds the sword of state in her right hand and has above her a haloed dove, representing the Holy Spirit, and a winged angel on either side of her. In the background, on her right, two angels lead her, while on her left there are three figures on horseback, perhaps representing her flight from Hunsdon. An army in the distance may well be her forces at Framlingham.

7 In the Michaelmas 1554 plea roll, Mary and Philip appear on their thrones, in their parliament robes and under a canopy of estate. Perhaps provocatively, Philip, as well as Mary, is crowned, and holds the sword of state, while she holds an orb and sceptre. There is no landscape background, and the gold crown, drawn on top of the letter 'P', also indicates joint sovereignty, an unwelcome prospect for many. The body-language of the two is very different. While Mary gazes intensely and magisterially forward, Philip appears almost to be lolling, as though relaxed in his new role as King.

8 The undated illumination of Mary touching a young woman, apparently for the skin-disease scrofula, also known as the 'King's evil', is rich in symbolism, both in the main picture and in its border. Mary sits beside a covered prayer-desk bearing a large book, probably a missal or breviary, while a priest, standing behind her wearing a surplice and gold stole, reads from another book. The woman is plainly dressed, and kneeling behind her in the manner of a sponsor, with his hands on her shoulders, is a tonsured cleric, apparently in a Benedictine habit and probably from the restored Westminster abbey community. Since the early Middle Ages, touching for the 'King's evil' had been a symbolic power of divinely sanctioned monarchy in France and in England, but the items in the border add to this. There are what appear to be 'cramp rings' which, when sanctified by a monarch's touch, were believed to help a woman in the pain of pregnancy and childbirth. There is an hour glass at the top of the Italianate picture and a skull at the bottom to emphasize mortality, while the pomegranates, and particularly the split one, are not only the personal emblem of Mary's mother Catherine, but also represent fertility. The irony of this juxtaposition is plain to all.

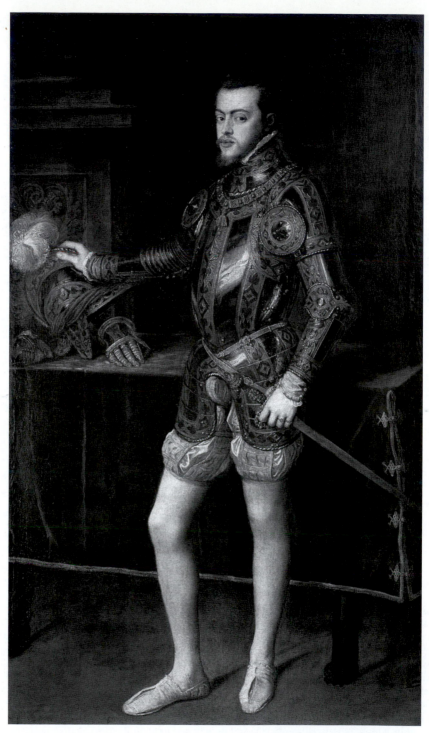

9 Painted by Titian, when Philip was on his European tour from 1548 to 1551, this masterly portrait encapsulates the vanity of a man who attracted girls everywhere he went as well as Philip's desperate desire to achieve personal glory in battle. The Habsburgs wanted the rest of Europe to see them in this way, whatever the reality.

10 Pompeo Leoni portrayed various members of the Habsburg family, and this silver, painted, bust of Philip, dated between 1556 and 1560, shows him as a man in his prime, serious and determined, as he lived through the stressful years of his marriage to Mary and his conflicts with France and the Papacy.

11 Hans Eworth, or Ewoutz, makes this interesting attempt at portraying the recently married royal couple. Some have mocked Philip's spindly legs, which were nonetheless much admired around Europe, and there is a certain stiffness in the figures, but the painter tries to convey the uneasy combination of monarchy with the domesticity that the unpretentious setting and the two little lap-dogs appear to suggest.

12 This anonymous portrait of Cardinal Reginald Pole, dated to *c*.1550 before he was appointed
for the second time as papal legate to England, derives from work by Sebastiano del Piombo,
who as well as being a fine painter was a papal official. Mary's counsellor certainly appears here
as the 'Englishman Italianate' which his successor as archbishop of Canterbury, Matthew Parker,
famously declared him to be.

13 Hidden behind a large Baroque altarpiece at the east end of Antwerp cathedral is this fine specimen of Flemish glass, commemorating the chapter of the Order of the Golden Fleece, which was held there in 1556 after Philip had become ruler of the Netherlands. He and Mary are shown crowned and wearing the robes of the Order. Philip has behind him his patron, Philip the Apostle, while Mary, who looks rather like her image on one of her coins, has with her the Virgin Mary and the baby Jesus. The couple's respective prayer-desks display their personal arms, while the infant Christ holds an orb to represent the universal rule over the world which the Habsburgs claimed. Mary and England are thus accepted and integrated into this grandiose but unsuccessful scheme.

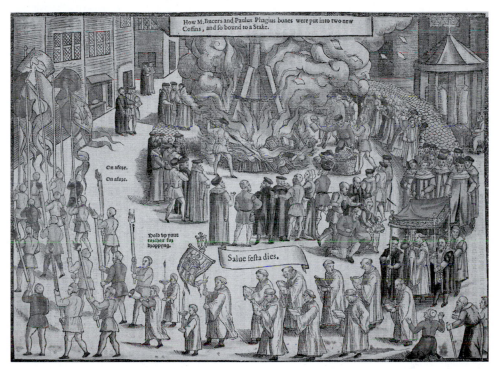

How M. Bucers and Paulus Phagius bones were put into two new Coffins, and so bound to a Stake.

On afore.

On afore.

Hold up your torches for dropping.

Salue festa dies.

14 The repressive side of Mary's religious policies is spectacularly represented by this woodcut, in the 1570 edition of John Foxe's *Acts and Monuments*. It shows the burning, in Cambridge Market place during the legatine and royal visitation to the University, of the personal remains and books of two Reformers who had been brought to Cambridge by Archbishop Thomas Cranmer, Martin Bucer and Paul Fagius. The picture conflates a succession of events into one drama, and there appears to be an attempt to portray known individuals in the procession, which includes banners, flaming torches for the burning, acolytes and singing clerks, the Blessed Sacrament in a monstrance under a canopy, and numerous members of the University. The festal hymn *Salve festa dies* (Hail thee, festival day) is being sung, but two bystanders in the bottom right-hand corner look horrified. What they are witnessing has many of the characteristics of a Spanish *auto de fe* of the period.

15 Framlingham castle, Suffolk, a stronghold of the Howard dukes of Norfolk, was in royal hands when, for a vital few days in July 1553, Mary used it as her base to prepare to fight, as she thought and expected, for the throne against the duke of Northumberland's army. In the event, there was no battle, but Framlingham was well prepared for attack, and it was there that Mary formed the inner core of her future government.

16 Both inside and out, Winchester cathedral has been a great deal changed since Mary and Philip were married there, on 25 July 1554, but the majestic outline of the building remains very much as it was, especially the transepts and the tower over the crossing.

17 Greenwich palace, on a south bank site now occupied by the old naval college, played a vital role in the lives of the Tudor royal family. Mary had a strong attachment to it, and particularly to the Observant Franciscan church, shown here with a narrow spire to the west of the palace itself. This building was still there in 1544, eight years after her father had dissolved that order in England, when the distinguished Antwerp artist Anthonis van den Wyngaerde made this drawing.

oner, by Sir Maurice Berkeley. After this, the remaining rebels also surrendered, and many were arrested.[44]

Mary had been badly frightened, and her first reaction seems to have been to seek vengeance, but her Council soon started disagreeing again, and she was once more subjected to conflicting advice on how severely the rebels should be punished. The whole episode also made a big impression abroad, where it seemed that Mary's regime had been shown to be insecure, while debate raged, both in England and abroad, over whether Wyatt and his fellow conspirators had been primarily 'heretical' or anti-Spanish. Reginald Pole, writing to his friend Cardinal Giovanni Morone from Brussels on 3 February 1554, linked the rebellion to Mary's planned marriage to Philip, though he still had few details of what had happened, and indeed was then still happening.[45] By the time Pole wrote on 9 February to Cardinal Innocenzo del Monte, Wyatt was in custody and more information was available, including details of the Rochester debacle and Mary's Guildhall speech. Pole's view, natural for one then resident in Habsburg Brussels, was that the French were behind the Kent rising, and that its main aim was to prevent the Spanish marriage. Knowing that Charles V's commissioners were then busy negotiating the relevant treaty with Mary's ministers, Pole now felt that it was vital that she should marry Philip, despite the opposition, in which up to then he had shared. She should do so not only to cement the Anglo-Habsburg alliance but also to assist the restoration of the Roman religion in England, and his own return to the country as legate.[46] Whatever impression of openness on this subject Mary may have given at the Guildhall, she, like Pole, knew that negotiations for her marriage to Philip were heading towards the point of no return.

Already, at the beginning of January 1554, Philip and Mary's alliance was being regarded in Rome as virtually a fact. On 1 January, Charles V's ambassador to the Holy See, Don Juan Manrique de Lara, spoke on the subject to Julius III, just after he had celebrated Mass for the Feast of the Circumcision of Jesus. In his delight, Julius went so far as to say that his contentment at the news was greater than it had been on the day of his own election to the Papacy. Among other things, he told Manrique that God was preserving Philip to do Him great service, and in particular to achieve the 'reduction' of England to the Roman obedience, which he regarded as a certainty. He immediately ordered a 'brief' (*breve*) to be drawn up, and despatched that same day to Charles to congratulate him on securing this marriage. Thus it was clear in Rome that Philip had had no personal role in the negotiations.[47] However, on 10 January, the Cardinal of Perugia wrote to Philip himself from Rome, saying that the

[44] Ibid., pp. 49–50; 'The Narrative of Edward Underhill', in *Tudor Tracts*, ed. A. F. Pollard (London: Archibald Constable, 1903), pp. 170–98.
[45] BAV MS Vat. Lat. 6754, fols 100r–101v [*CRP*, 2, p. 258 (no. 799)].
[46] BAV MS Vat. Lat. 6754, fols 101v–103v [*CRP*, 2, p. 259 (no. 801)].
[47] AGS E 879–95 (copies of the relevant papal brief in AGS E–01).

papal chamberlain (*cameriero*) was on his way to Spain to congratulate him on the marriage.[48] Then, while the Wyatt rebellion was still in progress, the Pope returned to the matter in further instructions to Monsignor Antonio Augustino, whom he was sending to England itself.[49] This document indicates that Julius was aware, at least in general terms, of the instability of Mary's kingdom at that time, and that it urgently needed to be brought back 'from perpetual damnation to the true way of salvation'. The marriage of Philip and Mary would play a vital role in this, along with the support of Julius himself and of foreign princes.[50] Most important of all, though, if Mary were to obtain her desired husband, was the attitude taken by Philip himself during the winter of 1553–4.

It is quite clear that the English conspirators were right to fear the imminent arrival of the Spanish prince in December or January. A series of notes, made at the Spanish Court, indicates that, by Christmas 1553, negotiations for the marriage were advancing rapidly and urgently. The anonymous writer records, in what appear to be the minutes of a meeting, possibly of Philip's Council, that on 24 December the Prince received various letters and also 'the minutes of the powers', which probably means those given to Charles V's commissioners to the English Court. The next note states that a letter received from England urged that the affair should be pressed forward with 'diligence', and that information should be obtained on how many men and horses Philip should take with him to England. To this was added a note that 'a person should be sent [presumably to Mary] with some jewel (*alguna joya*)'. Also on Christmas Eve, it was reported in the Court at Valladolid that the French were issuing communications and intelligence (*pláticas y intelligençias*) in an effort to obstruct the negotiation of the Anglo-Spanish marriage treaty. Charles V had also written to say that bribes (*dádivas*) should be used to overcome French diplomatic efforts, and that the ports, presumably in Spain, England and the Netherlands, should be secured. Interestingly, the minute adds that 'the marriage of Elizabeth should be undertaken', a comment which suggests that Mary's sister was regarded in Brussels as a security risk, at the very time when Wyatt and his allies were still hoping to enlist her in their plot. In a clear indication that, in December 1553, Charles thought his son's departure for England was, or should be, imminent, a further minute states: 'That His Highness [Philip] should immediately move closer to the coast, so that, hearing the advice of our ambassadors in England [Renard and his colleagues] he may depart'. Discussion then seems to have moved to the size of the military force (*gente de guerra*) that should accompany him. In addition, merchant ships should be enlisted in the navy to secure the Channel during Philip's passage.[51] On 7 January 1554, it was reported at

---

[48] AGS E 880–34.
[49] AGS Libro de Versoza 4, fol. 251r.
[50] AGS Libro de Versoza 4, fols 255–257v.
[51] AGS E 98–373.

the Spanish Court that more correspondence had been received from the Imperial ambassadors in England. Philip had seen it and, despite the legal protest that he had just filed, which is not mentioned in this document, now declared the matter of the marriage to be of the greatest importance, and that he was entirely well disposed towards it. His mood is described as 'very gallant and happy (*gallardo y alegre*)'. At this stage, before hostilities had broken out in England, the Prince proclaimed that he was eager for ambassadors to come from Mary, was keen for the marriage pledges (*albriçias*) to be arranged, and anxious to leave for England as soon as possible. The fears of his opponents in Devon and Kent were not, therefore, entirely unfounded, though it is impossible to know what Wyatt and his friends would have done, once Courtenay had had his interview with Gardiner, if they had known that Philip would not in fact arrive until the end of July. In any case, this Spanish document exudes a sense of urgency, and a strong desire on the part of the Prince to be at Mary's side.[52]

By 19 January, it was known in Valladolid that the terms of the marriage treaty had been agreed between Charles V's commissioners and the English Council. Charles V had confirmed them, and Philip was now awaiting a copy, to be despatched to him by sea. He was aware that the English wanted him to send his powers (*poder*), so that his representative could validly swear that when he married he would abide by the terms of the treaty. Significantly, the document states that although Mary's Council wanted him to maintain the laws and liberties (*leyes y fueros*) of England, 'the Queen assures him in secret of all the rest', this being a clear indication of her willingness to bypass her advisers in this matter of the heart. The French continued to cause trouble, but it is obvious that, in mid-January 1554, Philip was still generally expected to set out very soon for England.[53] He was certainly under pressure to do so from the Emperor's commissioners in London. On their behalf, the count of Egmont sent more than one urgent appeal from there on 21 January, by which time it was clear even to Mary's councillors that rebellion was in the offing.[54] On 1 February, the day of Mary's Guildhall speech, Egmont sent another letter to Philip from London, in which he reported on Wyatt's rebellion, and once again begged to know the Prince's departure date.[55] Between then and July, when Philip finally set out, he and his Spanish court were kept well informed of events in England, and left in no doubt as to Mary's desire to see her future husband as soon as possible.

At home in England, the immediate question was how the rebels, and near-rebels, should be treated. In contrast to what had happened in the previous July and August, a severe line was generally taken. About a hundred

---

[52] AGS E 808–1; Biblioteca del Palacio MS II – 2251, fol. 34 (letter from Ramón de Tassis to Cardinal Granvelle, 7 January 1554).

[53] AGS E 98–372.

[54] AGS E 808–2, 3.

[55] AGS E 808–9, 10.

men were executed, including leaders such as Wyatt himself and the duke of Suffolk. His daughter Jane and her husband Guildford were also put to death, and Elizabeth and Courtenay were imprisoned in the Tower.[56] Two of Mary's supporters wrote works of celebration: John Proctor's *The historie of Wyates rebellion* (London, 1554), and John Christopherson's *An exhortation to all menne to take hede and beware of rebellion* (London, 1554), interpreted her victory, as she seems to have done herself, as a manifestation of God's will, by which all her policies, including marriage to Philip, were vindicated. Thus the messages she received in one ear, from Spain, Brussels and Rome, appeared at last to correspond to what was actually happening in England. In reality, though, Philip's suit was no more popular after 7 February than it had been before. Wyatt was regarded as a martyr by many, indeed his severed head was illicitly removed from its pole at St James's apparently as a relic, and the Queen continued to receive conflicting advice on how to proceed against his posthumous fame.[57] Renard urged, with greater enthusiasm than ever, the execution of Elizabeth and Courtenay, whom he regarded as utterly compromised by the Wyatt affair and as a permanent threat to Prince Philip's security. The longer the Spanish party's arrival was delayed, the more frantic Renard became, and the more ready he was to sow dissension within the Council, between Gardiner and Paget, and between the councillors in general and the Queen. The second parliament of the reign was summoned for 5 April 1554, and proved to be acrimonious. The government was greatly discomfited by the acquittal, on 17 April, of Sir Nicholas Throckmorton, on the charge of rebellion. The action of this jury appears to reveal more than residual discontent in London against government policy.[58] Also, Mary had a public row with the peers over the passing of bills of attainder against Suffolk, Wyatt and their associates. These bills were introduced in the Commons on 23 April, had three readings there, and then received three more readings in the Lords on 4 May. However, the peers asked for changes, something that infuriated the Queen, and she also failed to gain parliamentary approval both for the disinheritance of Elizabeth and for the extension of the treason laws to protect Philip by name.[59] On top of all this, it was clear by this time that Mary's prince was dragging his feet, and Renard and Charles could not speed up his arrival in England. His initial plan, so much talked about in December and January, of coming quickly to England to support Mary, had evidently been abandoned, and then his wife-to-be took the traditional religious line of refusing to marry during the penitential season of Lent.

On 6 March, the betrothal *per verba de praesenti* finally took place, but Philip sent Mary no personal message, and was represented at the ceremony by the count of Egmont, who was Charles's man, and indeed had

[56] Loades, *Two Tudor Conspiracies*, pp. 89–127.
[57] *CSP Span* XII, p. 221; *Chronicle of Queen Jane*, p. 74.
[58] *CSP Span* XII, p. 221.
[59] Loach, *Parliament and the Crown*, pp. 91–2, 98, 102–3.

negotiated the marriage treaty. At about 1.30 in the afternoon, he was brought to meet the Queen and her Council at Westminster, in the presence of the Blessed Sacrament, as when Mary had first decided to marry Philip, at the end of the previous October. The two spouses' ratifications were exchanged and then, on her knees, Mary declared that she was marrying, not out of carnal affection, but solely for the honour and prosperity of her kingdom. This oath moved her councillors to tears, and afterwards she knelt again, to pray to God that she should be able to fulfil the terms of the treaty. Egmont then presented her with an engagement ring, which, significantly, was provided not by Philip, who had still not even written to her, but by the Emperor. Even so, she proudly showed it off to all present.[60] In mid-March, when Philip had still not written to Mary, and his father, too, was becoming anxious, an ambassador, Juan Hurtado de Mendoza, arrived from Brussels with a portrait of the Prince by Titian.[61] In fact already on 27 March, Philip, having been urged to bring reinforcements to the Netherlands, had told his father that he would set out with between 5,000 and 6,000 extra troops to help him, as well as a large retinue of his own for England. It would obviously take a long time to assemble such a force, and the focus of both father and son was evidently shifting from Mary's England to the Habsburg Netherlands.[62] This was ominous: the spouses were living in very different worlds, which would not easily be reconciled. Meanwhile, once the betrothal *per verba de praesenti* had taken place, an embassy, led by the earl of Bedford, was despatched to Spain to escort Philip to England, and in April Sir John Mason followed with a contingent of forty well-connected young Englishmen.[63] At the same time, preparations began in England to fit out both Mary's guards and Philip himself with suitably magnificent clothes.[64]

According to the eyewitness account, published in Zaragoza late in 1554, by Andrés Muñoz, the initial reaction of many of Philip's courtiers and retainers to the proposed English expedition was not enthusiastic, primarily because of the personal costs involved. The assumption seems to have been that the Spaniards who accompanied Philip to England would make no financial gain from the enterprise, and he tried to compensate for this by offering expenses payments (*ayudas de costa*). Philip's high steward (*mayordomo mayor*), the duke of Alba, was placed in charge of the English operation, and this proud, forceful and choleric military commander began by carrying out a full review of all the Prince's staff. No one was offered any direct reward if he agreed to go to England, but all were given the option of staying in Spain. Not surprisingly perhaps, those in Philip's privy chamber (*Cámara real*), as well as his intimate gentlemen

---

[60] *CSP Span* XII, p. 142.
[61] *CSP Span* XII, p. 162.
[62] *CSP Span* XII, pp. 103–5, 176; Rodríguez-Salgado, *Changing Face*, p. 84.
[63] *CSP Span* XII, pp. 170–1.
[64] *CSP Span* XII, p. 178; Vertot, *Ambassades*, ii, pp. 275–80.

servants (*gentiles hombres de la boca* – literally 'mouth', or 'bouche' of court), all volunteered to serve their master in the enterprise. The other officials were also interviewed individually, and their responses varied. Most of them did agree to go, but Muñoz is clear that most of them reacted as though, by going to Mary's remote and heretical kingdom, they would be heading for their own doom. In a somewhat desperate and melodramatic manner, they assured their master that they were 'ready and prepared to go, and die in his royal service', hardly the most optimistic of attitudes. Once the senior courtiers had made their decision, they in turn interviewed the Spanish and German troops at court, and as a result it was agreed that the Spanish royal guard should stay in Valladolid to protect Philip's heir, Don Carlos. They were apparently exempted from the English expedition on the grounds that they had already done their foreign duty when they accompanied Philip to Germany and the Netherlands in 1548–51. Those who agreed to go did so simply out of duty to the Prince and not apparently through any enthusiasm to see England. In the end, Philip had to order some of them to go, and appointed as his 'Captain of the Spanish Guard' the count of Feria, Gómez Suárez de Figueroa, who would become deeply involved in English affairs.

The reluctance of the Prince's servants to accompany him to England was not only due to their fear and suspicion of their destination. Because a long stay was evidently anticipated at this early stage, many, especially the bachelors, had to dispose of their property, and thus risk their entire future. According to Muñoz, when one servant told his master that he was going to sell all his possessions, the Prince replied, 'I'm not going for a wedding, but to fight', presumably in the Netherlands, though perhaps in England. In the event, ten years later, some of these courtiers were still paying off the debts they incurred then.[65] Although he was not after all to marry Maria of Portugal, Philip also agreed, at their request, to take with him some of the former Portuguese servants of his late mother, Isabella. He also took personal charge of settling the families of his married servants, sending the children to Alcalá de Henares, to be looked after there, and at this point he heard that English ambassadors were on their way. They landed on the north coast of Spain, at Laredo, and when they arrived in Valladolid they were given a lavish and festive reception, including chivalric tournaments and the Spanish war game, played with sticks on horseback and used to keep the cavalry in trim, the *juego de cañas*.[66]

Whatever would follow, the English adventure (*jornada*) seems to have been viewed, by Philip at any rate, in the spring of 1554, as a cause for optimism and delight. This would change within a few months. Since February, Renard had been keeping Philip informed of the state Mary was in economically, which was dire and which led her to request a loan from

[65] AGS *Diversos de Castilla* 6–65–8.
[66] Andrés Muñoz, *Viaje de Felipe Segundo a Inglaterra*, ed. Pascual de Gayangos (Madrid: Sociedad de Bibliófilos Españoles, xv, 1877), pp. 1–12.

Charles of 200,000 crowns.[67] Eventually, her main financial representative in the Netherlands, Sir Thomas Gresham, obtained a loan on the commercial market instead, but Philip still had to supply the sum involved from Spanish New World revenues. In view of this, the Spanish were naturally concerned that, having subsidized Charles's military action in Germany and elsewhere, they were now going to have to do the same for Philip in England.[68] Once Easter had come and gone, Mary was again willing to contemplate a wedding. At last, too, the Prince sent her, by the hand of the marquis of Las Navas, the jewel (a large diamond set in a rose) which had been talked about at the Spanish Court since the previous December. Philip had decided on 11 May to send a gift to Mary, but it was not until the beginning of June that Las Navas finally landed at Plymouth, amidst a tumult of artillery fire, to be met by Lord Admiral Howard. Even now, the Prince's efforts were trumped by his father, who sent Mary more jewels, and a set of Flemish tapestries depicting his own expedition to Tunis, back in 1535. These fine examples of Arras work would be stored in Whitehall Palace, once Philip and Mary reached London together.[69] When she learned of the arrival of Las Navas, Mary left London on 16 June to meet him at Guildford on the following day. She then travelled via one of the bishop of Winchester's castles, at Farnham, to another, Bishop's Waltham, to await her new husband's arrival.

Meanwhile, Philip now estimated that he would be travelling to England with a retinue of between 3,000 and 5,000, on board a large fleet which would be manned by up to 6,000 additional soldiers and sailors.[70] A factor delaying Philip's departure for England was the need to secure a regent to govern Spain and its overseas territories in his absence. In the event, his nineteen-year-old sister Juana, whose husband the Prince of Portugal had died on 2 January 1554, three weeks after she gave birth to the future King Sebastian, was drafted in to fill this vital post. In May 1554, having left her son behind in Lisbon, she presided over a meeting of the cortes of Castile at Valladolid and, at the same time (8–10 May), the count of Egmont and the earl of Worcester arrived in the city with documents for the formal ratification of the treaty and confirmation of the betrothal *per verba de praesenti* which had taken place two months earlier. Then at last, on 16 May, the Prince and his entourage left Valladolid and headed for Santiago de Compostela, the Galician shrine of Spain's patron saint, the Apostle James the Greater, arriving on 23 June. There the English ambassadors, the earl of Bedford and Sir John Mason, were awaiting him, and Philip finally signed the much-talked-about marriage contract on 25 June.[71]

[67] *CSP Span* XII, p. 115.
[68] *CSP Span* XII, p. 304.
[69] *CSPDM*, p. 51; *CSP Ven* VI, p. 898; *CODOIN*, iii, p. 521.
[70] AGS E 808–11 (Philip to Egmont).
[71] *CSP Span* XII, pp. 286–7.

A short but vivid account of Philip's voyage to England is given by Juan de Barahona (Varaona), in a letter which he wrote to a relative, Antonio de Barahona, then at home in Alcañices (Zamora).[72] He describes how Philip embarked at La Coruña on Thursday, 12 July and set sail the following day, at about eleven in the morning. He had about eighty ships with him, while about forty others remained in harbour there, under the command of Don Luis de Carvajal, in order to pick up the soldiers who had still not arrived. From 13–15 July, Philip was able to sail with a fair wind, though it almost reached gale force at times. On Monday 16 July, the lookouts spotted Cape Ouessant (Ushant) in France, and the next day came the first sight of England. Two days later, Philip's fleet met the thirty-eight galleons which had been despatched from England and Flanders to secure the Channel. The two fleets saluted each other with gunfire, and Philip sailed on past the Isle of Wight, where another salute was fired from the castle at the Needles. At four o'clock in the afternoon, the Spanish fleet dropped anchor between Southampton and the Isle of Wight. According to Barahona, this was the 'ysla de Viqz, que por otro nombre la llama Amadís la ynsula firme' (which Amadis calls by another name, Insula Firme). The allusion is to one of the most popular Spanish romances of chivalry, *Amadís de Gaula*, in which the hero travelled to such an island, off the coast of Britain.[73] That night, though, while Mary and her subjects were gearing up to receive the new king, continental affairs brusquely intruded. Apparently while he was still at sea, Philip received news that the French had captured two of his father's fortresses, Marienbourg and Dinant. Shocked by these two military defeats, Charles wrote to his son on 29 June, instructing him to despatch immediately the troops and money that he was bringing in his fleet. After all the delay, and with Mary desperate to meet her new husband, Philip now wrote to his father, begging for leave to go in person to the Netherlands after only ten days in England, with barely time for the wedding. In the meantime, he gave orders that none of the soldiers or horses on board his ships should disembark in England. Charles soon replied, saying that the French had now withdrawn, thus lessening the danger in Flanders, and telling his son to stay and enjoy his marriage, but to send the troops and cash to the Netherlands as soon as he could. Philip duly complied, keeping the whole army on board ship, and sending both men and money on to Flanders under the command of Don Alonso Pejón. Everyone was seasick and it was raining, but at least Mary's prince was now in English waters.[74]

[72] Juan de [Varaona] Barahona, *Viaje de Felipe II a Inglaterra en 1554 cuando fue a casar con la Reina Doña María* [Bibl. Escorial V–II–4, fols 444–9], ed. Martín Fernández Navarrete, Miguel Salva and Pedro Sanz de Baranda, in *CODOIN*, i, pp. 564–74, also ed. and trans. C. V. Malfatti, in *Accession [. . .]*, pp. 139–45, 79–89 (trans.).

[73] Garci Rodríguez Montalvo, *Amadís de Gaula*, ed. Juan Manuel Cacho Blecua, 2 vols (Madrid: Cátedra, 1987–88).

[74] Juan de Barahona, 'Dos cartas dirigidas a su tío Don Antonio de Barahona', I = Escorial MS V–II–4, fols 444–52.

Finally, on Friday 20 July, an ornate barge came out to Philip's ship from Southampton, with eight English nobles on board. They were courteously welcomed by the Prince, and then invited him to go ashore with them on the barge, which he duly did. Barahona says that the English peers much appreciated the fact that Philip placed this degree of confidence in them. The Prince of Spain boarded the barge with the duke of Alba and six or seven other Spanish nobles and told all the other grandees and nobles to follow, in other small craft. When Philip disembarked, artillery salutes were exchanged between the Spanish fleet and the shore batteries of Southampton. Once the English barge was alongside the jetty, the earl of Arundel went on board with a delegation of English nobles, which included Edward Stanley, earl of Derby, whom Barahona characterized as a descendant of another figure out of *Amadís*, Galvanes, king of 'Mongaza'. To the Spaniards, Mongaza was the Isle of Man, over which the Stanleys did indeed claim 'kingship', along with the neighbouring islands.[75] Arundel presented Philip with the insignia of the order of the Garter, these consisting of two heavily bejewelled blue bands, one to be worn round the leg on ordinary occasions and the other, even more elaborate, to be worn as a collar on special festivals. Mary had spent some time with a goldsmith at Gardiner's palace of Bishop's Waltham to ensure that these signs of honour were as splendid and correctly styled as possible. The royal Horse Guards were drawn up on the jetty as a guard of honour, dressed in the same livery as Philip's own guards, along with a delegation of the English nobility. Mary's own musicians played, and the master of the queen's horse, Sir Anthony Browne, presented the Spanish Prince with an elaborately caparisoned white jennet. Browne mounted Philip on this horse and, on foot in the Spanish style, led him to the church of the Holy Rood in Southampton, where he said his prayers, before adjourning to the house alongside, which had been elaborately decorated in his honour.[76] Philip and his entourage were no doubt meant to note, as they duly did, a red and white hanging, with gold thread, which referred to Mary's father as Supreme Head of the Anglican Church (*caput supremum ecclesiae anglicanae*).[77] The Spaniards were soon to see more signs of what had happened to the English Church in the two previous reigns.

Queen Mary's longed-for husband, Philip, loomed so large in the history of the rest of her reign and her life that it is important to consider the character of the man who came from Spain in July 1554 to marry her. If Mary herself has often had a 'bad press', the same has generally been at least as true of Philip. In 1855, the American historian J. L. Motley published what a much more recent biographer, Henry Kamen, has

[75] Barry Coward, *The Stanleys: Lords Stanley and Earls of Derby, 1385–1672* (Manchester: Manchester University Press for the Cheetham Society, 1983), p. 101.

[76] *CODOIN*, i, pp. 564–7; Barahona, 'Dos cartas', in *Accession*, ed. Malfatti, pp. 79–82, 139–41.

[77] BNM MS 1750, 'Papeles tocantes a Phelipe Segundo', ii, no. 7, fol. 95r.

described as 'the classic portrait of Philip as the incarnation of evil'.[78] For Motley, Mary's husband was a 'mediocrity, pedant, reserved, suspicious, his mind was incredibly small, . . . he was a bigot, grossly licentious, cruel . . . a consummate tyrant'. In reality, Philip inherited from his mother, Isabella of Portugal, a strong sense of self-discipline and composure, which meant that he almost never expressed his feelings openly in public, and generally appeared to others to be cold and aloof, in contradiction to common foreign stereotypes of the 'Iberian character'. Importantly, in view of his marriage prospects in 1553–4, he also inherited from his mother, and from her entourage, a deep love of Portugal, its people and culture, which had been a long-standing feature of his Trastamaran fore-bears. In particular, one of those Portuguese who had earlier come to Spain with his mother, Ruy Gómez de Silva, was one of his closest confidants and associates, and accompanied him to England.

Much has been made by some English historians of Philip's supposed lack of ability in languages, which is said to have prevented him from achieving anything much as King of England. In assessing more generally his character and ability, at the time of his marriage to Mary, it is worth looking at his education in more detail. Although rarely with him in person, Charles paid a great deal of attention to his son's educational progress, and this was hardly surprising given that he had taken the acute risk, in contrast to Mary's father, of not remarrying after the death of his wife Isabella in 1539, and hence depended totally on their only son to carry on the line. By February 1536, when the boy was eight years old, the Emperor received reports that his schooling was proceeding well, and he was able to read both Spanish (Castilian) and Latin with some skill. By March 1540, Philip's spoken Latin had improved; he was using it regularly in class, and was also beginning to compose in the language. By this time, he was playing the *vihuela*, a popular old Spanish form of the guitar, under the tutorship of Luis Narváez, and his Latin tutor, Juan de Zúñiga, told him that he must become a good Latinist since he was going to rule over people who spoke so many languages that he would need this effective tool of international communication. He was taught history and geography by the distinguished humanist Juan Ginés de Sepúlveda, who thought that it would be advisable for the Prince to speak to foreign ambassadors directly in Latin, so as to avoid the ambiguities which might arise from employing interpreters between different vernaculars. Philip never became a humanist himself, and was not a great intellectual, but he was certainly not lacking in skill, at least in Spanish and Latin, and had some competence in Italian and Portuguese.[79] From 1541, when he reached the age of four-teen and became marriageable by contemporary standards, the Prince of Spain acquired Christóval Calvete de Estrella as his tutor in Latin and

[78] Henry Kamen, *Philip of Spain* (New Haven, CT and London: Yale University Press, 1997), p. xi.
[79] Ibid., pp. 3–5.

Greek, and Honorato Juan in mathematics. It does appear that Philip was genuinely diffident in speaking languages other than Spanish, though his comprehension was probably very much greater than his oral ability.[80] One of Philip's traits, from childhood, was a deep love of music, both religious and secular, which went far beyond princely duty: from the 1540s to the end of his days, in 1598, he never travelled without his 'chapel', and he himself seems to have played the viol as well as the *vihuela*. Although he had problems with his health, and his fair hair and pale colouring made him seem sickly, he also had a strong taste for the manly pursuits which were then associated with nobility and royalty, in Spain as well as England. He loved jousts and tourneys and fully shared the popular taste of western Europeans for the romances of chivalry.[81] It remained to be seen how all these characteristics would manifest themselves when he came to England.

On Saturday, 21 July, Philip and his immediate entourage stayed in Southampton, being joined by the English household which had been chosen for him. Barahona recounts how it was on this day that the duchess of Alba, wife of Philip's high steward and military commander, disembarked at Southampton. It had not been Charles's policy for wives and families to travel to England, but no one could presumably gainsay the duchess, probably not even her normally proud and haughty husband. In deference to her rank at the peak of the Castilian upper nobility, she was met on the quayside by all the Spanish courtiers and a large number of their English counterparts. According to Barahona, her first experience of the less formal English court etiquette caused her initially to recoil when the earl of Derby, king of Man in the Amadís romance, came forward and moved to kiss her on the lips, but her aristocratic poise seems to have returned before a diplomatic incident could occur. It was, however, a sign of the problems in Anglo-Spanish relations, at the personal level, which would soon begin to emerge.[82] Sunday seems to have been a quiet day in Southampton for the Spanish party, apart from their attendance at Mass, which was observed by a large number of the English public. No contemporary source mentions whether or not Philip availed himself of the services of his own chaplains and other Spanish clerical advisers, though it is very likely that he did so, even if he also put in appearances at English churches. On Monday the 23rd, still in the pouring rain which had dogged them since their arrival, Philip and his entourage finally left Southampton for Winchester, where Mary was now lodged in the bishop's Wolvesey castle to await them. Philip wore a red felt cloak in a vain attempt to keep the rain off his black velvet and white satin clothes and his jewels. The Spanish were escorted by the English welcoming party which had originally met them, and Barahona estimated that there were 3,000 altogether,

[80] Geoffrey Parker, *Philip II*, 2nd edn (London: Cardinal, 1988), pp. 6–7.
[81] Ibid., pp. 9, 13.
[82] Barahona in *Accession*, ed. Malfatti, pp. 82, 141.

with an additional company of 300 archers, though he makes no comment on the reaction of the English public. Before they left Southampton, Bishop Gardiner himself had brought Philip a diamond ring from the Queen, and the Prince in turn despatched one to her, in the custody of his confidant Ruy Gómez de Silva. Before they reached Winchester, they were met by a further 200 horsemen, who were to escort them into the city. At the Hospital of St Cross, less than a mile to the south of the city, Philip changed his soaking clothes in the master's lodgings, and then the Anglo-Spanish party rode to the west door of the Cathedral, arriving at about six in the evening. There Bishop Gardiner and five other bishops were awaiting them in full pontificals, along with numerous canons, vested in copes, and a large crowd of onlookers, who pressed forward to see their king-to-be. Once the clergy had welcomed Philip, a *Te Deum* was sung in procession, as he was led into the choir for Sung Vespers, after which the royal party left to go to their lodgings in the former Prior's Hall, now the deanery, on the south side of the Cathedral.

After dusk, when they had had supper, came Philip's crucial first encounter with Mary herself. Accompanied by a large number of English and Spanish nobles, he walked to Wolvesey and entered by what Barahona describes as a 'secret door', climbing a winding staircase to the long gallery where the Queen was awaiting him. In Spanish accounts, the short walk from the deanery to Wolvesey was transformed into a magical adventure, in the midst of lush gardens and fountains, such as Amadís would have seen.[83] Mary was wearing a black velvet dress, decorated on the front with pearls, a black wimple embroidered with gold, and many jewels, and was accompanied by six councillors and six of her ladies. Mary came forward to greet him at the door, and they kissed each other on the mouth in the English manner, then walking hand in hand across the room to sit together under a canopy of estate. According to Barahona, who should be accurate in this respect, they spoke to each other for more than an hour, Philip in Spanish and Mary in French, which they would have found mutually comprehensible. Mary was about to be immersed once again in the flow of Spanish which had not surrounded her for more than twenty years. It was apparently at this point that she made her first attempt to teach Philip some English, so that he could say 'Good-night, my lords all' to the ladies and gentlemen of her Court. After their conversation, the couple stood up, and Philip introduced all the Spanish nobles and knights to the Queen. Once they had kissed hands, the couple parted, the Spanish returning to their lodgings.[84]

After this excitement, on top of the fatigue from the journey, Philip seems to have slept late in the deanery, then dined in state, and it was not until three in the afternoon that he left, with his English and Spanish courts, to visit the Queen once again. She had already sent him, that

[83] Muñoz, *Viaje*, p. 70.
[84] Barahona in *Accession*, ed. Malfatti, pp. 83–4, 141–2; *CSP Span* XII, pp. 319–22.

morning, two new suits, one of bejewelled, gold brocade and the other of crimson brocade. Philip walked on his own, so that the people might see him, though with a large aristocratic escort, and when he entered the courtyard of Wolvesey castle, a large orchestra began to play. Mary met her betrothed in one of the halls at Wolvesey, where they exchanged compliments before moving into the other hall, where they talked for a while, before Philip returned to his lodgings. After this, Philip asked two of his entourage, Don Antonio de Toledo and Don Juan de Benavides, to fetch Pedro Laso de Castilla, who was present as the ambassador of Charles V's brother, Ferdinand, king of the Romans, and also Don Hernando de Gamboa, who was representing Ferdinand's son, the king of Bohemia. Philip met these Habsburg embassies in the hall of the deanery, and received their credentials with due ceremony. After this he did the same for the ambassadors of Venice and Florence, acting very much as a king, even before he was married to Mary, let alone crowned in his own right. Finally, late that evening, he went to see the Queen again, duly kissing her ladies-in-waiting in the familiar English manner ('few attractive and many ugly ones,' according to Barahona), before finally retiring once more to his lodgings.[85]

With due diplomatic tact, the wedding of Mary of England and Philip of Spain took place on Wednesday 25 July, the feast day of St James the Greater, patron of Spain. Once again, the weather was rainy, and it is not known whether Philip and his courtiers were told of the Winchester legend that if it rained on 15 July, the feast of the translation of the relics of their Saxon patron St Swithun (d. 862), whose shrine in the cathedral had been destroyed in 1538 on Henry VIII's orders, it would do so for the following forty days. In order to provide maximum visibility for the congregation, a wooden walkway had been constructed, and covered with carpets, stretching from the west door of the cathedral to the entrance to the choir. It was about four feet high, and ended in a dais, about four yards square, which covered the whole of the central nave adjoining the choir screen. On this platform was an octagonal railed dais, where the marriage ceremony itself was to take place. The cathedral was decorated throughout with carpets, flags and standards, and Gianfrancesco Commendone says that it was kept closed until Philip arrived at midday.[86] However, the Scottish observer John Elder, who confirms that security was tight ('the dores beyng very straightlie kepte'), states that Philip in fact entered the cathedral at ten in the morning, accompanied by his English and Spanish courts in their most splendid attire.[87] Dressed in the French style to match Mary's clothes, he wore a bejewelled white doublet and breeches and an ornate golden mantle which had been given to him by the Queen, as well as the

[85] Barahona in *Accession*, ed. Malfatti, pp. 84, 142; John Elder, *The copie of a letter sente into Scotlande [. .]*, in Loades, *Chronicles*, p. 42.

[86] Commendone, *Accession*, pp. 51, 125; Barahona, in *Accession*, ed. Malfatti, pp. 85, 142.

[87] Elder in Loades, *Chronicles*, p. 42.

ceremonial collar of the order of the Garter, with which he had been presented the previous Friday. He walked down the nave on the 'catwalk', until he reached the platform.[88] He went to the far end of it and down a few steps on the left, to where a canopy had been prepared for him, and sat on a chair underneath it, in front of the rood loft. In the centre, there was a table in front of the screen and, to the right, looking from the west end, were another chair and canopy for the Queen. A chair still preserved at the cathedral is held to be the very one on which Mary sat.[89] This positioning clearly indicated Mary's superiority, as reigning monarch of England. As Philip awaited her arrival, he was accompanied by the ambassadors whom he had met the day before, seated according to precedence – the Emperor's, that of the King of the Romans, and those of Bohemia, Venice and Florence – as well as a few English and Spanish knights.[90] The French ambassador did not make an appearance. According to Elder, the Queen entered the west door of the cathedral at about 11.30 a.m., though the Tower chronicler suggests that Philip had to wait just half an hour.[91] Mary was accompanied by the leading noblewomen of the kingdom and was, in Commendone's phrase, 'richly dressed and adorned with jewels'.[92] Her train was carried by the marchioness of Winchester, assisted by the lord chamberlain, Sir John Gage.[93] According to the records of the royal wardrobe, Mary wore a dress in the French style, of rich, delicate cloth (*tissu*), with wide border and sleeves. Under this were a fashionable short-sleeved jacket known as a partlet, a high collar and a white satin kirtle.[94] The Queen's attire, though splendid and fashionable enough, may have been regarded as slightly subdued, and Commendone comments that her ladies and gentlemen were not as splendidly dressed as Philip's entourage.[95]

Seated on his chair at the eastern end of the nave, the Prince was at once alerted to Mary's arrival, and when she finally reached him she went to her place on the platform, beside the dais, and immediately began to pray, Commendone supposed, in thanks to God for bringing her to this moment at last. Then Gardiner and five other bishops, in full pontificals, emerged from the choir and climbed the five steps on to the railed dais, which Commendone thought looked like a pulpit, where the marriage ceremony would take place. They stood in the centre, with Gardiner, as

[88] *Chronicle of Queen Jane*, p. 167.

[89] Flora Winfield, ed., *The Marriage of England and Spain* (Winchester: Winchester Cathedral, 2004), pp. 21–2 (article by J. A. Hardacre).

[90] Commendone, *Accession*, pp. 51, 125–6; Barahona, in *Accession*, ed. Malfatti, pp. 85, 142.

[91] *Chronicle of Queen Jane*, p. 168.

[92] Barahona, in *Accession*, ed. Malfatti, pp. 85, 142; Commendone, *Accession*, pp. 51, 126.

[93] *Chronicle of Queen Jane*, p. 168.

[94] BNM MS 1750, fol. 99v; Porter, *Mary Tudor*, p. 323, with plate showing a reconstruction of the dress made by Tanya Eliott for the exhibition in Winchester Cathedral in 2004 commemorating the 450th anniversary of Philip and Mary's wedding.

[95] Commendone, *Accession*, pp. 51, 126.

diocesan bishop and also Lord Chancellor of England, in the most prominent place. Philip and Mary then joined the bishops, along with the
various foreign ambassadors, and also the earl of Bedford and Lord
Fitzwalter, who had earlier gone to Spain to 'fetch' the Spanish prince, as
well as the lord great chamberlain, the earl of Oxford. All others remained
outside the rail. As the royal couple and Gardiner stood ready to begin the
ceremony, Don Juan de Figueroa, a doctor of laws and councillor of
Charles V, as well as regent of the chancery of the kingdom of Naples,
came forward and presented letters patent to Philip, whereby the Emperor
conferred upon him the title and full rights of king of Naples. Once he
had received it from Figueroa, this fateful document was read out, in its
original Latin, by Gardiner, in his capacity as Lord Chancellor, and he
followed this with an explanation of the contents in English, for the benefit
of most of those present.[96] Philip's new rank entitled him to a sword of
state, and after some delay one was produced, to match Mary's as Queen
of England.[97] No doubt reflecting internally on his own previous opposition to the marriage, Gardiner then announced that the time had come
for the two parties to be married in person, according to the terms of the
articles which had, in Commendone's phrase, been 'approved by the
Emperor and ratified by the King [of Naples and very soon to be of
England] and accepted by the Queen'. Gardiner then proceeded to
display the marriage treaty itself, in its final Latin form, afterwards giving
a short commentary on it in English.[98] He stated that the articles of the
treaty were 'not ignorant to the wholle Realme and soe confirmed by
Parlament soe that there needed no further rehersal of this matter'. In his
speech about the treaty, he adopted a legalistic approach, stressing that it
had been approved by the 'whole estates of the said Realme of Spayne',
as well as by the English parliament.[99] Then, at last, he proceeded to the
marriage itself, first asking if anyone present knew of any reason of
kinship or preceding claim, which would prevent the two parties from
entering into marriage. According to Commendone, there was a pause
before those present answered that there was none (*nullus est*). Bishop
Gardiner then read out the dispensation from Pope Julius III, which
allowed these two close relatives to marry, thus effectively authenticating
both the marriage and the religious ceremonies involved.[100] So that all
those present should fully understand what was happening, the marriage
service, which for most people had traditionally taken place at the church
door, was conducted in both English and Latin, the former being

[96] Barahona, in *Accession*, ed. Malfatti, pp. 85, 142–3; Commendone, *Accession*, pp. 85,
126. The text of Charles V's resignation of Naples to Philip (AGS Patronato Real 42–13)
is reproduced in *Accession*, ed. Malfatti, pp. 156–7; see also P. T. Tyler, *England under the Reigns
of Edward VI and Mary*, 2 vols (London: Richard Bentley, 1839), ii, p. 432.
[97] College of Arms MS WB, fols 157r–158r; Samson, 'The Marriage', p. 218.
[98] Commendone, *Accession*, pp. 52–59, 126–9.
[99] College of Arms MS 1, 7, WB, fols 157r–158r.
[100] Barahona, in *Accession*, ed. Malfatti, pp. 86, 143.

recounted later, in writing by the Tower chronicler and the latter by
Commendone. When Bishop Gardiner asked who would give the Queen
away, four peers came forward – the marquis of Winchester and the earls
of Derby, Bedford and Pembroke, who acted for the whole kingdom, in
the obvious absence of any close male relatives. The congregation then
cried out in support of the Queen, and the exchange of vows took place
in Latin with a repetition in English. Perhaps reflecting their own religious
perspectives, sources differ on exactly how tokens were exchanged. The
Tower Chronicle has Philip placing the plain gold ring, which Mary had
chosen, on a bible held by Gardiner, to be blessed, as well as three hand-
fuls of fine gold, while for Commendone Philip's gold coins were laid upon
a missal held by the bishop. Mary's chief attendant, the fourteen-year-old
Lady Margaret Clifford, daughter of the earl of Cumberland and a relative of the Queen, then placed her similar tokens on the book, after which
the couple kissed, while the earl of Oxford held the Queen's hand, and
then the earl of Pembroke, bearing a sword, moved to stand before the
new King of England.

Once they were man and wife, the couple, accompanied by those who
had been with them on the platform before the rood screen, followed the
bishops into the choir, while trumpets sounded, and proceeded to their
places, under canopies at either side of the High Altar, on which the High
Mass was celebrated by Gardiner and two of his fellow bishops, with the
three others acting as servers. Mary is said, in a Spanish source, to have
gazed at the crucifix on the altar, but neither she nor Philip could have
avoided seeing behind and above it the gaps in Bishop William Waynflete's
fifteenth-century retro-screen, which had been deprived of its images in
Henry's reign.[101] At this most sacred moment in their lives, both were
powerfully reminded of the task of religious restoration which lay before
them. Philip's response, like that of his new wife, was to demonstrate his
devotion as visibly as possible, both to his compatriots and to his new English
subjects.[102] When the time came for the exchange of the peace, which in the
traditional service had been done with the passing of a token (pax), the King
left his place and went across to the Queen and gave her a kiss of peace. The
sources do not specify whether the couple received communion and, given
the Catholic usage of the period, it seems quite likely that they did not, thus
avoiding any awkwardness for Philip, who in principle should not have
received the ministrations of a bishop who was still formally in schism from
Rome. In any case, once the communion was over, Garter King of Arms
went to the foot of the High Altar, accompanied by heralds, and proclaimed
the 'style' of the King and Queen, in which their titles were combined in the
alternating manner which had been adopted in 1475 by Mary's grandparents and Philip's great-grandparents, Ferdinand and Isabella of Spain,
with precedence accorded to those of the Queen:

---

[101] BNM MS 9937 Florián de Ocampo, *Sucesos acaecidos, 1550–1558*, fol. 717.
[102] BREscorial MS V.ii.3, fol. 437r.

Philip and Mary, by the grace of God King and Queen of England, Naples, Jerusalem, Ireland and France, Archdukes of Austria, Dukes of Milan, Burgundy and Brabant, Counts of Habsburg, Flanders and Tyrol . . .

At the end of the Mass, which was presumably celebrated according to the use of Sarum, the Queen and her lay company received biscuits and spiced wine (hippocras), as a traditional social substitute for the consecrated elements which had been consumed by the clergy. A canopy was then brought to the foot of the altar by the leading peers of England, and under it Philip and Mary processed down the nave, out of the cathedral and to the wedding banquet in the east hall of Wolvesey castle. There, a raised platform had been built at one end, up several steps, and on this was the royal table, at which Philip and Mary sat with Bishop Gardiner, though he was placed some distance away from them. In the hall there was an impressive display on side buffets of gold and silver-gilt plate, which was not used for the serving of the lavish variety of courses on which the noble and knightly company no doubt fell with glee after the lengthy ceremonies in the cathedral. About 140 people sat down to eat, with the privy councillors and ambassadors at one table, and two more tables for the other English and Spanish guests, though some of the latter seethed because the service at the high table was performed entirely by English courtiers.[103] At the other end of the hall, a dais had been set up for the musicians, about whom Commendone tantalizingly says: 'who during the whole meal went on playing excellent music, as they had also done during the Mass'. During the banquet, a knight appeared, accompanied by four heralds, and made a speech celebrating the marriage, after which the King invited the English councillors to drink a toast. Once the meal was over, at about 5 p.m., the party went on into the night, in the west hall, with dancing and other revels, though at an early stage Philip and Mary retired to eat supper in a more secluded chamber.[104] Finally, Bishop Gardiner blessed the marriage bed, and the royal couple retired. The whole day had been a spectacularly cosmopolitan event, including, according to one anonymous Spanish participant, 'Spaniards, Englishmen [and women], Germans, Hungarians, Bohemians [Czechs], Italians', and even Martín Cortés, marquis of the Valley (of Oaxaca), who was the son of Hernán, the conqueror of Mexico.[105]

Philip was apparently up at seven on the morning of the 26th, starting his day with Mass, while Mary followed the English custom by spending that day in seclusion with her ladies.[106] Her husband, meanwhile, continued to transact continental business, as he had done even on the day before the wedding, no doubt profiting from the presence in Winchester, in addition to his Spanish court, of a significant group of ambassadors,

[103] BNM MS 9937, fol. 137v.
[104] Commendone, *Accession*, pp. 59–61, 129–31.
[105] BNM MS 9937, fol. 133v.
[106] Barahona, in *Accession*, ed. Malfatti, pp. 88, 144.

whose interests stretched as far as Italy and the Slav lands. On Friday 27 July, a tortured scene of divergent protocol took place in the Queen's lodgings. Mary sent two of her ladies-in-waiting, the countesses of Kildare and Pembroke, to fetch the duchess of Alba, who had asked to be allowed to kiss hands. According to Barahona, who may have been an eyewitness, Mary waited for her in one of the halls of the Bishop's Palace, standing up when her gentlemen escorted the duchess in. Mary seems to have been anxious to show gracious condescension to this senior Castilian peeress. She advanced to the middle of the hall to meet her visitor, who asked insistently to kiss her hands. The Queen had other ideas, however, attempting to kiss her in the English manner. Extraordinarily, given the stiffness and formality of the current Burgundian style at the Spanish court, the duchess is said to have grabbed Mary's hands and kissed them anyway. After this, Mary led her by the hand to a platform, where they were to converse, with the marquis of Las Navas interpreting her French and the duchess's Spanish. Once again, though, problems of protocol arose, which proved to be prophetic of the awkwardness of Anglo-Spanish relations in the succeeding months and years. Mary asked the duchess whether she wanted a high seat or a low one, and the latter replied that she wanted the Queen to sit, while she herself, with her lower status, would sit on the floor. In response to this, Mary herself tried to sit on the floor, but her clothes would not allow it, and instead she ordered two small stools to be brought. Even then, it took her a long time to persuade the duchess to sit on one of them, but eventually she did so and Mary apparently asked her many questions, probably about her new husband and about Spain, before the duchess left to return to her lodgings. Also on the 27th, the Queen received the ambassador of Ferdinand, King of the Romans, who gave her as a wedding present a diamond valued at more than 30,000 ducats.[107] Finally, on Sunday 29 July, the King and Queen appeared once more together in public, to dine with the earls of Arundel and Pembroke and, in the meantime, the Spaniards had paid a visit to the Great Hall of Winchester castle, to see its greatest treasure, the supposed Round Table of King Arthur.

Referring to this visit, Porter remarks that Philip and his party 'did what tourists do, and visited the local sights', in particular this one, but there was far more to the visit than that.[108] There is a clue in Juan de Barahona's description of the voyage of the Spanish fleet to England in July 1554. When referring to the Isle of Wight, he adds that 'by the people of the main island [England] it is also called Amadis', a reference to a cycle of chivalric romances which was immensely popular at the time throughout western Europe, especially in Spain.[109] The Spanish, from their avid reading and recounting of the romances which inspired all from king to peasant, thought England was the legendary land of Arthur, of the

[107] Ibid., pp. 88–9, 144.
[108] Porter, *Mary Tudor*, p. 326.
[109] Barahona, in *Accession*, ed. Malfatti, pp. 80, 139.

knights of his Round Table, and in particular of his beloved Amadis 'of Gaul'. Even in the heavy rain of St Swithun, Philip and his followers saw the Hampshire countryside as the very landscape of their chivalric dreams. As Muñoz wrote:

> He who devised and composed the books of Amadis and other similar books of chivalry, with imaginary countrysides and dwellings and enchantments, must without doubt have first seen the customs and strange ways in use in this realm, before he wrote about them. There is more to be seen in England than is written of in these books, because the dwellings that are in the country, the rivers, the fields, the beautiful flowered meadows, the cool fountains, are in truth a pleasure to see, and above all in summer.[110]

This rosy view would not last long, but it well represents the illusion which the hardy voyagers brought with them. By the mid-sixteenth century, the term 'Round Table' had developed three recognized meanings. Literally, as in the Winchester case, it meant a 'dining board', which would be laid on trestles and used for meetings and feasts. Secondly, as appears to be the case in Muñoz's writing, it could mean an institution, which might, according to the Arthurian texts, number up to 150 knights or more, who constituted an order in society on which the European orders of chivalry of the late Middle Ages and sixteenth century were modelled – notably the English order of the Garter and the Habsburg order of the Golden Fleece. Thirdly, the term 'Round Table' might refer, as in modern usage, to an actual meeting, in this case of the knights. Such 'round tables' might, in the Tudor period, consist of jousts, tournaments and other chivalric games and pursuits.[111] The recent meticulous study of the Winchester Round Table has concluded that it dates from the reign of Edward III, and was redecorated early in the sixteenth century, probably in or just before 1516, on the orders of Henry VIII. Thus the Spanish party saw, in 1554, a round table, painted in alternating segments of green and white (the Tudor colours), with a Tudor rose at the centre surmounted by the 'portrait' of a bearded king, purported to be Arthur himself. What has not always been observed is that, beyond the general chivalric tradition, Philip and his courtiers were returning to the scene of former Habsburg glory and at least apparent harmony between that dynasty and the Tudors.

Four significant episodes in the life of the house of Tudor took place in Winchester. In 1486, Prince Arthur, the older son of Henry VII and Elizabeth of York, was born and baptized there; in 1516 Henry VIII visited the city; in 1522 he returned with Charles, Emperor-elect, and

---

[110] Muñoz, *Viaje*, p. 113.
[111] John V. Fleming, 'The Round Table in Literature and Legend', in Martin Biddle *et al.*, eds, *King Arthur's Round Table: An Archaeological Investigation* (Woodbridge: The Boydell Press, 2000), pp. 10–12.

proudly displayed the restored and redecorated Round Table; and finally, in 1554, came the marriage of Henry VIII's daughter Mary and Charles's son Philip. Henry VII seems to have been convinced that the leading order of English chivalry, the order of the Garter, was closely connected with Arthur, and the connection was re-emphasized by his son Henry. New statutes were prepared for the Garter order in 1519–21, and put forward under the King's name at the Windsor chapter on St George's Day (23 April) 1522, in the presence of Charles of Burgundy and Spain, who, immediately after the meeting, accompanied the English King to Winchester to admire the Round Table. Thus, whatever the pragmatic reasons may have been for holding her wedding in Winchester, such as its nearness to Southampton and distance from turbulent London, by bringing her new husband here, Mary was closely following, in so far as a woman could, the tradition of her father and grandfather.[112] Philip was following his own family tradition. In 1506, on his way to sign the treaty of Windsor with Henry VII, his grandfather, Philip I of Spain, husband of Mary's aunt Joanna (Juana), had visited Winchester, and may well have seen the Round Table in its unrestored form. By then the Habsburgs, too, had a tradition of attachment to the figure of King Arthur which, at the beginning of the sixteenth century, took a remarkable form. In 1502, the Emperor Maximilian, great-grandfather of Mary's husband, began the planning for his personal monument, in the Hofkirche at Innsbruck. In the event he never occupied it, being interred instead at Wiener Neustadt, but in 1513 he had a statue made for it by Peter Vischler, which depicted, in the armour of the patron's own day, 'King Arthur of England'. Even more picturesquely, a drawing exists of another projected statue, which had been produced a few years earlier by Gily Sesselschreiber and purported to represent 'King Arthur of England, Count of Habsburg'.[113] With this background, it is hardly surprising that Mary and Philip's next journey, begun on 31 July 1554, took them to Windsor Castle, home of the order of the Garter.

In the meantime, the King and Queen visited Winchester College, where they left various traces of their presence. A celebratory ode, possibly written by the former warden of college, John White, who had recently become bishop of Lincoln but remained in Winchester for the celebration, was displayed in and around the cathedral during Philip and Mary's stay.[114] Its main theme was the opportunity provided by the marriage for Mary and Philip to produce an heir, while the Prince of Spain's English ancestry was also stressed. In addition, poems in Latin, composed by the scholars of the college, were collected in a bound manuscript volume and presented to the

---

[112] Pamela Tudor-Craig, 'Iconography of the Painting', in Biddle *et al.*, eds, *Round Table*, pp. 285, 310–11, 331–3.

[113] Martin Biddle, 'The Painting of the Table', in Biddle *et al.*, eds, *Round Table*, pp. 429, 447, 463–7.

[114] BL Cotton MS Vespasian F.III.23; also in *Chronicle of Queen Jane*, app. III, pp. 173–4.

royal couple.[115] Each pupil author's name is noted, as is the number of lines in his poem, the collection having been copied by one 'Purdie' for presentation to the King and Queen. The number of lines in the poems varies between an ambitious thirty-four and a humble two, and each boy's approach to the subject of celebrating the royal wedding, and the arrival of Philip as King, has its own individuality. Gabriel White, in his fourteen-line effort, while addressing the Queen 'Ave Maria', tactlessly refers to Philip as the spitting image of his father, the Emperor ('Caesaris ipsissima facies patris') (fol. 1r). The most prolific poet, Nicholas Hargreaves, employs a historical approach, referring to famous royal figures of Winchester, including Alfred, Canute and Harold, while Richard White shows off his Classical knowledge, alluding to Virgil's *Aeneid* (fols 3r–3v, 4r). In their enthusiasm, some of the schoolboy poets referred to the uniting of the English and Spanish crowns, Arkanwald Willerby asserting that Philip would be England's father, while Edmund Thomas alluded to the prospect of Queen Mary bearing a child and heir (fols 10v, 11r, 14v). The college accounts indicate that Philip and Mary gave money to William of Wykeham's foundation to celebrate their wedding. The King's 'almes' totalled £10 6s 8d and the Queen's £6 13s 4d, while the new bishop of Chichester, George Day, gave an additional pound. The choirmaster, Thomas Hyde, received £2 from this donation, while the seventy pupils of the school received £1 15s between them, and the sixteen Foundation choristers (queristers) 2d each. The authors of the Latin verses were paid 15 shillings in total, and the fact that the length of each poem was recorded in the presentation copy suggests that they may have been paid by the line.[116] The college bursar's accounts also record preparations for the royal visit, including the building of temporary accommodation on the college Meadow, which, given the adjacent water meadows south of the College, as well as the prevailing weather conditions, must have been a damp and insalubrious spot.[117] A fireplace in the Fellows' Library bears the monogram 'P', and may possibly be associated with the royal visit of 1554, but more certain is the connection with Warden John White's wooden 'Waterwork', or 'Painted Ceiling', now in Winchester's Westgate Museum. While the main ceiling appears to predate Mary's reign, its frieze, also on wooden boards, may have been added for the wedding and the royal visit to the college. In a style associated with the sixteenth-century Renaissance, the ensemble contains male and female heads and mythological figures, as well as biblical texts from the Book of Ecclesiastes.[118]

[115] BL Royal MS 12.A.xx.

[116] Winchester College Muniments Room, *Liber albus*, fol. 186v.

[117] Winchester College Muniments Room, MS 22210 *Custos domorum* (Bursar's Account, II, 1553–4).

[118] Elizabeth Lewis, 'A Sixteenth-century Painted Ceiling from Winchester College', *Proceedings of the Hampshire Field Club and Archaeological Society*, li (1995), pp. 137–65; Geoff Denford and Karen Parker, *The Westgate, Winchester, Medieval to Modern Times* (Winchester: Winchester City Council, 2005), pp. 8–11.

The efforts of the boy poets of Winchester might be compared with John Heywood's 'balade' in commemoration of the royal wedding.[119] In a poem of twelve stanzas, Heywood characterizes Philip as an eagle, presumably that of the Habsburgs, and Mary, perhaps inevitably, as a Tudor rose, while England is represented as a lion. The poem implies that there might have been violent conflict between the eagle and the lion, but asserts that the latter is:

No lion wilde, a lion tame
No rampant lion masculyne
The lamblike lion feminyne
Whose mild meeke propertie aleueth
This bird to light, and him asseur[e]th.

The tensions of the previous few months evidently underlie these verses, and the tone of the rest of the ballad is prayerful, offering thanks to God for the marriage and hopes for continuing unity in the future:

Whiche thanks full gyuen most thankfullie
To prayer fall we on our kneese
That it may lyke that lorde on hie
In helthe and welth to prosper theese
As faith for their moste high degreese
And hat all we, their subiects may
Them and their lawes, loue and obay.

And that betwene these twayne and one
The thre in one, one once to sende
In one to knit vs euerichone
And to that one, such mo at ende
As [t]his will only shall extende
Graunte this good god, adding thie grace
To make vs meete tobtayne this case.

The experienced Heywood represents the anxieties of the time more accurately than the schoolboy Latinizers.

In any case, during the early afternoon of that Tuesday, 31 July, the royal party travelled north to Basing House, the residence of the marquis of Winchester, where they stayed two nights before proceeding to Reading, spending the night there, and reaching Windsor on 3 August. By this time, Charles had made it absolutely clear to his son that, since the rains had affected the Continent as well and put an end to French incursions into Flanders, he might stay in England and enjoy his new married existence at

[119] Anon., *A Balade specifienge partly the maner, partly the matter, in the most excellent meeting and lyke mariage betwene our Soueraigne Lord, and our soueraigne Lady, the Kynges and Queenes highnes. Pende by John Heywod* (London: William Ryddell, 1554).

leisure.[120] At Windsor, Philip was duly installed in St George's Chapel as a knight of the Garter, close to the site, in the upper ward of the castle itself, where the 'Round Table' building projected by Edward III had once existed in part. Mary herself formally placed the collar of the order around his neck, but left him to preside over the chapter meeting, this being a man's role in her eyes.[121] In the first part of what passed for his honeymoon, though Habsburg business could never be forgotten for long, Philip did some hunting in Windsor Forest, before the couple moved to Richmond Palace on 11 August, no doubt for similar sport. There, news reached Philip that the French had returned to the fray, besieging Habsburg forces at Renty. As a result, Philip had, after all, to despatch some of his entourage to the Netherlands. On 17 August, the rest travelled with the native court to Southwark, ready for a formal entry into the capital on the following day.

When they were told that 'all suche triumphes and pageantes as wer devised in London agaynst their cumming thyther were finished and ended', the Eagle and the Rose sailed downriver on elaborately decorated barges, and disembarked at St Mary Overie Steps in Southwark. The King and Queen stayed that night with Bishop Gardiner at his riverside residence, Southwark (or Winchester) Place, and on the following day, at about two in the afternoon, set off in procession across London Bridge, in a triumphal enaction of what Sir Thomas Wyatt had vainly tried to do the previous February. Heads of executed rebels had to be removed from the bridge before the royal entry took place. Much attention was paid to the fact that Mary rode on the right and Philip on the left, indicating the superior status of England's Queen. They and their nobles, as well as the ambassadors, rode two by two, and were met on the bridge by the lord mayor of London, who presented the mace of his authority to the Queen as an act of submission, and duly received it back. After this, the procession headed into the City, led by the mayor, and with Philip and Mary each preceded by a sword. As they advanced, the guns of the Tower of London fired a salute. The preparation of the symbolic displays which greeted the King and Queen had been going on since May, and it was well understood that, with its highly dubious record in relation to Philip during the preceding months, the City had to work hard to prove its loyalty now. Two elaborate and expensive mythological giant figures, Corineus Britannus and Gogmagog Albionus, initially greeted the monarchs on London Bridge, bearing a Latin inscription which declared that the English must love Philip, who had been sent by God to be their king. The giants represented the medieval tradition, still current in the time of the Tudors, that Britain had been founded by Brutus, a Trojan not a Roman in this story, after the Greek capture of Troy. Corineus had been

[120] *CSP Span* XIII, pp. 7–13.

[121] Barahona, in *Accession*, ed. Malfatti, p. 89; Elder, in Loades, *Chronicles*, p. 43; Julian Munby, Richard Barber and Richard Brown, *Edward III's Round Table at Windsor* (Woodbridge: The Boydell Press, 2007).

an ally of Brutus in the defeat of the giants of Albion, led by Gogmagog, who had previously inhabited the British Isles. All this was duly noted by Spanish observers, such as Andrés Muñoz, who applied to the situation their knowledge of Arthurian tradition.[122] Most of the other displays which the royal couple met, on their way through London, focused on Philip, and on the historic Anglo-Spanish connections. The verses placed between the giants Corineus and Gogmagog give the flavour, here in a translation by Elder from the original Latin:

O noble Prince, sole hope of Caesar's [Charles V's] side
By God appointed all the world to guide,
Most heartily welcome art thou in our land . . .
But chiefly London doth her love vouchsafe,
Rejoysing that her Philip is come safe.[123]

On the Gracechurch Street conduit, the 'Nine Worthies' were painted, with a series of the highly popular proverbs and adages. The procession made a second stop at the 'Splayed Eagle', as in Heywood's poem, where various 'stories' were displayed, and the King was portrayed on horseback, 'all armed very gorgeously, and richly set out to the quicke'. Under this picture was written, in Latin: '*Divo Phi. Aug. Max. Hispaniarum principi exopatissimo*', which Elder translates thus: 'In honour of worthy Philip, the fortunate and most mighty Prince of Spain, most earnestly wyshed for'.[124] The triumphal arch contributed by the German Hanse merchants of their London headquarters, known as the Steelyard, included a mechanical statue of Philip on horseback, which reared and revolved as the King and Queen passed. A tableau on Cornhill showed four Philips – of Macedon, father of Alexander the Great; Philip 'the Arabian', who was alleged to have been the first Christian Emperor; and two of Philip of Spain's Burgundian ancestors, dukes Philip the Bold and Philip the Good. This display also included the Greek god Orpheus, in human form, marshalling other actors dressed as lions, wolves, foxes and bears. An elaborate genealogical device, in the style of a biblical Jesse tree, demonstrated Philip and Mary's common English descent, from Edward III through John of Gaunt. In a manner which would soon be imitated on their coins, at the top of this 'family tree' were the royal effigies facing each other, with the English Crown Imperial floating above them.[125] One awkward moment came when Gardiner spotted, in a pageant beside St Paul's, a painted figure of Henry VIII holding a book entitled *Verbum Dei*, shown as it appeared on the title page of the English 'Great Bible' of 1539. This was hardly surprising, given that two of the men chosen

[122] Muñoz, *Viaje*, pp. 80–2.
[123] Loades, *Mary Tudor*, p. 227.
[124] Elder, in Loades, *Chronicles*, p. 44.
[125] S. Anglo, *Spectacle, Pageantry and Early Tudor Policy* (Oxford: Clarendon Press, 1969), pp. 332–3.

by the Corporation, back in June, to 'devise' the pageant were Thomas Berthelet and Richard Grafton, who had successively printed English Bibles for the Crown, the latter, a noted evangelical, having been dismissed by Mary for printing Queen Jane's proclamation. Gardiner had this bible hastily painted out and replaced with a pair of gloves, such as were seen in many contemporary portraits. In addition to the *Verbum Dei* incident, hostile commentators immediately noted with disapproval the placing of the closed Imperial Crown of England above Philip's head, though not on it, but despite such notes of discord, the King and Queen seem to have had a happy day, which ended for them at Whitehall Palace.[126]

[126] Wriothesley, *Chronicle*, 2, p. 122; *Chronicle of Queen Jane*, p. 80; Richards, *Mary Tudor*, p. 166; *CSP Span* XIII, p. 53.

Chapter 8

A DUAL MONARCHY, 1554–1555

Now that Mary and Philip were married and had entered their capital as monarchs, they had to begin working out their system of government and establish the outline of their policies. As far as the Queen was concerned, the marriage itself had been a major aim, at least since September 1553, and that had been achieved, but in religion, which was perhaps her most fundamental concern of all, much remained to be done. The English Church had to be reunited with Rome, and Pope Julius III's cardinal legate to England, Reginald Pole, had to be admitted to begin work in the kingdom. Also, Philip's busy diplomatic activity, both before and after the wedding, clearly indicated that Mary's kingdom would have to adapt quickly to being not just a minor, though independent, offshore power, but also a link in a chain of Habsburg territories, in America as well as Europe, which was still expanding and had its own problems. Most immediately, Mary seems to have welcomed her new husband as a helpmate who would both provide her and England with an heir, preferably male, and relieve her of those duties of a sovereign which she did not think it fitting for a woman to perform. From Philip's point of view, the birth of an heir was equally important, seeing that his father was a widower and likely to remain so, while he himself had only one child, Carlos, from his first marriage to Maria of Portugal. Since Charles had by this time made it clear that he intended to renounce all his titles, and since their fate was still, in 1554, a matter of fierce dispute within the Habsburg family as well as outside it, Philip's future seemed then to depend very largely on how he played his role as King of England. He and his father saw the possibility, resulting from the Tudor marriage, of some kind of Anglo-Netherlandish state, which would more fully incorporate the historic insular kingdom of England, including Ireland as well as Wales, into the political structure of continental Europe. Yet, whatever his wife's personal attitude may have been, the marriage treaty severely restricted his ability to act as previous English kings had done. All the benefits and offices, lands, revenues, and 'fruits' of England were barred to him, and Mary retained absolute control of all public appointments, as well as her jewels.[1] Thus, in the autumn of 1554, it remained to be seen how the couple would get on politically, as well as personally.

---

[1] Hughes and Larkin, *Tudor Royal Proclamations*, ii, pp. 21–6; Glyn Redworth, ' "Matters Impertinent to Women": Male and Female Monarchy under Philip and Mary', *English Historical Review*, cxii (1997), pp. 597–613, at p. 598.

Despite her earlier misgivings about matrimony, Mary clearly invested a very great deal of her emotional capital in the marriage but her husband, though generally dutiful and solicitous, equally evidently did no such thing. To understand why, and gain an insight into the man who had emerged from Winchester Cathedral on 25 July 1554 as Philip I of England, it is necessary to go back to the previous decade and examine his first experience of foreign travel. The young Prince Philip of the 1530s had seemed to outside observers to be somewhat cold and reserved, but this *sosiego* (composure), as the Spanish called it, was in fact a consciously stoic posture, which demanded iron control of the emotions, especially in public, and resilience in the face of reverses. Yet in private all the Habsburg family was known for its passionate nature, its women being particularly strong and dominant. Philip too, behind his aura of charm and affability, was a strong, hardworking, determined and even aggressive man, who was certainly not overawed by his father and had a mind of his own.[2] Having become regent of the Spanish kingdoms and the New World colonies in May 1543, five years later Philip was to have his first experience of other Habsburg territories. Meanwhile, Charles V, having achieved a notable military victory over German Protestant princes at Mühlberg in April 1547, began to contemplate withdrawal from his immense dynastic and political commitments. His plans inevitably involved his son Philip, and early in 1548 he despatched the duke of Alba from the Netherlands to Spain with three commissions. One was to initiate a reform of the Spanish Court in accordance with Burgundian–Netherlandish arrangements, far more elaborate than those traditionally used, which were primarily Castilian in origin. Another was to deliver to Philip a set of instructions for the governance of the Habsburg dominions, which have become known as Charles's 'Political Testament'. The third, which was a crucial part of the Emperor's grand strategy, was to bring his son to the Netherlands, not immediately, but by means of a lengthy tour of what were meant to be his future dominions. On 2 October 1548, Philip left Valladolid with a large household, which included the duke of Alba and a number of others who would later accompany him to England, such as his beloved companion Ruy Gómez de Silva. He would not return to Valladolid, to pick up the reins of Spanish government once again, until 1 September 1551. A full eyewitness account of this extended 'Grand Tour' was provided by Juan Christóval Calvete de Estrella, and this may be supplemented by other sources, including an account by Philip's steward, Vicente Álvarez.[3] Even before they had left Spain, the Prince and his companions began what would prove to be a strenuous round of socializing

<hr/>

[2] Rodríguez-Salgado, *Changing Face*, pp. 7–9.

[3] Juan Christóval Calvete de Estrella, *El felicíssimo viaje del muy alto y muy poderoso Príncipe Don Phelippe [. . .]* [Antwerp, 1552], ed., with five studies by various authors, Paloma Cuenca (Madrid: Sociedad Estatal para la Conmemoración de los Centenarios de Felipe II y Carlos V, 2001); Vicente Álvarez, *Relation du beau voyage que fit aux Pays-Bas en 1548 le Prince Philippe d'Espagne*, ed. M.-T. Dovillée (Brussels: n.p., 1964); see also Kamen, *Philip of Spain*, pp. 35–49.

which would last throughout the whole trip. The tone was set in mid-October by a three-hour banquet consisting of about 150 dishes, which was offered by the cardinal archbishop of Trent in Barcelona, at the house of Philip's 'second mother' in childhood, Estefanía de Requesens. After delays caused by bad weather, as well as visits to various southern-French/Catalan towns, Philip and his party, travelling in a fleet of fifty-eight galleys under the command of the elderly Genoese admiral Andrea Doria, eventually landed at Savona on 23 November 1548, moving on to Genoa two days later. On 11 December the group advanced to Milan, of which Philip was duke. There, on New Year's Day 1549, the governor, Ferrante Gonzaga, laid on another elaborate feast, followed by dancing which went on until four the next morning. It is reported that Philip was particularly gallant towards the young ladies present, giving up his ducal chair to Gonzaga's daughter, and letting four other attractive women drink from his glass. A few days later, a chivalric tournament was held, in which Philip excelled, much to the delight and admiration of female spectators.[4]

The Prince of Spain's European tour continued in this vein, via Cremona and Mantua to Trent, where he arrived on 24 January 1549, while the Council of the Roman Church was suspended. By 21 March 1549, having passed through southern Germany, the Spanish prince was on Habsburg territory and there the entertainment and excesses became even more lavish. Charles was determined that his son should show himself to his future subjects, so in 1549 Philip spent several months touring the Netherlands, in a series of 'joyous entries' to towns that he would one day rule. In July and August he was in the southern provinces, then returned to Brussels, and toured the northern provinces in September and October. Once more, spectacular chivalric entertainments were laid on, until, at the end of May 1550, Philip was required to go with his father to the Imperial Diet, which would take place at Augsburg. According to Álvarez, his master spent his last night in Brussels, 31 May, 'on the tiles', chatting from the street to young ladies who were seated by their windows, dancing to bands in the moonlight, and not coming home to sleep.[5] Philip duly reached Augsburg, with his father, on 8 July 1550, and subsequently spent a year in southern Germany, struggling to accommodate himself to local customs, if his steward's account is to be believed.[6] For the rest of 1550, and into the following year, Philip continued to combine political business with a lively social life, but on 25 May he left Augsburg to begin his lengthy and long-drawn-out journey back to Spain. With his cousin, Ferdinand's son Maximilian, he finally entered Valladolid, which was effectively his capital, on 1 September 1551. His return to Spain does not, however, seem to have put a stop to his amorous activities. Although the evidence is not conclusive, there is a possibility that he had a relationship with a lady in Valladolid, Isabel Osorio, possibly the sister of the marquis of

[4] Álvarez, *Relation*, p. 43.
[5] Ibid., p. 119.
[6] Ibid., pp. 131–2.

Astorga, and may have had at least one child by her. According to some accounts, Philip actually acknowledged Isabel as his wife when he returned to Spain a widower in 1559, and provided for her and her family at least until her death, in 1590. Such a relationship might in part explain Philip's notarized repudiation of the terms of his marriage to Mary, even if he was not in fact a bigamist. But whatever the truth in this case, it is clear that Philip's philandering reputation preceded him to England, and Mary was quite right to quiz Simon Renard about this aspect of his character.[7] Even so, it is doubtful whether she ever became aware of her husband's continuing proclivities in this direction when he was not in England.

Once Philip returned to the regency of Spain, in September 1552, he sought, with the help of Ruy Gómez, to make the new system at court, with its separate Castilian and 'Burgundian' households, his own, and it was to a large extent this new personally chosen team that would form the heart of his household in England.[8] Yet, even with all their misgivings, the conscripts and volunteers for Philip's voyage to meet his new wife were probably not initially aware that an extra problem awaited them in England. According to a letter written at the time to his former jousting companion, the count of Egmont, Philip had planned to take a retinue of several thousand with him to England, and about 6,000 additional troops, who were destined for the Netherlands. These numbers may have seemed modest and reasonable to him, but looked like an invasion force to the nervous English.[9] In her great love and anticipation, however, and by agreement with her councillors, Mary had already organized for her new husband an almost complete household of her own subjects. This consisted of about 350 people, headed by her lord high steward, the earl of Arundel, who was to have charge of both monarchs' households. The heirs of seven leading English peers had been appointed to be Philip's gentlemen of the privy chamber (his English *Cámara real*), and they had been carefully chosen to include men who had experience of service at the courts of Philip's close relatives. Anthony Kempe had spent time with his aunt, Mary of Hungary, and Richard Shelley had recently returned from her service and that of Charles V's brother Ferdinand, King of the Romans. Both had linguistic skills, as did another of Philip's new gentlemen, Francis Basset, who was one of Bishop Gardiner's men. Mary had chosen two of her most faithful supporters, Sir John Williams and Sir John Huddlestone, to be Philip's Lord Chamberlain and Vice-Chamberlain respectively. Huddlestone was also appointed as captain of the hundred archers who would form Philip's English Royal Guard. All

---

[7] Kamen, *Philip of Spain*, pp. 47–50, 54–5; Agustín González de Amezúa, *Isabel de Valois, reina de España (1546–1568)*, 3 vols in 5 'tomes' (Madrid: Gráfica Ultra, 1949), i, p. 393; Luis Cabrera de Córdoba, *Felipe Segundo, rey de España*, 4 vols (Madrid: Real Academia de la Historia, 1874–76), iii, p. 367.

[8] Martínez Millán and Fernández Conti, 'La Corte del príncipe', pp. lxv–lxxi.

[9] AGS E 808 no. 11.

indoor posts were covered, though no special provision was made for kennels, mews and stables. On these matters, Mary's master of the horse, Sir Edward Hastings, was to liaise with his Spanish equivalent. In the sensitive English religious situation of the spring and summer of 1554, it was understood that Philip would be entirely responsible for his own Chapel Royal, including instrumentalists, as well as his chaplains and other preachers and clerical advisers. Crucially, Philip was to foot the bill for his entire English household, in addition to the pensions for various English nobles to which the Imperial ambassador, Simon Renard, had committed him.[10]

The ecclesiastical establishment which Philip brought with him to England in July 1554 was not only his joy and delight, particularly in musical matters, both religious and more secular, but also an important aspect of the Spanish presence in England in Mary's reign. As part of the reform of the Spanish Court, on 15 August 1548, the Feast of the Assumption of the Blessed Virgin Mary, a newly constituted chapel had begun its work for Philip in Valladolid as part of his new 'Burgundian' household. This derived from what had been, in the previous century, the most talented and influential school of Christian liturgical music in western Europe, to which the Habsburgs saw themselves as heirs, along with their dynastic inheritance from the Valois Burgundian dukes. As in all clashes of musical style and personnel, there was inevitable conflict with the Prince's existing Castilian chapel, but as with the rest of the Court, the two organizations had somehow to coexist in England. Not all the conflict involving Spaniards there concerned Mary's English subjects. Philip brought with him, from Coruña to Southampton, his familiar Castilian chapel, as well as the equivalent Burgundian chapel, which was equally well staffed with additional chaplains, choir men and boys, and an organist, as well as a second instrument-tuner. Outside the liturgical chapel itself, the Prince brought with him trumpeters and drummers, and perhaps a dancing-master, to instruct the royal pages. It should also be noted that the term 'tuner', used in the sources, was hardly adequate to describe the distinguished blind composer of keyboard, harp and *vihuela* music, Antonio de Cabezón, who seems to have been in England with Philip alongside his equally famous English contemporaries, such as Thomas Tallis, Christopher Tye and John Sheppard.[11] An inventory of 1602 from the royal palace in Madrid includes various English instruments – flutes, shawms and viols – which are labelled as having come from Queen Mary. There was evidently an exchange of instruments between England and Spain during Philip's time as her husband, involving the work of noted makers such as the Venetian

---

[10] *CSP Span* XII, pp. 297–9, 317 and n.; *RMT*, p. 93.

[11] AGS E 77–102 (1548 Chapel accounts); Luis Robledo Estaire, 'La música en la Corte madrileña de los Austrias. Antecedentes: las casas reales hasta 1556', *Revista de Musicología*, x (1987), 753–96.

Bassano family, who had been in London, at first in the former Charterhouse, since the time of Henry VIII.[12]

In order to understand Philip's approach to his new role as King of England it is necessary to be aware of the Habsburgs' general attitude to the exercise of monarchy. Although his father Charles may have harboured visions of some kind of supranational state, in reality the Habsburgs had acquired their many possessions largely by means of natural inheritance, rather than conquest. One consequence of this was that each of their territories had to be recognized as an independent entity, and very little sense of obligation was felt by one such territory towards another. A second result of the nature of the empires of Charles and his son was that each monarch was obliged to respect and observe the individual customs, privileges and institutions of his territories. He was invested with a separate and specific title to each, and when he was physically absent from the dependency concerned, as was inevitably the case in most of them for most of the time, he would maintain a semblance of his presence in the form of a viceroy, governor or lieutenant, who would exercise his relevant powers, of course under the monarch's personal supervision from a distance. When Philip married Mary, he was beginning the process of inheriting all these ideas and obligations, as well as a clear understanding that each Habsburg territory had an obligation to come to the aid of its sovereign in any other.[13] The consequences for England of this thinking would become ever plainer as Mary's reign approached its premature conclusion.

England, of course, presented an unprecedented challenge to the Habsburgs. In all their other domains, a Habsburg, at this time Charles, his brother Ferdinand or one of their dependants, was the sovereign of the territory concerned. Authority might be delegated, but it ultimately rested with the relevant Habsburg ruler. In the 'Land of Amadís', however, there was a historic and independent monarchy, which Philip and his companions themselves believed to go back to King Arthur, if not beyond, to the Roman empire and the origins of Christianity itself. Mary's husband would probably have recognized the severe limitations placed on his power, even if they had not been so clearly spelt out in the marriage treaty. Thus it is not at all surprising that, after the wedding on 25 July 1554, he treated his new wife with both gallantry and a degree of dependence. At this point, he had not yet received any of his promised inheritance in Spain, the Netherlands and America and, although he had been proclaimed King of Naples in Winchester Cathedral on his wedding day, England was in fact the first territory, outside Spain, in which he had any chance to exercise personal power. Mary, on the other hand, was both sovereign and very much present, a strong-minded Tudor and Trastamaran who had been

[12] Martin McLeish, 'An Inventory of Musical Instruments at the Royal Palace, Madrid, in 1602', *Galpin Society Journal*, xxi (1968), pp. 108–28. I owe this and other references on this subject to the kindness of Benjamin Hebbert.

[13] Rodríguez-Salgado, *Changing Face*, pp. 20–1.

prepared to fight to win her throne. Philip could do nothing in England without the consent of his wife and her Council, and found himself the unwilling pioneer of the role of consort to an English sovereign queen, which would only much later be developed by Victoria's Albert and Elizabeth II's own Philip. Given the state of monarchical values in the mid-sixteenth century, both husband and wife were feeling their way into their roles, and it is not surprising that there were some bumps on the road. Ominously, Mary did not use her prerogative to endow her husband with English lands and rents, even though this was not precluded by the marriage treaties.

When she married him in July 1554, 'Mary had long been deprived of family, honour and affection and Philip appealed both to her pride and to her need for love'.[14] On 12 August 1554, Ruy Gómez wrote to tell Charles's secretary Francisco de Erasso that Mary had effectively declared her love to Philip, in the manner of those traditional maidens of England whom she had claimed to imitate by wearing a plain gold ring at her wedding.[15] This kind of thing was not normally expected in sixteenth-century royal marriages, and Gómez's amusement must have been even greater if he knew about Isabel Osorio in Valladolid, as well as his master and companion's romantic adventures in Italy, Austria, Germany and the Netherlands in 1548–51. Spanish commentators were not impressed by Mary's appearance and, as they saw it, her unfashionable clothes, and were worried, along with other continental commentators, that she was already too old to bear the vital heir, who would probably inherit more than just the English throne. Ruy Gómez himself, in contrast, had been provided by Philip with a wealthy and lively thirteen-year-old bride, the future princess of Eboli, and therefore had occasion to rib his master, given that Mary was nearly three times his own wife's age. The Spaniards hoped that they might persuade the Queen and her ladies at least to dress more fashionably by continental standards.[16] Ominously for the future, Philip seems not to have returned Mary's affection even at the start of their marriage, and it became simply embarrassing that she expressed such deep love for him in letters to his father. Charles had, according to a letter he wrote to the duke of Alba, expected much worse behaviour from his son than in fact transpired. When he was told that things were going smoothly in England, he suggested that Philip must have changed dramatically since he had last seen him.[17]

Apart from his particular upbringing and his unequal political and personal relationship with his wife, Philip's view of England was also affected by the fact that he hardly knew, from one day to the next, how long his time there would last. Once the French besiegers of Renty were defeated, on 14 August 1554, his prospect of staying looked better, but on

[14] Ibid., p. 90.
[15] AGS E 808–143.
[16] Muñoz, *Viaje*, p. 106; *CSP Span* XI, pp. 532–3.
[17] AGS E 508–107; *CODOIN*, iii, p. 532.

20 August he was once again told by his father to set sail immediately for the Netherlands.[18] Then, just over a week later, Secretary Erasso was sent across to tell him to remain in England after all, which he duly did.[19] Given that it appeared, by September 1554, that he was not going to be able to gain his military spurs quickly on the Continent, as he so deeply desired, he had no choice but to devote himself to the government of England, as well as keeping a weather eye on the situation between the Habsburgs and France, and also seeking to get his wife with child. In these circumstances, the marriage treaty, which had been negotiated on his behalf and against which he had formally, though secretly, protested while still in Valladolid, began to show its teeth and claws.

Even if he had had more experience of governing non-Spanish territories than he did, Philip's assignment in England was always going to be a hard one. There had of course been a great deal of turbulence in the kingdom over the previous twenty years or so, but ancient institutions and procedures continued to function under Mary, and thus, in his inevitable absences, the default position was bound to be an entirely English government which, like the general public, recognized only Mary as its true sovereign, especially as her husband was married to her but not crowned. So he had ultimately to defer to his wife in governmental matters, and yet at the same time had to give her the support, if not the marital love, that she so desired. The English public generally expected this, whatever its misgivings about having a foreign king, whether Spanish or not. The marriage treaty stipulated that all governmental affairs were to be conducted in the traditional manner and by native Englishmen, but it soon became clear that Mary herself expected her new husband to play a full part in the governance of the realm. Almost immediately, on 27 July 1554, while the Court was still at Winchester, the Council decided, in order to help Philip, that 'a note of all such matters of Estate as shuld passe from hence shuld be made in Laten or Spanyshe'. On 13 August, Alba confirmed in a letter to Erasso in Brussels that some English business was indeed being transacted now in Spanish.[20] This evidently enabled Philip to take a more active part in English government, in addition to his increasing involvement in Habsburg affairs. According to the *alcalde de la Corte* (mayor of the palace) Briviesca, who was responsible for keeping order in Philip's Court, his master was in fact fully engaged in English matters from the start.[21] Indeed, the Spanish seemed to think that their master would supply all the lacks of a female ruler, taking charge of warfare and other 'matters impertinent to women'.[22] Philip was happy to

---

[18] AGS E 508–196.

[19] AGS Patronato Real 55–30.

[20] *APC*, V, p. 53; *CSP Span* XII, p. 2; AGS E 103 (1)–6.

[21] BPR 11–2286, fols 216–17 (letter to Granvelle, 21 November 1551).

[22] AGS E 1498 ('pudiesse governar la guerra y supplir otras cosas que son impertinentes a mugeres' at fol. 6r).

use his own financial resources to win support, immediately rewarding those councillors and other courtiers and gentlemen who had attended his wedding with payments totalling 30,000 ducats.[23] Then, on 23 August, he issued letters patent to twenty-one English councillors and other nobles, granting them annuities varying between £75 and £500.[24]

More significantly, Philip, greatly exceeding his powers under the marriage treaty, though with the full support of his wife, soon became involved in the reform of the Privy Council. In an autograph note, probably written soon after Philip's arrival in England, Mary ordered the Lord Privy Seal, William Paget, 'Furste to tell the kyng the whole state of the Realme, w[ith] all thynge appartaynnyng to the same, as myche as ye knowe to be trewe. Seconde to obey hys comandment in all thynge.'[25] Since Mary's accession, the Council, which Philip is said to have attended at least twice a week, on Tuesdays and Fridays, had become a somewhat unwieldy mixture of her loyalist retainers and career politicians.[26] The Queen still had her doubts about the loyalty of some of the latter, and was aware that something had to be done, even though attendances at individual meetings were generally quite small. Lord Paget had long been urging a reduction in numbers, to return to the situation under the two previous kings, and Philip now actively supported such a change. As a result, numbers were indeed reduced, but the new King could do nothing to heal the divisions in the Council, and in particular to mediate in the now bitter conflict between Paget and Bishop Stephen Gardiner. Indeed, Philip's arrival on the scene served only to make things worse in this respect, since Paget, who had been in favour of the marriage from early on and worked hard to achieve it, became the King's strong supporter, while Mary, with reluctance, continued to rely mainly on Gardiner. In fact, it seems to have been Philip's vigorous personality and action that did most to make his wife's government more efficient, and he was praised for this in later years. The duke of Alba thought that his master might even take full control of the realm, and said that he could not understand why he was willing to take a back seat on so many occasions, and behave like a temporary visitor, 'a poor traveller'.[27] The obstinate refusal of the English to have Philip crowned as King of England was felt by many, including the man himself, to be a dishonour to Spain and the Habsburgs in general, while another cause of friction, affecting both sides, was the new gold and silver coinage which began to be minted in England in 1554. The only existing model for Philip and Mary in these circumstances was the

[23] *CSP Span* XIII, p. 50.

[24] Loades, *Mary Tudor*, p. 231.

[25] BL Cotton MS Vespasian F III, no. 23.

[26] BREscorial V, iii, 3, fols 486v–487; *APC* V, p. 53.

[27] Rodríguez-Salgado, *Changing Face*, pp. 94–5, 98; Loades, *Mary Tudor*, pp. 136, 227; A. Weikel, 'The Marian Council revisited', in Jennifer I. Loach and Robert Tittler, *The mid-Tudor polity, c. 1540–1560* (London: Macmillan, 1980), pp. 52–73; *Epistolario del III duque de Alba, Don Fernando Álvarez de Toledo*, 3 vols (Madrid: Real Academia de la Historia, 1952), i, p. 7 (letter to Philip, 25 April 1555).

Castilian coinage of Isabella and Ferdinand, who were the couple's great-grandparents and grandparents respectively. While the Spanish fumed at the lack of recognition, by coronation, of Philip's royal authority in England, suspicious Englishmen were equally concerned to see the symbols of their kingdom's sovereignty being so closely associated with the image of the Prince of Spain and King of Naples, and the King placed on the right, in the position of superiority.

In reality, behind the immediate political issues which faced Philip and Mary in their first period of what was effectively joint government was the fact, already noted, that they were both experimenting in their new roles. The King was feeling his way in a country which was new to him, and long accustomed to being proudly self-sufficient, while his wife was experimenting as effectively the first female ruler of England, given the brief and very incomplete control that the empress Matilda had exercised in 1141, and the extreme brevity of the reign of Jane I. Before her marriage, the Queen had, of course, asserted her will at certain vital stages, by seizing the throne in the first place, and then by rallying her subjects to defeat Wyatt's rebellion. However, as in the case of Isabella and Ferdinand back in the 1470s, there was a strong tendency among her subjects, when Philip became King, to regard him as the effective ruler of the country because he was male. Another complicating factor was the lack of specific law governing succession by and from a female sovereign. England's claim to the French Crown was notoriously based on female succession, contrary to the patriarchal 'Salic' law which prevailed in France itself, but that claim assumed a female consort, in the case in question Edward II's wife Isabelle of France, and not a sovereign ruler. In the new situation of 1554, which Edward VI had tried so hard to prevent, some experts thought that normal English inheritance law should apply. This would mean that, while there was nothing to prevent a woman from inheriting an estate, in this case the kingdom itself, if she then married, that estate would automatically pass to her husband. He would hold it for his lifetime, whether she outlived him or not, but only if they had had children, and only after he died would it be handed on to his or her heirs, which might or might not be hers as well. A woman in such a situation was known in legal French as a *femme couverte* (literally a 'covered woman') and her rights were limited. In addition, most aristocratic titles in sixteenth-century England were handed down, in legal language 'entailed', through a male line. A woman could inherit such a title, and transmit it through her male heirs, but she could not normally use it herself. The question which preoccupied the lawyers in 1554 was this: given that the Crown of England was not an aristocratic title in the conventional sense, was it an 'estate'? Earlier in the year, opponents of the 'Spanish marriage' had tried to convince Ambassador Renard that it was, so that Mary's whole right to the kingdom would pass immediately to Philip when they married. The marriage treaty of course stipulated otherwise, denying the King any right to the Crown if Mary died before him without producing an heir.[28] It appeared that normal English common law was being applied in this case.

Legal doubts over this matter were apparently resolved in the parliament of April 1554 by the passing of two acts, one ratifying the marriage treaty, and thus giving it the force of statute law, while the other confirmed that the authority of a sovereign queen was exactly the same as that of a male ruler.[29] It was not so easy, however, to resolve the deep problems of gender in relation to monarchy which lay behind this earnest legal argument. This particularly applied to the situation and actions of the King and Queen themselves. Fundamentally, both of them believed that a ruler should really be a male war leader. Philip had a consuming desire to prove to his father that he could fight bravely and be victorious in battle, preferably against his family's primary historic enemy, France. Mary fully shared his values and attitude in this respect. Although her great-great-grandfather, Owen Tudor, had founded the dynasty by means of an illicit and scandalous liaison with the dowager queen Catherine of France, the role-models for her predecessors had been the royal warriors against France, including Edward, the Black Prince and, above all, the Lancastrian Henry V. Mary's father, Henry VIII, even before his brother Arthur's death made him heir to the throne, was deeply inspired by the example of the victor of Agincourt. Once king, he wanted to emulate him by conquering France and thus becoming the most feared king in Europe. Mary, like her half-brother before her, was strongly influenced by these ideals.

As noted earlier, on the eve of her coronation Mary could well have knighted her chosen candidates for the order of the Bath herself, but the intimacy with naked men at bathtime would probably have seemed improper even for a less disciplined and more carnal lady of her rank. There is no doubt, though, that her absence from the ceremonies, in which the earl of Arundel took the sovereign's role, did not correspond to what was generally expected of a monarch. Although she restored the traditional statutes and ceremonies both of this order and of the Order of the Garter, which Edward VI had tried to reform, once Philip arrived he seems to have slipped immediately and naturally into the chivalric role. As soon as he was installed as a knight of the Garter, at Windsor in August 1554, he was invited by his wife to take over the presidency of the chapter of the order. It followed naturally that he would use the organization of chivalric contests, as Henry VIII had done, to display his royal prowess and form bonds with the English aristocracy. It has not always been clear to English historians, but is evident from his exploits during his European tour of 1548 to 1551, that Philip loved these activities and was extremely good at them, not least in their romantic aspect.[30] As well as engaging in the exercises appropriate to the land of

[28] Hughes and Larkin, *Tudor Royal Proclamations*, ii, no. 398; Loades, *Intrigue and Treason*, pp. 178–9.

[29] Statute 1 Mary, 3 c. 1, 2, in *Statutes of the Realm*, ed. Luders and others, iv, pt 1, p. 222.

[30] *Pace* Loades, *Intrigue and Treason*, p. 191.

Arthur and Amadís, Philip and his Spanish knights introduced the English to the *juego de cañas*, with which their ancestors had kept their horsemanship up to standard during centuries of frontier warfare against the Muslim subjects of the emir of Granada. In this form of combat, sticks were used instead of lances, and lightly armed horsemen rode in the style of flat-racing jockeys (*a la jineta*), the emphasis being on speed and dexterity, not weight and brute force, as in the conventional joust. Such *juegos* were held on 25 November 1554 at Westminster and described by Henry Machyn, who refers to Spaniards riding in outfits of various colours, 'the kyng in red ... and with targets and canes in their hand, herlyng of rods on[e] at another'.[31] Subsequently, on 4 December, Don Fernando de Toledo, with a combined team of Spanish and English nobles, challenged another team to a fight on foot at the 'barriers', in the manner described in Sir Thomas Malory's *Morte d'Arthur*, and equally familiar to Iberian knights from romances in their languages. Philip again took part, as one of the answerers to Don Fernando's challenge, and was awarded a prize for swordsmanship by the judges, some of whom were English and others Spanish.[32] On 18 December 1554, another tournament was held at Philip and Mary's Court, in which English and Spanish knights fought on foot with spears and swords.[33] Just over a month later, on 24 January, there was another tourney 'at the tylt at Westmynstr', this time on horseback. Then, on 12 February 1555, to celebrate the wedding of Philip's English chamberlain, Lord Strange, a tournament, banquet, masque and *juego de cañas* were held at Whitehall, with much involvement of the King, who had clearly not lost his taste for such festivities. On 25 March, the Feast of the Annunciation to the Blessed Virgin Mary, or 'Lady Day', 'gret j[oustes]' were held at Westminster, in which, according to Machyn, Sir George Howard challenged an unnamed Spanish knight. Though the Queen was not apparently present on this occasion, 200 staves were broken, and older participants and spectators recalled the 'glory days' of Henry VIII. The last chivalric exercise held at Court during Philip's first sojourn in England seems to have been the one that took place on 20 April 1555, to celebrate the wedding of another of Philip's chamberlains, Lord Fitzwalter.[34]

These knightly entertainments appeared to display a cordial relationship between Philip and Mary's senior courtiers, but it became notorious, soon after the King's arrival in London, that things were not always so peaceful at a humbler level in and around the Court, especially when it was in Westminster. Since the abolition of the abbot of Westminster's former secular jurisdiction after the dissolution of the greater monasteries, that area had become notoriously lawless, and things were certainly not helped by the

---

[31] Machyn, *Diary*, p. 70.
[32] Loades, *Intrigue and Treason*, pp. 190–1; R. C. McCoy, 'From the Tower to the Tiltyard: Robert Dudley's Return to Glory', *Historical Journal*, xxvii (1984), 425–35.
[33] Machyn, *Diary*, p. 79.
[34] Ibid., p. 84; Loades, *Intrigue and Treason*, p. 192.

unfortunate duplication of offices between Philip's Spanish and English households. It has traditionally been assumed by English historians, not least on the basis of some of the propaganda surrounding Wyatt's rebellion, that there was a kind of 'natural' antipathy between the English and the Iberians, but earlier action and commentary on the subject did not suggest such a thing. Religious differences arising from Henry VIII's changes to the English Church, and in particular the executions of Sir Thomas More and Bishop John Fisher, undoubtedly scandalized Spaniards, and even more so the divorce of Queen Catherine. It is evident, though, that Philip, and hence his companions and retinue on the expedition to England, were under strict orders to be well behaved and conciliatory.[35] This was given as a reason for the prohibition on travel by accompanying wives, which was defied by the duchess of Alba and some others. Nevertheless, the Spanish, many of whom had been reluctant to travel north in the first place, seem on the whole to have become quickly disillusioned with Mary's kingdom, and especially with its inhabitants. An excellent source on this subject is the largely eyewitness account, published in Spain in 1554, of Andrés Muñoz, who indicates what he regards as the start of the trouble:

> After H[is] M[ajesty] went to England, none of his officials, whether among his leading officials or the rest, has served or is serving him, because the Queen had made and ordered the Household according to the custom of Burgundy, as H[is] M[ajesty] had brought it, and very much more accomplished in all offices; and thus those of the Chamber and stewards (*mayordomos*), Horse (*caballerizo*), gentlemen with bouche [of Court], as well as the rest, are all very prominent Englishmen. They regard themselves as men who know how to do what is required, since they do not cede any point of their pre-eminence. And it is believed [by the Spanish] that they will not allow H[is] M[ajesty] to have the Guard which he brought with him. For this reason, many people are confused, because apart from the expedition having been the most laborious that has been seen, as well as the disruption (*desbarato*) of the landing, [the English] want to subject them somewhat to their laws, because since [Philip's household] is so numerous, [and the] Spaniards [are] in their land, they want to be sure [of them].

As well as showing understanding of English concerns, Muñoz vividly conveys the Spaniards' discontent:

> The life the Spaniards are spending there is not very advantageous [to them], nor do they find themselves as well-situated as they would be in Castile; to this some respond that they would rather be in the stubble (*rastrojo*) of the kingdom of Toledo than in the forests of Amadís.[36]

[35] Pérez Martín, *María Tudor*, pp. 613–14 (AGS E 808).
[36] Muñoz, *Viaje*, pp. 77–8; Pérez Martín, *María Tudor*, pp. 630–5.

Elsewhere in his account, Muñoz says that his companions found the English 'white, pink and quarrelsome'. Avoiding mention of Philip's earlier exploits in Germany and the Netherlands, he remarks of the English that 'All their celebrations consist of eating and drinking, they think of nothing else'. Indeed, according to him, 'They have a lot of beer, and drink more of it than there is water in the river [Pisuerga] at Valladolid'.[37] Others, including Ruy Gómez, complained, in this case to Charles V, that Spaniards could not walk at night in the streets of London and Westminster for fear of attack and robbery.[38] The Protestant martyrologist John Foxe recounts a case which seems to illustrate well the tensions that arose in London when Philip and his court came to town:

> There was about the tyme that the Spanyardes began first to kepe a sturre in Englande [1554], one William [John in the 1576 edn, p. 1500] Tooly, a citezen and Poulter, in London, who conspired with certaine other of his societie to rob a Spanyarde at [the Palace of] S. Iames: and although the dede were heinous and wicked of it selfe, yet it was aggrauated and made greater then it was by other [factors], being committed against suche . . . a person, and against suche a countrey, whiche both the Quene and her whole courte semed highly to fauour.[39]

Foxe's main point is that, before he was hanged for the robbery, Tooly expressed Protestant sentiments. Thus Bishop Edmund Bonner of London became involved, having Tooly's body exhumed and burned for heresy. For this the convict might be regarded as a martyr for the reformed faith, but his case also gives a vivid impression of Anglo-Spanish tensions in London in the first few months of Philip's stay.[40] Given the circumstances of Tooly's death, it is perhaps ironical that a more balanced Spanish view of the situation was given by another heresy-hunter, the Dominican friar Bartolomé Carranza, in a letter in Latin which he sent from London to Cardinal Pole, on 1 September 1554. In it he commented on the abuse and ill-treatment that many Spaniards, both clerical and lay, were receiving from the English. He of course deplored this, but added that the Spanish had a proclivity for 'anger and bile (ad choleram et bilim)'. Thus some retaliated against the violence and insults, while others, as good servants of the King, overcame evil with good. However, Carranza's letter was mostly about religious policy, which would soon raise further tension among the English themselves, as well as between natives and Spaniards.[41]

In addition to his chapel, Philip brought to England a group of Spanish churchmen whose function, in some cases, would be to advise him and the

---

[37] Muñoz, *Viaje*, pp. 106–7, 118, 108, 119, 106; Pérez Martín, *María Tudor*, pp. 630–5.
[38] AGS E 808 no. 148 (27 and 30 July 1554).
[39] Foxe 1563, p. 1142.
[40] Foxe 1563, pp. 1142, 1145.
[41] Tellechea, *Legación*, pp.184–5; *CRP*, 2, pp. 333–4 (no. 928).

Queen on the reform and 'purification' of the English Church and its restoration (in Curial terminology 'reduction') to obedience to the Roman See. The new King had hand-picked these men in Spain earlier in the year, while he was recruiting his household for England. Like the secular courtiers, some of them stayed in England for a relatively short time. Among these were Dr Bartolomé Torres, who would later be bishop of the Canary Islands, and Archbishop Fernando de Valdés of Seville, who was also inquisitor-general of Spain. Others, however, were destined to spend several years in England. These included two Observant Franciscans, Fray (friar) Alonso de Castro and Fray Bernardo de Fresneda, who would act as chaplains and confessors to the King, and two Dominicans, Fray Juan de Villagarcía and Fray Bartolomé Carranza. In May 1555 they would be joined, at Carranza's request, by another Dominican, Fray Pedro de Soto, who had earlier founded the Catholic University of Dillingen, near Augsburg.[42] As there had been no religious orders in England since the late 1530s, the Spanish friars were not sure what their reception would be. According to Carranza's letter to Pole, dated 1 September 1554, they felt uncomfortable wearing their religious habits in public because they were sometimes the subject of attack in the streets around Westminster Abbey, where they resided in the precincts.[43] Nevertheless, they quickly became part of the English royal and ecclesiastical scene, and the importance of their contribution is increasingly being recognized.[44]

These Spaniards found that, although it was clearly the object of both Charles V and Philip that the Habsburgs should gain the credit for restoring Mary's kingdom to Roman Catholicism, the matter was of such fundamental concern to the Queen that such a policy had in fact been set in train a year before. Their efforts were crucially assisted by the fact that, at last, at the end of June 1554, Julius III had pronounced again on the still vexed question of English church goods in the hands of laypeople. He told Pole that he would not allow this issue to obstruct the saving of souls for Christ, and that he would place the onus of this on Mary herself. If she interceded on behalf of the owners of such goods, or of tenants of what were now crown lands but had formerly belonged to the Church, Pole would be allowed to leave the persons concerned in possession of them, without the need to feel scruples, although serious cases of abuse would have to be referred to the Pope himself. On 1 August, a papal bull was issued which embodied these provisions, after further consultations with Mary.[45] By this

[42] Tellechea, 'Bartolomé Carranza y la restauración católica inglesa (1554–1556)', in Tellechea, CyP, p. 29 and in Fray Bartolomé Carranza de Miranda: Investigaciones históricas (Pamplona: Gobierno de Navarra, 2002), p. 199; John Edwards, 'Spanish Religious Influence in Marian England', in CMT, p. 201.

[43] Tellechea, Legación, pp. 184–5; CRP, 2, p. 334 (no. 928).

[44] Edwards, 'Spanish Religious Influence', pp. 201–24; RCMT.

[45] CRP, 2, pp. 321–2 (no. 897), 328–9 (no. 916).

time Philip was in England as its King, but his father still seemed to be procrastinating. On 3 August, Charles's Chancellor, Granvelle, told Pole that the Emperor still did not want the Legate to go to England before he had consulted his son and his new daughter-in-law. He had that day sent an express messenger to do this.[46] On 11 August, Pole wrote to Mary to tell her about his latest consultations with the Pope over church property. Just when the Queen and her new husband were keen to advance rapidly with the Catholic restoration, Pole now threw a spanner into the works by saying that he could give neither a general nor particular dispensations to the 'possessioners' of such property without causing scandal to the Church, unless he first found out exactly what these goods were. He felt constrained to wait both for the reconciliation of the kingdom and for the examination of individual cases. However, he ended optimistically, assuring the Queen that a deal could be done with the possessioners, and adding that now she was married his own return to England should not be delayed any longer.[47]

As Pole also implied in that letter to Mary, he now had the support on the spot of Philip, in taking up his English legation in person. On 14 August 1554, the new King appointed two Spaniards, Don Fernando Francisco Dávalos de Aquina, marquis of Pescara, and Don Juan Manrique de Lara, to represent him at the Papal Curia, the latter already acting in that capacity for Charles V. No doubt this move was aimed, at least in part, at facilitating England's return to the Roman Church.[48] Yet it was not until 19 September that Philip wrote to Pole from Hampton Court, at last telling him to come to England as soon as possible.[49] In his reply, Pole took no trouble to conceal his irritation and impatience. He pointed out that he had been cooling his heels on the Continent for more than a year, and said sharply that since Philip had now inherited the title of 'Defender of the Faith', which Clement VII had first granted to Henry VIII, it was his particular duty to attend to the religious situation in England. Keeping the Legate out of the country was an offence to Christ, as well as the Pope. In fact, England would be in greater danger if he was not admitted, and he implied that Philip was being even more cowardly on the subject than his wife.[50] While Pole continued to express his frustration to all who would listen to him or read his letters, Mary wrote to him again. Her letter, dated at Hampton Court on 28 September 1554 and signed 'Cousin Mary the Quene', gives an insight into her psychological state at this time. This was evidently regarded as a significant document, since it was in Lord Chancellor Gardiner's own hand, with a postscript written by Mary herself. It makes clear that Philip and Mary wanted Pole in England in due course,

[46] *CRP*, 2, p. 329 (no. 917).
[47] *CRP*, 2, pp. 331–2 (no. 922).
[48] Tellechea, *Legación*, pp. 12–14 (no. V).
[49] *CRP*, 2, p. 337 (no. 938).
[50] *CRP*, 2, pp. 337–8 (no. 939).

but meanwhile they and their servants had scruples on which they required
his advice. These concerned the use for Catholic worship of churches
which had previously contained the services prescribed in Cranmer's
Prayer Books. Mary and her husband wanted to know if the dispensations
which they had received for their wedding in Winchester Cathedral
allowed them in good conscience to attend Catholic worship in other such
churches, hoping that Pole or Julius himself would settle the matter.[51] More
would be heard on this subject.

Pole was now working to achieve an ever better grip on affairs in
England, and especially on matters ecclesiastical. On 7 October, his secre-
tary, Niccolò Ormanetto, wrote on his behalf to Pole's agent Seth
Holland, who was representing him at the side of the 'Catholic Monarchs'
of England. In part Pole was responding to a letter from Friar Carranza.
This Spanish Dominican had written to him from London on 27
September 1554, expressing the concerns which were later articulated by
Mary, and also pursuing the central question of what would happen to the
property which had been confiscated from the Church by Henry and
Edward and was presently being held by the Crown or by individual
laypeople. Pole's message was that Rome wanted the property question to
be treated with caution and discretion. Julius III had made it clear to him
that he wanted this matter ultimately to be resolved in the Church's favour,
and did not anticipate that Philip and Mary would allow the situation
inherited from their predecessors to continue. Nevertheless, he wanted
spiritual issues to be given priority over economic ones. Above all,
Ormanetto wanted Holland to tell all the supporters of reunification at
Court, and in particular Carranza, to remain calm. Nothing must interfere with the return of Pole and the reconciliation of England.[52] Four days
later, on 11 October, Ormanetto wrote another letter, from Brussels, to
Seth Holland. This time he dealt with the scruples about ritual pollution
which had been raised with Pole by Carranza at the end of the previous
month.[53] Mary's concern was not only about churches which had been
used for Prayer Book worship, but also about the 'heretics' (i.e. willing
reformers and schismatics) who had been buried in those churches, or
their churchyards, during the two preceding reigns. In this context, Pole
seemed to make a distinction between the living and the dead. As long as
they had been personally absolved and reconciled, priests might freely
celebrate the Catholic sacraments, and others might attend their services.
However, the remains of deceased heretics and schismatics had to be
exhumed in accordance with canon law, though not if a public disturbance might thus be caused. Still fretting on the Continent, the Legate was
apparently ready now to condone the restoration of traditional services at
once, despite the still valid interdict, but warned that he would take action

[51] Tellechea, *Legación*, pp. 31–2 (no. XL); *CRP*, 2, p. 341 (no. 946).
[52] Tellechea, *Legación*, pp. 33–6, 115–19 (no. XXXII).
[53] Tellechea, 'Pole, Carranza y Fresneda', in Tellechea, *CyP*, pp. 186–7.

over the buried remains of 'heretics', and on other matters, when he finally reached England.[54]

On 14 October Pole wrote again to Julius, from Brussels, to report that now, at last, Charles V and Granvelle were optimistic about the English situation. Significantly, he assured the Pope that he was working for him, and would not be told what to do by Philip or Mary. He had met the Emperor, together with Granvelle and Girolamo Muzzarelli, on 10 October. It seems that Pole had finally come to understand the sensitivity of the church goods question. He now wanted Julius to remit the strictest penalties to which the possessioners were liable, but also felt that Philip and Mary should be empowered to reward those who had assisted in the reconciliation process. Charles V had acquired important experience of this kind of problem in Germany, and he did not think that all existing grants to laymen should be allowed to stand, but moderation should nonetheless be used. As Carranza had suggested earlier, the scope of the relevant papal brief might have to be widened. As the letter continues, it becomes ever clearer that Pole had not in fact changed his mind about the need to take back the possessioners' 'loot'. Now that Philip was in England and married to Mary, the Legate wanted parliament to deal with the property question as a matter of urgency. It was pointless to wait for all the opponents of reunification to change their minds, as this policy would mean that nothing happened.[55] On the same day, Pole wrote to another of his friends in Rome, Cardinal Innocenzo del Monte, with the news from England that parliament was due to meet again in mid-November. In addition he had heard of a sermon which Bishop Gardiner had preached on 30 September last, the Feast of St Jerome, in which the former Henrician loyalist had blamed himself for supporting the Royal Supremacy and had also criticized his fellow Englishmen who were currently treating the Spaniards badly. In an accompanying and more detailed account, Pole said that Gardiner specifically blamed Londoners, rather than the English in general, for anti-Spanish words and actions. The bishop of Winchester spoke of the 'iniquity' of times past in England and said that he personally had been purged of error by his time in gaol under Edward VI. Now, under Mary's rule, more and more people were acknowledging their errors and returning to the Catholic Church, a process which Gardiner compared to the repentance of the biblical Joseph's brothers for ill-treating him (Genesis 42: 21–3). The cardinal legate of England was not, of course, lacking in bitter memories of his own, and evidently enjoyed sharing these details with del Monte. On this same day, 14 October, which proved to be momentous, Philip and Mary despatched Seth Holland back to Pole with a letter telling him that they were sending Lord Paget and Sir Edward Hastings to the Netherlands to update him on the situation in England and escort him home.[56] The next day, they

[54] Tellechea, *Legación*, pp. 36, 119–20 (no. XXXIII); *CRP*, 2, p. 345 (no. 954).
[55] *CRP*, 2, pp. 345–6 (no. 955).
[56] *CRP*, 2, p. 347 (no. 957).

issued credentials to Mary's faithful confidant, the Imperial ambassador Simon Renard, to go to Brussels as well, to meet Pole.[57]

In his newly transformed situation, Pole was able to write to the Pope, on 19 October, to say that he had just been visited by Granvelle, Muzzarelli and Secretary Vargas, with the news that, at long last as the Legate would see it, Philip was actively trying to speed up his return to England. Even at this late stage, former church property was still the sticking point, and Philip was trying to broaden Pole's powers so that he could legally transfer (alienate) such goods to possessioners in good conscience, as well as ratifying the handovers which had taken place earlier.[58] Hard cases would not after all be referred to Rome, and flexibility now seemed to be the order of the day. Whatever his objections and scruples, Pole must have known that he would probably never see his native land again unless he agreed to all this. On 23 October, he responded by referring the question once again to Pope Julius. Renard had personally confirmed to him, on Mary and Philip's behalf, that the possessors of former church property were resisting Pole's return because they feared that, whatever conciliatory words were spoken, his legatine powers might be widened at any time, so that they would never feel secure in what they now regarded, with the sanction of English common law, as their own property. Pole was apparently desperate, and told the Pope that if necessary he would go to England as a private person, or else as a papal ambassador, as though to a non-Catholic country, rather than as a legate. On no account would he fail to follow the current plan, which was to arrive at Dover and be met by two or three of those whom he obstinately regarded as his fellow nobles, despite the Act of Attainder, which was still in force against him, as far as he knew.[59] His last few days of exile would be agonizing.

On 24 October 1554, Pole reported to del Monte in Rome that Paget was about to leave Brussels with about forty gentlemen, headed for England, and wished him to accompany them. Matters were urgent, as parliament was due to assemble on 12 November.[60] The next day, Pole told Julius of 'rapid' moves in England. Muzzarelli was to go there first, and return with a formal summons for him from Mary. There was still opposition in parliament to his return, however, and he in turn still had grave misgivings about what he regarded as 'buying' England's submission to Rome by means of concessions over what should be done with the church's property. He was deeply anxious and expected a difficult time when he returned.[61] On 27 October he wrote to Mary to thank her for what he described as her inspired decision to send Renard to Brussels. Having spoken to this confidant of the Queen, who had so much experience of England but from a continental perspective, he now felt reassured

[57] Tellechea, *Legación*, pp. 42, 125–6; *CRP*, 2, pp. 347–8 (nos 958–9).
[58] Tellechea, *Legación*, pp. 40, 120–1 (no. XXXIV); *CRP*, 2, p. 349 (no. 963).
[59] Tellechea, *Legación*, pp. 122–4 (no. XXXV); *CRP*, 2, p. 351 (no. 966).
[60] Tellechea, *Legación*, pp. 42, 124–5 (no. XXXVI); *CRP*, 2, pp. 352–3 (no. 968).
[61] Tellechea, *Legación*, pp. 42–4, 126–8 (no. XXXVIII); *CRP*, 2, pp. 352–3 (no. 969).

that he had not been excessively pressing and demanding in his dealings with Mary and her kingdom. Referring to her supposed pregnancy, news of which was just emerging, he produced another of his fulsome metaphors, that she had in fact been spiritually pregnant all along with her subjects, as spiritual children of a heavenly kingdom.[62]

As so often in times of crisis, Pole expressed his deepest feelings to Cardinal Morone, in a letter from Brussels dated 28 October 1554. He was evidently suffering from cold feet, affirming that if he were not received in the current parliament, he would never return to England. As he had told Renard when they met in Brussels, if he was indeed rejected he did not think that Philip and Mary would last long on their thrones. He did not doubt their sincerity, but was still agonizing over having to confirm some holders of church property in possession. He pointed out, though, that the English *praemunire* statute, which excluded foreign jurisdictions from England, including that of the Pope, would protect their position. He himself would not have given as many concessions in this matter as Pope Julius had done, and he did not want a deal concerning these goods to be made over his head between Rome and the English monarchs. Most intriguingly, he revealed to Morone that, while they were together in Brussels, Renard had opened to him, no doubt with royal authority, the possibility of his becoming archbishop of Canterbury in short order, despite the fact that Thomas Cranmer, though in prison, still held the office which had been initially granted to him by Pope Clement VII. The idea apparently was that Pole would then be able to lead the bishops personally in parliament, but Pole rejected this scheme until England was fully reconciled to Rome.[63] That day he also wrote to his faithful English servants Holland and Pyning, saying that he would arrive at Dover as a Roman cardinal, but not wearing the insignia of a legate, so as to avoid arousing unnecessary opposition. He was to be met by some of his surviving relatives and an escort of a hundred cavalry, for safety's sake. He repeated that he would not become archbishop of Canterbury unless the Pope gave his personal approval.[64]

As November began, Pole was still in Brussels, writing to del Monte to ask for more funds from Rome and confirming that the English monarchs were happy to receive him, whether attired as a legate or not.[65] In these final days before Pole's return to his native land, his correspondence clearly reveals the vital role which he was to play in the formulation of royal policy for the English Church. On 6 November, Julius replied to an earlier letter from Pole, saying that he had consulted twelve cardinals on the question of English property, as well as the court of Segnatura, which dealt with such matters. All agreed that it was more important to get the country back into the fold than to settle disputes over goods, but these

---

[62] *CRP*, 2, p. 354 (no. 971).
[63] *CRP*, 2, pp. 354-5 (no. 973).
[64] *CRP*, 2, p. 355 (no. 974).
[65] Tellechea, *Legación*, pp. 128-9 (no. XXXIX).

developments were to be kept from the English until a new papal bull was issued on the subject.[66] The next day, on the other hand, Julius did inform Charles V of all this in a brief (*breve*, a short letter), and also wrote to Philip and Mary, telling them of the new powers which he had given to Pole to deal with church goods.[67] At the same time Morone wrote again to Pole, acknowledging his friend's up-and-down emotions about returning to his homeland and trying to reassure him that the forthcoming bull really would allow him to sort out the property question satisfactorily. It was acceptable to sacrifice some goods for the sake of ransoming the kingdom, and Pole was allowed to be rather less scrupulous than he wished, because God would surely resolve the matter in His own time. Finally, everyone, including the Emperor, was fully behind what Pole was doing.[68] The countdown to the reconciliation of England to Rome was about to begin.

A significant step was taken on 10 November, when Philip and Mary issued letters patent to allow Pole to exercise his legatine authority in England.[69] The next day the Legate, still in Brussels, wrote again to Pope Julius. He said that the English monarchs had wanted him to be in London for the opening of the new parliament on 12 November, but Charles V thought that he should await the arrival of Paget and Hastings to be his escorts, and they had been due in Brussels on the 10th. Meanwhile, Granvelle had been told by Philip that Pole would be welcome in England without displaying his legatine insignia, but he would nonetheless be treated as legate by the King and Queen. The subject of church property was not to be mentioned at this stage. Pole told the Pope that he was happy with these arrangements. In fact, Paget and Hastings reached Brussels on 11 November, and it was then decided that Pole would go to Westminster as a papal ambassador rather than as legate. The party would leave for England on 13 November.[70] On that day, Pole reported to the Pope that he had had an audience of the Emperor on the 12th, during which he had at long last received some encouragement from that quarter. Charles told him that he had a better chance of restoring religion in England than he himself had ever had in Germany. Pole should consult Philip and Mary about everything, so as to ease himself back into the English situation. The Legate and his escort probably moved to Dilighem that night, and took six days in total to reach Calais and a futher four to get to London.[71] While waiting, no doubt anxiously, for Pole to arrive, Philip and Mary wrote to him again and, as they had received an optimistic report from Paget and Hastings, their tone was cheerful. On the same day, Mary herself penned a note to tell Pole that he would be met at

[66] *CRP*, 2, p. 357 (no. 978).
[67] AGS E 881–67; Tellechea, *El Papado y Felipe II*, 3 vols (Madrid: Fundación Universitaria Española, 1999–2002) i, 27 (no. XII).
[68] *CRP*, 2, p. 357 (no. 979).
[69] *CRP*, 2, p. 360 (no. 984).
[70] Tellechea, *Legación*, pp. 45–6, 131–4 (no. XLI); *CRP*, 2, p. 361 (no. 985).
[71] Tellechea, *Legación*, pp. 46–7, 136–8 (no. XLIII); *CRP*, 2, p. 361 (no. 986).

Dover by the new bishop of Ely, Thomas Thirlby, and by Anthony Browne, Viscount Montagu.[72] Then, on 22 November, just in the nick of time, parliament repealed the Act of Attainder under which the new legate should otherwise have been arrested as a traitor as soon as he set foot on English soil.[73]

In a letter to his regular correspondent, Cardinal Innocenzo del Monte, written in a Cranmerless Lambeth Palace on 25 or 26 November, Pole described his journey. He had arrived in the Pale of Calais on 19 November, where he was met by Marshal Sir John Fogge and Lieutenant William Lord Howard, with a force of cavalry. Amazingly, his passage the next day from there to Dover took only three and a half hours, indicating the fairest of winds. Pole, and Mary too when she heard of it, saw this as yet another sign of God's special favour. Having stayed in Dover castle overnight, and not in the dungeons, he was formally welcomed the following morning by Bishop Thirlby and Viscount Montagu, even though at this stage the Attainder Act was still technically in force. The two men handed letters from the King and Queen to the Cardinal, who was also met by the new archdeacon of Canterbury, Nicholas Harpsfield, who had replaced Thomas Cranmer's brother Edmund. There was also a welcoming party of canons of Canterbury. They asked him whether, when he reached the cathedral, they should receive him as a papal legate, and he stuck to his earlier decision to appear initially as a lower-ranking ambassador. On 22 November, the day of the repeal of his attainder, he was escorted to Canterbury to be welcomed by the cathedral authorities. From there, he sent Bishop Richard Pate, who had been with him on the Continent, to take his reply to his sovereigns. Two days later, the Legate and his party reached the Medway, ironically, in view of recent events in Kent, staying the night at Cooling castle, the home of Thomas Wyatt's uncle, Lord Cobham. There he was met by the earl of Shrewsbury and the elderly Bishop Tunstall of Durham, who informed him that he was no longer subject to attainder, and added that the King and Queen now wanted him to enter London in his full dress as legate.

The Queen's own barge conveyed the Cardinal from Gravesend to a landing-stage at Westminster. There he was met by the Lord Chancellor, Bishop Gardiner, and afterwards he was received by Philip, and finally by Mary herself. He handed over his letters of credence from the Pope, and told the King and Queen that he came not only as their vassal but also as the representative of Christ's Vicar on earth. After this celebratory meeting, Gardiner and others escorted Pole to a barge and took him across the river to his lodgings in Lambeth Palace. During the evening of 25 November and on the morning of the 26th, he received numerous callers. On his first evening at Lambeth, one of Mary's chamberlains came to invite him to a banquet in Whitehall Palace, in which the entertainments would include

[72] *CRP*, 2, p. 362 (no. 988); Tellechea, *Legación*, pp. 47–8, 143 (no. XLV).
[73] *CRP*, 2, pp. 312–13 (no. 988a, 1 Philip & 2 Mary, c. 18).

the Spanish cane-game, but offered the option of resting instead, which perhaps not surprisingly he accepted. The prevailing mood of exultation had evidently affected even the hard-bitten, and perhaps anxious, Gardiner, who spoke lyrically to Pole of the power of divine Providence expressed in having him come to the very palace in which Cranmer had resided while the English Church was being sent off on the wrong path.[74] It remained to be seen how long Mary's joy, and that of at least some of her subjects, would last. Now, the namesake of the Blessed Virgin would experience what was probably her 'fourth joy', after her arrival on the throne, her coronation, and her wedding to Philip – the reconciliation of her kingdom with Rome.

As these events of great moment for England were unfolding, Pole continued to keep his continental friends up to date. On Tuesday, 27 November he wrote to tell Cardinal del Monte how, that morning, Bishops Gardiner and Thirlby, as well as Paget, had waited upon him with details of the forthcoming parliamentary arrangements. The next day, Pole was to meet the Lords and Commons in Whitehall Palace and officially inform them that he had been sent on behalf of the Pope. He was to ask the Members formally whether they were ready to return to the Roman Church. On the 29th, the King and Queen would petition, on behalf of the kingdom, for absolution from schism, for the removal of ecclesiastical sanctions, and for the confirmation of existing church privileges which were in accordance with Catholic canon law. The plan was that on Friday 30 November, the Feast of Andrew the Apostle, Pole would grant all these petitions. The cardinal legate happily accepted these arrangements, and also readily agreed that on the following Sunday, 2 December, Gardiner should preach a sermon on the reconciliation with Rome.[75] Parliament duly met on Wednesday the 28th, and Pole gave an address to both Houses which survives in many versions, including several produced by the author himself. Some of his own autograph drafts and secretarial copies vividly display the immense emotional capital which he had invested in his voluntary exile under Henry VIII and his much-delayed return at Mary's invitation. Certain surviving versions would have taken several hours to deliver, as he relentlessly rehearsed his personal grievances against many of the lords spiritual and temporal who would be present when he delivered his speech. It seems, however, that the final, spoken version was much shorter and more to the point.[76] As agreed, Pole explained the reason for his coming back to England, and seems to have reduced the level of vitriol which may be found in his drafts, such as one which covers no fewer than fifty-five folios of a manuscript in the Vatican Library.[77] In this earlier version, which was evidently not entirely private, Pole not unexpectedly

---

[74] Tellechea, *Legación*, pp. 48–50, 139–42 (no. XLIV); *CRP*, 2, pp. 363–5 (no. 989), also *CRP*, 2, pp. 378–9 (no. 999), Henry Pyning's account.

[75] *CRP*, 2, p. 365 (no. 990).

[76] Full bibliographical references in *CRP*, 2, pp. 366–9 (no. 991).

[77] BAV MS Vat. Lat. 5968, fols 305r–359r.

launched an assault on the 'possessioners' of church property, who seem to have largely dominated his mind during his long wait to return to England. To them he said, in the draft, 'ye spoiled and altogether bereft [the Church], ye have of your owne doinge spoiled out of . . . venality'. He went on to condemn in detail every move in the expropriation of the English Church under Henry VIII. This was 'goddes property', but it was 'grabbed'. The owners were only in occupation ('possession'), and could never be the legitimate and permanent owners. Evidently deeply angry, and in a lecturing tone which he adopted very readily, Pole claimed that he did not understand how these people, who called themselves Catholic Christians, failed to question themselves before God about their behaviour.[78] Although the draft, or subsequent version, of Pole's speech in the Vatican Library is in English, as it might have been delivered, the Secret Archive of the Vatican contains a registered document in Italian which seems to be a version of what he actually said to parliament, in English, on 28 November 1554.

Here Pole begins by outlining his role as legate for Pope Julius III, to Mary as queen and to her whole kingdom. In the presence of the King and Queen, he first thanks the Lords and Commons for his welcome, and then descends to the personal, reminding them how he had been deprived of his native land and even prevented from communicating with his relatives. Now parliament had restored all his privileges to him, but he describes the measures thus repealed as having caused all the troubles of the years since they were enacted. He declared that he had always been well intentioned towards the Crown and the kingdom, and had never wanted to do anything other than serve them. He had now been restored to the nobility, to a rank which had been removed from him without any fault on his part. Going back in history, he spoke, as he so often did, of earlier times, from the conversion of Pope Eleutherius onwards, when England had been an outstanding part of the Church of God, naming kings who had been obedient to Rome and had prospered. When Saxon and other invaders had entered England, they had been incorporated into the pre-existing Church there, and subsequently English missionaries had converted pagans in Germany, Denmark, Norway and many other countries. As a result, England had been especially honoured and rewarded by popes, but Henry VIII's schism had ruined everything. The split with Rome, caused by Henry's lust, had taken the moral nobility away from England, leaving its people in a state of injustice and insecurity. Using material which he had rehearsed in letters over the preceding months, the Legate compared the England of Henry and Edward with other countries which had suffered the scourge of the Turks after separating themselves from the Roman See. Not only had the two previous kings broken with the Catholic Church, but they had denied its freedom to practise its faith, thus extinguishing England's liberty as well as its noble character. Now, though,

[78] Ibid., fol. 318v.

Mary was Queen. She had been through infinite dangers, and God was acting through her, as well as through Charles V, in her marriage to Philip. England's new King had been chosen by God, not to be like Saul, a man of blood and deceit, but like David, living in peace and sincerity. As for Pole himself, he had come in love and charity to be a good shepherd and kind father to the English. Back in the summer, Philip had sent his many troops away to the Netherlands rather than use them to quell dissent, but now he, Pole, had arrived as legate, with full power from the Pope to punish the disobedient. This was more than a shot across the bows of the parliamentarians, and Pole concluded by repeating the two parts of his commission from Julius. First, the English must return to God in repentance and humility, and if they did Pole had the power to open to them the gate of God's mercy. Secondly, they must repeal all the schismatical laws which remained on the statute book.[79]

On Friday 30 November 1554, the 'day of reconciliation' finally arrived. The momentous parliamentary ceremony is recorded in many versions.[80] According to an account written in London the day after, perhaps by Henry Pyning, which found its way into the Vatican Secret Archive, parliament had met on Thursday the 28th in its customary setting, the Palace of Westminster. Interestingly, given that Tudor parliaments normally tried to avoid divisions of either House, there was a vote, though this may have been intended as a public demonstration of assent. In the event, two Commons members, out of 440, had the courage to vote against reunion with Rome, but this did not derail the para-liturgical act which followed the next day. After the vote, Gardiner and Pole sorted out the details of proceedings on Friday the 30th. As a result, in the morning of St Andrew's Day, the chapter of the order of the Garter met at Westminster, beginning with a solemn mass in Westminster Abbey, then still staffed by a dean and chapter. This service was also attended by about 500 other English people and 600 of Philip's servants. The ceremony finished at about two in the afternoon, after which the King dined in the palace. Meanwhile the earl of Arundel, as lord high steward, and six Garter knights with an escort, accompanied the Cardinal to the Palace of Westminster. He was now fully vested as a Papal Legate, and he was met first by Philip and afterwards by Mary. The three sat on a dais, under a gold cloth of estate, the Queen in the middle, with Philip on her left and Pole on her right, the representative of the Vicar of Christ taking precedence even over the sovereign Queen. When the formal parliamentary session began, Philip's household was allowed to remain in the chamber, by the King's special permission. Bishop Gardiner, as Lord Chancellor, read out the resolution of both Houses which had been passed on the previous day, and handed it to the Queen. She then asked Pole, in English not Latin, to give the absolution.

[79] Tellechea, *Legación*, pp. 52–4, 147–51 (no. XLVIII = ASV Stato. Inghilterra, 3, fols 156r–158v).

[80] Full bibliographical references in *CRP*, 2, pp. 369–70 (no. 993).

In response, the Legate had various papal documents read, including a bull addressed specifically to Mary and another specifying his own powers to act on behalf of the Pope. Then, after a short address in which he once more referred to England's true Christian past, he absolved the kingdom of the sin of schism in the name of the three Persons of the Trinity. There were then 'Amens', and Mary is recorded as having wept throughout. The proceedings ended with the singing of the *Te Deum*.[81]

Not surprisingly, joyous letters were soon radiating around Catholic Europe. On the day itself, Pole wrote to Charles V and to the Cardinal of Naples, Gianpietro Carafa, who had once been his friend but later, as Pope Paul IV, would cause him and Mary many problems. On this day of reconciliation, Pole harked back to the 1530s when he and Carafa had been active in planning Catholic reform together. In his excitement and exaltation, he told Carafa that England could now become an example to others of a reformed Catholic province, in accordance with their common ideals.[82] It remained to be seen whether this would really happen. In the meantime, while there seem to be no surviving written expressions of Mary's joy – and indeed she had to retire from public view immediately, no doubt to recover from her emotional reaction – her husband's letter to the Pope remains in the Vatican archives. It was written in Spanish from London, evidently in Philip's own hand and without the aid of a secretary, soon after the absolution ceremony had finished. The language is personal, excited, and not entirely tidy. Signing himself 'Most humble son of Your Holiness, the King', instead of the normal style, 'I the King (*Yo el Rey*)', Philip reported that the Legate had duly absolved the kingdom 'at the Queen's intercession and mine'. His ambassador to the Holy See, Juan Manrique de Lara, would give Julius details in due course, but Philip wanted to tell him at once that 'the Queen and I, as such true and devoted children of Your Holiness, have received the greatest contentment that can be expressed in words' from the reconciliation.[83] Like a modern media event, news of the happenings in Westminster on that St Andrew's Day was systematically and enthusiastically spread around Europe.[84] How long would this delight and exaltation last, and who exactly would share in it?

---

[81] *CRP*, 2, p. 374 (no. 994), pp. 378–82 (no. 999), pp. 375–7 (no. 995).

[82] *CRP*, 2, pp. 377–8 (nos 996–7).

[83] Tellechea, *Papado*, i, 28.

[84] Corinna Streckfuss, 'England's Reconciliation with Rome: A News Event in Early Modern Europe', *Historical Research*, lxxxii (2009), pp. 62–73.

Chapter 9

BATTLE FOR ENGLAND'S SOUL,
1553–1558

The reconciliation ceremony in Westminster on 30 November 1554 naturally raises questions concerning Mary's personal religious faith, which had
produced such a drastic action. Apart from referring to the label 'Bloody
Mary', given to her largely as a result of the work of the Protestant martyrologist John Foxe, to such permanent effect, most scholars seem to have felt
that the job was done if they described her as 'Catholic' or 'traditionalist'.[1]
Her obstinate and almost self-destructive clinging to the Mass during her
half-brother's reign certainly supports such an interpretation, but actions of
this kind, however essential and profoundly felt, do not give a rounded view
of a person's religious faith and life. Nor did the dogged resistance expressed
in country houses necessarily indicate what Mary would do when she
obtained power over the whole English Church. Given that religion was
very obviously a – if not the – essential core of Mary's character and life,
it is essential to look closely at what her thoughts and feelings were about
public and private religion. A good start can be made by examining her
custom of worshipping before the Blessed Sacrament in the form of the
consecrated bread, or Host, something she was often reported as doing at
vital stages of her life such as when deciding finally to marry Philip of Spain.

The use of the wafer, the Host, outside the context of the celebration of
the Eucharist did not become part of the practice of the Western Catholic
Church until the fourteenth century. From then on, though, the custom
developed of holding separate services, known as the 'Exposition of the
Blessed Sacrament', in which a previously consecrated Host was displayed
on the altar in a vessel called a monstrance. This enabled Christians to
spend more time gazing at the Host, and praying and meditating in front
of it, than was possible or permitted during the Mass. There might be
hymns, prayers and readings to assist worshippers, and the service of
Exposition commonly ended with a priest blessing the people with the Host
enclosed in the monstrance. This ceremony became known as Benediction.
The details of Mary's personal arrangements for worship are still rather
uncertain, despite some fragments of evidence given by chroniclers and
ambassadors, who were not apparently experts in formal Christian worship
or liturgy. It does seem, however, that, during the period between her

---

[1] Recent examples include Carolly Erickson, *Bloody Mary: The Life of Mary Tudor*
(London: Robson Books, 2001) and Jasper Ridley, *Bloody Mary's Martyrs: The Story of
England's Terror* (London: Constable, 2001).

mother's death in 1536 and her accession to the throne, she was rarely if ever without the wherewithal for Catholic worship, including the Mass and other Eucharistic devotions. The houses in which she lived had private chapels, she employed chaplains of a similar persuasion to herself, and she thus participated in the kind of 'privatized' devotion which until then had been traditional among the upper classes of England and other countries. Once she became Queen, observers sometimes remarked that she took this devotion further than many of her devout contemporaries. Charles V's ambassador Simon Renard notes that, in late October 1553, she had the Blessed Sacrament in her room.[2] Given that he describes her doing the kind of things that the faithful normally did during services of Exposition, it is probable that she had some kind of oratory, with an altar, in the privy chamber in addition to the facilities of the royal chapel. This practice was criticized by Philip's ecclesiastical adviser Bartolomé Carranza in a sermon preached at Court in Lent 1555.[3] Much more publicly, an anonymous Spanish observer recorded that, during the wedding itself, she spent her time gazing at the sacrament. He does not specify whether this was the Host consecrated by Bishop Gardiner on the High Altar of Winchester Cathedral during the nuptial Mass or, more probably, the reserved Sacrament suspended above it in a pyx, as was traditional until the Council of Trent decreed, in 1563, that it should be in a box, or 'tabernacle' fixed to the altar.[4] Evidently Mary's approach to the Sacrament of the Altar represented a profound Christian faith which could not be compromised, either in adversity or prosperity. The many frustrations of her life might be channelled into her devotion to the Lord's Body.[5] In order to understand how Mary understood this, a look at her spiritual upbringing is needed.

Fortunately, for those who seek a deeper understanding, there is a genuine literary link between Mary and her mother, placing her in a powerful spiritual tradition which had grown up in late medieval Europe and which had particularly influenced the three centres of the Tudor–Trastamaran–Habsburg alliance: England, Spain and the Netherlands. In 1534, just before she was transferred from Buckden to Kimbolton, where she would die, Catherine sent two books of spiritual consolation in Latin to her daughter Mary, from whom she was by then irrevocably separated. One was a letter by St Jerome, the fourth-century translator of the Latin Bible known as the Vulgate, while the other was the *Vita Christi* (Life of Christ) by Ludolf of Saxony.[6] Ludolf was first a Dominican friar and then a Carthusian monk, becoming prior of the Charterhouse in Koblenz

---

[2] *CSP Span* XI, 327.

[3] Tellechea, 'Un tratadito de Bartolomé Carranza sobre la Misa', *Archivio Italiano per l'Historia della Pietà*, xi (1998), 145–79, at p. 164, translated in Edwards, 'Bartolomé Carranza de Miranda's "Little Treatise on How to Attend Mass" (1555)', *Reformation and Renaissance Review*, xi (i) (2009 [2010]), pp. 91–120.

[4] *CSP Span* XIII, 7.

[5] Compare Loades, 'The Personal Religion of Mary I', *CMT*, p. 29.

[6] James Carley, *The Books of Henry VIII and his Wives* (London: British Library, 2004), p. 110.

between 1343 and 1348, the year of the Black Death plague in Germany, and afterwards the order's prior in Strasbourg. His 'Life of Christ', which soon became a spiritual classic, is a meditation rather than a biography, containing prayers, moral and doctrinal commentary, and numerous quotations from the early Christian theologians, or Fathers of the Church. This *Vita* was quickly put into print when that technique arrived, and Mary's mother Catherine will surely have learned of it from her own mother Isabella, who had it both in Latin and in a Castilian Spanish translation.[7] As well as this personal gift from her mother, Mary was supported, in the 1530s, by a sympathetic friend who shared her spiritual approach and survived well into her reign as Queen. This was Henry Parker, eighth Baron Morley, who translated religious works for her as well as sending New Year copies of them, with flattering prefaces, to her father. Some time in the 1540s, Morley presented Mary with a manuscript copy of a commentary on the Psalms by the fourteenth-century English mystic Richard Rolle, who was born in Yorkshire, studied at Oxford, later became a hermit, and advocated in his writings a subjective and emotional approach to Christianity. In his preface to Rolle's commentary, Morley apologized for offering Mary an 'old boke', but said that it was redeemed by its contents. He relied on her 'excellent wytt' to discern the spiritual riches within this manuscript.[8] As for Ludolf, who was a near contemporary of Rolle and wrote in a similar way, Lambeth Palace Library has a copy of his *Vita Christi*, which was printed in Paris in 1534 precisely at the time of Catherine's gift of the work to her daughter. Whether or not this is the copy which Mary received from her mother, its form and style indicate that it was bound by the anonymous binder who had worked personally for Edward VI and continued in Mary's reign. It is most likely that it was in fact the copy presented to Mary in 1557 by the then royal printer John Cawood.[9] Also, on New Year's Day 1556, Morley had given Mary a treatise on the miracles attributable to the Eucharist, which celebrated her role in restoring the Catholic faith in England.[10]

Ludolf's book, like Thomas à Kempis's (of Kempen's) *Imitatio Christi* (Imitation of Christ), is apparently more often cited than read by historians, but its meaning is great in Mary's life as she herself understood that life. It would be very easy to see an attachment to Ludolf and Thomas's books as an example of what tends today to be called 'traditional' religion. Both texts are 'medieval' in date, an anachronistic concept which is of little use in understanding the religious life of Mary and her contemporaries. Looking forward, though, it is clear that the founder of the Society of Jesus

[7] Francisco Javier Sánchez Cantón, *Libros, tapices y cuadros que coleccionó Isabel la Católica* (Madrid: Consejo Superior de Investigaciones Científicas, 1950), pp. 26, 60.

[8] Carley, *Books*, pp. 61–4.

[9] Ibid., p. 110.

[10] Richard Rex, 'Morley and the Papacy: Rome, Regime and Religion', in Marie Axton and James P. Carley, *'Triumphs of the English': Henry Parker, Lord Morley, Translator to the Tudor Court* (London: British Library, 2000), pp. 87–105.

(Jesuits), Ignatius of Loyola, a friend of Pole, was deeply influenced, in particular, by Ludolf's Life of Christ, which he read when he was recovering in his family castle of Loyola, in 1521, from wounds acquired in Charles V's army while defending Navarre against the French.[11] Thus Mary, far from being out of touch with the forthcoming Catholic 'Counter-Reformation', was at least indirectly influenced by one of its founding texts. Ignatius's 'Spiritual Exercises', which are a major inspiration of the order he founded and of innumerable retreat houses to this day, copied and developed, from his own experience, the vivid imagining of Christ's life and death, as described in the Gospels, which are characteristic of Ludolf and Thomas's works. Given what is now known of Mary's religious life, it seems clear that she was convinced that she had a personal relationship with her Saviour Jesus Christ, such as the reformers and evangelicals of her own time, and of subsequent centuries, have generally claimed for themselves. This is the perspective from which her excellent Renaissance humanist credentials should be viewed.

One significant handicap in attempting to discover Mary's full religious identity is the almost complete lack of personal writings which can be ascribed to her. The British Library does, however, have an autograph copy of a prayer ascribed to St Thomas Aquinas. Written in a lavishly illustrated devotional Book of Hours, it is entitled: '[T]he prayer of Sainte Thomas of Aquine translated out of Latine into Englyshe by ye moste exselent Prince[s]s [crossed out, with "lady" overwritten] Mary daughter to the moste hygh and myghty Prynce and Prynces[s] [not crossed out] Kyng Henry the VIII and [Quene Kateryne hys wyfe (crossed out)] in the yere of oure lorde god mccccc.xxvii [1527] and the xi yere of here age'. In the manner of the traditional Catholic liturgical offices, the prayer is written in the first person singular, thus making the young Mary pray it personally. In it Aquinas, and by extension the translator herself, ask God:

> to grant me to covyt w[i]th an ardent mynde those thingys whiche may please the[e], to serche them wysely, to know them truly and to fulfyll them perfytely to the laude and glory of thy name. Order my lyuynge that I may do that whiche thou requirest of me, and geve me grace that I may know yt and have wyll and powre to do it.[12]

The prayer's content shows that Mary was brought up in orthodox Catholic devotion, with a moral earnestness which she would display when she eventually reached the throne. It could also be said that, in the religious context of the late 1520s, the prayer looked both backwards and forwards. Written by one of the greatest scholastic theologians of the Middle Ages, it also in a small way represented the revival of Aquinas's

---

[11] John W. O'Malley, *The First Jesuits* (Cambridge, MA: Harvard University Press, 1993), p. 46.
[12] BL Additional MS 17012, fol. 192r; Carley, *Books*, p. 109.

theology, known as 'neo-Thomism' which was taking place in the period when Mary translated it. Especially strong in Spain, this intellectual movement would later arrive in her court in the persons of Philip's ecclesiastical advisers, and in particular of three members of Aquinas's Dominican order: Carranza, Villagarcía and De Soto.

As a young adult in the 1540s, Mary made a more notable contribution to religious development in England through her association with her father's last Queen, Catherine Parr. Despite coming from conventional gentry stock of no great academic distinction, Catherine seems to have taken to the humanistic atmosphere of her new husband's court with enthusiasm. Notably, in 1545, she produced a devotional work entitled 'Prayers or medytacions wherin the mynde is styrred patiently to sufre al afflictions here'. Intended for distribution among her ladies, the book contained prayers from various sources, including the executed bishop of Rochester, John Fisher. The 'meditations' referred to in the title came from the *Imitation of Christ* of Thomas à Kempis. It has often been suggested that Catherine Parr and her circle showed evangelical sympathies which heralded the reforming zeal of Edward VI and his advisers, but whatever the truth of that, in the main her devotional collection represented a certain kind of mainstream Catholic spirituality.[13] In this, Mary herself was deeply involved. Catherine seems to have regarded her stepdaughter as an academic mentor, and it was at this time that Mary undertook an important project, the translation from Latin into English of Erasmus's 'Paraphrase' of St John's Gospel. The Dutch humanist's lengthy paraphrases of, or commentaries on, the New Testament were all to be thus translated and, although she had to drop out of the project, apparently because of ill-health, Mary's initial participation involved her directly in work on a text which would be much favoured in the following reign. On the advice of Cranmer and others, the Erasmus *Paraphrases* in English were ordered by Edward's government to be placed in all parish churches. Like their author, they both predated and cut across the growing denominational divisions of sixteenth-century Europe. Thus it appears that, up until her accession to the throne in 1553, Mary represented both a kind of Catholic humanism which contained the values of the previous generation, and the influence of what happened at the Council of Trent between 1545 and 1552, which affected both Catholics and Protestants. Significantly, when Queen herself, Mary immediately took into her own library a large number of Catherine Parr's books, and continued thereafter to be a strong patron of Christian humanist publication.[14] It is certainly arguable that, until July 1553, Mary showed no sign of special devotion to the Papacy or to traditional activities of which her father had come to disapprove, such as

[13] For the 'Protestant' interpretation of Catherine Parr's spirituality, see James, *Catherine Parr*, especially pp. 202–10.

[14] Carley, *Books*, pp. 138–41; Lucy E. C. Wooding, *Rethinking Catholicism in Reformation England* (Oxford: Clarendon Press, 2000), pp. 106, 117–19.

pilgrimages to shrines and the veneration of saints' relics. The Christian humanist circle in which she was brought up, which was greatly influenced by Erasmus and Vives, had little use for such things.[15] It remained to be seen whether her own ideas would be put into practice, now that her 'good cousin' Pole had arrived to advise her.

Until quite recently, Pole's papal legation to restore and run the English Church, with the widest possible powers given to him by Julius III, has tended to be viewed negatively, by English scholars at least. He was 'the Pope's alter ego' and his 'resident agent in north-western Europe', and he has been seen as dominated by irrelevant Italian experience, addicted to running away from difficulty and conflict, and better at small-group work and spiritual direction, especially with women, than at government and leadership on a large scale. It is said, as though this were a bad thing and hence constituted a criticism, that his twenty years of exile in Italy led him to see the English Church as 'only a part of the international Church', which of course it had been until the Henrician schism, and hence he was totally out of sympathy with the English bishops whom Mary had restored before his return. He is accused of having used inappropriate Italian methods, whatever those were, and of fatally underestimating the strength both of English patriotism and of heresy in the country.[16] His fundamental problem, as it turned out, was none of these but rather the shortage of time available to carry out such a comprehensive and difficult programme.[17] He has until now been generally regarded as legalistic and obsessed with ritual and ceremony. Knowledge that he employed Italians, such as Niccolò Ormanetto, Gianbattista Binardi and Antonio Fiordibello, as well as the Hungarian Andras Dudic, in addition to Englishmen who included John Clerk, Nicholas Harpsfield, Thomas Stemp/Stymp and Seth Holland, has only made him seem, in many minds, even more exotic and out of touch.[18] Yet he became one of the central figures in Mary's life, and his activity as legate requires another look, as does his relationship with his relative and Queen, once they were dealing face to face and not by correspondence.

Even though Mary had managed to get her chosen new and restored bishops put in place by April 1554, they still needed to be fully absolved for their schism and 'heresy' once Pole was in England. This proved to be one of the first of many cases in which the absolute nature of Roman canon law

[15] Loades, 'Personal Religion', pp. 19, 25–6, 29.

[16] Mayer, *PP&P*, pp. 252–3; Rex Pogson, 'Cardinal Pole: Papal Legate to England in Mary Tudor's Reign', Ph.D. thesis, University of Cambridge, 1972, pp. 26–7, 40, 52, 120, 308; Pogson, 'Reginald Pole and the Priorities of Government in Mary Tudor's Church', *Historical Journal*, xviii (1975), pp. 3–21, at 6, 7–9.

[17] Pogson, 'Cardinal Pole', pp. 223, 232, 248; Mayer, *PP&P*, p. 253. This view has been elaborated by Eamon Duffy in *Fires of Faith: Catholic England Under Mary Tudor* (New Haven, CT and London: Yale University Press, 2009).

[18] Pogson, 'Revival and reform in Mary Tudor's Church: A Question of Money', in Christopher Haigh, ed., *The English Reformation Revised* (Cambridge: Cambridge University Press, 1987), pp. 139–56, at p. 154; *CRP*, i, pp. 24–9, 37.

did indeed make pastoral and political sensitivity difficult to achieve. In outline, the position was as follows. Bishops who had been consecrated according to the Roman rite and under papal authority, before the split, and had subsequently adopted heresy and/or married (Cranmer had secretly married even before his consecration) were removed from office. Bishops who had been consecrated using the Roman rite, but during the schism, might be absolved, and allowed to continue as bishops, if they abjured their previous errors. In contrast, those who were consecrated using the new ordinal of Edward VI were in no circumstances allowed to continue in office. As for the lesser clergy, the great majority who had been ordained using the Roman rite were permitted to continue as clergy if they abjured their errors and received absolution. As in the case of using, without reconsecration, churches which had also been used for reformed worship, there seems to have been something of a fudge concerning those clergy who had been ordained using the Edwardian ordinal. Nevertheless, particularly in 1555, Pole paid a lot of attention to regularizing the diaconal and priestly orders of individuals in England, Wales and Ireland. The non-Roman ordinals of the English Church were never recognized, though, by Pole or anyone else at Rome, a situation which persists to this day.[19] As far as ability to celebrate the Sacraments and minister to Christians was concerned, the situation of the clergy during and after the Marian restoration was clearly set out by Bartolomé Carranza in the catechism which he wrote originally for the English Church, and published in Antwerp in 1558. Those who were ordained into the Catholic Church, and then left it through heresy and schism, retained the authority which they had had before to consecrate the bread and wine in the Mass, although they personally sinned when they did so outside the Catholic Church. But even though their celebration of the Sacraments was valid, Catholics should not receive the consecrated elements from them if they had not first been individually absolved.[20] This severe Spanish Dominican constantly bolstered Pole's conscience in such matters but, in a series of documents issued in January and February 1555, the Legate nonetheless allowed various senior clergy to exercise a full Catholic ministry as bishops and priests.[21] As had been anticipated in earlier discussions between Pole and Rome, the job of issuing the appropriate documents of absolution proved too demanding for the small staff at Lambeth Palace. Therefore, between 29 January and 7 March 1555, Pole issued a large set of documents, in standard form, to the cathedral deans and chapters and other officials of the English and Welsh dioceses of the province of Canterbury, with implicit extension to the province of York over which he had legatine authority, delegating to them his papal power to

---

[19] Hutchings, *Reginald Cardinal Pole*, pp. 86–7; R. William Franklin, ed., *Anglican Orders: Essays on the Centenary of* Apostolicae Curae, *1896–1996* (London: Mowbray, 1996).

[20] Bartolomé Carranza, *Comentarios sobre el catechismo christiano*, ed. J. I. Tellechea, 2 vols (Madrid: Biblioteca de Autores Cristianos, 1972), ii, p. 224.

[21] *CRP*, 3, pp. 26–9 (nos 1042–5), 35–8 (nos 1055–6), 40 (nos 106–70), 41 (no. 1072).

absolve former heretics and schismatics. However serious their offences, they were to be absolved if they humbly sought forgiveness and did penance. The offences concerned included presiding over non-Roman services, ordaining clergy while in heresy and schism, taking oaths to kings as Supreme Head rather than to the Pope, and making irregular presentations (appointments) to clerical livings, whether by their own nomination or that of laymen. Those who might be absolved, if they showed proper contrition, included members of religious orders who had abandoned their monasteries and convents, becoming secular priests and occupying benefices. Copies of Pole's powers from Rome were included in many of these letters, and the recipients were authorized to delegate their authority in these matters to parish priests, if the pressure of business made this necessary.[22]

Also mentioned in these documents addressed to the dioceses was the vexed question of clerical marriage. It is perhaps hard for many readers in a much later century to understand the passions which were aroused by the marriage of priests, though it still remains a lively issue for some members of the Roman Catholic Church. In the context of Mary's religious restoration, it was one of the most contentious issues, as far as the ordinary English and Welsh public was concerned, though less so in Ireland, where the Henrician and Edwardian reformations had scarcely taken hold. Henry and his two daughters, though not apparently his son, seem to have found the idea of married clergy utterly abhorrent. Thus Thomas Cranmer kept his own marriage, in Nuremberg in 1532, secret from most, and the same applied to his younger brother Edmund, who had become archdeacon of Canterbury and provost of Wingham by February–March 1534. By 1535, he too had broken his priestly vow of celibacy and fathered a son, named Thomas after his uncle. In 1538, clerical celibacy was one of the subjects which caused English negotiations with some German Protestants to fail. The issue would not go away and, in the following year, Henry expressed a willingness to have it examined by the universities. Nonetheless the 1539 Act of Six Articles still required celibacy, and the 1543 doctrinal formulation known as the 'King's Book' went even further, prescribing the death sentence for clergy caught breaking their vows in this respect. Perhaps not surprisingly, Archbishop Cranmer, who kept his own wife in complete privacy most of the time, did not attend the relevant debate in the House of Lords.[23] Thus until the old King died, England's clergy, and those of Wales and Ireland, had to regard any lapse from traditional Catholic celibacy as liable to end their lives, and not only cause them social shame and separation from their partners. Perhaps it was in reaction to this climate of fear that, at the beginning of Edward's reign, in 1547, the ordinary clergy in the lower house of the Convocation of Canterbury

[22] *CRP*, 3, pp. 33–5 (no. 1054).
[23] MacCulloch, *Cranmer*, pp. 69–73, 109, 219–20, 238, 240, 243, 249, 274, 455; Diarmaid MacCulloch, *Tudor Church Militant. Edward VI and the Protestant Reformation* (London: Allen Lane, 1999), pp. 5–6.

voted overwhelmingly in favour of being allowed to marry. As a result a bill to that effect was quickly passed by the Commons, but defeated in the Lords. Nevertheless, from then on, Cranmer started living openly as a married man, and by the end of 1547 documents issued from Lambeth Palace were beginning to refer explicitly to clergy wives, if only in select cases.[24] Eventually, during his trial in 1555, Cranmer admitted publicly that, even before Henry VIII died, he and his wife had had a son and two daughters. Although he offered no details, his daughter Margaret seems to have been born in the late 1530s, marrying after 1555. Son Thomas was still a boy when Elizabeth succeeded Mary on the throne, and seems to have been born during Edward's reign.[25] Early examples of open and legal clerical marriage in England were not always wholly inspiring. A case close to the heart of Mary's Lord Chancellor, Stephen Gardiner, was Cranmer's chaplain John Ponet, who succeeded Gardiner as bishop of Winchester when the latter was despatched to the Tower of London for resisting further reform. Parliament finally made clerical marriage a legal option in 1549, but before that, on 4 November 1548, Ponet and his wife gained a joint dispensation from Cranmer's faculty office to eat meat and drink milk in Lent, thus indicating that they were at least cohabiting. Unfortunately, by 1550, when they were ensconced in Wolvesey Palace at Winchester, it had become clear that Ponet's wife was a bigamist, being already married to a Nottingham butcher. In July 1550, in a public act which was highly embarrassing to the supporters of the 'new religion', and not least to Cranmer himself, Ponet and his 'wife' were legally separated at a consistory hearing in St Paul's Cathedral. Ponet did not have to pine for long, though, as on 25 October of that year he married again, in Croydon parish church, near one of the archbishop's palaces. This time Cranmer supervised the whole thing closely, as Ponet married Mary, daughter of Peter Hayman, a solid member of the Kentish gentry who assisted the archbishop in financial matters.[26]

It seems that, at the end of 1548 or the beginning of 1549, the duke of Somerset had secured a sufficient political consensus for marriage to be permitted to clergy of the Church of England. Thus when Mary came to the throne there was a considerable number of married clergy, about whom she and Pole were deeply concerned. The main concentrations seem to have been in south-east England and Wales. The reformers' strongest argument against clerical celibacy naturally came from the New Testament, and in particular from Paul's first letter to Timothy. Part of this text was commonly painted on the now whitewashed walls of Edwardian churches, obliterating earlier paintings: '[The enemies of the Gospel] forbid marriage . . . which God created to be received with thanksgiving by those who believe and know the truth' (1 Timothy 4: 3–4). As promised

[24] Ibid., p. 77.
[25] MacCulloch, *Cranmer*, p. 361.
[26] Ibid., pp. 492–3.

in the voluminous correspondence which preceded his arrival in England, Pole quickly tackled the question of the married clergy.[27] One of the powers issued on 29 January 1555 from Lambeth Palace to bishops and other senior clergy was to absolve and restore the orders of those clerics who had married, as long as they abandoned their wives and lived outside the dioceses in which they had previously worked.[28] The documents of course give no indication of the domestic and often public anguish which was caused by these expressions of what the official Church regarded as its mercy. The strong feelings which surged around this issue, not least within Mary and Pole, are well represented in the work of Thomas Martin, an Oxford theologian who had gone into exile under Edward VI, and denounced his reforms from Paris. On Mary's accession, he returned to England and became chancellor of Winchester diocese under Gardiner. In 1555, he took part in the visitations of Oxford and Cambridge and was later successively made master of requests and a master of chancery. In 1557 he became a commissioner for heresy, having already taken part in the trials of Bishops Cranmer and Hooper, as well as those of Rowland Taylor and John Cardmaker.

In his book *The marriage of priestes*, Thomas Martin, a civil lawyer and protégé of Gardiner, combined Christian teaching with polemic against those of the clergy who had married during the previous reign. In answer to the reformers' claims for 1 Timothy as sanctioning clerical marriage, he asserted that it was for the bishops and no others to interpret the Bible.[29] He criticized the Eastern Churches for having married priests, asserting that they had fallen away from the strict standards of the early Church Fathers. He used successive condemnations of clerical marriage by medieval popes, beginning with Gregory VII in the late eleventh century, to justify his stance, even, contrary to history, calling married priests a 'novelty'.[30] He lashed out against the clergy of his own day who had married, saying that they should attend solely to the altar and not be distracted by sexual relationships, which they were driven to only by lust. He sarcastically added that these reformed clerics found Purgatory on earth with their wives, even though they did not believe Catholic teaching on the subject.[31]

As had been indicated to Pole even before he set foot in England, one of the most urgent problems in Mary's plan to restore Catholicism was the

---

[27] *CRP*, 2, pp. 228–9, 254–7, 264, 269–70 (nos 794, 796–812, 822).

[28] *CRP*, 3, pp. 35–6, 59, 68–70, 74, 78–81, 90, 94, 97, 100, 103, 126, 128, 136, 141,167, 191 (nos 1055, 1110, 1137, 1149a, 1160, 1162, 1171, 1192, 1201, 1205, 1214, 1225, 1285, 1286, 1291, 1320a, 1333, 1380, 1424).

[29] William Wizeman, S. J., *The Theology and Spirituality of Mary Tudor's Church* (Aldershot: Ashgate, 2006), pp. 32, 36, 40, 58–9.

[30] Thomas Martin, *A traictaise declaring and plainly prouying that the pretensed marriage of priestes and professed persons is no marriage* (London, 1554), sigs N3r–v, Q4r–v, KK1r, I 2r–4v; Wizeman, *Theology and Spirituality*, pp. 123–4, 130.

[31] Martin, *Marriage*, sigs π A3r–v, R3v; Wizeman, *Theology and Spirituality*, p. 139.

fact that the churches had for several years been used for the services of the 1549 and 1552 Prayer Books. No one seems to have paid much attention to this issue for the first year of Mary's reign, when there was a de facto restoration of Henry VIII's 'national Catholic' Church, but Philip's religious advisers had other ideas. In his letter to Pole, dated 27 September 1554, Friar Bartolomé Carranza had reported that 'our priests' (meaning the Spaniards) were having scruples about celebrating Catholic services in the English churches. They were particularly worried about those in which 'heretics' had been buried, with non-Roman rites. Their argument in such cases was logical, if severe: if Catholics were to have no communion with heretics when they were alive, how could they do so when they were dead, with the ritual pollution of their presence remaining? The whole of England was still under interdict until it was reconciled to Rome, so that, strictly, no Catholic services at all should have been held. This would evidently have been intolerable to Mary, leaving her more or less where she had been under Edward VI, but the ever meticulous Carranza felt that he had to ask his friend Pole for a ruling.[32] Mary shared this concern, and in her letter to Pole, dated 28 September 1554, she indicated that English priests who already regarded themselves as Catholics were now conducting traditional services, despite their dubious situation in canon law. Like Carranza, the Queen also raised the question of heretics buried in churches and churchyards.[33] Pole's initial reaction was that all the churches concerned had to be reconsecrated, and 'heretical' remains removed from them and their surroundings, before the reconciliation could take place.[34] This was not done by the time of Pole's arrival, and there was other ground to be made up as well.

England's cathedrals and parish churches had changed a great deal in how they looked, as well as how they were used, between Henry's divorce of Catherine and the accession of their daughter. On 20 November 1534, the Acts of Supremacy had been put into statute, making Henry head of the Church of England instead of the Pope. Subsequently, in June 1535, the King's secretary and 'vicegerent' for spiritual affairs, Thomas Cromwell, had ordered the removal from missals and other service-books of all references to the Pope: prayers for him were henceforth banned. On 11 August 1536, an Act of the Convocation of Canterbury, which was presumed also to apply to the province of York, abolished some traditional holy days – saints' days and other festivals on which Christians were required to attend church and specially elaborate services were held. Abandoned were all those which fell during the law terms kept by the King's courts at Westminster, which covered about half the year, and also those during the harvest period, between 1 July and 30 September. The only special celebrations still allowed were St George's Day (23 April), the Birth of St John the

---

[32] Tellechea, *CyP*, pp. 186–7; *CRP*, 2, p. 339 (no. 941).
[33] Tellechea, *Legación*, pp. 31–2, 130–1 (no. XL).
[34] *CRP*, 2, p. 345 (no. 954).

Baptist at Midsummer (24 June), and All Saints' Day (1 November). Services might still be held on the other feast days, but the bells were not to be rung, there were to be no solemn processions, there should be no obligation to attend, and most people were now expected to do their normal work. In addition, this session of Convocation ordered that Christian doctrine should henceforth be taught to children in English and not Latin, and the rector or patron of each parish church should now provide a bible, either in Latin or English, to be read by the public. The 'Great Bible' in English was placed in churches all over England and, more spectacularly, the government ordered a serious assault on the keeping of 'images' or statues of saints in churches, and the funding of lights to burn before them out of reverence. After this, the only heavy candles which were permitted to burn continuously were those before the reserved sacrament in the pyx and the figures of Christ on the cross, with Mary and St John the Evangelist on either side, which remained on the 'rood' (cross) screen between the clergy's part of the church, to the east, and the 'nave' which was occupied by the lay congregation. Although the Latin mass continued to be celebrated, there had thus been considerable disruption of parish life even before the imposition of the first English Prayer Book in 1549.[35] One sometimes forgotten consequence of the many changes that had taken place under Henry and Edward was that, by the time Mary began her restoration of the Mass, a large proportion of her subjects had either never knowingly experienced that way of worship, let alone understood its meaning, or else had never had that possibility, because of their date of birth. Someone who was twenty in the summer of 1553 could never have known England as subject to the Pope, while a fifteen-year old would have been just nine when Henry died. He or she would thus have known nothing but the turmoil of Edward's time, and heard of older ideas and practices only from older people.[36] Mary's beloved Mass would have to be taught more or less from scratch, even to the better disposed and more traditionally brought up among England's youth.

The reconciliation of England to Rome would not, of course, have happened without Julius's last-minute concessions to the possessors of former church property. Both Charles and Philip had put on pressure, through their ambassadors, to persuade the Curia to allow Pole greater latitude to dispense individuals to remain in possession of what they had been granted by the Crown under Henry and Edward. The scale of the problem was vast since the English Church had been subjected to very severe depredations between the 1530s and Mary's accession and a significant amount of this property still remained in royal hands. The loss of the monasteries was the most conspicuous change to the English

[35] Eamon Duffy, *The Voices of Morebath: Reformation and Rebellion in an English Village* (New Haven, CT and London: Yale University Press, 2001), pp. 84, 88–9, 91, 94–101.

[36] Susan Brigden, 'Youth and the English Reformation', *Past and Present*, xcv (1992), pp. 37, 43.

landscape, also affecting Wales and Ireland. About 800 religious houses, of varying sizes and belonging to a number of orders, had been confiscated. The dioceses and parishes were not safe either, since Henry VIII had effectively declared open season for the grabbing of their property as well. The bishops' London residences were a particular target of royal and aristocratic greed. For instance, Henry's boyhood friend, Charles Brandon, duke of Suffolk, received Norwich Place, formerly the London residence of the bishops of Norwich. Things became even worse under Edward VI. Lord Protector Somerset's massive Thames-side Somerset House obliterated no fewer than three former bishops' residences, Worcester, Llandaff and Carlisle, and involved the destruction by explosives of the former Hospitallers' priory church of St John's, Clerkenwell. Then, under the presidency of the duke of Northumberland, all remaining church property was nearly confiscated, as guild and chantry goods indeed were. The plan failed for political reasons, mainly to do with Northumberland's growing unpopularity in 1552–3, but it would have involved the paying out of pittances to 'preaching ministers', with the effective winding up of bishops' and cathedral establishments. It is hard to assess the scale of actual deprivation of the clergy as a whole in the early 1550s, but rural clergy were by then increasingly involved in legal action to retain control over their 'glebe' lands and to be allowed to continue collecting tithes, the latter being effectively impossible to raise in the towns after 1549, when the new Prayer Book came in. Under Edward, the clergy's complaints were ignored, but their indignation burst out in the more sympathetic climate of Mary's reign. A poem of 1553 in support of the Commonwealth (*Respublica*) of England reflected the clergy's sense of grievance, in particular against the despoiled bishops who received compensation from the Crown in the form of the former livings of lesser men:

> Bare pa[r]sonages of appropriations,
> Bought from Respublica and first empowr'd;
> Then at the highest extent to bishops allowed,
> Let out to their hands for fourscore and [nineteen] year.[37]

In fact, the bishops were in a bad way as well, financially, when Mary came to the throne. Unprecedentedly high levels of taxation and inflation in the previous two reigns meant that those who remained in post in 1553 between them owed to the Crown the colossal sum of £9,825 10s 5¼d which should have been paid at Christmas 1552. This was clearly a matter of personal conscience to Mary, and she acted at once, without the need for Pole's urgings, which he, of course, freely offered. First, the Crown resumed its traditional patronage of the cathedrals. In particular, it

---

[37] *Respublica*, ed. W. W. Greg (London: Early English Text Society, old series, ccxxvi, 1952), III, v; Felicity Heal, *Reformation in Britain and Ireland* (Oxford: Clarendon Press, 2003), pp. 201–6.

restored the bishopric of Durham, which had been abolished under Edward VI in part as a financial measure. Then, bishops were dispensed from paying to the Crown the traditional taxes of first fruits and tenths, which had been sent to the Papacy before Henry VIII's schism and were supposed to be some kind of thank-offering for receiving high office in the Church. This new arrangement was of course supported by Pole, with the money being handed to the bishops themselves in compensation for their earlier economic losses. After they had used some of it to pay pensions to the surviving ex-members of religious orders, they were to put the rest towards current expenses. In addition, and quite typically, Mary took up an instrument of her brother's government, the issuing of royal commissions for ecclesiastical affairs, but for a very different purpose. This was to work painstakingly to regain the property of the Church which had disappeared into private hands. As in so many other cases, Mary was destined to suffer frustration and disappointment in this area, but her purpose was clear enough.[38]

The fullest representation of Mary and Pole's ideas for the reform of the English Church on Catholic lines was the Synod held at London and Westminster, which began on 11 November 1555. The decree announcing this assembly of the bishops and other leaders of the clergy received its first reading in the House of Lords that day and proceedings began at once despite some opposition among the peers.[39] Pole presided as papal legate, though not yet archbishop of Canterbury, but he naturally had his programme approved by Pope Paul IV, who had succeeded Julius in the previous May, and he was also advised on the spot by Bartolomé Carranza.[40] On 11 December, Pole's friend Cardinal Morone wrote to him to confirm that the Pope wholly approved of his plans for the Synod and would be sending a brief to confirm this.[41] The main planks of Pole's programme were as follows:

Personal residence of bishops in their dioceses and parish priests in their parishes.

The correction of various vices and abuses, first among the clergy and then among the laity.

The need for Catholic preaching and a good Christian example to be set by the clergy.

A return to traditional liturgical ceremonies which had been banned under Edward VI, such as the application of ashes on Ash Wednesday and the carrying of palms or other branches on Palm Sunday, as well as personal veneration of the cross on Good Friday.

[38] Pogson, 'Revival and Reform', pp. 145–7.
[39] *CRP*, 3, pp. 193–4 (no. 1430).
[40] *CRP*, 3, p. 206 (no. 1451); Tellechea, *CyP*, p. 62.
[41] *CRP*, 3, pp. 209–10 (no. 1458).

The restoration of churches for Catholic worship.

The preparation of a new English translation of the New Testament to replace that of William Tyndale and the 'Great Bible'.

The preparation and publication of a new Catechism, to be used primarily by the clergy as a teaching aid, and a book of homilies to be read in parishes by clergy instead of the collection which had been in use under Edward VI.

The establishment of a seminary in each diocese to train new clergy.[42]

The voluminous records of Carranza's trial by the Inquisition, in Spain and then Rome, between 1559 and 1576, clearly indicate that this Spanish Dominican was constantly present at the Synod sessions and had considerable influence as an adviser. In this respect he appears to have carried on as he had done in Charles V's team during the first two phases of the Council of Trent, in 1545–6 and 1551–2. Pole presided over these sessions, and gave addresses in English to the assembled fathers.[43] Carranza, on the other hand, was Philip's eyes and ears at their deliberations. Indeed, Don Antonio de Toledo was despatched by the King from Brussels to instruct Carranza to attend, while later the friar himself, by then archbishop of Toledo, told the inquisitors in his homeland that he had been ordered by Philip to remain in England for this reason, and not join him in the Netherlands, as most of the other Spaniards did during 1556–7.[44] In view of Pole's excited letter to his long-standing colleague Gianpietro Carafa, dashed off on the afternoon of the absolution and reconciliation of England, it is not surprising that, with the recipient now pope, the proceedings of the Synod should have been sent to Rome with such pride. While the Council of Trent remained suspended, what was happening in England may have seemed the best current hope, anywhere in Europe, for the implementation of the agenda of Catholic reform. In fact, the London decrees were not published in Rome until 1562, by which time Pole was dead and Carranza in prison, and then only after heavy revision.[45] In February 1556, and with Carranza's support, Pole prorogued the Synod, so that the bishops might return to their dioceses and carry out formal visitations to discover the true situation on the ground. In the event they would never reconvene, since the Synod was prorogued again on 10 November 1557, and did not meet in 1558 because of 'dearth in the country'.[46] The subsequent life of the English synodal decrees would be within the worldwide Catholic Church, since in its revised version they largely constituted the relevant decrees of the Council of Trent.[47] In the meantime, the

[42] Tellechea, *CyP*, p. 63.
[43] BAV MS Vat. Lat. 5968, fols 2r–4v.
[44] Tellechea, ed., *Fray Bartolomé Carranza*, iii, p. 25.
[45] Tellechea, 'El formulario de visita pastoral de Bartolomé Carranza, Arzobispo de Toledo', in *CyP*, p. 321.
[46] *CRP*, 2, pp. 227–8, 401 (nos 1492, 1931).
[47] Tellechea, 'Formulario', in *CyP*, pp. 306–7.

programme of restoration and reform in the English Church had to continue.

Preaching was stressed in the Westminster decrees as a way of teaching Catholic doctrine and counteracting the previous and current efforts of the reformers. In this respect, the 'generation gap' in Catholic teaching in England was recognized by the monarchs and by church leaders. Pole's ideas on the subject had been formed largely on the Continent, during the ferment of the 1530s when the divisions between 'Catholic' and 'Protestant' had not yet coagulated. Back then, it seemed that the youthful population of Europe was open to be won, and would fall to those who most purely adhered to the values of the New Testament Church and put them over most effectively to the population at large. In many ways, the situation in Mary's England would have seemed very similar. Thus preaching was a natural and prominent part of the reform programme about which Pole had gleefully written, on the 'Day of Reconciliation' in 1554, to Gianpietro Carafa. In England, the Legate also had the active support of Spanish representatives of the Dominicans, whose real name, 'Order of Preachers' indicates their primary purpose. In particular, he had been able to join forces with Bartolomé Carranza, whom he had known at Trent and who, while being a distinguished theologian, was also no mean preacher. Probably during the second period of that Council, in 1551–2, Carranza had set down his ideas on the duties of a bishop in his 'Mirror for Pastors'. In it, he put preaching second after a bishop praying for his people, and even before the administration of the sacraments, including the Mass. In the context of Mary's England, the views of Trent on the subject of episcopal preaching were almost frighteningly pertinent, and although they would not be formally promulgated until 1563, Carranza put them in his 'Mirror' and brought them with him to England. The Tridentine Fathers wanted all diocesan bishops personally to proclaim scripture and Catholic doctrine on Sundays and major festivals, as well as on fast days in Advent and Lent. Ominously for some of Mary's bishops, Carranza thought that those who failed to do this were 'dumb dogs who do not know how to bark' (Isaiah 56: 10), an old image but alarmingly relevant in English conditions in 1554–8. Carranza was also an expert on the historic councils of the Church, and pointed out in his 'Mirror' that the Eleventh Council of Toledo, in the seventh century, had decreed that a bishop should leave other tasks in order to preach, since his people should never be left hungry for the Word of God. In advance of coming to England with Philip, Carranza had severely criticized those bishops of his own time who failed in this duty, preferring litigation to preaching.[48]

[48] Bartolomé Carranza, *Speculum pastorum: Hierarchia ecclesiastica in qua describuntur officia ministrorum Ecclesiae militantis*, ed. Tellechea (Salamanca: Universidad Pontificia de Salamanca, 1992), pp. 22, 72–8, 225–32.

Although they would later seem to fall out on the subject, Pole was in this respect deeply sympathetic to his Spanish friend's ideas, and fully appreciated the urgent need to bring a large proportion of Mary's subjects back to the Catholic faith. While he still had no episcopal post in England, he inevitably concentrated on the nuts and bolts of legatine business, concerned with money and appointments, but things changed once he replaced Thomas Cranmer as archbishop of Canterbury. He had been alerted in December 1555 that Pope Paul IV (Gianpietro Carafa) wanted to make him archbishop, but this would happen only after Cranmer was dead. Knowing that the denouement of the trial of Cranmer in Oxford was due before the end of March 1556, though not, of course, expecting the dramatic form it would take, Pole began to plan his own ordination as both priest and bishop, since up to then he had been just the cardinal deacon of Santa Maria in Cosmedin, in Rome. In accordance with Tridentine ideas on episcopal residence, another subject on which his friend Carranza had expressed strong views in print, he planned to go to Canterbury by 23 March 1556, in order to celebrate his first mass as archbishop in his cathedral on the following Passion Sunday. But in the event, Mary kept him in London, partly for political reasons connected with further threats of conspiracy and rebellion. Thus he received a Roman patent to take possession of the material property ('temporalities') of the archbishopric of Canterbury on 17 March, formally accepting it on the very day of Cranmer's death by burning, 21 March 1556. On the 22nd, he was ordained bishop in the restored Observant Franciscan house beside Greenwich Palace, in the presence of the Queen. On 25 March, the Feast of the Annunciation to Mary, Pole received the pallium, the symbol of his office as 'metropolitan' archbishop, in one of the Canterbury parishes in London, St Mary Arches. On this occasion, according to his secretary, Marcantonio Faita, the congregation begged him to preach to them, and he appears to have done so spontaneously. He later wrote down several versions of what he had said, and the results indicate that he spoke of the desperate need for better spiritual food in England. He explained what a legate and bishop was supposed to do, and used the Queen's patron saint, the Virgin Mary, whose festival it was, to indicate how lay Christians should respond. Just as Mary had received from the Archangel Gabriel God's message that she should bear His Son (Luke 1: 26–38), and accepted it despite her misgivings, so English men and women should accept the restoration of the Roman Church. Preaching remained on Pole's mind during and after the Synod of Westminster. When, on 1 April 1556, he accepted, with at least a show of reluctance, the chancellorship of Cambridge University, left empty by the death of Bishop Gardiner the previous November, he expressed admiration for the preaching tradition there, including members of that university who had preached before Mary in Lent of that year.[49] Although it took eighteen months from his

[49] *CRP*, 3, pp. 244–5 (no. 1533); Mayer, *PP&P*, pp. 245–9.

arrival in England for Pole to preach his first sermon, apart from his addresses to the Synod, he gave at least twelve sermons in the remaining years of his life, while his Protestant successor, Matthew Parker, preached only nine in twenty-five years. Sometimes Pole used the preaching of others in a targeted way, notably in Worcester, where the earlier efforts of bishops Latimer and Hooper needed to be counteracted. In 1555, he had issued legatine preaching licences to a former Benedictine, George London, to preach first at Worcester and then more generally.[50]

Although the plan agreed at the Synod was to set up a new system of training for the clergy through new institutions called diocesan seminaries, which were to be located in cathedral cities, in the meantime Oxford and Cambridge universities remained the main immediate sources of recruits. This was an area in which Mary had taken rapid and immediate steps, long before her marriage and the reconciliation with Rome. On 20 August 1553 she wrote to both universities in an attempt to enlist them in her enterprise of restoring true religion. They should 'by there doings as by there preachyng instruct and confirm the rest of her subjects'.[51] In the previous two reigns, Oxford and Cambridge had become all too accustomed to direct royal intervention, being purged of staff, and nearly closed down altogether, in effect, by Henry VIII in 1545–6, when their colleges were initially lumped in with the chantries. So to begin with, Mary's support must have seemed to usher in a new era of security and respect from the Crown. The Queen was being generous, since both universities had earlier declared her parents' marriage illegitimate and hence agreed in their learned opinion that she was a bastard, though this view seems to have been more strongly and widely held in Cambridge than in Oxford, where fewer fellows with Protestant views left their jobs, and the country, when her restoration plans became clear.[52] Now, Mary needed academic support as much as the dons needed hers, and it was clearly on instruction from her that the Council adopted a generally conciliatory attitude towards them.

In religious thought and practice, which were fundamental to the role of both universities, there was a perception that Cambridge had been far more deeply affected by reformed ideas than Oxford. Since the duke of Northumberland had been chancellor of Cambridge, his execution left a vacancy, which was filled by his predecessor Bishop Gardiner. In March 1554, Gardiner demanded that Cambridge academics swear an oath of conformity to Catholic religion, something that was not required of their equivalents in Oxford. Cambridge had evidently also been compromised, in the eyes of Mary and her supporters, by Northumberland's resort there in July 1553, and by the sermon preached at that time in the university church,

[50] *CRP*, 3, pp. 49, 80 (nos 1096, 1166).

[51] 11/1/201 [*CSPDM*, p. 7], in Claire Cross, 'The English Universities, 1553–58', *CMT*, p. 57, and Andrew Hegarty, 'Carranza and the English universities', in *RCMT*, p. 155.

[52] Christopher Haigh, *English Reformations: Religion, Politics and Society under the Tudors* (Oxford: Clarendon Press, 1993), p. 188.

Great St Mary's, by the vice-chancellor, Edwin Sandys, in support of Jane Grey as queen. Sandys duly arrived in the Tower, but the chancellor of Oxford, Sir John Mason, seemed to be running a tighter conservative ship and although, as bishop of Winchester, Gardiner was the Visitor of three of its colleges, New College, Magdalen and Corpus Christi, he seems to have had very little to do there. In both universities, the celebration of mass resumed in the autumn of 1553 and Piero Martire Vermigli, the Italian ex-friar who was ironically named after the first inquisitor martyr of the thirteenth-century Dominican Inquisition, was removed from the Regius (royal) chair of Theology at Christ Church, Oxford. His ex-Dominican opposite number in Cambridge, the Strasbourg reformer Martin Bucer, had died in 1551, before he could be removed from office, but would not escape a macabre form of retribution, in the form of exhumation and burning, before the end of Mary's reign. In both universities, but especially in Cambridge, numerous heads and fellows of colleges left their posts, and many fled the country to avoid investigation and punishment. Thus it was natural that the compulsory theological 'disputation' involving Bishops Latimer, Ridley and Cranmer, in April 1554, should have been held in Oxford. After this, in May of that year and apparently as a reward for its loyalty and devotion, Mary granted three rectories, then in crown possession, to Oxford University. The resulting income transformed the institution's financial situation. The wealth of the university, as opposed to that of the individual colleges and halls, was thereby trebled, and a restoration of the central teaching buildings, the Schools, took place as a result. In the summer of 1554, Mary turned her attention to Cambridge. Apparently in celebration of her marriage, and perhaps of the earlier defeat of the Wyatt rebellion, she virtually refounded her father's Trinity College there. It was turned into a choral foundation with the function of a chantry for souls, and thus became part of the religious changes which would become even more significant when Cardinal Pole intervened as papal legate. Whereas, up to then, the initiative in the universities had been taken by Mary herself, Pole immediately set about reintegrating them into the Catholic university system on the Continent.[53]

It was agreed at the English Synod that, to further the restoration of the teaching of Catholic scholastic theology at Oxford and Cambridge, and to assure the universities' proper function in the new context, formal visitations should take place in both. By now, in addition to Gardiner, Mary could take the advice of her husband and of Pole, as well as that of the churchmen who had come over with the King from Spain. Later, during his trial by the Inquisition in Spain, Friar Bartolomé Carranza had a question about these visitations put to the witnesses whom he had chosen for his defence, including Philip himself. Question 54 of his own interrogatory asked various courtiers and churchmen who had been with him in England to confirm that

---

[53] Cross, 'Universities', pp. 57–66; Hegarty, 'English Universities', pp. 155–7.

by the order that had been made by the said synod [of Westminster], by the Most Serene queen and the Legate, persons of life, letters and example had been deputed to go and visit the said universities, among whom was named the said Most Reverend [Archbishop] of Toledo [Carranza].

According to this account, Carranza took part in the visitation of Oxford, here clearly described as both legatine and royal, examining thirteen colleges to ensure that sound doctrine was being taught in them. This fact was duly confirmed by Philip and others.[54] In addition, some Spaniards obtained academic posts in Oxford, though none apparently in Cambridge. Thus Carranza's Dominican pupil Juan de Villagarcía succeeded Vermigli at Christ Church, while his companion in the order of Preachers, Pedro de Soto, took up a readership in Theology at Pole's old college, Magdalen. From the beginning of 1555, Mary tended to leave more public initiatives concerning the universities to Pole and his advisers. In April 1556, the cardinal archbishop agreed to become chancellor of Cambridge, and in the next few months both universities received a formal legatine visitation, with royal support, beginning with Oxford. After the virtual refoundation of Trinity College Cambridge, which Mary had carried out before Pole's arrival, two new colleges were founded in Oxford. In 1555, Sir Thomas White, a London merchant taylor and former lord mayor, obtained licence from Mary's Council to establish the college of St John the Baptist on the site of the dissolved monastic St Bernard's College. Then, in 1558, Sir Thomas Pope, a friend of the late Sir Thomas More, who had made his money as a lawyer in Chancery, obtained the remains of the former Benedictine Durham College to set up, alongside St John's, the College of the Most Holy Trinity. There was a certain irony in this since, from 1536 to 1540, Pope had been the first treasurer of the Court of Augmentations, which administered confiscated church property. As executor to More's successor as lord chancellor, Sir Thomas Audley, Pope also helped to complete the foundation of Magdalene College, Cambridge, on the site of the former Benedictine Buckingham College. Also in Cambridge, in Mary's time, Dr Caius reformed Gonville Hall on Catholic lines, as what would become known as Gonville and Caius College.[55] In the long run, Mary's efforts, and those of her supporters, to found or refound colleges would long outlast those of Pole and his English and Spanish allies to restore Catholic syllabuses.

---

[54] Tellechea, *CyP*, pp. 94, 99, 101, 102, 104, 105, 110, 112, 113.

[55] Cross, 'Universities', pp. 66–72; Hegarty, 'English Universities', pp. 160–2; Tellechea, *CyP*, pp. 94–9, 102, 110; McConica, 'The Rise of the Undergraduate College', pp. 1–68, at p. 43; Peter Cunich, 'Benedictine Monks at the University of Oxford and the Dissolution of the Monasteries', in *Benedictines at Oxford*, ed. Henry Wansborough, OSB, and Anthony Marrett-Crosby, OSB (London: Darton, Longman & Todd, 1997), pp. 155–81 at pp. 176–9; Andrew Pettegree, 'A. G. Dickens and his Critics: A New Narrative of the English Reformation', *Historical Research*, lxxvii (2004), pp. 39–58, at pp. 47–8.

It is perhaps ironical that the new colleges in Oxford should have been founded on the sites of defunct monastic institutions. Thus they fulfilled one of the desires of the humanists and reformers, that education should replace 'vain' monkery, but of course their founders had a very different religious aim in mind. It would be wrong to see such activity simply as an example of Mary's harking back to her father's ways. Pole, too, with all his continental experience and papal powers, certainly regretted the dissolution of the English religious houses, but thought that the parishes were clearly the highest priority in the circumstances of the 1550s.[56] Nevertheless, some efforts to restore the religious orders would be made in Mary's reign, although she, like Pole, has often been suspected of lacking fervour in this area, as well as in the matter of restoring shrines and relics. Thus despite these doubts in high circles, some attempt was indeed made in Mary's reign to revive the religious life in England. At times the Queen was personally involved, although the results achieved by the time of her death were very limited. There were many obvious difficulties. The property of the former religious houses had, of course, been wholly confiscated by the Crown, and Henry VIII and Edward VI's governments had spent much of the resulting revenue on warfare, and distributed large amounts of the property among laypeople. Another major issue concerned personnel. By the time of Mary's accession, large numbers of monks, friars and nuns had accepted pensions from the Crown, but many of the surviving men had become secular priests with parishes, and some of them had married. It was relatively simple for the exiles, who had not broken their religious vows or abandoned the Catholic faith, to return home and live in community, but those who had remained in England required legatine absolutions which were more complicated than those issued to ordinary parish clergy. Then there was the question of finding sites on which the community life might be resumed. In the circumstances, it is perhaps surprising that so much was achieved, and such restoration was always on the agenda for Mary and Pole, even though it never came near to being the highest priority.

Mary inherited from both sides of her family a strong attachment to the Observant Franciscans, and this quickly showed itself in the restoration of that order's house alongside Greenwich Palace. She had been baptized there and also had direct control over it, as she did over the former Observant house at Richmond, though the latter was not restored. Two of the most notable Franciscans, William Peto and Henry Elson, had chosen exile, and during Edward's reign Mary had corresponded with Peto in Rome.[57] Now they returned and were able to move into their former house at Greenwich, and the arrival of Pole in November 1554 did no harm to their cause, since Peto had by then been in the Legate's retinue for some years. He and other exiled English Franciscans had lived in the Hospice of St Thomas (Becket) the Martyr in Rome, of which Pole had been warden

---

[56] Compare Wooding, *Rethinking Catholicism*, pp. 137–8.
[57] *CSP Ven* VI, ii, no. 938.

since 1538. It is possible that Mary's relations with Peto cooled somewhat when he opposed her marriage to Philip, but this did not prevent the restoration at Greenwich, after the buildings had been repaired. The friars were installed by Bishop Maurice Griffin of Rochester on Palm Sunday, in April 1555, effectively as a new community, Paul IV having wound up all pre-existing foundations in England to allow the maximum flexibility in restoring the religious life. The Greenwich Franciscans would turn out to be the largest community in Mary's England. They began with twenty-five friars and had grown further by November 1555. The community apparently consisted of former English friars who had renewed their vows, with some Spaniards and perhaps some Netherlanders. The importance of the Greenwich community to Mary is indicated by the funds and property which she lavished upon it. The accounts of the royal surveyor of works record that she spent no less than £1,551 8s 6d on the Greenwich house, also leaving it £500 in her will dated 30 March 1558. Important public occasions took place in the Franciscan chapel, notably the consecration of Pole as bishop, carried out there by Archbishop Heath of York and others on 22 March 1556. Mary also used the Franciscan church for her private devotions.[58] In contrast, an attempt by some former friars to restore the main conventual Franciscan house in London, Greyfriars, to that order's use was unsuccessful, in part apparently because of Spanish intervention. In Edward's reign it had been occupied by a new orphanage and school, Christ's Hospital. As a result of the Franciscans' petition to the Crown to regain the house, Philip's Franciscan confessor Alfonso de Castro and the Dominican Oxford professor Juan de Villagarcía dined there at high table with the children in hall. Villagarcía is said to have been overcome by emotion at the sight, and to have observed that he would rather serve the orphans than be steward to the King. Christ's Hospital was saved, and the Franciscans were somewhat miffed. There was greater success in Southampton, where the Observant Franciscan friary had been refounded before January 1557, partly with friars from Greenwich. Its previous lay 'possessioner', Thomas Bowes, a tenant of the earl of Pembroke, was compensated with a licence to export cloth.[59]

The leadership in the restoration of the Dominicans to England rested with Bartolomé Carranza who, before he arrived in England, had been empowered by the Dominican general to restore the order's English province. Even before the Spaniards' arrival in July 1554, at least sixteen English Dominicans had readopted the habit, notable among them being William Perrin, who would later become prior of the restored St Bartholomew's Smithfield, where the order which had pioneered the Papal Inquisition in the thirteenth century lived alongside the site of so many burnings of heretics. The community of Dominican nuns who had formerly

---

[58] Keith Duncan Brown, The Franciscan Observants in England, 1482–1559', D. Phil. thesis, University of Oxford, 1986, pp. 222–31.

[59] Ibid., pp. 231–3.

lived at Dartford was refounded in King's Langley and a brief attempt was also made, in 1557, to establish a female community in Oxford. In the case of the Dominicans, the main initiative seems to have come from Pole and Carranza, rather than Mary herself. In Oxford, this seemed natural, given that two Dominicans, Villagarcía and de Soto, now held posts in the university, but by this time the former priory in Littlegate Street was in the hands of the mayor. Pole summoned Villagarcía to arrange the financing of a restoration, and in May–July 1557, now with Philip in Flanders, Carranza kept in touch with developments. By September 1557, the house was indeed restored and occupied, but only by very few friars, including Brother Richard from London. Carranza seems to have thought that Mary, like her Trastamaran mother and grandmother, would take particular care of the nuns. In a letter from Brussels dated 26 September 1557, he urged Villagarcía to make sure that the grievances of the Oxford Dominican nuns were dealt with, or else they would complain to the Queen. He also revealed an intimate knowledge of Oxford, which some have supposed him not to have. He remarked to Villagarcía that Magdalen College, where de Soto had his post but Carranza's inquisitor's nose may have told him that Protestantism had not been entirely rooted out, was not a suitable place for a Dominican to live. Lincoln College, on the other hand, was apparently too expensive. In any case, the Dominican houses in Oxford would not last much longer and an attempt to refound one in Cambridge failed, though the Franciscans briefly occupied the site which had been planned for Dominicans. Interestingly, Carranza told his Dominican (and Thomist) brother Juan de Villagarcía that it would not be good for Cambridge to be subjected to Scotist theology, which was a Franciscan approach. For Carranza, this was not apparently the way to purge that university of reformed teaching. In his subsequent Inquisition trial, his supporting witnesses, including Philip, confirmed his activity in the restoration of his own and other orders.[60]

Individual houses of other orders were also refounded. These included the Charterhouse at Sheen, where Pole had received his early education, and the house of Bridgettine nuns at Syon, which had recently been occupied by the duke of Northumberland. Both had strong royal connections and therefore naturally qualified for Mary's personal interest, though Pole was a prime mover in both cases. Other orders, notably the Augustinian 'eremitical' ('hermit') friars and canons, did not succeed in re-establishing themselves, but two other prominent restorations did take place in the capital.[61] One of these was the former priory of the Knights of St John of Jerusalem (Hospitallers) at Clerkenwell. Given the strategic importance of this order in the battle against the Ottoman Turks in the Mediterranean, particularly from their bases in Malta and Rhodes, it is not surprising that Pole, on behalf of Paul IV, took a special interest in restoring the Knights' English possessions. To

[60] Mayer, *PP&P*, p. 286; Tellechea, *CyP*, pp. 93, 97, 98, 102–4, 106, 109–11, 113, 116–17, 258–65.
[61] Tellechea, *CyP*, p. 66; Mayer, *PP&P*, pp. 260, 287.

make the point more strongly, one of Philip's closest advisers in England was Don Antonio de Toledo, prior of the Spanish military orders and grand commander of the Hospitallers in León, in northern Spain. Although the Clerkenwell house remained legally dissolved under English law, by 1556 its goods were gradually being extracted from their possessioners, even though its church had been pillaged by the late duke of Somerset. There was a poignant aspect to this question, however. Perhaps ironically, the Clerkenwell priory, having been confiscated at the dissolution of the order in England, had in 1547 been granted by Edward VI's Council to Mary herself, under the terms of her father's will. She used its domestic accommodation as her London residence when paying her rare visits to her brother's Court, and perhaps that is why, despite pressure from her husband, Pole and the Pope, it was not until May 1557 that Clerkenwell was returned to the Knights. Only at the beginning of 1558 did the order receive back all its English and Irish property, by royal letters patent.[62] The magnitude of this affair could not, however, compare with the restoration of the Benedictine community in Westminster Abbey, at the very heart of government.

In this case also, it is hard to tell whether Pole or Mary herself played the crucial role. There is no doubt that the Legate took a personal interest in bringing the Benedictines back to England, once he had sized up the situation there. Towards the end of 1555, he tried to persuade monks from the community at Monte Cassino in Italy to come to England for that purpose, but they never arrived.[63] Although Henry VIII's attempt to make Westminster a separate diocese had lapsed, the former abbey still had a dean and chapter, and acted as a secondary cathedral for the bishop of London. In September 1556, Pole approved the arrangements for the dean and chapter to surrender the Church to the Crown in return for alternative revenues. Mary's role had been to receive, on 19 March 1555, the former abbot, John Feckenham, who had latterly been dean of St Paul's. He and fifteen of his brothers had waited upon the Queen, dressed in the Benedictine habit, and had apparently moved her greatly, so that she asked Gardiner and three other councillors to arrange their restoration. Eventually, in September 1556, the dean and canons moved out and the monks moved back in, though they only obtained full legal possession in the following November. This Monastery of St Peter was a new foundation according to canon and common law, but was very much modelled on what had gone before. The former dean, Hugh Weston, had protested bitterly, but the monks would remain in place until the summer of 1559, when Elizabeth finally removed them.[64] Although some attempt was made to refound Glastonbury and St Alban's Abbeys, Westminster was the only Benedictine foundation to reappear during Mary's reign.

[62] Mayer, *PP&P*, pp. 284–9; *CRP*, 3, p. 174 (no. 1392), p. 417 (no. 1968), 4, pp. 313–22.

[63] *CRP*, 3, pp. 199, 438 (nos 1436, 2020).

[64] Mayer, *PP&P*, p. 284; Tellechea, *CyP*, pp. 259–60; Knighton, 'Westminster Abbey Restored', *CMT*, pp. 77, 80–1.

Those who believe that both Mary and Pole had a somewhat backward view of Catholicism which led them to avoid new developments in the Church have tended to cite the 'failure' to invite Ignatius of Loyola's Society of Jesus into England. This fact is sometimes held to be an example of how they missed the new currents of what is still commonly, if controversially, known as 'Counter-Reformation' religion. This is somewhat unfair. From his arrival in England until the Jesuit founder's death in 1556, Pole corresponded regularly, though not frequently, with Ignatius, who seems in fact to have offered to train students for England, rather than send full members of his society to work there.[65] Ignatius and Pole had known each other since about 1540, when the latter was papal legate in Viterbo, in the Papal States in central Italy. Even then Ignatius and his earliest companions had consulted Pole about a possible mission to England, and it seems that the founder of the Jesuits did himself pay a brief, unobtrusive visit to the England of Henry VIII at that time. But the difficulties of the Marian restoration and the Queen's early death, as well as the turmoil in the order which followed Ignatius's death, delayed the arrival of the Jesuits in England until Elizabeth's reign. Even without Jesuit intervention, attention had to be paid to spreading the Catholic message once more in England.

When studying the past, scholars perhaps naturally tend to concentrate on the media with which they make their own living, which in most cases means printed text. Thus a massive amount of effort has gone into examining the minutiae of the reformers' disputes and propaganda. In contrast, Mary and her supporters have often been accused of neglecting print, and thus, on the assumption that the printed word is everything, losing the battle for the hearts and minds of the great majority of the English population.[66] It now appears that this view was and is largely based on a failure to examine the evidence available. In fact, Mary's government worked hard to proclaim its views and gain public support for them, in both secular and religious matters. There was indeed a Marian printing strategy, aimed at religious renewal in England on Catholic lines. In the traditional manner, it was expected that change would emanate from the academic world, hence the great concentration on 'purifying' the universities and the attempt to reorganize clergy training.[67] Given the central roles of the Queen and Pole in the campaign to bring England back into the Catholic fold, it is not surprising that, as in continental countries,

---

[65] *CRP*, 3, pp. 24, 100, 119, 182 (nos 1036, 1215, 1266, 1413); Mayer, 'A Test of Wills: Pole, Loyola and the Jesuits in England', in T. M. McCoog, ed., *The Reckoned Expense: Edmund Campion and the Early English Jesuits* (Woodbridge: The Boydell Press, 1996), pp. 21–8, at pp. 21–2; T. M. McCoog, 'Ignatius Loyola and Reginald Pole: A Reconsideration', *Journal of Ecclesiastical History*, xlvii (1996), pp. 257–73.

[66] E. J. Baskerville, *A Chronological Bibliography of Propaganda and Polemic between 1553 and 1558* (Philadelphia, PA: American Philosophical Society, 1979), pp. 6–11; Loach, 'The Marian Establishment and the Printing Press', *English Historical Review*, ci (1986), pp. 135–49.

[67] Wizeman, *Theology and Spirituality*, pp. 47–9; Wooding, *Rethinking Catholicism*, pp. 114–17.

including the Habsburg domains, secular mechanisms were combined with ecclesiastical instruction and sanctions in order to control printing and publication. Thus while the Westminster Synod urged the censorship of books on the Inquisitorial pattern then used, for example, in Spain, perhaps the most important move made by Mary's government in this area was the granting of a new charter to the London Stationers' Company on 3 June 1557. Evidently in an attempt to establish long-term arrangements for the industry, Philip and Mary thus placed control of the entire craft of printing in the hands of that company.[68] Given that many of the printers involved had formed an essential part of the religious reform programme in the previous reign, this move may seem surprising, but a more detailed examination of what was produced, and who printed and published it, during Mary's reign suggests that her policy might have been perfectly viable, had external circumstances beyond her control not dictated otherwise.

Religious works were the priority, after normal governmental needs had been met in the form of proclamations, letters patent, acts of Parliament, and so on. Various types of Christian publication may be distinguished. These are sermons, including selections of homilies, systematic doctrinal teaching in the form of catechesis, direct polemic against Protestantism, and spiritual or devotional works. The authors of these works included bishops, professional theologians, former or restored members of religious orders and conservative 'secular' clergymen.[69] Particularly interesting were the printers who managed to 'convert' from Protestant to Catholic work, two notable examples being John Weyland and John Day. Both men became heavily involved in one of the main licensed printing activities in Mary's reign, which was the publication of the devotional works known as primers. Such books, which contained the Hours, or liturgical offices, as well as other prayers, and very often illustrations, had continued to be the staple of upper-class Christian devotion well into the sixteenth century. In this respect, the English market had traditionally been catered for largely by continental printers, especially in France and Flanders, but reformers in Henry and Edward's reigns had recognized the importance of primers. Hence they began to produce replacement books, containing more 'wholesome' doctrine, as well as purging from existing works what was now regarded as 'popish' material. Almost as soon as Mary came to the throne, a campaign was begun to reverse this process. Weyland, who had done similar work under Henry VIII, returned from uncontroversial stationery and scribal activity to printing and began to produce Catholic primers and other religious books. He recruited John Day, a protégé of Sir William Cecil who had been active in printing and publishing for Edward VI's governments, and would later serve Elizabeth in a similar

[68] Andrew Pettegree, *The Stationers' Company and the Development of the English Printing Industry* (London: Stationers' Company, 2009), pp. 1–16, at p. 3; Edwards, *Inquisitors*, pp. 177–84.
[69] Wizeman, *Theology and Spirituality*, pp. 25–43.

way. In Mary's time, though, once Day had returned to London from a secret press in Cecil's zone of control in the East Midlands, he engaged in work for Weyland on the Sarum primers. Paradoxically, although it is estimated that about half of London's printers fled to the Continent on Mary's accession, production of Catholic primers actually increased to about twice the pre-Edwardian level, thus, at least in part, repatriating this important section of the book trade.[70] On a more positive note, Mary was also the subject of published works of praise, which might have been more effective had it not been for two of her central policies, which negated their effect in the eyes of many – her marriage to Philip and her violent enforcement of Catholic orthodoxy. The written and printed word was not the be-all and end-all.

Recently, more thorough, but not totally sympathetic, attention has been given to the public ceremonies and events which were intended by Mary and her government, and indeed sometimes seem to have served, to improve her image with her subjects. Into this category come the great public events of her life such as her coronation and her wedding, as well as jousts, masques and music-making, which were strongly revived during her reign, especially when Philip was in England. There was, however, a darker side to the public pageantry which spilled out of Mary's Court. One aspect of this was the use of judicial execution, most notably in the cases of the duke of Northumberland, soon after the accession, and those of Jane Grey, Guildford Dudley and Thomas Wyatt and some of his supporters, after the failed rebellion of January 1554.[71] Much resented by some was Mary's effort to gain strength and popularity by her revival of traditional public worship, which had been first truncated and then largely banned under Henry and Edward. The restoration of the Mass was accompanied by the reintroduction of liturgical processions, in which the Latin prayers known as litanies were sung. These formerly popular parish ceremonies were now held once again before celebrations of High Mass on Sundays and major saints' days. Particularly significant in this context was the strong attempt, initially on the part of the Spanish churchmen in Philip's household, but thereafter by Bishop Bonner and others, to restore the liturgical outdoor processions that had traditionally accompanied, in England as on the Continent, the summer festival of Corpus Christi, which celebrated Christ's gift of Himself in the Mass. At least according to his own account and that of numerous witnesses of his subsequent trial by the Spanish and Roman Inquisitions, the main instigator of this revival was Bartolomé Carranza. On Corpus Christi Day 1555, a solemn procession of the Blessed

[70] Elizabeth Evenden, *Patents, Pictures and Patronage: John Day and the Tudor Book-Trade* (Aldershot: Ashgate, 2008), pp. 40–4; Duffy, *Stripping of the altars*, pp. 526–9, 539–43; Duffy, *Marking the Hours: English People and Their Prayers, 1240–1570* (New Haven, CT and London: Yale University Press, 2006), pp. 163–66; Loach, 'Marian establishment', p. 137.

[71] Kevin Sharpe, *Selling the Tudor Monarchy: Authority and Image in Sixteenth-Century England* (New Haven, CT and London: Yale University Press, 2009), pp. 256–7, 301–5.

Sacrament took place at Kingston upon Thames, where, in the previous year, Wyatt and his men had crossed the river before attacking London. The consecrated Host, displayed in a monstrance, was carried by a royal chaplain from Toledo Cathedral, Cristóbal Becerra. Philip and Mary were across the Thames in Hampton Court at the time but did not attend, no doubt because of the Queen's confinement. It appears that all the personnel and liturgical apparatus came from the King's own chapel and household. In 1556, a similar procession was held on Corpus Christi day itself at Bishop Bonner's palace of Fulham, while on the Sunday following he himself carried the sacrament in such a procession at Whitehall Palace. The intended symbolism was clear: Christ in the form of the consecrated bread of the Eucharist was to reoccupy all those crucial places which had been desecrated by rebellion and heresy under Henry and Edward.[72] Inside the churches, a programme of restoration of the necessities of Catholic worship, and removal of relics of the liturgies of the previous reign, continued steadily throughout the reign. Clearly there was religiously motivated resistance in some parishes, notably in London and Kent, but delays in restoring altars, liturgical vessels, vestments and rood screens surmounted by images of Christ on the cross with Saints Mary and John beside Him, seem generally to have been due more to financial considerations and excessive pressure on craftspeople with the necessary skills than to doctrinal objections.[73]

In a sense, Mary's attitude towards those who would not accept her ideas on religion is the central question of her whole life. She was blamed at the time, and sometimes still is, for not producing a child after she had wickedly married a 'Spaniard', but the real damage to her reputation comes from the burning of nearly 300 Protestants during her short reign. To being too old and increasingly ugly is added the charge that she was a religious fanatic and bigot, and in thrall to two foreign powers, Spain and Rome, which did not have the 'true', Protestant, interests of the English at heart. But even leaving these common stereotypes aside, a real problem remains. How did Mary come to back a campaign against individuals which led to their publicly enduring a horrible death? Mary had, after all, been known in her youth not only as beautiful to look at but also as possessed of an idealistic and 'pure' Christian humanist, religious nature. These ideas were strongly opposed to the religious and secular violence which was then tearing Europe apart. At the centre of her religious life, Mary had a deep devotion to Christ both in His personal sufferings, as recorded in the Bible, and as He was present to her in the consecrated bread of the Eucharist, which she kept constantly by her as a focus for prayer and contemplation,

[72] Edwards, 'Corpus Christi at Kingston-upon-Thames', in *RCMT*, pp. 139–51.

[73] Ronald Hutton, 'The Local Impact of the Tudor Reformation', in *The English Reformation Revisited*, ed. Christopher Haigh (Cambridge: Cambridge University Press, 1987), pp. 114–38, at pp. 127–31; Duffy, *Stripping of the Altars*, pp. 527–8, 533, 543–9; Duffy, *The Voices of Morebath*, pp. 155–66.

in the form of the reserved or exposed sacrament. She fully shared the intense attachment to the saving sufferings of Jesus, in particular His trial and Crucifixion, which had been a central theme of Christian belief and practice all over western and central Europe up to and including her own lifetime. This core belief and attachment affected people who ended up on both sides of the Catholic–Protestant divide which was hardening during her reign. There was in fact no real conflict among Europe's rulers and religious leaders over the centrality of Christ's sacrifice on the cross. His sufferings were described in agonizing detail in the Gospels, interpreted in the rest of the New Testament, and re-enacted in the traditional liturgies of the Church, especially during Holy Week, which had flourished in England, as elsewhere, up to Henry VIII's reign, and which had been gradually restored when Mary became Queen.

One might suppose that this form of religious devotion, together with ideas from predominantly pacifist Christian humanism with its intimate involvement in Christ's suffering, would have led to compassion, rather than violence, in royal policy towards those who had followed Thomas Cranmer and his allies in their intepretation of the Gospel, and of what Christ did on the cross. Why was this not the case? In recent years it has been suggested that the hermetically sealed denominational narratives – Catholic, Lutheran, Reformed, Anabaptist – of those who died for their faith in the sixteenth century need to be treated as equivalent, without ignoring or downgrading the particular religious feeling and emphasis which underlay their suffering and death.[74] Henry VIII had over thirty English men and women, some with a Catholic and some a Protestant orientation, executed for religious offences, the former category, with the exception of Friar John Forest, being convicted of treason, and the latter burned as lapsed heretics.[75] Mary in effect added adherents of Cranmer's reforms to the list of potential victims, which seems to be the right word to use in this context. In her time, religious knowledge among the general population, and not just the educated elite, whether lay or clerical, was amazingly extensive and sophisticated by twenty-first-century standards. People generally thought they knew very well how a good person should die, and what the death of a bad Christian or 'heretic' should be like. Yet there is ample evidence, not least from foreign ambassadors' reports and from John Foxe's *Actes and monuments* ('Book of martyrs'), that people in the crowds which witnessed the burnings of heretics in Mary's reign were also very sure who was a martyr and who was not, though they might differ in their views of each individual case. Words like 'martyr' and 'heretic' are slippery, though, and need to be looked at more closely.

[74] See Brad S. Gregory, *Salvation at Stake: Christian Martyrdom in Early Modern Europe* (Cambridge, MA: Harvard University Press, 1999), *passim*.

[75] Peter Marshall, 'Papist as Heretic: The Burning of John Forest, 1538', *Historical Journal*, xli (1998), pp. 351–74, at p. 356.

Put simply, 'martyr' is a version of the Greek for 'witness'. In the first three or four Christian centuries, when followers of Jesus's 'Way', as members of the Church, had been persecuted by 'pagan' authorities, 'martyr' was used to describe those brave or foolhardy individuals who died a horrible death for their faith, often in public arenas. Both concepts – witnessing for one's faith, even to death, and the violent and cruel form of that death – had become fully part of the religious life and the procedures of the Church long before Mary's time. 'Heresy', also a Greek word by origin, meant 'choice', but had come to mean, in the religious context, 'wrong choice'. To it had become attached a set of unsavoury concepts involving anti-social behaviour and disease. 'Wrong' religion was thus an infection which had to be cauterized or cut out of the individual and of society. Those among sixteenth-century scholars who, like their medieval predecessors, engaged in the generally harmful and misleading practice of dredging for appealing texts in the Bible and taking them out of their contexts, could easily develop ideas about 'sheep' (Christians) who became diseased and infected the rest of the flock (the Church). By Philip and Mary's time, such people were commonly dealt with by an 'Inquisition'. This word, from the Latin *inquisitio*, was used to mean a legal inquiry, and from the thirteenth century it began to be applied to heresy. Specalized tribunals of churchmen, with papal authority, operated in some parts of Europe, notably Spain and, from 1542, Rome, to identify and try heretics. By 1500, a complex set of laws and procedures had evolved to deal with such cases and it was accepted that although the Church itself, through its clergy and lay officers, could not shed blood, lapsed heretics, in particular, could and should be handed over to secular authorities, who would administer the death penalty, usually by means of fire. This would purge church and society of their sin and, according to the prevailing Augustinian theology, send their souls to eternal damnation, as indicated by Jesus in Matthew's Gospel (25: 46).[76]

Without awareness of all this, it is impossible to explain Mary's readiness to adopt such methods in 1554–5, and persist with them until her death. In the summer of 1553, she had at least appeared to outsiders to be willing to allow the reformed services of the 1552 Book of Common Prayer to continue, if only for a time, alongside the beginnings of the restoration of Catholic worship. It is commonly understood that, to begin with, she and her closest advisers, especially Gardiner and Bonner, thought that if they took the reforming leaders out of circulation, notably Bishops Cranmer, Latimer, Ridley and Hooper, their followers would quickly return to the old faith. It soon emerged, however, that this approach would not work, and even though the kingdom was still technically in schism from Rome, the Queen and her advisers chose the traditional remedy of an Inquisition. The problem was that the old English heresy laws, which were part of statute not canon law, had been removed in the previous reign. Apart from a brief experiment under Edward II, England had never had a specialized tribunal for heresy on

---

[76] Edwards, *Inquisition*, pp. 17–47.

the continental model. Instead, such 'error' and dissent had been investigated
either by diocesan bishops and their officials or by a papal nuncio or legate.
Before 1381, when the self-styled peasants famously rose against the government of Richard II, such cases were normally dealt with on the model
offered by the New Testament, which involved admonition and, if necessary,
excommunication (Titus 3: 10). The Peasants' Revolt badly frightened the
government, though, and from 1382 onwards those accused of heresy, then
generally of the Lollard or Wycliffite variety, were liable to immediate arrest
by the secular authority. In 1388, these authorities, both local and national,
became even more deeply involved, actively seeking out heretics themselves
and not just arresting and punishing them when they had been found by the
Church. This mix of secular and ecclesiastical influences would become even
more significant when, in 1397, parliament rather than the Church's
Convocations took the main initiative, enacting heresy law as statute. By this
time, canon law, which crossed national boundaries, normally required the
death penalty for those who relapsed into heresy, having once given it up, and
the highly insecure and nervous Lancastrian regime of Henry IV enacted
this provision in a new law.[77] The resulting statute, *De haeretico comburendo* (On
the burning of the heretic, 2 Henry IV c. 15), provided that anyone accused
of heresy might be arrested by secular law officers, should subsequently be
dealt with by the Church, and should then be handed back to the secular
authorities for punishment, if canon law so permitted. In such cases, the
diocesan bishop should hand the prisoner over to the King's Court, apparently on the understanding that if he abjured, or recanted his 'error', he
would be fined and released. If, however, he refused to abjure before the
bishop or his commissioners, he would be regarded as having relapsed into
heresy, and be delivered, under the terms of canon law, to the courts of his
shire or borough for execution by burning.[78] Trials of heretics took place
under this statute in subsequent reigns, and it remained on the statute book
until its repeal under Edward VI. The only addition in this area was made
by Henry V, who, after the further fright of Sir John Oldcastle's rebellion of
1414, issued a new proclamation, specifically against Lollards, which also
remained on the statute book into the Tudor period.[79]

    The Tudor move towards royal supremacy over the Church in England
certainly did not bring an end to the use of heresy laws. The parliamentary
legislation in force in Henry VIII's reign was of course already native, and
could continue to operate without reference to the bishop of Rome. This

[77] R. N. Swanson, *Church and Society in Late Medieval England* (Oxford: Basil Blackwell,
1989), pp. 338–9.
[78] Chrimes and Brown, *Select Documents*, pp. 204–5, 215; J. L. Kirby, *Henry IV of England:
A Biography* (London: Constable, 1970), pp. 114–15.
[79] Norman P. Tanner, *Heresy Trials in the Diocese of Norwich, 1428–31* (London: Camden
Society, 4th series, xx 1977), pp. 7, 9, 22; Paul Strohm, *England's Empty Throne: Usurpation and
the Language of Legitimation, 1399–1422* (New Haven, CT and London: Yale University Press,
1998), p. 145; R. N. Swanson, *Catholic England: Faith, Religion and Observance Before the
Reformation* (Manchester: Manchester University Press, 1993), pp. 267–8.

indeed happened, with the result that the English public continued to link religious diversity and nonconformity with the likelihood of violent and public retribution, in this case for reformers. In reaction to Henry's burning of some of these, Edward VI's first parliament repealed the heresy laws of Richard II, Henry IV and Henry V. In 1549, Bishop Edmund Bonner of London, an opponent of this measure, was removed from office for refusing to continue enforcing general ecclesiastical discipline after the introduction of the first English Prayer Book, and he was replaced by Nicholas Ridley on 12 April 1550. Bonner had refused to tell his flock, on government orders issued in August 1549, that anyone who thereafter used the 'old ceremonies' was in the very act of doing so rejected by God. The certainty of Edward's councillors and bishops that they totally knew the divine will, as Henry too had appeared to claim on occasion, had its effect in the following year, when a royal commission of thirty-two bishops, theologians and canon and civil lawyers was set up to draft new canon law to replace the Catholic code which was then still in force despite the split with Rome. Had the duke of Northumberland not quarrelled with Cranmer, a type of Protestant Inquisition would have been in place when Mary came to the throne. Whereas the now repealed heresy laws had defended the Catholic faith and targeted Lollards and other dissenters, the draft code of 1552–3 was directed at the eradication of traditional belief and practice. A dualist distinction was made throughout between 'scriptural truth', which the commission members apparently thought that they could perfectly discern, and 'diabolical' traditional faith and practice. Those who disagreed with the 'evangelicals' were dismissed as blind and idolatrous, and the old heresy-hunting simply acquired new potential victims. Catholics and Lutherans were added to the traditional list of heretics and were threatened with joining Arians, Pelagians and Anabaptists on death row. Edward's government-appointed commissioners for heresy, who included those who had drafted the new canon law, planned to punish all who opposed the new Book of Common Prayer, or Books, since the first lasted barely three years. The bark of the proposed Edwardian mechanism for the investigation and punishment of heresy might well have been worse than its bite, but this was never demonstrated in practice.[80]

Two unfortunates, Joan Boucher and the émigré George van Parris, were actually burned by the Edwardian authorities, supposedly for adhering to the catch-all Anabaptist heresy, with Cranmer acting as inquisitor-general, but using common law powers connected with treason, as Elizabeth would later do. Thus it has been possible for idealists of the Protestant cause reasonably to see Edward's reign as an era of at least comparative religious freedom.[81] So it was, in the sense that the government failed to get a grip, but the procedures set out in the canons drafted in 1551–2 would have had a very different

[80] Jones, *English Reformation*, pp. 101–2, 121–4.
[81] MacCulloch, *Tudor Church Militant*, pp. 141, 197.

result if the Lords had not rejected them, at Northumberland's urging. Following the traditional approach of continental handbooks for inquisitors, such as the then still operative works of the Frenchman Bernard Gui and the Catalan Nicolau Eymerich, the Edwardian draft code listed specific heresies which had to be identified.[82] Now added to the list were transubstantiation, clerical celibacy, belief in the supremacy of the Roman See and, as part of an intra-Protestant feud, 'errors' concerning the doctrine of predestination. There was also an addition to the traditional forms for the denunciation of Christians as heretics. To investigation (also referred to as 'inquisition') and 'accusation' was added 'evangelical denunciation', this last apparently allowing the authorities to dispense with such tiresome procedural niceties as the preparation of evidence, as in a normal trial. As in the old laws, 'obstinate' heretics, for whom excommunication was ineffective, were to be handed over to what continental Catholic Inquisitions called the 'secular arm' for punishment, which might in the Edwardian case be permanent exile or life imprisonment, or any other penalty which seemed suitable to the magistrate. It is not clear whether or not this punishment might include burning, but the resemblances between what Cranmer was planning and what Mary did are strong, and add their own twist to what the 'bloody' Queen presided over subsequently.[83]

Once England had been reconciled to the Roman See, parliament, meeting in January 1555, re-enacted the heresy laws of Richard II, Henry IV and Henry V, which empowered royal commissioners to arrest heretics. The death penalty was reinstated for this offence as well as the confiscation of goods and lands from those convicted, and hence from their families. As a first step thereafter, on 22 January 1555, Bishop Gardiner required all those Protestant preachers then imprisoned to come to his house at St Mary Overie church, in Southwark, where he promised them the Queen's mercy if they abandoned their 'heretical' views. Mary set out her own views on the subject at about this time in a memorandum to her Council written in January or February 1555. According to one version, she said:

> Touching the punishment of heretics, me thinketh it ought to be done without Rashness, . . . while to do justice to such as by learning would seem to deceive the simple. And the rest so to be used that the people might well perceive them not to be condemned without just occasion, whereby they both understand the truth and Believe to do the like.[84]

---

[82] Bernard Gui, *Manuel de l'Inquisiteur*, ed. and trans G. Mollat, 2 vols (Paris: Société d'Éditions 'Les Belles Lettres', 1964; Nicolau Eymerich, *Le manuel de 'Inquisiteur*, ed. and trans. Louis Sala-Molins (Paris: Mouton, 1973).

[83] MacCulloch, *Cranmer*, pp. 474–5; James C. Spalding, *The Reformation of the Ecclesiastical Laws of England, 1552* (Kirksville, MO: Truman State University Press, 1992), *Sixteenth Century Studies*, xix, pp. 1–34, 59–82; Torrance Kirby, 'Lay Supremacy: Reform of the Canon Law of England from Henry VIII to Elizabeth I (1529–1571)', *Reformation and Renaissance Review*, viii (2006), pp. 349–70.

[84] BL Harleian MS 444, fol. 27.

Whatever the apparent moderation of this statement, Mary in fact let loose, in January 1555, a set of mechanisms which would prove hard to control and which would lie as a cloud of oppression over the rest of her reign. The first to be burned was a noted Protestant preacher, John Rogers, who died at Smithfield, on the northern edge of the city of London, on 4 February. Thereafter a general offensive started against those who either were already known to the authorities or else were brought to their attention, generally by neighbours and local justices of the peace. It is striking that the geographical distribution of the trials and burnings was very patchy.[85] The overwhelming concentration was in London, Middlesex and Essex, with other significant groupings in Kent and Sussex, and a noticeable but lesser number of cases in East Anglia, no doubt reflecting the strength of support for reformation in those areas, in contrast with other parts of the country. The centre of the activity was Bonner's London diocese, in which over a hundred people died by burning in 1555-8, nearly a third of the total. This does not suggest a systematic national campaign, but rather a spasmodic settlement of grudges with at least a religious pretext, as was common on the Continent, too, in the period. What must never be forgotten is the sheer calculated horror of this kind of trial and execution.[86]

While a mixture of ecclesiastical and secular persons and agencies was clearly involved in the trial of numerous English people for heresy, the balance of responsibility for what happened is still a highly controversial subject. Even before the re-enactment of the heresy laws, and despite the so-called 'toleration' edict of August 1553, it is clear that Mary and her inner circle did not intend reformed Christianity to continue for long in her kingdom. In particular, Stephen Gardiner and Edmund Bonner, whom she had instantly freed from the Tower and then restored to their sees, shared her concern to root out what they regarded as corrosive and evil Protestant heresy. Of the two, Gardiner, as lord chancellor as well as bishop of Winchester, took the lead initially. In the latter half of 1553, he, the Queen herself and others who, though still schismatics, thought of themselves as Catholics, took a view of the dynamics of heresy which was traditional in the Western Church. This was that most Christians would not make the 'wrong choice' about religion unless they were misled by a small number of evil individuals. In the English context, these heresiarchs were thought to be Cranmer and his strongest supporters, and so they were fairly rapidly taken out of circulation. It appears, though, that when the burnings began in February 1555 Gardiner, at least, became disillusioned. His view that if someone had to die in this way the Church had failed was entirely correct in terms of current Catholic thought, since the

---

[85] For details of this distribution, see the definitive maps by Thomas S. Freeman in Duffy, *Fires of Faith*, pp. 124-7.

[86] Loades, *The Oxford Martyrs* (London: Batsford; Bangor: Headstart History, 1992), pp. 144-5.

object of all heresy tribunals, in England as on the Continent, was in fact
to save souls, wherever possible. Not all Mary's prominent advisers understood this, though, and William Paget, for example, accused Gardiner,
with whom he had fallen out over the Spanish marriage, of going soft. Yet
Paget had previously opposed the restoration of the heresy laws by parliament, helping to delay this move from April–May 1553, when the relevant
bill was rejected by the Lords, to December of the following year.[87] The
same could never be said of Bishop Bonner of London. In the 1540s, he
had been active in book censorship and the repression of dissident religion, and once released from prison in 1553 he fully supported a similar
policy. Like Mary, he was described by Foxe as 'bloody', and if the
Protestant martyrologist's documentation can be relied on, he was a
forceful and somewhat idiosyncratic inquisitor, who nonetheless desired
that heretics would return to the Church. Not only did Bonner use his
diocesan court to examine suspects who were brought to him, frequently
by the secular authorities, but he even took some of them back to his episcopal palace at Fulham for long rambling sessions of interrogation and
debate.[88] Whatever may be said about others, there can be no doubt that
Bonner played one of the most prominent parts in the attempted repression of Protestantism in Mary's England, though with active support from
lay councillors, heresy commissioners, justices of the peace and jurors.[89]

Given that Philip joined Mary in July 1554, before trials and burnings
for heresy began in England under Roman authority, it is inevitable that
the question of Spanish influence has been raised. The new King came
from a country where an Inquisition, which apparently had his full
support, had been active since 1478, when it had been established by Pope
Sixtus IV at the request of Philip's great-grandparents, Ferdinand and
Isabella. Yet Foxe treats the subsequent repression as an entirely English
affair, and although the Spaniards are mentioned briefly in more modern
literature on the subject, they are still generally held to have been either
irrelevant or a force for moderation.[90] In this respect, most of these writers
follow Foxe, who credits Philip's Franciscan confessor, Alfonso de Castro,
with having preached a sermon urging a gentler approach soon after the
burnings began in February 1555. Given Castro's track record at the time,
this is strange. Like the Dominican Carranza, the Franciscan had attended
the first phase of the Council of Trent and, also like Carranza, he had
produced a kind of 'position monograph', intended to advise the Fathers
on a particular matter of substance. Thus, before coming to England,
Castro published, in several editions, a book entitled *On the just punishment*

[87] *CSP Span* XI, p. 335, XII, pp. 152, 200; Loades, *Mary Tudor*, p. 324; Edwards, 'A
Spanish Inquisition? The Repression of Protestantism under Mary Tudor', *Reformation and
Renaissance Review*, iv (2000), p. 63.
[88] See, for example, the case of Thomas Haukes, in Foxe (1563), pp. 1148–51.
[89] Gina Alexander, 'Bonner and the Marian Persecution', in Haigh, *The English
Reformation Revised*, pp. 157–75.
[90] Prescott, *Mary Tudor*, p. 384; Loades, *Mary Tudor*, p. 323.

of heretics, which suggests that, when he preached at Philip and Mary's Court in February 1555, he was one of the leading exponents of up-to-date Catholic thinking on how to deal with heretics on the basis of his work in canon law, for which he was best known. It is possible that Friar Alfonso may have toned down his message for some political reason arising from the English situation, but his earlier book is utterly uncompromising in its defence of orthodoxy. Like other writers of the period, he sees the Catholic Church as perfect and unchanging, so that for him a heretic is anyone who does not believe and teach what the Church perpetually believes and teaches. Heretics are like sons who have rebelled against their fathers, and thus have forfeited all their filial rights. One implication of this is that they should not be allowed free access to scripture and certainly should not be permitted to comment on it. Indeed, Castro strongly advocates ecclesiastical censorship of all suspect books, something in which Carranza had previously been involved in Spain, and which was at the time being developed there in the form of inquisitorial indexes of forbidden books. Particularly interesting is what Castro had to say, in 1549, about the processes which the Church should use to deal with heretics. Here may be found the background to what he preached in London in February 1555. In his book, he urges that heretics should be admonished, if possible in private, before being punished. There should be no public disputation with such people because they were avid for publicity and would be far more likely to admit their errors in private.[91] The outcome of Cranmer's trial would support this view.

Turning to Bishop Bonner of London, it might be argued that, in his 'fireside chats' with suspected or actual heretics, he was in his own way following Castro's advice, and this raises the question of the Spanish role in everyday heresy-hunting in Mary's England. On this subject, perhaps ironically – though entirely in accordance with its own highly developed professional standards – it was the Spanish Inquisition that collected the best evidence. In the early 1560s, Friar Bartolomé Carranza was defending himself against accusations of 'Lutheran' heresy. The best form of defence in such a case was to prove one's own zeal against precisely that kind of heresy, and so it was natural that among the questions which he chose to have put to his defence witnesses were several concerning his activity while in England. Number 59 in Carranza's questionnaire asked witnesses to confirm that, when he was in England, he had worked with 'the commissioners who exercised the office of inquisitors', that three in particular, Bishop Bonner, Dr Story and Richard Rochester, had been frequently in his lodgings at Westminster, and also that he himself had often been in Bonner's consistory (*audiencia*) when prisoners were present for examination. Witnesses, including King Philip himself, were also asked

---

[91] Alfonso de Castro, *De iusta haereticorum punitione libri III* (Salamanca, 1547; Venice, 1549); Virgilio Pinto Crespo, *Inquisición y control ideológico en la España del siglo XVI* (Madrid: Taurus, 1983), pp. 235–58.

to confirm that Carranza had frequently worked with Pole in these matters, and that a large number of heretics were, with his agreement and advice, 'relaxed' for burning, and many others were given penances and reconciled. This terminology is entirely that of the Spanish Inquisition, in which Carranza had been working since 1539. Only a few of Carranza's witnesses gave answers to this question, but they were significant people. The Toledan royal chaplain Cristóbal Becerra, who had carried the sacrament in the Corpus Christi procession at Kingston in June 1555, said that he had been present at the meetings to which Carranza referred, and King Philip himself confirmed this, while his beloved companion and favourite Ruy Gómez de Silva added further detail. He said that the meetings had happened 'by order of the Queen, with the knowledge of the King O[ur] L[ord]'. Another courtier, Luis Venegas, confirmed that Carranza had been, in matters of heresy, 'the main person from whom the Queen sought advice', adding that he had heard that Carranza was unhappy with Pole, 'because he saw him as being softer than he would have wished in the punishment of such things'.[92]

Carranza also asked his supporting witnesses to answer questions from the Spanish Inquisition on individual cases. Chronologically, the earliest is that of Thomas alias William Flower, or Branche, who on Easter Sunday 1555 stabbed a priest while he was administering communion in St Margaret's church, Westminster. Here it is interesting to compare Foxe's account with the version included in Carranza's Inquisition trial. With considerable circumstantial detail, Foxe describes someone who appears to have been a mentally disturbed former Benedictine monk, who heard a 'voice' which told him to attack a minister of what he now regarded as the evil idolatry of the Mass. On that Easter Day, he had first crossed from Lambeth to attend mass at St Paul's Cathedral. There, unbidden by his inner 'voice', he had done nothing, but he had returned home and then gone out again, armed with a woodman's knife, to St Margaret's where he had stabbed a vested priest in the head and hands while he was distributing Easter communion. Not only was the priest dangerously wounded, but his blood fell on the hosts in the ciborium which he was holding. As a result of this profanation, the people had to leave for a service in another church, where they might receive what for most was their only communion of the year. Foxe has the accounts of witnesses, some of whom restrained Flower, who later told a fellow prisoner in Newgate gaol that he repented of the violence. He would not, however, concede to Bonner that the Mass was a valid sacrament, and died what Foxe called a martyr's death by burning, in the ironically named 'Sanctuary' between St Margaret's church and Westminster Abbey. Question 48 in Carranza's list describes Flower as a 'sacramentarian', one who rejected the Catholic doctrine of the Mass, and adds that his victim was a former member of the Dominican order. This seems to be crucial to Carranza's action in the

[92] Tellechea, *CyP*, pp. 95, 100, 102, 105, 110.

case, which was corroborated by several witnesses in his Spanish trial. He asked his defence witnesses to confirm that he personally had gone to Hampton Court Palace to see the King and Queen and urge them to strong action. As a consequence, according to the phrasing of the question, within three days (on 24 April 1555), Flower had had his right hand, which had done the deed, cut off at the door of St Margaret's, before being burned to death in the 'Sanctuary'. Carranza adds that he subsequently arranged for the wounded priest to be re-admitted to the Dominican order and moved to its restored house at Smithfield, where an unnamed man was detailed to care for him while his injuries healed. Numerous witnesses, including, significantly, the King, confirmed the essentials of Carranza's story, which sheds bright light on the religious attitudes and tensions which surrounded the Court at the time.[93]

Crucially, Carranza's subsequent and corroborated claim to have taken a leading role in precipitating heresy trials under Mary included his activity in the case of Archbishop Cranmer. It is now generally agreed that Mary was determined to punish as severely as possible her old adversary, who had aided and abetted her father in all the damage he had done to her mother and to her. Cranmer could legally have been executed before Christmas 1553 as a convicted traitor to the Crown, but the Queen wished him to die as a heretic, which could not be done until England was restored to the Roman obedience. He had been instituted as archbishop, even if under false pretences, by Clement VII, and only one of that pope's successors could canonically deprive him of the see of Canterbury. In most accounts of Cranmer's lengthy final ordeal at Oxford, attention is drawn to the attempts by the two Spanish Dominican university post-holders there, Juan de Villagarcía and Pedro de Soto, to argue him out of his Protestant views and persuade him to recant them in writing. Apart from being a spiritual victory in Catholic eyes, such an outcome would have been an immense boost for the religious policies of Mary and her government, and might have avoided the burnings which in fact continued to the end of the reign. The actual result is well known, and it is very probable that Villagarcía and de Soto were bitterly disappointed that they had failed, by their lights, to save Cranmer's soul. What is not normally noted is the role of their Dominican brother Carranza in arriving at the denouement of 21 March 1556, when the former archbishop was burned to death in the then town ditch of Oxford, now Broad Street. Once again, it is Carranza's defence in his trial by the Spanish Inquisition which provides the evidence. Two of his questions concerned the last days of Cranmer. Number 57 asked witnesses to confirm that, in December 1555, when Philip was in Flanders and Carranza still in England, sentence against the archbishop had been given in Rome, declaring him to be 'a heretic, and as such he was relaxed'. According to the rules of the Inquisition, this should have meant that he was handed over to the secular authorities to

[93] Foxe (1563), pp. 1129–33; Tellechea, *CyP*, pp. 93, 97–9, 101–3, 105–11, 113–15, 117.

be burned, without further legal process. That, of course, was not how things turned out, since a disorderly and irregular 'trial' was then held in the Oxford University church of St Mary the Virgin. In question 57, Carranza states that 'because there was great difficulty in the execution of the sentence, the aforesaid most reverend [archbishop] of Toledo [Carranza] insisted and worked hard for the sentence to be carried out, as it was carried out and [Cranmer] was burned'. The clearest confirmation of this came from the royal chaplain, Cristóbal Becerra, who said he knew that all this had happened, 'because he was in the Court, where it was done'. Becerra added that while Mary and her advisers were hesitating over the execution of the Roman sentence, Carranza had preached a sermon at Greenwich, where Mary was at the time, on the subject of true and false penitence. It seems to have been a typically powerful utterance, in which he declared Cranmer's apparent recantation to be false, and urged that the Roman sentence should be carried out as soon as possible.

Question 58 asked witnesses to confirm that when the news of Cranmer's burning reached the Queen, on the night of 21/22 March 1556, she immediately had Carranza woken and told, although it was after midnight. Such was the closeness of the pair and the extent of the friar's involvement in the battle against heresy. This question also contains Carranza's own treatment of his Greenwich sermon, which was preached before Mary herself in the Franciscan church there. Becerra's testimony is unclear on the subject, but Carranza states that the sermon was given after Cranmer's death (perhaps there were two), and suggested that he had died like Judas, Christ's betrayer. Significantly, Carranza says that he also referred to the strength of the continuing support in England for Cranmer and his views, saying that he himself was regarded by Protestants as waging war against them 'in the Council of the King and of the Queen'. In question 60, he indeed asked his witnesses to confirm that he had been threatened by Protestants with assassination because of his labours to have them punished. All these points were confirmed by significant witnesses, including Becerra and the count of Feria in England, and Ruy Gómez de Silva, who was by then in the Netherlands.[94]

Given the support which Carranza received in these matters back in Spain in the early 1560s, even though he was then on trial for heresy and might have been burned himself, it seems hard to deny that Carranza was central to the violence against reformed believers in Mary's England. Whatever the other Spaniards may have thought, he seems to have urged Mary, at crucial moments, to further repression. The English heresy laws and judicial procedures for the arrest and trial of suspects may have had some unique features, but the Carranza trial records clearly indicate that he and his compatriots regarded Mary's heresy commissioners as doing an inquisitorial job and, back home, used the standard terminology of the

---

[94] MacCulloch, *Cranmer*, pp. 583–605; Tellechea, *CyP*, pp. 95, 97, 99–100, 102–5, 107, 110, 112–13, 115.

Spanish 'Holy Office' to describe what had happened in England. Indeed, this point seems to find confirmation in an illustration in one of John Day's Elizabethan editions of Foxe's martyrology. This coloured line-drawing shows the burning in Cambridge Market Place in 1557 of the bones and books of the reformers Martin Bucer and Paul Fagius. The scene shown, which appears to conflate separate events, bears a strong resemblance to a Spanish *auto de fe*, except in one important respect. In Spain burnings normally took place away from the main scene of a public *auto*, after the completion of the procession and preaching. Nevertheless, the Cambridge burnings of bones and books, for which Carranza later claimed some responsibility although he seems not to have been present, indicate all too clearly that Mary's England was indeed beginning, in this respect, to integrate itself with continental practice.[95]

Pole, on the other hand, evidently aroused some doubt, among the Spanish as well as in Paul IV's Rome, concerning his zeal for punishing heretics. It certainly can be argued that, in this respect at least, Mary's beloved 'cousin' was not her main adviser and support, though his own diocese of Canterbury saw some of the severest persecution.[96] As for Mary herself, it seems impossible to deny her crucial responsibility for what happened. In her 1555 directions to the bishops, she advocated the entirely traditional approach of combining instruction of the ignorant with punishment of the guilty, and Pole repeated this policy in his circular to the bishops, issued in September 1555 in preparation for the Synod which began later in that year.[97] Not only did Mary herself intervene publicly, on more than one occasion, to ensure that the trials and burnings continued, but some of the most severe action was taken by members of her inner core of supporters in East Anglia and the south-east, such as Robert Rochester and Edward Waldegrave, as well as those who had hastily joined her cause in July 1553, for example John de Vere, earl of Oxford, and Richard, Lord Rich.[98] Numerical comparisons with such state and ecclesiastical violence in other countries cannot divert attention from the horror of what happened in each and every case.

[95] Foxe, 1570, p. 2151; Tellechea, *CyP*, pp. 96, 100, 103–5, 107, 112, 114.
[96] Dermot Fenlon, 'Pole, Carranza and the pulpit', *RCMT*, pp. 87–9; Patrick Collinson, 'The Persecution in Kent', in *CMT*, pp. 309–33.
[97] Gilbert Burnet, *The History of the Reformation of the Church of England* (London: W. S. Orr, 1850), ii, p. cclxxiv.
[98] Anna Whitelock, 'In Opposition and in Government: The Household and Affinities of Mary Tudor, 1516–1558', Ph.D. thesis, University of Cambridge, 2004, pp. 241–9.

Chapter 10

ENGLAND THREATENED, 1555–1557

It is still sometimes suggested today, as it was by her enemies at the time, that one reason for Mary's grim determination to pursue heretics to the end, despite the undoubtedly harmful effect of this violence on the popularity and success of her government, was the sadness and even bitterness she felt because she could not conceive a child. Certainly, when Cardinal Pole had finally reached Westminster and met her, in November 1554, he greeted her in a way which might seem blasphemous to many twenty-first-century Christians but would probably not have appeared so at the time. He apparently spoke to her as the Archangel Gabriel addressed the future mother of Jesus in Luke's Gospel (1: 28), but in the adapted form used habitually in the short devotion known as the Angelus, which might be attached to the Mass or said as part of the rosary. Pole said, 'Hail Mary, full of grace, the Lord is with thee'.[1] It is not recorded that he continued with the next sentence, 'Blessed art thou among women and blessed is the fruit of thy womb Jesus', but he hardly needed to. The allusion would have been understood by all, given that the Queen was believed to be pregnant, a story which had been circulating since the beginning of October. In fact, the month of religious reconciliation, November 1554, also saw the beginning of what proved to be a tragic tale, with serious implications for the future of England.

Whatever the marriage treaty of 1553–4 may have said, the burden placed on Mary by her marriage at Winchester in July 1554 was to ensure the dynastic continuity of her husband's family as well as her own. As the 'pregnancy' went on, many observers recognized that there would be trouble in England if Mary failed to produce an heir. In April 1555, Mary had gone to Hampton Court Palace for the traditional royal lying-in. On 23 April, she watched from her window the St George's Day parade of the knights of the Garter, which had been transferred from Windsor. She was seen and cheered by the English public, but then retired from view. It may well have been in part to demonstrate Christ's Eucharistic presence in her support that Carranza and his compatriots organized their Corpus Christi procession across the river at Kingston, in June of that year. In the meantime, ladies came from all over England to attend the Queen in her 'birth

---

[1] John, Elder 'Letter describing the arrival and marriage of King Philip, his triumphal entry into London, [. . .] the legation of Cardinal Pole, etc (London, 1 January 1555)', in *The chronicle of Queen Jane*, ed. Nichols, appendix, p. 153; *CRP*, 2, p. 380 (no. 998).

chamber', which was elaborately furnished, largely closed to the outside world, even excluding most natural light, heated with fires and equipped with all the paraphernalia thought necessary for a royal baby. By the end of April, though, the realization began to spread that things were not going smoothly. Male physicians were brought into the female world in which Mary was living, and worries that had been around for some time, concerning her age and state of health, became ever more urgent, at court and in the country at large. Doubters generally kept quiet, but some individuals apparently spoke on the subject with the French ambassador Antoine de Noailles as early as March 1555.[2] At the beginning of April, in an attempt to reassure and encourage the Queen, three small children were brought to her who had recently been born to a woman of her age; and Mary was not, after all, required to produce triplets.[3] In preparation for a happy outcome, letters were prepared in French, leaving the word *fil* to be amended as *fils* or *fille*, according to the gender of the expected heir.

A particularly harrowing episode took place on May Day 1555. On the night of 30 April, a rumour 'leaked' from Hampton Court to London that the Queen had given birth to a son. No doubt encouraged by their own desires for Mary and for the country, the city authorities chose to believe the story and celebrations began. The shops were shut for a May Day holiday, the beginning of the special month of the Queen's patron, St Mary, and bell-ringing, liturgical processions and singing of the normally celebratory *Te Deum* were ordered. People wishfully imagined to themselves how beautiful the child would be and there were street parties and celebratory bonfires both in London and elsewhere in the country. By the afternoon of May Day, it was known in London that the rumour was false, but unfortunately the news had by then reached Brussels, where Charles and his court were ready enough to believe in an event which was at least as important to the Habsburgs as it was to the Tudors.[4]

Mary, however, in her confinement at Hampton Court, seems to have contrived to remain hopeful after that, believing still that the *Magnificat* applied to her. Not only was she convinced that, like her patron the Blessed Virgin, she was highly favoured by God, but she also believed that she would triumph because, having overcome the duke of Northumberland in 1553, she was one of the 'humble and meek' whom God made to vanquish the mighty. It is distressing to imagine what it was like in the stuffy and over-heated chamber as the late spring and summer of 1555 drew on. It must have been hard for Mary's ladies to keep cheerful and for the midwives to repress their fears, and there was inevitably male interference in their normal sphere of operation. Foreign ambassadors in London avidly collected gossip and distributed it on the Continent, while professional medical men increasingly intervened, with ever more far-fetched

---

[2] Vertot, *Ambassades*, iv, pp. 225–7.
[3] *CSP Ven* VI, i, p. 42.
[4] *CSP Ven* VI, i, p. 72; Tyler, *England under Edward VI and Mary*, ii, pp. 469–70.

prognostications. Ominously, Mary's belly had become less swollen by mid-May. Some desperately interpreted this as a hopeful sign, believing that the birth would occur either at the new moon (23 May), or at its 'occultation' or obscuring, on 4–5 June.[5] When nothing happened on 23 May, gossip began to spread in an even less inhibited fashion. Unsurprisingly, given the threat which an heir for Philip and Mary would pose to France, Ambassador Noailles had a paid informer in Mary's inner circle, who reported that two of the women closest to her, one of them known as a skilled midwife, no longer believed that she was pregnant, or that she ever had been. Mary had a warm and close relationship with her servants, though, and many of them still tried to tell her that she would indeed come to term, probably, on a revised estimate, in a month or two. Perhaps inevitably, such encouragement did not prevent the Queen from falling into what looks like depressive behaviour. She had previously been coming out of confinement for regular walks, but now stopped doing so. She apparently spent hours on cushions on the floor of her chamber with her knees drawn up to her chin which would have been impossible if she was heavily pregnant.[6] By early June, lurid rumours were circulating again, including a story current in Italy that she had in fact already given birth, but to a lump of inanimate flesh rather than a baby. In England prayers and processions continued to be made for a successful outcome, but in Brussels, by June, it was commonly believed that Philip's Queen was not pregnant, and she felt constrained to tell her Council to write to her ambassador there, Sir John Mason, ordering him to rebut this story. As often happened in such cases, a rumour also circulated in England that Mary's agents were searching London for a suitable baby, to be falsely put in place as her infant prince.[7] None of this helped to secure stability in the kingdom, or England's reputation abroad. At the end of July 1555, Mary's women and the doctors were still trying to assure her that she would come to term in August or even September, but in early August the penny seems finally to have dropped for her. Then things became even more grim than they had been before, since she knew all too well that the whole of Europe would see her humiliation, and many would surely gloat. On 4 August her Court transferred from Hampton Court to the much smaller Oatlands, nearby, where her 'birthing' retinue could not be fitted in. The prayers and processions were stopped, and Mary resumed her normal governmental duties. Philip left for the Netherlands on 29 August.

At the time and ever since, observers and scholars have tried to divine what was actually happening medically during the Queen's long and fruitless ordeal. As early as March 1555, the French ambassador had heard a story that Mary had a tumour inside her rather than a foetus.[8] It is

---

[5] *CSP Ven* VI, i, p. 89.
[6] Vertot, *Ambassades*, iv, pp. 341–3.
[7] *CSP Ven* VI, i, p. 162.
[8] Vertot, *Ambassades*, iv, pp. 225–7.

notoriously difficult, and probably impossible, to extract from sixteenth-century evidence details of symptoms which are usable in modern diagnosis. In terms of historical explanation, it has naturally been suggested that Mary's yearning for a child, which is well attested in human as well as dynastic terms, may have caused a delusion, and one which many of her subjects, as well as observers abroad, found it convenient to support, at least for a time. Given her known health problems, it is indeed possible that Mary suffered from a tumour, as the French ambassador suspected, but her deep religious fervour should also be considered as a factor. As their correspondence in 1553–4 clearly shows, both Mary and Cardinal Pole implicitly believed that she had become Queen through the direct intervention of God. If one miracle had brought her to the throne and a second had made Philip her husband, why should a third not bring her a child? In this spirit, and making the parallel between her and the Blessed Virgin, of which she and her Catholic advisers were so fond, the prayers for her safe delivery stressed her humility and chastity. In current medical discussion of the subject of pseudocyesis, or phantom pregnancy, there is a tendency to regard the condition, which still occurs from time to time, as a sign of mental illness. Interestingly, Mary's case is commonly quoted as a 'historic' example, though accurate pregnancy tests have made such an event much more unlikely in the contemporary world. In defence of Mary's doctors as well as her midwives, it is still observed that some medical practitioners continue, in a small minority of cases, to diagnose pregnancy in women when there is none. Also, in a parallel with Mary and her contemporaries, it is still observed that pseudocyesis is more likely to occur in social circles which strongly associate pregnancy with a woman's personal worth. Thus social pressure and personal desire are still today regarded as important preconditions for a 'false pregnancy' and these are clearly present in Mary's case. What appears to follow is that any potential symptom of pregnancy is seized upon by the potential mother, and given the overwhelming longing for the birth of an heir in Mary's case, depression, at least in the early stages, seems an unlikely cause of her imaginings. With the available evidence, it is impossible to determine any physical symptoms which might indicate a reason for Mary's belief about the state of her body between the autumn of 1554 and the summer of the following year, but the outcome was undoubtedly devastating for her in various ways. It may well be true, as Milo Keynes has suggested, that an underlying medical condition was largely responsible for many of the symptoms which Mary is recorded as displaying from her teenage years onwards, such as severe headaches and deteriorating eyesight, as well as her failure to conceive. The condition in question is prolactinoma, or a tumour of the pituitary gland.[9]

According to a letter written by Pole to Mary at the end of August, before Philip left for the Netherlands, his Franciscan confessor, Bernardo

[9] Milo Keynes, 'The Aching Head and Increasing Blindness of Queen Mary I', *Journal of Medical Biography*, viii (2000), pp. 102–9.

de Fresneda, had given the Queen an image of Christ, which may have been a figure or a crucifix. This was evidently intended to offer her consolation, and in his letter Pole paraphrased a text from the prophet Zechariah: 'And a fountain will open for the House of David'. He also provided a prayer for Mary to use before the image in question, and the full text from Zechariah, which Pole cites, though only partially, in his customary manner which assumed a good knowledge of the biblical text, seems to imply a return to ritual purity (in the Vulgate Latin, *menstruatae*) as though after childbirth. Although at this distance such an allusion may seem unduly insensitive in the circumstances, it is not untypical of the way in which the Cardinal dealt with the Queen in spiritual matters.[10]

Writing to Philip on 2 September 1555, Pole indicates that the King had given him the primary duty of caring for Mary in his absence. Accordingly, he tells Philip that, more than anything else apart from his return, she wants to receive letters from him. She believes that her husband is held in God's Providence, but she is evidently battered and desolate as a result of recent events. Pole thinks that Philip had been wise to urge her to immerse herself in government duties, and says that Mary was following her husband's instructions implicitly. Thus on 31 August she had sent some people to confer with Pole about government business, and she had been very busy with administration on 1 September.[11] By 15 September, Pole had received a reply from Philip, and now wrote from Greenwich to say that he was glad the King thought he was doing a good job in looking after Mary. Characteristically, in describing how the Queen was spending her time, he uses another scriptural allusion, saying that she was 'Mary' in the mornings and 'Martha' in the afternoons. According to Luke's Gospel, Jesus and His disciples went into an unnamed village and were invited by Martha into her house. While she carried on with her domestic duties, her sister Mary sat at Jesus's feet and listened to His teaching. When Martha complained about her sister's idleness, Jesus rebuked her, saying that Mary 'has chosen the better part, which will not be taken away from her' (Luke 10 : 42). In this way, Jesus was traditionally seen by the Church as praising the contemplative over the active life, and in his letter Pole appears to be telling Philip that his wife spent the morning at her devotions, and the afternoons on governmental business. He adds that Queen Mary was using her work to relieve her sadness at her husband's absence, and that only the thought of his return consoled her.[12]

In addition to making the Cardinal personally responsible for Mary during his absence, Philip left a new system of government, which would

---

[10] *CRP*, 3, pp. 156–7 (no. 1355): the full Vulgate text of Zechariah 13: 1 is: 'In die illa erit fons patens domui David et habitantibus Ierusalem, in ablutionem peccatoris et menstruatae' ('On that day a fountain shall be opened for the House of David and the inhabitants of Jerusalem, to cleanse them from sin and impurity').

[11] *CRP*, 3, pp. 159–60 (no. 1362).

[12] *CRP*, 3, pp. 165–6 (no. 1378).

enable him to keep a grip on events in England. Although specific documentation does not survive, it is clear that he had continued to take an active role between July 1554 and his departure for Brussels in August of the following year.[13] Before he left, he established, with his wife, a new form of council, known as the 'Select Council' (in Spanish, *Consejo escogido*). This apparently consisted of the existing inner, working, core of the old Council, and its membership remained unchanged until the King returned, in 1557. The Select Council seems to have largely relegated its predecessor to formal proceedings, though the members of the new body were required to report to the Privy Council each Sunday.[14]

While this administrative reform was taking practical shape, on 24 September Pole wrote again to Philip, giving a similar picture of Mary's life though adding that she was throwing herself into what would turn out to be futile preparations to send ships to bring or escort her husband home.[15] By the time of Pole's next recorded letter to Philip, written from Greenwich on 8 October, Lord Chancellor Gardiner, the mainstay of Mary's government, was ill. Maybe because of that, as well as her general distress and depression, the Queen was now working beyond midnight, which worried Pole in terms of her health.[16] On 15 October, he received another letter from Philip, thanking him for sending news of Mary and undertaking to write to her more often: the infrequency of his letters had evidently been a complaint of hers, relayed by the Cardinal. The King urged Pole to carry on trying to persuade his wife to slow down and, on 26 October, the archbishop wrote to say that Mary appreciated Philip's concern and took it as a sign of his love for her.[17] On 11 November Pole once again relayed Mary's wish that her husband should return, to make her content and to help with the religious restoration of England. She was feeling ever more strongly about this, but all was in God's hands, and in the meantime more letters from Philip would help to keep her going.[18] It would be many months before Philip would respond to his wife's pleas and return.

By the end of 1555, it was clear that Philip was making or at least influencing important decisions through the Select Council. Not only did he carefully annotate the reports of meetings and decisions which were sent to him regularly, in Latin, by the principal secretary, Sir William Petre, but he also intervened in major appointments. In September of that year,

[13] *APC* V, p. 53; G. A. Lemasters, 'The Privy Council in the Reign of Mary I', Ph.D. thesis, Cambridge, 1971; Loades, 'Philip II as King of England', in *Law and Government Under the Tudors: Essays Presented to Geoffrey Elton*, ed. C. Cross, D. M. Loades and J. J. Scarisbrick (Cambridge: Cambridge University Press, 1988), pp. 177–94.

[14] *CSP Ven* VI, i, pp. 182–4, *CSP Ven* VI, ii, p. 1068; BL Cotton MS Titus B ii, fol. 160; RMT, pp. 195–6, 198–9; Redworth, 'Matters impertinent', pp. 601–5.

[15] *CRP*, 3, p. 168 (no. 1382).

[16] *CRP*, 3, pp. 175–6 (no. 1396).

[17] *CRP*, 3, pp. 183–4 (no. 1414).

[18] *CRP*, 3, pp. 193–4 (no. 1430); Pérez Martín, *María Tudor*, pp. 703, 707–8, 715–17, 719–20.

he delayed for twelve months the recall to London of the English ambassador in Brussels, Sir John Mason, to resume his place on the Privy Council and perhaps to become chief secretary.[19] Then he blocked Chancellor Gardiner's plan to replace St Leger, as Lord Deputy of Ireland with Edward, Lord Clinton, whom he wanted as admiral of the English fleet.[20] Most significantly, when Gardiner died, in November 1555, he effectively chose the new Lord Chancellor of England in an episode which reveals the ambiguities both of Anglo-Spanish rule and of religious identity and loyalty in Mary's reign. When the bishop of Winchester died, after a long illness, it was rumoured at court that the Queen initially wanted to replace him with Bishop Thomas Thirlby of Ely. Along with Gardiner, Thirlby had supported the Royal Supremacy but had then fallen out of royal favour under Henry VIII, who excluded both as executors of his will in 1544, and then again under Edward VI when he opposed some of the changes involved in the first and second English Prayer Books, including the removal of the elevation of the Eucharistic Host. He had been rehabilitated as a bishop by Mary while England was still in schism, but was nonetheless received in Rome as Philip and Mary's ambassador after the reconciliation of England.[21] He would, however, become Lord Chancellor. Instead, Philip consulted Pole, both before Gardiner's death on 11 November and after it, on the 28th. The replies were noncommittal, and the King also consulted the Select Council.[22] William Paget was evidently anxious for the job, but was opposed in one of Bartolomé Carranza's many crucial interventions in English affairs. The records of the friar's later Inquisition trial reveal that he wrote to Philip to protest that Paget should not be chancellor, since it was the duty of Catholics to avoid anyone 'who may have been a heretic, or [to] whom the heretics want [the post] to be given'. When interviewed, back in Spain, by the Inquisition, Philip confirmed this account, and Paget received the consolation office of Lord Privy Seal.[23] Instead, Archbishop Nicholas Heath of York succeeded Gardiner, although he, too, like all English bishops in this period, had an ambiguous record in relation to Catholicism and the Roman See. He had come from the stable of Cranmer and Cromwell and negotiated for Henry with German Lutherans in the late 1530s before adopting a more conservative position during the turmoil of Edward's reign. Like Thirlby, he had been restored by Mary, in this case as bishop of Worcester, before reconciliation, but must have put himself right with the Papacy in order to

[20] C. Brady, *The Chief Governors: The Rise and Fall of Reform in Tudor Ireland* (Cambridge: Cambridge University Press, 1994), pp. 27–8.
[21] *CSP Ven* VI, i, 252; *CRP*, 4, pp. 523–5; MacCulloch, *Cranmer*, pp. 136, 310, 323, 363, 396, 398, 406–9, 423, 457–8, 521, 591–3; Bernard, *King's Reformation*, p. 592; Alec Ryrie, *The Gospel and Henry VIII: Evangelicals in the Early English Reformation* (Cambridge: Cambridge University Press, 2003), pp. 214–19; Loades, 'Mary's Episcopate', in *CMT*, pp. 126–30.
[22] *CRP*, 3, pp. 193–4 (no. 1430) and p. 201 (no. 1441).
[23] Tellechea, *CyP*, pp. 96 (question 63), 101, 103.

be translated to York in June 1555.[24] In the meantime, events had taken place in Rome which would drastically affect Philip, Mary and England.

The central figure in Mary's plans was Pole, her 'good cousin' and counsellor. When Pope Julius III died, on 23 March 1555, the 'cardinal of England' was immediately recognized as one of the strongest candidates to replace him. The newly consecrated archbishop of Canterbury had been regarded as *papabile*, in Italian terminology, since the 1540s, even before the opening of the Council of Trent, where he was one of Paul III's legates. On 19 July 1547, during the interval between the first and second phases of the Council, Charles V's then ambassador in Rome, Juan Hurtado de Mendoza, reported to his master on Pole's suitability as a candidate. He regarded the Englishman as excellent and even ideal in many ways, but, ominously, thought his theological orthodoxy somewhat uncertain, particularly in the area of salvation by faith as well as works.[25] At that time, Pole was governor of the papal territory of Bagnoregio, where he was frequently resident between 1547 and 1553, although he was still also governor in Viterbo. He would eventually set out on his long and vastly delayed journey to England from his base there, in the Augustinian convent at Bagnoregio. On 10 November 1549, Pope Paul III died, the College of Cardinals took over the government of the Roman Church, and Pole was the immediate favourite to succeed him. In conclave on 4 December 1549, the Cardinal of England gained twenty-four out of the twenty-eight votes required for victory. As his vote was so much stronger than anyone else's, Cardinal Alessandro Farnese proposed that, rather than proceeding to a further ballot, the cardinals should elect Pole at once by acclamation, or 'adoration', as this procedure was known in Roman curial terminology. At first, Pole agreed to this, but he quickly changed his mind, even though local and foreign bankers, who always took a close professional interest in papal elections, still regarded his victory as a 90–95 per cent certainty. At the session on 5 December, however, Cardinal Gianpietro Carafa of Naples, the future Pope Paul IV, raised the concerns which the Imperial ambassador had mentioned in 1547 concerning Pole's doctrinal orthodoxy. Carafa, with the authority of the Roman Inquisition, which he had revived for Paul III in 1542 and now presided over, declared the Englishman a heretic. The 'secret' conclave, which seems not to have been particularly secret in practice, then saw efforts by Pole's supporters to gain the extra four votes required for his election, by whatever means they could, legal or otherwise. Nonetheless, in the next ballot their candidate failed again by four votes. It is easy to blame Carafa and the Inquisition for this, but it may also be that Pole scuppered his own efforts by obstinately refusing to campaign. Certainly, while one of Carafa's inquisitorial colleagues tried to damn him, another spoke in his defence. The truth is that although Pole's fate would eventually be

[24] MacCulloch, *Cranmer*, pp. 69, 83, 106–7, 161, 174–5, 310, 334, 337, 379, 405, 408, 423, 456; Ryrie, *Gospel*, pp. 215, 218, 219; Loades, 'The Marian Episcopate', in *CMT*, pp. 34–6.
[25] Tellechea, 'Pole, Carranza y Fresneda', in Tellechea, *CyP*, p. 124.

immensely important to Mary's England, at the time of the 1549 conclave, which stretched into 1550, proceedings were dominated, in the traditional fashion, by a conflict between the French and Imperialist lobbies. Even so, Pole remained the most likely candidate until as late as 5 February 1550, but two days later, Giovanni Maria Ciocchi del Monte was finally elected as Julius III.[26] About ten years later, in their treatise *Il conclavista*, two curial staff members, Felice Gualtaro and Cipriano Saracinello, would write that Pole had finally been beaten by a combination of the French lobby and his condemnation by the Cardinal of Naples as 'suspect in the Catholic faith'. They placed the main blame on Carafa, though, for suborning enough of Pole's votes to let in del Monte, by deploying the threat to the Englishman's potential supporters of guilt, in the eyes of the Inquisition, by association with the supposed 'Lutheran' heretic.[27] By the time that they wrote this, Gualtaro and Saracinello had seen Gianpietro Carafa active in two further conclaves, in the second of which he secured his own election as Pope, to the eventual detriment of Pole.

The next two papal elections took place between March and May 1555, when the restoration of Catholicism and repression of Protestant ideas and practice were fully under way in England. Julius III, who had strongly supported and assisted this process, died on 23 March 1555, and was buried in St Peter's two days later. On 5 April, Gianpietro Carafa, as dean of the College of Cardinals, sang the Mass of the Holy Spirit which preceded the locking of the doors for the conclave. Thirty-seven cardinals were enclosed, which meant that the victor would require at least twenty-five votes, and on 9 April Marcello Cervini, cardinal of Santa Croce, was elected, unusually keeping his baptismal name as Pope Marcellus II. It seemed that, on this occasion at least, the Imperialists, who for this purpose included Mary, had managed to block the French candidate, who was the cardinal dean himself.[28] Pole's friend, Cardinal Giovanni Morone, writing from Augsburg, had warned of Julius's mortal illness, but the recipient, who was the new archbishop of Canterbury, must have been greatly encouraged by the new Pope's first letter to him, written on the day after his election.[29] Marcellus told Pole that he needed the help of all princes to solve the problems of the Christian Republic (Commonwealth), and said he was drawing particular consolation from the piety of Philip, Mary and the cardinal archbishop.[30] On 28 April, Pole wrote to Marcellus, expressing delight at his election, and expectation of further 'reformation' of the Church. He promised full collaboration with the new Pope, and on the same day expressed similar sentiments in a letter to Mary. He wrote that Marcellus's election was a joy for the whole of Christendom, and he was sure that the Queen

[26] Mayer, *PP&P*, pp. 165, 167, 175–6.
[27] AGS E – Libros de Versoza, 2, fol. 23r.
[28] AGS E – Libros de Versoza, 5, fols 159r–165r.
[29] *CRP*, 3, pp. 75–6 (no. 1153).
[30] *CRP*, 3, pp. 86–7 (no. 1184).

would feel the same. Marcellus, he said, would bring consolation to Christians through his 'goodness and doctrine'.[31] On 8 May, Pole expressed similar views in a letter to the Jesuits' founder, Ignatius of Loyola, but by then Marcellus was dead.[32]

In his treatise *De summo Pontifice* ('On the supreme pontiff'), written at the time of the conclave of Julius III, Pole had expressed the view that a pope needed *imbecillitas*, meaning weakness, or vulnerability, rather than stupidity, as well as *sapientia* (wisdom), and it seemed to him that Marcellus possessed both qualities. Yet many may have thought that, instead of writing enthusiastically from England about Marcellus, Pole should have gone to Rome and been elected Pope himself. On 5 April 1555, Charles V had written from Brussels to his son Philip in London, regretting Julius III's death, and praising him for his concern for the good of the Church in general and the house of Habsburg in particular, this evidently including his involvement with England. As might have been expected, the ill and exhausted Emperor, who was about to cede all his authority to Philip, did not forget his dynastic obligation to work for a pro-Habsburg Pope who would frustrate the aims of the French. He told his son that he had duly consulted his sister Mary of Hungary, and other advisers, as a result of which the Habsburg shortlist of candidates was drawn up. Omitting Marcello Cervini, who was actually elected, it was headed by Pole, who was followed by Rodolfo de Carpi and Giovanni Morone. However, this Habsburg think-tank saw Pole as being better at goodness than government and, professing his own ignorance of the English situation, Charles told Philip that he did not know how to advise Pole on the subject of going to Rome for the conclave: he was therefore happy to let the cardinal himself decide. Three days later, Philip replied from Hampton Court, telling his father that he had done what was necessary in Pole's case. The cardinal archbishop had replied that, if he went to Rome, he would be just one vote in support of some other candidate, that he could be elected in his absence, if the majority of the cardinals wanted that, but that it was more important, in the situation of England in the spring of 1555, that he should stay there as legate.[33] Both he and Philip must have known that Pole was thus excluding himself from the papal throne, and the message was not lost on continental observers, of whom there were many. Marcellus only had time to send one friendly, if formal, document to Philip and Mary, informing them of his election, before the College of Cardinals met again to choose the second new pope of the year.[34]

The winner on this occasion, Gianpietro Carafa, came from a distinguished noble family in Naples, had been a keen reformer of 'abuses' in the

[31] *CRP*, 3, pp. 91–2 (no. 1193), p. 92 (no. 1194 = AGS Libros de Versoza, 5, fols 17v–18r).
[32] *CRP*, 3, p. 100 (no. 1215).
[33] Manuel Fernández Álvarez, ed., *Corpus documental de Carlos V*, 5 vols (Salamanca: Ediciones Universidad de Salamanca, 1970), iv, pp. 38–9.
[34] Tellechea, *Papado*, i, pp. 39–40 (no. XX).

Church since his early years, and was bishop of the Italian see of Chieti from 1504 to 1524. In 1514 he had been in England, as an envoy from Pope Leo X to Henry VIII, in a futile attempt to break up the anti-French league which had recently been formed by the Tudors, Habsburgs and some Italian states. On that occasion he was ignored by Henry and outmanoeuvred by Cardinal Wolsey and Bishop Richard Fox of Winchester.[35] In 1520, he was on the papal commission which considered the case of Martin Luther, and in 1524 he resigned his bishopric in order to found the reforming Theatine order, with Tommaso del Vio Cajetan. In 1536 he returned to the episcopal bench as cardinal archbishop of his native Naples, with unfortunate results for the Habsburgs and for Mary. Having thwarted Pole's election as pope in 1550, and having been pipped by Marcellus in April 1555, Carafa now had another chance, at the age of seventy-nine, to exploit his position as dean of the College of Cardinals.[36]

According to a letter written from Rome to Charles V, on 25 May 1555, by the Cardinal Archbishop of Santiago de Compostela in Spain, the Habsburg supporters went into action immediately. Charles's current ambassador there, Don Juan Manrique de Lara, was in Pope Marcellus's chamber when he died. Immediately afterwards, Manrique called the Spanish cardinals together, and told them of the Emperor's will concerning the choice of the next pope. The Habsburg shortlist was the same as it had been earlier in the year, with Pole as first choice, followed by Carpi and Morone, in that order. Knowing that the French would be similarly engaged in support of Carafa, who in the crucial role of dean of the College had a great opportunity to influence or even control the election, the Cardinal of Santiago at once started negotating with those Italian cardinals whose votes might come the way of the Habsburgs. It is evident that Charles V and Manrique did not anticipate that Pole would come to Rome for the conclave. Victory for their cause was unlikely, therefore, though it is clear that the Habsburgs did not, as has sometimes been asserted, neglect this election and thus let Carafa in.[37] An anonymous Italian account of this conclave, copied later for Philip by Juan de Versoza, states that it was largely a matter of accident and fortune that the new Pope Paul IV was elected. As in the case of his predecessor Marcellus, the election was dominated by rivalry between the French and the Imperialists, the latter being opposed to Carafa. Pole was out of consideration because, as was generally accepted, he had to remain in England to deal with the difficult religious situation there. According to this Italian commentator, Pole's absence weakened the Imperial side, but even so, there was lengthy debate before Carafa could be elected.[38] In their version of events, Gualtaro and Saracinello used Paul IV's conclave as an example of the ups

[35] *LP* I, no. 2610; Scarisbrick, *Henry VIII*, pp. 51, 53.
[36] *Oxford Dictionary of the Christian Church*, ed. F. L. Cross and E. A. Livingstone, 3rd edn (Oxford: Oxford University Press, 1998), p. 1239.
[37] AGS E 882–151.
[38] AGS E – Libros de Versoza, 2, fols 165r–171v.

and downs of such gatherings. They regarded Carafa's success as a prime example to future *conclavistas* of how one individual could dominate matters. Specifically, they noted that, as dean of the College of Cardinals, Carafa succeeded, both in Marcellus's conclave and his own, in persuading his colleagues to rule out in advance the use of the procedure of 'adoration', which might have secured Pole's election back in 1549. These hard-bitten curialists regarded Pole's earlier high-mindedness as a prime example of how to lose a papal election.[39]

Once elected, Paul IV immediately indicated the policies which he intended to follow, to the advantage of Henry II of France and to the clear detriment of Philip and Mary. On 24 May 1555, the day after the white smoke went up, he sent one letter to Charles V in Brussels and another to Philip and Mary in London. To Charles he indicated that he might replace Pole as legate for peace between the Habsburgs and France, while he assured the English monarchs that he had no intention of reducing Pole's standing there, as he would in fact later do, by removing his specific, personal powers as legate *a latere* and leaving him with those of an *ex officio legatus natus*, as archbishop of Canterbury.[40] Indeed, despite their earlier personal and doctrinal conflicts in Rome, there seems to have been a kind of initial honeymoon in relations between Pole and the new Pope. Paul sent letters to Pole in the same post as those to Charles and Philip and Mary. He told the legate that he would like to have him in the Curia to advise him, and was awaiting the English ambassadors who had originally been sent to his predecessor.[41] Pole replied on 6 June, apparently impressed that he had learned of Paul's election on Pentecost (Whitsunday, 2 June) and seeing the news as a gift of the Holy Spirit. It is quite clear that he saw the new Pope in terms of the Catholic reform in which they had worked together in Italy years before. He was convinced that the spirit of Carafa's Theatines would now renew the Church in general, and the Curia in particular. He would do anything he could to help, and Philip and Mary's ambassadors, then approaching Rome, would give him details of the situation in England.[42] As a gesture of goodwill, as well as a messenger with news of the church situation in England and Wales, Pole soon afterwards sent to Rome the bishop-designate of St Asaph, Thomas Goldwell, who was a member of Carafa's Theatine order.[43] A few days later, on 30 June, Paul wrote again to Pole, in a tone of continuing cordiality. He told the English cardinal that, especially since he had reached the papal throne at such a great age, he desperately wished that he had his advice on the spot in Rome. Despite his notoriously pro-French views, he professed himself certain that the best hope of peace in Europe, and particularly between France and the

---

[39] AGS Libros de Versoza, 2, fols 14r–23r.
[40] Tellechea, *Papado*, i, pp. 43–5 (nos XXI, XXII).
[41] *CRP*, 3, p. 105 (no. 1231).
[42] *CRP*, 3, p. 107 (no. 1237).
[43] *CRP*, 3, pp. 111–12 (no. 1250).

Habsburgs, lay with Mary, Philip and their cardinal.[44] Things would in fact turn out rather differently.

The sequence of events which would eventually lead to the English loss of Calais to France, in January 1558, in fact began years earlier, and far away in the southern Italian kingdom of Naples. One of the high points of the festivities in Winchester Cathedral on 25 July 1554 had been the cere-monial reading, by the regent of Naples, Don Juan de Figueroa, of Charles V's grant of that kingdom to his son Philip. This had ensured that Mary, as sovereign ruler of England and Ireland, and also with a claim to France, would be marrying a royal equal, and not just the Prince of Spain. Naples was, however, a papal fief, which meant that, at least in the eyes of the Roman Curia, Philip, and hence Mary when she married him on that day, should have been invested not by Charles but by Pope Julius III or his representative. The error or omission would revive an ancient conflict over control of the 'nearer' and 'further' Sicilies (from Rome), these being Naples and Sicily itself. Spanish rule over the island kingdom had generally been accepted since the time of Mary's grandfather, and Philip's great-grandfather, Ferdinand of Aragon (d. 1516). The French, however, on the basis of an Angevin claim dating back to the thirteenth century, most certainly did not acknowledge Trastamaran, and then Habsburg, rule in Sicily itself or in the mainland kingdom of Naples, which covered most of southern Italy. The French claim to the 'Two Sicilies' had been the primary cause of conflict in Italy at least since 1494, when Charles VIII invaded the peninsula.[45] Belatedly, on 1 October 1555, by which time Philip was back in Brussels after his wife's phantom pregnancy, a document was drawn up in the Imperial chancery, whereby he accepted investiture with the kingdom of Naples from Julius III, swearing allegiance to the Holy Father. Philip signed it in Spanish, 'El Rey' (the King).[46] With his customary tact, Julius III had formally invested Philip as King of Naples on 23 October 1554, nearly three months after the wedding, and yet the new King's oath of allegiance to the Pope as suzerain took almost a year longer than that to materialize.[47] The bitterly anti-Spanish and anti-Habsburg Carafa would not be so accommo-dating. He was acutely aware that, by making his oath of allegiance, Philip had effectively, as well as legally, become the Pope's vassal in Naples. He had also accepted, if only implicitly, the agreement which had been made by Ferdinand and Pope Julius II, whereby successive Spanish rulers were required to perform such an act.[48] Pope Carafa, however, nonetheless threatened to sue both Charles and his son for disobedience to their over-lord in the kingdom of Naples, Sicily and Jerusalem, titles which English heralds had proudly proclaimed for Philip and Mary at their wedding.[49]

[44] *CRP*, 3, pp. 115–16 (no. 1260).
[45] Edwards, *Ferdinand and Isabella*, pp. 109–14.
[46] Tellechea, *Papado*, i, pp. 52–3 (no. XXVII).
[47] Ibid., p. 25 (no. X).
[48] Ibid., p. ix.
[49] Ibid., p. xii.

Even so, things briefly seemed to go smoothly at the beginning of Paul IV's reign. At long last, and when Mary was expected by many to give birth to a child very soon, a Franco-Imperial peace conference opened at La Marque, in the Pale between Calais and Gravelines, on 23 May 1555. A special conference venue had been built, in which no delegation had to meet another outside formal sessions.[50] Pole had worked hard for this, and led a team of English mediators. The supposedly forthcoming birth directly affected the course of the conference by stalling negotiations, since a child for Philip and Mary would greatly strengthen the Habsburg position, while if mother and child died, the supposedly pro-French Elizabeth would succeed, thus reopening many issues. While deeply satisfied initially that something had come of his efforts as peace legate since the summer of 1553, Pole had to report to Pope Paul from Calais, on 9 June, that the La Marque conference had broken up and that he was returning to England to await further orders.[51] On or about 24 June 1555, he gave Paul a fuller account of the abortive meeting. At the opening session, on Ascension Day, he, as the Pope's legate, and Mary's representatives, who were formally acting only for England, sat at the head of a large, if hardly Arthurian, round table, with the Habsburg delegation on their right and the French on their left. Henry II's team was led by those great rivals, the Cardinal of Lorraine and Constable Anne de Montmorency, while the duke of Medinaceli and Chancellor Granvelle spoke for the Emperor and his family. On the next three days, the French and Imperial delegations met separately with Pole and Mary's representatives, who were led by Lord Chancellor Gardiner. Much time was spent on the problems of the two major powers in Italy, and although attempts were made at face-to-face negotiations, the French eventually left, and the effort was abandoned.[52] Peace would not be made between the two major European powers in Mary's lifetime, but in the meantime, Pope Carafa went on the warpath as well, though at first England seemed not to be in the firing line.

On 30 June 1555, soon after the failure of the La Marque conference, Paul IV sent a lengthy letter to Philip and Mary, containing an account of their ambassadors' arrival in Rome, the first such event since Henry VIII's reign, and after the death of four popes. Their primary duties were to give the King and Queen's thanks for the papal pardon which had been issued by Julius III and to swear England's obedience to the Apostolic See. In an eloquent and well received speech, Bishop Thirlby of Ely assured the Pope that Mary and Philip's kingdom had truly returned to the Roman Church. A few days later, his ambassadorial colleague, Sir Edward Carne, presented all the relevant documents which had been issued by Julius III, so that they could be reissued in Paul's name. On the day after that, a special consistory of cardinals was held in the Pope's summer palace of San Marco, during

[50] Redworth, 'Matters Impertinent', p. 610.
[51] *CRP*, 3, p. 109 (no. 1242).
[52] *CRP*, 3, pp. 112–13 (no. 1251).

which the old documents were read again and measures taken to store them. There seems to be no doubt that, at this stage, just over a month after his election, Pope Carafa was still extremely enthusiastic about what Philip, Mary and Pole were doing in England, speaking highly of both monarchs and of the see of Canterbury, which was still legally in the possession of the imprisoned Thomas Cranmer.[53] By 12 August, though, Paul IV, in one of those violent changes of mood and policy for which he became renowned, was writing to Pole virtually ordering him to abandon his legation in England and return to Rome The Venetian ambassador in London, Giovanni Michieli, reported home that Pole placed himself in the Pope's hands at this stage, but if he did so this proved to be no more than a gesture.[54] In fact, real trouble for Europe in general, and for Mary and her regime in particular, was just about to begin in earnest.

In the 1550s, the overwhelming fear of both French and Habsburgs was encirclement. France wanted to weaken or even destroy Charles and Philip's power in Spain, the Netherlands, Germany and Italy, but always portrayed her own military action as 'defensive', even when it involved invading Habsburg territory on her frontiers. In return, Charles and Philip claimed that France was hampering their efforts to fulfil their Christian duty to fight against the enemies of the Catholic faith, whether Protestant or Muslim. There was some basis for these assertions, but behind them lay the Habsburgs' overwhelming desire for military glory, which, whatever their other exploits, was only truly gained by fighting against the French. Thus the hopes of Mary and her peacemakers were unlikely to be fulfilled. As in her father's day, the viability of military campaigns was primarily assessed in terms not of cost and size, although these factors were of course taken into account in practice, but of how much 'honour' and glory they would generate. In particular, to obtain true fame and reputation, it was not enough for a battle or siege to be won; the ruler had to take part personally in the action. Up to and during his marriage with Mary, this was perhaps Philip's main preoccupation. Reputation in this area could easily be lost, and had to be worked on constantly, and as Charles prepared to hand over to him most of his titles and responsibilities, he inevitably inherited his father's ambitions and major policy goals. As soon as he became Holy Roman Emperor, in 1519, Charles had demanded recognition as the leader of Christendom, but France obstinately refused to accept this, basing its own claim to supremacy on its wealth, population, fertile lands and tradition of acting as the leading defender of the Roman Church. French kings and their advisers asserted, not without foundation, that the Empire, despite its maddening resilience, was in truth little more than a symbol, because the Imperial title was elective, and what would otherwise have been the most powerful state in Europe was torn apart by princely rivalries, now rendered even more destructive by religious

[53] Tellechea, *Papado*, i, pp. xxvii, 46–9 (no. XXIV).
[54] *CRP*, 3, p. 145 (no. 1339).

divisions. Both Francis I and his son Henry II thus saw it as their duty to impose their just and righteous supremacy over the Habsburgs by force of arms, with the result that war between them was the normal state of affairs and intervals of peace no more than occasionally necessary interludes. Although both the French and the Habsburgs claimed to abhor 'hegemony', both were in fact seeking just that. In this situation, secondary powers such as England were constrained to work for an ephemeral and generally spurious 'balance of power' and in this respect Pole was no more successful than Wolsey had been in the reign of Mary's father.[55]

Another political 'law' of mid-sixteenth-century Europe was that no stable continental settlement could be obtained without resolving disputes in Italy. Whoever controlled Italy would be supreme, and this inevitably involved the kind of efforts to manipulate papal elections which went on in 1555. Charles V's chancellor in the 1520s, Mercurino Arborio de Gattinara, had declared that dominance of Italy meant domination of the world, but, for many decades, the result had been constant meddling in the Italian peninsula by France, Spain and the Empire. During his time as King of England, Philip was finding his political feet, and defining his own identity against his father, with unfortunate results for Mary and her Kingdom. Other vital factors in the events of 1555 were Charles's own character and how it was perceived around the capitals of Europe. The Emperor's self-image, as depicted by Titian in his portrait now in the Prado gallery in Madrid, was of a majestic, noble warrior devoted to the safety and unity of Christendom, but most of his politically aware contemporaries regarded him as greedy, aggressive, amoral and happy to trample on the rights of others. They also feared that Philip would prove to be a chip off this particular block, as he gradually took over the Habsburg territories in the Netherlands, Spain and Italy. Once the La Marque peace conference broke up in failure, and Paul IV began to show his teeth, it became increasingly likely that, for the foreseeable future, the fate of Europe would be decided in Italy, and that England, through the marriage of Mary and Philip, would be dragged along behind.

By the time that Philip abandoned his desolate, childless wife to return to the Netherlands in August 1555, it was known all over the Continent that his father was planning, in a manner unprecedented in the history of the Holy Roman Empire and of European monarchy in general, to start disposing of his various titles. This encouraged his many enemies to begin attacking various Habsburg territories in revenge for the ill-treatment which they had received from him in earlier years. Significantly, at the time of his marriage to Mary, Philip was seen as weak, precisely because he had not yet been 'blooded' in battle. Now, it was thought by the French and others, was the moment to strike, before the new regime could establish itself. These views were powerfully expressed by Pope Paul IV, who was happy to tell people that he regarded Charles as a cripple in body and soul,

[55] Rodríguez-Salgado, *Changing Face*, pp. 28–31.

and that he thought little better, if at all, of his son. Pope Carafa's enthusiastic initial messages to England after his election should be read with this overall picture in mind, one which would place Philip's wife in evergrowing danger. Given the political layout of Europe at the time, it was generally supposed that the north-western territories of Italy and its borders, Piedmont, Savoy and Milan, were the most likely flashpoints, and this proved to be the case. Even before Paul IV's election, Henry II of France had begun military action in Italy in order to exploit the weaknesses of the Habsburgs. In March 1555, his troops captured Ivrea and Casale, on the road to Genoa and Piacenza, thus threatening the Habsburg winter quarters in the east of Piedmont. These moves succeeded in exposing a disagreement between Charles and his son over who should command their army and how to retaliate against the French. The massive Habsburg financial crisis of the 1550s inevitably intruded. Lack of money delayed the duke of Alba's arrival at the front from England, once he had been chosen as commander, and there was a stalemate until June 1555, by which time Paul had been elected and things looked even brighter for the French. In that month, Alba finally set off for Italy, short of cash and time but with 23,000 infantry. He soon became bogged down, though, and in the meantime the main action moved to southern Italy.[56]

Gianpietro Carafa's accession to the papal throne had the immediate effect of encouraging Henry II of France to move his troops south from Milan towards Naples, since he knew that he now had an ally in the Papal States, which straddled central Italy. In addition, it was not long before Paul IV, still fuming over Philip's investiture with Naples, began to take actions of his own which helped the French and harmed the Habsburgs. He made his warlike nephew, Carlo Carafa, cardinal secretary of state, and decided that he should 'inherit' the archbishopric of Naples from his uncle.[57] This immediate provocation to the Habsburgs was followed by a papal investiture to the Neapolitan fief of Camerino, which bypassed Philip. Also, in August 1555, the Neapolitan archbishopric of Trani was vacant, and Paul apparently blamed Philip for not filling it. The Pope produced his own candidate, whose name cannot be established, and his request for this favour reached England just before Philip left for the Netherlands. On 18 August 1555, Reginald Pole had written from Richmond to Carlo Carafa, telling him that Philip was concerned not to appoint a non-Neapolitan to Trani and the issue had still not been settled by the time of the King's departure. Apparently riled by the Pope's request, Philip would not accede to it, even though Pole had assured him of the excellent qualities of the proposed papal candidate. At the end of September 1555, Pole found himself still entangled in this dispute, telling Carlo Carafa that he felt thoroughly uncomfortable as pig-in-the-middle between Philip and Paul.[58] At

---

[56] Ibid., pp. 31–40, 137–45.
[57] *CRP*, 3, p. 133 (no. 1308).
[58] *CRP*, 3, pp. 152–3, 158–9, 171 (nos 1345, 1359, 1386).

about this time things got even worse, with the outbreak of a direct military conflict between the Habsburgs and the Papacy. The problem began in a typically complicated and local way, with moves by Paul IV against Roman aristocrats whom he perceived to be favourable to Charles and Philip. Count Sforza of Santa Fiora and his two brothers responded by seizing two papal galleys from Paul's territory. The Pope inevitably blamed the Habsburgs for this, accusing the Sforza of treason, and arresting Cardinal Alessandro Sforza as a hostage for the ships' return. This was duly achieved by the end of September, but even Pole, in England, became involved on his King's behalf. In a letter to Carlo Carafa, dated 10 October 1555, he stated that the fugitive galleys had been commanded by Cardinal Guido Ascanio Sforza, and had indeed subsequently fallen into Habsburg hands. Pole, who was at the time preoccupied with caring for the Queen, told the papal secretary of state that, though the boats had been restored and Cardinal Guido released from Habsburg custody, he himself was very upset about the whole business, adding pointedly that he, Philip and Mary were all hoping the Pope would now return to the real business in his hands, which was church reform. Although, in a letter dated 23 October, Pole was able to tell Paul that Mary and the English court rejoiced at the freeing of Cardinal Sforza, and the improvement in relations between Rome and the Habsburgs, it would not be long before further conflict erupted.[59]

To begin with, the Pope engaged in a war of words against the Habsburgs, accusing them of aspiring to 'monarchy', which in the sixteenth century meant totalitarian rule over Europe. He went beyond the most severe political critics of Charles, though, by accusing him of being an enemy of Christ, and even, incredibly, of deliberately fomenting heresy in Germany in order to undermine the Roman Church. Then words turned to action, when he formally accused both Charles and Philip of rebellion and felony, excommunicating them, absolving their subjects of obedience to them, and appointing himself as 'protector' of their subjects. These measures appear not to have applied to England, but did nothing to stabilize Mary's regime there. Needless to say, Paul's moves delighted the French, as he no doubt intended. They began talks with the Papacy, which led in October 1555 to an offensive and defensive treaty and 'Holy League', which also included the duchy of Ferrara, with at least the hopes that Venice might join as well. The underlying assumption of this enterprise was that the Habsburg presence in Italy was relatively weak, and hence there would be rich pickings for the allies. Siena and some Milanese territory would go to the Papacy, once it had been captured from the Habsburgs, while the historic duchy of Milan itself, together with the kingdom of Naples, would go to Henry II of France, who would grant them to his sons Francis and Charles, respectively. The Pope, as its feudal overlord, would authorize the French invasion of Naples, and Sicily would be partitioned between Henry II and the Papacy. After all this had

[59] Rodríguez-Salgado, *Changing Face*, pp. 146–7; *CRP*, 3, p. 177 (no. 1401), p. 182 (no. 1412).

been achieved, Medici Florence would be 'liberated' from its Habsburg ducal protectorate and re-established as a pro-French and pro-papal republic. In practical terms, Henry of France would provide an army of 12,000 infantry, and pay 350,000 écus to Pope Paul, who would himself assemble 10,000 infantry, 1,000 cavalry, and 150,000 écus in funds. Evidently, Paul IV's approach to Mary, her Church and kingdom, from the autumn of 1555 onwards, cannot be understood without awareness of these papal manoeuvres, which dwelt constantly on the minds of the Queen and her husband, and also preoccupied Reginald Pole. Philip's initial response, which directly involved Pole as legate for peace, as well as counsellor and moral supporter of the Queen, was to try to call the Pope's bluff by requesting that he support a revival of peace negotiations with France, after the La Marque fiasco, Inevitably, given what had recently been going on between Paul and the French, the papal response was negative, and subsequent communications between London, Brussels and Rome reflected this increasingly dangerous situation.[60]

There could no longer be any doubt that Paul IV was a violent enemy of the Habsburgs and their allies. On 8 October, he harangued the Imperial, English and Venetian ambassadors in Rome on the subject of the prerogatives of the Roman See, reminding them of the horrors of the 1527 sack of Rome, for which he held Charles V responsible. Then, about a week later, he was heard to describe all Spaniards as *marranos*, an abusive Spanish term for those judged to be false converts from Judaism to Christianity, also announcing that he planned to punish the whole Spanish nation, and having to be calmed by his nephew, the count of Montorio.[61] In July 1555, Paul had issued his bull *Cum nimis absurdum*, which established a Jewish ghetto in Rome for the first time, and introduced various other restrictive policies towards the Jews of the Papal States.[62] On 27 July, his nephew Cardinal Carlo had gleefully reported to Pole that, as part of his campaign for peace and reform, the Pope had taken the easy steps of forcing the Jews of Rome into a ghetto, making them wear the traditional yellow hats of medieval anti-Jewish laws, and restricting their money-lending activities.[63] In sixteenth-century Europe, it was always easy to tar the Spanish with the 'Judaizing' brush, and Philip was vulnerable to such tactics. Mary and the English, however, were not, since in 1290 Edward I had pioneered the practice of expelling a nation's entire Jewish population. Another of Paul IV's anti-Habsburg measures would, however, have a direct effect on England. In November 1555 he revoked the commissions of all his legates and nuncios in Charles and Philip's territories, except for Pole, whose exemption was confirmed in the following month.[64] This

[60] Rodríguez-Salgado, *Changing Face*, pp. 147–8.
[61] Mayer, *PP&P*, pp. 303–4.
[62] Kenneth Stow, *The Jews in Rome, 1551–1557*, 2 vols (Leiden: Brill, 1997), ii, pp. 742–3.
[63] *CRP*, 3, p. 136 (no. 1320).
[64] Mayer, *PP&P*, p. 304; *CRP*, 3, p. 217 (no. 1471).

action may or may not have been a warning to Pole, and by implication to Mary as well as Philip, but in any case it ushered in a period of growing insecurity for Catholic leadership in England.

On 25 October, one of the greatest events in Philip's life, from which Mary his wife was absent, took place in Brussels. Amidst great ceremony, Charles invested his son with authority over the 'Circle of the Netherlands', which at his request had been made into a separate political unit, neither Imperial nor French, in 1548. Three days before, Charles had handed over to Philip the governance of the highly prestigious chivalric order of the Golden Fleece. It would have been expected that Philip's Queen would be with him, just as she was soon to be included beside him in stained-glass windows in leading churches in Antwerp in the south and Gouda in the north, but circumstances made that impossible.[65] Philip's new role served only to redouble the vigour of his family's enemies, in Paris and Rome. On 28 November 1555, Paul wrote to Philip, shamelessly exhorting him to keep the peace of Europe, and particularly to avoid war with France: the existing conflict was strictly between Charles and France. But as so often, though without explicitly stating his francophile feelings, the Pope expressed himself strongly, saying that, if the English King and prince of Spain started a war with France (the contrary possibility was not mentioned), 'believe Us, dearest son, there will be no victory, no one will triumph with the praise of it'.[66] On the same day, the Pope wrote to Mary, as usual praising her and Pole for their work to restore the Church, but pointedly urging her to make an equally great effort to stop her husband and father-in-law making war in Europe. His own pro-French war plans were not, of course, mentioned.[67] Nevertheless, from then until the end of 1555, the Pope did at least appear to be genuinely pursuing peace. In various documents, issued on 11 and 14 December, he arranged and facilitated the succession of Pole to Cranmer as archbishop of Canterbury.[68] Before these letters reached him, Pole expressed concern, in another to Paul dated 15 December, that the Pope should really want and work for peace, following this up with the despatch of an envoy, Vincenzo Parpaglia, to Brussels in that cause.[69] Indeed, just before Christmas 1555, Paul seemed to be anxious to show his favour to Pole and Mary in their enterprises, reassuring Pole that he still had his full legation, praising and exhorting the English bishops and Synod, and promising every help in the full restoration of the 'primitive' Church in England.[70] The New Year would bring cold reminders of the true situation facing Mary and her kingdom.

[65] Irene Smets, *The Cathedral of Our Lady in Antwerp* (Ghent: Ludion, n.d.), p. 46; www.sintjan.com (Sint Janskerke, Gouda (Goudseglazen)).

[66] Tellechea, *Papado*, i, pp. 56–7 (no. XXXI, '[. .] crede nobis, fili charissime, nulla erit victoria, nullus triumphus cum ea laude'); *CRP*, 3, pp. 202–3 (no. 1442).

[67] Tellechea, *Papado*, i, pp. 58–9 (no. XXXII).

[68] *CRP*, 3, pp. 210–12 (nos 1459–61).

[69] *CRP*, 3, pp. 212, 215 (nos 1463, 1468).

[70] *CRP*, 3, p. 217 (no. 1472).

Faced with the threat of attacks on his lands and interests in Italy, and particularly in Milan, Naples and Sicily, Philip opted for negotiation. In February 1556 he proposed a truce with France, to be negotiated by Pole and his own ambassador in Rome, with the Pope acting as mediator. Much to the surprise of most, the actual result was a truce, signed in that month at Vaucelles between Charles as Emperor and Henry II, without papal intervention but instead with mediators provided by Mary, who were no doubt accepted by the French in order to keep England out of any subsequent conflict. Once again, Pole headed the English mediation team, though Philip took no direct part in proceedings. The French had begun by demanding ratification of the status quo, which involved Habsburg acceptance of their incursions into Italy, while the Imperialists wanted a return to the situation before hostilities broke out. With his mind as ever on church matters, Pole proposed that a final settlement should await the resumption of the General Council at Trent, which the French were happy to accept, as their existing gains would thus be consolidated. Both sides inevitably accused the English of bias against them, but the truce was achieved, mainly because financial problems forced Charles and Philip to accept the loss of honour and reputation involved. It was evident that both Henry of France and Pope Paul regarded the Vaucelles truce as no more than a chance to regroup, but observers also wondered whether Philip would ever actually fight a war against the Pope. In general terms, all the theologians he consulted maintained that such a conflict could never be 'just', in terms of the Christian laws of war, especially as a pre-emptive strike on the Papal States seemed inevitable in the circumstances.

For Mary and England, such an outcome would self-evidently be catastrophic, whatever the rights and wrongs of the situation, and the English were not alone in being worried. The distinguished Spanish Dominican theologian Diego de Soto went so far as to advise Philip that to make war on a pope, however bad and even heretical he might be, risked destroying the Christian faith altogether. Philip's star commander, the duke of Alba, who had ample experience of fighting in Italy, also totally opposed such a campaign, preferring the less extreme options of placing economic sanctions on the Papal States and imprisoning any Spanish churchmen at home who opposed the seizure of church assets there to fund military activity in Italy. In his view, it was better to achieve fame by enduring injustice than to be declared a heretic for fighting the Pope. If these were important considerations in Spain, how much more would they weigh in England, where the very existence of the Catholic Church was still highly controversial. Philip's dilemma continued for some weeks, as both principle and pragmatism came into play. One camp, which included Philip himself, thought that it would be dishonourable not to fight on behalf of his Italian allies, especially as he personally had still not won his spurs in battle, while pragmatists, including Alba, pointed out that troops and funds were lacking for an effective campaign. Meanwhile Paul IV tried to discredit Philip and his allies, saying that there could be no justification for a war against the head of Christendom.[71] Hostilities did not in fact break out until the autumn of 1556, but in the meantime, a masquerade of a peace process continued. In April, Pole was quietly removed from his 'peace' legation on the Continent, which was becoming increasingly embarrassing for him and particularly for Mary, as conflict loomed between her husband and the Pope. He was replaced by Cardinal Scipione Rebiba, an ally of Carlo Carafa.[72] Like so much else in England at that time, the kingdom's relations with the Papacy continued to stagnate during the summer of 1556. The same could not, however, be said for the French.

It soon became clear that the truce of Vaucelles had solved none of the long-standing issues between France and the Habsburgs, and the Papacy was ready to take full advantage. When news of the truce reached Rome, on 14 February 1556, Paul IV had gone into one of his rages, not least because the agreement seemed to negate his recent alliance with Henry II. On the surface at least, and perhaps genuinely in part, the Pope still proclaimed that he wanted peace throughout Europe, and he announced that he would send legates to both courts to pursue this cause. In fact, Scipione Rebiba remained with Philip, but Paul's nephew Carlo, who in truth was committed to driving the Habsburgs out of Italy altogether and was therefore hardly an impartial broker, arrived at Henry's Court in Fontainebleau on 14 June 1556. Not only did he find his hosts divided over how to proceed, but by then the French King and his advisers had become riskily involved in English affairs. The French ambassador in London, Antoine de Noailles, had long tried to foment discontent and rebellion against Philip and Mary's regime, but opportunities of this kind increased in 1555–6, as the violent campaign to repress Protestantism continued and fears grew in England that the country would become embroiled in continental wars. Ever since Mary came to the throne, English political and religious dissidents had attempted to stir up trouble at home from bases in France. Early in 1556, Sir Henry Dudley's conspiracy had seemed more serious than most. Unusually for him, Henry II explicitly authorized Noailles to negotiate with Dudley, and their dealings continued even after the Vaucelles truce. In March, Dudley and several other conspirators crossed to France and met King Henry at Blois. He urged them to go on with their plot, and said that he would directly supply them with troops and funds if the truce did indeed collapse. It is striking, though, that, when, soon afterwards, one of the conspirators leaked their plans to the English authorities and revealed the personal involvement of the French King and his London ambassador, Mary did not react by declaring war. She may have felt that her support at home was insufficiently strong, but in any case, in contrast with her reaction to Wyatt's rebellion in 1554, she did not even act on the rebels' confessions. Nevertheless, from then

[71] Rodríguez-Salgado, *Changing Face*, pp. 148–53.
[72] Tellechea, *Papado*, i, pp. xxx, 162–3 (no. XXXV); Mayer, *PP&P*, p. 306.

onwards, the French could never be sure that war with England would not break out at some stage, if events on the Continent precipitated it.

Despite Cardinal Carlo Carafa's warlike presence, up until July 1556 Henry II's foreign policy continued to be dominated, as it had been for some months, by the Constable of France, Anne de Montmorency, who had various reasons for wanting peace with the Habsburgs to continue. In particular, his son François was their prisoner, from the campaigns earlier in the year, and the country, like its neighbours in that time of high inflation, was short of financial resources. However, the duke of Guise and his brother, the cardinal of Lorraine, though currently out of the royal favour, still advocated a more aggressive policy in Italy, sharing the Pope's desire that the Vaucelles truce should be broken. To them, Paul's hostility to Philip and his allies offered an ideal opportunity for French expansion in Italy. In the meantime, Carlo Carafa at least publicly played the part of a peacemaker. On 5 July, though, while acting as godfather to Henry II's short-lived daughter, the cardinal legate gave a public harangue against the Spanish which was worthy of his uncle in Rome. This reflected the Pope's efforts at that time to start his own conflict with the Habsburgs. He excommunicated two pro-Habsburg Roman aristocrats of the Colonna family, confiscating their estates as a provocation, especially as he re-granted them to another of his own nephews, Giovanni Carafa. He then sent papal troops to Palaiano, which the Habsburgs regarded as being under their protection. Soon after, on 7 July 1556, he had a courier arrested, who was carrying a letter to the duke of Alba, now viceroy of Naples, suggesting that Paul IV would need to be dealt with by 12,000 battle-hardened troops. During this period, the Pope on several occasions denounced the Habsburgs and all their works to the Venetian ambassador in Rome, whom he regarded as a confidant. Paul called Charles and Philip heretics and threatened to dethrone them and give their titles to Henry II. The Pope may have been encouraged in these excesses by his nephew Carlo's reports from France, which suggested that the French King would defend the Papacy at any cost. Also, as there continued to be hitches in the release of his son, Constable Montmorency was now becoming more aggressive towards the Habsburgs. Contrarily, though, the Guise cardinal of Lorraine now transformed himself into a peace campaigner, urging the Pope not to make Palaiano a pretext for all-out war.[73]

In the midst of all this aggressive posturing, amazingly and implausibly, on 8 June Paul wrote to Philip to praise him for his efforts in the cause of peace. More honestly, on the 24th of that month, Pole, now isolated, like his Queen, from continental events, wrote again to Philip, urging him not to go to war over Naples, and reminding him that the kingdom was a papal fief and that he must obey the supreme pontiff, whatever he thought of him.[74] On 14 July, Pole wrote to Morone, giving his views on the European

[73] Baumgartner, *Henry II*, pp. 179–82.
[74] Tellechea, *Papado*, i, pp. 65–6 (no. XXXVI); *CRP*, 3, p. 269 (no. 1589).

situation. He was still urging peace, and said that Mary very much disliked being caught in the middle, between her husband and the Pope. He wanted Philip to settle as soon as possible the issues concerning infringement of papal jurisdiction.[75] Pole's letter crossed, though, with one from Morone, dated 18 July, in which he said that he still hoped for peace but feared there would be war. Then, on the 25th, Henry II heard from Brussels that François de Montmorency might now be ransomed for the reduced price of 50,000 *écus*, which made his father even keener to keep the peace, and at the end of July the King seemed to agree with him. Paul IV, though, via his nephew Carlo, asked for a contribution of 300–400 French *gens d'armes*, 8,000–12,000 Swiss, and 350,000 *écus* in funds. The French line continued to be that the truce of Vaucelles should not be broken. Cardinal Carafa was reminded that his uncle had already received large amounts of money from France, and that two French captains, Montluc and Strozzi, were already based in Rome. Henry had also sent 800 Gascon infantry, who had reached the Eternal City at the end of July. Carlo Carafa left the French Court more or less empty-handed, on 17 August, but soon afterwards Henry did agree to place the requested 350,000 *écus* in a reserve, to be held in Venice until required. At that time, the French ambassador in Brussels thought that there would be no campaign that autumn because of the Habsburg financial crisis. Also, at the beginning of September, Henry II was influenced further against war in Italy by the defection to the Habsburg side of Ottavio Farnese, duke of Parma, whose family felt let down in various ways by the French. At the same time, François de Montmorency was finally released, and in early September the Constable was still urging peace on Paul IV. It was by then too late. Meanwhile, on 19 August, Cardinal Morone had told Pole that personally he was so fed up with the situation that he would rather join an austere cloistered community like the Carthusians or Camaldolensians, or even be in England. He did not think it was practical for Mary to offer mediation at this stage.[76] Given the difficulties in Italy, of which he was all too well aware, Morone must have been fairly desperate, and he had reason to be, since in September the war finally started, when Philip at last decided that he must launch a military action against Rome itself.

Alba set out from Naples on 1 September 1556, with a somewhat inadequate army of 10,000 men. The Colonna family though, who had quarrelled with Paul IV, brought extra forces and things initially went well, when the fighting began in early October. Several papal fortifications outside Rome were captured, and panic grew in the city itself, as it looked as though the 1527 sack would indeed be repeated. Philip and Alba's pre-emptive strike had succeeded, and Paul was forced to negotiate. In the meantime, on 23 September 1556, reports of what was happening in the Papal States led Henry II to decide finally to intervene. Montmorency had argued in council

---

[75] *CRP*, 3, p. 278 (no. 1615).
[76] Baumgartner, *Henry II*, pp. 182–4; *CRP*, 3, pp. 280–1, 292 (nos 1624, 1658).

that Alba's move did not actually break the truce of Vaucelles, and urged him to send the Pope money rather than troops, but the Constable's opponents, including the Guises, now argued that their King had a duty to defend Paul against Alba's aggression: this was a matter of honour for the 'Most Christian King'. On the 28th, Henry made his decision to send troops, disingenuously claiming that he was simply defending the Pope and was not thereby breaking the truce of Vaucelles. Also, the gendarmerie was mustered and the northern frontier fortifications of France itself were inspected, though Henry hoped somewhat optimistically that the truce on the Franco-Netherlandish border would survive, even if the French became involved in fighting the Spanish in Italy. This was a matter of great concern in England, since it was rightly expected that Philip would request help from Mary if fighting broke out in France and Flanders. The army despatched by Henry to Italy, under the command of François, duke of Guise, consisted of 6,000 French infantry, 6,000 Swiss, 500 lances, 600 light cavalry and twenty-five guns. Not least because his newly released son needed a papal dispensation for his forthcoming marriage, Constable Montmorency continued to oppose the war, exploiting every difficulty, and there were many, that occurred in the campaign, to argue for peace. Queen Catherine of France, however, was entirely in favour of the war.

While Spanish Habsburg war aims were clear enough, to defend the kingdom of Naples and subdue the Papacy, according to correspondence at the time between the duke of Guise and Henry, the French plan was to place Prince Charles on the throne of Naples, with Guise acting effectively as regent (*père et administrateur*: father and administrator). Although he would not be king, the duke would inevitably much strengthen the fame and influence of the house of Guise. To begin with, it looked as though the French and the Papacy would win easily, and Paul's imagination, as usual, ran away with him. He talked of giving Naples and Milan to two of Henry's younger sons, bringing them to Italy and having them brought up as Italian patriots, who would banish French and Spanish interference for ever. This was in addition to his previously expressed desire to depose Philip as a heretic, and grant his titles, in the grand manner of a medieval papal monarch such as Innocent III (reigned 1198–1216), to Henry of France. In November 1556, the duke of Alba captured Ostia, thus cutting Rome off from the sea, and, not being entirely sure of the French king's resolve, Carlo Carafa accepted Alba's offer of a ten-day truce, on 28 November 1556. Avoiding massive devastation like that of 1527, a further forty-day truce was agreed by Alba and the Pope, which the latter hoped would give time for a French army to arrive to support him. Henry was extremely annoyed when he heard the news, and his mistrust of the Carafas and doubts about the Guise expedition grew further. Most of the advocates of the Italian war had gone on the campaign, and the influence of the more cautious Montmorency was growing again at home.

All this had put Pole in an impossible position and, in addition, on 28 November 1556, Morone wrote to inform him that the Pope now demanded that he leave Mary to her own devices and come to Rome.

Having to make a truce with the Habsburgs, even if it was just a temporary expedient, seems to have sent Paul into another of his desperate moods. According to Morone, he blamed Philip for everything, and Pole's attempt to support peace efforts and beg sympathy and praise for Mary in her difficulties were in vain. The Pope was so angry that the cardinals had thought it best not even to let him see Pole's latest letters. He was now announcing to all and sundry that he would rather be martyred than have peace without honour and that, if the Vicar of Christ was not respected, nothing could be done about threats from the Protestants or the Turks.[77] Despite all this, it is clear that Pole was against the war in principle, and had constantly urged Philip to patch up his quarrels with the Pope, showing reverence to the pontifical office even if he could not respect its holder. Yet Philip had given him strict instructions to care for Mary, and his presence in England, now as archbishop of Canterbury as well as legate, seemed as essential as ever. Thus his response was to send his faithful messenger Henry Pyning to represent him at the Curia, and try to arrange necessary new appointments to the English episcopal bench.[78] As 1556 came to an end, it was clear to the Queen and her supporters that Philip must return to England as soon as possible, and that there should be no more continental warfare involving him, the Pope and France. These hopes, like so many, were to be dashed. Instead, as Mary's sad, still childless Christmas approached, things seemed to be getting worse. On 12 December, Morone wrote again to Pole, telling him that Paul now thought Philip actually wanted to overthrow the Papacy, and seemed to imply that he too blamed Philip for the whole problem in Italy. Paul IV was now attacking Mary herself for supposedly supporting her husband financially, which she was not doing at this stage, and was threatening not to appoint bishops to vacancies, something that would be disastrous for the restoration of the English Church. The only bright spot was a letter from Henry Pyning in Rome, dated 23 December, in which he reported that new efforts, now involving Venice, were being made to make peace in Italy.[79]

Crucial as these developments would prove to be for the future of Mary and her government, more domestic concerns were also looming. Successive bad harvests in 1554–6 had led to massive grain price rises, acute shortages and epidemics in England and Wales.[80] Politically and strategically, there was also deep concern over Ireland. In June 1541, an Irish parliament had made Henry VIII King, instead of lord, of Ireland, and since then the English lord deputy had been, apart from short intervals during Edward VI's reign, Sir Anthony St Leger. He had generally pursued a policy of negotiation rather than confrontation with the Gaelic

[77] *CRP*, 3, pp. 336–7 (no. 1778); Rodríguez-Salgado, *Changing Face*, pp. 157–8.

[78] *CRP*, 3, pp. 339–40 (no. 1783).

[79] *CRP*, 3, pp. 342–3, 344–5, 346, 348 (nos 1789, 1794, 1797, 1804).

[80] C. S. L. Davies, *Peace, Print and Protestantism, 1450–1558* (Frogmore: Paladin, [1976] 1977], pp. 245–6.

clans of 'wild' Ireland beyond the Anglo-Irish Pale around Dublin. In March 1554, a royal commission had found serious fault with government officials there, and the practice of issuing much-debased coins specifically for Ireland, just at a time when successful efforts were being made to improve the quality of the English currency, had caused further economic disruption. In 1556, St Leger had been replaced as lord deputy by the earl of Sussex, who claimed that he would bring the Irish clans to order. While this may have seemed desirable in the long run, from the English point of view the immediate effect was to threaten further destabilization in Ireland, which might readily be exploited by the French and the Scots.[81]

Meanwhile, on the Continent, Guise and his French forces continued on their march into Italy, reaching Turin on 28 December. He spent two weeks there drawing up plans, with the help of local advice, and meanwhile, as 1557 began, it seems that Philip was making a serious attempt to end the conflict permanently. Alba advised him that Habsburg resources were close to being exhausted, and he was even willing to let Carlo Carafa have Siena, although this would alienate his allies in Medici Florence. Nevertheless, peace talks with the Papacy were abandoned in January when the French army finally crossed the Alps into Italy itself. Naples was of course the French goal, but the commander of the Franco-papal forces, Hipolito d'Este, duke of Ferrara, tried to persuade Henry to order an attack on Milan first, as Charles VIII had done in 1494. The French King was adamant, though, and in March, skirmishes on the border between the Papal States and Naples turned into outright war. The French were successful at first, but stout resistance in the little town of Civitella gave Alba time to reinforce his garrisons in the area. The invaders were forced back, and the Roman aristocratic exiles, led by Colonna, then mounted a counter-attack on Rome itself. Alba once again prevented a sack of the city, but the Habsburg and Neapolitan success brought this particular French adventure to an end.[82] Subsequent developments would be even more dangerous to England, and the origin of this trouble lay back in January, even as Guise and his army were moving into Italy. Before then, an envoy from the Carafas had reached the French Court to explain why they had made a truce with the duke of Alba in late 1556, and why Henry should nonetheless pursue his Italian campaign. Then, on 31 January 1557, the truce of Vaucelles was declared to be null and void, but this was because of events on the Franco-Netherlandish front, rather than what was happening in Italy. Early on 6 January, troops commanded by Admiral de Coligny attacked the fortress of Douai, no doubt hoping that the garrison would be distracted by the Feast of the Epiphany on that day. The defenders were alert, however, and the French withdrew, instead destroying a smaller fortress at Lens. It is not clear whether these attacks were made on Coligny's own initiative or on the orders of the King, but afterwards Henry certainly engaged in damage limitation. The Venetian ambassador in Paris

---

[81] *RMT*, pp. 248–49, 254–6; Heal, *Reformation in Britain and Ireland*, pp. 146–7, 166–72.
[82] Rodríguez-Salgado, *Changing Face*, pp. 157–9.

suggested that the raids were the culmination of a period of tension on the Franco-Netherlandish border. As a result of French border closure, some Flemish livestock had been trapped in Picardy, and the attacks on Douai and Lens may well have been in retaliation for Habsburg raids, which had been intended to 'rustle' these animals back to Flanders. It also seems clear, though, that Henry, in January 1557, was still anxious not to provoke a general war on his northern frontier, a policy which Mary and her Council would have gratefully supported. As evidence, on 10 January Constable Montmorency wrote on the King's orders to the governor of the fortress of Péronne, telling him to take no initiative until the situation became clearer. Nevertheless, there was a drift towards war, as further incidents took place on the frontier, and this was inevitably supported by the Carafa, who desperately wanted a war to the death against the Habsburgs. Thus Cardinal Carlo wrote again to Henry II, encouraging him with a claim that Venice was about to join their 'Holy League' against Philip. This was not true, but on 27 January, buoyed up by that communication, Henry ordered the arrest of the Habsburg ambassador in Paris and placed an embargo on French trade with the Netherlands. The truce of Vaucelles was formally ended shortly afterwards.[83]

Like other countries, France had been severely affected by bad weather and poor harvests in 1556, and the royal finances were not in good shape. Nonetheless, a war fund was assembled at the Louvre Palace in Paris. If this expenditure was to be recouped, it was essential that the French should capture Naples and install Henry's second son as its king. He received conflicting advice on which Italian territory should be attacked first. Some urged that Milan should be the first target, others Florence, while Paul IV naturally wanted the French to expel Alba and his forces from the Papal States and invade the kingdom of Naples. Henry went along with the Pope, and ordered the duke of Guise to proceed at once to Rome, which however, when he arrived there on 2 March 1557, he found totally unprepared for war against the Habsburgs. Another problem was that, by March, with the main campaigning season about to begin, he also had to worry seriously about his northern frontier, as all his best troops and commanders were in Italy. He tried to make a border truce with Philip's local commander in Flanders, and also to ensure that Mary did not provide aid to her husband.

Meanwhile, in late 1556 and early 1557, the English ambassador in Paris, Nicholas Wotton, had reported various French plots against the Calais Pale and in support of English dissidents, some of whom now lived there, and Henry expressed the view that Mary was unlikely to intervene on the Continent since she had so many problems to deal with at home. The Anglo-Burgundian, now Habsburg, alliance had always caused difficulties for France, and the English were still feared there as soldiers, even if they were now believed to be less powerful than they had been

[83] Baumgartner, *Henry II*, pp. 185–8.

during the Hundred Years War. Although the new French ambassador in
London, Gilles de Noailles, brother of Antoine, reported that Mary was
very unlikely to intervene, he nonetheless organized some diversions just
in case. He urged the Scots to invade northern England and sent several
hundred Gascon troops there to resist any English reprisals. Then he
seems to have supported the raid on Scarborough by Thomas Stafford, on
28 April 1557. Stafford was grandson of the last duke of Buckingham, who
had been executed by Henry VIII in 1521, and was the son of Cardinal
Pole's sister Ursula. He was thus a claimant to the English throne itself,
and had spent over a year in France, seeking support for an expedition. He
managed to meet Henry in March 1557, though the French King afterwards denied any involvement in the expedition, which included about a
hundred English exiles and several French ships and crew. Once they had
captured the half-ruined and lightly garrisoned Scarborough castle,
Stafford had himself declared lord protector, as the 'true' duke of
Buckingham. In his lengthy proclamation, he claimed that he knew, from
Spanish correspondence intercepted at Dieppe, that when Philip was
crowned King of England, something which would never in fact happen,
the Spanish would be granted twelve English castles. He also claimed that
Mary, being half-Spanish anyway, hated the English, and would allow the
Spaniards to mistreat them just as they did the Turks, Jews and Moors, no
doubt alluding in this case to the Inquisition as well as military action. In
the event, local troops, who had already assembled under the earl of
Westmorland to resist the Scots, quickly mopped up the rebels, and
Stafford was executed in London at the end of May. Three other ring-
leaders were also executed there, and twenty-seven more, including four
Scots, died similarly in Yorkshire. The faithful John Heywood celebrated
Philip and Mary's victory in 'A breefe balet touching the traytorous
takynge of Scarborow Castel', which concluded:

> Our soueraigne lord, and soueraigne lady both.
> Lawde we our Lorde, for their prosperitee,
> Beseching him for it, as it now go[e]th,
> And to this daie hath gone, that it may bee:
> Continued so, in perpetuitee.
> We lettyng theyr Scarborow castells alone,
> Takyng Scarborow wa[r]nings euerychone.[84]

France is not explicitly mentioned in the ballad, but the message to
England seems clear enough. The French claimed that the Stafford expedition had in fact been en route for Scotland, but whatever the truth it
certainly precipitated Mary and her Council into reversing their deeply
held policy on continental military involvement, a result that Philip, even

---

[84] (London: Thomas Powell, 1577).

by dint of returning to England in person, had up to then been unable to achieve.[85]

In London on 7 June, war was duly declared on France, the grounds being that Henry II had supported every rebellion and intrigue against Mary's government, including Stafford, and that English ships had been seized. When Mary's herald simultaneously reached the French court to deliver the declaration, he was kept waiting for two days, and subjected to typical mockery of a female ruler, which went totally against the laws of war and rules of diplomacy. Henry disparaged Mary publicly, as a mere woman incapable of waging war without orders from her husband, and refused to allow her herald to read out the English justifications of war. Henry had, in fact, largely brought the ensuing conflict on himself through his aggression in Italy and then in Douai and Lens. While still heavily committed in the Papal States and Naples, he now had hastily to strengthen his defences in Picardy. Up to then, Henry had thought that Philip was no more capable than he of starting a war in the north. Both sides were suffering from a bad economic situation and their best troops were already committed in Italy. Nonetheless, at the end of May 1557 Henry appointed Constable Montmorency as commander on the Flanders front, instead of Antoine de Bourbon, and announced that he would be sending 30,000 extra troops there. Because of the 1556 famine, he would not be able to field a provisioned army until July 1557, and he let it be known that he did not expect a major battle that year. In the meantime, however, things were not going well for the French in Italy. There was no unity of purpose between the Papacy and its French allies in Rome, and Guise was unwilling to invade Naples immediately, as Paul IV wanted, because his army was smaller than Alba's and also badly supplied. When he heard of this, Henry ordered the duke of Guise not to invade the southern kingdom, but before his letter arrived, the French commander had succumbed to papal pressure and sent his army southwards, joining his troops on 5 April. Alba then proceeded to wear the French down, by fighting a war of attrition and refusing to engage them in a field battle, and by now even the Guise cardinal of Lorraine was urging Henry to withdraw his brother from Italy. The Pope was now in his eighties, and there were rumours that he was beginning at last to make his peace with the Habsburgs. If Paul died, it was felt that there were not enough French and pro-French cardinals in the conclave to secure a friendly replacement, and the fear was that Guise's army might be trapped by a new, hostile Pope. Finally, on 28 May, Montmorency, on the King's behalf, ordered the duke of Guise to abandon his attack on Naples altogether, and bring his troops north against Florence, Siena or Milan, though securing Rome before he left. This delay gave time for a papal envoy to reach the French Court with fervent assurances which led to the issuing by Henry, on

[85] John Strype, *Ecclesiastical Memorials Relating Chiefly to Religion and its Reformation under the Reign of King Henry VIII, King Edward VI and Queen Mary*, iii pt 2 (Oxford: Clarendon Press, 1716), III, ii, pp. 67–9; *RMT*, pp. 304–8.

8 July 1557, of contrary orders to Guise to remain in central Italy after all, protecting Rome indefinitely.[86]

By this time, things were hotting up in northern France, where the harvest was the best for some years. Funds were voted for the French army, and an inventory of church goods was made with a view to confiscation and melting-down for war. During July, there was much speculation that Henry would command the northern army himself, but on the 28th, Constable Montmorency left to take control in Picardy, while the King devoted himself to fund-raising and victualling. Philip seems to have had 40,000–50,000 troops in the field by then, while Montmorency had just over half that number. Meanwhile, despite his desperate desire to gain personal honour in battle, Mary's husband was not present with the army, leaving his ally Emmanuel Philibert, duke of Savoy, in command. The French supposed that the Habsburg army was aiming to capture Marienbourg or Rocroi, but these were merely feints, the real aim being to advance into the heart of Picardy. On 1 August, various Habsburg contingents arrived outside the lightly defended town of Saint-Quentin, on the River Somme, 120 kilometres north-east of Paris. There they coincided with the Dauphin François's 100 lances, whose commander was not with them. These *gens d'armes* joined the local militia and repelled the Habsburg attack, and when he heard the news, Montmorency sent reinforcements to Saint-Quentin, which was strategically placed on the road to Paris. Emmanuel Philibert reacted to this by sending his main army to the town, but 800 French troops, commanded by Admiral Coligny, nonetheless managed to slip in first as reinforcements. Henry duly blamed his lieutenants for having left Saint-Quentin with too small a garrison, and on 7 August the Constable brought his main army forward from Laon, apparently with the intention of reinforcing and defending the town, rather than taking the Habsburg army head-on. On 10 August, troops commanded by one of Montmorency's nephews, François d'Andelot, tried to enter Saint-Quentin under covering fire from the main French forces. At about nine in the morning, French artillery opened up on Emmanuel Philibert's troops on the south-western side of the town, driving them back from the river and marshes there. The plan was to clear the way for d'Andelot's forces to cross the Somme on rafts, but there were not enough, and these few were positioned too far away from the town to be effective. So by the time the French got close, the Habsburg troops had returned to their defensive positions in large numbers and their withering fire killed or wounded most of the attackers, leaving d'Andelot and only 200 men to enter the town. Belatedly, Constable Montmorency ordered the retreat, but in the confusion of battle a large contingent of Philip's cavalry slipped through French positions without being identified until it was too late. The strange inertia which can affect the most experienced commanders in battle seems to have fallen upon the Constable at this point. He failed to speed up the French retreat in order to protect his

---

[86] Baumgartner, *Henry II*, pp. 188–92.

artillery in the rear, which was in any case inadequate. His troops were outnumbered and overwhelmed, with some inexperienced French infantry companies mingling with better disciplined German units behind them, thus preventing an orderly withdrawal and opening the way for a massacre of the French army, which went on until five in the afternoon.

This was a catastrophe for French military pride. Fifty-six out of fifty-seven company standards were captured by the Habsburg forces, more than 2,500 French soldiers were killed, and 7,000 more were captured, including Constable Montmorency himself and a number of other noble commanders. Despite all this, about half the army escaped south, and when the King, who was nearly 60 kilometres away in Compiègne, was given the news the next day, he immediately ordered the Court to retreat to Paris, since the capital was undefended. Henry himself stayed in Compiègne for a couple more days, in order to assess the damage and take what measures he could. The consequences were drastic for France. Not only were a large number of Henry's best officers, other than those still in Italy, removed from the field and subjected to expensive ransom demands, but the way to Paris itself lay open, had Philip wished to proceed there. Although many blamed Montmorency for the defeat, the King felt honour-bound to ransom him, too, at whatever cost. Crucially, he also decided that the duke of Guise should be recalled from Italy, though even the addition of his troops would not have enabled the French to match the Habsburg forces. Henry's decision would have a huge effect on England, as well as the Continent, but Philip's actions were equally important in determining the fate of Mary and her Crown.[87] By becoming involved in a war on two fronts, the French King had clearly overreached himself, and his capital was at the mercy of Philip, who had joined his army only after the main action was over, but could nonetheless regard himself as 'blooded' at last in battle. In the event, Philip did not exploit his victory by going on to Paris, but there was panic in the city for a while. Nevertheless, the whole of Europe was extremely impressed by his victory, which had nearly not happened, since Philip had initially delayed Emmanuel Philibert's assault so that he could be personally present to take the glory.[88] After the 'battle of St Lawrence' (10 August 1557), and the capture of Saint-Quentin itself on the 27th of that month, English involvement on the Habsburg southern border with France would create new and dangerous problems for Mary and her regime.

At the beginning of 1557, while Henry II of France was meditating on further military adventures, Cardinal Pole had continued to be under pressure from Paul IV, and Mary from her husband, as England uneasily and awkwardly tried to forge a new identity as a subsidiary power in continental politics while still conserving, as far as possible, its sovereign independence. In January, Pole was told by his servant Henry Pyning what the Pope intended to do, or at least was willing to say, concerning the Habsburgs and

[87] Ibid., pp. 192–6.
[88] Rodríguez-Salgado, *Changing Face*, p. 178.

their future actions. In a letter dated 15 February 1557, the archbishop of Canterbury told Carlo Carafa that Ruy Gómez de Silva, then on his way from the Netherlands to Spain, had fully revealed Philip's desires and plans during a stop in London. He assured Carlo that Habsburg intentions towards the Papacy were entirely pacific and friendly, and hoped that the arrival in Rome of Charles and Philip's ambassador, Don Francisco Pacheco, would serve to reassure the Pope.[89] In April 1557, Pole was still writing to Paul, on Mary's behalf, to tell him how upsetting the conflict in Italy was. Philip had, after all, played a major part in the restoration of Catholicism in England, and Pole deeply regretted that the current dispute with the Papacy had gone on so long. He respectfully asked that the Pope should console all Christian people, and expressed his certainty that Philip would behave, as always, like a good son of the Church.[90] It was soon clear, though, that things were not going smoothly in Rome. On 8 May, Morone wrote to Pole, saying that the Pope would not negotiate a settlement with the duke of Alba and expected a more emollient negotiator, who would apologize for the Habsburg invasion of papal territory. He added that Paul still regarded Mary very favourably, though he was anxious that she and her kingdom should give no support to Philip in the war. In this letter, Giovanni Morone,who himself had reason enough to fear the Carafa pope because of religious disagreements, declared that he was still hopeful of a peaceful settlement on the Continent, which would also secure England's position as a Catholic power.

In fact, on 25 May, Pole wrote to Paul in reaction to a thunderbolt. He told the Holy Father that he was horrified to have been suddenly deprived, on 10 April, of his powers as legate, even, apparently, those which he had received automatically with the office of archbishop of Canterbury, though this was uncertain. Naturally, this development had greatly saddened Mary, and he assured Paul that he had her full support and that of her Council, who saw the Canterbury legation as an English right as much as a papal one. Not unreasonably, he told the Pope that his action had left the ship of the English Church without a captain, and could only give comfort to the enemies of the Roman See. He loyally declared that he would assist any new legate who might be appointed to England, but said that there was bound to be trouble if he was not quickly replaced in that office.[91] On the same day, Pole wrote to Carlo Carafa, setting out his views at greater length and basing them on the report he had recently received from his messenger Henry Pyning, detailing what had passed between Philip and the Pope. Expressing himself strongly, Pole showed great distress at the rupture, which had badly wounded the Body of Christ, the Church. He assured Carlo that he had worked hard to persuade Philip to reconcile himself to the Pope, which the King assured him he very much wanted to do. Like

---

[89] *CRP*, 3, pp. 367–8 (no. 1848).
[90] *CRP*, 3, p. 405 (no. 1939).
[91] *CRP*, 3, pp. 433–5 (no. 2010); Mayer, *PP&P*, p. 309.

Philip's new representative in Rome, Don Francisco Pacheco, he urged that Mary would be 'the very best instrument' to restore relations between her husband and the Pope. When it came to the revocation of Pole's legation in England, the Cardinal Archbishop suggested that Pope Paul must be very badly informed about the situation in that kingdom, but he once again declared his loyalty to the Apostolic See, to death if necessary.[92] In a reply dated 20 June 1557, Paul recognized that Pole had taken hard the revocation of his office as legate, and claimed that he saw himself as a father to Mary, though, in a manner which would hardly have increased his popularity with her Council, he referred to England as a 'prodigal son', whom he had welcomed back after a period of dissolute separation from his family (Luke 15: 11–32). While assuring Pole that he was aware of his 'right and sincere mind', Paul nonetheless summoned him back to Rome, and announced that he was going to replace him as legate with the elderly Observant Franciscan William Peto, then in retirement at Greenwich. Pole's activities as counsellor and support to Mary, in her husband's absence, and as archbishop in the conflictive diocese of Canterbury, seem to have been at least momentarily forgotten in this pronouncement.[93]

It seems fair to say that, during the series of events which culminated in the English declaration of war against France in 1557, Pole tried to behave correctly towards the Holy See. In March, when Philip returned to England to seek his kingdom's military aid, Pole avoided any public meeting with the King, in an effort not to compromise his position as papal legate, even moving for a time from London to Canterbury to avoid involvement. Nevertheless, the suspicions which soon afterwards led Paul IV to end his legation seemed at least partly justified when Pole met Philip secretly, although he claimed that this was only to discuss a peace plan rather than to support a new war effort by England.[94] Inevitably, Pole defended both Philip and Mary to the Pope for their steadfast work in the restoration of the Catholic faith in England, and in late March or early April 1557, he had drafted a letter on the subject for the monarchs.[95] Things soon changed for him, however, when he heard that his old friend Cardinal Giovanni Morone had been arrested on 31 May by the Roman Inquisition on heresy charges. Not only did this arrest threaten Pole's intimate circle, but it took out of circulation Philip's main adviser and negotiator in the Curia.[96] Along with Pole's recall to Rome, it also devastated Mary, as though recent events at home had not done enough damage to her mind and soul. The Pope's removal of Pole's legatine powers, apparently as a result of personal rivalry and suspicion dating back to the late 1530s, seemed to undermine, and even condemn, all her efforts to make England a fully Catholic country once

---

[92] *CRP*, 3, pp. 435–6 (no. 2011).
[93] *CRP*, 3, 450–1 (no. 2048).
[94] *CSP Ven* VI, ii, pp. 858, 862.
[95] *CRP*, 3, p. 405 (no. 1939); Mayer, *PP&P*, p. 308.
[96] *CSP Ven* Vi, ii, p. 993; Mayer, *PP&P*, p. 308.

again, and even to cast doubt on the authenticity of the whole enterprise. Notoriously, accusations of heresy such as these, especially in high circles of the Church, involved networks as well as individuals, and if there was guilt by association, which was the lifeblood of inquisitorial procedures, who was to say that Paul would not turn on the Queen herself?

The paradox of the events which followed will have seemed to many contemporaries to be a ghastly inversion and parody of all that had happened in the English Church under Henry VIII and Edward VI, and when the time and the test came, Mary behaved as Queen of England, rather than as a devotee of the Papal See. When, at the beginning of July 1557, Paul's nuncio reached the boundary of the Calais Pale with letters recalling Pole to Rome for what looked like Inquisition investigation, he was initially refused entry, in complete defiance of Catholic diplomatic protocol. The papal move coincided with Philip's departure, so painful for Mary, to take up the reins of power in the Netherlands. Despite another failure to become pregnant, she was healthy enough to accompany her husband on his journey, staying with him in Sittingbourne and Canterbury and reaching Dover on 6 July. Early the next morning, they parted on the quayside, with Mary left behind, forlorn. The papal letters eventually arrived from Calais, some of them addressed to the Queen and others to Pole, but Mary initially tried to keep them all in her own possession, just as many of her royal predecessors would probably have done in the circumstances. Once he heard this news, later in the month, Pole wanted to, or at least felt that he had to obey, apparently hoping to clear his name of heresy in Rome. But Sir Edward Carne, who was still Mary's ambassador in Rome, warned that the Archbishop was indeed very likely to end up in the Inquisition's prison and, on this basis, as well as her own natural pride and indignation at the charges against him, Mary used her royal authority over a subject, just as she might have done previously under the Royal Supremacy, to forbid him to leave the kingdom. On 26 July, she personally wrote a strong protest to the Pope against the withdrawal from England of a man who was so vital to the Catholic future of the English Church.[97] At the same time, and probably without any further pressure being applied, Peto told the Pope that he was too old and lacked the capacity to replace Pole as legate. Also, in a manner highly reminiscent of her father, and indeed of her Trastamaran ancestors, Mary instructed Carne to tell Paul IV that any heresy charges against her archbishop must be tried within her kingdom.[98]

Apparently in August 1557, and in response to his recall to Rome, Cardinal Pole composed what has become known as his 'Apologia', a justification of his actions and beliefs as a Catholic Christian in the face of the doubts and accusations of the Pope.[99] In a remarkably uninhibited and at times bitter

[97] *CSP Ven* VI, ii, pp. 1161, 1166, 1240.

[98] *CSP Ven* VI, ii, p. 1248.

[99] Inner Temple Library, Petyt MS XLVI, fols 391–426, transcribed and edited in Tellechea, *CyP*, pp. 201–41, summary in *CRP*, 3, pp. 462–9 (no. 2076).

way, this document reverted from the England of 1557 to the Italian world of the 1530s, in which Pole and Gianpietro Carafa had worked together, with the now arrested Morone among others, in an optimistic mission to reform the Catholic Church and end its split with the Lutherans and Swiss Reformers. In it, Pole shows a clear sense of personal betrayal, claiming that no Pope had ever before treated a cardinal so badly. Significantly, Pole's approach in the 'Apologia' displays the fierce English patriotism of his royal and aristocratic forebears. For himself, he reproached Paul for condemning him unheard, though it was of course Mary who prevented him from going to Rome for interrogation. Principally, though, he speaks for England, pointing out to the Pope, in no uncertain terms, what dreadful consequences would follow if he left his post and went to Rome. Only disaster could ensue if his old friend, now his bitter enemy, continued on his current path. Bravely, and perhaps somewhat innocently, Pole defended himself by means of attack, in a manner which no doubt would have fascinated observers all over Europe, including Philip and Henry II of France, had they known of it. For Pole, Paul was proceeding not by divine example but in imitation of secular rulers, something which was expressly condemned in the Gospel (John 18: 36). Pole also criticized Paul for linking him, in terms of heresy, with Morone. Unattractively, and perhaps disingenuously, Pole tried to disentangle himself from association with his old friend in this respect, suggesting that Morone might have transgressed subsequently to any personal contact between the two. Pole was on stronger ground with his next point, which was a protest against the removal of his powers as legate *a latere*. The job of a legate in England was a hard one, but he had accepted it as a duty to the Church. Now, though, he had been condemned not only unheard but even without any specific accusation being made against him. Having set out his defence, Pole then went on the offensive against the Pope. Pulling no punches, he accused Paul of being disrespectful, unjust, impious, and likely to cause yet another schism in England, like the one he, Pole, had just managed to end, though only after great struggle.

Pole, especially in his drafts of documents, tended to pile on words, and provide what he regarded as a watertight justification for everything that he had done. In this case, he next recounted the English part in recent events, and in particular what had happened after Philip had left Mary on Dover quayside. He confirmed that she had withheld the Pope's letters from him, and had not talked to him about their contents. Inevitably, Pole heard about such a sensational post, and had artfully asked the royal secretary, Sir William Petre, if any correspondence had come for him from Rome. Petre dissembled, no doubt fearing his royal mistress's anger, but then the Queen herself gave in and told him that she had indeed received Paul's missives, and had already sent a stiff reply to Rome. He could have the letters when they returned to London from Kent. A few days later they had met again in London, and Mary told him everything she knew, clearly indicating to him her distress and anger. This was an afternoon meeting, and the next morning Mary's messenger, newly returned from Rome, came to see the Archbishop, though the Queen had once again held on to the letters which the messenger had brought from Paul IV. A few days later, these too were handed over to Pole. According to the 'Apologia', Mary did not tell Pole that she had in the meantime informed Philip of what was happening. Pole was then told by the Queen's messenger that a nuncio was on his way to London with more letters and 'orders' for him and Mary. It was still clear to Pole at this stage, presumably in early August 1557, that Mary was determined to deal with the whole problem without involving him. In the event, the papal nuncio was detained at Calais on Mary's orders until her own messenger had been to Rome and back, presumably in the hope that Paul's earlier letters would be withdrawn. In her customary simple way, she believed that the Pope would be bound to see the rightness of her cause. When Pole found out about Mary's manoeuvres, he went in person to her and the Council, to beg them to let the nuncio in as soon as possible. However, both Queen and councillors in turn urged him not get involved, so that Mary would be free to act. Crucially, they asked Pole to continue functioning as a legate, until the brief (*breve*) definitively removing him from office was received. They told him of Ambassador Carne's report that the Pope had stated that he should not be 'worried' until he actually received that brief, but unsurprisingly Pole would not accept this unless the nuncio was allowed free access to London, which Mary and the Council certainly did not want. Ever a stickler for canon law, Pole said that, in the circumstances, he refused to continue acting as legate, and it was in the midst of this confusion that he had decided to send Niccolò Ormanetto to Rome to give the Pope proper information, and perhaps change his mind. Ormanetto duly left England at the end of July 1557, at which time Pole told the Pope that he was confident of being saved by his record to date.

At this stage in the 'Apologia', and no doubt growing ever angrier with his former friend Carafa, Pole turned to the Morone case. He told Paul that, after Morone's arrest, he felt threatened if he returned to Rome. Now mentally back in the curial world with which he was so familiar, he criticized Paul for not taking the case to the consistory, instead going directly to the cardinal inquisitors. The Pope had given him no information, but he had heard from his own sources in Rome that Paul had reported earlier private conversations with Pole to the Inquisition, Carafa expressing the view that Pole was 'tainted' by his association with the late 'heretic' Marcantonio Flaminio. Not surprisingly, Pole then went over the old ground of the Conclave of Julius III in 1549–50, which, not without some basis, he held to be the main origin of Pope Carafa's hostility to him. Pole had evidently been far from unaware of the then Cardinal of Naples's activities at that time, and fully understood that both men gave the highest priority to the doctrinal purity of the Church. Pole, however, argued as forcefully as his Queen that Carafa was totally misjudging the English situation. With hindsight, it would be hard to gainsay his statement in the 'Apologia' that, as a result of the Pope's action against him in

April–July 1557, Rome now appeared to be 'inconstant' and capricious to Englishmen as English reform under Henry and Edward was still seen as being in Rome. On the subject of Mary, Pole did not mince his words. She had relied on her husband and the Pope to support her, but now she was desperate. As far as Pope Paul was concerned, Pole concluded by admitting that, out of loyalty, he had too often kept silent in the face of what he regarded as provocation and errors, but that time had now passed, and the Church needed loyal protest rather than misguided silence. In reality, Paul IV never received this diatribe, and it seems unlikely that it could have had a positive effect if he had.[100]

Despite this crisis of personal relations between Pole and the Pope, which was certainly not a figment of the former's imagination, in June 1557, while tension was building, the highest monthly total of burnings in the whole of Mary's reign, twenty-eight, took place. The programme would continue more or less unabated until the Queen's death. There were between five and ten burnings in each month between July and September 1558, and even more in November of that year, though none after Mary's death on the 17th.[101] Also, it is clear that, despite Pole's unwillingness to continue acting as legate when his powers had been revoked by the Pope, such business continued to be transacted in his courts right up to his own death, on the same day as the Queen. Thus appeals from lower ecclesiastical tribunals continued to be heard regularly, both in his papal legatine court and in his archiepiscopal Court of Arches.[102] Pole's legatine prerogative also continued to be used in other matters. On 13 August 1557, Pole gave Mary and Philip his approval (*significavit*) as legate *a latere* for the excommunication of William Goodwin, a Londoner.[103] Evidently, for Pole, as for his archiepiscopal predecessor Thomas Cranmer, service to the Crown could trump loyalty to the Papacy. More intriguingly, Paul IV continued to make episcopal appointments to England, though it is not clear whether these were simply cases already in the curial system and therefore not affected by Paul's current rage against Pole. During August 1557, the brilliant Catholic controversialist Thomas Watson was appointed to the see of Lincoln, while the civil lawyer David Pole (apparently no relation of Cardinal Reginald) was nominated to Peterborough.[104] In the meantime, the victory at Saint-Quentin had to be digested and, this time, there was some genuine English military achievement to be recognized.

When Philip had returned to the Continent, on 6 July 1557, he took with him a well-equipped English army, under the command of the earl of Pembroke. Notionally it consisted of 10,000, but the actual number seems to have been just over 7,200. One of its more intriguing aspects is

[100] Tellechea, *CyP*, pp. 201–9, 213, 219–23, 225–41.
[101] See Thomas Freeman's figures in Duffy, *Fires of Faith*, p. 129.
[102] Mayer, 'The Success of Cardinal Pole's Final Legation', in *CMT*, p. 153 (table 5.3).
[103] *CRP*, 3, p. 472 (no. 2083a).
[104] Loades, 'The Marian Episcopate', in *CMT*, p. 47.

that among the officers were men who had a dubious political past, including not only Andrew, Henry and Robert Dudley, as well as Sir Peter Carew and Sir Nicholas Throckmorton, who had been associated with the Wyatt rebellion of 1554. The strategy seems to have been to keep loyalists at home and export dissidents, while giving a boost to the whole English military class by allowing it another crack at the French. Pembroke, as commander (lieutenant) of the field army, was also given oversight of Calais and the Pale. While Philip headed for the besieged Saint-Quentin in his desperate search for personal military glory, Pembroke stayed at Calais, reorganizing its garrison and keeping his troops busy, while they impatiently awaited what they no doubt hoped would be their own Agincourt. Problems quickly arose, as there were now too many troops within the Pale, and on 29 July Pembroke wrote to tell Philip that some might have to be sent home if they were not used quickly, which would be a great disappointment and waste of scarce resources.[105] In the event, Pembroke was summoned the next day to join the King at Saint-Quentin with the bulk of his army, leaving 500 men at Guisnes, and a hundred each at Hammes and on the Calais causeway. Nonetheless, the vital 'battle of St Lawrence' at Saint-Quentin took place in the absence of the English as well as Philip. Pembroke had been constantly urged to hurry, but he managed to miss the action by hours. However, he and his men were involved in the siege of the town itself which lasted until 27 August. This time the English were very much part of the action, and were highly praised for their bravery and skill, at least, by one of Philip's men, Juan de Pineda.[106] The road to Paris having not been taken, by October 1557 Pembroke's army, like the other Habsburg units, was stood down to winter quarters. A muster on 15 September had indicated that there were still about 200 nobles and other officers and 5,839 men fit for active service.[107] While many assumed that the Franco-Habsburg conflict would resume in 1558 at the latest, with continuing papal support for the French side, European diplomacy was about to take a different course.

On 14 September 1557, out of the blue to outsiders, and after Mary's messenger had been kept cooling his heels in Rome for seven weeks, Paul IV made peace with Philip.[108] Perhaps somewhat chastened by the combination of his own spell at the mercy of the duke of Alba and the spectacular defeat of his main allies at Saint-Quentin, Pope Carafa bowed to the inevitable. The way was now open for a real 'peace process' between France and the Habsburgs, but there was no obvious advantage to England in this development. Not only was an English army, not for the last time in history, stranded uselessly across the Channel, but, given the

---

[105] *CSP Span* XIII, p. 307.
[106] *CSP Span* XIII, p. 317.
[107] BL Stowe MS 571, fols 87–93.
[108] Rodríguez-Salgado, *Changing Face*, p. 161.

continuing threat to Calais, which was only increased by French rage at the Saint-Quentin defeat as well as the danger of joint Franco-Scottish action on behalf of Mary, queen of Scots and heiress to France, the English homeland had to remain on expensive military alert. The timing was unfortunate since Mary had by now fallen out with parliamentarians, mainly over church property and revenues. In any case, shire musters in May and July had revealed an alarming state of unpreparedness. Even while the main English army was in action on the Continent, there is evidence of resistance at home to press-gangs, and rumour of a mutiny in the fleet during August. In addition, the 1557 harvest was poor, and there was strong resistance to a forced loan under the privy seal, which was ordered in September and collected only with significant difficulty. In view of the threat from Scotland, where French troops were already stationed, the northern defences also had to be strengthened, particularly at Berwick-upon-Tweed and Carlisle.

What is more, apparent peace between her husband and the Pope certainly did not mean a relaxation of pressure on Mary's archbishop. The English ambassador, Sir Edward Carne, supposed that the new agreement between the Pope and Philip involved the restoration of Pole to his full lega-tion in England, but in fact papal relations with England deteriorated even further. Mary's messenger was still waiting to be received in Rome, and the Pope would barely address a word to Carne. Approaches to Paul from the duke of Alba were equally unsuccessful and it seemed that the 'peace' had only made things worse. The truth was that Pope Carafa, with his long and intimate knowledge of both men, still closely associated Pole with Morone, whose Inquisition trial was about to begin. On 4 October Morone was formally charged, and the Cardinal of England was directly implicated.[109] With its customary hardness of style, the Roman Inquisition's compendium of trials contains a section headed 'Discipline of Pole' (*Disciplina Poli*). In its eighteen charges, which were never actually put to him, Mary's strength and stay was accused of being averse to the Catholic faith, of preaching heresy and of urging others to do so, this last making him a heresiarch. He was accused of being an abettor (*fautor*) of heresy, who gave financial support to heretics, read and distributed heretical books, and had heretics in his house-hold. Amazingly, Pole was also charged with neglecting to punish English heretics. According to this indictment, he had promised to 'reform' himself, but this was mere pretence, and he in fact kept to his earlier beliefs, about which the Pope knew all too much. Given his public comments, there can be no doubt that the motivation for these charges came from the Pope himself. As Morone's trial dragged on through the autumn, Pole remained in ecclesi-astical limbo, safe on the other side of of the Channel under Mary's protec-tion, but with his status unresolved.[110] In this dismal time for Mary, with an

[109] Anne Overell, *Italian Reform and English Reformations, c. 1535–c. 1585* (Aldershot: Ashgate, 2008), p. 162.
[110] Mayer, *PP&P*, pp. 331–4.

absent husband and no child, and her whole project for rule under threat, St Andrew's Day 1557 was in danger of becoming a somewhat muted celebration. Two years earlier, this feast had been designated 'Reconciliation Day', to celebrate the papal absolution of the kingdom and its restoration, or 'reduction', to the Roman obedience. On the third anniversary of that solemn event, it seems that a sermon was preached by Pole before the Queen, the Court, the legal profession and the mayor and aldermen of London. The text only survives in a later and incomplete edition, and Pole notoriously changed and redrafted his writings, including sermons, but internal evidence in the surviving version, and in particular the otherwise unlikely references to St Andrew, suggest that this was indeed the context of the sermon's delivery.[111] In the gloomy circumstances of November 1557, it was felt that a splash had to be made, particularly in London. In accordance with the relevant decree of the Westminster Synod, the ceremonies of that Tuesday morning began with a procession, solemn Mass and sermon at St Paul's Cathedral, attended by a priest from every parish in London. In the evening, after various other ceremonies at Whitehall Palace and Westminster Abbey, Pole preached in the Chapel Royal.

The Cardinal, himself now effectively almost as much in schism as Henry and Edward's bishops had been, took his text from Matthew's Gospel, in which Jesus's precursor, John the Baptist, preached repentance to the people of Israel: 'Bear fruit worthy of repentance . . . Even now the axe is lying at the root of the trees; every tree therefore that does not bear good fruit is cut down and thrown into the fire' (Matthew 3: 8, 10). This passage, particularly ominous coming from the mind of a former cardinal inquisitor who now presided over the burning of Protestants in England, yet poignant in that he was himself evading trial for heresy in Rome, introduced a sermon on repentance. Allusion was also made to Jesus's calling of Andrew by the Sea of Galilee, which formed part of the Gospel reading at that day's masses (Matthew 4: 18–22). What followed was in effect yet another 'Apologia', this time for the entire Catholic restoration in England, with a rigorous assessment of the spiritual state of the kingdom, especially of London, and an outline of what still needed to be done. Addressing a congregation of lawyers, councillors and courtiers, he tackled the ever vexed question of church property. Pragmatically, he told them that they would not be required to hand back their former ecclesiastical possessions as their own 'fruits of repentance', but he nonetheless urged them to restore ex-monastic churches to use, in order to supplement the creaking parish system. However, he also somewhat provocatively reminded his listeners that they only held these properties by the concession of the Church. Somewhat unflatteringly, he compared the 'possessioners' to a greedy child who had been given an over large apple by its mother. Seeing that the fruit was too big and would do the child harm, she asked for at least a little piece of it

[111] Strype, *Ecclesiastical Memorials*, iii, pt 2, pp. 482–510; Eamon Duffy, 'Cardinal Pole's Preaching', in *CMT*, p. 187 n. 31.

back. The 'mother' here was evidently, and conventionally, the Church, and the 'child' was a beneficiary of the monastic and chantry dissolutions, but Pole now warned that Christ, like the 'angry father' in a family setting, might come, take the apple away, and throw it out of the window. Pole did not think the Church would behave like this, but hoped for voluntary concessions. Given the current state of his relations with Paul IV, this was a brave thing to say. It is almost as though Pole was inviting the English authorities into some kind of agreement with him, to ensure that the English Catholic Church flourished, whatever happened on the Continent. If they helped him, he would help them.

The Cardinal then turned to the controversial question of medical and social provision in the capital. In an attempt to compensate for the loss of former monastic and chantry foundations, and to face the very serious health and economic problems which confronted England as well as other countries, five new hospitals had been founded in London under Edward VI: St Bartholomew's, St Thomas's, Bethlehem, Bridewell and Christ's Hospital. Supporters of reform used these institutions as a weapon to beat Catholics, whom they accused, given the undistinguished record of the former monasteries in this respect, of being more concerned with convents than hospitals. Pole weighed into this controversy in his sermon, pointing out that Protestants had no monopoly of social concern, and suggested that his wealthy and powerful congregation, including Mary herself, might use some of their own gains from the Church to fund such provision. Emotionally, he pointed out, from considerable experience, that while there were fewer than ten hospitals and religious houses devoted to the relief of the poor in London, there were hundreds in the major Italian cities such as Milan and Rome. He regarded this failure as characteristic of the reform in England, which had also despoiled the clergy on the pretext that some of them led vicious lives. These were consequences of schism, along with the undermining of morals and order, contempt for the sacraments of the Church, and heresy in general. In his usual eloquent, if verbose, manner, Pole attacked the Henrician schism and urged Londoners to be more grateful for their reconciliation to Rome, even to the extent of acknowledging the value of the burnings which had taken place there, including the deaths of people from outside the city. Having eulogized John Fisher, and particularly Thomas More, whose collected works had recently been published by John Rastell, Pole then attacked those, among them perhaps some who were seated before him, who still refused to accept Mary's church settlement.[112] He reminded the congregation that he himself had been jeered in Cheapside when he first rode through the city with the Queen in 1554 and realized that support for the Protestants had still not entirely gone away. He went on to blame the young, particularly apprentices and their employers, for much of this resistance. Indeed, he was more

---

[112] On Rastell's edition of More, and the unpublished biography of him by Nicholas Harpsfield, see Duffy, *Fires of Faith*, pp. 179–87.

inclined to blame the adults for what was happening, and went on to attack the notion that those burned for heresy were true Christian martyrs, ending with an emotional appeal for Catholic orthodoxy and loyalty.[113]

What Pole's influential listeners made of his oration is not explicitly known, but his text vividly portrays the beleaguered and difficult situation in which he and Mary found themselves at the approach of Christmas 1557. There were more burnings before the end of the year, but both Philip and the English Council believed that there would be no more military action, either in Flanders or on the Scottish border, until the spring of 1558. The fleet was laid up and the troops settled down in winter quarters. A kind of equilibrium seemed to have been reached in Europe, but the peace was soon to be shattered, in a way which would hasten the decline of Mary and her regime.

---

[113] Duffy, 'Pole's preaching', pp. 188–98.

Chapter 11

THE 'PROVIDENTIAL QUEEN' RELEASED, 1558

As the new year of 1558 dawned, there was no reason to suppose that by the end of it Mary and Cardinal Pole would be dead, and Philip no longer King of England. Yet in later legend, Mary I was laid in her grave with the word 'Calais' engraved on her heart, so how was that city lost? Unlike Philip and the English, the French did not settle down for the winter in November 1557. It had been a while before King Henry became sure that the Habsburg armies would not attack him again after Saint-Quentin, let alone advance on Paris. Still, he kept a large army in Picardy, and was anxious to use it rather than disband it. In addition, thanks to the uneasy peace in Italy, his best officers, including the duke of Guise, were now available to fight on the northern front. Thus, as 1557 drew to its close, the badly defended English territory of Calais and its Pale began to look an ever more attractive target. Since the end of the long and acrimonious Hundred Years War (in fact from 1337 to 1453), this was England's last possession in France, Boulogne having been sold back under Edward VI, after a brief occupation begun by Henry VIII in 1544. The English were clearly not expecting a winter attack, but for Henry II of France the capture of Calais would go a long way to expunging the dishonour of the Saint-Quentin defeat. From the French point of view, there was a danger that an attack on Calais would bring England and Philip closer together, but if the territory was lost by Mary, the most likely result would be greater dissension between them, as indeed proved to be the case. The campaign was carefully planned by Guise and his brother, the Cardinal of Lorraine. It was a risky enterprise, since the winter was severe, and there was inevitable suspicion, after French victory had been achieved, that there had been English collusion, an accusation which did not improve the atmosphere in England.

In the nature of things, the necessary preparations could not be kept totally secret, and by 11 December there were rumours of an attack, fuelled by the fact that one of Guise's officers from the Italian campaign, Pietro Strozzi, had been seen reconnoitring Calais and its defences. A few days after that, French troops, split into small units so as not to attract attention, headed north, but by 17 December no news of this had reached Brussels. On 22 December, the first details were given by one of Philip's spies to Lord Grey at Guisnes, in the Calais Pale, and he duly passed the warning to London, saying that he did not take it seriously, but that in any case he did not have the men and supplies to resist a strong assault.

Crucially, the rivers and watercourses, on which the Pale relied for defence against land attack, froze over that winter. His own spies had apparently found nothing. The Calais garrisons had been run down after their re-inforcement in the previous August, but at last, on Christmas Eve, Mary wrote to the lord deputy of Calais, Thomas, Lord Wentworth, instructing him to cease the disbandment of his forces. After this, it became alarm-ingly obvious locally that a major attack was being mounted. On 27 December, the Calais council reported that only Hammes had an adequate garrison, and supplies were short everywhere. It was decided that, if and when the French arrived, all forces would withdraw to Calais itself. The danger was now crystal clear, and requests for help for the enclave were reaching England daily. But the Council had virtually no forces at its disposal, and on 29 December it decided to despatch the earl of Rutland, with those who could be scraped together, although this order was rescinded on 31 December and then reinstated on 2 January 1558. It was too late by then, and when Rutland reached Dover on 3 January he was told that the French were now in occupation of the Channel beaches, and there was no access to Calais from the sea. On 31 December, realizing that no help was forthcoming from England, Lord Wentworth had at last written to Philip, who delayed his response to him until the end of the Christmas festivities, on 5–6 January. On the latter date, the Feast of the Epiphany, 200 of his arquebusiers, from Gravelines, tried to enter the Pale, but were repulsed by French forces. In fact, Philip had been monitoring the situation in Calais very closely over the Christmas season. Subsequent events and actions, recorded in Spanish archive material, show that, despite never returning to England in person, he continued to spare no effort on behalf of his wife and their island kingdom.

On 2 January 1558, Philip wrote from Brussels one of his customary letters to the English Select Council. In it, he stated as a certainty that Calais was going to be invaded by the French and urged the councillors to make every effort to defend the territory properly. He demanded that his wife should be fully informed of what was happening, and that defen-sive preparations be made on both sides of the Channel. He reminded the councillors that a French attack on Calais was just as much a danger to him as it was to England.[1] This letter to London may well have been in response to a report which Philip had received that day, from Wentworth, in which the deputy in Calais reported that no fewer than 20,000 French troops, including infantry and cavalry, were now drawn up facing the town, on the other side of the causeway, and artilley was expected to be stationed there shortly. Wentworth was clear that Henry II's army intended to besiege the town and, in the absence of help from England, he begged Philip to send him between 300 and 400 arquebusiers, under the command of 'some gentleman of honour and reputation'.[2] The next day, one of

[1] AGS E 811–20 (copy).
[2] AGS E 811–17 (Spanish translation from French).

Philip's Spanish subjects reported to him from Calais that the French attack had begun.[3] Too late, on 7 January, Philip wrote to Luis de Carvajal, telling him to get his fleet clear of Calais harbour, but this had already been done, and early that morning, after a bombardment, the town surrendered. Wentworth and about 2,000 of his men were captured, and many citizens of Calais fled to England. The whole of the Pale had not as yet been lost, and on 10 January Edward Dudley wrote to Philip from Hammes, professing his deep loyalty to his King and appearing to imply that Wentworth had not handled things well. He begged Philip to send troops to help save Hammes, and interestingly referred also to a hundred unde-ployed troops in Calais itself, who had been sent there at Mary's personal expense.[4]

Immediately after the fall of Calais, and perhaps partly as a result of Dudley's letter to Philip, the lord deputy was accused of more than mili-tary incompetence. It also began to be suggested that he had betrayed Calais because he was a Protestant, supposedly in league with others of the same persuasion who were living there to avoid Mary's clutches. It is true that, on previous occasions, English dissidents had at least contem-plated the subversion of the enclave as a means of destabilizing the Queen's government, but there is no evidence that Wentworth was in this category, and subsequent accusations of treason against him seem to have been an effort at face-saving by the Council. Whatever the truth, there was no doubt that Mary and her husband had lost a great deal of face as a result of the Calais debacle.[5] Philip and his advisers soon came to the conclusion that there had indeed been some kind of illicit communication between Wentworth and the French, but incompetence and complacency seem to be better explanations of the lord deputy's conduct than treason. Until it was too late, he had refused to believe that the French military activity was directed against Calais rather than the Habsburg Netherlands. He had suggested to Philip that Hesdin was the French target, and hence asked his King for help much too late, although it had been offered weeks earlier. Before the assault actually came, Philip had sent an envoy, Juan de Ayala, to London to beg for reinforcements. Ayala knew Calais from the previous summer's campaign, but the Council preferred to believe Wentworth and did nothing. By the time that Mary ordered a force to be sent to Calais, outlying Rysbank had fallen and, with the troops already on board, the ships' crews mutinied, showing a lack of military ardour which went down very badly at Philip's Court. On 12 January, with Calais itself lost, the English government disbanded the expedition rather than ask Philip for a continental base. This suggested to many that Mary and her advisers were prepared to abandon Calais at least for the time being, hoping that Guisnes and Hammes would hold out

[3] AGS E 811–19.
[4] AGS E 811–23 (English original), 22 (Spanish translation).
[5] *RMT*, pp. 316–18.

until a full expedition could be mounted in the spring. There seems to
have been no coherent English plan. On 17 January the disbandment
order was reversed, on the 19th the levy was reduced, and on 27 January
all forces were finally disbanded.[6]

In contrast, Philip acted decisively, as a king of England should. Despite
Wentworth's dithering, he had sent in a company of arquebusiers on
3 January, and after that his fleet had tried to reinforce Calais from the sea.
On 19 January, he received detailed eyewitness reports on the situation in
Calais and the Pale from Spaniards who had escaped. According to them,
Henry II had between 16,000 and 18,000 infantry there, including
German and Gascon units as well as French, about 4,000 cavalry and
thirty artillery pieces. They confirmed that the main attack on Calais had
indeed happened on 2 January, adding that most of the French army was
now elsewhere in the Pale and noting that the duke of Guise had carefully
kept his troops out of Habsburg territory. Begging for reinforcements to
help the English, they also reported the surrender to France of the castle
at La Marque, where the abortive peace conference had been held a few
years earlier.[7] On 20 January, Philip wrote to Cardinal Pole, whose role as
guardian of Mary continued to be crucial. The King referred to 'the pain
and emotion' which the loss of Calais had caused him, and told Pole that
he was about to send his trusted emissary, the count of Feria, 'to inform
the Queen of everything which is occurring to me about this business, and
communicate to her and discuss with her everything which must and can
be done to remedy what has happened . . .'.[8] The next day, Philip wrote
again to the Select Council in London, saying that he could not express in
words his grief at the fall of Calais (*nullis verbis exprimere possimus*), and
urging it to co-operate with Feria when he arrived in London.[9] At about
this time, Philip wrote to Feria himself, telling him that the Pale was
steadily falling into French hands, though stiff resistance was being put up
in Guisnes, where the garrison had already repelled two attacks and both
needed and deserved reinforcement. The implication seems to be that the
King expected England to undertake this and Philip also mentions that he
had written to Mary herself the day before, though he feared that his
correspondence with her was not getting through, for whatever reason.[10]
Nevertheless, Habsburg agents were still evidently expecting Philip to try
to retake Calais rapidly, since a Spaniard sent him a detailed, expert report
on how specialists in trench-building and crossing watercourses (*gastadores*)
might enable such an operation to take place. In his view, the best prospect
was for a counter-attack to be made from the seaward side, and he

---

  [6] *CSPDM*, pp. 97–8; C. S. L. Davies, 'England and the French war, 1557–9', in *The Mid-Tudor Polity, c. 1540–1560*, ed. Jennifer Loach and Robert Tittler (London: Macmillan, 1980), pp. 159–85, 174.

  [7] AGS E 811–18.

  [8] AGS E 811–16 (Spanish copy).

  [9] AGS E 811–18 (Spanish copy).

  [10] AGS E 811–16 (copy).

expressed admiration for English seamanship in this respect, although shallow water would cause difficulties.[11] On 24 January, the King wrote again to Feria, to report that he had just received the earl of Sussex and the comptroller of Mary's household in Brussels, and urging the count to leave for England without delay.[12]

During the attacks on Guisnes, some of Captain-General Luis de Carvajal's soldiers from the Habsburg fleet fought alongside the English garrison, which was under the command of Lord Grey, in what proved to be the only active military resistance to the French annexation. In addition, Philip sent to Spain for a levy of 2,500 men, who were intended as a reserve which the English could call upon.[13] Also, perhaps after he heard of the mutiny in the English fleet, Emmanuel Philibert of Savoy sent some of his own ships to England to fetch troops, but none were awaiting them, and the Council had no information for his commanders on how, if at all, the Calais Pale was to be reinforced. All this, not unnaturally, caused great frustration on the Habsburg side, and did nothing for England's military credibility abroad.[14] It seems, nevertheless, that Philip was still deferring to his wife, and was unwilling to criticize her or her government directly. In public at least, he put the English lethargy and inefficiency down to inexperience and lack of organization. He seems to have believed, wrongly as it turned out, that an army of 10,000 was being raised in England for Calais. As was his right as King of England, Philip wanted larger forces than this for immediate retaliation against France: 17,000 infantry, 3,000 cavalry and 4,000 sappers. He himself would provide 32,000 infantry and 11,000 cavalry. However, when Calais fell and England appeared to make no response, he accepted advice to delay any joint offensive until the main campaigning season, beginning in the spring of 1558.[15] The loss of Calais had severely affected the Habsburg lands as well as England. There had previously been hopes for renewed peace after the victory of Saint-Quentin, but Henry's victory at Calais had brought conflict near again. From the French point of view, the capture of Calais partially expunged the setback in Italy in 1557, as well as the Saint-Quentin defeat, and just as Philip was deciding on a new campaign, Henry II made an announcement of military action to his States-General. Philip, on the other hand, felt deeply his personal responsibility for dragging his English wife and subjects into war and thus precipitating this damaging loss. He accepted that he must help England regain Calais, but nonetheless thought Mary's government was responsible for losing the territory in the first place, through apathy and a refusal to heed clear warnings. On 31 January, Philip replied from Brussels to two of Feria's letters, one written in Dunkirk on

[11] AGS E 811–13 (undated).
[12] AGS E 811–17 (copy).
[13] Real Academia de la Historia Salazar y Castro, A–48, fols 233, 234; AGS E 129–20,21.
[14] *CSP Span* XII, p. 336.
[15] AGS E 8340 – fol. 318; *CSP Span* XIII, pp. 332–3; AGS E 128 fol. 355.

the 24th and the other in Gravesend on the 25th. He reiterated that the count's main job, when he reached London, was to ensure that Mary's promised troops were duly sent to join those which he had ready on the Continent. It was the crisis of the affair, in which the French would either be defeated or win the day in the Pale (*levantar a los enemigos o darles la jornada*). Importantly, he adds, in one of his many highly informative letters to his trusted relative the count, that he did not want Mary to try and raise more military finance at this stage, which suggests that he was fully aware of her current political difficulties. As though conversing with Mary herself rather than Feria, he added that, while the English troops already agreed would be very useful, he had enough of his own to defend his borders. In any case, he appreciated her 'diligence' in this matter, and her support for his cause, though he quite understood if there were no more funds to send further reinforcements. His faith in his wife was not to be gainsaid.[16]

The count of Feria eventually arrived in London when the news of Calais had been digested, but, when he met the Queen and Council soon afterwards, he was indeed told that England could not afford a major campaign. The principle of unripe time was invoked by the councillors, who estimated that 20,000 men from England would be necessary, at a cost of £520,000. The national budget was inadequate, and unrest and an outbreak of 'sweating sickness' would make the levying of troops difficult, if not impossible. Feria, however, whose skill in English was exceptionally good among Philip's men, had other sources outside the Council chamber, and they told him that Mary's advisers had deliberately inflated the likely scale and cost of a Calais expedition. Gradually, and despite his natural proclivity for the native land of his future wife, Jane Dormer, he too came to the conclusion that Mary's government was not really serious about regaining Calais, and in any case wanted Philip to bear the costs of any action entirely from his own resources. Yet Philip would doggedly persist in his attempts to control England, and thus keep the kingdom involved in continental affairs, until his wife's death in November 1558.[17]

In the meantime, in February 1558, there appeared to be a change of heart in London. On 2 February, Feria wrote another lengthy report to his master. Philip had apparently been ill earlier and Feria told him that Mary had been delighted to hear news of an improvement in his health. She had undertaken to call a council meeting, which he would be able to address, while Pole, whom he had also consulted, was 'deeply involved in his business with Rome'. At this time, the Council (Feria does not specify whether full or select) was apparently meeting regularly in Pole's lodgings. On 28 January it had expressed appreciation to Feria of Philip's efforts to save Calais and his subsequent involvement. At a meeting on 1 February, concern had been voiced at the presence of French troops in Scotland, and it was also said that

---

[16] AGS E 811–24 (copy).
[17] *CSP Span* XIII, pp. 349–51; *CODOIN*, lxxxvii, pp. 41–2.

more English forces were needed to secure Ireland. Worry was expressed about the security of the Isle of Wight and other offshore islands, in the face of the French and Scottish threats. It was said that the French had a fleet of eighty ships in Dieppe, but Calais was not specifically discussed. It was, however, decided that the defences of the south coast of England should be reinforced. On 31 January, Mary had given Feria a memorandum containing detailed defence plans, which involved a fleet of a hundred warships, of various sizes, and fifty supply vessels. These meetings and consultations indicated a European political and military agenda which would dominate the rest of Philip and Mary's reign in England. The English councillors made known to Feria their concerns about possible military alliances between France, Denmark and the German Hanseatic League, which would be inimical to both English and continental Habsburg interests. The perceived danger was that Henry II would obtain extra warships from these Baltic powers. To secure the Scottish frontier, in particular, Mary and her government wanted Philip to recruit 3,000 German troops, such as had been deployed on British soil in the previous reign, as well as 500 cavalry. Admiral Lord Clinton told Feria that the German infantry should sail from Amsterdam and land in Newcastle upon Tyne, for use on the Anglo-Scottish border, while the cavalry should land in Dover, presumably for use directly against the French. The problem, of course, was finance. According to Feria, both Mary and her council were expressing concern at this time about possible spying by the many Frenchmen who were resident in England. They had been put under surveillance, but the count told Philip that many of them had become naturalized as his and Mary's subjects and would therefore not be affected by any expulsion order.

At this stage, Feria was still convinced that the Queen and her advisers were genuinely keen to raise these extra military forces, though one of his ideas fell flat when he put it to the earl of Sussex. He suggested to the earl that English lords might supply their retinues to serve the Crown, as their Castilian equivalents would have done, but was told that 'all [the lords] of this Kingdom together would not serve with [even] a hundred horse, and as many infantry'. This revealing political and cultural clash between England and Spain led Feria to conclude this despatch by stating the view that, while they were concerned to protect their own territory, the English were not interested in recovering Calais.[18] From this time onwards, the count became increasingly pessimistic about Spanish prospects in England. In a report from London, dated 12 February, he said that public opinion, at least in the capital, was not at all friendly towards Philip, and that he did not expect the current parliament to vote funds, since 'everything they do is confusion and passion, one with another'. Despairing, he now suggested to Philip that he should appoint someone to oversee military preparations, since this would be better late than never and was the only chance of success.[19] Whatever the problems

---

[18] AGS E 811–25.
[19] AGS E 811–26.

and tensions, Feria's despatches make it very clear that he was deeply involved in the inner core of Mary's government, and in this respect was fully representing Philip himself. On 15 February, the King duly confirmed to the count his enthusiasm for military preparation on both sides of the Channel.[20] Three days later he wrote again, expressing pleasure that his wife had appointed commissioners for war and finance, and that she had agreed to send some naval ships to Dunkirk to monitor traffic in and out of Calais, the loss of the historic wool exchange (Staple) having damaged the English business community, something which concerned both monarchs. Philip's continued close involvement in Mary's government is illustrated by his observation, in this letter, that he should not be accused of meddling in the appointment of a new admiral of the fleet, his candidate being Clinton.[21] At the same time, the King took an active interest in Mary's plan to reward Lord Grey for his resistance to the French at Guisnes.[22]

By the time that Feria reported to Philip on 10 March 1558, he had apparently lost patience with the English government and was feeling desperate:

> Before God, I cannot do any more here, nor do I know what to do with these people. Your Majesty understands, that from night till morning and from morning till night, there are changes in everything they decide, and there is no way to get to understand them, in the state in which they are ... And ... I believe it would be better to abandon them in the power of whoever will treat them as they deserve ... The Queen Our Lady says that she is doing everything she can, and she really has spirit and good will for the things that need the most work.

Feria added that Cardinal Pole, her main support on behalf of her husband, was 'a dead man' and, interestingly, that if he and Philip's other main representative in London, Juan de Figueroa, were not content with what the Council was doing, they complained directly to the Queen.[23] Meanwhile, with the matter of Calais still unresolved, Philip started peace negotiations with France at Câteau Cambrésis.[24] These talks were naturally Philip's main priority during March, but the English agenda also continued to receive attention. In particular, the German troops for the Scottish border were duly recruited, and by 6 April were near Brussels, en route to embark for England.[25]

In May, Philip, having had his way over the appointment, summoned Edward, Lord Clinton, to Brussels, but there was further delay and when

[20] AGS E 811–31.
[21] AGS E 811–32, 37 (3 March 1558).
[22] AGS E 811–36.
[23] AGS E 811–34.
[24] AGS E 811–38, 43 (8–24 March 1558).
[25] AGS E 811–47.

the new admiral eventually arrived he told the King that Mary's navy was unfit for service in a full campaign, though it could patrol the Channel and might take part in minor raids. It still seemed to Feria that Mary and her government had definitively abandoned Calais to its fate, though this was clearly not the Queen's wish.[26] Even so, Philip continued to hope, at least in public. Now acting as an English king and not a Habsburg ruler, he ordered the navy to be refitted for action in July, and told Mary's government to provision it up to September of that year. He was on the defensive in any case, and his uncertainty about the English prevented him from formulating a fully coherent plan. Nonetheless, on 1 May, Feria sent his King a coded letter from Greenwich in which he suggested that it would not in fact be too difficult to recapture Calais, using an Anglo-German army, though he thought this should be entirely Philip's operation.[27] England's contribution, if any, was to be naval, with Philip expecting Mary to ensure that the ships were produced, while it now appeared that the much talked-of German contingent was expected to go to Gravelines with a view to attacking the Calais Pale.[28]

In the event, it was the duke of Guise who, characteristically, took the initiative, attacking Thionville in June, while other French forces raided Dunkirk, Bergues and Saint-Winocque, their main aim being to prevent English forces from establishing bases. All this seems to have seriously panicked Philip, who feared that another French victory at this stage might bring crashing down the whole Spanish–Netherlandish edifice which he and his father had constructed in recent years. He made another desperate plea for English naval forces to be sent to the Flemish coast, and was horrified when he heard that Mary's fleet had instead, despite Feria's efforts, been sent much further west to Alderney, which had recently been attacked by France. The message was clear: when push came to shove, Mary's ancestral Norman lands had priority even over Calais, and certainly over Philip's continental ambitions and needs. Thus the main English fleet found itself in the Channel Islands and not at Gravelines, where it was meant to be assisting the Habsburg forces, though some of Mary's ships did take part in that action.[29] Relations between Philip and the English government were not improved when the Spanish naval commander Luis de Carvajal, without English help, succeeded in luring the French raiders into a trap while they were sacking Bergues. Their commander, Termes, was captured, along with 3,000 of his men, and 1,500 Frenchmen were killed. After this, Henry II and Philip could feel that they were 'level on points', with Bergues cancelling out Calais, and both regrouped, hoping for a decisive battle later that year which could

[26] *CSP Span* XIII, pp. 349–52; *CODOIN*, lxxxvii, pp. 5–11, 45, 47, 48, 60.
[27] AGS E 811–55.
[28] AGS E 811–57 (14 May 1558), 56 (31 May 1558).
[29] *CODOIN*, lxxxvii, pp. 48, 69–70, 73: *CSP Span* XIII, p. 403; Davies, 'England and the French War', p. 181.

lead to a 'good peace'. Thus England was largely marginalized in a way which would further darken what turned out to be Mary's final months.

It is difficult to avoid the conclusion that the weak or non-existent English intervention after the loss of Calais was down to lack of political will rather than a shortage of financial and military resources. English wars were generally paid for by means of special parliamentary subsidies, but neither the Queen nor her Council had wanted to summon a new parliament in 1557. There was an ugly mood among much of the political class, caused in part by resentment of Mary's religious policies, and it was thought better to try other measures, such as selling crown lands and arranging loans abroad, as mid-sixteenth-century states normally did. Mary feared, however, that the sale of lands which had been confiscated from the nobility, and in particular from the late duke of Northumberland, would upset the aristocracy further at an inopportune time. Eventually, in March 1558, Mary did announce that the Crown would borrow £100,000 abroad to fund war, and after this she asked Philip to arrange a further loan of £400,000 for her at Antwerp, but her highly able and experienced representative there, Sir Thomas Gresham, found that the interest rates on offer were too high, and England withdrew from the market. There seems to have been a philosophical clash on this subject between Philip and the English, in which the latter were determined to stick to 'sound finance', while the former, like other major European powers, was happy to run national finances on the basis of systematic and large-scale indebtedness, in accordance with the budgetary habits of later centuries. At the end of Mary's reign, the English Crown would have a debt of £300,000, which seemed crippling in London but derisory on the Continent. What Mary's men, such as Lord Treasurer Winchester and Sir Thomas Gresham, saw as prudence, Philip and his advisers, including the count of Feria in London, regarded as disloyalty bordering on treachery. This was an unfortunate contrast between two financial systems since the English Crown, unlike the Habsburgs, lacked the regular tax revenues on which state debt-financing might have been based.[30] The mismatch would certainly not be resolved before Mary's death, and would only worsen under her successor. In the meantime, defensive preparations went ahead in England.

There was also a more personal agenda, shared by the King and Queen. When the count of Feria went to London, early in 1558, as well as seeking military assistance he was commissioned by Philip to find out whether his wife was in fact pregnant.[31] A few days earlier, Philip had acknowledged Cardinal Pole's information to this effect, in words which hardly suggest cold reserve:

> . . . the pregnancy of the most serene Queen, my very dear wife, [causes me] much greater joy and contentment than anything which is

---

[30] Rodríguez-Salgado, *Changing Face*, pp. 178–87.
[31] AGS E 811–24 (Philip to Feria, Brussels, 31 January 1558).

dear to me here [in Brussels], because it is the thing that I have most wanted in the world, and is so important for the good of Religion and of our Kingdoms. And so I have given, and am giving, to our Lord the thanks which should be given for this goodness and mercy which He has done, and I greatly thank you for the special uplift which you have given me . . .[32]

Philip seems to have found it easier to say such things to other men, such as Pole and the count of Feria, than to say them to Mary herself. On 22 February, for instance, Feria told his master that she was 'pained' because letters from him had been delayed by his illness.[33] Both the count and the Cardinal would often write in this vein during 1558. Meanwhile, Mary's second supposed pregnancy received very much less publicity and credence in England and abroad than the first, so that little is known about it. Evidently the Queen's hopes had been raised by her time with her husband between March and July 1557, but the latter part of that year seems to have passed without any public discussion of the birth of an heir. Philip no doubt kept his disappointment to himself, as was his custom, though at the end of January, Mary had felt sure enough in her own mind to send the news in a personal letter to her husband, saying that it consoled her somewhat for the loss of Calais, and that she too thought that a child was the best thing for the kingdom and for religion.[34] This time, there were no preparations for a confinement, and Feria, possibly with the help of his future wife Jane Dormer, who was one of Mary's inner circle, soon came to the conclusion that the 'pregnancy' was make-believe, and the rest of Europe thought the same.[35] The prospect of an heir for Mary and Philip in England and the Netherlands was thus as illusory as English military aid for the Habsburg war against France. In her customary stolid and determined manner, Mary, probably alone, continued to believe that she would come to term, despite the apparent lack of visible signs such as swelling of her body. Thus on 30 March, notionally nine months, by a fine and desperate calculation, after she had supposedly conceived, she took the common step, for a noblewoman entering childbirth, of making a will. The text was explicitly related to the future birth of an heir of her body, and couched in full accordance with the marriage treaty of 1554. In it, she made no specific arrangement for the succession, though she stipulated that no heir of her body and Imperial crown should interfere with any of the terms of this document.[36] On 1 April, Philip actually wrote personally to his wife, in a somewhat stiff and perhaps bashful way. 'Now I do so moved only by the great desire and care which I have to see Your Majesty's

[32] AGS E 811–16.
[33] AGS E 811–29 (copy).
[34] *CSP Span* XIII, pp. 340–1.
[35] *CSP Span* XIII, p. 363.
[36] Loades, *Mary Tudor*, pp. 370–80, at p. 377 (BL Harleian MS 6949).

affairs as well placed and established as are my own.' He urged Mary to be assured that she would always find him 'as true and good a brother' (*sic*) as he had always been to her.[37] In equally stoic fashion, Feria told Philip on 6 April, at Mary's request, that she was well, and occupied with the services of Holy Week.[38] From Antwerp on 24 May 1558, Philip felt able to speak more freely to Pole, thanking him for the news that Mary was in good spirits, this bringing him out of the 'care which [her distress over the pregnancy] had given him, which was not small'. The text of this letter strongly suggests that as late as 19 May, when the Cardinal wrote to Philip, it was still believed that Mary was indeed coming to term, though this idea was quickly abandoned thereafter. Even so, her husband pleaded urgent and major business as the reason why he could not come to England.[39] Soon afterwards, Feria was able to tell the King categorically that his wife's supposed symptoms had been illusory.[40]

While this personal tragedy continued for her, both Mary and Pole had to pursue their struggles with the unsympathetic and intractable Pope. Thinking objectively and on a European scale, rather than from the specific point of view of England, on 2 February 1558 Pole wrote to Cardinal Carlo Carafa, who was now acting as Paul IV's legate in Brussels, expressing the opinion that there were at last greater hopes of peace. His main reason for saying this was that the Pope had apparently begun to view Philip in a better light. On 3 January 1558, Paul had replied in a friendly fashion to a personal letter from Philip, in which the King had assured him that all conflict between them was over and that in future he would be wholly loyal to the Holy See. In return, Pope Carafa assured Philip that he now regarded him as fully part of the European peace process. This remarkable reversal was confirmed on 7 January, when Paul wrote again, praising Philip for preventing a gathering of Protestant leaders at Worms, telling him that he was now behaving like a true 'Defender of the Faith' and Catholic king.[41] However, this change did little or nothing to improve England's situation in relation to the Papacy, and on 30 March 1558, as Mary was making her will, Pole wrote to Paul from Greenwich. This letter, which unlike his 'Apologia' does seem to have reached its addressee, continues in a similar vein to the earlier document. In it he tells the Pope that he has to trust him still, despite everything that has happened, and that he has accepted the removal of his English legation, though he reproaches Paul for refusing to hear Sir Edward Carne or even his own brother Carlo Carafa, on the subject. Somewhat disingenuously, Pole tells the Pope that he has heard a rumour that a trial has started

[37] AGS E 811–44 (copy).
[38] AGS E 811–46 (copy).
[39] AGS E 811–50 (copy).
[40] *CSP Ven* VI, ii, p. 1142.
[41] *CRP*, 3, pp. 503–4 (no. 2174); Tellechea, *Legación*, pp. xxxii–xxxiii, 69–74 (nos XXXIX, XL).

against him, and responds with a typically dramatic biblical analogy. This was the episode (Genesis 22: 1–19) in which God told the patriarch Abraham to sacrifice his only son Isaac as a test of faith, in the event saving the boy and substituting a ram at the last minute. Pole sees himself in Isaac's role and the Pope as the father who is willing to sacrifice him. He accuses Paul of tearing his life away when he questioned his faith. Pole has seen the fire, sword and wood of the Genesis story, and has no doubt that he is the intended victim, yet he denies that he has ever done anything to justify such action and says that, on the contrary, he has done a great deal for the Church. He had been enthusiastic when Paul was elected Pope, and had himself restored the true Church in England through his own efforts as well as those of Mary and Philip. When he was first made a cardinal in Rome, he had said that he came as a lamb, or sacrificial victim, but now he prays that, like Isaac, he will be freed at the last minute. He characterizes the martyred bishop of Rochester, John Fisher, as the ram which was sacrificed, implying that there is no need for a further victim and expressing the devout wish that the Pope will now treat him as a right-eous man and friend, rather than a suspected heretic.[42]

Any hope Pole had that he and England might gain greater favour in Rome, and that the reconciliation of Paul IV and Philip might last, was dashed when a new dispute arose between the Pope and the Habsburgs. On 14 March 1558, in the final step of his grand retirement strategy, Charles V passed his Imperial crown to his brother Ferdinand at a Diet in Frankfurt am Main. Ever since the Habsburg family compact had been made in 1551, the Electors of the Holy Roman Empire, as well as other German princes, several of them Protestant, had been concerned at the way in which the Habsburgs rode roughshod over Imperial law and protocol. Now, it was Pope Paul's turn to be angry, undoing the good work for peace that Philip had done in the autumn of 1557. In the March 1558 consistory of cardinals, Pope Paul expressed his fury at Charles's action, and it was agreed that a collection should be made of archival documents, many of them centuries old, on relations between the Papacy and the Empire, a subject which had always been controversial and had split the Christian powers of Europe many times before. The issue came to a head with the arrival in Rome, on the night of 12–13 May, of the new Imperial ambassador, Martín de Guzmán. Paul refused to receive him as Ferdinand's envoy, but gave him a private audience as an individual Catholic, explaining the problems which had been caused by Charles's abdication. The Pope also asked the cardinals for their opinions on how he should proceed, and in particular whether Ferdinand's election as emperor should be declared invalid. The resulting 'votes' show an overwhelmingly negative attitude to the Habsburgs, though Paul was persuaded by them to avoid any drastic action, having himself opened the way for such a conclusion by asking the cardinals what would be best, in the circumstances, for the good and tranquillity of Christendom.

---

[42] *CRP*, 3, pp. 520–8 (no. 2211).

Nevertheless, the issue rumbled on until Charles died, at the Jeronymite monastery of Yuste in south-western Spain, on 21 September 1558.[43] Even after that, the Imperial question remained unresolved into the reign of Mary's successor.

In the summer of 1558, none of the problems which had beset Mary's reign seemed any nearer resolution. Calais was not retaken, bad harvests and epidemics were still affecting the population, opponents of the religious settlement were still being burned, and England appeared largely irrelevant to continental power politics. Most crucially, and most personally for the Queen, she and her husband had no heir from their bodies, and no alternative successor had been designated. In these circumstances, the role of Mary's half-sister Elizabeth became ever more important. While many in England assumed that, as in 1553, Henry VIII's will would come into effect when Mary died so that Anne Boleyn's daughter would succeed to the throne, it was recognized that Philip, as King of England, would have a say. His attitude to this is intriguing. Once again, everything came back to Mary's failed 'pregnancy' in 1555. It seems that when Philip left England for the Low Countries at the end of August in that year, he had already come to a personal conviction that he would never father a future king or queen of England. This changed the way in which the Habsburgs saw their involvement in England, which was henceforth regarded as a temporary rather than a permanent asset. It could therefore be said that the inevitability of Elizabeth's succession became clear when Mary left the birthing chamber in Hampton Court and moved to Oatlands. As Philip re-immersed himself in continental affairs, and in particular the organization of his father's heritage, he seems to have changed his attitude towards Elizabeth. Since there would be no child for him and Mary, meaning that if he wanted the English throne he would almost certainly have to fight for it, the younger sister now became a much better prospect, who should be conciliated rather than regarded as simply a heretical rebel.

Even so, whatever Philip may initially have thought about Elizabeth, many in England assumed that he was threatening her right to the throne, and this became a pretext for conspiracies. Advised of this, he had reacted to the Dudley conspiracy of 1556 by urging his wife to drop her enquiries into Elizabeth's involvement, which seems in fact to have been real. Instead, it was to be said officially that her servants acted without her knowledge in this case. Reluctantly, on 6 June 1556, Mary had sent her half-sister a jewel and a reassuring message, and also removed the guard on her house at Ashridge. By this time, it is clear that Philip, already looking to the future, had decided that Elizabeth should not be antagonized, even though she and Mary showed no sign of becoming reconciled. By the summer of 1556, there was no prospect that parliament would make any alteration to the 1544 Succession Act, and it was almost univer-

---

[43] Tellechea, *Paulo IV y Carlos V: la renuncia del Imperio a debate* (Madrid: Fundación Universitaria Española, 2001) [BAV Vat. Lat. 7042].

sally accepted, though not of course by Mary, that Elizabeth would eventually become Queen. Philip, ever the realist and pragmatist, knew that antagonizing Henry VIII's younger daughter would only make it more likely that she would undo his wife's work and, given the level of support which she had in the country, he now believed that any attempt to disinherit her might provoke a civil war. This was to be the grim reality of Mary's situation in her final years. Whether or not the Queen had a child, the dangers of pregnancy made the succession an urgent matter, and in this context the issue once again arose of marrying Elizabeth off, preferably to a safe Catholic prince. To Philip and his continental advisers, the obvious candidate seemed to be his faithful ally Emmanuel Philibert, duke of Savoy.[44]

Previously, when pressure on her to marry was less severe, Elizabeth had appeared to be open to the possibility of marrying Emmanuel Philibert, whom she had met when he came to England in 1554, but in the autumn of 1556, although relations between her and her sister at least seemed to have warmed somewhat, she made her opposition clear. In one respect things were simplified when the most likely English candidate for her hand, Edward Courtenay, died in Padua on 18 September 1556. At this stage, it is not clear from the evidence whether Mary agreed with Philip's plan for Elizabeth, but by the following year they were certainly strongly disagreeing on the subject, to the permanent detriment of their relationship. At the beginning of 1557, Emmanuel Philibert came in person to England to plead his cause, but it is uncertain how keen he really was. His sterling service to the Habsburgs had arisen out of his loss of his native land to the French, and Philip was demanding as a price that, if he did marry Elizabeth, the duke of Savoy would have to surrender to him the Savoyard lands west of the Alps, including Nice and Villefranche. In any case, Emmanuel Philibert's English mission failed, and the result was further acrimony between Mary and her husband. At some time in January or February 1557, she told Philip that she had been against marriage for Anne Boleyn's daughter ever since she was born, and professed not to understand her husband's argument that she must support the Savoy marriage as a matter of faith and conscience. Mary also suggested that parliament's consent would be necessary for her sister's marriage and this greatly irritated Philip, who saw this argument as obfuscation. Mary reacted badly, warning that she would become 'jealous' of her husband if he did not come round to her point of view. In the end, the exasperated Mary told him that if he wanted to arrange for her sister to marry Emmanuel Philibert, he would have to come to England and organize it himself. In March 1557 Philip duly did so, primarily, to gain help for his war with France, but the marriage plan for Elizabeth was also very much on the agenda. He brought with him two formidable ladies, the duchesses of Lorraine and Parma, whose job was to bring Elizabeth, and perhaps Mary, to agreement. Both Tudors remained obdurate, however, Mary never

[44] *CSP Span* XIII, p. 285; *CSP Span* XIII, p. 120.

becoming convinced of the merits of the scheme, while Elizabeth accepted the French view that by marrying Emmanuel Philibert, and thus giving him a kingdom in exchange for his lost duchy, she would effectively become dependent on Philip and his family. Finally, Philip admitted defeat, and after this he simply resorted to 'wooing' Elizabeth in order to make her at least a political if not a personal friend. In May 1557, the outgoing Venetian ambassador, Michieli, once more reported that Elizabeth was generally expected in England to be the next queen, and was protected, presumably from Mary's wrath, by Philip. The same view seems to have been held in Brussels.[45] In these circumstances, it is not surprising that subsequent overtures from Sweden were unsuccessful.

In May 1558, an embassy arrived in London from King Gustavus Vasa, seeking Elizabeth's hand for his son, the duke of Finland, but not only were the Swedes virtually Lutheran by then, which could not have pleased Mary even if she had been willing to let her sister marry at all, but they committed the diplomatic faux pas of approaching Elizabeth directly at Hatfield, receiving a rebuff from her too, which was no doubt heartfelt as well as correct. Nonetheless, Mary later decided that it would be unfair for the Council to rebuke the Swedish ambassador formally. The Lord Chancellor and lord treasurer were to have a quiet word with him instead.[46] In a letter from London dated 18 May, the count of Feria had made it clear that he thought he should have gone to visit Elizabeth before he left England for the Netherlands, adding that Juan de Figueroa held the same view. Feria had used Lady Clinton, the admiral's wife, as a contact with Elizabeth because, as he wrote to Philip, they had grown up together.[47] The proposed visit did not happen, apparently so as not to offend the Queen, but Philip and his agents were evidently very interested in at least sounding out the likely successor to the throne. By this time, though, an ominous development had taken place in Paris. On 25 April 1558, the other prominent candidate for the English succession, Mary, Queen of Scots, had married the future Francis II of France. By one route or another, Mary of England's nemesis was approaching.

In political terms, things should have improved for England in the summer of 1558. Both Philip and Henry of France were seeking one more victory before they settled down to make peace, but the war was winding down. Even so, in July, the French mounted an attack on Habsburg Dunkirk, and this time the English participated in its defence. On the 13th of the month, Captain John Malen attacked the French with ten ships, and succeeded in driving them off. Once Philip had achieved victory at Gravelines and Henry at Thionville, there were no further major actions by either side, a fact which should have been to Mary's advantage. England had at last regained some military credibility on the Continent,

---

[45] *CSP Ven* VI, 2, p. 1057; *CSP Span* XIII, pp. 372–3.
[46] AGS E 811–63 (count of Feria to Philip, 6 June 1558).
[47] AGS E 811–54.

and was unlikely to receive any further demands for forces from Philip.[48] Things at home, on the other hand, allowed little opportunity for profit from the international situation, and one important factor was the recurrence of disease. In 1557, what would today be called a new virus became rife in England which, unlike the all too familiar sweating sickness, often took a long time to kill. Then the summer of 1558 brought the country its greatest mortality crisis of the sixteenth century, which would ultimately be a factor in the deaths of the Queen and her cardinal. The disease, apparently a form of influenza, affected nearly half of England, reducing the labour force available to bring in the harvest, and particularly affecting the upper classes. In August, the Court itself was touched, at Hampton Court Palace, and one of the victims was Jane Dormer. Mary sent her to London with a royal physician in attendance. By the time the Queen joined her in September Jane had recovered, but Mary announced that she was now ill herself.[49]

Meanwhile, the Church in England remained unreconciled with Paul IV, who regarded William Peto as his legate in the country, until the friar's death that summer, and still apparently believed that Pole was a heretic. This can only have deeply grieved Mary, and naturally it greatly afflicted Pole himself. Pope Carafa's intransigence also disrupted the running of the Church in England and Wales through the failure of Rome, in 1558, to ratify new appointments to the vacant sees of Salisbury, Hereford, Bangor and Gloucester.[50] Significantly, nevertheless, it now appears that, despite his loss of powers from the Papacy, Pole continued throughout 1558, until his death on 17 November, to receive business in his court of audience, as *legatus a latere*, and Court of Arches, as archbishop of Canterbury and *legatus natus*. The evidence seems to indicate that both the lawyers involved in the work of these courts, and litigants seeking absolution or dispensation in ecclesiastical matters, were happy to function as though Pole was still fully linked with Rome.[51] Interestingly, as late as 11 October 1558, Pole issued a *significavit*, as *legatus a latere*, confirming the excommunication of one Thomas More for not paying costs in a plea which had been heard by the archdeacon of Canterbury, Nicholas Harpsfield, sitting as legatine auditor of causes. Even with Peto dead, this was a resolute defiance of the legal situation as it had been defined by Paul IV.[52] In this respect, at least, the Church in England seems, with Mary's tacit approval, to have reverted to operating as a 'national' Catholic Church, as it had done in her father's time. Meanwhile, the burnings continued within Pole's province of Canterbury, though concentrated in the same areas as in earlier years. The peaks were in June and July 1558,

[48] Loades, *Mary Tudor*, p. 303.
[49] Porter, *Mary Tudor*, p. 401.
[50] *CRP*, 3, pp. 533, 534, 542, 555 (nos 2220, 2227, 2248, 2277).
[51] Thomas F. Mayer, 'Cardinal Pole's Concept of *Reformatio*', in *RCMT*, pp. 77–80; Mayer, 'The Success of Pole's Final Legation', in *CMT*, pp. 149–75.
[52] *CRP*, 3, p. 572 (no. 2287a).

with seven fatalities in each month, and a final effort, as things turned out, took place in November, with five being burned in Canterbury just a week before Mary's death.[53] There has been some debate over the direct role of Pole in heresy trials, but there is no doubt that he was supervising things closely in 1558, not least in his own diocese of Canterbury. He had issued a strong warning to this effect, as well as attacking the credentials of Protestants as Christian martyrs, in his St Andrew's Day sermon in London the previous year, and it is possible to speculate that his fervour in this matter in 1557–8 may at least in part have been due to his indignation at the loss of his legation and the accusation by the Pope and the Roman Inquisition that he was himself a heretic and a protector of heretics. If this is so, it was perhaps inevitable that the violent repression would go on, even as it became clear that things would change when Elizabeth succeeded. That depended, however, on the fate of the Queen, as well as that of the now ailing cardinal archbishop.

When Mary returned to London, at the end of August 1558, she entered her apartments in her favourite St James's Palace and never left them alive. This was not, of course, a likely or predictable outcome at the time, but her existing health problems seem to have been compounded by the influenza epidemic. She began at this point to suffer increasingly from fevers, with growing physical weakness adding to her existing depression at her personal and public situation. Her decline proved to be gradual but remorseless, although it was not until the end of October that those around her began to fear that she would not survive. In 1558 and 1559, an extraordinary number of Europe's leading figures left the political scene through death. Mary was particularly affected by the death, on 21 September, of her mentor Charles V, with her own former adviser Bartolomé Carranza at his bedside. A month later, and while the news of the Emperor's death was still permeating Europe, Charles's sister, Mary of Hungary, also died, as she was preparing to return to the Netherlands from Spain. These intimate losses were not confirmed to Philip until 1 November, and by that time it had been made clear to him that his own wife was mortally ill as well. He seems to have decided, however, that arranging the obsequies in Brussels for his father and aunt, as well as the continuing search for peace with France, would prevent him from coming to London. Emmanuel Philibert, no doubt still smarting from his encounter with England's royal family, as well as the long-term loss of his duchy of Savoy, was refusing to continue acting as regent of the Netherlands, and this added to Philip's burden. Nonetheless, Philip was still King of England, and as his wife floated in and out of delirium he knew that he must do all he could to secure a smooth succession there. If he did not, France and Scotland were waiting, newly inspired by the marriage alliance of Mary, Queen of Scots and the Dauphin, and although the Pope now at last appeared to be friendly, he could certainly not be relied on to remain so. Another reason for Philip's not coming to London

---

[53] Duffy, *Fires of Faith*, p. 129; Collinson, 'The Persecution in Kent', in *CMT*, p. 320.

was that a peace conference with France started at Cercamp on 8 October. Instead, he decided to send, for the third time in 1558, his special envoy Gómez Suárez de Figueroa, count of Feria.

In the meantime, Mary herself had belatedly begun to make arrangements for the future. In her will, dated 30 March, she had explicitly prepared for childbirth, providing only for the heir of her body to succeed her. She had made Pole her leading executor, had left £1,000 as alms for the poor, and had made legacies to the newly restored religious houses – the Carthusians at Sheen, the Bridgettines at Syon, the Observant Franciscans at Greenwich and Southampton, the Benedictine monks of Westminster, the Dominican friars of St Bartholomew, Smithfield and the nuns of the same order at Langley – as well as the Hospital of the Savoy and the universities of Oxford and Cambridge. On 28 October, now seriously ill, she added a codicil, witnessed by, among others, her physician Thomas Wendy. The world of the sick and dying can, in one way, become more confined, but in another it expands, and now Mary finally acknowledged that she would bear no child, and would have to accept Elizabeth as her successor. Yet even now, she could not bear to name her half-sister, instead referring to her just as 'my next heire and Successour', whom she instructed to carry out the terms of her will and testament.[54] On 5 November, parliament reassembled, somewhat depleted by the epidemic, and quickly turned to the question of the succession. Probably as a result of pressure from parliament, which was communicated to her in a lucid period, on 7 November Mary summoned the Speaker of the Commons, William Cordell, to her bedside. The next day, the comptroller of her household, her old East Anglian retainer, Sir Thomas Cornwallis, and the secretary of the Privy Council, John Boxall, travelled to Hatfield House to tell Elizabeth that her half-sister had finally named her as heir to the throne. The future countess and later duchess of Feria, Jane Dormer, later claimed that at this stage she herself took some of Mary's jewellery to Elizabeth, together with a request, in accordance with her will and codicil, that she would pay Mary's debts and ensure that the English Church remained Catholic. It soon became clear that Elizabeth's assurance on this matter was insincere, to say the least.

In early October, Philip had two main agents in London, Alonso de Córdoba and Christophe d'Assonléville, and it was the latter who wrote from Westminster, on 10 October, to inform him of Mary's condition. He said that he had been asked by the Council of the Netherlands to find out about current English policy, particularly towards Denmark, Sweden and the Hanseatic League, and duly reported on this. However he also gave an optimistic message about Mary's health:'Sire, the Queen is feeling better now than she has done since the beginning of her illness, as is the Cardinal [Pole] also. May God order an end to these great illnesses.'[55] Then, on 22 October, Philip wrote to Alonso de Córdoba, acknowledging two letters

[54] Loades, *Mary Tudor*, pp. 370–83.
[55] AGS E 811–14.

from him, dated 14 and 16 October, from which, along with earlier correspondence, he had learned of the Queen's serious illness, saying that Don
Alonso might imagine 'the pain and deep feeling' with which he had
reacted to this news. Philip expressed his appreciation for the ambassador's efforts, but told him that he had decided to send the count of Feria
back to London to see the Queen on his behalf. The count would bring a
doctor with him, something that Don Alonso had evidently requested.[56]
Also on 22 October, Philip wrote in Latin to Mary's English doctors,
thanking them for their devoted care so far and urging them on to further
efforts.[57] In the same post went a letter to Pole, in Spanish, announcing the
despatch of Feria, 'to serve the Queen in this her illness, because I cannot
go in person'. The King added that he would have loved to see Pole free
of the quartan fever, and begged him to accept his affection as genuine.[58]
Feria's departure was delayed for a few days by over-optimistic news that
Mary had recovered, but on or about 5 November he was at Arras, and he
arrived in Dover on the 7th or 8th.

   While Feria was still in transit, on 6/7 November, d'Assonléville wrote
again to Philip, reporting on the first day's proceedings in the new parliament. The question of the succession to Mary was openly discussed, and
the value to England of the alliance with the Netherlands was questioned.
While some councillors, at least, accepted the need to remain linked to
Flanders, the ambassador thought that the general public (*vulgaire*) did not
see things that way. He said that the Queen was having some intervals of
remission from her illness, but still suffered from occasional 'paroxysms'
(*paroxis*). He added that the people were taking a less optimistic view of her
health than her doctors did. The next day d'Assonléville added that
Mary's councillors had gone to see her on the 6th, and brought before her
their current political agenda. They also tried to persuade her to say
explicitly that Elizabeth should succeed her, but were aware that she
would not accept this unless the current state of the English Church was
conserved.[59]

   The count of Feria reached London on the 9th, and the report on
his visit is contained in a despatch which he wrote for Philip on
14 November.[60] Although his detailed instructions from Philip do not
survive, it seems that, as a close counsellor, he expected to operate at the
highest level and, since he brought his household, to stay in England for
some time. He was no doubt also planning to marry Jane Dormer, a
wedding which Mary hoped, almost to the last, that she could attend. Also
with him was the Franciscan Bernardo de Fresneda, who had been with

   [56] AGS E 811-12 (copy).
   [57] AGS E 811-87 (copy).
   [58] AGS E 811-88 (copy).
   [59] AGS E 811-89.
   [60] M. J. Rodríguez-Salgado and Simon Adams, 'The Count of Feria's Dispatch to Philip
II of 14 November 1558', *Camden Miscellany*, xxviii (London: Royal Historical Society, 1984),
pp. 302-44, pp. 319-27.

Philip, as his confessor, in England in 1554–5, and had evidently been deputed to look into Mary's physical and spiritual well-being. In this he wasted little time, since on 10 November he sent a letter to Brussels, addressed not to Philip himself, but to the royal favourite, Ruy Gómez de Silva. In it he stressed that Philip must pay close and immediate attention, both to Mary herself and to the question of the English succession. He may have thought that Ruy Gómez could penetrate his master's preoccupation with continental matters, and in the process gives a vivid picture of Mary in her last days. He tells Gómez that 'the Queen neither wishes nor thinks anything but what His Majesty [King Philip] wants, and orders her', and tells the favourite that he may be sure that she has lost her vitality (*ánimo*) because her husband has not written to her for so long. If Philip does write to her, which he should do urgently, telling her how she should conduct the government of England, this would 'revive her greatly and give her strength, because she is so faint-hearted that she does not dare speak a word of love, if there is not within it the very clear will and intention of her husband'. If Philip does give his wife instructions, he must also give her plenty of freedom to decide how to put them into effect, since 'the others', by whom Fresneda presumably means the Council, are now allowing her very little latitude, and are putting sinister interpretations on her actions, 'as the Devil is'. His impression, seeing Mary's situation after a considerable absence, is that she is now treated with very little respect by the Court and Council, indeed 'much less than is proper for royal dignity and authority'.[61] Fresneda's personal and political account was filled out and elaborated in the count of Feria's report to Philip, dated 14 November, just three days before Mary died.

On 10 November, while the Franciscan confessor was sizing up the Queen's situation, Feria met her Council. The earl of Pembroke was absent and William Paget ill, but the count informed those present of Philip's wish for the succession to his dying wife. In this connection, he said that the King particularly wanted to know what dealings the Council had had with 'madama Ysabel' (Elizabeth). He reminded them that 'many days ago' Philip had asked them to take action in this matter, and he rebuked them, including Mary herself in this reproach, for not having listened to their ambassador in Brussels, Sir John Mason, who was fully apprised of Philip's views and a great 'favourite' of Elizabeth's. Feria told the Council that he had come specifically to meet the Princess, 'and serve her as His Majesty's sister', and also to clear the way for her to obtain the Crown, 'without disturbance or anxiety among those from whom these things might be expected', by which he no doubt meant the French and Scots, as well as her English opponents. Both England in general and Elizabeth in particular had many enemies, and trouble could be expected from them, so that firm action at this stage, before the Queen died, was essential. On the subject of Elizabeth, the councillors gave Feria a 'succinct' answer, saying that they

[61] AGS Consejos y Juntas de Hacienda 34–482.

had done their best and hoped to God that there would indeed be no disturbance in the kingdom. The discussion then turned to the Cercamp peace conference, which an English delegation was attending, along with the French and Habsburg representatives. Feria told his master that, in general, 'those councillors are very frightened of what Madam Elizabeth will do with them'.

The count then reported to Philip on his subsequent visit to Elizabeth herself, apparently at Lord Clinton's Brocket Hall near Hatfield. He had dinner with the Princess and Clinton's wife. Then the two adjourned for a wide-ranging business meeting in the presence of just a few of Elizabeth's ladies, the point apparently being that they only understood English, so that the discussion could take place in Spanish, which Elizabeth spoke fluently. They read together Philip's instructions for Feria's mission, and Elizabeth assured him of her 'good friendship' for his master. She then proceeded to give her reasons for this. Specifically, Philip had literally got her out of gaol after Wyatt's rebellion in 1554, while, more generally, the Tudors had always been friends of the house of Burgundy, and of their successors, the Habsburgs. Before Feria's return to England, and in case Mary died before he arrived, Philip had already sent his ambassadors, Alonso de Córdoba and Diego de Azevedo, to see her at Hatfield and assure her of his friendship. Now Feria personally reassured Elizabeth that Philip would treat her as his sister, and as Mary's legitimate successor, adding that the Princess knew, as did the whole of England, that he had been working for this outcome for some time. When he saw her in the previous June, Feria had found Elizabeth very cordial, but now he began to see the steel in her nature, which he compared with that of her father. Although she was not open on the subject, he gained the distinct impression that she would not allow Mary's religious settlement to remain once she became Queen. Elizabeth was, however, happy to talk freely about her personal and political situation. She told Feria that she resented her sister being Queen and believed that the people were actually behind her, not Mary; with which the Spaniard agreed. In a parallel with the situation at the end of Edward's reign, although Feria does not allude to this, and also in defiance of the aristocratic values of the period, Elizabeth said that 'the people has placed her in the state in which she is'. He had to tell Philip that in this respect she thought she owed nothing either to him or to the English nobility, even though they had all undertaken to support her as Queen. Strikingly, in an allusion to the continuance of strong religious dissent in the country, and to the counter-productive effect of the religious persecution, Feria told Philip that if Elizabeth went for the throne, the 'heretics' (Protestants) would rise from their graves to support her. In the true Tudor manner, she informed Feria that she would not be governed by anybody, and in his view she was now totally prepared to rule, and knew exactly who was for her and who was against her.

The discussion then turned to the question of her marriage. Elizabeth smiled at talk of Philip's earlier efforts to hitch her to Emmanuel Philibert of Savoy, but the count assured her that Philip had only wanted Mary to treat her well, 'as her sister and heiress', and had never wanted to force her into any such marital arrangement against her will. Elizabeth pointedly replied that her sister had lost the good will of the nation by marrying a foreigner, implying that she intended to do no such thing. Feria naturally objected to this, and the Princess again went through her reasons for being grateful to Philip. Feria then told her that the King would come and see her again soon, when 'the Queen got well again or died'. If Mary died sooner rather than later, Elizabeth should summon the count at once, as he was under orders to go to her in such circumstances. No doubt anxious to secure her new government without foreign interference, she replied that she did not want him to do this, but he should rather await her summons when she was ready. Her excuse was that 'the English were resentful of her socializing with foreigners'. Feria agreed with this, but said that, undoubtedly because of his known relationship with Jane Dormer, 'they now counted me as English'. There were many signs in this interview, good and bad, of future Anglo-Spanish relations.

The report then turned to other political matters. Feria told Philip that things in England were

> in the worst state that they can be for Your Majesty; because, though Your Majesty was able for the last four years to dispose of Madam Elizabeth, marrying her to whomever he liked, now she will marry whomever she wants, without Your Majesty being a party to reaching any other result, except by means of a new negotiation, and buying all these [English] Councillors, because they will sell themselves to whoever pays them best.[62]

Elizabeth felt that she owed nothing to Philip or Mary in becoming Queen, and Feria believed that the English would fight for her if necessary. When Mary and parliament had recently accepted her as heir to the throne, Philip was not even mentioned. Feria had the impression from meeting her that Elizabeth wanted to remain friendly with both Philip and Henry II of France, without becoming too tied to either. He still thought, though, that she was marginally more pro-Habsburg than pro-French. She had not liked his reference at Brocket Hall to Philip's pensioners in England, apparently seeing the continuance of this arrangement as an intrusion, but Feria thought that any attempt by her to interfere could only induce greater sympathy for Philip among the recipients. Although Philip had never succeeded in creating his own political 'party' in England, since his arrival there in 1554 he had been providing fairly regular incomes for some of his and Mary's leading courtiers, including the earls of Arundel, Pembroke, Derby and Shrewsbury, as well as Lord Dacre and Sir William Petre.[63] Feria was now trying to obtain all the correspondence that Mary

[62] Rodríguez-Salgado and Adams, 'Count of Feria's Dispatch', p. 325.
[63] Ibid., pp. 315–16; Prescott, Mary Tudor, pp. 344–5.

had received over the last few years from Philip, which he believed her to have kept, so that it would not fall into the wrong hands after she died. But once this despatch had been sent, on 14 November, Mary had very little time to live.

At the very end of his report, the count of Feria gave Philip an essential piece of information for a Catholic husband: 'Last night (13 November), they anointed the Queen our Lady, and today she is better, although there is very little hope for her life'.[64] Since the early days of the Church, blessed oil, normally of the olive, had been used as part of Christian care for the sick and dying: 'Are any among you sick? They should call for the elders of the Church and have them pray over them, anointing them with oil in the name of the Lord. The prayer of faith will save the sick, and the Lord will raise them up' (James 5: 14–15). In the case of those regarded as close to death, the use of this oil had, by Mary's day, become one of the 'last rites' of the Church, along with the making of confession and the administration of Holy Communion. In this way, the soul began to be accompanied out of this world by its fellow Christians, on a journey that would include both the last moments of life and death itself, in the liturgy of the Office for the Dead. In Mary's case, the time after the anointing was spent, drifting in and out of consciousness, in the company of her faithful ladies, including Jane Dormer and Susan Clarencius, who had served her for so long. Accounts suggest that, at this stage, she was not in physical pain, but told of dreams and visions. In particular, she said that she had seen herself with groups of children, who were singing to her like angels. This may have been the dream of a childless woman who had longed all her life for a family, and it may also have been a kind of rehearsal in her own mind of her funeral Mass, which was soon to come. A 'common' or core passage of the requiem speaks of angels leading the departed soul to Paradise (*in Paradisum deducant eam Angeli*). Mary was surrounded by attentive nursing and spiritual care in her last hours, and on the morning of 17 November, which must initially have seemed much like any other, Mass was celebrated at six in her privy chamber. It is said that although her ladies sobbed through the service, she took her part in a firm, strong voice, returning to the 'manly' Spanish register of her earlier years. No one seems to have noticed exactly when she slipped away, but it was after the Mass had ended. From then onwards, events moved fast, with none of the secrecy which had been associated with the deaths of her father and brother. Her coronation ring was quickly taken to Elizabeth at Hatfield to indicate beyond doubt that the Queen was dead and parliament, then in session, was informed within hours. About twelve hours after her death, her 'good cousin' Reginald died too, at Lambeth Palace, having suffered from fevers, and probably influenza, for some months. An era was indeed ending.[65]

[64] Rodríguez-Salgado and Adams, 'Count of Feria's Dispatch', p. 327.
[65] Henry Clifford, *The Life of Jane Dormer Duchess of Feria*, ed. J. Stevenson (London: Burns and Oates, 1887), pp. 69–80.

Mary lay in state in her privy chamber at St James's Palace until 13 December, when she was moved in procession to Westminster Abbey for the funeral liturgy and burial. Elizabeth had no expense spared, the cost being over £7,700, and she chose the elderly lord treasurer, the marquis of Winchester, to arrange the ceremonies. Anne Boleyn's daughter must have been aware that he had also, as comptroller of Henry VIII's household, organized the funeral of Mary's mother Catherine at Peterborough, in January 1536. On the 13th, Mary was taken to the Abbey with, above her coffin, a coloured effigy robed as for her coronation. She was accompanied by her household servants, gentlemen mourners, King Philip's remaining servants, the English royal standard carried by the marquis of Winchester, and the symbols of male, chivalric monarchy – sword, helmet and suit of armour. The chief mourner, Margaret Douglas, countess of Lennox, followed the coffin, accompanied by secular clergy and religious and, as was customary in such cases and not as a snub, the new queen was not present. At the door of Westminster Abbey, the cortège was received by the abbot and four bishops, in copes and mitres. When the coffin and effigy had been brought into the church on their hearse, the office started, with the censing of the body and the singing by the Benedictine community of the first of the liturgical offices for the dead. Vigil and offices were held overnight, and on the morning of 14 December a High Mass of requiem was sung, and the symbols of Mary's earthly monarchical power were offered back to God – and, of course, eventually to her successor. During the Mass, Mary's military regalia were given back to God by being placed on the altar after the offertory and the symbols of her royal authority were removed from her effigy. She was buried in a vault which had been opened in her grandfather King Henry VII's Chapel, at the east end of the Abbey, and her senior household officials broke their staves of office and threw them into the grave. Only after this, when the heralds proclaimed her as Queen, was Elizabeth truly held to have succeeded her sister on the throne. In her will, Mary had asked that her mother's remains be translated from Peterborough Cathedral and buried alongside her. This never happened, and although her funeral took place, like her mother's, in a Benedictine setting, there was one important difference. During a series of requiems, Catherine had been denounced as a false queen by John Hilsey, who had then recently succeeded John Fisher as bishop of Rochester, and even claimed that she had belatedly acknowledged that her marriage to King Henry was invalid.

The sermon at Mary's funeral was very different, and not at all pleasing to Elizabeth. It was preached by John White, bishop of Winchester, who, while warden of Winchester College, had welcomed Mary and Philip to that city and college at the time of their wedding, and had always been their supporter. Frequently moved to tears while he spoke, the bishop said some fine and unexceptionable things about Mary, praising her character, and in particular her patience in enduring all that had come to her during her reign:

She was a King's daughter, she was a King's sister, she was a King's wife. She was a Queen, and by the same title a King also . . . Howsoever it pleased God to will her patience to be exercised in the world, she had in all estates the fear of God in her heart, . . . [and] she had the love, commendation and admiration of all the world . . . She used singular mercy towards offenders. She used much pity and compassion towards the poor and oppressed. She used clemency amongst her nobles . . . I verily believe, the poorest creature in all the city feared not God more than she did.

Some of these points were debatable enough, but White's chosen biblical texts proved to be even more controversial. Both were from the 'Wisdom' book Ecclesiastes, the first being:

And I thought the dead, who have already died, more fortunate than the living, who are still alive, but better than both is the one who has not yet been, and has not yet seen the evil deeds that are done under the sun. (4: 2–3)

The other proved even more contentious: 'But whoever is joined with all the living has hope, for a living dog is better than a dead lion' (9: 4).[66] No doubt White was referring to Mary's Christian faith and fortitude, as one should when accompanying a soul on its journey to the Lord, but Elizabeth seems to have, wilfully or accidentally, chosen to regard the second text as referring to Mary as the 'dead lion', leaving her, by the same token, as the 'living dog'. It cannot have helped that the duke of Northumberland had quoted this same passage just before his execution. In any case, White had thereby made his own retirement speech as a diocesan bishop. Elizabeth put him under house arrest at once and, although he was released on 19 January 1559, she deprived him of his see in the following June. This proved to be the shape of things to come.[67]

In his report on 14 November, the count of Feria had mentioned his visit to Pole, saying that the Cardinal was suffering from 'quartan' fever, one which recurred every four days, adding that he was 'so weak that I think he must die'. By then, Feria had already been to see Elizabeth, and he told Pole that he had spoken up for him to Elizabeth, as Philip had ordered him to do. This had apparently given Pole some encouragement out of his general depression, and he told Feria of a letter, which had fallen into the hands of the French, in which he had asked Philip to look after his Italian servants after his death, since he did not expect them to be well treated in Elizabeth's England. Pole's pessimism, of course, proved to be entirely justified. Meanwhile, both he and Mary were naturally given the full preparation and

---

[66] Strype, *Ecclesiastical Memorials*, III, ii, pp. 277–87.

[67] Ibid., pp. 142, 548; *Harleian Miscellany* (1813), x, pp. 259–60; Loades, *Mary Tudor*, pp. 311–13.

burial rites of the Catholic Church, but it is perhaps interesting to see in what devotional framework their respective wills were formulated. Although Mary left benefactions to various religious communities and asked them to pray for her soul, unlike her father she made no provision for Masses to be said specifically for her.[68] In particular, it appears from the various surviving records of Reginald Pole's will that he too excluded such donations and requests, thus making a silent comment on the traditional system of gifts and Masses for the souls of the departed.[69] In any case, Elizabeth was primarily concerned with the living, in religion as in other matters.

At the human level, of course, Mary was remembered. Philip is quoted as having shown 'reasonable regret' for his wife's death, which indicates all too clearly his lack of emotional attachment to her.[70] In England, the printer Richard Lante published, as a broadsheet, *The Epitaphe upon the death of the most excellent and oure late vertuous Quene, Marie, deceased, augmented by the first Author*.[71] The anonymous author was as unstinting as Bishop White in praise of the dead Queen:

> . . . Witness, alas, may Marie be, late Queen of rare renown,
> Whose body dead, her virtues live, and doth her fame resowne . . .
> She never closed her ear to hear the righteous man distrest,
> Nor never spared her hand to help, when wrong or power oppress.
> Make for your mirror (Princes all) Marie, our mistress late . . .
> Farewell, O Queen! O pearl most pure! That God or nature gave,
> The earth, the heaven, the sprites, the saints cry honor to thy grave.

Like White's funeral sermon in Westminster Abbey, this anonymous 'Epitaph' did not amuse the new Queen. The unfortunate Lante was arrested and imprisoned for printing it and, once at liberty again, he not surprisingly added a new stanza to the subsequent version of the text, which corresponded better, if somewhat unsubtly, to the favoured political mood of Elizabeth's first year on the throne:

> Marie now dead, Elizabeth lives, our just and lawful Queen,
> In whom her sister's virtues rare abundantly are seen.
> Obey our Queen, as we are bound, pray God her to preserve,
> And send her Grace life long, and fruit, and subjects true to serve.

Lante's own anxiety shows all too clearly in these verses.

Mary's successor came to the throne after careful preparation, and considerable co-operation from members of the previous administration.

---

[68] Loades, *Mary Tudor*, pp. 377–83.
[69] *CRP*, 3, pp. 558–71 (no. 2286, 4 October 1558).
[70] *CSP Span* XIII, p. 440.
[71] London, 1558 (?), in *Old English Ballads, 1553–1625, Chiefly from the Manuscripts*, ed. Hyder E. Rollins (Cambridge: Cambridge University Press, 1920), pp. 23–6.

Within a very few days of Mary's death, Elizabeth's government was complete, the new power in the land being her secretary, William Cecil, who had worked closely with her at Hatfield during the previous reign.[72] In some cases, notably that of the lord treasurer, William Paulet, marquis of Winchester, existing office-holders were retained, but Mary's devout Catholic servants were removed.[73] Elizabeth's accession also had important effects on European politics. The future of England in general, and the question of Calais in particular, were bones of contention between Philip and Henry of France which threatened to undermine their efforts to make a general peace in the autumn and winter of 1558/9. The issues which had arisen while Mary was dying were not instantly resolved by the advent of her sister as Queen. Many on the Continent still regarded Anne Boleyn's daughter as illegitimate, the French had proclaimed Mary, Queen of Scots as the new Queen of England, and Elizabeth's regime was initially seen as unstable, thus encouraging predators. Elizabeth had the perceived disabilities of a female ruler and lacked experience. She was also an unknown quantity in the vital matter of religion, though many shared the count of Feria's view that she was likely to revert to a form of Protestantism, which she indeed did in the following year. Ultimately, neither Henry II of France and his successors nor Philip were able to dominate England, but in the meantime the Spanish, in particular, had to readjust quite rapidly to a new situation, in which they were the marginal ones.

[72] Alford, *Burghley*, pp. 80–2.
[73] Loades, *The Life and Career of William Paulet (c. 1475–1572): Lord Treasurer and First Marquis of Winchester* (Aldershot: Ashgate, 2008), pp. 135–7.

Chapter 12

REGIME CHANGE

In the second half of 1558, Elizabeth had worked hard, while still at Hatfield House, to prepare her new government. Mary's administration was divided on policy matters, and there was plenty of discontent in the country which her successor could exploit. Even so, a great deal of uncertainty remained. It is perhaps not surprising that she refused to discuss the details with the count of Feria when he visited her a few days before Mary's death, but the worried toings and froings at that time, between Hertfordshire and Westminster, indicated the reality of the tensions and anxieties involved for most or all of the English political class. Tudor monarchy was, of course, highly personal, and a change of regime was as likely to cause a clear-out then as it is today, when there is a change of president in the United States of America. Given the personalities and beliefs of Mary and Elizabeth, there was an additional worry. Although, in 1558 just as five years earlier, no one really knew beforehand what the new Queen thought and was intending to do about religion, Feria gained the distinct impression that Elizabeth would move in a Protestant direction.[1] Although things did not become entirely clear for several months, Gómez Suárez's judgement in this case proved to be entirely accurate.

By the time that Mary was in her tomb in Westminster Abbey, the political landscape had changed even more radically than it had when she succeeded Edward, or when he had succeeded his father, but the full extent of the upheaval did not appear immediately. Among the leading officers of the Court and royal household, the earl of Oxford initially continued as lord great chamberlain, the earl of Arundel as lord high steward, Sir John Mason as treasurer of the chamber, Richard Ward as cofferer of the chamber, Sir Edward Waldegrave as master of the great wardrobe, and Sir Thomas Cawarden as master of the revels.[2] Within a few months, though, many of these men would be gone, along, naturally, with Mary's ladies and her most zealous Catholic supporters among the lower ranks of court and household. To begin with, William, Lord Howard of Effingham replaced Sir Edward Hastings as lord chamberlain, and Sir Edward Rogers became vice-chamberlain instead of Sir Henry Bedingfield. Sir Thomas Parry, who was one of Elizabeth's closest collaborators 'in opposition', succeeded Sir Thomas Cheney as treasurer of the household and also Sir Richard Freston

---

[1] Rodríguez-Salgado and Adams, 'The Count of Feria's dispatch', pp. 321–2.
[2] Loades, *Intrigue and Treason*, pp. 309–11.

as comptroller of the household. Inevitably, Sir Henry Jerningham, who had helped so much with Mary's East Anglian coup, lost his job as master of the horse to Sir Robert Dudley, whose pro-Elizabethan dissidence had been partially purged by his service with Philip in the recent Franco-Habsburg war, but now received its reward. Unsurprisingly, in view of what was to come for the English Church, the dean of the Chapel Royal, William Hutchenson, was replaced by George Carew. The most crucial new appointment was that of Sir William Cecil, the future Lord Burghley, as secretary, but there were also major changes in the royal Council. As with the Court and household, some privy councillors survived, in fact about a third of the membership under Mary. William Paulet, marquis of Winchester, would carry on for many years as lord treasurer, Lord Clinton stayed on as lord high admiral and Sir Henry Sidney remained as lord justice of Ireland. Other councillors retained by the new Queen were the earls of Derby, Shrewsbury and Pembroke, the new chamberlain Lord William Howard, Sir John Mason, Nicholas Wotton, Sir William Petre and Archbishop Nicholas Heath of York, though the last two left shortly after-wards, Petre to retirement and Heath because of Elizabeth's religious plans. Among those removed were Sir Edward Hastings, Sir Richard Freston, and the secretary to the Council, Archdeacon John Boxall. The result was that two-thirds of Mary's Council departed, leaving a mixture of clear Protestant supporters and ten 'national Catholics', in the manner of Henry VIII. New councillors were Sir Ambrose Cave, Sir Thomas Parry and Sir Nicholas Bacon, who became lord keeper of the privy seal, although the Queen kept the Great Seal of England in her own hands.[3] Also added to the Council were William Parr, now restored as marquis of Northampton after punishment for supporting Jane Grey, Francis Russell, earl of Bedford, Sir Francis Knollys, Sir Edward Rogers and Sir Richard Sackville.[4] One of the most intriguing cases during the transition is that of William, Lord Paget. Just before Mary's death, he told the count of Feria that he wished to continue in the royal service under her successor, though he was ill with quartan fever at the time of Gómez Suárez's visit.[5] His removal from the office of lord privy seal may seem puzzling, in that he was a long-standing friend of William Cecil, but his political views and actions in Mary's reign had been somewhat self-contradictory. Once Philip was in England, Paget had spoken up for Elizabeth to him, as a 'well-willer', thus incurring the profound suspicion of Marian loyalists, and Ambassador Renard and the count of Feria suspected him for this reason almost as much as William, Lord Howard of Effingham. Despite this, Paget may have been damned in Elizabeth's eyes by his active part in securing Mary's marriage to Philip, and possibly by his conservative views on religion. In any case, he suffered from

[3] Ibid., and David Loades, *Elizabeth I* (London: Hambledon and London Books, 2003), pp. 126–7.

[4] Loades, *Elizabeth I*, p. 128.

[5] Rodríguez-Salgado and Adams, 'Count of Feria's Dispatch', p. 325.

Elizabeth's drastic reduction of the size of the Privy Council. There is subsequent evidence that he did not take kindly to enforced retirement, since in March 1559 he was still seeking office, perhaps in Wales, by writing to the influential Sir Thomas Parry.[6] In this he was unsuccessful.

Apart from their own political and religious preferences, and their personal attitudes towards the new Queen, some leading courtiers may have been influenced in part by the policy followed by Philip in England at the end of the old reign and in the beginning of the new. In November 1558, as well as taking the political temperature in the Privy Council and in the mind of 'Madama Ysabel', the count of Feria was commissioned to look into Philip's remaining personal property in England with a view to possible salvage. In his despatch, dated 14 November of that year, the count referred to 'some jewels' of which he had heard his master speak. These had apparently been given by Mary to her husband and had previously belonged to her father, Henry VIII. Feria thought that the objects in question included a dagger, and that the King wanted them to be secured in a chest. He now asked for further details of the goods involved, and in the end Philip received his property after Mary's death. A detailed list of these jewels survives in Spain's Simancas archive, and they appear to be the jewels left to Philip in Mary's will, dated 30 March 1558.[7] The collection contained ninety 'gold objects and stones and pearls and clothes which His Majesty ordered to remain in England, all in a chest which was bought in London', among them being Philip's Garter insignia.

A much more significant matter, in political terms, was the question of the annual pensions which Philip had been paying to leading Englishmen since his arrival in the country in July 1554. According to the accounts of the then Spanish treasurer-general, Domingo de Orbea, and his agent in London, Francisco de Lixalde, on 23 August of that year, after earlier approaches and suggestions from the Imperial ambassador, Simon Renard, and from William Paget, Philip had tried to secure much needed goodwill by granting such pensions to twenty-two individuals, seventeen of them members of the Privy Council, and the others, courtiers and military men. By the end of Philip and Mary's reign, there were twenty-five names on the list, again seventeen of them being councillors. Up until 1557, these pensions had been paid regularly, in six-monthly instalments, but problems arose when Philip became involved in his expensive war against France. During his visit to England in early 1558, the count of Feria reminded Philip of the arrears, having no doubt heard some grumbling in the highly sensitive period after the loss of Calais. As a result, some money was paid, notably to Lord Clinton and Lord William Howard, who had provided naval assistance during his recent campaigns

[6] Ibid., p. 315 and p. 315 nn 2, 4; Loades, *Elizabeth I*, pp. 124, 126–7, 344; David Starkey, *Elizabeth: Apprenticeship* (London: Chatto & Windus, 2000), pp. 231, 314.

[7] AGS E 811–33; Rodríguez-Salgado and Adams, 'Count of Feria's Dispatch', p. 324; Loades, *Mary Tudor*, p. 311.

against the French. However, when Feria returned to England in November 1558 the rest of the arrears had still not been paid, and he quickly decided that something must be done about this if England was not to be lost to Habsburg interests, since some of the money had been owing for eighteen months or two years. Worse, Philip's remaining skeleton household in England had not been paid since 1556. Feria, still thinking that there were hopes of keeping Elizabeth within the Habsburg fold, advised his master to settle and end the old pensions and draw up a new list, containing those who were likely to have influence in the new government, such as William Cecil, Lord Robert Dudley, the earl of Bedford and Sir Thomas Parry. He even mentioned the subject in his Brocket Hall interview with Madama Ysabel in November 1558, but unsurprisingly he received a dusty reply. At last, in March 1559, Philip was able to send Feria 60,000 ducats of Spanish cash with which he was instructed to pay existing pensions up to the end of 1558, and his remaining English household just to the end of 1557. Various detailed accounts, drawn up by Feria and Lixalde, still survive at Simancas.[8] Still evidently retaining some hopes of Elizabeth and her regime, he also gave the count full discretion to decide whether new pensions should be offered and paid in future to Englishmen, and if so whether they should be used to buy influence or else to reward Catholic loyalists. In the event, strategic aims had to give way to financial reality. A fiscal crisis in Habsburg lands meant that English pensions could not be paid from Netherlandish funds, which had all been mortgaged already, and there was no more Spanish cash to fill the gap. As the recently deceased Charles V's dream of an Anglo-Spanish-Netherlandish triangle vanished, Feria was reduced to paying Philip's long-suffering English household up to the end of 1557, as instructed, and using his permitted discretion to pay off those pensioners whom he regarded as being of greatest value or merit – Lord Paget, the marquis of Winchester, Admiral Lord Clinton, Lord William Howard, Viscount Montagu and Sir Henry Jerningham. After this, the pensions lapsed amidst a *fin-de-siècle* air among the former government.[9]

The transition to Elizabeth's regime is chronicled in some detail in the correspondence between the count of Feria and his King. Philip, having lost his father, his aunt and his wife in succession, spent the Christmas season in the monastery of Grunendal, but remained in touch with events in England as well as on the Continent. Feria reported to him on 21, 25 and 26 November, and he replied on 28 December, in at least three missives.[10] On the same day he also wrote to the new Queen, apparently in Spanish, using careful and diplomatic phrasing, apparently in an effort to secure correct, if not warm, relations with her.[11] The next day, however,

[8] AGS E 811–67, 90, 107, 118, 119, 120, 121, 122, 124, 125, 128, 130, 131, 132, 133.
[9] Rodríguez-Salgado and Adams, 'Count of Feria's Dispatch', pp. 315–17; *CODOIN*, lxxxvii, p. 173.
[10] AGS E 811–101, 102, 103.
[11] AGS E 811–14.

Feria sent a long report to Philip in which he gave a clear indication of the problems that Elizabeth would cause, both to Mary's legacy and to future Anglo-Spanish relations. He began with religious matters. On Christmas Day 1558, the bishop of Carlisle, as celebrant of the High Mass, which was still the rite used in the Chapel Royal, was told by the Queen not to elevate the Host at the consecration. Acording to Feria, 'The bishop replied that Her Majesty was lady of the person and the life, but not of the conscience' and, in response to this defiance, Elizabeth had left the chapel after the Gospel reading, 'so as to avoid the canon and the adoration of the Sacrament', something that a Catholic ruler would have been most unlikely to do. At the Mass of the Holy Innocents, on 28 December, when a more compliant celebrant omitted the elevation, the Queen had remained for the whole service. Continuing in code, Feria said that it was his great desire to give heart to English Catholics, 'so "That Woman" [Elizabeth] has problems with the wickednesses that she is beginning to do', doing as much as he could without 'breaking with her or making her annoyed with me'. He expressed the hope that Philip would take action with the Pope to prevent Mary's successor continuing with her current religious policy. He also added that he understood Paul IV to be planning to declare Elizabeth a bastard, and offer her throne to Mary, Queen of Scots. According to Feria, it was being said in London that Henry II of France had already agreed all this with the Pope some days before, and while the plan was not being put into effect, the new Queen's support in the country was growing all the time. The next section in Feria's report gives a valuable insight into the religious and political climate in England during the early days of Elizabeth's reign. In uncoded writing, he says that the English had an ancient prophecy for every occasion, and that it was now being said 'that That Woman would reign for a very short time, and that Your Majesty would return to reign here'. However, Feria, by now thoroughly disillusioned with the English, apart presumably from his new wife Jane, adds that 'the true prophecy is that this kingdom is such a friend of novelties, and That Woman is beginning to govern in such a way that it can very reasonably be expected that she will make a change every hour. And among the people it is beginning to be said that she is fickle, and as she is hitting them with [taxation] subsidies, they are becoming even more discontented.' He also points out that many of the political class, who expected jobs under Elizabeth, were disappointed because they had not been given them, while others were angry at being removed. Feria clearly wishes to convey the impression to Philip that the new regime was highly unstable and might well be short-lived.

Feria also gave Philip the London gossip about Elizabeth's religious changes and also her supposed marital prospects. He said that at vespers on Christmas Eve, the late Emperor had been duly prayed for, but the Pope was not. The count indicates that, in this service, some of Henry VIII's liturgical changes had been restored, such as the clergy saying the Lord's Prayer in English 'with the people, which is the custom of the heretics'. At Mass, some passages, including the Lord's Prayer, were now being said in English, not Latin, and the English litany of Edward VI's time had already been reprinted. Some of Elizabeth's new chaplains were married and some '*sospechosos*', this being the Spanish Inquisition's normal term for those suspected of heresy. As for the possibility of the Queen marrying, the prime candidate was thought to be Duke Adolphus, brother of the King of Denmark, there being no barrier now to a union with a Lutheran dynasty. As for Calais, Feria wrote in code that the English were wobbling about regaining the territory, something which up to then had blocked his peace talks, now at Cercamp, with France. This added to the air of uncertainty which, according to the Spanish count, surrounded Elizabeth and her court. To confirm this, and in an interesting implied comparison with the previous reign, he concluded with the news that the Queen had recently called her ladies-in-waiting together and told them to stop leaking government business.[12] Perhaps Feria felt that he was in danger of losing some of his inside sources.

The subsequent lives of Mary's most passionate supporters, who either were not trusted by Elizabeth or felt that they could not work with her, are not only interesting personal stories, but also reveal much about the future religious and political character of England. Outstanding among the loyalists of the previous regime was Jane Dormer, who had served the Queen since just before her accession, being younger than many of Mary's closest supporters. Uniquely among the English, and apparently despite strong opposition from her family, Jane married a Spaniard, the count of Feria. In the autumn of 1558, believing that she would pull through her illness, Mary had asked the couple to delay their wedding so that she could attend it, but in the event it took place after her death, on 29 December 1558. The count was kept in England until May 1559, to clear up Philip's business there, after which the couple moved first to Flanders and then to Spain, joining the Court at Valladolid. They took with them twelve monks and three lay monastic brothers from England, and quickly became supporters of those who could not stomach Elizabeth's religious changes, and settled on exile. Gómez Suárez de Figueroa and Jane were granted the titles of duke and duchess of Feria in 1567. The duke died in 1571, but the duchess lived until 1612. When the Jesuit-run English College of St Alban the Martyr was established in Valladolid in 1589, to train priests for mission work in England, Duchess Jane became one of its leading supporters. Her activity was conspicuous enough to be debated in the English House of Lords, in 1593, in part on the initiative of William Cecil, Lord Burghley. Undeterred, Jane Dormer continued to give financial support to students at the Valladolid college, and invited them to her home, much information about her being offered in a posthumous biography by one of her servants, Henry Clifford.[13] Less

[12] AGS E 811–105.
[13] Javier Burrieza Sánchez, *Valladolid: Tierra y caminos de Jesuitas: Presencia de la Compañía de Jesús en la provincia de Valladolid, 1543–1767* (Valladolid: Diputación de Valladolid, 2007), pp. 225, 264; Porter, *Mary Tudor*, p. 411; Richards, *Mary Tudor*, p. 237; Clifford, *Life of Jane Dormer*.

fortunate was Mary's former confidante Susan Clarencius, who received no government licence to travel abroad, but nonetheless accompanied Jane Dormer and her elderly grandmother to the Netherlands and then to Spain. Elizabeth and her advisers seem to have thought that Susan might return, since in October 1559 she was granted lands and wardships in Essex, but she stayed with the count and countess of Feria, dying in Spain in about 1564.[14]

Sir Francis Englefield, who had served Mary since at least 1549, and who resigned his offices at court when she died, also left England for Flanders, and then Spain, in the spring of 1559. Although she required him to resign, Elizabeth nonetheless gave him licence to go abroad on the understanding that he would return if summoned, which suggests that there was not a total rift between them. However, being loyal to the Roman Church, he feared for his safety in England and stayed abroad for the rest of his life. His estates were eventually confiscated by the Crown and given to one of the Queen's favourites, the earl of Leicester. During the 1570s and '80s, he became involved in plots against Elizabeth, and in 1593, parliament enacted a bill of attainder against him. Like Jane Dormer, he became heavily involved, after 1589, with the English College at Valladolid, but he was also politically active, becoming English secretary to Philip. With one of the Jesuit founders of the College, the noted controversialist Robert Persons, and others, he did genealogical work in an attempt to demonstrate that the true heir to the English throne, after Elizabeth, was Isabel, daughter of Philip II and his third wife, Isabelle de Valois. Not surprisingly, this and other actions, some involving the English College, led to denunciation by Elizabeth of all Catholic plotters, in Valladolid and elsewhere abroad, in 1591, and unfavourable mention of Englefield in the Lords debate of 1593. The response of Sir Francis was to become, in 1594, a benefactor of the College of St Alban, and of other English Catholic exiles. Because of threats then being made by the English government to nationals teaching or training in continental seminaries, he also asked his master, Philip of Spain, through his ambassador in Rome, to seek further physical protection for these men in general, and Robert Persons in particular. Englefield died in 1596, leaving all his goods to the English College and asking to be buried in its chapel. This was the year in which the earl of Essex's expedition attacked Cádiz and a statue of the Blessed Virgin Mary was damaged by English troops, being later brought to the chapel of the English College in Valladolid, where it remains, as the *Virgen vulnerata* ('Wounded virgin').[15]

Those clergy and laypeople who wished to continue with the Church in England as Mary left it were soon faced with a return to a slightly revised

---

[14] Porter, *Mary Tudor*, pp. 411–12.

[15] Ibid., p. 412; Burrieza, *Una isla de Inglaterra en Castilla* (Valladolid: El Real Colegio de San Albano, 2000), pp. 13–14, *Valladolid: Tierra y caminos*, pp. 222–3, 236, 264, and *Virgen de los ingleses, entre Cádiz y Valladolid: Una devoción desde las guerras de religión* (Valladolid: El Real Colegio de San Albano, Ayuntamiento de Valladolid, Ayuntamiento de Cádiz, Universidad de Valladolid, 2008).

version of Edward VI's Book of Common Prayer. Perhaps above all other
Tudor monarchs, Elizabeth gave full force to the concept of 'royal
supremacy'. The main effect of this was to make conformity, manifested
in attendance at services in the parish churches, rather than explicit
doctrinal correctness, the yardstick of true religion. The year or so after
the new Queen's succession saw an almost complete change of the bench
of bishops, as well as a large exodus from the Oxford and Cambridge
colleges, but only a minor change (about 5 per cent) in the rest of the
clergy. The Acts restoring the Royal Supremacy and the Prayer Book were
passed with ease in the Commons but only with great difficulty in the
Lords, while the parallel convocations, or assemblies, of the provinces of
Canterbury and York overwhelmingly opposed them. Observers in
Valladolid, Brussels and Rome, who had become so closely involved with
English affairs in the previous reign, were as puzzled by these developments as many in England itself. The reaction of the new Medici Pope,
Pius IV, who succeeded Mary and Pole's nemesis, Paul IV Carafa, on
Christmas Day 1559, after a delay which had lasted since 18 August, is
interesting. The lengthy conclave, which eventually chose Pius IV, no
doubt reflected both the lack of Gianpietro Carafa's guiding hand and the
turmoil in the Church which had only grown in recent years. In the
absence of any clear direction from Crown or bishops in England, and of
any ruling from the Papacy on Elizabeth's 'settlement', confusion reigned.
There was even a rumour, convenient for those of Mary's clergy who had
no wish to be removed from their posts once again, that the new Pope
would actually tolerate the Anglican liturgy as long as Elizabeth accepted
his jurisdiction in her kingdom. Some who hoped for this outcome drew
encouragement from the fact that the restored English litany now omitted
the Edwardian petition to God for deliverance from 'the tyranny of the
bysshop of Rome and al hys detestable enormities'. Others felt able to
believe that they could live with the Prayer Book because of its more
conservative features, such as the churching of women after childbirth,
and a royal injunction for the use of unleavened bread in the form of
wafers for communion. Other things which seem to have been dear to the
Queen's heart were the retention of bishops and cathedral chapters,
though in greatly reduced economic circumstances, the use of copes in the
greater churches, as well as the traditional surplice which was required
everywhere, the survival of Latin services in Oxford and Cambridge
universities, though now from the Prayer Book, and the retention of
choral foundations, which resulted in the survival of choral music in
church services, with composers such as Thomas Tallis and William Byrd
now setting English instead of Latin liturgical texts. In reality, though, as
may be expected given the explicitly reformed statements which the Book
of Common Prayer contained, notably on the Eucharist as a memorial
and not in any sense a sacrifice, such notions of conservatism and orthodoxy cut no ice in Rome. In 1562, some anxious English noblemen
managed to approach Pope Pius through the Portuguese and Spanish

ambassadors, to ask for a ruling on whether Catholics could attend Prayer Book services without sin. Some Catholics in England even seem to have thought that they might attend 'Calvin's supper', as the Anglican Eucharist was known in polemical Catholic circles. Pius was absolute in his decision. Any attendance by Catholics at Church of England services, especially Holy Communion, would indeed be a mortal sin. At about the same time, this issue was put to a committee of the Council of Trent, which had begun its third and final phase, and its decision was the same. However, for reasons which are not entirely clear but may have involved a continuing hope that Elizabeth would send bishops to the Council as well as Iberian concern for continuing good relations with England, these rulings were not published. The reigning confusion in the English parishes thus continued, with growing variations between the more conservative or 'Catholic' ones and those which were more reformed. Mary's religion, though, was not completely lost, even in England.

So what of Mary's nature and legacy? Mary still has a bad reputation, centuries after the conflicts and controversies in which she engaged. As late as 1977, Geoffrey Elton thought it just and appropriate to sum her up as 'arrogant, assertive, bigoted, stubborn, suspicious and (not to put too fine a point on it [indeed not]), rather stupid, . . . devoid of political skill, unable to compromise, set only on the wholesale reversal of a generation's history'.[16] Eleven years later, John Guy took a very similar view: 'Despite the efforts of modern historiography to boost her reputation, Mary I will never appear creative . . . [In 1558,] she was thirty-seven, tested and toughened by her experiences, pious, yet amiable and generous, she was politically self-deceived'.[17] Yet despite the difficulties of reaching into any historical character, however high and mighty, which were alluded to at the beginning of this book, a great deal has emerged about her. Not all of it will have been expected, given the traditions of biographical writing about her, even as they have been partly revised in recent years. Those who have seen her as a simple housewife at heart are in one sense not wide of the mark. One reaches a long way into Mary's character by focusing as she did, on her family – mother, father, siblings – and on her husband. Much of her life centred on all of them. Even so, she was born to sovereignty and, as the events of 1553 showed, she firmly believed that it was her destiny to rule. Her notions of the status and power of monarchy were as exalted as those of her father, and once she reached the throne she fully exercised the royal prerogative, as Henry and Edward had left it. Thus, while it is clear that one of the major problems of her life was the unwillingness of many in the sixteenth century to accept a woman as their executive sovereign, the necessary stress, in much recent work on her life, on the problems created by the fact that she was a woman should not obscure her own primary

---

[16] Geoffrey Elton, *Reform and Reformation: England, 1509–1558* (London: Edward Arnold, 1977), p. 377.

[17] Guy, *Tudor England*, pp. 226–7.

concern, which was to govern her kingdom as effectively and successfully as possible, for God and for her people, just as a man would have done. Given the highly personal nature of European monarchy during her lifetime, it was of course impossible to separate the personal from the public, and historians should not try to do so now. In particular, Philip of Spain represented for her not only married life and the prospect of motherhood, but also an epoch-making strategic alliance for England with a major European power. The deep tension which ran through Mary, typically in this period, was between the hierarchical values, with herself at the top of the tree, which she inherited as Queen, and the position as a humble lay disciple of Christ, inferior even to the lowest-ranking ordained person, which was hers as a member of the Catholic Church. The extraordinary liberties which Cardinal Pole sometimes took in his correspondence with her may have reflected this fundamental paradox, as well as the fact that they were royal relatives. Another feature of the religious mentality which Mary, in this respect at least, shared even with her bitterest Protestant opponents, and one which is unpalatable to virtually everyone who studies the matter in the twenty-first century, is her willingness, whatever her love of finery, music, dancing and even gambling, to accept that a Christian's physical body was much less important than his or her immortal soul. Such a view did not, of course, lead inevitably to a policy of violent repression, but in the turbulent circumstances of Mary's reign it is unlikely that England could have avoided the actions against religious dissenters which, at the time of her accession, were already being vigorously applied on the Continent, notably in the Netherlands, France and Spain. That Mary's policy in this respect represented a specific response to a specific problem is suggested by other evidence, which shows her to have been in every other way a kind and affectionate woman with strong familial and maternal instincts. This made her childlessness all the more tragic, but nevertheless appeared in her personal love and favours towards her servants, and particularly to the children of others.

Mary evidently took the patronage and support of her namesake, Mary the mother of Jesus, extremely seriously, and it is possible, in some respects, to 'map' her life on the hymn, or canticle, which the evangelist Luke records as the biblical response to the Archangel Gabriel's announcement that she would bear God's son (Luke 1: 46–55). The Magnificat was silently prayed at home, and said and sung in Catholic churches all over England and Europe, the Book of Common Prayer prescribed it for evensong, or Evening Prayer, and it featured prominently in the devotional books which Mary herself used. Mary indeed magnified the Lord when she became Queen in 1553, and when she married Philip in 1554. She believed that God had looked with favour on the lowliness of His servant, when He ended the years of faith and devotion which she had lived through, while she was so often excluded from the court and power, between 1536 and 1553. Although she was not to be called blessed throughout all generations, like her patron, as Queen she was constantly reminded by Cardinal Pole that God had done great things for her, by bringing her to both throne and marriage. She believed, as the Blessed Virgin said, that those who truly feared God would receive His mercy, 'from generation to generation'. In particular, she believed that the duke of Northumberland and the Greys, and Thomas Cranmer and his allies and successors in the Church, were those who had been 'brought down' by God, and that she was the 'lowly' one who had been 'lifted up' by God, to the English throne. Finally, in terms of Mary's Magnificat, she was convinced that her restored, Catholic England was the 'Israel' whom God promised to help. Nevertheless, as in most human existence, some of Mary's hopes – accession to the throne, marriage – were fulfilled, and hence were her 'joys', in terms of traditional devotion to the Blessed Virgin, but she also experienced her own 'sorrows' – childlessness, separation from her husband, a still-divided kingdom and the loss of Calais. After her death, still more of her achievements would be attacked, undermined or destroyed.

Partly in the sixteenth century and partly in more recent times, Mary's historical clothes have been stolen by Elizabeth. For many, despite some scholars' recent efforts, Mary's achievement as England's first recognized sovereign queen has been effectively usurped by her half-sister. This process was evidently under way by the time that John Foxe produced the first printed edition of his *Actes and monuments*, in 1563. He began thus the sixth volume of his mighty compilation:

> Hauing thus by the power of the allmightye plainly and truli displaied the cruell practises and horrible persecutions of quene Maryes raigne, freelye and boldlye describinge her tragicall storye . . .; and nowe orderly coming to the florishing, and long wished for reigne of the most noble, vertuous, and renowned Syster of the sayd Marye, this our drede and souereigne mistres and gouernesse Quene Elizabeth: I thought my traueled penne not a litle refreshed with ease and gladnes, not so much for that hauinge nowe ouerpassed the bitter and sorowfull matters of such terrible burning, imprisoning, murdering, famishing, racking, and tormenting, and spitefull handelinge of the pitifull bodies of Christes blessed saintes; as also for that we are now entringe into the time and reigne of such a worthy Princes[s], and Quene, the remembraunce and story wherof, ministreth not so much vnto me matter to write vpon, as also delectacion to laboure and trauaile aboute the same.[18]

Foxe would acquire a less rosy view of Elizabeth as her reign went on, but the reputation of Mary and her regime took an immediate dive in the works of political commentators and other writers of the time. By 1559, the older sister was being compared with evil and violent Old Testament women, most notably Jezebel and Athaliah (2 Kings 8, 11; 2 Chronicles 22, 23), and with Roman emperors who persecuted Christians, such as

[18] Foxe, 1563, p. 1720.

Caligula, Nero, Domitian and Diocletian, as well as the Jewish Herod who massacred the 'Holy Innocents'.[19] Mary's reign has continued to be portrayed thus in most writings and other media up to the present, notably in Shekhar Kapur's film *Elizabeth* (1998), in which it is 'defined on the basis of her childlessness. Her inner Court is represented as dark, foreign and feminine', and Kathy Burke plays the Queen herself as 'a hysterical, unattractive woman', while Cate Blanchett's Elizabeth is pretty, happy and portrayed in idyllic country settings.[20]

In view of all this, it is right that this particular account of Mary's life should end with a summary of her achievements, and not Elizabeth's. In terms of internal and external threats, Mary's reign was never tranquil. Even where open conflict did not break out, as on the Continent in 1557 and 1558, it was always latent. Even so, unlike her father and brother, she did not become involved in a major and bloody war with the neighbouring kingdom of Scotland. Conflict on the Anglo-Scottish border did arise in connection with English declaration of war against France in June 1557. On 18 July of the previous year, a formal peace among border raiders (reivers) was simultaneously declared at Carlisle and Dumfries, after a particularly serious English raid on Scottish territory earlier in the month. The pro-French policy of Marie de Guise, as regent for her daughter Mary, Queen of Scots, was unpopular with much of the Scottish political class, but nonetheless she responded to the 18 July Peace by consulting her French advisers, notably Henry II's ambassador, Henri Cleutin, seigneur d'Oysel, with a view to undermining this 'peace'. Marie's attempt, with French help, to start a full-scale war against England failed, however, and the same happened again in the summer of 1557, despite some activity then on the border, in which Scottish artillery and French troops were involved. Philip did not in any case want war between England and Scotland, and the French lost enthusiasm for such a conflict after their defeat at Saint-Quentin in August 1557. Thus there were no major English atrocities in the northern kingdom in Mary's time to match those committed in the previous two reigns, though the border was never totally peaceful.[21] While the loss of Calais was a blow to English pride, Mary's successor did nothing, apart from emitting some dramatic speech, such as threatening to have the heads of her delegates at the 'peace' conference of Cercamp and Câteau Cambrésis cut off if they failed in this respect, to regain this last possession of the English Crown on the Continent, where the point was not lost on observers. Mary, who was often compared to her patron, the Virgin

[19] Paulina Kewes, 'Two Queens, One Inventory: The Lives of Mary and Elizabeth Tudor', in *Writing Lives: Biography and Textuality, Identity and Representation in Early Modern England*, ed. Kevin Sharpe and Steven N. Zwicker (Oxford: Oxford University Press, 2008), pp. 187–207, at p. 189.

[20] Michael Dobson and Nicola Watson, *England's Elizabeth: An Afterlife in Fame and Fantasy* (Oxford: Oxford University Press, 2002), pp. 254–5.

[21] *Calendar of State Papers Scotland: Mary I*, pp. 417, 421; *APC* VI, p. 137; *CSP Span* XIII, pp. 311–12, 315–17; *RMT*, pp. 309–11.

Mary, married and tried to have children, being no 'Virgin Queen' like Elizabeth, but instead a serious dynast who, despite everything, secured a peaceful succession. In many respects, there was continuity between the Marian and Elizabethan regimes. The navy, which Henry VIII had begun to establish systematically, was further developed in Mary's reign. Philip had not been impressed with Mary's fleet when he first saw it in 1554, but reform and reorganization began immediately. Early in 1555, the keels of the *Philip and Mary* and the *Mary Rose*, a replacement for Henry VIII's lost ship of the same name, were laid down, and by June 1557 twenty royal ships were ready to assist in the war against France. Mary's navy seems to have had a competent command structure, and finance of the service was reorganized. In January 1557, the lord treasurer, the marquis of Winchester, took charge of the issue of warrants to the treasurer of the navy, Benjamin Gonson, for repairs, refurbishment, fitting, victualling and wages for seamen and workers on land. A basic annual budget of £14,000 was allocated, actually falling to £12,000 once Elizabeth had come to the throne.[22] There was also some continuity of personnel, in Court, in government, and to some extent even in the clergy, which allowed expertise to be developed continuously under the two queens. Those who had fled from England for religious reasons quickly returned when Elizabeth came to the throne, but many of them had fallen out, while abroad, over the proper ordering of churches and their worship, and they brought their conflicts back to England, with many questioning the 1559 settlement on the basis of the Book of Common Prayer. Both continuity with the Edwardian Church and continuing criticism from the Catholic and reformed margins would be features of the new reign.[23]

Yet Mary's personal and specific contributions to her country's history went well beyond institutional efficiency and continuity. When conditions for her were equal, she was an active cultural patron, who loved good music and drama, as well as commissioning the obligatory portraiture. She gave vital help to Oxford and Cambridge universities, which might otherwise have closed, and although her restoration of the link with Rome seemed to end with her death, it has never left the ecclesiastical, or even the secular, agenda. Mary's reign lasted only just over five years, and Elizabeth's about nine times as long. In this respect it is legitimate to speculate, given the count of Feria's pessimism in December 1558, not only on what the older sister would have done in a reign of that length, but also on what would have happened if Elizabeth had died of the smallpox from

---

[22] BL Cotton MS Otho E: 321 42, ix, fol. 88; T. Glasgow, Jr, 'The navy in Philip and Mary's war, 1557–8', *Mariner's Mirror*, lii (1967), pp. 23–27, and 'The maturing of Naval Administration, 1556–64', *Mariner's Mirror*, lvi (1970), pp. 3–27; Loades, *Mary Tudor*, pp. 280, 293; *RMT*, p. 239; Geoffrey Moorhouse, *Great Harry's Navy: How Henry VIII Gave England Sea Power* (London: Phoenix, [2005] 2006), pp. 298–300; BL Lansdowne MS 4, fol. 182.

[23] Haigh, *English Reformations*, pp. 195–6, 236, 238, 241; Heal, *Reformation in Britain and Ireland*, pp. 252, 332; Collinson, *From Cranmer to Sancroft*, p. 77.

which she suffered in the autumn of 1562. After nearly four years on the throne, despite having succeeded to it more peacefully and straightforwardly than any previous English ruler since Henry VI in 1422, she was beset by many problems which might easily have toppled her, given the general turbulence of those years in Europe. The question of Elizabeth's marriage, while pressing, was nowhere near resolution, her religious 'settlement' was still unstable, and she suffered just as much as her predecessor from doubts about a woman's capacity to fulfil the role of an executive sovereign, and also from the existence of rivals, above all Mary, Queen of Scots, who were still circling.[24] It is impossible to be specific about what would have happened to the English monarchy if Elizabeth had died then, but, despite all the pains and failures of Mary's life, it may be that her personal motto, first set before her by her childhood tutor, Juan Luis Vives and subsequently usurped by Elizabeth, was and is ultimately appropriate to its original possessor:

Veritas temporis filia: 'Truth is the daughter of time', or perhaps, 'The truth will out'.

[24] Starkey, *Elizabeth: Apprenticeship*, pp. 235–6; Loades, *Elizabeth I*, pp. 131–2, 140–4.

BIBLIOGRAPHY

PRIMARY SOURCES

I Manuscripts

Archivo General de Simancas, with numbers of *legajos* (bundles):
    Consejos y Juntas de Hacienda: 34.
    Diversos de Castilla: 6.
    Estado: legajos 01, 77, 98, 103, 128, 129, 376, 508, 807, 808, 811, 879, 880, 881, 8340,
        Libros de Versoza 2, 5.
    Patronato Real: 7, 53–1, 55.
Archivio segreto vaticano,
    Secretaria Stato: Inghilterra 3 (see also Tellechea, *La legación del Cardenal R. Pole*, in 'II
        Printed', below).
Biblioteca apostolica vaticana MSS (microfilm in the Knights of Columbus Vatican Film
    Library, St Louis University):
    Vatican Latin manuscripts: Vat. lat. 5869, 5967, 5968, 6754, 7042 (see also Mayer, *The
        correspondence of Reginald Pole*, in 'II Primary' sources', below).
Biblioteca Nacional de España, Madrid (Sala de Cervantes):
    MSS 1750, 9937.
Biblioteca del Palacio Real, Madrid:
    MSS II–2251, II–2286.
Biblioteca Real de San Lorenzo del Escorial:
    MSS V.II.3, V.II.4.
British Library [BL]
MSS
    Additional 17012, 34320.
    Cotton: Otho C.V; C.X, E.321–42; Titus B ii, Vespasian D.XVIII, F.III.23; Vitellius,
        C.1, C.2.
    Egerton 616.
    Harleian 444, 787, 1703, 3504, 5087, 6949.
    Lansdowne 4, 1236.
    Royal 12.A.xx, 16.C, 17.C.
    Stowe 571.
College of Arms
    MSS 1, 7, WB.
Corpus Christi College, Cambridge, Parker Library:
    MS 418.
Inner Temple: Petyt MSS IV, 538/47, XLVI.
Real Academia de la Historia, Madrid: Colección Salazar y Castro [SyC]
    MS A–48.
Trinity College Cambridge, Wren Library: C.17.25.
Winchester College Muniments Room:
    MSS 22210, 22211 (Domus, or Bursar's, accounts), vols II, III, 22992 *Liber albus*.

II Printed

Acts of the Privy Council [APC], vols IV–VII (1552–8), ed. John Roche Dasent (London: HMSO, 1891–2).

Allen, P. S., and H. M. Allen, eds, *Letters of Richard Fox, 1486–1527* (Oxford: Clarendon Press, 1929).

Álvarez, Vicente, *Relation du beau voyage que fit aux Pays-Bas en 1548 le Prince Philippe d'Espagne*, ed. M.-T. Dovillée (Brussels: n.p., 1964).

Anon., *Certayne questions demanded and asked by the noble Realme of Englande, of her true natural chyldren and Subiectes of the same* (Zurich?, 1555).

Anon. [Italian], *Coronación de la inclita y serenissima reyna María de Inglaterra*, anonymous Spanish translation (Medina del Campo: Matheo y Francisco del Canto, 1554), in Garnett, ed., *The Accession of Queen Mary*, pp. 69–75, English trans., pp. 117–23.

Anon., *A diary of events regarding [. . .] the rebellion of Thomas Wyatt*, ed. C. V. Malfatti, in *The Accession, Coronation and Marriage of Mary Tudor as Related in Four Manuscripts of the Escorial* (Barcelona: Sociedad Alianza de Artes Gráficas and Ricardo Fontà, 1956).

Anon., *A glasse of the truthe* (London: Thomas Berthelet, 1532).

Archer, Ian W., et al., eds, *Religion, Politics and Society in Sixteenth-Century England*, Camden Society, 5th series, xxii (2003).

Barahona [Varaona], Juan de, *Viaje de Felipe II a Inglaterra en 1554 cuando fue a casar con la Reina doña María*, ed. Martín Fernández Navarrete, Miguel Salva and Pedro Sanz de Baranda, in *Colección de documentos inéditos para la historia de España [CODOIN]*, i (Madrid: Imprenta de la Viuda de Calero, 1842), pp. 564–74, trans. in *Accession*, ed. Malfatti, pp. 79–89.

Bedouelle, G., and F. Le Gal, eds, *Le Divorce du roi Henri VIII* (Geneva: Librairie Droz, 1987).

Cabrera de Córdoba, Luis, *Felipe Segundo, rey de España*, 4 vols (Madrid: Real Academia de la Historia, 1874–6).

Calderón de la Barca, Pedro, *La Cisma de Inglaterra [The Schism of England]*, trans. Kenneth Muir and Ann L. Mackenzie (Warminster: Aris & Phillips, 1990).

Calendar of State Papers Domestic series of the reign of Mary I, 1553–1558, preserved in the Public Record Office, revised edn, ed. C. S. Knighton (London: Public Record Office, 1998).

Calendar of State Papers, Scotland: Mary, ed. J. Bain and others (London: HMSO, 1861), vol. I.

Calendar of State Papers, Spanish, I, ed. G. A. Bergenroth (London: Longman & Co., 1862); vol. IX, ed. Martin A. S. Hume and Royall Tyler (London: HMSO, 1912); vols X–XIII, ed. Royall Tyler (London: HMSO, 1914–54).

Calendar of State Papers, Venetian, vols II, III, IV, VI, ed. Rawson Brown (London: HMSO, 1867–81).

Calendar of the Patent Rolls preserved in the Public Record Office, Edward VI, ed. H. C. Maxwell Lyle, 6 vols (London: HMSO, 1924–9).

Calvete de Estrella, Juan Christóval, *El felicissimo viaje del muy alto y muy poderoso Príncipe Don Phelippe [. . .]. .*[Antwerp, 1552], ed., with five studies by various authors, Paloma Cuenca (Madrid: Sociedad Estatal para la Conmemoración de los Centenarios de Felipe II y Carlos V, 2001).

Carranza de Miranda, Bartolomé, *Comentarios sobre el catechismo christiano*, ed. José Ignacio Tellechea Idígoras, 2 vols (Madrid: Biblioteca de Autores Cristianos, 1972).

—— *Speculum pastorum: Hierarchia ecclesiastica in qua describuntur officia ministrorum Ecclesiae militantis* (Salamanca: Universidad Pontificia de Salamanca, 1992).

Castro, Alfonso de, *De iusta haereticorum punitione, libri III* (Salamanca, 1547; Venice, 1549).

Chrimes, S. B., and A. L. Brown, eds, *Select documents of English constitutional history, 1307–1485* (London: A & C Black, 1961).

Christopherson, John, *An exhortation to all menne to take heed against rebellion* (London, 1554).

Chronicle of Queen Jane and of the first two years of Queen Mary, The, ed. J. G. Nichols (London: Camden Society, xlvii, 1850).

Chronicle of the Grey Friars of London, ed. J. G. Nichols (London: Camden Society, 1st or old series, 1851).

Clifford, Henry, *The life of Jane Dormer, Duchess of Feria*, ed. J. Stevenson (London: Burns and Oates, 1887).

Colección de documentos inéditos para la historia de España, ed. M. F. Navarrete and others, 112 vols (Madrid: various publishers, 1842–95), vols I, III, LXXXVII.

Commendone, Giovanni Francesco, *Successi delle attione del Regno d'Inghilterra incominciando del Re Edoardo VI, fine al sponsalitio seguito tra il Ser[enissi]mo Principe Philippo di Spagna e la Ser[enissi]ma Reina Maria* [Escorial MS X–III, fols 133–240], in *Accession*, ed. Malfatti.

Crowley, Robert, *An epitome of chronicles . . . continued to the reign of Queen Elizabeth . . .* (London: 1555).

Díaz Plaja, F., *La historia de España en sus documentos. El siglo XVI* (Madrid: Instituto de Estudios Políticos, 1958).

Elder, John, 'Letter describing the arrival and marriage of King Philip, his triumphal entry into London, [. . .] the legation of Cardinal Pole, etc. (London, 1 January 1555)', in *The Chronicle of Queen Jane*, ed. Nichols, appendix, pp. 139–40 [also in Loades, *Chronicles of the Tudor Queens*, pp. 42–4].

Ellis, Henry, *Original letters illustrative of English history*, 3 vols (London: Harking, Tiphook and Lepard, 1824–46).

Elyote, Sir Thomas, *The Book Named the Governor*, ed. S. E. Lehmberg (London: Dent, 1962).

English Historical Documents, v, *1485–1558*, ed. C. H. Williams (London: Eyre & Spottiswoode, 1967).

Epistolario del III duque de Alba, Don Fernando Álvarez de Toledo, 3 vols (Madrid: Real Academia de la Historia, 1952).

Eymerich, Nicolau, *Le manuel de l'Inquisiteur*, ed. and trans. Louis Sala-Molins (Paris: Mouton, 1973).

Fernández Álvarez, Manuel, ed., *Corpus documental de Carlos V*, 5 vols (Salamanca: Ediciones Universidad de Salamanca, 1970).

First and Second Prayer Books of Edward VI, The (London: The Prayer Book Society, 1999).

Florio, Michelangelo, *Historia de la vita e de la morte de l'Illustrissima Signora Giovanna Graia* (Middelburg, 1607).

Foxe, John, *Actes and monuments of these latter and perillous dayes . . . commonly known as Book of Martyrs* (London: John Day, 1563, 1570, 1576, 1583): [www.hrionline.ac.uk/johnfoxe/]

Garnett, Richard, *The accession of Queen Mary, being the contemporary narrative of Antonio de Guaras, a Spanish merchant resident in London [. . .]* (London: Lawrence and Bullen, 1892).

Grey, A., *A Commentary on the Services and Charges of Lord Grey of Wilton* (London: Camden Society, xl, 1840).

Guaras, Antonio de, *Relación muy verdadera de Antonio de Guaras criado de la Serenissima y Catholica reyna de Inglaterra [. . .] como doña María fue proclamada por Reyna, y de todos obedescida, y de su coronación, etc.*, in Garnett, ed., *The accession of Queen Mary [. . .]* (London: Lawrence and Bullen, 1892), pp. 33–75.

Gui, Bernard, *Manuel de l'Inquisiteur*, ed. and trans. G. Mollat, 2 vols (Paris: Société d'Éditions 'Les Belles Lettres', 1964).

Hall, Edward, *The union of the two noble and ilustre famelies of Lancaster and York*, ed. Henry Ellis (London: J. Johnson and others, 1809).

Harleian Miscellany: a collection of scarce, curious, and entertaining pamphlets and tracts [. . .]. Selected from the library of Edward Harley, Second Earl of Oxford [. . .], 10 vols (London: Printed for John White, and John Murray, Fleet-Street, and John Harding, St James's-Street, 1808–13).

Haynes, Samuel, ed., *A collection of state papers . . . left by William Cecil, Lord Burghley* (London: William Bowyer, 1740).

Hearne, Thomas, *Sylloge epistolarum*, in Titus Livius, *Vita Henrici Quinti* (Oxford: Sheldonian Theatre, 1716).

Heywood, John, *A balade specifienge partly the maner, partly the matter, in the most excellent meeting and lyke mariage betwene our Soueraigne Lord and our Soueraigne Lady, the Kynges and Queenes highnes. Pende by John Haywood* (London: William Rydell, 1554).

——, *A breefe balet [ballad] touching the traytorous takynge of Scarborow Castel* (London: Thomas Powell, 1577).

Hogarde [Huggard], Miles, *The assault of the sacrame[n]t of the altar* (London, 1554).

—— *A treatise entitled the Pathwaye to the towre of perfection* (London, 1554).

Hughes, P. L., and J. F. Larkin, *Tudor Royal Proclamations*, 2 vols (New Haven, CT and London: Yale University Press, 1964–9).

Kingsford, C. L., ed., *The First English Life of King Henry the Fifth* (Oxford: Clarendon Press, 1911).

Letters and Papers: Foreign and Domestic: Henry VIII [LP], vol. I, 2nd edn, ed. R. H. Brodie (London: HMSO, 1920): vols III parts 1–2, IV parts 1–4, ed. J. S. Brewer (London: HMSO, 1867–76), vols VI–XIII, ed. James Gairdner (London: HMSO, 1886–93).

Letters of denization and acts of naturalization for Aliens in England, 1509–1603 (Lymington: Publications of the Huguenot Society of England, 1893).

Loades, David, ed., *The Chronicles of the Tudor Queens* (Stroud: Sutton, 2002).

Machyn, Henry, *The diary of Henry Machyn, citizen and Merchant-Taylor of London, from A.D. 1550 to A.D. 1563*, ed. J. G. Nichols (London: Camden Society, old series, xlii, 1848).

Madden, F., ed., 'The petition of Richard Troughton', *Archaeologia*, xxii (1831), pp. 18–49.

—— *The Privy Purse expenses of Princess Mary, daughter of King Henry VIII* (London: William Pickering, 1831).

Malfatti, C. V., ed., *The Accession, Coronation and Marriage of Mary Tudor as Related by Four Manuscripts of the Escorial* (Barcelona: Sociedad Alianza de Artes Gráficas and Ricardo Fontá, 1956).

Martin, Thomas, *A traictaise declaring and plainly prouying that the pretensed marriage of priestes, and professed persons, is no marriage [. . .]* (London, 1554).

Mayer, Thomas F., ed., *The Correspondence of Reginald Pole [CRP]*, 4 vols (Aldershot: Ashgate, 2002–8). (*A calendar*, i, *1514–1546*, ii, *1547–1554*, iii, *1555–1558*, iv [with Courtney B. Walters], *A biographical companion: the British Isles*).

Muñoz, Andrés, *Viaje de Felipe Segundo a Inglaterra*, ed. Pascual de Gayangos (Madrid: Sociedad de Bibliófilos Españoles, xv, 1877).

North, Jonathan, ed., *England's Boy King: The Diary of Edward VI, 1547–1553* (Welwyn Garden City: Ravenhall Books, 2005); also in *Literary remains of Edward the Sixth*, ed. J. G. Nichols, 2 vols (London: The Roxburghe Club, 1857–8).

Palencia, Alfonso de, *Crónica de Enrique IV, Guerra de Granada*, ed. and trans. Antonio Paz y Melia, *Biblioteca de Autores Españoles*, vols cclvii, cclviii, cclxvii (Madrid: Editorial Atlas, 1973–5).

—— *Cuarta década de Alfonso de Palencia*, ed. and trans. José López de Toro, 2 vols (Madrid: Real Academia de la Historia, 1970–4).

Pollard, A. F., *Tudor tracts* (London: Archibald Constable, 1903).

Proctor, John, *The historie of wyattes rebellion, with the order and manner of resisting the same* (London, 1554).

Respublica [attr. Nicholas Udall], ed. W. W. Greg (London: Early English Text Society, old series, ccxxvi, 1952).

Rodríguez Montalvo, Garci, *Amadís de Gaula*, Books 1–4, ed. Juan Manuel Cacho Blecua, 2 vols (Madrid: Cátedra, 1987–8).

Rodríguez-Salgado, M. J., and Simon Adams, 'The count of Feria's dispatch to Philip II of 14 November 1558', *Camden Miscellany*, xxviii (London: Royal Historical Society, 1984), pp. 302–44.

Rollins, Hyder E., ed., *Old English Ballads, 1553–1625, Chiefly from the Manuscripts* (Cambridge: Cambridge University Press, 1920).

Rymer, Thomas, and others, *Foedera*, etc. (Hagae Comites [The Hague], 1641–1713), vols xiii, xv.

Spalding, James C., *The Reformation of the ecclesiastical laws of England, 1552* (Kirksville MO), *Sixteenth Century Studies*, xix.

Statutes of the Realm, ed. A. Luders and others, 11 vols (1810–28; Dobbs Ferry: Transmedia Publishing Co., 1972).

Strype, John, *Ecclesiastical Memorials Relating Chiefly to Religion and its Reformation under the Reign of King Henry VIII, King Edward VI and Queen Mary*, iii, pt 2 (Oxford: Clarendon Press, 1716).

Tanner, Norman P., *Heresy Trials in the Diocese of Norwich, 1428–31* (London: Camden Society, 4th series xx (London: Royal Historical Society, 1977)).

Tellechea Idígoras, José Ignacio, ed., 'El formulario de visita pastoral de Bartolomé Carranza, arzobispo de Toledo', in Tellechea, *CyP*, pp. 303–51.

—— *El Papado y Felipe II*, 3 vols (Madrid: Fundación Universitaria Española, 1999–2002).

—— *Fray Bartolomé Carranza: documentos históricos*, 7 vols (Madrid: Real Academia de la Historia, 1962–94).

—— *La legación del Cardenal R. Pole (1553–54). Cuando Inglaterra volvió a ser católica* (Salamanca: Centro de Estudios Orientales y Ecuménicos 'Juan XXIII', 2002).

—— 'Un tratadito de Bartolomé Carranza sobre la Misa', *Archivio Italiano per l'Historia della Pietà*, xi (1998), pp. 145–79.

Vertot, René Aubert de, *Ambassades de Messieurs de Noailles en Angleterre*, 5 vols (Leiden: Chez Dessaint et Saillant, Durand, and others, 1763).

Wingfield, Robert, 'The *Vita Mariae Angliae* of Robert Wingfield of Brantham', ed. and trans. Diarmaid MacCulloch, *Camden Miscellany*, 4th series, xxviii (London: Royal Historical Society, 1984), pp. 181–301.

Wriothesley, C., *A Chronicle during the Reigns of the Tudors from 1485 to 1559, by Charles Wriothesley, Windsor Herald*, ed. W. D. Hamilton, 2 vols (London: Camden Society, 2nd or new series, xi, 1875–7).

SECONDARY SOURCES

Aguirre Rincón, Soterraña, 'La música de la época de Isabel la Católica'; la Casa Real como paradigma', in *Arte y cultura en la época de Isabel la Católica*, ed. Julio Valdeón Baruque (Valladolid: Ámbito Ediciones, 2003), pp. 281–321.

Alcalá, Ángel, and Jácobo Sanz, *Vida y muerte del príncipe don Juan: Historia y literatura* (Valladolid: Junta de Castilla y León, 1999).

Alexander, Gina, 'Bonner and the Marian Persecution', in Haigh, *The English Reformation Revised*, pp. 157–75.

Alford, Stephen, *Burghley: William Cecil at the Court of Elizabeth I* (New Haven, CT and London: Yale University Press, 2008).

—— *Kingship and Politics in the Reign of Edward VI* (Cambridge: Cambridge University Press, 2002).

Alsop, J. D., 'A regime at sea: the navy and the 1553 succession crisis', *Albion*, xxiv (1992), pp. 577–90.

Anglo, S., *Spectacle, Pageantry and Early Tudor Policy* (Oxford: Clarendon Press, 1969).

Aram, Bethany, *La reina Juana: Gobierno, piedad y dinastía* (Madrid: Marcial Pons Ediciones de Historia, 2001).

Arnold, Janet, ed., *Queen Elizabeth's Wardrobe Unlock'd* (Leeds: W.S. Maney & Son, 1988).

Azcona, Tarsicio de, *Isabel la Católica: Estudio crítico de su vida y su reinado*, 3rd edn (Madrid: Biblioteca de Autores Cristianos, 1993).

—— *Juana de Castilla, mal llamada La Beltraneja* (Madrid: Fundación Universitaria Española, 1998).

Bascher, Armand, 'List of the French ambassadors in England', in *Report of the Deputy Keeper of the Public Records* (London: HMSO, 1876).

Baskerville, E. J., *A Chronological Bibliography of Propaganda and Polemic between 1553 and 1558* (Philadephia, PA: American Philosophical Society, 1979).

Baumgartner, Frederic J., *Henry II, King of France (1547–1559)* (Durham, NC and London: Duke University Press, 1988).

Benito Ruano, Eloy, *Gente del siglo XV* (Madrid: Real Academia de la Historia, 1998).

Benson, Pamela Joseph, 'The new ideal in England: Thomas More, Juan Luis Vives and Richard Hyrde', in Pamela Joseph Benson, *The Invention of the Renaissance Woman: The Challenge of Female Independence in the Literature and Thought of Italy and England* (University Park, PA: Pennsylvania State University Press, 1992), pp. 157–81.

Bernard, G. W., *The King's Reformation: Henry VIII and the Remaking of the English Church* (New Haven, CT and London: Yale University Press, 2005).

——, and S. J. Gunn, *Authority and Consent in Tudor England: Essays Presented to C. S. L. Davies* (Aldershot: Ashgate, 2002).

Betteridge, Thomas, 'Staging Reformation Authority: John Bale's *King Johan* and Nicholas Udall's *Respublica*', *Reformation and Renaissance Review*, iii (2000), pp. 34–58.

—— *Tudor Histories of the English Reformation, 1530–83* (Aldershot: Ashgate, 1999).

Biddle, Martin, and others, eds, *King Arthur's Round Table: An Archaeological Investigation* (Woodbridge: The Boydell Press, 2000).

Bindoff, S. T., 'A kingdom at stake, 1553', *History Today*, iii (1953), pp. 642–8.

—— *Tudor England* (Harmondsworth: Penguin Books, 1950).

Boyle, Andrew, 'Hans Eworth's Portrait of the Earl of Arundel and the Politics of 1549–50', *English Historical Review*, cxvii (2002), pp. 25–47.

Braddock, R. C., 'The Character and Composition of the Duke of Northumberland's Army', *Albion*, vi (1974), pp. 13–17.

—— 'The Duke of Northumberland's Army Reconsidered', *Albion*, xix (1987), pp. 13–17.

Brady, C., *The Chief Governors: The Rise and Fall of Reform in Tudor Ireland* (Cambridge: Cambridge University Press, 1994).

Brigden, Susan, 'Youth and the English Reformation', *Past and Present*, xcv (1992), pp. 37–67.

Brown, Keith Duncan, 'The Franciscan Observants in England, 1482–1559', D.Phil. thesis, University of Oxford, 1986.

Burnet, Gilbert, *The History of the Reformation of the Church of England* (London: W. S. Orr, 1850).

Burrieza Sánchez, Javier, *Una isla de Inglaterra en Castilla* (Valladolid: El Real Colegio de San Albano, 2000).

—— *Valladolid. Tierra y caminos de jesuitas. Presencia de la Compañía de Jesús en la provincia de Valladolid 1543–1767* (Valladolid: Diputación de Valladolid, 2007).

—— *Virgen de los ingleses, entre Cádiz y Valladolid. Una devoción desde las guerras de religión* (Valladolid: El Real Colegio de San Albano, Ayuntamiento de Cádiz, Ayuntamiento de Valladolid, 2008).

Bush, M. L., *The Pilgrimage of Grace* (Manchester: Manchester University Press, 1996).

Cadden, Joan, *Meanings of Sex Difference in the Middle Ages: Medicine, Science and Culture* (Cambridge: Cambridge University Press, 1993).

Cárdenas y Vicent, Vicente de, *El Saco de Roma de 1527 por el ejército de Carlos V* (Madrid: Revista *Hidalguía* and Consejo Superior de Investigaciones Científicas, 1974).

Carley, James, *The Books of Henry VIII and his Wives* (London: British Library, 2004).

Chambers, D. S., *Popes, Cardinals and War: The Military Church in Renaissance and Early Modern Europe* (London and New York: I. B. Tauris, 2006).

Childs, Wendy R., *Anglo-Castilian Trade in the Late Middle Ages* (Manchester: Manchester University Press, 1978).

Chrimes, S. B., *Henry VII*, 2nd edn (New Haven, CT and London: Yale University Press, [1972] 1999).

Cocke, Thomas, and Donald Buttress, *900 Years: The Restoration of Westminster Abbey* (London: Harvey Miller, 1995).

Collinson, Patrick, *From Cranmer to Sancroft* (London: Hambledon Continuum, 2006).

—— *The Birthpangs of Protestant England: Religious and Cultural Change in the Sixteenth and Seventeenth Centuries* (Basingstoke: Macmillan, 1988).

—— 'The Persecution in Kent', in *CMT*, pp. 309–33.

Coward, Barry, *The Stanleys: Lords Stanley and Earls of Derby, 1385–1672* (Manchester: Manchester University Press for the Cheetham Society, 1983).

Cross, Claire, 'The English Universities, 1553–58', in *CMT*, pp. 57–76.

Cunich, Peter, 'Benedictine Monks at the University of Oxford and the Dissolution of the Monasteries', in Wansborough and Marett-Crosby, *Benedictines in Oxford*, pp. 155–82.

Davies, C. S. L., 'England and the French War, 1557–9', in *The Mid-Tudor Polity, c.1540–1560*, ed. Jennifer Loach and Robert Tittler (London: Macmillan, 1980), pp. 159–85.

—— *Peace, Print and Protestantism, 1450–1558* (Frogmore: Paladin, [1976] 1977).

—— 'The Pilgrimage of Grace Reconsidered', *Past and Present*, xli (1968), pp. 54–76, reprinted in *Popular Protest and the Social Order in Early Modern England*, ed. Paul Slack (Cambridge: Cambridge University Press, 1984), pp. 16–36.

Denford, Geoff, and Karen Parker, *The Westgate, Winchester, Medieval to Modern Times* (Winchester: Winchester City Council, 2005).

Dickens, A. G., 'Robert Parkyn's Narrative of the Reformation', *English Historical Review*, lxii (1947), pp. 58–83 [= Dickens, *Reformation Studies* (London: Hambledon, 1982), pp. 287–312.]

Dobson, Michael, and Nicola Watson, *England's Elizabeth. An Afterlife in Fame and Fantasy* (Oxford: Oxford University Press, 2002).

Doran, Susan, ed., *Henry VIII: Man and Monarch* (London: British Library, 2009).

Doran, Susan, and Thomas Freeman, eds, *Mary Tudor: Old and New Perspectives* (Basingstoke: Palgrave Macmillan, forthcoming).

Dowling, Maria, *Fisher of Men: A Life of John Fisher* (Basingstoke: Macmillan, 1999).

—— *Humanism in the Age of Henry VIII* (London: Croom Helm, 1987).

Duffy, Eamon, 'Cardinal Pole's Preaching: St Andrew's Day 1557', in *CMT*, pp. 176–200.

—— *Fires of Faith: Catholic England under Mary Tudor* (New Haven, CT and London: Yale University Press, 2009).

—— *Marking the Hours. English People and their Prayers, 1240–1570* (New Haven, CT and London: Yale University Press, 2006).

—— 'Rolling back the Reformation', *London Review of Books*, 7 February 2008, pp. 27–9.

—— *The Stripping of the Altars: Traditional Religion in England, 1400–1580*, 2nd edn (New Haven, CT and London: Yale University Press, 2005).

—— *The Voices of Morebath: Reformation and Rebellion in an English Village* (New Haven, CT and London: Yale University Press, 2001).

Duffy, Eamon, and David Loades, eds, *The Church of Mary Tudor* (Aldershot: Ashgate, 2006).

Durme, M. van, *El cardenal Granvela (1517–1586): Imperio y revolución bajo Carlos V y Felipe II*, 2nd edn (Barcelona: Editorial Teide, 1957).

Earenfight, Theresa, ed., *Queenship and Political Power in Medieval and Early Modern Spain* (Aldershot: Ashgate, 2005).

Echevarria, Ana, *Catalina de Lancaster, reina regenta de Castilla (1372–1418)* (Hondarribia: Editorial Neres, 2002).

Edwards, John, 'A Spanish Inquisition? The repression of Protestantism under Mary Tudor', *Reformation and Renaissance Review*, iv (2000), pp. 62–74.

—— 'Bartolomé Carranza de Miranda's "Little treatise on how to attend Mass (1555)"', *Reformation and Renaissance Review*, xi, i (2009 [2010]), pp. 91–120.

—— 'Corpus Christi at Kingston upon Thames: Bartolomé Carranza and the Eucharist in Marian England', in *RCMT*, pp. 139–51.

—— *Ferdinand and Isabella* (Harlow: Pearson Longman, 2005).

—— *Inquisition* (Stroud: The History Press, [1999] 2009).

—— 'Spanish Religious Influence in Marian England', in *CMT*, pp. 201–24.

—— *The Inquisitors: The Story of the Grand Inquisitors of the Spanish Inquisition* (Stroud: Tempus, 2007).

—— *The Spain of the Catholic Monarchs, 1474–1520* (Oxford: Blackwell, 2000).

Edwards, John, and Ronald Truman, eds, *Reforming Catholicism in the England of Mary Tudor: The Achievement of Friar Bartolomé Carranza* (Aldershot: Ashgate, 2005).

Elston, Timothy G., 'Widowed Princess or Neglected Queen? Catherine of Aragon, Henry VIII and English Public Opinion, 1533–1536', in *Queens and Power in Medieval and Early Modern England*, ed. Carole Levin and Robert Bucholz (Lincoln, NB and London: University of Nebraska Press, 2009), pp. 16–30.

Elton, Geoffrey, *Reform and Reformation: England, 1509–1558* (London: Edward Arnold, 1977).

Erickson, Carolly, *Bloody Mary: The Life of Mary Tudor* (London: Robson Books, 2001).

Evenden, Elizabeth, *Patents, Pictures and Patronage: John Day and the Tudor Book Trade* (Aldershot: Ashgate, 2008).

Fenlon, Dermot, 'Pole, Carranza and the Pulpit', in *RCMT*, pp. 81–97.

Fernández de Córdova Miralles, Alfonso, *Alejandro VI y los Reyes Católicos: Relaciones político-eclesiásticas (1492–1503)* (Rome: Edizioni Università della Santa Croce, 2005).

Ferreira Priegue, Elisa María, 'El papel de Galicia en la redistribución de productos andaluces vistos a través de los archivos ingleses', in *Actas del II Coloquio de Historia Medieval Andaluza, Hacienda y Comercio* (Seville: Publicaciones de la Excma Diputación de Sevilla, 1982), pp. 241–7.

Franklin, R. William ed., *Anglican Orders: Essays on the Centenary of* Apostolicae Curae, *1896–1996* (London: Mowbray, 1996).

Gammon, S. R., *Statesman and Schemer: William, First Lord Paget of Beaudesert* (London: David & Charles, 1973).

García, Angelina, *Els Vives: Una familia de jueus valencians* (Valencia: Eliseu Climent Editor, 1987).

Glasgow, T., Jr, 'The Maturing of Naval Administration, 1556–64', *Mariner's Mirror*, lvi (1970), pp. 3–27.

—— 'The Navy in Philip and Mary's War, 1557–8', *Mariner's Mirror*, lii (1967), pp. 23–7.

Gómez-Salvago Sánchez, Mónica, *Fastos de una boda real en la Sevilla del Quinientos (Estudio y documentos)* (Seville: Universidad de Sevilla, 1998).

González de Amezúa, Agustín, *Isabel de Valois, reina de España (1546–1568)*, 3 vols in 5 'tomes' (Madrid: Gráfica Ultra, 1949).

Gordon, Bruce, *Calvin* (New Haven, CT and London: Yale University Press, 2009).

Gregory, Brad S., *Salvation at Stake: Christian Martyrdom in Early Modern Europe* (Cambridge, MA: Harvard University Press, 1999).

Gregory, Philippa, *The Constant Princess* (New York: Simon & Schuster, 2006).

Groot, Wim de, ed., *The Seventh Window: The King's Window Donated by Philip II and Mary Tudor to Sint Janskerk in Gouda(1557)* (Hilversum, North Holland: Verloren, 2005).

Gunn, S. J., 'A Letter of Jane, Duchess of Northumberland, in 1553', *English Historical Review*, cxiv (1999), pp. 1267–71.

—— *Charles Brandon, Duke of Suffolk, c.1484–1545* (Oxford: Basil Blackwell, 1988).

—— *Early Tudor Government, 1485–1558* (Basingstoke: Macmillan, 1995).

Gunn, Steven, and Linda Monckton, eds, *Arthur Tudor, Prince of Wales: Life, Death and Commemoration* (Woodbridge: The Boydell Press, 2009).

Guy, John, *A Daughter's Love: Thomas and Margaret More* (London: Fourth Estate, 2008).

—— *Tudor England* (Oxford: Oxford University Press, 1988).

Haigh, Christopher, *English Reformations: Religion, Politics, and Society under the Tudors* (Oxford: Clarendon Press, 1993).

——, ed., *The English Reformation Revised* (Cambridge: Cambridge University Press, 1987).

Harbison, E. Harris, *Rival Ambassadors at the Court of Queen Mary* (Princeton, NJ: Princeton University Press, 1940).

Harris, Barbara J., *English Aristocratic Women, 1450–1550* (Oxford: Oxford University Press, 2002).

Heal, Felicity, *Reformation in Britain and Ireland* (Oxford: Clarendon Press, 2003).

Hegarty, Andrew, 'Carranza and the English Universities', in *RCMT*, pp. 153–72.

Hickerson, Megan L., *Making Women Martyrs in Tudor England* (Basingstoke: Palgrave Macmillan, 2005).

Hillgarth, J. N., *The Spanish Kingdoms, 1250–1516*, ii, *1250–1410: Precarious Balance* (Oxford: Clarendon Press, 1976).

Himsworth, Sheila, 'The Marriage of Philip II of Spain with Mary Tudor', *Proceedings of the Hampshire Field Club*, xxi (1962), pp. 82–100.

Hoak, D. E., *The King's Council in the Reign of Edward VI* (Cambridge: Cambridge University Press, 1976).

—— 'Two Revolutions in Tudor government. The formation and organisation of Mary's Privy Council', in *Revolution Reassessed*, ed. C. Coleman and D. Starkey (Cambridge: Cambridge University Press, 1986), pp. 87–115.

Hoyle, R. W., *The Pilgrimage of Grace and the Politics of the 1530s* (Oxford: Oxford University Press, 2001).

Hutchings, Michael, *Reginald, Cardinal Pole, 1500–1558: The last* [Catholic] *Archbishop of Canterbury* (Midhurst, UK: The Saint Joan Press, 2008).

Hutton, Ronald, 'The local impact of the Tudor Reformation', in Haigh, ed., *The English Reformation Revised*, pp. 114–38.

Ives, Eric, *Anne Boleyn* (Oxford: Oxford University Press, 1986).

—— *Lady Jane Grey: A Tudor mystery* (Malden, MA and Oxford: Wiley–Blackwell, 2009).

—— *The Life and Death of Anne Boleyn* (Oxford: Blackwell [2004] 2005).

Jack, Sybil M., 'Northumberland, Queen Jane, and the Financing of the 1553 Coup', *Parergon*, n.s., 6 (1988), pp. 137–48.

James, Susan, *Catherine Parr: Henry VIII's Last Queen* (Stroud: The History Press, 2008).

Jansen, Sharon L., *Dangerous Talk and Strange Behaviour: Women and Popular Resistance to the Reforms of Henry VIII* (Basingstoke: Macmillan, 1996).

—— *The Monstrous Regiment of Women: Female Rulers in Early Modern Europe* (New York and Basingstoke: Palgrave Macmillan, 2002).

Jones, Edwin, *The English Nation: The Great Myth* (Stroud: Sutton, 1998).

Jones, Norman, *The English Reformation: Religion and Cultural Adaptation* (Oxford: Blackwell, 2002).

Jordan, W. K., *Edward VI, the Young King: The Protectorship of the Duke of Somerset* (London: Allen & Unwin, 1968).

Kamen, Henry, *Philip of Spain* (New Haven, CT and London: Yale University Press, 1997).

Kantorowitz, E. M., *The King's Two Bodies: A Study of Medieval Political Theology* (Princeton, NJ: Princeton University Press, 1957).

Katz, David S., *The Jews in the History of England, 1485–1850* (Oxford: Oxford University Press, 1994).

Kelly, H. A., *The Matrimonial Trials of Henry VIII* (Stanford, CA: Stanford University Press, [1976] 2004).

Kelso, Ruth, *Doctrine for the Lady of the Renaissance* (Urbana IL: University of Illinois Press, 1956).

Kewes, Paulina, 'Two Queens, one Inventory: The Lives of Mary and Elizabeth Tudor', in *Writing Lives: Biography and Textuality, Identity and Representation in Early Modern England*, ed. Kevin Sharpe and Steven N. Zwicker (Oxford: Oxford University Press, 2008), pp. 187–207.

Keynes, Milo, 'The Aching Head and Increasing Blindness of Queen Mary I', *Journal of Medical Biography*, viii (2000), pp. 102–9.

Kim, Hyun-Ah, *Humanism and the Reform of Sacred Music in Early Modern England: John Merbecke the Orator and* The Book of Common Praier *noted* (1550) (Aldershot: Ashgate, 2008).

Kirby, J. L., *Henry IV of England: A Biography* (London: Constable, 1970).

Kirby, Terrance, 'Lay Supremacy: Reform of the Canon Law of England from Henry VIII to Elizabeth I (1529–1571)', *Reformation and Renaissance Review*, viii (2006), pp. 349–70.

Kirby, T. F., *Annals of Winchester College from the Foundation in the Year 1382 to the Present Time* (London: Henry Frowde, 1892).

Knecht, R. J., *Renaissance Warrior and Patron: The Reign of Francis I* (Cambridge: Cambridge University Press, 1994).

Knighton, C. S., 'Westminster Abbey Restored', in *CMT*, pp. 77–123.

Laynesmith, J. L., *The Last Medieval Queens: English Queenship, 1445–1503* (Oxford: Oxford University Press, 2004).

Lemasters, G. A., 'The Privy Council in the Reign of Mary I', Ph.D. thesis, Cambridge, 1971.

Levin, Carole, and Robert Bucholz, eds, *Queens and Power in Medieval and Early Modern England* (Lincoln, NB and London: University of Nebraska Press, 2009).

Levine, Mortimer, *Tudor Dynastic Problems, 1460–1571* (London: George Allen & Unwin, 1973).

Lewis, Elizabeth, 'A Sixteenth-century Painted Ceiling from Winchester College', *Proceedings of the Hampshire Field Club and Archaeological Society*, li (1995), pp. 137–65.

Liss, Peggy K., *Isabel the Queen: Life and Times*, 2nd edn (Philadelphia, PA: University of Pennsylvania Press, 2004).

Loach, Jennifer, *Edward VI*, ed. George Bernard and Penry Williams (New Haven, CT and London: Yale University Press, 1999).

—— *Parliament and the Crown in the Reign of Mary Tudor* (Oxford: Clarendon Press, 1986).

—— 'The Marian Establishment and the Printing Press', *English Historical Review*, ci (1986), pp. 135–48.

Loach, Jennifer, and Robert Tittler, eds, *The Mid-Tudor Polity, 1540–1560* (London: Macmillan, 1980).

Loades, David, *Elizabeth I* (London: Hambledon and London Books, 2003).

—— *Henry VIII: Court, Church and Conflict* (Kew: The National Archives, 2007).

—— *Intrigue and Treason: The Tudor Court, 1547–1558* (Harlow: Pearson Longman, 2004).

—— *Mary Tudor: A Life* (Oxford: Blackwell, 1989).

—— *Mary Tudor: The Tragical History of the First Queen of England* (Kew: The National Archives, 2006).

—— 'Philip II as King of England', in *Law and Government under the Tudors: Essays Presented to Geoffrey Elton*, ed. C. Cross, D. M. Loades and J. J. Scarisbrick (Cambridge: Cambridge University Press, 1988), pp. 177–94.

—— *The Life and Career of William Paulet (c. 1475–1572), Lord Treasurer and First Marquis of Winchester* (Aldershot: Ashgate, 2008).

—— 'The Marian Episcopate', in *CMT*, pp. 33–56.

—— *The Oxford Martyrs* (London: Batsford, 1970; Bangor: Headstart History, 1992).

—— 'The Personal Religion of Mary I', in *CMT*, pp. 1–29.

—— *The Reign of Mary Tudor: Politics, Government and Religion in England, 1553–58*, 2nd edn (London and New York: Longman, [1979] 1991).

—— *Two Tudor Conspiracies* (Cambridge: Cambridge University Press, 1965).

McConica, James, 'The Rise of the Undergraduate College', in James McConica, ed., *The History of the University of Oxford*, III, *The Collegiate University* (Oxford: Clarendon Press, 1986), pp. 1–68.

McCoog, Thomas M., 'Ignatius Loyola and Reginald Pole: A Reconsideration', *Journal of Ecclesiastical History*, xlvii (1996), pp. 257–73.

McCoy, 'From the Tower to the Tiltyard: Robert Dudley's Return to Glory', *Historical Journal*, xxvii (1984), pp. 425–35.

MacCulloch, Diarmaid, *Thomas Cranmer: A Life* (New Haven, CT and London: Yale University Press, 1996).

—— *Tudor Church Militant: Edward VI and the Protestant Reformation* (London: Allen Lane, The Penguin Press, 1999) [= *The Boy King: Edward VI and the Protestant Revolution* (Berkeley, Los Angeles: University of California Press, 1999)].

McIntosh, J. L., *From Heads of Household to Heads of State: The Preaccession Households of Mary and Elizabeth Tudor* (Columbia: Columbia University Press, 2008).

McLeish, Martin, 'An Inventory of Musical Instruments at the Royal Palace, Madrid, in 1602', *Galpin Society Journal*, xxi (1968), pp. 108–28.

Marshall, Peter, 'Papist as Heretic: The Burning of John Forest, 1538', *Historical Journal*, xli (1998), pp. 351–74.

Martínez Millán, Juan, and Santiago Fernández Conti, 'La Corte del príncipe Felipe (1535–1556)', in Calvete de Estrella, *Felicíssimo viaje*, pp. li–lxxi.

Mattingly, Garrett, *Catherine of Aragon*, 2nd edn (London: Readers Union and Jonathan Cape, [1942] 1944).

Mayer, Thomas F., 'A Test of Wills. Pole, Loyola and the Jesuits in England', in T. M. McCoog, ed., *The Reckoned Expense: Edmund Campion and the Early English Jesuits* (Woodbridge: The Boydell Press, 1996), pp. 21–8.

—— *Cardinal Pole in European Context: A Via Media in the Reformation* (Aldershot: Ashgate Variorum, 2000).

—— 'Cardinal Pole's Concept of *Reformatio*: The *Reformatio Angliae* and Bartolomé Carranza', in *RCMT*, pp. 65–80.

—— *Reginald Pole, Prince and Prophet* (Cambridge: Cambridge University Press, 2000).

—— 'The Success of Cardinal Pole's Final Legation', in *CMT*, pp. 149–75.

Moorhouse, Geoffrey, *Great Harry's Navy: How Henry VIII Gave England Sea Power* (London: Phoenix, [2005] 2006).

—— *The Pilgrimage of Grace: The Rebellion that Shook Henry VIII's Reign* (London: Weidenfeld & Nicolson, 2002).

Munby, Julian, Richard Barber, and Richard Brown, *Edward III's Round Table at Windsor* (Woodbridge: The Boydell Press, 2007).

Murphy, Virginia, 'The Literature and Propaganda of Henry VIII's First Divorce', in *The Reign of Henry VIII: Politics, Policy and Piety*, ed. Diarmaid MacCulloch (Basingstoke: Macmillan, 1995), pp. 135–58.

Noreña, Carlos, *Juan Luis Vives* (The Hague: Martinus Nijhoff, 1970).

O'Malley, John W., *The First Jesuits* (Cambridge, MA: Harvard University Press, 1993).

Overell, Anne, *Italian Reform and English Reformations c. 1535–c. 1585* (Aldershot: Ashgate, 2008).

Oxford Dictionary of the Christian Church, 3rd edn, ed. F. L. Cross and E. A. Livingstone (Oxford: Oxford University Press, 1998).

Park, Katharine, 'Medicine and Magic: The Healing Arts', in *Gender and Society in Renaissance Italy*, ed. Judith C. Brown and Robert C. Davis (London and New York: Longman, 1998), pp. 129–49.

Parker, Geoffrey, *Philip II*, 2nd edn (London: Cardinal, 1988).

Pérez Martín, María Jesús, *María Tudor: La gran reina desconocida* (Madrid: Ediciones Rialp, 2008).

Pettegree, Andrew, 'A. G. Dickens and His Critics: A New Narrative of the English Reformation', *Historical Research*, lxxvii (2004), pp. 39–58.

—— *Marian Protestantism: Six Studies* (Aldershot: Ashgate, 1996).

—— *The Stationers' Company and the Development of the English Printing Industry* (London: Stationers' Company, 2009).

Pierce, Hazel, *Margaret Pole, Countess of Salisbury, 1473–1541: Loyalty, Lineage and Leadership* (Cardiff: University of Wales Press, 2003).

Pinto Crespo, Virgilio, *Inquisición y control ideológico en la España del siglo XVI* (Madrid: Taurus, 1983).

Pogson, Rex, 'Cardinal Pole: Papal Legate to England in Mary Tudor's Reign', Ph.D. dissertation, University of Cambridge, 1972.

—— 'Reginald Pole and the Priorities of Government in Mary Tudor's Church', *Historical Journal*, xviii (1975), pp. 3–21.

—— 'Revival and Reform in Mary Tudor's Church: A Question of Money', in Haigh, ed., *English Reformation Revised*, pp. 139–56.

Pollard, A. F., *The History of England from the Accession of Edward VI to the Death of Elizabeth, (1547–1603)* (London: Longman, Green, 1915).

Porter, Linda, *Mary Tudor: The First Queen* (London: Portrait [Piatkus Books], 2007).

Prescott, H. F. M., *Mary Tudor: The Spanish Tudor* (London: Phoenix, [1940] 2003).

Redworth, Glyn, *In Defence of the Church Catholic: The Life of Stephen Gardiner* (Oxford: Blackwell, 1990).

—— 'Matters Impertinent to Women: Male and Female Monarchy under Philip and Mary', *English Historical Review*, cxii (1997), pp. 597–613.

—— '¿Nuevo mundo u otro mundo?: conquistadores, cortesanos, libros de caballerías y el reinado de Felipe el Breve de Inglaterra', in *Actas del Primer Congreso Anglo-Hispano*, iii, *Historia*, ed. Richard Hitchcock and Ralph Penny (Madrid: Editorial Castalia, 1994), pp. 113–25.

Rex, Richard, 'Morley and the Papacy: Rome, Regime and Religion', in Marie Axton and James P. Carley, eds, *'Triumphs of English': Henry Parker, Lord Morley, Translator to the Tudor Court* (London: British Library, 2000), pp. 87–105.

—— *The Theology of John Fisher* (Cambridge: Cambridge University Press, 1991).

—— *The Tudors* (Stroud: Tempus, 2002).

Reynolds, Anne, 'The Papal Court in Exile: Clement VII in Orvieto, 1527–28', in *The Pontificate of Clement VI: History, Politics, Culture* (Aldershot: Ashgate, 2005), pp. 143–61.

Richards, Judith M., *Mary Tudor* (London and New York: Routledge, 2008).

—— 'Mary Tudor as "Sole Quene"? Gendering Tudor Monarchy', *Historical Journal*, xl (1997), pp. 895–99.

—— 'To Promote a Woman to Beare Rule', *Sixteenth Century Journal*, xxviii (1997), pp. 101–21.

Ridley, Jasper, *Bloody Mary's Martyrs: The Story of England's Terror* (London: Constable, 2001).

Robinson, W. R. B., 'Princess Mary's Itinerary in the Marches of Wales, 1525–1527', *Historical Research*, lxxi (1998), pp. 233–52.

Robledo Estaire, Luis, 'La música en la Corte madrileña de los Austrias. Antecedentes: las casas reales hasta 1556', *Revista de Musicología*, x (1987), pp. 753–96.

Rodríguez-Salgado, M. J., *The Changing Face of Empire: Charles V, Philip II and Habsburg Authority, 1551–1559* (Cambridge: Cambridge University Press, 1988).

Rodríguez Villa, A., *El emperador Carlos V y su corte según las cartas de Don Martín de Salinas, embajador del infante don Fernando (1522–1539)* (Madrid: Real Academia de la Historia, 1903).

Russell, P. E., *English Intervention in Spain and Portugal in the Time of Edward III and Richard II* (Oxford: Clarendon Press, 1955).

Ryrie, Alec, *The Gospel and Henry VIII: Evangelicals in the Early English Reformation* (Cambridge: Cambridge University Press, 2003).

Samson, Alexander, 'Power Sharing: the Co-monarchy of Philip and Mary in Principle and Practice', in *Tudor Queenship: The Reigns of Mary and Elizabeth*, ed. Alice Hunt and Anna Whitelock (Basingstoke: Palgrave Macmillan, forthcoming).

—— 'The Marriage of Philip of Habsburg and Mary Tudor and Anti-Spanish Sentiment in England', Ph.D. thesis, University of London (1999, revised, 2009).

Sánchez Cantón, Francisco Javier, *Libros, tapices y cuadros que coleccionó Isabel la Católica* (Madrid: Consejo Superior de Investigaciones Científicas, 1950).

Savage, Henry, ed., *The Love Letters of Henry VIII* (London: Allan Wingate, 1949).

Scarisbrick, J. J., *Henry VIII*, 2nd edn (New Haven, CT and London: Yale University Press, [1968] 1997).

—— *The Reformation and the English People* (Oxford: Basil Blackwell, [1984] 1989).

Schwartz, Stuart B., *All Can be Saved: Religious Toleration and Subversion in the Iberian Atlantic World* (New Haven, CT and London: Yale University Press, 2008).

Screech, M. A., *Laughter at the Foot of the Cross* (London: Penguin Books, 1997).

Shagan, Ethan, *Popular Politics and the English Reformation* (Cambridge: Cambridge University Press, 2003).

Sharpe, Kevin, *Selling the Tudor Monarchy: Authority and Image in Sixteenth-Century England* (New Haven, CT and London: Yale University Press, 2009).

www.sintjan.com (Sint Janskeke, Gouda, goudesglazen).

Skidmore, Chris, *Edward VI: The Lost King of England* (London: Weidenfeld & Nicolson, 2007).

Smets, Irene, *The Cathedral of Our Lady in Antwerp* (Ghent: Ludion, n.d.).

Starkey, David, *Elizabeth: Apprenticeship* (London: Chatto & Windus, 2000).

—— *Henry, Virtuous Prince* (London: Harper Press, 2008).

—— *Six Wives: The Queens of Henry VIII* (London: Chatto & Windus, 2003).

Stow, Kenneth, *The Jews in Rome*, ii, *1551–1557* (Leiden: Brill, 1997).

Streckfuss, Corinna, 'England's Reconciliation with Rome: A News Event in Early Modern Europe', *Historical Research*, lxxxii (2009), pp. 62–73.

Strohm, Paul, *England's Empty Throne: Usurpation and the Language of Legitimation, 1399–1422* (New Haven, CT and London: Yale University Press, 1998).

Suárez [Fernández], Luis, *Isabel I, Reina* (Barcelona: Ariel, 2000).

Surtz, Ronald E., *Writing Women in Late Medieval and Early Modern Spain* (Philadelphia, PA: University of Pennsylvania Press, 1995).

Swanson, R. N., *Catholic England: Faith, Religion and Observance before the Reformation* (Manchester: Manchester University Press, 1993).

—— *Church and Society in Late Medieval England* (Oxford: Basil Blackwell, 1989).

Tellechea Idígoras, José Ignacio, 'Bartolomé Carranza y la restauración católica inglesa (1554–1558)', in Tellechea, *Fray Bartolomé Carranza y el cardenal Pole: Un navarro en la restauración católica de Inglaterra (1554–1558)* (Pamplona: Diputación Foral de Navarra, 1977), pp. 15–118.

—— *El papado y Felipe II*, 3 vols (Madrid: Fundación Universitaria Española, 1999–2002).

—— 'El formulario de visita pastoral de Bartolomé Carranza, Arzobispo de Toledo', in Tellechea, *CyP*, pp. 303–51.

—— *Fray Bartolomé Carranza de Miranda: Investigaciones históricas* (Pamplona: Gobierno de Navarra, 2002).

—— *La legación del Cardenal R. Pole (1553–54): Cuando Inglaterra volvió a ser católica* (Salamanca: Centro de Estudios Orientales y Ecuménicos Juan XXIII, 2002).

—— *Paulo IV y Carlos V: la renuncia del Imperio a debate* (Madrid: Fundación Universitaria Española, 2001).

—— 'Pole, Carranza y Fresneda: cara y cruz de una amistad y de una enemistad', in Tellechea, *CyP*, pp. 119–97.

Tighe, W. J., 'The Gentlemen Pensioners: The Duke of Northumberland and the Attempted Coup of 1553', *Albion*, xix (1987), pp. 1–11.

Tittler, R., *The Reign of Mary I* (Harlow: Longman, 1981).

Tittler, R., and S. L. Battley, 'The Local Community and the Crown in 1553: The Accession of Mary Tudor Revisited', *Bulletin of the Institute of Historical Research*, lvii (1984), pp. 131–9.

Tyler, P. T., *England under the Reigns of Edward VI and Mary*, 2 vols (London: Richard Bentley, 1839).

Varela, Consuelo, *Ingleses en España y Portugal, 1480–1515: Aristócratas, mercaderes e impostores* (Lisbon: Edições Colibri, 1998).

Wansborough, Henry, OSB, and Anthony Marett-Crosby, eds, *Benedictines in Oxford* (London: Darton, Longman & Todd, 1997).

Weikel, A., 'The Marian Council Revisited', in *The Mid-Tudor Polity*, ed. Loach and Tittler, pp. 52–73.

Weir, Alison, *Innocent Traitor* (London: Hutchinson, 2006).

Weiss, Charles, *Papiers d'État du Cardinal de Granvelle*, 9 vols (Paris: 1841–52) (Collection de documents inédits sur l'histoire de la France).

Weissberger, Barbara F., *Isabel Rules: Constructing Queenship, Wielding Power* (Minneapolis: University of Minnesota Press, 2004).

Whitelock, Anna, 'A Woman in a Man's World. Mary I and Political Intimacy, 1553–1558', *Women's History Review*, xvi, no. 3 (2007), pp. 323–34.

—— 'In Opposition and in Government: The Household and Affinities of Mary Tudor, 1516–1558', Ph.D. dissertation, University of Cambridge, 2004.

—— *Mary Tudor: England's First Queen* (London: Bloomsbury, 2009).

Whitelock, Anna, and Diarmaid MacCulloch, 'Princess Mary's Household and the Succession Crisis, July 1553', *Historical Journal*, l (2007), pp. 265–87.

Williams, Glanmor, 'Wales and the Reign of Queen Mary I', *Welsh History Review*, x (1981), pp. 334–58.

Williams, Patrick, *Philip II* (Basingstoke: Palgrave Macmillan, 2001).

Winfield, Flora, *The Marriage of England and Spain* (Winchester: Winchester Cathedral, 2004).

Wizeman, William, SJ, *The Theology and Spirituality of Mary Tudor's Church* (Aldershot: Ashgate, 2006).

—— 'The Virgin Mary in the Reign of Mary Tudor', in *Studies in Church History*, xxxix, *The Church and Mary*, ed. R. N. Swanson (Woodbridge: The Boydell Press, 2004), pp. 239–48.

Wooding, Lucy [E C.], *Henry VIII* (London and New York: Routledge, 2009).

—— *Rethinking Catholicism in Reformation England* (Oxford: Clarendon Press, 2000).

INDEX